A Contemporary
Cuba Reader

A Contemporary Cuba Reader

Reinventing the Revolution

Edited by
Philip Brenner, Marguerite Rose Jiménez,
John M. Kirk, and William M. LeoGrande

ROWMAN & LITTLEFIELD PUBLISHERS, INC.
Lanham • Boulder • New York • Toronto • Plymouth, UK

ROWMAN & LITTLEFIELD PUBLISHERS, INC.

Published in the United States of America
by Rowman & Littlefield Publishers, Inc.
A wholly owned subsidiary of The Rowman & Littlefield Publishing Group, Inc.
4501 Forbes Boulevard, Suite 200, Lanham, Maryland 20706
www.rowmanlittlefield.com

Estover Road, Plymouth PL6 7PY, United Kingdom

British Library Cataloguing in Publication Information Available

Library of Congress Cataloging-in-Publication Data

A contemporary Cuba reader : reinventing the Revolution / edited by Philip Brenner . . .
[et al.].
    p. cm.
  Includes bibliographical references and index.
  ISBN-13: 978-0-7425-5506-8 (cloth : alk. paper)
  ISBN-10: 0-7425-5506-2 (cloth : alk. paper)
  ISBN-13: 978-0-7425-5507-5 (pbk. : alk. paper)
  ISBN-10: 0-7425-5507-0 (pbk. : alk. paper)
  1. Cuba—History—1990– I. Brenner, Philip.
  F1788.C67 2008
  972.9106'4—dc22

                              2007017602

Printed in the United States of America.

∞™ The paper used in this publication meets the minimum requirements of American
National Standard for Information Sciences—Permanence of Paper for Printed Library
Materials, ANSI/NISO Z39.48-1992.

Contents

A special feature of *A Contemporary Cuba Reader* is a dedicated webpage, http://www.rowmanlittlefield.com/isbn/0742555070, that will give readers access to a variety of resources as a companion to the book itself. The site will include annotated links to resources, where material ranging from declassified documents, significant speeches, and government reports (from both Havana and Washington) to art work and music can be accessed. The reader will be able to obtain basic political and economic data about Cuba, view the most recent news reports (from a variety of perspectives), see historical documents, and stay on top of events in the country.

Preface

In 1990, Cuban president Fidel Castro announced that Cuba was entering a "Special Period in a Time of Peace"—a period of extreme hardship that led to a dramatic reversal in the quality of life for most people on the island. The collapse of the socialist trading bloc in 1989, and the subsequent break-up of the Soviet Union, caused the Cuban economy to decline by nearly 30 percent in four years.

Since then, Cuba has been undergoing an extraordinary transition process that has reinvented the Cuban Revolution. Everything in Cuba has been touched by the changes: the economy (in which sugar is no longer king), internal politics, Cuba's international relations, its culture (music, films, writing, dance, and art), and new ways in which race, class, gender, and religion affect social relations among Cubans. When Castro unexpectedly announced on July 31, 2006, that he was relinquishing temporarily all of his leadership responsibilities, the news seemed to portend changes even greater than those of the prior sixteen years.

Yet one year later, as we write this preface, the pace of change has remained steady. As Castro had designated, his brother, Raúl Castro, continued to serve as president, head of the Cuban Communist Party, and commander-in-chief of the armed forces. In effect, a peaceful transition of power had occurred in Cuba. In May 2007, Fidel Castro essentially confirmed that his abdication of authority was no longer temporary. Writing in the main Communist Party newspaper, *Granma*, he acknowledged that his medical problems of July 2006 had required several operations. "Initially," he noted, "it was not successful and this implicated a prolonged recovery period." But the life-threatening problems of the previous year had passed, he reported, and he was again eating food normally. The improvement in his health, though, did not mean he would resume his leadership posts. He pointedly remarked, "Nowadays I do what I should be doing, especially reflecting and writing about issues which, to my mind, have some importance and transcendence. I have a lot pending."[1]

There is little doubt that Fidel Castro played the central role in determining the character, the successes, and the failures of the Cuban Revolution. Yet this was not

"Castro's revolution." The calm that ensued after he stepped down suggested both that he was replaceable and that the revolution he led had been forged by the Cuban people who continued to support its fundamental goals. As we highlight in the introduction, contemporary Cubans carry with them the legacy of many prior generations who were determined to build a Cuba independent of foreign domination—whether by Spain, the United States, or the Soviet Union—and at least since 1959 to foster an ethos of egalitarianism.

Our intention in this book is to give the reader an appreciation for the way in which that legacy combined with the Cuban spirit of boundless energy, creativity, and patience to reinvent the revolution. The Special Period thus has taken on a dual meaning. It was a time of enormous suffering and desperate survival that certainly will become part of Cuban legend. It was also a time of renewal and rebirth, a period made special by the death of the old revolution and the emergence of a new Cuba.

Several people have assisted us as we worked on *A Contemporary Cuba Reader*. In particular, Philip Brenner thanks Bea Reaud and Kathryn Werner for their research assistance; Marguerite Jiménez thanks Patrick Quirk for his help in several ways; John M. Kirk thanks Emily Kirk for her research assistance; William LeoGrande thanks Kim Moloney, Michael Danielson, Melissa Del Río, and Farah Jamal for their research assistance. We have benefitted from the advice and contributions given to us by numerous colleagues at American University, Dalhousie University, the National Security Archive, and the University of Havana. Officials at the U.S. Interests Section in Havana and the Cuban Interests Section in Washington, D.C. have facilitated our travel and research. Our families have been generous with their support and patience. Above all, this book would not have been possible without our editor at Rowman & Littlefield, Susan McEachern. She engaged in this project with the spirit of a team captain, who combined good judgment and professionalism with collegiality, and with the commitment to producing a book true to the editors' objectives and better than it would have been had many of the editors' preferences prevailed.

NOTE

1. Fidel Castro Ruz, "Reflections by the Commander in Chief: For the Deaf Who Won't Listen," *Granma*, May 24, 2007, at www.granma.cubaweb.cu/english/news/art52.html, accessed May 24, 2007.

Credits

Sinclair, Minor, and Martha Thompson. "Going Against the Grain: Agricultural Crisis and Transformation." Oxfam America (June 2001).

Henken, Ted. "*Vale Todo* (Anything Goes): Cuba's *Paladares*." *Cuba in Transition* 12, 2002: 344–353.

Eckstein, Susan. "Dollerization and Its Discontents: Remittances and the Remaking of Cuba in the Post-Soviet Era." *Comparative Politics* 36 (April 2004). Reprinted by permission.

Castro Ruz, Fidel. "Neoliberalism, Global Inequality, and Irreparable Destruction of Our Natural Habitat: Message to the 11th United Nations Conference on Trade and Development."

Domínguez, Jorge I. "Cuba and the *Pax Americana*: U.S.-Cuban Relations Post-1990," in *Between Compliance and Conflict: East Asia, Latin America, and the "New" Pax Americana*, eds. Jorge I. Domínguez and Byung-Kook Kim (New York: Routledge, 2005): 193-217.

Erisman, H. Michael. "Cuba's Counter-Hegemonic Strategy." In *Cuba's Foreign Relations in a Post-Soviet World*, University Press of Florida, 2000: 22–48.

Fisk, Daniel W. "Advancing the Day When Cuba Will Be Free." Remarks to the Cuban American Veterans Association, Miami, Florida, October 9, 2004.

Sweig, Julia E. "Fidel's Final Victory." Reprinted by permission of *Foreign Affairs*, (January/February 2007). Copyright 2007 by the Council on Foreign Relations, Inc.

Smith, Wayne. "Wanted: A Logical Cuba Policy." *Center for International Policy*, 1997.

Roy, Joaquin. "The European Union Perception of Cuba: From Frustration to Irritation." *FOCAL Background Briefing* (September 2003).

McKenna, Peter, and John M. Kirk. "Sleeping with an Elephant: The Impact of the United States on Canada-Cuba Relations." *Cuba, the United States, and the Post-Cold War World*, edited by Morris Morley and Chris McGillion, 2005: 148–179. Reprinted with permission of the University Press of Florida.

Eckstein, Susan, and Loren Barberia. "Cuban Americans and Their Transnational Ties." *The International Migration Review* 36, no. 3 (Fall 2002).

Williams, Robin C. "In the Shadow of Plenty, Cuba Copes with a Crippled Health Care System." Reprinted from *CMAJ* 01/Aug/97; 157(3), Page(s) 291–293 by permission of the publisher. © 1997 Canadian Medical Association.

Uriarte, Mirén. "Social Impact of the Economic Measures." In *Cuba: Social Policy at the Crossroads: Maintaining Priorities, Transforming Practice*. Oxfam America, 2002.

Domínguez, María Isabel. "Cuban Youth: Aspirations, Social Perceptions, and Identity. In *Changes in Cuban Society since the Nineties*, Woodrow Wilson Center Report on the Americas no. 15, eds. J.S. Tulchin, L. Bobea, M. Espina Prieto, and R Hernández (Woodrow Wilson International Center for Scholars, 2005).

Gasperini, Lavinia. "The Cuban Education System: Lessons and Dilemmas." *World Bank Country Studies, Education Reform and Management Publication Series* 1, no. 5 (July 2000): 1, 2, 5–8, 23, 28.

Vigil, María López. "Heroines of the Special Period." In *Cuba: Neither Heaven Nor Hell*. EPICA, 1999: 43–61, 75, 161–166.

Pagés, Raisa. "The Status of Cuban Women: From Economically Dependant to Independent." Granma International Online, Special Weekly Supplement, 2000.

de la Fuente, Alejandro. "Recreating Racism: Race and Discrimination in Cuba's Special Period. *Cuba in the 1990s: Economy, Politics, and Society*, a special issue of *Socialism and Democracy* 15, no. 1 (Spring 2001).

Oberg, Larry R. "The Status of Gays in Cuba: Myth and Reality." Cuban Libraries Solidarity Group, 2006.

Crahan, Margaret E. "Civil Society and Religion in Cuba: Past, Present, and Future." In *Changes in Cuban Society since the Nineties*, Woodrow Wilson Center Report on the Americas no. 15, eds. J.S. Tulchin, L. Bobea, M. Espina Prieto, and R Hernández (Woodrow Wilson International Center for Scholars, 2005).

Ortega Alamino, Cardinal Jaime. "There Is No Homeland without Virtue." *Miami Herald*, March 3, 2003.

Kirk, John M. "A Black Woman from Cuba, That's All." In *Culture and the Cuban Revolution: Conversations in Havana*. John M. Kirk and Leonardo Padura Fuentes. University Press of Florida, 2001. Reprinted with permission of the University Press of Florida.

Fuentes, Leonardo Padura. "Living and Creating in Cuba: Risks and Challenges." In *Culture and the Cuban Revolution: Conversations in Havana*. John M. Kirk and Leonardo Padura Fuentes. University Press of Florida, 2001. Reprinted with permission of the University Press of Florida.

Finn, Maria. "Visions of Dollars Dance Before Cuban Artists' Eyes." Copyright © 2003 by The New York Times Co. Reprinted with permission.

Fernández, Enrique. "Ballet: Split with Cuba Still Brings Pain." *Miami Herald*, September 17, 2005.

Chanan, Michael. "Wonderland." In *Cuban Cinema* (University of Minnesota Press, 2004): 444–473.

History as Prologue

Cuba before the Special Period

Imagine your reaction if you had to substitute sugar water for food every third day for a year, and as a result you lost your eyesight because of a vitamin deficiency (as happened to fifty thousand Cubans temporarily), and lost twenty to twenty-five pounds (the average for Cubans in 1993–1994). Imagine oil imports dropping by 70 percent over a four-year period (1989–1993), so that you could not drive your car and buses ran infrequently because of gasoline shortages. Picture yourself undergoing an operation at a formerly reliable hospital, where now several doctors and nurses were absent because of transportation problems, and there were hardly any anesthetics, medicines, or bandages. In 1990, few Cubans imagined they would ever live this kind of life, even when Cuban President Fidel Castro announced that the country was entering a "Special Period in a Time of Peace."

As the Soviet Union plodded to its ultimate demise, it could no longer sustain large losses on the products which Cuba had purchased at subsidized prices, such as oil. Worse, the collapse of the Eastern bloc's trading system, through which Cuba had conducted 85 percent of its international commerce, forced it to find new trading partners who provided far less favorable terms than its former socialist allies. As international trade plummeted between 1990 and 1993, Cuba's gross domestic product (GDP) declined by 30 percent.[1]

Until 1990, Cuba had developed to the point where infectious diseases had been eradicated and its rate of infant mortality was comparable to that of advanced industrial nations; where there were more doctors per capita than in any other country, and free universal health care was available throughout the island; where universities had been established in every province, education through graduate school was free, and racial and gender disparities were disappearing because of educational opportunities. Though Cuba was still a poor country by standard measures of GDP, it was an egalitarian society where most people considered themselves to be middle class, and could reasonably hope that their children's lives would be better than their own. In the first thirty-two years of the revolution, the great majority of Cubans also had gained an intangible but discernible sense of dignity, in part because of Cuba's prowess in international sports competitions, the worldwide recognition of Cuban artists, writers, dancers, and filmmakers, and the respect other Third World countries accorded to this small nation that had repeatedly and successfully defied the hovering giant ninety miles away.

Few regimes could have survived the sudden and epochal decline that Cuba endured at the start of the Special Period. But its adaptation to the new conditions altered the very nature of the Cuban Revolution, significantly impacting the political and economic organization of the country, daily life and culture, and Cuba's foreign relations. This book examines those changes and the way in which they transformed the revolutionary state between 1991 and 2007. Such an examination necessarily includes a review of the way in which the country's prior experiences prepared Cubans for survival and instilled in them a tradition of independence. That is the purpose of this introduction.

Two patterns have repeated themselves during Cuba's last five centuries: (1) an external power (Spain, the United States, or the Soviet Union) has tried to dominate Cuba and prevent it from developing; and (2) Cubans have struggled to be independent of the dominant external power. Until recently, Cuba was vulnerable to control because its economy depended on one major export product—sugar. Yet its dependency with each great power had its particular characteristics. While some Cubans benefited during the first two periods (1500–1898, 1903–1958), and most Cubans benefited during the last period (1959–1991), Cuba's dependent relationships and its continuing reliance on sugar exacerbated the severe problems it faced at the start of the Special Period.

FIRST FOUR CENTURIES OF DEPENDENCY

Christopher Columbus "discovered" Cuba on his first voyage across the Atlantic in 1492, claiming it on behalf of the Spanish Crown. Prior to Columbus's discovery, native tribes of Cuba—largely Arawak and Ciboneys—had lived in peace for centuries, in basic harmony with their neighbors and nature. The Spaniards outlawed the tribes' religious practices, stole their collective property, and made them slaves for the benefit of the Crown. In contrast to the indigenous population of mainland Spanish America, the native peoples of Cuba virtually disappeared within a generation of Spain's arrival, wiped out by overwork, disease, and mass suicides.[2] A notable exception were the Taino Arawaks, who waged a fierce struggle against the Spanish. Their example of resistance is still celebrated in Cuba, and Taino tribal leader Hatuey is a national hero.

For much of its time as a colony, Cuba languished as a backwater in the Spanish Empire. It possessed few minerals of real worth; its value lay in the strategic location it provided Spain. The Spanish Crown maintained a monopoly on all of Cuba's trade, stifled attempts to develop indigenous industry, and imposed high taxes on all imports and exports. As in other colonies, political control in Cuba remained with governors and administrators from the mother country, and Spanish soldiers enforced colonial rule. The Crown rewarded Spanish settlers who came to live in the "most lovely land that eyes have ever seen," as Columbus described Cuba, with immense tracts of land. In the mid-eighteenth century they began to transform their agricultural production from basic food staples to sugar, in response to European popular demand. Sugar was cultivated most efficiently on large plantations, and its harvesting was a labor-intensive process. With profits waiting to be earned and a shortage of workers on the island, Spain legalized slavery, and an active trade in African slaves began in 1763. Slave traders brought approximately 750,000 Africans to Cuba in the next one hundred years. In 1862, Afro-Cubans accounted for more than half of the 1.4 million people on the island, and Cuba produced one-third of the world's sugar supply. Slavery did not end in Cuba until 1886.

The Spanish colonial government encouraged the racial divide that slavery produced, doling out almost all prestigious positions in the military and government to whites born in Spain, known as the *peninsulares*—those born on the peninsula of Spain. Children born in the "colonies" to Spanish parents—the *criollos*, or creoles—were branded with an original sin of inferiority despite being "white." The end result was an extraordinarily racist society, in which one's status, privileges, and rights were based upon the color of one's skin and the location of one's birth. Spanish Catholic bishops accommodated and reinforced this standard by allowing only white Spanish priests—many of whom were "parachuted" in for limited-term appointments—to officiate in Cuban churches.

Between 1810 and 1821, people throughout the mainland of Spanish America successfully struggled to end colonialism in most of the region, developing national boundaries more or less along the lines of the current configuration of Latin America. But not in Cuba. It became the refuge for the Spanish warriors defeated in the wars of independence, who tended to reinforce the authoritarianism, rigidity, and racism already prevalent in Cuba. The consequent tension was heightened by Cuba's uneven development, which produced great disparities in wealth between Cubans and between regions. This volatile mixture came to a head in 1868, when Cubans began a ten-year war for independence that would unfold over the following ninety years.

The Ten-Year War

Agitation for independence had been building for nearly two decades, particularly in the eastern part of the island, when plantation owner Carlos Manuel de Céspedes proclaimed Cuba's freedom from Spain on October 10, 1868. Joined by other planters, he freed his slaves and declared the *Grito de Yara* (Cry of Yara)—a call for revolution. Starting with less than two hundred volunteers, the rebel army (called the *mambises*) grew within a few months to twelve thousand, gathering small farmers, laborers, and freed slaves. This was a conservative revolution in most aspects other than ending slavery, as the planters resented the increases in Spanish taxes and sought political power for themselves. Though western sugar plantation owners, who depended on slavery, opposed the revolutionary effort, it was able to accumulate many successes. The rebels defeated superior Spanish forces in several battles, they captured cities such as Bayamo, and they established a new government and democratic constitution. But both the rebels and the Spaniards were exhausted after ten years of fighting, which left fifty thousand soldiers and civilians dead. In February 1878 they signed a treaty which freed some slaves, promised future reforms, and left Cuba as a Spanish colony. Unwilling to accept continued foreign rule, rebel officers led by Antonio Maceo penned "The Protest of Baraguá," a pledge to continue the independence war. Cuban leaders today still refer to Baraguá as a symbol of defiance against external dominance.[3]

Maceo had to abandon the fight within a few months, after the Spanish military captured and exiled him. He did not return to Cuba until March 1895, one month after the renewed independence war began. Yet he had been working with others such as General Máximo Gómez to plan for the war. In 1892 José Martí gathered the opposition under the banner of the Cuban Revolutionary Party, as he coordinated preparations for the coming struggle. The son of poor Spanish immigrants, Martí began his first attacks on Spanish colonial rule in *La Patria Libre* (*Free Fatherland*), a newspaper he started in 1869 at the age of sixteen. Jailed for his political activities, he was then exiled to Spain in 1871. In 1881 he moved to New York, where he worked as a journalist, covering U.S. politics for several Latin American newspapers, and wrote poetry and novels.

Cuba was experiencing a severe depression in 1895, in part caused by a U.S. tariff on sugar imposed the year before. This contributed to the widespread support the rebels received. They started their campaign in the east (Oriente Province), and by the end of the year the struggle for independence had engulfed the entire island. Martí was killed in combat on May 19, 1895, only six weeks after returning to Cuba with General Gómez. Yet his concept of *Cuba Libre* continued to inspire the new *mambises*. It also set the stage for an inevitable clash with the United States. As historian Louis Pérez explains:

> At the time of Martí's death in 1895, *Cuba Libre* had come to signify more than separation from Spain. . . . [S]o unyieldingly did [*Cuba Libre*] proclaim the primacy of Cuban interests, that it placed separatists squarely on a collision course with the United States. The *independentista* formula was simple: Cuba for Cubans—the one eventuality which nearly one hundred years of North American policy had been dedicated to preventing.[4]

Meanwhile, Spain fought back against the revolutionaries with enormous brutality, razing villages and driving Cubans out of their homes. The two-hundred-thousand-soldier Spanish garrison at first seemed sufficient to counter the *independentistas*. But by 1898 the army's morale was low, and Spanish repression had stimulated support for the revolutionaries. Both Madrid and Washington assessed that the rebels would likely win the war by year's end.

"A Splendid Little War"

The U.S. declaration of war against Spain, in April 1898, did not result merely from a sudden burst of popular passion—fueled by the "yellow" journalism of William Randolph Hearst and Joseph Pulitzer's competing newspapers—after a U.S. battleship exploded in Havana harbor killing 260 U.S. seamen. Many factors contributed to the U.S. intervention. U.S. business barons, for example, feared that a rebel victory would mean a Cuba run by Cubans, which might undermine their holdings and privileged trade deals. Even before the war, the United States had supplanted Spain as Cuba's main trading partner.[5] It was in response to concerns about property owned by Americans—and perhaps about the lives of U.S. citizens—that President William McKinley had dispatched the U.S.S. *Maine* to Cuba in January. Yet there also were U.S. political leaders who convinced themselves that intervention would be a humane and selfless action, because an independent Cuba could not govern itself.[6] The "splendid little war"—as Secretary of State John Hay described the 1898 conflict—resulted in the transfer of the Philippines, Guam, and Puerto Rico from Spain's colonial control to that of the United States. Of course, Cuba also was a U.S. prize from the war.

The *Maine*'s explosion, on February 15, 1898, occurred as the rebels were preparing their final offensives. U.S. engagement in the conflict effectively stole from Cubans the fruits of their thirty years of fighting. Four months after the United States declared war, it signed a bilateral peace treaty with Spain, without any Cuban participation. The name commonly applied to the conflict in the United States—"Spanish-American War"—betrays an ignorance about the limited importance of the U.S. contribution in securing victory. It also obscures the U.S. suppression of Cuban hopes for full independence. In Cuba, the conflict is known as the Cuban War of Independence.[7]

DE FACTO COLONIALISM: CUBA'S SPECIAL RELATIONSHIP WITH THE UNITED STATES

Though Cuba was nominally independent from 1903 to 1959, it was a de facto colony of the United States, which gave it little opportunity to overcome its dependence on sugar. The United States withdrew its occupation forces from Cuba in 1902 on the condition that the new constitution would include the Platt Amendment, a provision which permitted U.S. unilateral intervention on the island. During the period when the Platt Amendment was in force, from 1903 to 1934, the United States occupied Cuba with troops on three different occasions. At the same time, U.S. corporations and investment banks gained control of Cuba's basic infrastructure. Louis Pérez has succinctly delineated Cuba's dilemma in 1903, observing that

> Cubans had achieved self-government without self-determination and independence without sovereignty. . . . Peace was an anticlimax, for separation from Spain did not signify independence for Cuba. Foreigners again ruled Cuba, again in the name of Cubans, but, as before, for their own ends.[8]

The U.S. occupation began on January 1, 1899. Leonard Wood, the second U.S. governor-general, revealed in a letter to President McKinley the patronizing attitude the new rulers had toward their subjects. He wrote that "we are dealing with a race that has steadily been going down for a hundred years and into which we have to infuse new life, new principles and new methods of doing things."[9] Indeed, while the Platt Amendment was couched in the language of protecting liberty, life, property, and stability on the island, historian Lars Schoultz explains that its purpose was to "maintain control over people whom they [U.S. officials] considered unfit for self-government," without continuing military occupation of the island.[10] In developing the Platt Amendment as a mechanism for intervention, Senator Orville Platt and Secretary of War Elihu Root manifested President McKinley's vision that Cuba and the United States should have a "special relationship" with "ties of singular intimacy."

In practice, the special relationship stifled Cuban development. Spurred by concessions the occupation government granted to U.S. investors, the North American hold over Cuban sugar plantations quickly led to U.S. domination of Cuba's non-sugar industries. Sugar operations were quite large, and the *centrales* became thoroughly integrated small cities which linked key sectors of the Cuban economy, most of which were controlled by U.S. firms. Consider that in the mid-1920s, as a result of ties between sugar mills and railroads, U.S. companies owned 22 percent of Cuba's land area.[11] Moreover, U.S.-Cuban trade agreements opened Cuba to inexpensive manufactured goods, which suppressed the creation of an indigenous manufacturing sector. The U.S. sugar quota, which specified how much sugar Cuba could sell at a subsidized price, became the most important determinant of year-to-year survival for Cuba's sugar workers, and for Cuba's economic planning. A "wrong" decision which might upset one U.S. senator could lead to a filibuster against Cuba's quota. And so, for example, though Cuba had the potential to produce tomatoes and even tomato ketchup commercially, both were imported from the United States because of U.S. tomato growers.

By the mid-1950s, 90 percent of Cuba's telephone and electrical services, 50 percent of public service railways, 40 percent of raw sugar production, and 23 percent of nonsugar industries were U.S.-owned. The United States was Cuba's largest export market, and the main source for its imports: 59 percent of the value of Cuban exports—including 80 percent of its exported sugar—went to the United States. Notably, 76 percent of Cuba's imports originated in the United States. This reflected, in part, U.S.-owned firms buying from their own subsidiaries. As important, Cuba needed to import basic foods, because its dependence on sugar for hard currency reduced its ability to produce rice, wheat, and flour. One-third of U.S. rice exports were sold to Cuba in the 1950s.[12]

As U.S. businesses rapidly took root in Cuba, demand for the services of English-speaking Cubans increased. This led members of the Cuban elite to send their children to U.S. universities, and even high schools, so that they subsequently could take up management positions with U.S. companies on the island. Not surprisingly, the Cuban upper class came to identify with U.S. cultural values. During the first half of the twentieth century, the Americanization of the creole middle class followed the accelerating conversion of the elites, and Cuban society as a whole became imbued with a North American perspective. Baseball became the national pastime. The use of U.S. products conveyed a sense of higher status, and soon anything American was deemed better than anything Cuban—from the arts to the design of buildings to business strategies. Louis Pérez well describes the profound influence this process of acculturation had on Cubans' worldview:

> The well-being of many people, specifically as it related to economic development and prosperity, which also implies social peace and political order, was increasingly linked to the United States: entry to its markets, access to its products, use of its capital, application of its technology. . . . These were complex social processes, for they involved the incorporation of a new hierarchy of values into Cuban life. Tens of thousands of Cubans of all classes—children and adults, men and women, black and white—were integrated directly into North American structures at virtually every turn; as customers, clients, coworkers, as employees and business partners, in professional organizations and voluntary associations, at school and in social clubs, in

church and on teams. . . . This process of negotiation, often irrespective of outcome, was arguably the single most decisive determinant of an emerging national identity.[13]

During the period of the special relationship, a limited form of democracy did emerge on the island, but it was one that Cubans associated with corruption and foreign domination. U.S. Marines occupied Cuba from 1906 to 1909, for a short time in 1912, and from 1917 to 1922. In 1933, U.S. President Franklin Delano Roosevelt (FDR) feared that the unpopularity of Cuba's president—the dictatorial Gerardo Machado—might lead to instability and a radical government. He dispatched a personal emissary, Ambassador Sumner Welles, who persuaded Machado to resign, and arranged for his replacement by a reformer who would comply with U.S. requests.

Within weeks a popular uprising—sparked by a sergeants' revolt with Fulgencio Batista in the lead—ousted the U.S.-approved president and established a provisional government. The new government proclaimed it would bring about national "economic reconstruction" as it began "the march toward the creation of a new Cuba founded . . . upon the most modern concept of democracy."[14] Welles made clear his disapproval of the revolutionaries' chosen leader, Ramón Grau San Martín, but was rebuffed. In turn, FDR refused to recognize Grau's government. Welles then worked behind the scenes to entice key backers, particularly Batista and the military, to defect from the revolutionary coalition, which lasted only four months. Batista continued to be a dependable U.S. surrogate for the next quarter century. Cubans learned that FDR's "Good Neighbor Policy" meant only that the United States would not intervene *militarily*. The U.S. success in suppressing Cuban nationalism, though, led nationalist populism to become the dominant theme of Cuban politics in the following twenty-five years, which legitimated the revolutionaries in 1959 who invoked radical nationalism.

When Batista overthrew the constitutional government in 1952, ending Cuba's experience with "democracy," there was little public outcry. Nelson Valdés observes, in the first chapter of this book, that many in the Cuban elite had abandoned the concept of a distinctive Cuban national identity. In addition, the mass of Cubans associated democratic elections with the theft of Cuban nationalism, either by the mafia or the U.S. government. The revolutionary movement which triumphed in 1959 derived its legitimacy, in part, from its devotion to Cuban nationalism. This placed the new regime on an inevitable collision course with the United States.

THE 1959 REVOLUTION

Active opposition to the Batista dictatorship was organized in several groups, and was spread across the island, especially in the cities. Each group of revolutionaries had distinctive goals, but together they shared a desire to rid Cuba of corruption, modernize the country, and raise living standards for the vast majority of the population. It was not until mid-1958 that the combined revolutionary organizations came together as a unified force, though they did not acknowledge anyone as their single leader. The July 26th Movement had become the largest and most dynamic group, gaining increased support as it won military victories in the summer of 1958. The Movement took its name from the date in 1953 on which Fidel

Castro and some 160 others stormed the Moncada garrison in Santiago, in a failed attempt to spark a general uprising to overthrow the Batista dictatorship. As founder of the rebel army and head of the July 26th Movement, Castro quickly became the natural leader of the revolutionary government when Batista fled the country on December 31, 1958. In its first post-Batista edition, the private, popular weekly magazine *Bohemia* described Castro as a "national hero."[15]

A seemingly upwardly mobile lawyer, Castro was a graduate of the elite Belén high school, which educated Cuba's upper classes, and his father was a plantation owner, though not a rich one. His first wife, Mirta Díaz-Balart, was the daughter of Rafael José Díaz-Balart, a wealthy and prominent conservative lawyer who became transportation minister in Batista's cabinet from 1952 to 1954. Yet Castro also had been a leader of the activist student movement at the University of Havana, a member of the leftist Ortodoxo Party, and an ardent supporter of the party's charismatic leader, Eduardo Chibás. The 1956 platform of the July 26th Movement could have been interpreted as either a radical manifesto or a list of modest changes aimed at "national affirmation, human dignity, and democratic order," goals which earlier reformers historically had promised.[16] With this profile, it is no wonder that U.S. intelligence analysts were uncertain at first whether Castro would try to radically transform the system or institute only modest reforms that would not fundamentally alter the structure of power on the island or with the United States.

The answer came quickly, as the new government initiated major changes in 1959 and 1960. The March 1959 Agrarian Reform Law reduced the maximum landholding size to one thousand acres, and the excess land was largely distributed to landless farm workers. Forty percent of Cuba's rural property was nationalized. The Urban Reform Law cut rents substantially. Cubans with more than two pieces of property were obliged to hand over the excess to the government, which then reclassified them as social property, transforming houses, for example, into day care centers. In other cases, the government quickly erected apartment buildings to deal with the enormous housing shortage.

These reforms produced little new wealth. Instead, they entailed a massive redistribution from the rich to the poor in Cuba. The wealthiest 10 percent of the population lost much of its property, privilege, and political power. They were forced to pay new luxury taxes; their private schools and clubs were closed; private beaches were opened to the public; private clinics were forced to treat indigent patients. In turn, urban Afro-Cubans and all those in rural areas received immediate benefits, because historically they had suffered the greatest unemployment and had received the fewest public services. More than 40 percent of the Cuban workforce in 1958 was either underemployed or unemployed. Sugar cane workers, who made up approximately 25 percent of the national labor force, averaged less than four months of work a year, and Cuba's official unemployment rate in 1958 was 16 percent.

In addition to tangible relief, the revolutionary government set in motion processes which would create new opportunities for the previously dispossessed. It passed new laws banning discrimination on the basis of race or gender; it began to train doctors so that good health care would be universal, and it set out to strengthen the education system. The 1961 literacy campaign engaged a large number of educated Cubans in the revolutionary process, sparking their idealism and opening their eyes to the vast inequalities in the country. University classes were suspended as students and professors went throughout the country over a nine-month period to teach adults how to read. They succeeded in reducing illiteracy from 23.6 percent of the population to 3.9 percent.

Blacks and mulattos constitute a much higher proportion of the population in Cuba than in the United States. The 1953 census recorded 26.9 percent of Cuba as black or mulatto; in the 1981 census it was 34 percent.[17] Racial discrimination before 1959 may have been less a result of interpersonal prejudice than in the United States, though it was entrenched in the way Cuban institutions functioned. Lourdes Casal, a seminal scholar on the subject of racism in Cuba, points out that several factors softened the expression of racism. "[T]he most important leaders of the Cuban independence struggle such as José Martí (white) and Antonio Maceo (black)," she wrote, placed great emphasis on "racial unity and integration."[18] Still, schools for darker-skinned Cubans—when they were available—were vastly inferior compared with those for whites. Afro-Cubans had the worst living conditions, and held the lowest-paid jobs. There was some social mobility for nonwhite Cubans, and Cubans elected Fulgencio Batista, a light-skinned mulatto, as president in 1940. But the white, upper-class Havana Yacht Club denied membership to Batista while he was in office from 1940 to 1944.

Polarization Emerges

As the pace of change accelerated, an ideological gulf emerged between moderate and radical reformers. The struggle against Batista had brought together groups with diverse agendas. Without a common enemy, their differences came to the forefront. Some moderates joined the campaign because they were appalled by Batista's violent repression and disregard for human rights; others had focused on his regime's corruption and willingness to give the mafia effective carte blanche over part of Cuba's tourist industry. Some genuinely believed that the enormous gap between the country's rich and poor could be closed significantly through liberal democratic reforms. To these moderate Cubans, Castro and the July 26th Movement were "betraying" the goals that led them to join the revolution. On the other hand, some so-called moderates invoked democracy merely to protect their property and privilege. Saul Landau comments that they

> had little interest in ending the state of dependency with the United States, and absolutely no inclination to channel their wealth to the services of the majority. This was the essence of the class war that confronted Castro and the revolutionaries by spring 1959.[19]

In fact, the class war was only the first of three simultaneous conflicts Castro expected the revolution would need to fight. The second emanated from the close ties between Cuban property owners and U.S. capital, and from the extensive investments U.S. corporations had made in Cuba. These were the very bonds the radical nationalists aimed to cut, in the hope that decisions about Cuba's economy could be made in Havana, not New York or Washington. The United States had almost never allowed a country in its sphere of influence to act so independently. The revolutionary leadership viewed the 1954 U.S.-engineered coup in Guatemala, which overthrew the democratically elected government of Jacobo Arbenz, as the model of what to expect. Castro made some attempt to blunt the negative U.S. reaction he expected. On a goodwill trip to the United States in April 1959, he offered to repay owners of confiscated lands a price that was greater than their assessed values in tax records, and promised to deliver eight million tons of sugar to the United States at a lower than market price. But many of his speeches in 1959 and 1960 were rife with derisive and insulting remarks which were seemingly intended to taunt the United States.

The third conflict was cultural. It involved overcoming sixty years of neocolonial acculturation to U.S. values which implicitly denigrated Cuban identity, and Cubans themselves. This struggle was the most difficult because it occurred at an ideological, unconscious level, where the enemy was ingrained in each person's conception of the Cuban character. Most often the clash manifested itself as a contest over the meaning of civilization. Defenders of the old order argued that the extent to which Cuba had become civilized could be ascertained by the availability of modern technology and even luxuries which would enable a person to live comfortably. In contrast, Castro argued, the level of civilization should be evaluated by the percentage of people who were illiterate and unemployed, and by the number of children with parasites. In effect, Louis Pérez points out, the revolutionaries sought "to rearrange in usable form the standards by which to measure civilization and in the process summon a vision of an alternative moral order."[20]

Victory in all three conflicts entailed sacrifices. It cost the middle and upper classes wealth, privileges, and status. Workers and peasants were deprived of normalcy: their values were challenged, and demands for their nonpaid "social labor" disrupted routines of daily life. Clashes with the United States involved the loss of life and caused the economy to suffer. Anticipating these costs, the revolutionary leadership reasoned that victories would require Cubans to sustain great leaps of faith which could be undermined if there were disunity and dissent.

The determination to create and maintain unity led the revolutionary government to close down newspapers, nationalize television and radio stations, and cancel promised elections. Efforts to develop a disciplined party apparatus led to the arrest of some who had fought against Batista but did not want to accept Castro's leadership. Ultimately these measures left an indelible imprint on the Cuban Revolution. Justified at first by the necessity to galvanize the mass of Cubans and enable them to develop a revolutionary consciousness, repression became routinized by the seeming demands of national security.

To be sure, the Cuban Revolution had serious enemies. Counterrevolutionaries, centered in the Escambray Mountains and located throughout the country, fought tenaciously from 1960 to 1966. In that period, more than two thousand insurgents and five hundred Cuban soldiers were killed in battle. One counterrevolutionary veteran, Lino Fernández, told a conference in 1996 that the insurgency was essentially a military operation, not a political one, because the fighters believed that the Cuban government could only be overthrown by force, not by political means.[21] The United States began to support the counterrevolutionaries in 1960, and attempted to overthrow the regime by mounting the unsuccessful April 1961 Bay of Pigs invasion. In the wake of that spectacular failure, President John Kennedy authorized the Central Intelligence Agency to wage a multifaceted "low intensity" war against Cuba, code-named Operation Mongoose, which included plans for an invasion by U.S. Marines.[22] The possibility of a U.S. attack has been ever-present since then, because the United States designates Cuba as one of six "terrorist states," and several

U.S. laws stipulate that Cuba is an "enemy" of the United States. A small country like Cuba, adjacent to the world's most powerful nation, does not have the luxury to view such designations casually, as if they have no meaning. Ricardo Alarcón de Quesada, President of Cuba's National Assembly, remarked to us in a 2006 interview that he "awakes every day anticipating a U.S. attack on the horizon."

Yet over time, as national security came to eclipse other priorities, some threats became exaggerated, fear replaced hope, and petty officials were given license to engage in spiteful acts of cruelty. The height of repression came in the early 1960s. Following the Bay of Pigs invasion, the Cuban government rounded up and arrested tens of thousands of people. While most were released quickly, in 1965 Castro acknowledged that twenty thousand political prisoners continued to be incarcerated.[23] Late in that year, the military began to "draft" thousands of people whom the regime designated as "socially deviant": homosexuals, vagrants, and Jehovah's Witnesses and other religious missionaries. They were placed in prison-like camps named Military Units to Aid Production (UMAP)—ostensibly to be reeducated—and ordered to do nonremunerated labor. The UMAP program lasted for two years. Castro disbanded it in 1967 after the Cuban National Union of Writers and Artists protested the drafting of many writers and university professors.[24]

Still, the early years of the revolution produced an enormous outpouring of vibrant cultural expression. For example, the official newspaper of the July 26th Movement, *Revolución*, included a literary supplement every Monday—*Lunes de Revolución*—which quickly gained international acclaim from the world's leading avant garde authors. *Lunes* focused on all of the arts. In addition to the magazine, *Lunes* created a record company, it started a publishing house which emphasized works by new Cuban writers who broke with traditional themes, and it produced a weekly television program that featured modern plays, jazz, and experimental films.[25] In effect, *Lunes* became the forum for debates about Cuban culture.

The explosion of creativity inevitably ran the risk of challenging the government's plan for unity. In June 1961, Castro made clear the limits of tolerance had been reached. During the course of a three-day meeting with "intellectuals," he laid down a new dictum. The revolution, he said, must give an opportunity to all writers and artists, even to those who were not "genuine revolutionaries," to express themselves freely and to use of their "creative spirit." But this freedom would be available only if their creative work was consistent with the revolution. Castro tersely summarized the rule by declaring, "within the revolution, everything; against the revolution, nothing."[26] The trouble was that he did not provide clear parameters as to what lay within and what strayed outside the borders of permissible dissent. Without guidelines, enforcement became arbitrary. Writers and artists feared that the pronouncement was intended to stifle, not to endorse, freedom of expression, and their interpretation was reinforced in November when Castro shut down *Lunes de Revolución*.

As the Cuban revolutionaries implemented their plans, disaffected Cubans voted with their feet and left Cuba. The first wave of émigrés (1959–1962) consisted largely of landowners, wealthy business people, former Batista government officials, managers, small proprietors, and professionals such as doctors, engineers, and skilled technicians. Many went to the United States, where those with professional training were especially welcomed, as part of a U.S. strategy to undermine the Cuban Revolution by depleting the island of people who had technical expertise. By November 1965, when Castro opened the door to unrestricted emigration, 211,000 Cubans had departed. In the next six years, an additional 277,000 emigrated from Cuba.[27]

Debate Over the "New" Cuban Man (Material vs. Moral Incentives)

At its core, the Cuban Revolution included a socialist humanist vision, which contributed to its international appeal. The vision was based on an Enlightenment belief that human beings are perfectible and it is their institutions which make them imperfect. Simply stated, socialist humanists contend that people become alienated from their full potential when a society's institutions, and its consequent relationships, lead them to pursue self-gratification and individual survival. They assert that humans are capable of transcending individualism and selfishness, and of acting with a social conscience for the benefit of the whole society, under the right conditions.

Scholars have tended to identify Ernesto Che Guevara as the main proponent of the socialist humanist vision among the founding leaders of the revolution. Indeed, Guevara did call for the development of new Cuban citizens—the term he used was *new man*—who would eschew "the satisfaction of their personal ambitions" and "become more aware every day of the need to incorporate themselves into society."[28] Guevara's "ultimate aim," economist Bertam Silverman explains, was "to consciously use the process of socialist development as a force to create a new morality."[29] The transition, Guevara asserted, involved reeducation that should take place not only in schools, but also through extensive processes of socialization, politicization, and acculturation, implemented by revolutionary leadership and sustained by nationwide citizen participation. People needed to learn the meaning and practice of the new morality gradually, through their daily activities and relationships. This would require, in Guevara's view, the use of "moral incentives" to motivate people, rather than "material incentives," which would tend to reinforce individualism.

In practice, the use of moral incentives is usually accompanied by inefficiency. Appeals to a common purpose are less likely to engender consistent hard work than differentiated rewards to individuals. For a poor country like Cuba, reduced production affects the availability of basic necessities, and so it would tend to undermine popular support for the revolution itself. The dilemma—posed by the debate over the reliance on material or moral incentives—is one that continues to frame Cuban development decisions even today, as Mirén Uriarte highlights in her chapter in this volume.

Those on one side of the debate focus on the goal of meeting Cubans' basic needs. They argue that the use of material incentives is necessary in order to produce enough wealth so that all Cubans receive adequate food, health care, education, transportation, and social services. Those on the other side emphasize the goal of instilling Cubans with a new morality based on egalitarianism and social consciousness. They argue that cradle-to-grave welfare socialism, without the concurrent or prior development of the new morality, reinforces individualism and inevitably generates inequalities which make realization of the egalitarian goal impossible.

Notably, the latter position did not lose its potency when Guevara left Cuba in 1965. Fidel Castro continued to be a forceful advocate for a new Cuban morality, often invoking Guevara's name to rail against evidence of greed and selfishness. Indeed, at key junctures he implemented significant changes in Cuba's economy in order to restore what he viewed as a balance between material and moral incentives. In March 1968, following a January purge of "old" Communist Party members who favored material incentives, he nationalized fifty-five thousand small businesses, and called for a "revolutionary offensive" to "complete the job of making our people fully revolutionary." Cubans had to learn to develop their revolutionary consciousness from "each event . . . each new experience."[30]

Similarly, in 1986, Castro shut down private farmers' markets and denounced the distributors of agricultural produce who earned sums far greater than ordinary workers. At the same time, he criticized managers of state enterprises for applying capitalist principles—favoring the production of higher-priced goods which earned more money for their firms over the production of goods needed for social projects—and "people who confuse income earned through work with what can be got through speculation." These practices had to be "rectified," Castro asserted, by returning to the fundamental principles of the Cuban Revolution. "There are some," he said, "who think that socialism can be brought about without political work . . . I believe that the problems must be resolved morally, honorably and with principles."[31]

To some extent, Cuba was able to reconcile the first goal—providing universal and quality health care and education, adequate affordable housing and food for everyone, and universal access to basic necessities such as electricity and clean water—with the second goal, developing a new Cuban morality, when its economy was productive and the Soviet Union provided large subsidies. Within twenty years of overthrowing the Batista regime, the revolutionary government had eradicated epidemic diseases and reduced the rate of infant mortality to the same level as the United States. Rural poverty essentially had been eliminated, in part because of a conscious effort to locate new production facilities in previously downtrodden areas, and to increase wages of agrarian workers and provide them with housing, roads, schools, health clinics, and electricity.[32] At the same time, the government attempted to instill a new morality by creating free boarding schools in the countryside. Students at these schools spent part of each day cultivating and harvesting crops. The intention was twofold: to break down urban prejudices about *campesinos* by integrating children in city and rural locales, and to induce a sense of responsibility for the common good by engaging in nonremunerated "social labor."[33]

The 1986 Rectification campaign began as the Soviet Union introduced *perestroika*, a restructuring of its economic planning process to place greater reliance on market mechanisms. Rectification was a pointed rejection of the Soviet model, and implicitly of Soviet leadership. Cuba's Communist Party leaders blamed the stagnation of Cuba's economy in the late 1970s and early 1980s on their own blind adherence to Soviet practices.[34]

Four factors mainly accounted for the early1970s growth spurt. First, a new generation of Cuban specialists had graduated from universities and were able to do the work of the professionals who departed in the early 1960s. Second, the world price for sugar jumped to historic levels—$0.70 per pound briefly in 1974—which enabled Cuba to earn hard currency from surplus sugar and to buy modern technology from European firms. Third, material incentives were introduced to spur productivity. Workers could increase their salaries by working overtime at higher wage rates, and more productive workers could earn the right to buy refrigerators, air conditioners, and other consumer durables. Fourth, in 1972 Cuba joined the Council for Mutual Economic Assistance (CMEA), the socialist trading bloc headed by the Soviet Union. Cuba was designated as a commodity producer for the CMEA countries, providing sugar, citrus, nickel, and cobalt to its new partners. In turn it was able to import machinery and manufactured goods from them at subsidized prices, defer loan repayments, and obtain new loans with low rates. Though the products from the Soviet Union and eastern European countries tended to be of low quality, they provided Cuban leaders with the means to begin an effort at diversifying the economy.

In both the 1968 and 1986 cases, Cuba's economic decisions were in part a reaction to pressures from the Soviet Union, and they reflected Castro's determination to maintain as much independence for Cuba as possible. But just as Cuba's special relationship with the United States from 1903 to 1959 created conditions which influenced the course of the Cuban Revolution, so its relationship with the Soviet Union from 1960 to 1991 reduced Castro's options.

FOREIGN RELATIONS AFTER 1959

Testing the Limits of Soviet Tolerance

Despite his reputation for rashness and braggadocio, Soviet Premier Nikita Khrushchev was quite wary about disturbing the United States in the Western Hemisphere. The Soviet Communist Party had ordered its affiliated parties in Latin America to distance themselves from any attempts to forcibly overthrow or destabilize their governments. Most Cuban communists, who were organized as the Popular Socialist Party before 1959, also followed this Moscow line and had little if any contact with the revolutionaries. The Soviets thus did not know much about Fidel Castro and the July 26th Movement, and they were not anxious to support rebels who would neither take orders from Moscow nor were likely to survive U.S. hostility. It took until February 1960 for a Soviet trade delegation to arrive in Havana, though it was a prominent one, headed by Deputy Premier Anastas Mikoyan. Shortly afterwards the two countries reestablished diplomatic relations, which Batista had broken in 1952.

In the spring of 1960 the Soviets began to supply Cuba with a few light arms, artillery and mortars, tanks, anti-aircraft rockets, and technical assistance. But only after the Bay of Pigs invasion, when it was clear the revolutionary government had popular support and staying power, did the Soviets promise to send more sophisticated weapons.[35] Of greater importance, when President Dwight Eisenhower barred any further U.S. importation of Cuban sugar in July 1960, the Soviet Union purchased the sugar that Cuba had expected to export to the United States. This began a trading relationship in which Cuba remained dependent largely on its production of sugar. By the 1980s, sugar export earnings from sales to the Soviet Union and Eastern European countries accounted for approximately the same percentage of total exports as they had to the United States in the 1950s.[36] In addition, Soviet sales of petroleum to Cuba at below market prices were a form of foreign assistance on which Cuba came to depend.

Still, Cuba's relations with the Soviet Union were never as congenial as U.S. officials and the western media portrayed them. In fact, tension between the two countries was so great in 1968 that Raúl Castro publicly charged Aníbal Escalante with treason for conspiring with Soviet officials—presumably with the approval of Soviet leaders—to replace Fidel Castro as first secretary of the Cuban Communist Party. Escalante had been in the Popular Socialist Party leadership prior to 1959, and had maintained close ties to Moscow party officials in the 1960s.

The bitterness that Cuba's leaders felt towards the Soviet Union can be traced to October 28, 1962, the day on which the Cuban missile crisis is commonly said to have ended with an understanding between the U.S. and Soviet heads of state. (The so-called Kennedy-Khrushchev agreement stipulated that the Soviets would withdraw all offensive weapons from Cuba, and the United States would pledge not to invade or support an invasion of Cuba.) The Cubans interpreted the agreement as a Soviet capitulation to U.S. threats, and judged that the Soviet Union would be unwilling in the future to put itself at risk to protect Cuba. "We realized how alone we would be in the event of a war," Castro remarked in a speech to the first full meeting of the Communist Party's Central Committee in January 1968. From the Cuban perspective, the Soviet Union had made Cuba even more vulnerable than before the missile crisis. Not only had the Soviets signaled to the United States that its guarantee of protecting Cuba was hollow, but Khrushchev also was asking Cuba to return weapons to the Soviets that the Cubans believed were necessary for their defense. Castro's palpable contempt was evident in 1968 as he characterized the Soviet leaders as "feeble-minded bureaucrats."[37]

After the missile crisis, the two countries locked horns on several issues, as Castro tried to demonstrate that Cuba could not be controlled by a domineering Soviet Union. In 1963, despite Soviet requests, Cuba refused to sign both the Limited Test Ban Treaty and the Tlatelolco Treaty, which declared Latin America as a nuclear-free zone. Guevara, speaking on behalf of the Cuban government at a 1965 conference in Algeria, castigated the Soviets for their regressive ideological views and for their immorality in not adequately supporting liberation movements.[38] In January 1966, Cuba frontally challenged the Soviet Union's claim to be the natural leader of the Third World. It brought together five hundred delegates from Africa, Asia, and Latin America at the first Tricontinental Conference, to initiate an organization that would be dedicated to promoting and supporting armed liberation struggles on the three continents. Soviet leaders had repeatedly admonished Castro to back away from supporting armed struggle. As retribution for their imperious warning, Castro did not invite any communist parties to be represented at the conference. Then in October 1967, Guevara was killed fighting against the Bolivian government. It was a terrible blow to Castro, who blamed his comrade's death on the Bolivian Communist Party, and by implication on their Soviet puppet masters.[39]

Cuba Joins the Socialist Camp

At that point, though, Castro recognized that Cuba and the Soviet Union had come close to a breaking point. He had no other options but to reduce the tension and cease his open challenges to Soviet leadership. This was underscored by a Soviet decision to provide Cuba with less oil in 1968 than it was expecting to receive. On January 2, 1968, Castro reported that troublesome news to the Cuban people. In the first instance, he said, the shortfall would require new controls on the use of gasoline, great efforts to conserve oil, and a reliance on alternative sources of fuel to run sugar mills. But he held out the hope that the hardships would be temporary, lasting for at most three years. By achieving the goal of a ten-million-ton sugar harvest in 1970, he asserted, Cuba would earn enough hard currency to be self-reliant. It would no longer need to make undignified, "incessant requests" for advance shipments of oil. The ten-million-ton harvest thus embodied a political goal as well as an economic one. Cuba could truly be independent if the plan were successful.[40]

As a consequence, virtually the entire economy was subordinated to the task of meeting this target, which would have been a record harvest. Ultimately, some 8.5 million tons were gathered. Although that also set a record, it represented a pyrrhic victory. Several other sectors of the economy suffered major losses, because so many workers had been diverted from their regular jobs to harvest sugar, and scarce resources were directed towards achieving the singular goal. The failure of the ten-million-ton campaign led directly to Cuba's decision to become a junior partner in the CMEA.

As Cuba tied its economic planning more closely to the Soviet Union, it also began to link its armed forces and intelligence services to the corresponding Soviet agencies. Despite such integration, though, Cuba took its own counsel on foreign policy. Most scholars have concluded that Cuba was neither a puppet of nor a stalking horse for the Soviet Union. While Cuba's choices often coincided with Soviet interests, there were several notable disagreements between the two countries. In early November 1975, Cuba sent the first contingent of what would be a thirty-five-thousand-soldier deployment to Angola, to support the Popular Movement for the Liberation of Angola (MPLA), one of the three parties already engaged in a civil war to determine who would rule the country after independence. Castro did not inform Soviet leaders about the Cuban troop movement, fearing that they were likely to oppose it. Indeed, the Soviets were not pleased, because their first priority was advancing détente with the United States. Soviet-Cuban engagement in the Angolan civil war, they accurately guessed, was likely to upend delicate negotiations with the United States, which was backing the forces opposed to the MPLA.[41]

In contrast, Third World countries—especially those in Africa—lavished praise on the Cubans. Cuba's support for the MPLA, and its willingness to fight against the apartheid regime in South Africa, was a key reason that the Nonaligned Movement (NAM) selected Cuba to be the location for its 1979 summit. The host country also serves as chair of the NAM until the next summit, and Castro saw this as an opportunity to forge unity among poorer countries of the world. He planned to encourage oil-rich countries in the "South" to use their resources for South-South cooperative programs, which he viewed as an essential step to reduce their dependency on the advanced industrial nations.

Cuba's Internationalism

The divergent Soviet and Cuban perspectives—one from the vantage point of a small nation and the other from the vantage point of a superpower—were painfully evident to Castro in December 1979, when the Soviet Union invaded Afghanistan. The invasion vitiated Cuba's ability to serve as an effective NAM leader, because Afghanistan was a NAM member and nonintervention was a core NAM principle. Castro had not even been informed in advance about the intervention. But he felt constrained to support the Soviet action by not condemning it, which was a position exactly opposite the one that NAM countries expected their chair to take. The asymmetry between Cuba and the Soviet Union, which had contributed to their friction in the 1960s, continued to generate tension for the next twelve years, until the Soviet Union collapsed.[42]

In particular, disagreements over support for liberation struggles in Central America and southern Africa during the 1980s led to public displays of hostility. For example, Castro did not attend the 1985 funeral of Soviet President Konstantin Chernenko, to show his displeasure with the low level of support the Soviet Union was providing the Sandinista government in Nicaragua.[43]

Cuba's commitments to the MPLA's victory in Angola, to the success of the Southwest Africa People's Organization in its struggle for Namibia's independence, and to the consolidation of Sandinista rule in Nicaragua, were not based on expedient short-term calculations or spontaneous bursts of revolutionary zeal.[44] They developed slowly, starting in the 1960s, and were deeply rooted in the Cuban revolutionaries' belief that internationalism served Cuba's immediate and long-term interests. In the short term, Cuba's military contributions to liberation struggles, technical assistance to newly independent states, and education and health care to people from the Third World would generate goodwill and needed allies. Ultimately, as more countries shared Cuba's views, its internationalism would have contributed to the creation of stronger South-South coalitions. As political scientist Michael Erisman explains in his chapter in this volume, such coalitions could effectively reduce each country's vulnerability and enable them to implement policies that support a "counterdependency politics."

Internationalism also brought ordinary Cubans into contact with the deep poverty many Third World people suffer, and so new generations of Cubans who had no memory of the 1950s would gain an appreciation for the achievements of the revolution. By the mid-1980s, approximately 15,000 Cubans—1 out of every 625—were working in civilian foreign-aid missions in more than thirty countries. At the same time, twenty-four thousand students from eighty-two countries were enrolled in Cuban high schools and universities.[45]

Challenging the United States

It may be impossible, now, to deconstruct the ideological underpinnings of U.S. policy toward the Cuban Revolution in the early years. Conventional wisdom holds that the policy was shaped by Cold War ideology. Washington was in the grip of a Cold War mindset that framed foreign policy decisions in terms of a bipolar, zero-sum view of the world: a country was either for the United States or for its enemy, the Soviet Union. There was no room for an independent country of the sort Cuba hoped to be.

Cuba did not even establish diplomatic relations with the Soviet Union during the first year after the revolution. But U.S. policymakers still were worried about the revolutionary government, in part because of its charismatic chief, Fidel Castro. Vice President Richard Nixon reported in a confidential memo, after his April 1959 meeting with Castro, that the Cuban leader "has those indefinable qualities which make him a leader of men. Whatever we may think of him he is going to be a great factor in the development of Cuba and very possibly in Latin American affairs generally."[46]

By the end of the year, the Central Intelligence Agency was developing schemes to assassinate Castro and overthrow the Cuban government.[47] In a November 1959 memo to President Dwight Eisenhower, Secretary of State Christian Herter provided the justification for the subversive plans. Cuba threatened the United States, he observed, because Castro "has veered towards a 'neutralist' anti-American foreign policy for Cuba which, if emulated by other Latin American countries, would have serious adverse effects on Free World support of our leadership."[48]

In effect, Cuba challenged the legitimacy of U.S. dominance in the Western Hemisphere. Castro made his opposition to U.S. leadership explicit in September 1960, openly proclaiming Cuba's duty to make revolution in the hemisphere. But his "First Declaration of Havana" came four days after the Organization of American States (OAS) approved the Declaration of San Jose (August 28, 1960), in which the hemisphere's foreign ministers implicitly condemned Cuba for permitting Soviet and Chinese "extra-continental intervention" that "endangers American solidarity and security."[49] Whether the initial concern, then, was over the apparent threat to U.S. hemispheric hegemony or was in fact the so-called Soviet threat, Cold War assumptions had gained full rein over U.S. policy by mid-1960. There was no longer any question as to whether Cuba was in the Soviet camp, because the two countries had negotiated a trade agreement in February and reestablished diplomatic relations in the spring.

At this point Cuba was not yet ruled by a Communist Party. Castro first declared the character of the Cuban Revolution to be "socialist" only on the eve of the 1961 Bay of Pigs invasion. Within months of the failed U.S.-sponsored attack, Kennedy authorized the CIA to undertake a more ambitious effort to overthrow the revolutionary regime. Code-named Operation Mongoose, the project had four components: (1) terrorism—CIA agents and assets based in Florida would conduct raids in Cuba to sabotage factory equipment, burn down fields, contaminate processed sugar, and provide weapons to counterrevolutionaries who would undertake their own "military" actions; (2) political isolation—the United States was able to pressure enough OAS members in January 1962 to gain the necessary votes to suspend Cuba from the organization; (3) economic strangulation—in February 1962 Kennedy instituted a full embargo on all transactions between Cuba and the United States, including food and medicine; (4) military intimidation—the U.S. Navy conducted several unusually large exercises in the Caribbean in 1962, including one which involved the practice invasion of an island named "Ortsac," that is, "Castro" spelled backward. There was also an associated project, which ran concurrently with Mongoose, to assassinate Castro.[50] Castro interpreted all of this activity as a certain prelude to a U.S. invasion. He sought Soviet assistance to defend Cuba, and Khrushchev offered ballistic missiles. The resulting October 1962 missile crisis confirmed the Kennedy administration's worst fears about how the Soviet-Cuban connection could undermine U.S. security. Subsequently, Cuba's supposed threat to the United States, because of its close ties to the other superpower, remained a core assumption of U.S. policy until the Soviet Union imploded in 1991.[51]

Still, there were three brief periods during the Cold War when the glimmerings of a U.S.-Cuban *modus vivendi* surfaced. In 1963, Kennedy used unofficial emissaries to probe the possibility of restoring relations between the two countries. But these efforts ended shortly after Johnson became president. In 1974, Secretary of State Henry Kissinger initiated secret negotiations between U.S. and Cuban officials aimed at what appeared to be a normalization of relations. The next year, as a signal of good faith, the United States voted with a majority of members in the OAS to lift the 1964 hemispheric-wide embargo against Cuba. President Gerald Ford then relaxed the U.S. embargo to permit subsidiaries of U.S. corporations in third countries to trade with Cuba.[52] Cuba's response to the conciliatory U.S. moves, Kissinger believed, was decidedly hostile. He viewed its support for the MPLA in Angola later that year as an assault on U.S.-Soviet detente. In December 1975, President Gerald Ford announced that Cuba's Angola operation "destroys any opportunity for improvement of relations with the United States."[53]

The third opening occurred during the first two years of the Carter administration. Shortly after his inauguration President Jimmy Carter expressed a hope to alleviate tensions between Cuba and the United States.[54] A few weeks later, Carter announced that he would not renew the ban on travel to Cuba by U.S. citizens, and that U.S. citizens would be permitted to spend money in Cuba related to their travel. He also approved negotiations with Cuba over maritime boundaries and fishing rights, and an agreement was finalized in April 1977. In September the two countries opened diplomatic missions in each others' capitals.

However, by mid-1978 the Cold War intruded again. Cuba had deployed more than twenty thousand troops to Ethiopia to support that country's conflict with Somalia over the Ogaden desert. While not enamored of Somalia, U.S. officials were concerned that the Cuban presence in Ethiopia would provide a foothold for the Soviet Union on the horn of Africa. Moreover, Carter's national security adviser, Zbigniew Brzezinski, relentlessly urged the president to interpret Cuban behavior in terms of the Cold War, because he believed that the Soviets were using the Cubans as a "military proxy" in Africa to serve their own expansionist aims.[55] Carter acknowledged in his memoir the influence Brzezinski had on his thinking: "Originally from Poland, he [Brzezinski] had made a special study of the Soviet Union and Eastern Europe. . . . I was an eager student, and took full advantage of what Brzezinski had to offer."[56]

As the president began to adopt Brzezinski's worldview, he painted himself into rhetorical corners, quickly responding to each new Cuban "challenge" with a tough stance, even when the reality turned out to contradict his allegations. Wayne Smith, who was in charge of the State Department's Cuba desk at the time, recalls that in 1978 and 1979 Cuba made sincere efforts to be cooperative, but these were rebuffed.[57] On October 4, 1979, Carter issued PD-52, a presidential directive which ordered key national security agencies to devise ways "to contain Cuba as a source of violent revolutionary change."

Thus when President Ronald Reagan took office, the U.S. hostility towards Cuba that already was in place provided firm ground from which to launch a more threatening policy. Secretary of State Alexander Haig established the tougher orientation in February 1981, asserting that the United States must "deal with the immediate source of the problem [in El Salvador]—and that is Cuba."[58] Cuba took the threat seriously. It responded by creating a 1.5-million-person "Territorial Troop Militia" to defend the island with a Swiss-like strategy of a "people in arms."[59] In fact, the Reagan policy offered more continuity than change. The U.S. president tightened the embargo, launched *Radio Martí*, a station which transmitted propaganda broadcasts to the island, and generally closed the door to any discussions with Cuban officials. However, the United States did engage in negotiations with

Cuba about migration issues in 1984, and it acceded to Cuba's presence at multi-party talks in 1988 that ended the fighting in Namibia.

After 1988, Cuba's significance as a U.S. national security threat largely disappeared. With the danger gone, the rationale for U.S. policy toward Cuba evaporated. To President George H. W. Bush, the change meant that Cuba was no longer a foreign policy issue. It had become a domestic policy on which he had to placate a tenacious ethnic lobby. And so he turned the policy over to Congress, where the Cuban American National Foundation (CANF) had gained considerable clout.

Before the 1980s, the Cuban exile community played only a small role in shaping U.S. policy. Anti-Castro Cubans did not have an organization that operated in the commonly accepted manner of other ethnic lobbies until 1981, when CANF was founded with the assistance and encouragement of Reagan administration officials.[60] Structured much like the effective American Israel Public Affairs Committee (AIPAC), CANF received guidance from AIPAC to broaden its focus beyond Cuba. At the time there were just over one million people in the United States who were born in Cuba or were of Cuban descent. Largely concentrated in south Florida and northern New Jersey, they could not hope to influence policy merely by the power of their votes in a few congressional districts. Moreover, even then the Cuban-American community did not have a monolithic position on U.S. policy towards Cuba. Notably, in 1978 a group of Cuban Americans formed The Committee of 75, to engage in a "dialogue" with Cuban officials on behalf of Cubans in exile. The Committee focused on humanitarian issues, such as the release of political prisoners and the right of Cubans outside of the country to return for family visits. Beginning in 1979, the Cuban government granted visas to people entering Cuba to see families; more than one hundred thousand Cuban Americans visited the island in 1979–80.[61]

Beyond Cuban Americans' votes, CANF relied on campaign contributions shrewdly spent by its political action committee, and the power of a few well-placed senators and representatives who valued CANF's support, to influence Congress. As the Special Period started, CANF had effectively gained control of U.S. policy, and was determined to restructure the policy in order to push the revolutionary regime into the abyss toward which it was tipping.

THE NEW CUBAN REVOLUTION

In the roughly 120 years prior to the Special Period, from 1868 to 1990, Cuba went through several stages of decolonization. The first thirty-year period involved the destruction of Spanish colonialism's bonds. But as Marc Frey, Ronald Preussen, and Tan Tai Yong demonstrate with case studies of Southeast Asian decolonization, formal independence is only a first step. They explain that

> decolonization in Southeast Asia is best regarded as a process . . . that did not end with transfers of formal power in the 1940s, 1950s and 1960s. Cultural emancipation and economic developments, for instance, should be seen as integral parts of a transition to postcolonial orders—and steps in these directions have had complex and open-ended timelines.[62]

For Cuba, the five decades after formal independence were marked by the struggle against a neocolonial relationship with the United States. Both economically and politically, Cuba was dependent on its northern neighbor, unable to chart its own future. Governments rose and fell based on the blessings of Washington. Prosperity depended upon trade and investment from the United States. Breaking these bonds of informal subordination was high on the agenda of Fidel Castro and his revolutionaries when they seized power in 1959, but the road to real national independence proved harder than any of them anticipated. For the Cuban economy to survive the severing of economic ties to the United States, it needed a new patron to buy its sugar and provide it with manufactured goods. For the Cuban state to survive the antagonism of successive governments in Washington, it needed a new ally to provide it with military assistance. But as Cuba forged a new relationship with the Soviet Union, it discovered that its freedom of action was still encumbered by the legacies of colonialism and neocolonialism. The Soviets were a more distant partner, less able to direct Cuba's destiny, but Soviet patronage was not without its price. The collapse of the Soviet Union made clear the continuing weakness of Cuba's monocultural export economy and its vulnerability to the United States.

In this sense, the Special Period, for all its pain, marked the first time since colonization that Cuba stood as a fully free and independent country, no longer dependent on the patronage of a major power. Now that Cuba's economy has largely recovered from the trauma of the Soviet collapse, the Special Period is coming to a close. Cuba stands at the beginning of a new period, defined by the challenges of exploring new possibilities for economic development and managing a political transition from the generation that made the revolution to a group of leaders born after 1959. For good or ill, the choices Cubans will make are more likely than ever before to be their own.

NOTES

1. Jorge I. Domínguez, "Cuba's Economic Transition: Successes, Deficiencies, and Challenges," in *The Cuban Economy at the Start of the Twenty-First Century*, ed. Jorge I. Domínguez, Omar Everleny Pérez Villanueva, and Lorena Barberia (Cambridge: Harvard University Press, 2004), 19.

2. There were an estimated 112,000 natives on the island in 1492, and fewer than 3,000 by the mid-1550s. Louis A. Pérez, *Cuba: Between Reform and Revolution* (New York: Oxford University Press, 1995), 30.

3. For example, see "Discursos pronunciados en el Acto Solemne, el 20 de Junio del 2002. Intervención de Ricardo Alarcón de Quesada, Presidente de la Asamblea Nacional del Poder Popular," www.cuba.cu/gobierno/documentos/2002/esp/a200602e.html (accessed February 10, 2007).

4. Louis A. Pérez, Jr., *Cuba and the United States: Ties of Singular Intimacy* (Athens: University of Georgia Press, 1990), 80–81.

5. Jules Robert Benjamin, *The United States and Cuba: Hegemony and Dependent Development, 1880–1934* (Pittsburgh, Pa.: University of Pittsburgh Press, 1977), 4–5; Pérez, *Cuba and the United States*, 61.

6. Louis A. Pérez, Jr., *Cuba between Empires, 1878–1902* (Pittsburgh, Pa.: University of Pittsburgh Press, 1983), 138.

7. Carlos Alzugaray Treto, "Is Normalization Possible in Cuban-U.S. Relations after 100 Years of History?" Research Report No. 6 (Havana: Instituto Superior de Relaciones Internacionales, 2002), n.p., also at www.isri.cu/Paginas/Investigaciones/Investigaciones/Investigaciones06.htm (accessed February 10, 2007).

8. Pérez, *Cuba: Between Reform and Revolution*, 192.

9. Lars Schoultz, *Beneath the United States: A History of U.S. Policy toward Latin America* (Cambridge: Harvard University Press, 1998), 145.

10. Schoultz, *Beneath the United States*, 148.

11. Leland Hamilton Jenks, *Our Cuban Colony: A Study in Sugar* (New York: Vanguard Press, 1928), 286.

12. Thomas G. Paterson, *Contesting Castro: The United States and the Triumph of the Cuban Revolution* (New York: Oxford University Press, 1994), 35; Leland Johnson, "U.S. Business Interests in Cuba and the Rise of Castro," *World Politics* 17, no. 3 (1965): 443, 453; Robin Blackburn, "Prologue to the Cuban Revolution," *New Left Review*, no. 21 (October 1963): 59–60.

13. Louis A. Pérez, Jr., *On Becoming Cuban: Identity, Nationality and Culture* (Chapel Hill: University of North Carolina Press, 1999), 7, 157.

14. As quoted in Luis E. Aguilar, *Cuba 1933: Prologue to Revolution* (New York: Norton, 1972), 163–64.

15. Julia E. Sweig, *Inside the Cuban Revolution* (Cambridge: Harvard University Press, 2002), 165–82.

16. "Program Manifesto of the 26th of July Movement," in *Cuba in Revolution*, ed., Rolando E. Bonachea and Nelson P. Valdés (Garden City, N.Y.: Anchor Books, 1972), 113–40.

17. Lourdes Casal, "Race Relations in Contemporary Cuba," in *The Cuba Reader: The Making of a Revolutionary Society*, ed. Philip Brenner, William M. LeoGrande, Donna Rich, and Daniel Siegel (New York: Grove Press, 1989), 475; Alejandro de la Fuente, "Recreating Racism: Race and Discrimination in Cuba's Special Period," in this volume.

18. Casal, "Race Relations in Contemporary Cuba," 477.

19. Saul Landau, "Asking the Right Questions about Cuba," in *The Cuba Reader*, xxiii.

20. Pérez, *On Becoming Cuban*, 482.

21. James G. Blight and Peter Kornbluh, eds., *The Politics of Illusion: The Bay of Pigs Invasion Reexamined* (Boulder, CO: Lynne Rienner, 1998), 10–13; Jorge I. Domínguez, *Cuba: Order and Revolution* (Cambridge: Harvard University Press, 1978), 345–46.

22. Brig. Gen. Lansdale, "Review of Operation Mongoose," Memorandum for the Special Group (Augmented), 25 July 1962, Office of the Secretary of Defense, declassified January 5, 1989, 8, in *The Cuban Missile Crisis 1962: A National Security Archive Documents Reader*, ed. Laurence Chang and Peter Kornbluh (New York: New Press, 1992), 47.

23. Domínguez, *Cuba: Order and Revolution*, 253.

24. Larry Oberg, "The Status of Gays in Cuba: Myth and Reality," in this volume; Domínguez, *Cuba: Order and Revolution*, 356–57.

25. William Luis, "Exhuming *Lunes de Revolución*," *CR: The New Centennial Review* 2, no. 2 (Summer 2002): 254–57.

26. "Discurso Pronunciado por el Comandante Fidel Castro Ruz, Primer Ministro del Gobierno Revolucionario y Secretario del PURSC, Como Conclusión de las Reuniones con los Intelectuales Cubanos, Efectuadas en la Biblioteca Nacional el 16, 23 y 30 de Junio de 1961," www.cuba.cu/gobierno/discursos/1961/esp/f300661e.html (accessed February 14, 2007).

27. Susan Eckstein and Lorena Barberia, "Cuban Americans and Their Transnational Ties," in this volume; Felix Roberto Masud-Piloto, *From Welcomed Exiles to Illegal Immigrants: Cuban Migration to the U.S., 1959–1995* (Lanham, Md.: Rowman and Littlefield, 1996), 58–59.

28. Ernesto Che Guevara, "Man and Socialism in Cuba," in *Man and Socialism in Cuba: The Great Debate*, ed. Bertram Silverman (New York: Atheneum, 1971), 343–44.

29. Bertam Silverman, "Introduction: The Great Debate in Retrospect: Economic Rationality and the Ethics of Revolution," in Silverman, *Man and Socialism in Cuba* (New York: Atheneum, 1971), 15.

30. Fidel Castro, "Speech Delivered on March 13, 1968, at Ceremonies Marking the 11th Anniversary of the Attack on the Presidential Palace, at the University of Havana," in *Fidel Castro Speaks*, ed. Martin Kenner and James Petras (New York: Grove Press, 1969), 271, 283.

31. Fidel Castro, "Speech Delivered on the 25th Anniversary of the Bay of Pigs Victory, April 19, 1986," in *Cuban Revolution Reader: A Documentary History*, ed. Julio García Luis (Melbourne, Australia: Ocean Press, 2001), 243–45.

32. Susan Eva Eckstein, *Back from the Future: Cuba under Castro* (Princeton, N.J.: Princeton University Press, 1994), 129–37, 151–54.

33. Marvin Leiner, "Cuba's Schools: Twenty-Five Years Later," in *Cuba: Twenty-Five Years of Revolution, 1959–1984*, ed. Sandor Halebsky and John M. Kirk (New York: Praeger, 1985), 27–36.

34. Max Azicri, *Cuba Today and Tomorrow: Reinventing Socialism* (Gainesville: University Press of Florida, 2000), 24–31, 55–59; Eckstein, *Back from the Future*, 41–47.

35. Carlos Lechuga, *In the Eye of the Storm: Castro, Khrushchev, Kennedy and the Missile Crisis*, trans. Mary Todd (Melbourne, Australia: Ocean Press, 1995), 18; Aleksandr Fursenko and Timothy Naftali, *One Hell of a Gamble: Khrushchev, Castro, and Kennedy, 1958–1964* (New York: W.W. Norton, 1997), 146.

36. Marifeli Pérez-Stable, *The Cuban Revolution: Origins, Course, and Legacy*, 2nd ed. (New York: Oxford University Press, 1999), 88.

37. James G. Blight and Philip Brenner, *Sad and Luminous Days: Cuba's Struggle with the Superpowers after the Missile Crisis* (Lanham, Md.: Rowman and Littlefield, 2007), 36, 60.

38. Ernesto (Che) Guevara, "Speech in Algiers to the Second Seminar of the Organization of Afro-Asian Solidarity, February 25, 1965," in *Che Guevara Speaks*, ed., George Lavan (New York: Pathfinder Press, 1967), 107–8.

39. Fidel Castro, "A Necessary Introduction," in *El Diario del Che en Bolivia* (Havana: Editora Política, 1987), xvii–xviii.

40. Departamento de Versiones Taquigraficas del Gobierno Revolucionario, "Discurso Pronunciado por el Comandante Fidel Castro Ruz, al Conmemorarse el IX Aniversario del Triunfo de la Revolución, en la Plaza de la Revolución, el 2 de Enero de 1968," www.cuba.cu/gobierno/discursos/1968/esp/f020168e.html (accessed on February 17, 2007).

41. Piero Gleijeses, *Conflicting Missions: Havana, Washington, and Africa, 1959–1976* (Chapel Hill: University of North Carolina Press, 2002), 260, 305–7.

42. Mervyn J. Bain, "Cuba-Soviet Relations in the Gorbachev Era," *Journal of Latin American Studies* 37 (2005): 773–76.

43. William M. LeoGrande, "Cuba," in *Confronting Revolution: Security through Diplomacy in Central America*, ed. Morris Blachman, William M. LeoGrande, and Kenneth Sharpe (New York: Pantheon, 1986), 253.

44. William M. LeoGrande, *Our Own Backyard: The United States in Central America, 1977–1992* (Chapel Hill: University of North Carolina Press, 1998), 15, 24–25. Eckstein, *Back from the Future*, 186–88.

45. Jorge I. Domínguez, *To Make a World Safe for Revolution: Cuban Foreign Policy* (Cambridge: Harvard University Press, 1989), 171–75; H. Michael Erisman, *Cuba's Foreign Relations in a Post-Soviet World* (Gainesville: University Press of Florida, 2000), 98–99.

46. Richard M. Nixon, "Rough Draft of Summary of Conversation between the Vice-President and Fidel Castro," April 25, 1959, reprinted in Jeffrey J. Safford, "The Nixon-Castro Meeting of 19 April 1959," *Diplomatic History* 4, no. 4 (Fall 1980): 431.

47. Peter Kornbluh, "Introduction: History Held Hostage," in *Bay of Pigs Declassified*, ed. Peter Kornbluh (New York: New Press, 1998), 9; Paterson, *Contesting Castro*, 258.

48. U.S. Department of State, "Memorandum from the Secretary of State to the President: Current Basic United States Policy toward Cuba," *Foreign Relations of the United States, 1958–1960*, Volume VI: Cuba (Washington, D.C.: Government Printing Office, 1991), Doc. No. 387, 657.

49. "First Declaration of Havana," in *Cuban Revolution Reader: A Documentary History of 40 Key Moments of the Cuban Revolution*, ed., Julio García Luis (Melbourne, Australia: Ocean Press, 2001), 45–51.

50. Blight and Brenner, *Sad and Luminous Days*, 16–18, 155–56.

51. McGeorge Bundy, "Memorandum for the Record," in *Foreign Relations of the United States, 1961–1963*, Vol. XI: Cuban Missile Crisis and Aftermath (Washington, D.C.: Government Printing Office, 1997), Doc. No. 377, 889; Gregory F. Treverton, "Cuba in U.S. Security Perspective," in *U.S.-Cuban Relations in the 1990s*, ed. Jorge I. Domínguez and Rafael Hernández (Boulder, Colo.: Westview, 1989), 71.

52. Peter Kornbluh, "JFK & Castro: The Secret Quest for Accommodation," *Cigar Aficionado*, September/October, 1999; Peter Kornbluh and James G. Blight, "Dialogue with Castro: A Hidden History," *New York Review of Books*, October 6, 1994.

53. Henry Kissinger, *Years of Renewal* (New York: Simon & Schuster, 1999), 785–87; "Ford Says Angola Acts Hurt Detente, Cuba Tie," *New York Times*, December 21, 1975, 3.

54. Austin Scott, "Carter Outlines Basis for Better Ties with Cuba," *Washington Post*, February 17, 1977.

55. Zbigniew Brzezinksi, *Power and Principle: Memoirs of the National Security Adviser, 1977–1981*, rev. ed. (New York: Farrar, Straus, and Giroux, 1985), 180–90.

56. Jimmy Carter, *Keeping Faith: Memoirs of a President* (New York: Bantam Books, 1982), 51.

57. Wayne S. Smith, *The Closest of Enemies: A Personal and Diplomatic Account of U.S.-Cuban Relations since 1957* (New York: Norton, 1987), 128–40, 141–42.

58. Richard Halloran, "From Washington and El Salvador, Differing Views on Fighting Rebels," *New York Times*, February 21, 1981.

59. Philip Brenner, "Change and Continuity in Cuban Foreign Policy," in *The Cuba Reader*, ed. Brenner, LeoGrande, Rich, and Siegel (New York: Grove Press, 1989), 263–265.

60. Patrick J. Haney and Walt Vanderbush, *The Cuban Embargo: The Domestic Politics of an American Foreign Policy* (Pittsburgh, Pa.: University of Pittsburgh Press, 2005), 32–36.

61. Masud-Piloto, *From Welcomed Exiles to Illegal Immigrants*, 73–78.

62. Marc Frey, Ronald W. Pruessen, and Tan Tai Yong, "Introduction," in *The Transformation of Southeast Asia: International Perspectives on Decolonization*, ed. Marc Frey, Ronald W. Pruessen, and Tan Tai Yong (Armonk, N.Y.: M.E. Sharpe, 2003), viii.

PART I

FIDEL CASTRO AND THE CUBAN REVOLUTION

There is a tendency in the United States to personalize foreign policy. The complexities of another country seem easier to understand when they are reduced to the characteristics of one person. Consider the way U.S. presidents regarded Iraq as if it were merely the personification of Saddam Hussein, or how Venezuela has been transformed into little more than Hugo Chávez.

Similarly, U.S. officials, the U.S. media, and many Americans have embodied Cuba in the person of Fidel Castro. Of course, an accurate analysis of Cuba during the Special Period must give Fidel Castro his due. The very maintenance and evolution of the Cuban Revolution since 1991 have been entwined with his leadership. But Nelson Valdés and Saul Landau explain, in the two articles which follow, that however important Castro has been during the last fifty years, the revolution was not merely a reflection of Castro's personality and personal predilections. It grew from below, was shaped by the relationship between leaders and followers, and was constrained by both the circumstances in which the country found itself and the pressures it experienced from outside.

Valdés and Landau have closely studied the transformation of Cuba and Fidel Castro from nearly the beginning of the 1959 Revolution. Both view Castro as "a larger than life leader"—as Landau evocatively describes him—as the kind of person whom sociologist Max Weber depicted in developing the political notion of "charisma" more than one hundred years ago. Moreover, both stress that Castro's charisma bears little relation to the "packaging and marketing of U.S. politicians as commodities or brands," as Valdés notes, or to the way U.S. politicians communicate with the electorate via television.

Valdés focuses on the content of the Cuban Revolution, and observes that Castro's charismatic authority has depended on the values he espoused and the policies he helped to implement. These reflected a moral code which had emerged from a popular politics on the island and a particular moment in Cuban history. That morality defined the essence of Castro's charisma, and has been more important than his personality or style.

Castro has often been denigrated as merely another Latin America *caudillo*. But in fact he did institutionalize his charisma and develop what Valdés calls "double charisma"—a situation where one leader continues to mobilize and inspire the populace while a second leader develops his own authority through the institutions created by his larger-than-life partner. Raúl Castro was the second leader, and the legitimacy of his authority was one reason the transition in power after July 31, 2006, was so uneventful.

Landau also emphasizes that Castro's ability to lead cannot be separated from the content of the policies he pursued or from its historical context. But contemporary Cubans have experienced a history quite different from the one that the Moncada generation knew. A new Cuba requires new relationships, Landau contends, which would be based less on charismatic leadership than on full political participation by all Cubans.

❶

The Revolutionary
and Political Content of
Fidel Castro's Charismatic Authority

Nelson P. Valdés

Fidel, Fidel, que tiene Fidel que los americanos no pueden con él.

Chant by crowd, September 28, 1960, Revolution Square

Fidel Castro and "the Cuban Revolution" have often been characterized as one and the same. Many writers have asserted that he was the revolution, and so the revolution was little more than the embodiment of his personal qualities. Understandably, then, Fidel Castro's personality has been a central topic in the study of Cuba's changing political, economic and social processes since 1959. In effect, such analyses focused attention on the man while ignoring the policies that his exercise of power produced.

This chapter departs from that conventional wisdom. It proposes that Fidel Castro's charismatic authority has been entwined with both the revolutionary changes he fostered and the context in which his leadership unfolded. His charismatic authority would not have been possible without the revolutionary practices which the Cuban populace embraced.

The approach here avoids the often subtle denigration of Cubans which most studies of Fidel Castro's personality and character inevitably convey. They suggest that Cubans have a predilection for personalistic politics, in contrast to the more "advanced" Europeans and North Americans who support political institutions. Consider, for example, Raymond Duncan's claim that "Cuban party history, like that of its sister republics, reflects the importance of personalities (personalism) endemic to Latin American politics, where charismatic leadership and the role of individual leaders, rather than the party ideology or platform, guide political action."[1]

Even if such descriptions were valid, they do not constitute explanations. An analysis of political leadership should begin with the larger social and cultural matrix within which it is embedded; otherwise, we descend into reliance on such questionable premises as traits inherent in a group, class, or nation. What informs personalism or *caudillismo*? Since culture is not a thing unto itself, one cannot treat such matters as "givens" or by-products of national character or Cuban cultural essentialism.

DEFINITION OF CHARISMA

Max Weber was the first to use the concept of charisma in a systematic way, and his approach continues to be widely accepted. "The term charisma," he wrote, "will be applied to a certain quality of an individual personality by virtue of which he is set apart from ordinary men and treated as endowed with supernatural, superhuman, or at least specifically exceptional powers or qualities." According to Weber such qualities were "not accessible to the ordinary person, but are regarded as of divine origin or as exemplary, and on the basis of them the individual concerned is treated as a leader."[2]

Charisma implies a social relation between leader and followers. Ian Robertson appropriately notes that charisma is "an extraordinary attribute of individuals that enables its possessors to lead and inspire without the necessity of formal authority."[3] The question, then, is what are the circumstances which convince people to follow a charismatic leader? Is the special social relation followers have with such a leader disclosed to them by some supernatural agency, or is the trust of the followers earned by the person who becomes a charismatic leader? Here lies the profound difference between a description of charismatic leadership which asserts that the essence of charismatic leadership lies solely in a leader's extraordinary inherent qualities, and a description which assumes that a follower accepts the leadership of a charismatic individual because of the leader's actions and the consequences of that behavior. Such consequences depend on their context, as Weber explains in asserting that charismatic authority can emerge only under special circumstances.

Charismatic leadership becomes a possibility in times of institutional crisis and breakdown. The unique circumstance which leads to the disappearance of political authority based on a codified legal-rational system or on traditional institutions opens the opportunity for the emergence of charismatic authority. When the old order cannot be preserved because its institutions do not function or do not exist while social and political forces external to the system increase their pressure, the *charismatic moment* appears. Such was the case on December 31, 1958, the eve of the revolutionary triumph.

Notably, Fidel Castro said on the morning of January 1, 1959, that Cubans found "with the military downfall of the Batista regime, nothing was left. There was no legislative power in the classic sense, no judicial power, nothing."[4] Traditional mechanisms of social control had broken down and no substitutes were evident. The whole bourgeois state machine built after 1940 had come to an end. The old order's institutional vacuum determined the breakdown and demise of the old order itself, and the appearance of a new type of authority. Certainly, revolutionaries led by a unique political leader seized the opportunity. But personal leadership without a crisis of authority would not have produced charisma.

Prior to that charismatic moment, Fidel Castro was an astute political leader who managed to seize political power in two years and one month after initiating a guerrilla war campaign. His revolutionary strategy helped to create the charismatic moment, but it was a propitious symbolic event that transformed him into the island's charismatic revolutionary leader. On January 8, 1959, as Fidel spoke to a crowd at the old military headquarters in Havana, several doves landed on his shoulder and on the podium as he spoke. Especially to Cubans immersed in the country's popular religiosity of Santeria, that was the sign, the confirmation, of the revolutionary leader's uniqueness. The sacred symbols of popular religiosity touched the profane world of politics.[5] The concatenation of structural conditions, institutional crisis, authority vacuum, and the appearance of a commonly shared sign were contingencies which interacted and reinforced the process by which ordinary leadership evolved into charisma. Those exceptional external cultural circumstances were matched by the unique qualities of Fidel Castro.

WEBER'S CHARISMA OR MACHIAVELLI'S PRINCE?

Max Weber was silent about the personal attributes that a charismatic leader should have. Instead he focused on the social relations between the leader and followers, and the interpretation the followers make of the leader, observing that

> charisma is to be considered an uncommon quality of an individual personality. . . . It invests that personality with . . . extraordinary powers which are not accessible to other individuals. These qualities are thought to be either of divine origin or exemplary personal characteristics, and therefore designate the individual as leader. How the relevant quality might be "objectively" assessed . . . is obviously immaterial: of sole importance is how the charismatically ruled assess this quality.[6]

The Weberian tradition of understanding [*verstehen*] is solely concerned with the subjective interpretation that followers have of a leader's actions, the interactions between leader and followers over time, and the dynamics of exercising charismatic power.

While some scholars have referred to Fidel's leadership qualities as charismatic, the theoretical underpinnings of their analyses are closer to Niccoló Machiavelli's descriptions of *The Prince* (1505) than Weber's paradigm. They characterize Fidel Castro in the same manner as Machiavelli portrayed his vision of the ideal prince: a leader guided only by ambition and the cunning application of power to preserve his rule. The analysts' unstated political agenda in applying Machiavelli's cynical realism to Fidel Castro is that the comparison naturally raises doubts about the stated motivations behind the revolutionary's actions.[7]

A variant of the Machiavelli approach, which has become fashionable since Edward González and David Rondfeldt introduced it in 1986, are pop psychological speculations about Fidel's unconscious. "Castro continues to exhibit the same ambitions and behavioral patterns," González and Rondfeldt confidently conclude from afar, "that have characterized his rule for more than a quarter of a century. The reasons for such constancy are in his extraordinary mindset and a mode of behavior that has served him well since childhood." Without any first-hand knowledge of their subject, they argue that two concepts drawn from Greek mythology, hubris and nemesis, form a "complex" which "reflects two of Castro's most basic drives: his unrelenting ambition for power and his continuing animosity turned toward the United States."[8]

STYLE VS. SUBSTANCE

Analysts often assume that the interaction between Fidel Castro and the Cuban population is based on emotions rather than ideas or policies. The Hollywood style of packaging and marketing of U.S. politicians as commodities or brands has become so pervasive that it seems natural to explain Cuban politics with the same "logic." In doing so, authors depoliticize revolutionary charisma, and strip it of political content, message, values, ideas, specific interests, and goals. Charisma becomes a cliché that substitutes style for message. Thus, they focus on Castro's oratorical skills, not the content of his speeches, as if he mesmerized people by his voice, diction, cadence, manner, and movements. Moreover, without evidence, they presume that he successfully moves followers only by appealing to their emotions, and that the values he conveys are irrelevant. But that can hardly be the case. For followers, leading by example is essential for them to continue believing in the legitimacy of leadership based on charisma. The leader must embody the values he espouses. In this way the content of his message is more important than the style in which it is delivered.

Anecdotes abound of the way Fidel's behavior has moved his followers. His personal example has elicited energy and dedication from others, because of the message it conveys, which reinforces the substance of his speeches. Some of the most important messages are

- Cuba has the right to sovereignty, and to full political and economic independence, free from foreign control;
- The Cuban people should make all the decisions about their own social, economic, and political institutions with no foreign interference;
- The Cuban people have the right to determine how all their resources ought to be used;
- Cuba is a country with a political, intellectual, and cultural history equal to any other;
- The unity of the Cuban nation is essential in order to preserve its independence;
- All the basic material, health, and cultural needs of the Cuban people should be met through state policies;
- Social equality is fundamental and should be secured;
- Political representation depends on mass participation and mass mobilization; the political system has its own unique institutions that respond to the country's needs;
- Internationalism and solidarity with other countries, particularly underdeveloped nations, are an ethical responsibility as well as a political necessity; and
- Everyone needs to participate as fully as possible in society.

Until 1991, Fidel's charismatic leadership was reinforced by the revolution's benefits, which were conscientiously distributed to all segments of the population. The Soviet Union provided economic resources to sustain these benefits. Without a Soviet Union and its assistance, that situation drastically altered. From the start of the so-called Special Period, Fidel resorted to a manner of policymaking he seemed to have abandoned years earlier. As social, economic, and political problems deepened, the *Comandante* increased the number of his speeches, as he explained problems in detail, using examples from nineteenth-century history to provide lessons. He stressed the necessity of acquiring a solid and deep political awareness.[9] In addition, he appeared more involved than ever, concentrating his energies on problem solving.

DEATH AND RESURRECTION OF POLITICAL AND MORAL CHARISMA

By 1959, corruption, political violence, and gangsterism had destroyed Cuba's legitimate political authority. There was a deep and widespread desire for drastic changes. The *fidelistas* were able to take command precisely because they were based in a pre-existing moralistic movement that denounced and fought against selfish interests. José Martí initiated the populist movement in order to unite every sector of Cuban society against the Spanish colonial regime. That language and paradigm did not change much during the first half of the twentieth century.[10] And to the surprise of the doomsayers, the revolution led by Fidel Castro survived.

Political leaders and revolutionaries spoke the language of ethical regeneration. Cuban revolutionary populism espoused the exact opposite of individualist self-serving materialism. The populist message negated the very premises of individualist ideology because the personal had to be sacrificed for the benefit of the community—i.e., the nation. Neither individualism nor narcissism was considered a positive value.

Legitimacy derived from service, not from self-interest. By proclaiming that "the Partido del Pueblo Cubano has been created in order to fulfill the great historical objectives of the Cuban people by means of a moral revolution in public life," Eduardo Chibás, the leader of the Ortodoxo Party, helped to raise political expectations of a population that had grown weary of sinecures, corruption, and nefarious politics.[11] Chibás promised his followers a moral regeneration. In 1951, just before national presidential elections, Chibás committed suicide, leaving his movement without its charismatic leader. At that opportune juncture, General Fulgencio Batista carried out a military coup and brought an end to the Cuban constitutional order, thus ending legal/rational authority.

Fidel Castro and a handful of young *ortodoxos* merged those engaged in a variety of anti-Batista struggles, taking on the leadership of Chibás's followers. The death of one charismatic leadership led to the appearance of a new one. Fidel spoke the same language of supporting a radical break with the past by relying on selfless revolutionists willing to sacrifice their lives if necessary. He did not need to proselytize or convince the Cuban people. A significant segment of Cuba's adult population was already waiting for another Chibás who would rally the people around the guiding principle of "vergüenza contra dinero" (shame against wealth).

Fidel did not inherit that role; through audacity and hard work he took it. He was able to keep it in part because he did not violate the movement's secular ideology. Ethical populism was consonant with charismatic leadership as long as the leader was not individualistic. Fidel evoked this theme in a 1998 speech:

> I concede that at a certain time, certain people can play a certain role. However
> . . . I believe the role that any man has played at any time has always depended on

circumstances that had nothing to do with the man himself. . . . Previous conditions are required for which no man can take credit . . . The association of historical events with specific people has long been rooted in the propaganda and even in the conception of reactionaries, imperialists and enemies of the Revolution. Thus they speak about Castro's Revolution, they personalize it: Castro did this, Castro did that.[12]

To be sure, Fidel Castro's personal traits contributed to his charisma. Friend and foe alike have acknowledged his intelligence and photographic memory, and that he is self-assured and creative, deliberate, audacious, persistent, assertive, courageous, enthusiastic, and fearless. Gabriel García Márquez, the Nobel Prize novelist and a friend of the revolutionary leader, has observed, "It is impossible to find anyone more addicted than he to the habit of *conversation*."[13] He is also a listener, although this is a quality that is seldom mentioned. If one happens to have knowledge about a subject matter of his interest, Fidel will grill the person for hours with questions. Yet, these traits alone would not engender charisma. They are likely to be found in anyone who is successful in politics, regardless of ideology.

CONTEXT AND AWARENESS OF HISTORY

Fidel Castro was a product of his country's history as well as a student and analyst of it. He excelled in history and geography in primary school.[14] The Jesuits educated him from the fifth grade until the end of high school, requiring him to read Cuban and world history, biographies, and the classics of Spanish literature, as well as the Bible. In his last year of secondary school, he read two large volumes of the political writings of José Martí. By the time he was twenty years old he managed to be one of the custodians of Cuba's liberty bell, the very relic that was used in 1868 to initiate the Cuban War of Independence. In 1947 he got the bell moved from Manzanillo to Havana in order to ring it again, calling on Cubans to fight against government corruption and graft.

He used historical references to legitimate his actions. They also provided a common political framework which he used to proselytize and educate. At the University of Havana, he read history of law, political history, the Marxist classics (Marx, Engels, and Lenin), and biographies of Hannibal, Alexander the Great, Julius Ceasar, Napoleon, and Simón Bolívar. His understanding of Bolívar came from Martí's works, which he memorized.

At his trial after the failed attack against the Moncada Barracks on July 26, 1953, he spoke in his own defense and cited Martí verbatim, without notes, seventeen times. His argument provided a narrative history of the country leading to up that day in the courtroom. Then, he shouted: "Condemn me, it does not matter. History will absolve me!"[15] Thereafter, Martí's political influence would remain as a permanent presence in every facet of the Cuban revolutionary regime. Several biographers have asserted that Fidel modeled his oration on one that Hitler gave in 1923. They betray their ignorance, because it was Martí, in his trial for conducting activities against Spanish colonialism, who declared, "La Historia no habrá de declararnos culpables" [History will not declare us guilty"].[16]

In prison and mostly in solitary confinement from August 1953 to May 1955, Fidel read an average of 14 hours a day. He read works by Karl Marx, Sigmund Freud, Romain Rolland, Fyodor Dostoyevsky, Victor Hugo, Curzio Malaparte, Benedetto Croce, Gustave LeBon, Ortega y Gasset, Honoré de Balzac, Karl Mannheim, Juan José Arévalo, Luis Cardoza Aragón, and Max Weber, including the Spanish version of Weber's three-volume classic, *Economy and Society* (1914).[17] Volume three includes the section on charisma.

EXERCISING REVOLUTIONARY CHARISMA: TIMING, AUDACITY, AND PREDICTION

Fidel Castro's interest in historical details enables him to see parallels to problems he confronts. In his political decisions and activities he has demonstrated an uncanny capacity to comprehend complex situations, second-guess the reaction of others, and preempt their actions. Blas Roca, secretary-general of the pre-1959 Communist Party (Partido Socialista Popular), described this dimension as the "capacity to see far ahead." Ernesto Che Guevara observed that Fidel

> possesses the qualities of a great leader: . . . his ability, for example, to assimilate knowledge and experience in order to understand a given situation as a whole without losing sight of the small details, his immense faith in the future, his broad vision in foreseeing events and acting ahead of them, always seeing further than his companions.[18]

A number of examples illustrate this quality.

Rebel Victory: Fidel did not come down from the mountains on January 1, 1959, and jump onto an airplane headed for the capital. Instead, as historian Richard Gott recounts,

> With a sense of theater, and an intuition that the passions aroused by victory should be allowed a few days to cool, Castro set out on a stately pilgrimage from Santiago to Havana. . . . He traveled the length of the island for a week, sometimes in an open jeep, sometimes on top of a tank, stopping frequently to greet the enthusiastic crowds.[19]

The guerrilla columns moving from east to west, from countryside to capital, symbolically completed the liberation begun by Máximo Gómez and Antonio Maceo in the 1890s. The salt of the earth, the *guajiros*, were bringing political freedom to the metropolis, and in the process every hamlet and town from the Sierra Maestra to Havana was placed in the hands of revolutionaries. Before Fidel's forces entered the center of administrative, political, and economic power, the rest of the country had been absorbed into the revolution. The *guerrilleros* repeated their message at each stop: the revolutionary cause had triumphed; it was not the victory for a particular organization but a "people's victory." Fidel's "pilgrimage" thus set the basis for a new revolutionary administration at the grassroots, as he personally called on the population to become part of the process.

Bay of Pigs: Two days before the April 17, 1961, Bay of Pigs invasion, Central Intelligence Agency contract employees bombed most of the airports on the island. Seven Cubans were killed in the raids. The following day, at the mass funeral of the victims, Fidel Castro stressed to the huge crowd the necessity to defend the nation, and he declared for the first time that the character of the Cuban revolution was "socialist."[20] In doing so he united socialism and Cuban nationalism. Defending the homeland thus meant defending the revolutionary commitment to socialism. On the fortieth anniversary of the Cuban victory over the invaders, Fidel explained why he announced the socialist character at that moment. He was about to send Cubans into a potentially ferocious and bloody battle with the United States. Under these circumstances, he recalled, "It was essential to seek out loftier objectives in the political and social development of Cuba." He needed the populace to feel connected to earlier generations whose "blood and tears spilled throughout almost a hundred years of struggle for independence and justice," and to be inspired by a goal greater than "the rebuilding of a neocolonialist, capitalist and bourgeois society."[21]

9/11 and War: When the terrorist attacks occurred on September 11, 2001, Castro changed a planned speech on the economy into an offer of assistance to the U.S. government, for example, to enable U.S. airplanes to land on Cuban territory. He also offered some advice. The United States should not go to war, he cautioned, because war would not solve the problem of terrorism. But as bellicosity rose in the United States in the ensuing weeks, he warned the Cuban people that the coming war would be a terrible mistake for the United States. "Whenever there is a tragedy like this," he said,

> I see no other way but to remain calm . . . and not to start trying to hunt people down by throwing bombs just anywhere. I reiterate that none of the world's problems, not even terrorism, can be solved with the use of force, and every act of force . . . is going to seriously aggravate the world's problems. . . . [T]his international struggle against terrorism . . . can only be won, among other ways, by putting an end to State terrorism and other repulsive forms of killing, by putting an end to genocide, and by seriously pursuing a policy of peace and respect for moral and legal standards.[22]

U.S. officials responded by lambasting Castro for not endorsing the bombing of Afghanistan. In 2003, they scornfully denounced him for the arrest of 75 alleged dissidents. Like a skillful "blackbelt," Castro absorbed these thrusts and turned them back on the United States, successfully portraying the self-proclaimed global leader as a bully. The image resonated with Third World countries, who rallied to small countries' defense by selecting Cuba for a seat on the U.N. Human Rights Commission, and by naming Cuba as the host for the 2006 summit of the Non-aligned Movement.

THE IMPORTANCE OF INSTITUTIONALIZATION

While the United States experimented with several methods of "regime change" in Cuba, the preferred one continued to be liquidation of the charismatic leader. Cuban officials claim there were 638 plots or attempts on Castro's life from 1959 to 2005; the U.S. government has acknowledged only nine, claiming the attempts ended in 1966. The CIA also planned to remove what its analysts believed was the very source of Fidel's charisma—his beard—with a powder devised specially for this task.

This approach to regime change is rooted in the vacuous assumption that the Cuban revolution was little more than a manifestation of Castro's psychopathology, and that the termination of the revolution would follow immediately from his demise. For example, President Dwight D. Eisenhower remarked, in an October 1959 press conference, that any problems between the United States and Cuba were the result of one man's oversized ambition. "I have no idea," he said,

> of discussing possible motivations of a man, what he is really doing, and certainly I am not qualified to go into such abstruse and difficult subjects as that. I do feel this: here is a country that you would believe, on the basis of our history, would be one of our real friends. . . . You would think they would want good relationships. I don't know exactly what the difficulty is."[23]

In the face of this facile U.S. strategy, the Cuban government took counter-measures to frustrate all assassination plots, and to develop political institutions necessary for continuing the revolutionary regime without a charismatic leader. Some analysts have confused the succession of the revolutionary leader with the institutionalization of the revolution itself. The two processes are interconnected, but the revolutionary leadership addressed the question of succession before it began the process of institutionalization (although the formal succession guidelines have been revised three times since 1959).

Castro understood from the start that a revolutionary regime which draws its legitimacy and stability only from a charismatic leader inevitably faces the problem of continuity. As early as January 21, 1959, at a mass rally, Fidel designated his brother as his successor: "To take precautionary measures, because we should expect anything [from our enemies], so I will propose to the collective leadership of the 26th of July Movement, that *compañero* Raúl Castro become the Second Chief of the 26th of July Movement organization." Raúl would take over thanks to his revolutionary credentials, and qualifications as an organizer and leader, not because of familial relations. The massive crowd roared its approval. Fidel responded: "So now the enemies know: You can attack me when you want, there will be no problems. And, moreover, if you also kill Raúl, behind him there will be another leader, and behind that one another, and another."[24]

On May 1, 1960, Fidel repeated his designation of Raúl as successor, this time to two additional roles Fidel occupied, Prime Minister and leader of the revolution. In both cases, the designation fit a process outlined by Max Weber and explained by Reinhard Bendix. Confirmation by acclamation of the designated successor means "the beginnings of a representative system."[25]

Within two years of taking political power a slow process of political "routinization of charisma" unfolded, in order to unite disparate revolutionary forces, and to operate according to codified rules. Begun in 1961, the complex process of unification—which sectarian conflicts, insufficient technical and political knowledge, and the paucity of people with experience made especially difficult—came to fruition in 1965 with the creation of the new Communist Party of Cuba [PCC]. It integrated the 26th of July Movement, the *Partido Socialista Popular* and the *Directorio Revolucionario*, and was buttressed by mass organizations, which Fidel organized, and the military, which Raúl Castro controlled. Repeating the same message to each new revolutionary cadre, Fidel emphasized the importance of institutionalization:

> Today the mass of people have faith in the Revolution and they deposit their trust on the leaders; but tomorrow it no longer will be a matter of faith on men, it will be a matter of reliance on principles, reliance on institutions. Because men can be one way or some other way, today a set of leaders and tomorrow another set. But trust and faith should be based on something that should not change: principles and institutions.[26]

Still, the Castro brothers believed that in the early years of the revolution, institutions could not substitute for rule by charismatic authority. In 1974, Raúl Castro described their reasoning:

> In those early years it became necessary to fight the successive and ever more violent aggressions of imperialism and the counterrevolution. To function in that situation and face the tasks of those days we needed an agile and operative apparatus that exercised the dictatorship on behalf of the working people, concentrating legislative, executive, and administrative powers in one structure, enabling us to make rapid decisions without delay.[27]

While the PCC had written rules, formal structures, and a clear process for selecting members, it was only in 1975 that the party's membership could vote for its leaders. That was a decisive moment in the process of institutionalization for two reasons. First, not everyone in Cuba could become a member of a vanguard/cadre organization. Thus, the plebiscitarian nature of ratifying the charismatic leader shifted from the undifferentiated mass of the population to a cadre organization. In a formal sense, this shift terminated the connection between charismatic authority and followers. The PCC, Raúl Castro remarked, did not occupy a leading position because of a popular election, and it was not the product of votes cast by the working class. The leaders intended it to be selective, claiming that the best and brightest among the mass of Cubans would become members. Second, the charismatic leader would be required to operate within a formal organization and to follow its statutes. Notably, when Fidel and Raúl were respectively elected as First and Second Secretaries of the Central Committee at the 1975 PCC Congress, Fidel downplayed his personal importance and emphasized the political organization's institutionalization process.[28]

A similar and almost parallel effort to routinize charisma within the government occurred a decade after the founding of the PCC. Cubans approved a constitution in 1976 after an elaborate two-year process which included often heated open meetings in each *municipio*. In effect, they began a progressive transformation of charismatic authority to legal-bureaucratic authority, with codified procedures and well-defined areas of responsibility for the machinery of state. In fact, Cuban leaders dubbed 1977 as the "Year of Institutionalization." It should be noted that institutionalization is a transitional phase during which a state dominated by a charismatic power becomes a state based on legalized power, and the charismatic authority defines and elaborates the rules and regulations of the new political structure. Institutionalization is the formalization of new authority. "Men die," Fidel said in 1976. "The Party is immortal."[29] Indeed, as early as 1966 he identified the unacceptable costs of a charisma–mass mobilization governing model. "The revolutionaries," he said in a speech on August 29,

> who initiate revolutionary processes tend to have a lot of prestige with the people, they enjoy huge authority with the people, and with that authority they usually can do a lot of good, but they can also do a lot of harm. We hope that in future times few or no one should have the authority that some of us had at the beginning, because it is dangerous that men should have so much authority.[30]

The routinization of charisma within the Communist Party affected the relationship between the leader and followers of a cadre organization, a minority of the Cuban population. The routinization of charisma within the government affected the leader's relationship to the entire population over the voting age of sixteen. Under the Cuban system, there is popular election for representatives at the municipal, provincial, and national levels. The National Assembly selects the executive branch. The Council of Ministers, on paper, answers to the national legislature. Both the party and governmental processes of institutionalization were coordinated by the Castro brothers, who repeated a pattern—called "double charisma"—found in other historical experiences.

Double charisma is the practical solution to a problem which arises as institutionalization occurs. One person cannot play two essential roles. The first is as the leader who mobilizes and inspires, who takes on a semi-prophetic persona and serves as the public image of the revolution. The other leader is the organizer, involved in detail, procedures, daily decisions. The former has been called the "charisma of the outer call"; the other is the "charisma of an inner consolidation." Sociologist Michael A. Toth explains,

> It is this second leader who is able to turn the corner from charisma to routine, accomplishing it under the aegis of the more unearthly charisma of the first leader. It is this first charisma which Weber described; the charisma of inner consolidation remains to be adequately defined, although the literature is suggestively prescient enough to make adumbration at least plausible. [31]

CHARISMA NEEDS ORGANIZATION

The charismatic ruler requires organization in order to operate. His successor is chosen precisely because he is known as the organizer, the one who can build and show how to run successful organizations. It is a common aphorism that charismatic rulers tend to be anti-bureaucratic. But this adage should be questioned. Charismatic rulers may very well target inefficient bureaucrats rather than any bureaucracy. The anti-bureaucracy campaigns in Cuba (1964–1970), for example, took place during those periods of time when there was a significant shortage of labor in the countryside.

Fidel Castro's goal-oriented leadership has been possible because he has depended, on a daily basis, on assistants and organizers. The charismatic leader needs an immediate organization to work with. Such a unit is neither a party nor state agency, but functionally connects to both. Fidel Castro holds several positions of responsibility, each with a different role. Within the government, he is President of the Council of State, President of the Council of Ministers, and Commander in Chief of the Armed Forces. He is also the First Secretary of the Communist Party and consequently a member of the PCC Political Bureau and Secretariat. Of necessity, he has delegated several tasks to confidantes who work closely with him, a group of approximately twenty persons who serve as "gatekeepers," personal assistants, and sounding boards, and who also work on specific projects. They are called his *Grupo de Apoyo* [GdeA], a name given to them in the 1980s when they became a formal organization.

Before 1959, Fidel relied on two or three core assistants. Once the guerrillas attained power, and his responsibilities multiplied, the size of the group increased. Led by Celia Sánchez, it consisted of people who had been in the guerrilla movement, such as René Vallejo and Jesús Montané, or who had played a role in the Ortodoxo Party, such as Luis Buch and Conchita Fernández.[32] By the mid-1980s most of Castro's initial associates had departed from the informal *Grupo de Apoyo*. Some obtained ministerial posts, as the institutionalization of the state and the party continued apace. The older ones had retired or died, though Antonio Núñez Jímenez, José Naranjo Morales (Pepín), and José Miyar Barruecos (Chomy) continued to work with him.

The new team members were younger, and generally they had not engaged personally in the armed struggle against Batista. They were recruited from the Union of Young Communists and the Federation of University Students on the basis of their talents and skills. Their importance was highlighted when Fidel named Felipe Pérez Roque as Foreign Minister in 2002. Only thirty-four at the time, he had been a leader of the Union of Young Communists and the Federation of University Students, and a member of the GdeA. To some extent, the GdeA operates as a super auditor and executive enforcer. The *Grupo* can cut across lines of authority, deal directly with ministers, and give orders to those beneath the ministerial level in an agency. The GdeA can enter any office at any time or attend any meeting, and it keeps close watch over the government machinery.

RAÚL'S "SUCCESSION"

Raúl Castro has shown significant administrative and organizational skills. His peers accord legitimacy to his leadership because they judge that it was earned on the basis of merit. In the early years, the two brothers arrived at a clear division of labor—one handled political matters, the other military ones. While either would be able to lead in both realms at exceptional times, political practice and necessity evolved into an informal network of interlocking but separate powers and responsibilities occupied by both brothers and their appointed close comrades.

Yet Raúl Castro cannot merely replace Fidel Castro. The "successor" will not be able to replicate the founder. Raúl cannot become the charismatic leader Fidel Castro was, for reasons beyond the obvious differences in their personalities. Charismatic leadership requires a charismatic moment, when order has broken down, and followers who hunger for such leadership and willingly participate in the process of legitimating charismatic authority. Another reason, generally overlooked, is that there is no "equivalent Raúl" for Raúl Castro, someone who could do for him what he did for his brother. That means Raúl will need to find others to perform numerous roles. The interlocking network of power in the hands of just two persons will become ever more dispersed.

Raúl Castro pointedly acknowledged this reality just six weeks before his brother relinquished command "temporarily." On June 14, 2006, at a ceremony marking the 45th anniversary of the creation of the Cuban military's Western Command, he said that the succession process would not involve the search for another charismatic leader. Fidel Castro would be replaced by a collective leadership made up of national leaders from within the Communist Party. "The Commander in Chief of the Cuban Revolution," he proclaimed, "is solely and uniquely the Communist Party, as an institution that brings together the revolutionary vanguard and is a sure guarantee of Cuban unity in all times, can be the worthy inheritor of the confidence deposited by the people in its leader."[33]

Fidel Castro has left his mark on the histories of Cuba, Latin America, Africa, and Asia. It is more than remarkable that his revolutionary experiment survived despite the opposition of every U.S. president since 1959. He managed to integrate Latin American political and intellectual traditions with Marxism, in the process challenging Eurocentric premises. He helped build a nation-state with a clearly defined identity. He has excelled as strategist and as tactician. His speeches have provided a political education for people around the globe, even for those who disagreed with him. Yet his contributions on social policies remain to be fully analyzed and understood. The uniqueness of the social, economic, and political systems he helped shape has not been fully appreciated yet. History will judge Fidel Castro after he dies. Only then will it be clear whether the institutions, policies, and ideas that he created and defended survive him. But that will depend, as he well understands, on the people of Cuba.

NOTES

1. W. Raymond Duncan, "Nationalism in Cuban Politics," in *Cuba, Castro and Revolution*, ed. Jaime Suchlicki, (Coral Gables: University of Miami Press, 1972), 27.

2. Max Weber, *The Theory of Social and Economic Organization* (New York: Oxford University Press, 1947), 358–359.

3. *Encyclopedia of Sociology*, (Connecticut: The Dushkin Publishing Group, Inc., 1973), 37.

4. Fidel Castro, "Conversation with University Students at University of Concepción, Chile," *Granma Weekly Review* (Havana), November 28, 1971, 14.

5. For an elaboration of this process, see Nelson P. Valdés, "Cuba's Fidel Castro: Charisma and Santería" in *Caribbean Charisma: Reflections on Leadership, Legitimacy and Populist Politics*, ed. Antón Allahar (Boulder: Lynne Rienner Publishers, 2001), 216–217, 221–222.

6. Wolf Heydebrand, ed., *Max Weber: Sociological Writings* (New York: Continuum, 1994), 32–33.

7. For examples, see Georgie Anne Geyer, *Guerrilla Prince: The Untold Story of Fidel Castro* (Boston: Little Brown and Company, 1990), xii; Ramón E. Ruiz, *Cuba, The Making of a Revolution*, (New York: W. W. Norton and Company, 1970), 17; Tad Szulc, *Fidel: A Critical Portrait* (New York: Morrow, 1986), 23.

8. Edward González and David Rondfeldt, *Castro, Cuba and the World* (Santa Monica, Calif.: RAND Corporation, 1986), v. See Leycester Coltman, *The Real Fidel Castro*, (New Haven: Yale University Press, 2003), for a more recent example of such a superficial psychological analysis.

9. Discurso pronunciado por el Comandante en Jefe, Fidel Castro Ruz, Primer Secretario del Comité Central del Partido Comunista de Cuba y Presidente de los Consejos de Estado y de Ministros, con delegados a la Conferencia Sindical de los Trabajadores de América Latina y el Caribe sobre la deuda externa, durante la sesión de clausura del evento, 18 de Julio de 1985. See www.cuba.cu/gobierno/discursos/1985/esp/f180785e.html.

10. Nelson P. Valdés, *Ideological Roots of the Cuban Revolutionary Movement*, Occasional Paper, No. 15, 1975 (Scotland: University of Glasgow, Institute of Latin American Studies).

11. Luis Conte Agüero, ed, *Eduardo Chibás, el Adalid* (Mexico: Editorial Jus, 1954), 629.

12. Speech in Dominican Republic, August 24, 1998; transcription prepared by the Cuban Council of State. Available at www.cuba.cu/gobierno/discursos/1998/ing/f240898i.html.

13. Gabriel García Márquez, "A Personal Portrait of Fidel," in *Fidel, My Early Years* (Melbourne: Ocean Press, 2005), 11.

14. Aldo Isidrón, et al., *Antes del Moncada* (Habana: Editorial Pablo de la Torriente, 1986), 17.

15. The speech is reprinted in Rolando E. Bonachea and Nelson P Valdés, eds., *Revolutionary Struggle, 1947–1958* (Cambridge, Mass.: The MIT Press, 1972), 164–221.

16. José Martí, *Obras completas* (La Habana: Editorial Ciencias Sociales, 1975), Vol. 4, 306.

17. Claudia Furiati, *Fidel Castro, la historia me absolverá* (Barcelona: Plaza Janes, 2003), 201, 203.

18. Rolando E. Bonachea and Nelson P. Valdés, *Che: Selected Works of Ernesto Guevara* (Cambridge, Mass.: MIT Press, 1969), 58.

19. Richard Gott, *Cuba, A New History* (New Haven: Yale University Press, 2004), 167.

20. Fidel Castro, "Proclamation of the Socialist Character of the Cuban Revolution," in Julio García Luis, ed., *Cuban Revolution Reader: A Documentary History of 40 Key Moments of the Cuban Revolution* (New York: Ocean Press, 2001), 65–69.

21. Speech delivered by Commander in Chief Fidel Castro Ruz, President of the Council of State and the Council of Ministers of the Republic of Cuba, on the 40th Anniversary of the proclamation of the socialist nature of the Cuban Revolution, held on 23rd Ave. and 12th St. in Havana City. April 16, 2001. See www.cuba.cu/gobierno/discursos/2001/ing/f160401i.html.

22. Speech given by Dr. Fidel Castro Ruz, President of the Republic of Cuba, the day of the tragic events that occurred in the United States. September 11, 2001. See www.cuba.cu/gobierno/discursos/2001/ing/f110901i.html.

23. See www.presidency.ucsb.edu/ws/index.php?pid=11569.

24. Discurso pronunciado por el Comandante Fidel Castro Ruz, en la Magna Concentración Popular, Palacio Presidencial, 21 de Enero de 1959. Departamento de versiones taquigráficas del Gobierno Revolucionario. See www.cuba.cu/gobierno/discursos/1959/esp/f210159e.html.

25. Reinhard Bendix, *Max Weber: An Intellectual Portrait* (New York: Anchor Books, 1962).

26. Discurso pronunciado por el Comandante en Jefe Fidel Castro Ruz, Primer Secretario del Partido y Primer Ministro del Gobierno Revolucionario, en la clausura del acto de la Juventud en Las Villas, *Revolución* (Habana) October 22, 1964, 6.

27. Raúl Castro, Discurso de clausura del seminario impartido a los delegados del Poder Popular electos al iniciarse la experiencia en Matanzas, 23 de Agosto de 1974. Author's personal copy. English translation by the author.

28. Fidel Castro, "Closing Speech," in *First Congress of the Communist Party of Cuba*, Moscow: Progress Publishers, 1976, 290.

29. Discurso pronunciado por Fidel Castro Ruz, Presidente de la República de Cuba, en la sesión solemne de Constitución de la Asamblea Nacional de Poder Popular, el 2 de Diciembre de 1976. See www.cuba.cu/gobierno/discursos/1976/esp/f021276e.html.

30. Discurso pronunciado en la clausura del XII congreso de la CTC-R, efectuada en el teatro de la CTC-R, el 29 de agosto de 1966. Departamento de versiones taquigráficas del Gobierno Revolucionario. See www.cuba.cu/gobierno/discursos/1966/esp/f290866e.html.

31. Michael A. Toth, "Toward a Theory of the Routinization of Charisma," *Rocky Mountain Social Science Journal 9*, no. 2 (April 1972): 93–98.

32. Luis M. Buch and Reinaldo Suárez, *Gobierno revolucionario cubano, primeros pasos* (La Habana: Editorial Ciencias Sociales), 2004.

33. www.granma.cubaweb.cu/secciones/raul-45ejercito/raul03.html, accessed February 2, 2007.

2

July 26. History Absolved Him.
Now What?

Saul Landau

Televised contemporary events marginalize the role of history. TV broadcasts death from Lebanon, Gaza, and Israel, but paid scant attention to the fifty-third anniversary of Cuba's revolutionary beginning. On July 26, 1953, Fidel Castro led 150-plus men to capture the Moncada Barracks in Santiago de Cuba. This act of nationalist voluntarism failed. The revolutionaries had hoped the heroic act would catalyze an island-wide uprising. In January 1959, however, Fidel's guerrilleros took control of the island.

As Cubans celebrated the fifty-third anniversary of the Moncada attack, they again confronted Fidel Castro's famous words. "History will absolve me," he concluded his defense. His accomplishments more than absolve him. But the age of revolutionary innocence that fostered the Cuban revolution has ended, as 9/11 dramatized.

Fidel remains a larger-than-life leader who never relied on TV spots or political "handlers" to preach his messages to Cubans and millions of others around the world. People listen because he has something to say. His agenda—justice, equality, ending poverty, facing the perils of environmental erosion—retains urgent cogency. Compare his presentation to the "lite ideas" offered by major power heads of state!

From the 1960s on, critics have ignored Fidel's noble ideas and focused their barbs at Cuba's rationing system and chronic shortages. The anti-Castroites systematically neglect to compare the island's life with that of its neighbors, whose health and living standards rank far worse. Unlike residents of other South American countries, post–Batista era Cubans did not fear death squads or "disappearances."

Cuba does not have a free press or political parties, which has led to problems that Cuba faces today—the absence of critical public dialogue. These deficiencies, however, do not detract from the accomplishments.

The revolution converted an informal U.S. economic colony (until 1958) into a proud nation whose citizens danced on the stage of contemporary history. In the heady days of the 1960s and 1970s, students returned from studying abroad to join those at home in building hospitals, schools, roads, and day care centers. The revolution also gave Cubans rights only dreamed of by other Third World people. Not just education and health care, the right to a job and pension, but the chance to change history.

In 1993, at Nelson Mandela's inauguration after the demise of the apartheid system, the new South African President embraced Fidel Castro: "You made this possible," he whispered audibly, referring to the 1987–1988 Cuban military defeat of the apartheid South African forces at the battles of Cuito Cuanavale.

In Africa, from the 1960s through the 1980s, Cuban troops played historical roles in safeguarding Algerian, Angolan, and Ethiopian integrity. In solidarity, Cuba sent 1,500 soldiers to fight alongside Syrian troops in the 1973 Middle East War. Cuban doctors and technicians offered aid to Vietnam in the 1960s and 1970s. Cuban doctors are the first to volunteer to help earthquake and other disaster victims all over the world. Indeed, Pakistanis will remember the contribution Cubans made to their recent earthquake victims.

Cuban artists, intellectuals, writers, athletes, and scientists have also engraved their works and feats in the annals of many countries throughout the world. Cuba has more doctors abroad than the entire World Health Organization. Its doctor-patient ratio is similar to that of Beverly Hills.

Other third world revolutions and independence movements in small nations did not achieve this level of success. After imperial powers looted their resources and brains for centuries, they "gave" them independence; in some cases, the colonized won it. The "beneficent" former rulers allowed them ten or twenty years to "shape up" into fully operating capitalist "democracies." The imperialists did not replace stolen resources or share technology; they offered no easy credit or beneficial terms of trade. The one option—"get IMF'd," as the late Jamaican Prime Minister Michael Manley called it.

Cuba's good fortune, having a veritable insurance company ready to write a long-term development policy, meant the Soviet Union would provide for infrastructure and the know-how necessary for development. In spite of the hideous warts of the Soviet system, it worked. Cuban infant mortality and life expectancy reached first world levels. Cuba has a literacy rate equal or better than the United States.

The Cuban Revolution was a success. What is it now?

In 1990, the Soviet Union dissolved. Cuba lost its aid and trade partner. Its leaders reluctantly compromised—dollarization and tourists—to survive in a U.S.-sponsored hostile climate. Facing severe hardships, tens of thousands of Cubans placed their destinies in the fate of rafts or, later, in the hands of smugglers, and the uncertain seas that separate the island from Florida.

Before the USSR's dissolution, however, Cuba had already begun to lose its revolutionary purity. Heroic guerrilla warriors often turned into poor heads of ministries and worse politicians. They did not build democratic transition into their model, by transferring their power in a compact of trust to the very generations they educated. Instead, the leaders who enjoyed certain material privileges began to lose close contact with the people. Paternalism, inherited from centuries of Spanish culture, also began to erode the spontaneous rapport and enthusiasm of the early years.

In 1968, while I was filming *Fidel*, a PBS documentary, Fidel told me that "socialist democracy should assure everyone's constant participation in political activity." This insight is incompatible with fatherly control—even for people's "own good." Paternal attitudes sapped initiative from Cuban society. By "giving" people what they needed without demanding mature responsibility and by maintaining control of virtually all projects, the Communist Party and government helped depoliticize the very people they had educated.

The 1959 revolutionaries swore to fulfill the goals of the 1860s and 1890s independence leaders who began the struggle for nationhood. Fidel expanded their vision into one of communist consciousness: full political participation for each citizen. In 2006, much of the population does not respond to calls for communist consciousness, or participate in meaningful politics.

Instead, visitors to the island hear *"No es fácil"* (It's not easy), a preface to a laundry list of complaints. In fact, government salaries don't allow most Cubans to live at levels to which they've grown accustomed. The black market, therefore, remains vital.

Cubans consume—not as much as they want—but don't produce goods that bring in foreign exchange. Both producers and those in the service sector, however, don't suffer from the kinds of job stress Americans experience.

"Hard work at boring jobs, that's capitalism," a Cuban friend told me. "Socialism doesn't erase people's energy in meaningless tasks that don't benefit them or society."

The people who continue to risk their lives to leave the island for an uncertain existence are the human face of Cuban socialism. Young Cubans, on and off the island, demonstrate high levels of culture, except when political themes arise; their eyes glaze.

After I returned from Vietnam in March, a Cuban friend asked about that country.

"Prospering," I said.

"Imagine, the Americans bombed them into the Stone Age and they're prospering. Not a bomb has fallen on Havana and yet we live like we're in the Stone Age."

This habitual whine should be taken with the proverbial grain of salt. Cuba's investment in human capital did initially stimulate political consciousness. Cubans defended their revolution against a relentless U.S. dirty war, because they understood their cause—and their enemies. An anti-imperial and a class struggle!

Through the 1970s, Cubans remembered the murderous practices and invidious capitalism of the prerevolutionary era. Today, 75 percent of the population doesn't remember Batista's cruelty or U.S. neocolonialism. Lacking vivid memory and without having political input, they have grown tired of party jargon and slogans that bear little relationship to their reality.

This disturbs me because Bush's July Cuba plan calls for the resumption of U.S. control in the post-Castro era, privatizing its economy and reshaping its politics structure to make it compatible with current administration views of democracy. The United States would even show Cubans how to manage their schools and farm efficiently. As of July 2005, Bush had already appointed a transition coordinator—without even bothering to invade Cuba, as he ordered for Afghanistan and Iraq.

The "Made in Washington" blueprint shows the mind-altering glue inherent in imperial memory. In Washington, the policy crowd sticks to old economic claims on Cuba. The July plan should remind Cubans that they will lose free education, health, and housing and start paying heavy prices for these services. Cubans should imagine life under real-estate-hungry Miami exiles. How hard and meaningless their work lives would become when their labor went to enrich a true parasite class!

Bush's recolonization of Cuba plan offends Cubans. But that ugly road is possible if cynicism deepens on the island. Will Fidel have the will to wage yet another campaign, a movement for socialist democracy? A good start premise would be the recognition that educated Cuban citizens merit trust and thus power to make choices as well as participate in the policies that guide their nation. It would put renewed meaning into "patria o muerte!"

PART II

POLITICS

Cuban politics before 1959 was always circumscribed by the predominant power of the United States. From the intervention in 1898, the imposition of the Platt Amendment in 1903, and repeated interventions in the first two decades of the century, to the coup that short-circuited the 1933 revolution and installed Fulgencio Batista in power, Cubans were never truly masters in their own house. As U.S. Ambassador Earl E. T. Smith was fond of declaiming, Washington's emissary in Cuba was "the second most important man in Cuba, sometimes even more important than the president." Throughout the first half of the twentieth century, Cuba's nominally democratic institutions repeatedly failed to deliver responsive, honest government. Politicians campaigned for office promising the sky, then delivered corruption and repression. By the 1950s, Cuban political institutions had scant legitimacy.

Fidel Castro did not invent the anti-American strain in Cuban nationalism, but he reflected it, amplified it, and made it a core tenet of his political appeal. As Nelson Valdés points out, Fidel's charismatic authority derived as much from the policies he championed as the style of his leadership. The revolution of 1959 swept away all the old institutions of government, including the constitution of 1940 and the electoral institutions it created. The revolution was, nevertheless, extraordinarily popular. Its initial legitimacy came from overthrowing the hated dictator Batista, who engaged in indiscriminate repression as the revolutionary wave rose against him. That legitimacy was reinforced by early policies that redistributed income from rich to poor, raising the standard of living of a majority of Cubans, and by rhetoric that defied the United States, in effect declaring Cuba's second independence.

During the first decade of revolutionary government, Cuban politics had a chaotic quality. Government agencies were created, merged, divided, and abolished routinely. Most of the ministries inherited from the old regime were dissolved. As the government nationalized the economy, a whole new government bureaucracy sprang from the initial seed of the National Institute of Agrarian Reform. Key decisions were made by Fidel Castro and his "revolutionary family," a small group of trusted advisers, most of whom fought together in the mountains during the insurrection. Fidel roamed the country, stopping in on government operations far and wide, as if he could manage the whole country personally. In power, the veterans of the insurrection tried to run the country the way they had fought the war. "Guerrilla administration" was ad hoc, pragmatic, flexible, and somewhat disorganized.

Early on it became clear that the revolutionary government would tolerate no opposition. Moderates from the prerevolutionary political parties who had opposed Batista were initially included in the new government. But their pro-capitalist, pro-U.S. instincts were not in keeping with the vision the Fidelistas had for Cuba's future. By the end of 1959, most had been eased out. Independent institutions, from unions to newspapers and radio stations, were brought under state control. Opponents found it easier to leave for the United States, in the expectation that Washington would do what it had always done—decide Cuba's political future. Thousands who stayed were jailed until the 1970s.

In the 1970s, under the influence of the Soviet Union, Cuban political institutions began to take on the familiar shape of established Marxist-Leninist polities. The Cuban Communist Party, founded in 1965 through the merger of groups that had fought against Batista, was a small and ineffectual institution in the late 1960s. By the late 1970s, however, it had grown in size and maturity to take on the leading role in politics. Cuba adopted a new constitution in 1976, providing more permanence to state institutions, and creating for the first time elected legislative assemblies at the local, provincial, and national levels—the Organs of People's Power.

The decade of the 1980s was one of gathering storms for Cuba's political system. It began with the 1980 Mariel boatlift. Propelled by deteriorating economic conditions on the island, 125,000 Cubans opted to flee to the United States. A series of corruption scandals marked the decade, culminating with the 1989 trial and imprisonment of several senior military and security officials for drug smuggling—and the execution of four officers, including Cuba's legendary Division General Arnaldo Ochoa. In the Soviet Union, the 1980s was a decade of transition. Mikhail Gorbachev's policies of *perestroika* and *glasnost* struck a chord among some Cubans. Cuba had, after all, been following the Soviet model in both political organization and economic management. If these policies were now under critical scrutiny in the homeland of socialism, why should they remain above criticism in Cuba? The collapse of European communism, first in Eastern Europe and then in the Soviet Union, intensified the urgency of Cuba's internal debate.

When European socialism collapsed, many prognosticators foresaw the imminent demise of Castro's Cuba. Yet Cuban socialism defied the conventional wisdom and survived. In retrospect, there were manifest differences between Cuban and European communism. Cuba had an authentic revolution that began with broad support, whereas communism arrived in most of Eastern Europe in the knapsack of the Soviet Red Army. Cuban nationalism bolstered the legitimacy of a government in conflict with the United States, whereas European nationalism corroded the legitimacy of regimes beholden to the Soviet Union. The standard of living in communist Europe paled in comparison to that of the West, whereas Cuban conditions compared favorably with much of Latin America and the Caribbean. European communist regimes were led by colorless bureaucrats who had long since lost faith in their own ideology, whereas Cuba was still led by the founding generation who made the revolution—foremost among them Fidel Castro himself.

One key reason Cuba survived was that Castro did not repeat Mikhail Gorbachev's mistake of combining the disruptions of economic transformation with a political opening. Even Cuba's modest economic reforms took place within the context of unremittingly tough political controls. Washington lent Fidel an unintended helping hand by ratcheting up the pressure, hoping to speed his demise. Instead, it once again gave Castro a convenient external enemy to rally Cuban patriotism. The Special Period spawned greater discontent among ordinary Cubans than ever before, but they had few opportunities to demonstrate that discontent.

The two most important institutions in the Cuban political system have been the Cuban Communist Party (*Partido Comunista de Cuba*, PCC) and the Revolutionary Armed Forces (*Fuerzas Armadas Revolucionarias*, FAR). In this section, William LeoGrande describes how the PCC developed from a small organization with a fractious leadership in the 1960s, to the dominant decision-making institution in the 1970s and 1980s. Led initially by the same "revolutionary family" that made the revolution, the party has gradually become more institutionalized and brought new generations of aspiring politicians into senior positions. In the 1990s, the party was the principal venue for elite debate over how to survive the collapse of the Soviet Union. After a brief flurry of discussion, however, the party closed ranks at the 1991 Party Congress. Several officials noted for a willingness to expand the scope of acceptable political expression were replaced, as Castro opted for maintaining tight political control during the ensuing economic crisis. The party will face its toughest test when Fidel Castro finally passes from the scene and his successors have to establish new rules of the political game for resolving disagreements when Fidel can no longer serve as ultimate arbiter.

The FAR have been Cuba's most stable and reliable institution—not because the military has played an independent political role, but rather because, as Hal Klepak explains, it has been Cuba's best organized, most efficient, and most respected revolutionary institution. Since the earliest years, the military has been a source of skilled managers, staffing many agencies of the civilian bureaucracy. In the 1970s, it won accolades at home and abroad for its role in Africa, defending Angola from South Africa's intervention and defending Ethiopia from Somalia's invasion. Most importantly, of course, the armed forces successfully carried out their central mission—defending the revolution from the subversive efforts of the United States. Since the late 1980s, the armed forces have also been a bellwether of economic change. Even before the collapse of European socialism and the advent of the Special Period, the armed forces had begun experimenting with Western management and accounting methods, hoping to improve the productivity of military industries. In the 1990s, these methods began to be applied throughout the state sector of the economy under the "Enterprise Perfecting" plan (*Perfeccionamiento Empresarial*).

The Special Period hit the Cuban armed forces particularly hard since they received all their military equipment without cost from the Soviet Union. With spare parts suddenly available only for purchase, and petroleum too scarce to be spared for military maneuvers, the military was forced to mothball most of its heavy equipment and reduce its size from over two hundred thousand to fewer than sixty thousand troops. Even then, the military was ordered to generate revenue to cover a significant portion of its own budget, by growing its own food. One of the most lucrative enterprises for the military proved to be the rest and recreation facilities built originally for Soviet military troops and advisers. The military renovated the facilities and opened them to international tourists under the name *Gaviota*, which remains one of Cuba's largest tourist businesses. Raúl Castro has led the FAR since 1959, and the loyalty of its top officers to him and to the present government is unquestioned. The respect with which the military is regarded by ordinary Cubans, its effectiveness as the defender of the *patria*, and the fact that it holds a monopoly of arms all make it centrally important in any succession scenario.

Rafael Hernández takes up the issue of democracy from a Cuban point of view. Cuban political culture differs from that in the United States, he argues—differences that predate 1959. Cubans see social justice as a critical element of democracy in a way that North Americans do not. While conceding that Cuba does not have competing political parties or the freedom of association and expression available in Western democracies, Hernández argues that political space expanded during the Special Period. Cubans today are better informed, have greater freedom to travel, and are developing a more robust civil society. State institutions are still not as open as they should be, but the ongoing threat of U.S. hostility makes Cuban leaders reluctant to risk a political opening.

In their article on Cuban local government assemblies, Cuban social scientists Haroldo Dilla Alfonso and Gerardo González Núñez note that these were the first elected state institutions. The secret, multicandidate elections from among nominees selected at neighborhood meetings have important elements of grassroots democracy. In a survey of voters, Dilla and González found that voters picked candidates based upon their personal reputations as civic-minded citizens. In creating the Organs of People's Power in the mid-1970s, the party leadership aimed to bolster its legitimacy by acknowledging the importance of elections as a mechanism for periodically renewing the regime's mandate, and by encouraging popular input to local government. By the late 1980s, however, the assemblies were suffering from serious public disaffection. Municipal assemblies had few resources at their disposal, and so could not effectively respond to popular demands.

Indeed, the government's shrinking capacity to provide resources to Cuban society during the Special Period has led to a flowering of civil society. Nongovernmental organizations were allowed to organize, new social networks developed out of market reforms in the economy, and religious institutions enjoyed a resurgence. The nature of civil society in Cuba has become the focus of much debate. Damián Fernández reviews the diversity of civil society organizations, from government-sponsored mass organizations that occasionally take an independent position in defense of their members, to community groups focused on self-help, to cultural organizations pushing the boundaries of expression, to the dissident groups operating on the margin of the law. Perhaps most importantly, the introduction of market mechanisms into the economy in the 1990s, albeit limited, has created social networks outside the control of government. Nevertheless, Fernández takes a relatively pessimistic view of these developments, seeing in them at best the emergence of a proto-civil society, existing at the sufferance of the state, and unlikely to pose any challenge to it.

What do ordinary Cubans think about politics? The Cuban government conducts polls periodically, but rarely releases the results and almost never asks overtly political questions. In 1994, however, the government allowed CID-Gallup to conduct an independent poll in Cuba. Pollsters asked Cubans what had been the "major achievement" of the revolution. Education (29 percent) and health care (14 percent) led the list of responses, and equality (9 percent) was fourth. Fifty-eight percent of respondents said that there had been more achievements than failures since 1959, but 31 percent said there had been more failures.

The poll also asked, "In a society, what do you consider most important for everyone? Should the law promote economic and social equality, or should the law promote individual freedom?" Half the respondents said equality; 38 percent said freedom. When asked "who should run the farms and factories of Cuba," 51 percent said the government should; 36 percent said they should be run privately. Yet 53 percent said they would be at least somewhat interested in setting up their own private business if the government allowed it, suggesting that Cubans want to preserve key features of their socialist system while at the same time hoping for greater personal opportunity and freedom.

A shorter CID-Gallup poll in 2006 found that Cubans continued to see themselves as more committed to equality (71 percent) and fairness (79 percent) than to democracy (47 percent). Health care and education remained points of pride, with over 90 percent of respondents saying that these services were freely available to all, and over 70 percent expressing satisfaction with them. The only political question in the 2006 survey asked whether respondents approved of the government's leadership; 47 percent said they approved, 40 percent disapproved, and 13 percent did not answer.

Organized opposition to Fidel Castro's government has been sparse since the mid-1960s. The efficiency of state security and the ease of migrating to the United States made it more attractive to oppose Castro from Miami than from Havana. Dissident organizations began to appear in the late 1980s and, though beset by harassment and arrests, they continued through the Special Period. Conventional wisdom held that these small, isolated groups had little capacity to reach beyond their own ranks with a message of opposition. In 2002, however, a Christian activist, Oswaldo Payá, surprised everyone by collecting more than eleven thousand signatures on the Varela Project's petition demanding democratic reform. Tim Padgett's profile of Payá describes how he came to lead the most effective domestic opposition to Fidel Castro in half a century. The dissidents' ability to work together and mobilize people far beyond their own numbers suggested strength greater than any opposition the Cuban government had faced before. Fidel Castro responded to the Varela Project's petition by mobilizing over 90 percent of the population to sign petitions for a constitutional amendment making socialism inviolable.

Castro has always had a low tolerance for dissent. By his own admission, thousands of opponents were imprisoned in the early years of the revolution for opposing its socialist trajectory. To critics of Cuba's human rights record, he points to the advances in social and economic rights Cuba has made since 1959. Castro's argument against multiparty democracy has always been rooted in Cuban history and nationalism. He traces the need for a single party not to Lenin, but to José Martí. When Cubans have been divided, Castro reminds his countrymen, outside enemies have been able to compromise Cuban sovereignty—first Spain and then the United States. Political unity is therefore a necessary condition of national independence. For almost half a century, this nationalist appeal has had sufficient resonance for Cubans that they have not demanded a more open politics. Time will tell whether it will retain that resonance once the generation that founded the revolutionary government has passed from the scene.

3

"The Cuban Nation's Single Party"

The Communist Party of Cuba Faces the Future

William M. LeoGrande

"Men Die, but the Party Is Immortal," read the banner headline in *Granma*, official organ of the Communist Party of Cuba. As suggested by this article from 1973, a time when the party was being strengthened as part of the "institutionalization" of the revolution, the Communist Party was intended to be the organizational guarantor of the continuity of Cuba's socialist system.[1] But the history of the Cuban party has always been atypical. It did not lead the struggle against Fulgencio Batista's dictatorship in the 1950s, and it did not direct the political system in the 1960s and 1970s. Since the collapse of the socialist camp, the Cuban party has looked and sounded more like the party of the Cuban nation (and Cuban nationalism) than the vanguard of the revolutionary working class.[2] The party's challenge in the years to come is to find a way to accommodate its leadership of Cuban politics to the island's rapidly changing economic and social reality.

ORIGINS OF THE COMMUNIST PARTY OF CUBA

Inaugurated in 1965, the Communist Party of Cuba (*Partido Comunista de Cuba*, PCC) was created *after* the triumph of the revolution it was intended to lead. Built during the 1960s among veterans of three revolutionary organizations that fought against Batista's dictatorship, the PCC did not preside over Cuba's transition to socialism or direct the new political system that followed.[3] During the revolution's critical early years, it was the Rebel Army (later, the *Fuerzas Armadas Revolucionarias*—FAR) that provided the political apparatus through which Fidel Castro and his closest compatriots governed the nation.

Creation of the new Communist Party followed Castro's declaration of the socialist character of the revolution during the Bay of Pigs invasion. Domestically, Castro sought to forge a political instrument that would unify the fractious revolutionary family and mobilize supporters. Internationally, he sought to demonstrate to the Soviet Union that Cuba was, indeed, a member in good standing of the socialist camp, worthy of Soviet economic assistance and military support. But the party-building process got off to a rocky start. The first effort, the Integrated Revolutionary Organizations (*Organizaciones Integradas Revolucionarias*, ORI) was dismantled in early 1962 after a faction of old communists from the Popular Socialist Party tried to capture control of it by filling its ranks with PSP members to the virtual exclusion of veterans from Castro's 26th of July Movement.[4]

The second attempt, the United Party of the Socialist Revolution (*Partido Unido de la Revolución Socialista*, PURS) was shaken by another crisis when two leading members of the former Communist Party were implicated in the infamous 1957 murder by Batista's police of revolutionary students at 7 Humboldt Street. Only Castro's intervention prevented the revolutionary leadership from shattering into warring factions.[5] Yet another crisis erupted in 1968, when a small group of party members (a "microfaction") was caught soliciting Soviet diplomats to replace Castro because of his unorthodox economic views.[6]

As a result of this turmoil, the leaders of the revolution were reluctant to turn over too much authority to the new party apparatus for fear that their efforts to institutionalize Fidel Castro's charismatic authority might dissipate it instead. Major policy decisions continued to be made by Castro and a small circle of trusted lieutenants, most of whom had fought together in the Sierra Maestra. When the new Communist Party was finally launched in 1965, this inner circle was formally installed as the party's Political Bureau, but the change was more a matter of name than process. Castro continued to make major policy decisions in consultation with the same people. The more elaborate decision-making machinery of the party, including the 100-member Central Committee, remained unused for most of the next decade. The PCC did not convene its First Congress until 1975, before which it had neither a program nor statutes. Its small size (just 55,000 members in 1969, or 0.6 percent of the population) made it the smallest ruling Communist Party in the world by a wide margin, and it had party organizations in only 16 percent of the nation's work centers, covering less than half the labor force.[7] Only in the 1970s did the PCC develop into an organization strong enough to assert real direction over the Cuban political system. By the time of the PCC's Founding Congress in 1975, it had grown to 202,807 members (2.2 percent of the population). By the late 1970s, the PCC had taken on the leading role in politics typical of ruling communist parties.[8]

During the ten years (1975–1986) from the first to the third party congresses, the PCC grew in size, organizational capacity, and administrative authority. Membership grew substantially, from 211,642 members in late 1975, to 434,143 in 1980, and 523,639 in 1985. Party bodies met regularly, and the apparatus developed a system for controlling the appointment of cadres to all major posts in the government and mass organizations.[9]

The dominant theme at the PCC's Second Congress in 1980 was continuity. The congress reaffirmed the validity of the program adopted at the First Congress and most of the supporting resolutions. The bulk of the discussion both before and during the congress focused on social and economic development.[10] The party's work, as Castro noted in his main report, had been "directed towards boosting and consolidating the Economic Planning and Management System, improving the mechanisms of economic leadership, and raising the quality of production."[11]

In the mid-1980s, Mikhail Gorbachev's perestroika and glasnost stimulated more open debate about the future of state socialism throughout the communist bloc, and Cuba was no exception. Party ideological chief Carlos Aldana would later confess to being among those smitten by Gorbachev's ideas, until he was set straight by Fidel.[12] Castro, too, saw the economic failings of the Soviet planning model—the inefficiency, the tendency to produce corruption, the erosion of ideology by the individualism of material incentives. But where Gorbachev saw the need for more radical economic restructuring to give fuller scope to the market, Castro saw the limited market reforms of the 1970s as the source of the problem, not the solution. Thus the Cuban version of perestroika was to reverse course, limiting and scaling back the use of market mechanisms and reemphasizing, once again, the political-ideological element of economic command.

The Third Congress in 1986 marked the launch of the Rectification campaign, a major retreat from the Soviet-sponsored socialist-economic management system (System of Economic Management and Planning, SDPE) installed in the mid-1970s and praised during the Second Congress. Criticizing the SDPE for fostering inefficiency, corruption, and profit-minded selfishness, Castro called for the "rectification of errors and negative tendencies" in the economic management. The campaign focused on recentralizing economic planning authority, and dismantling SDPE material incentives and market mechanisms.[13] The free farmers' markets launched in 1980 were closed, wage inequalities were narrowed, and voluntary labor was touted once again—all echoes of the radicalism of the late 1960s.

By putting politics in command over economic policy, the Rectification campaign implicitly meant a more assertive role for the PCC. Principal responsibility for economic policy moved from the Central Planning Board (*Junta Central de Planificación*, JUCEPLAN) to a special "Central Group" of the PCC's Political Bureau.[14] The top planning official, Humberto Pérez, was dropped from his alternate membership in the Political Bureau at the Third Congress. In the PCC Central Committee, 37 percent of the full members and 47 percent of the alternates were replaced—the largest turnover in the party's elite bodies since its founding. The new leaders promoted to the Political Bureau included the leaders of mass organizations and provincial PCC secretaries, in line with the Rectification theme of focusing on ideological work led by the party.[15]

THE COMMUNIST PARTY IN THE SPECIAL PERIOD: THE FOURTH CONGRESS

At the end of the 1980s, the Cuban regime was rocked by a bewildering rush of events, both domestic and international. At home, the arrest, trial, and execution of General Arnaldo Ochoa and his co-conspirators for cocaine trafficking, and subsequent corruption trials, struck a heavy blow to regime legitimacy. During a period when the standard of living for ordinary Cubans had been falling and Fidel Castro had been exhorting people to emulate the selflessness of Che Guevara by working harder for less, the scandals revealed that a significant number of senior officials were living luxuriously through corruption.[16]

Abroad, the European communist states were experiencing a flowering of economic and political reform spurred by Gorbachev's policies of glasnost and perestroika, which ran directly counter to Cuba's retreat from market mechanisms. There was a vigorous, albeit somewhat veiled, intellectual debate in Cuba over the merits of Gorbachev's reforms until the summer of 1989, by which time Castro's negative verdict on the experiments had been registered unequivocally.[17] Then the sudden collapse of European communism triggered an economic cataclysm in Cuba, prompting an uncharacteristically vigorous debate over the future of the revolution.

Held at the beginning of Cuba's "Special Period in a Time of Peace," the PCC's Fourth Congress endorsed a series of economic and political reforms designed to bring Cuba safely through the trauma of the demise of the socialist bloc. The Special Period's economic measures were analogous to a wartime economic crisis plan; its political measures went under the general rubric of "perfecting" and "revitalizing" Cuba's political institutions.

As in 1970, after the failure of the ten-million-ton sugar harvest, the Cuban leadership reacted to the crisis both by revising economic policy and trying to rebuild regime legitimacy by making political institutions more responsive to popular demands. From the outset, however, the basic strategy was to undertake only the reforms absolutely necessary to guarantee the survival of the existing order, although the political leadership was not always in agreement about how extensive the requisite reforms needed to be. A transition away from either socialism (i.e., state control of the commanding heights of the economy) or Leninism (one-party rule with limited freedoms of expression and association) was never seriously contemplated, as symbolized by Castro's slogan of the time, "Socialism or death!"[18]

Starting in late 1993, the government adopted a series of structural economic reforms, including the reintroduction of free farmers' markets, the transformation of most state farms into cooperatives, the legalization of self-employment in most occupations, the reduction of subsidies to state enterprises, the reduction of price subsidies on nonessential consumer goods, and the legalization of dollars. Outside analysts disagreed as to whether these limited reforms were sufficient to produce stable, long-term growth, but their success at reversing the slide in Gross Domestic Product (GDP) meant that Cuba's political leadership was able to forego more drastic changes.

In the political realm, reforms were less dramatic. Fidel Castro's political diagnosis was that Cuba had copied too closely the economic and political models of the European socialist states, thus reproducing in Cuba a form of socialism that was highly bureaucratized and apolitical, in the sense that the party focused its efforts too much on economic management and not enough on the "political work" of sustaining its ideological hegemony.[19] This was Castro's rationale for Rectification, his explanation for the eventual collapse of the European regimes, and his motive for limiting political reforms during the Special Period.[20]

To counter the political weaknesses they saw in Europe, the Cuban leaders sought to reform their political institutions by making them more responsive. For the PCC, the first wave of change was the introduction of secret ballot elections for party leaders at the base (in the workplace "nuclei") in early 1990. Prior to that, elections had been by open nomination and a show of hands. Subsequently, new municipal and provincial leaders were elected (in the usual way, from slates of preselected nominees), producing a 50 percent turnover in municipal leaders and the replacement of two of the fourteen provincial secretaries.[21]

Next came a major downsizing of the party bureaucracy preceding the Fourth Party Congress. The number of departments in the Central Committee staff organization was reduced from nineteen to nine, and the staff was cut by 50 percent. The

Party Secretariat was abolished as a separate organization (though later reinstated), with its organizational responsibilities distributed to individual members of the Political Bureau. Provincial committee staffs were cut as well, and overall, some two-thirds of the positions in the PCC's paid apparatus were abolished. In the posts that remained, a significant number of the incumbents were replaced.[22]

The March 1990 call for the Fourth Party Congress sought an unprecedented openness in debate, not just among party members but among the entire populace, so as to foster greater participation and build "the necessary consensus" for the government's policy response to the Special Period.[23] But the call was so extraordinary that people did not know how to respond, and the leadership halted the discussions after just a few weeks because the grassroots meetings were producing little more than hortatory praise for the party and the revolution. "We're just not used to debating," explained party ideological chief Carlos Aldana.[24] In June, debate resumed under the guidance of a new Political Bureau statement emphasizing the virtues of open discussion. But the revised call set limits, noting that the discussions were intended to provide "political clarification" and that the socialist character of the Cuban system and leading role of the party were not open to debate.[25] Party conservatives thought the debate process, despite its limitations, was still too vigorous.[26]

Eventually, some three million participated in the pre-congress discussion, producing over a million suggestions.[27] There was sharp debate on issues such as whether to allow religious believers to join the Communist Party, and on whether free farmers' markets, abolished during Rectification, ought to be resumed.[28] The principal political criticisms voiced concerned the sclerotic bureaucratism that had overtaken local government and the mass organizations.[29] One of the more popular suggestions was to have Provincial Assembly and National Assembly delegates directly elected rather than picked by the Municipal Assembly delegates.[30]

Debate continued at the Fourth Congress itself when it opened in October 1991, and for the first time, some votes on proposed resolutions were not unanimous. The party statutes were amended to redefine the PCC as the party of the "Cuban nation" rather than the party of the working class, and the new statutes emphasized its ideological roots in the ideas of José Martí as well as Marx and Lenin.[31] The prohibition on party membership for religious believers was lifted, and the process for choosing new party members was simplified so that more members could be drawn from work centers based on a vote of their coworkers (rather than requiring sponsorship by existing members or prior membership in the Youth Communist Union).[32] Over the next five years, these changes produced a flood of new members as the PCC's ranks grew from 611,627 at the Fourth Congress to 780,000 in 1997 on the eve of the Fifth Congress. By 1997, 232,000 people, one-third of the PCC's total membership, had joined the party since the beginning of the Special Period.[33]

The Fourth Congress also adopted the suggestion that all delegates to People's Power assemblies be directly elected by their constituents and called for the strengthening of the National Assembly's work commissions.[34] But it rejected proposals made in the pre-congress meetings that candidates be allowed to campaign and thereby present contrasting policy views. Nor did it endorse the idea of allowing competing policy views in the state media.[35] On the economic front, the congress endorsed a liberalization of rules governing foreign direct investment and the legalization of self-employment, but it rejected reopening the free farmers' markets (though as the economic crisis deepened, this decision would be reversed).[36]

DIVISIONS IN THE PARTY: REFORMERS VS. HARDLINERS

The limited reforms produced by the Fourth Congress were the result of an internal struggle in the PCC between a reform faction, led by party ideological chief Carlos Aldana, UJC First Secretary (later Foreign Minister) Roberto Robaina, and economic manager Carlos Lage, on the one hand, and a conservative faction (*los duros* or "hardliners," as they are known in Cuba) led by José Ramón Machado Ventura and José Ramón Balaguer, on the other. The reformers pushed for the use of market mechanisms to speed economic recovery, and greater political space for dissenting views that were not manifestly counterrevolutionary. The conservatives argued that rapid economic change would undercut the party's political control and that any political opening in the midst of economic crisis risked setting off a torrent of criticism that might sweep away the regime, as happened in Eastern Europe and the Soviet Union.[37]

A delay of several months in convening the Fourth Congress was attributed to the unresolved internal debate between reformers and conservatives. "There is a major struggle between the forces represented by Aldana and those of Machado Ventura, and Fidel hasn't decided between them," explained an unnamed Cuban government official.[38] When the congress did convene, radical reform proposals, particularly creating a prime minister position separate from the first secretary of the party, thereby devolving some of Castro's authority to other decision makers, were not on the agenda. The leadership had decided that major political changes were too risky in light of Cuba's economic problems. "For the revolution to be perfected, it must first close ranks," Carlos Aldana explained after the close of the congress.[39] Nevertheless, the reformers fared reasonably well in the new leadership line-up; Carlos Lage and Abel Prieto, head of the National Union of Writers and Artists (UNEAC), were added to the Political Bureau, joining Aldana and Robaina.

After the congress, the locus of debate between reformers and conservatives shifted to the local and national OPP elections scheduled for late 1992 and early 1993. The most significant change in OPP recommended by the Fourth PCC Congress and implemented by the constitutional changes in 1992, was allowing direct election of provincial and national People's Power delegates. But when the new electoral law was finalized in October 1992, it dashed any hopes for a significant opening of OPP to alternative voices. The ban on campaigning was retained and the nomination of provincial and national assembly candidates was entrusted to Candidacy Commissions. Through an elaborate process of consultation and suggestions from mass organizations, municipal assemblies, and local work centers, the Constituency Commissions produced slates of nominees with just one candidate per seat. Voters only had the choice of voting yes or no.[40] Thus the election process at the provincial and national levels avoided the possibility of even implicit policy differences among candidates of the sort that could occur in local contests.

The cause of party reformers was dealt a severe blow in September 1992 when Carlos Aldana, the most powerful Cuban politician besides the Castro brothers, was dismissed from the Political Bureau, ostensibly for involvement in illegal financial dealings.[41] Aldana's dismissal changed the balance of power within the top echelons of the party in favor of the conservatives. His position as chief of ideology for the Central Committee was taken over by conservative José Ramón Balaguer, who was also promoted to the Political Bureau.[42]

As the economy deteriorated in 1992 and 1993, the Cuban leadership's tolerance for political dissent contracted along with it. Raúl Castro emerged as the pivotal figure in the regime's response. Despite being hostile to the idea of political liberalization, he was a persistent advocate of economic reforms, applying the management experiments underway in the armed forces since 1986 to the state sector of the civilian economy. These reforms, adopted under the rubric of the Enterprise Perfecting Plan (*Perfeccionamiento Empresarial*), involved significant decentralization of management authority and increased use of market-based incentives.[43] In 1993, as food shortages worsened, Raúl finally convinced Fidel to allow the reopening of private farmers' markets as a means of stimulating food production. Providing enough for people to eat had become a matter of national security. "Beans are more important than cannons," Raúl argued.[44]

But on political issues, Raúl was intransigent. In the midst of a government crackdown on the small dissident movement that followed the Fourth Congress, he warned that the government might revive the Revolutionary Tribunals used to try accused counterrevolutionaries in the early 1960s.[45] In March 1996, Raúl presented a report from the Political Bureau to a plenum of the Central Committee in which he outlined, with considerable candor, the political and ideological challenges posed by the collapse of European communism, Cuba's terrible economic decline, and the regime's necessary concessions to the market and private sector. All this had created "feelings of depression and political confusion," he acknowledged. The party needed to wage a "battle of ideas" to explain these events, lest people lose faith in socialist values and be seduced by capitalist consumerism. "We must convince the people, or the enemy will do it."[46]

As an object, negative lesson, he singled out the Central Committee's own research centers, especially the Center for the Study of the Americas (CEA), which had fallen prey to U.S. efforts at "internal subversion." Moreover, he extended his critique to every institution of intellectual pursuit. He warned against the mass media taking an overly critical attitude—an error that eroded party authority in Eastern Europe and the Soviet Union, paving the way for the restoration of capitalism. The party would need to "examine" all these institutions, he concluded, in order to thwart U.S. schemes to turn them into "fifth columnists."

Party conservatives were able to gain the upper hand because of heightened tension between Cuba and the United States. Raúl's March 1996 speech came just a few weeks after the Cuban air force shot down two Brothers to the Rescue planes, which prompted the quick passage of the Helms-Burton bill, further tightening the U.S. embargo and writing it into law. But even before the shoot-down, Cuban leaders had been increasingly concerned that Washington might exploit the growing diversity of Cuban society to subvert the revolution. Discontent and demoralization were real, for all the reasons Raúl Castro outlined, and the proliferation of groups and social sectors not directly under party control—small farmers, entrepreneurs, the churches, NGOs—created openings that the enemy might exploit.

STABILIZING THE STATUS QUO: THE FIFTH CONGRESS

The Fifth Congress held in 1997 offered an opportunity to assess the effectiveness of the party's and government's response to the crisis of the Special Period. Two main resolutions were discussed in the preparatory meetings—one on economic policy and one on politics. The economic resolution called for greater efficiency and continued growth of the tourist sector as the leading source of hard currency; it offered no new reforms.[47] The political resolution, entitled, "The Party of Unity, Democracy and the Human Rights We Defend," argued in defense of Cuba's one-party system led by the Communist Party, in favor of socialist democracy based on mass participation rather than the bourgeois "liberalism" of contention among diverse interests, and for human rights based on social justice rather than unfettered political liberties. In short, it presented a brief for the political status quo. The document portrayed the revolution of 1959 as a direct continuation of the struggle for independence and national sovereignty stretching back to 1868, and the Cuban Communist Party as the "legitimate heir" of José Martí's Cuban Revolutionary Party. Disunity among the revolutionary forces led to defeat in 1878, to U.S. domination after 1898, and to the collapse of the 1933 revolution. Unity required, as in the time of Martí, a single party to prevent the United States from reimposing neocolonial capitalism on Cuba.[48]

The Fifth Congress elected a new Central Committee of only 150 members, far below the 225 elected at the Fourth Congress. The downsizing was intended to make the body more efficient and to prevent it from being infected with any "ideological viruses," explained Raúl Castro, who apparently had a major role in the selection process. "What happened to the socialist countries of Eastern Europe and the Soviet Union is not going to happen here," he added.[49] Apparently, the diversity of views inside the party that produced differences between reformers and hardliners, although submerged since Aldana's dismissal, persisted. Reformers suffered yet another blow, when Foreign Minister Roberto Robaina was fired for poor performance in 1999 and was replaced by Felipe Pérez Roque, Castro's chief of staff, a reputed ideological hardliner.[50]

The reaffirmation of the limited reform strategy made at the Fifth Party Congress suggested that Castro and his top lieutenants were generally convinced they had weathered the worst of the economic and political maelstrom following the Soviet Union's collapse. The gradual recovery of the economy and the absence of further outbreaks of public disorder after 1994 served as evidence of their strategy's success.

TOWARD THE FUTURE

Despite the changes forced on the Cuban Communist Party over the preceding decade, at the turn of the century it was still led by the charismatic founder of the revolution, who kept alive the flame of radical nationalism and social justice. Fidel Castro's authority was unassailable within the revolutionary leadership. At moments when the revolution was riven by sharp cleavages, Castro's authority provided the glue to hold the elite together—through the conflicts between the urban wing of the 26th of July Movement and the Rebel Army, between the veterans of the Sierra and the old communists, between the armed forces and the Interior Ministry in the aftermath of the Ochoa affair, and between reformers and hardliners during the Special Period.

Since Castro could reach out and resolve any policy issue he chose, elite decision making inevitably involved lobbying Fidel. Other leaders had to compete for Castro's time and attention, striving to get him to focus on their priority issues and to decide in their favor.[51] Policy conflicts among elite factions were thus channeled upward to Fidel for resolution, rather than causing permanent splits or expanding in scope to draw in potential allies from state and party institutions or the mass public.

When Castro departs, this will all change. Raúl Castro will assume the formal mantle of leadership as head of the party and government, but despite a strong managerial record as Minister of the Revolutionary Armed Forces, Raúl lacks his older brother's charisma and keen political instincts. He may inherit the regime's top titles, but he will not enjoy the authority to demand conformity from fellow leaders.

On a number of issues, the post-Castro leadership will undoubtedly be in accord. They will be determined to maintain Cuba's independence and national sovereignty—that is, to prevent the island from falling once again into political and economic dependence on the United States. They will also agree on the need to maintain the social achievements of the revolution, especially the ones that enjoy the highest level of popular support—the advanced system of health care and education. But as the new leadership faces tough policy choices, debate will surely intensify, spurred by those who favor more thorough-going economic reforms and greater political liberalization. After winning some key battles in the early 1990s, the reformers have been frustrated by Fidel's intransigence. Pent-up demands for further change will be hard to contain when Castro no longer stands as an insurmountable bulwark against it.

How will Castro's heirs settle on the new rules of the political game? If history is any guide, the new leadership will be more collective, not only because no one can fill Fidel's boots, but because surviving elites generally prefer a process that is more rule-guided and hence less arbitrary than the past. Raúl Castro himself has anticipated as much. "Many other comrades and I will have authority," he remarked in a 2001 interview. "However, we want the party to have it, which is the only thing which can guarantee continuity, the unity of the nation. Within that unity we can have differences and everything we might want to air."[52]

Collective leadership typically means that intra-elite debates, at least within the Political Bureau of the party, become more vigorous, meaningful, and are decided by voting. Leadership politics shifts from everyone lobbying the founding father to coalitions lobbying one another, and paying special attention to the undecided. Political resources like bureaucratic position take on new importance. Stalemates are possible, and losers may be tempted to expand the scope of conflict in hopes of prevailing by bringing new allies into the contest.[53] More open policy debate among Castro's heirs will likely spark more open debate among the public. Some members of the elite—the reformers, most likely—will want to foster greater space for public discussion as a way of strengthening their hand in intra-elite argument.

Fidel Castro's immense personal authority at the dawn of the revolutionary government was rooted in his personal courage, political savvy, and heroic achievements as the leader who made the revolution. Historically, the revolutionary regime has drawn legitimacy from Fidel Castro, not the other way around. For Castro's heirs, the situation will be reversed. Their right to govern will derive from the legitimacy of the institutions over which they preside, not from their personal virtues, which can only appear weak and pallid in comparison to Fidel's. To meet the challenge of legitimacy, Castro's heirs might well follow the pattern set by the successors to regime founders in Eastern Europe, appealing to culturally resonant themes, especially nationalism.[54] In Cuba, of course, the party and revolutionary government have steeped themselves in the symbols of Cuban nationalism from the very beginning. In recent years, nationalist themes featuring José Martí have gotten greater play than Leninist ones.

The Cuban Communist Party has already made significant progress in addressing one succession issue that stymied both the Soviet and Chinese regimes for years—the issue of generational leadership succession. The first hint of change came at the PCC's Third Congress, which for the first time removed a number of "los históricos" (the historic leaders of the revolution) from the Political Bureau and Central Committee. The Fourth Party Congress went even farther in this regard. Of the eleven new people added to the twenty-five-member Political Bureau, all were under fifty years old. The new Central Committee of 225 was made up of 126 new members and 99 incumbents, only 23 of whom were members of the founding Central Committee in 1965. The average age of the new Central Committee was just 47.[55] The Fifth Party Congress elected a Central Committee that was younger still, and only half the size of the previous body.[56] On the new Political Bureau, Fidel Castro was the oldest member, and the average age was just 53. The National Assembly has experienced a similar process of incorporating younger leaders. The 1993 election produced an Assembly with 83 percent new members, with an average age of 43, which remained unchanged through the elections in 1998.[57] "There has already been a tangible transfer of power [to the next generation]," explained Foreign Minister Felipe Pérez Roque, "and that has been done by Fidel."[58]

The Cuban Communist Party is faced with a polity in flux. Even the limited economic reforms forced on the regime by the need to re-enter the global economy are having significant social reverberations and changing the political terrain of the future. As market reforms weaken the Communist Party's control over the economy, its political monopoly becomes frayed as well. Emergent entrepreneurs, both farmers and small businessmen, depend less and less on the state for their well-being. As they accumulate wealth and grow increasingly indispensable to the health of the economy, their desire for less government interference is certain to take a more explicitly political direction.

As Cubans increasingly interact with populations abroad, through tourism, family visits, and professional cooperation, the danger of "ideological contamination" increases. The proliferation of non-governmental organizations (NGOs) in recent years has created social networks independent of party supervision and direction. Even those that have been spawned by the government itself for the purpose of soliciting hard currency from foreign NGOs create mechanisms through which a growing number of Cubans will come into contact with people—and ideas—from abroad.

The government can try to quell these stirrings, but it cannot eliminate them because they are the unavoidable by-product of the economic concessions to capitalism Cuba has been forced to make. The market has eroded the scope of state and party control, creating what an observer of Eastern Europe called "islands of autonomy" in civil society which serve, albeit fragilely, as "safe spaces" within which people forge new social relationships and networks of communication, acquire consciousness of their common interests, and develop the capacity for politics outside the regime.[59] The future of the Cuban Communist Party will depend on whether it takes the leading role in adapting itself and the Cuban polity to these emerging social forces, or is swept aside by them.

NOTES

1. Castro first used the phrase in his July 26, 1973, speech commemorating the attack on Moncada barracks (which produced the headline quoted: *Granma Weekly Review*, August 5, 1973) and he has repeated it frequently in the years since.

2. The characterization of the party in the title of this chapter as the "single party of the Cuban nation," is from Alberto Alvariño Atienzar, "The Cuban Nation's Single Party," *Granma International*, May 13, 1997.

3. The three organizations were Fidel Castro's 26th of July Movement, the student-based Revolutionary Directorate, and the old communists of the Popular Socialist Party.

4. Castro's denunciation of the ORI was delivered in three speeches, on March 13, March 18, and March 22, 1962, reprinted in Fidel Castro, *Fidel Castro Denounces Sectarianism* (Havana: Ministry of Foreign Relations, 1962).

5. Fidel Castro, "Declaración del Primer Ministro...en el jucio contra el delator de los mártires de Humboldt 7," *Obra Revolucionaria* 7 (March 24, 1964): 5–47.

6. Raúl Castro, "Report to the Central Committee on the Activities of the Microfaction,"*Granma Weekly Review*, February 11, 1968.

7. For a more detailed discussion of the PCC's weakness in the 1960s and early 1970s, see William M. LeoGrande, "Party Development in Revolutionary Cuba," *Journal of Interamerican Studies and World Affairs* 21, no. 4 (November 1979): 457–480.

8. William M. LeoGrande, "The Communist Party of Cuba Since the First Congress," *Journal of Latin American Studies* 12, no. 2 (November 1980): 397–419.

9. Communist Party of Cuba, *Second Congress of the Communist Party of Cuba: Documents and Speeches* (Havana: Political Publishers, 1981): 77–84; Marifeli Pérez-Stable, "'We Are the Only Ones and There Is No Alternative': Vanguard Party Politics in Cuba, 1975–1991," in Enrique A. Baloyra and James A. Morris (eds.), *Conflict and Change in Cuba* (Albuquerque: University of New Mexico, 1993): 67–85.

10. Almost half of Fidel Castro's "Main Report" to the congress focuses on economic and social development plans, and the congress resolution on this subject is 123 pages long. Communist Party of Cuba, *Second Congress of the Communist Party of Cuba.*

11. Communist Party of Cuba, *Second Congress of the Communist Party of Cuba*, p. 80.

12. Mimi Whitefield and Andrés Oppenheimer, "No. 3 Man in Cuba Is Booted," *Miami Herald*, September 24, 1992; Howard W. French, "Cuban's Exit Hints at Trouble at Top," *New York Times*, September 27, 1992.

13. Sergio Roca, "The Comandante in his Economic Labyrinth," in Baloyra and Morris (eds.), *Conflict and Change in Cuba*, pp. 86–109.

14. Fidel Castro, *Main Report: Third Congress of the Communist Party of Cuba* (La Habana: Editora Política 1986): 38–39.

15. Jorge I. Domínguez, "Blaming Itself, Not Himself: Cuba's Political Regime After the Third Party Congress," in Sergio Roca (ed.), *Socialist Cuba: Past Interpretations and Future Challenges* (Boulder, CO: Westview, 1988): 3–10; Rhoda Rabkin, "Cuba: The Aging of a Revolution," in Roca (ed.), *Socialist Cuba*, pp. 33–56.

16. Juan M. del Aguila, "The Party, the Fourth Congress, and the Process of Counterreform,"in Jorge F. Pérez-López (ed), *Cuba at a Crossroads: Politics and Economics after the Fourth Party Congress* (Gainesville, University of Florida Press, 1994: 19–40.

17. Jorge I. Domínguez, "The Political Impact on Cuba of the Reform and Collapse of Communist Regimes," in Carmelo Mesa-Lago, (ed.), *Cuba after the Cold War* (Pittsburgh: University of Pittsburgh Press, 1993): 99–132.

18. Castro first used the slogan in January 1989 in two speeches commemorating the triumph of the revolution, but it only became a routine closing to his speeches in December after the collapse of the Eastern European communist regimes.

19. According to the "Resolution on the Program of the Communist Party of Cuba," adopted at the Fourth Party Congress in 1991, under the SDPE, "the political work and the actions of the revolutionary vanguard were reduced to mere formalities." The text of the resolution is in Gail Reed, *Island in the Storm: The Cuban Communist Party's Fourth Congress* (Melbourne, Australia: Ocean Press, 1992):101–110.

20. On the origins of Rectification and the collapse of socialism in Europe, see Castro's opening address to the Fourth Party Congress in Reed, *Island in the Storm*, pp. 25–79.

21. "Asambleas de balance en las organizaciones de base del Partido," *Granma*, January 6, 1990. Marifeli Pérez-Stable, *The Cuban Revolution: Origins, Course, and Legacy* (New York: Oxford University Press, 1999):169.

22. Susan Eckstein, *Back From the Future: Cuba Under Castro* (Princeton, NJ: Princeton University Press, 1994): 114.

23. Pérez-Stable, "'We Are the Only Ones and There Is No Alternative'," p. 81; "Llamamiento del Partido," *Granma Resumen Semanal*, March 25, 1990.

24. "Se require una participacíon consciente y activa," *Granma*, April 13, 1990; Reed, *Island in the Storm*, p. 14–15.

25. "Acuerdo del Buró Político sobre el proceso de discusion del llamamiento al IV Congreso," *Granma*, June 23, 1990.

26. Roca, "The Comandante in His Economic Labyrinth," in Baloyra and Morris (eds.), p. 102.

27. Reed, *Island in the Storm*, p. 17.

28. Eckstein, *Back From the Future*, p. 115.

29. Reed, *Island in the Storm*, p. 17–18. Eckstein, *Back From the Future*, p. 115.

30. Reed, *Island in the Storm*, p. 17.

31. Compare "Statutes of the Communist Party of Cuba," in *Second Congress of the Communist Party of Cuba*, p. 128, to the "Resolution on the Rules of the Cuban Communist Party" in Reed, *Island in the Storm*, p. 88.

32. "Resolution on the Rules of the Cuban Communist Party" in Reed, *Island in the Storm*, pp. 88, 89, 94.

33. Max Azicri, *Cuba Today and Tomorrow: Reinventing Socialism* (Gainesville: University Press of Florida, 2001): 338 fn.18; Fidel Castro Ruz, *Informe Central, Discurso de Clausura: V Congreso del Partido Comunista de Cuba* (La Habana: Editora Política 1997): 68.

34. "Resolution on Improving the Organization and Functioning of People's Power," in Reed, *Island in the Storm*, p. 122.

35. Jorge I. Domínguez, "Leadership Strategies and Mass Support: Cuban Politics Before and After the 1991 Party Congress," in Pérez-López, *Cuba at a Crossroads*: 1–18.

36. Domínguez, "Leadership Strategies and Mass Support," in Pérez-López, *Cuba at a Crossroads*.

37. A number of analysts have described the factional cleavages in the PCC: Eckstein, *Back From the Future*, pp. 257-58; Reed, *Island in the Storm*, p. 21; Andrés Oppenheimer, *Castro's Final Hour* (New York: Simon and Schuster, 1992): 379–80; Edward González, *Cuba: Clearing Perilous Waters?* (Santa Monica, CA: Rand, 1996): 39–42.

38. Pablo Alfonso, "Dispute Delays Party Session, Official Says," *Miami Herald*, March 29, 1991.

39. Oppenheimer, *Castro's Final Hour*, pp. 383–99.

40. The nomination process is discussed in detail in Arnold August, *Democracy in Cuba and the 1997–1998 Elections* (Havana: Editorial José Martí, 1999): 299–317.

41. James Canute, "Top Cuban Ideologue Dismissed over Scandal," *Financial Times* (London), October 13, 1992; no author, "Aldana Says Business Gaffe Led to Ouster," *Miami Herald*, September 29, 1992.

42. Andrés Oppenheimer, "Cuban Expelled from Party," *Miami Herald*, October 27, 1992; Reuters, "Cuba Replaces Official with Close Castro Ties," *Los Angeles Times*, September 24, 1992.

43. Oppenheimer, *Castro's Final Hour*, 385–86.

44. Larry Rohter, "Cubans Find the Army Rising as the Party Sinks," *New York Times*, June 8, 1995.

45. Lee Hockstader, "Cuba Steps Up Intimidation of Dissidents," *Washington Post*, January 21, 1992.

46. Raúl Castro, "The Political and Social Situation in Cuba and the Corresponding Tasks of the Party," *Granma International*, March 27, 1996.

47. "Resolución Económica del V Congreso del Partido Comunista de Cuba," online at www.cuba.cu/politica/webpcc/resoluci.htm.

48. "The Party of Unity, Democracy and the Human Rights We Defend," *Granma International*, May 1997. ("El Partido de la Unidad, la Democrácia y los Derechos Humanos Que Defendemos," at www.cuba.cu/politica/webpcc/unidad.html.

49. Serge F. Kovaleski, "Castro Appears Strong, Cuban Economy Weak," *Washington Post*, October 11, 1997; Juan O. Tamayo, "Raúl Castro Takes on a Higher Profile," *Miami Herald*, December 17, 1997.

50. Serge F. Kovaleski, "Cuba Replaces Foreign Minister With Top Aide to Castro," *Washington Post*, May 29, 1999.

51. Reformers in the PCC acknowledge as much with the refrain, "With Fidel, everything; against Fidel, nothing." Quoted in Eusebio Mujal-León and Joshua W. Busby, "Much Ado About Something? Regime Change in Cuba," *Problems of Communism* 48, no. 6 (November-December 2001): 6–18.

52. Vanessa Bauzá, "Looking at Cuba's Future: Who Is Raúl Castro?" *South Florida Sun Sentinel*, July 1, 2001.

53. E. E. Schattschneider, *The Semisovereign People* (New York: Holt, Rinehart and Winston, 1960).

54. Andrrzej Korbonski, "Leadership Succession and Political Change in Eastern Europe," *Studies in Comparative Communism* 9, nos. 1–2 (Spring-Summer 1976): 3–22.

55. Domínguez, "Leadership Strategies and Mass Support," and Juan M. del Aguila, "The Party, the Fourth Congress, and the Process of Counterreform," both in Pérez-López (ed), *Cuba at a Crossroads*, pp. 19–40.

56. Mark Fineman, "Castro Points to His Brother as Successor," *Los Angeles Times*, October 12, 1997.

57. David Clark Scott, "Castro's Foreign Office Choice: Sign of a New Generation?" *Christian Science Monitor*, April 1, 1993; Interview with Ricardo Alarcón in Cynthia Tucker, "Communism after Fidel Castro," *Atlanta Journal and Constitution*, July 8, 2001.

58. Scott Wilson, "The Face of Cuba's New Generation," *Washington Post*, September 12, 2000.

59. The concept of "islands of autonomy" is from Valerie Bunce, *Subversive Institutions: The Design and Destruction of Socialism and the State* (Cambridge: Cambridge University Press, 1999).

4

Cuba's Revolutionary Armed Forces

Last Bulwark of the State!
Last Bulwark of the Revolution?

Hal Klepak

INTRODUCTION

Few would doubt that Cuba's *Fuerzas Armadas Revolucionarias* (FAR) have been or still are an essential element of the state apparatus of the government of Fidel Castro. But the nature of that utility is rarely addressed. Instead, often rather glib analyses make comments on the vital role they play in propping up the state in its difficult moments or suggest the FAR are evolving in this way or that but without looking more deeply into the organization's role in support of that state and government.

This chapter will look at the nature of the internal role they have played and are currently playing in the service of the state and the revolution. It will be argued that while they have always been a lynchpin of both, especially as at the present when things are going badly, they remain first and foremost Cuban national armed forces and may well survive as such through any transition. This argument will be made beginning with a brief look backwards at the uses to which the FAR have been put since the "triumph" of the revolution in January 1959, emphasizing their remarkable flexibility in responding to President Castro's requirements from them over the period 1959–1990. Then we will discuss the particular challenges of the Special Period, declared in the summer of 1990 and still with us to this day, again with a view to analyzing the FAR's ability to respond to even more varied, and arguably more difficult demands over that period. We will then be able to ask the question as to what extent they can play a key role in any transition as a result of their remarkable utility in the present stage of the revolution and Cuba's history.

THE FAR FROM 1959 UNTIL 1990

The Cuban revolutionary armed forces date their official existence from the arrival of the yacht *Granma*, carrying just over eighty insurgents from exile in Mexico, to the coast of Oriente province in the east of Cuba, in November 1956. This was the real beginning of the continuous and organized armed struggle that was to topple the Batista government in the first week of January 1959, and bring to power that of the commander of the expedition Fidel Castro Ruz.

After impressive growth and increasingly effective fighting, this armed force was by the summer of 1958 able to advance in two columns down the length of Cuba while other columns continued the struggle in and around the hills of the Sierra Maestra, the island's highest mountain range near where the 1956 landing had taken place. Besting the corrupt Batista army in battle after battle, it was a hardened and intensely loyal force that moved on to capture the capital of Havana in the first two days of the new year, 1959.

Since the Batista army (and his police and secret police) had been disbanded and entirely replaced by the *Ejército Rebelde* (Rebel Army), the latter became the only armed force available to defend the regime and the country. Not surprisingly and following firm Latin American custom, Fidel appointed in October 1959 his own brother Raúl as Minister of the FAR (the Ministry of the Armed Forces was named MINFAR) and retained the post of commander-in-chief (always termed *comandante* in Cuba, the title by which people refer to Castro in all walks of life on the island).

Over those same early months of the Castro government, the armed forces were tasked with a bewildering number of jobs within the new structures of the state. Castro needed people he could trust in positions of importance, especially those such as agrarian reform where opposition was soon strong and always vocal. But elsewhere in the political reorganization of the government and for the increasingly state-administered economy, military personnel in whom Fidel felt he could rely were called in. Given the small size of the force, only a few thousand in January 1959, these demands were hard to fill and very young men indeed took over portfolios for which they had sometimes little but usually no training. Loyalty to the *comandante* and to his revolutionary program counted for more than efficiency in these trying but heady days. Under these conditions the Communist Party, for some months growing in its influence on the Cuban state, began obviously to take an even greater role in the running of the island. The military were to be asked now to take on the task of building a real professional army capable of deterring United States attack, but in its event of either defeating it or at least making it an undertaking of such cost that Washington would rue the day it took it on. In this they would soon be able to count on steadily increasing amounts of Soviet assistance in the form of advisers, training opportunities, doctrine, equipment, and weapons. In this professionalization process, slowly but surely the FAR's personnel moved out of non-military tasks.

It is important to note, however, that this transformation was never completed. Military officers still held many posts of a strictly non-military nature in later years and the FAR could be asked at any time to undertake tasks normally done by civilian authorities. Indeed, in the great but ill-starred ten-million-ton sugar harvest planned for 1970 the FAR returned to national prominence as an essential element of the agricultural program. And it was rare throughout all these years when some element of the military forces was not engaged in activities of a non-professional nature.

Cuba's militarized status in the Americas, facing an overwhelming grouping of states led by the United States and anxious to overthrow the revolution and reverse its program, was occasioned as well by the "export of revolution" phase of Cuban foreign policy, when the FAR trained and otherwise assisted any number of insurgent movements in Latin America. While the number of personnel actually sent overseas at this stage was very small indeed, the numbers of other Latin American insurgents trained in Cuba was impressive. The real expansion of the forces, however, to yield large and professional regular forces and vast reserves, took place in stages, perhaps the most impressive of which was the adoption of the *Guerra de Todo el Pueblo* (War of All the People) strategy in the very early 1980s.

In the wake of President Reagan's electoral victory in the 1980 elections, combined with ever clearer indications that the USSR was not only not going to be willing to actually fight for Cuba in the case of a crisis with the United States, but also was not going to be continuing with its lavish defense hand-outs to the Cubans, Havana had to find a deterrent strategy more in keeping with the country's own capabilities. This required a new strategy and the expansion of the regular force to almost 300,000 strength, and the reserves in all their categories to several times that figure. Thus Cuba became an even more vastly militarized society, more so than even in the years of direct threat just after the revolution came to power.

The last years of the Cold War saw many changes for the FAR, again demonstrating their exceptional flexibility in serving the Castro government in a variety of fields. If the early 1980s were already showing that the Soviet connection was becoming if not a weak reed certainly a weaker reed, Cuba's economic conditions were requiring new thinking as well. In the mid to late-1980s Cuba entered a period of economic "Rectification" brought on by increasing problems of inefficiency, absenteeism, and excessive centralization. Fidel was apparently losing confidence in Soviet-style management techniques and gave Raúl the go-ahead to implement his own thinking in restructuring the military industries of the country.

If he succeeded, the intention was that these methods applied in military industries should be employed more globally in addressing Cuba's economic woes. Deemed the "System of Enterprise Perfection" (or Improvement), the new approach emphasized decentralization, streamlined and effective modern management techniques, flexibility, discipline, hierarchy, a chain of command along military lines, dedication, and competitiveness as an openly desirable goal. Officers were sent abroad, usually not to the Soviet Union, to study modern management techniques. And many of these, and other, officers were placed in charge not only of military industries but increasingly of civilian ones as well. More dramatic change still was on its way and the armed forces were to be called, perhaps in as striking a fashion as ever in their history, to lead the way in the struggle to save the revolution from a context as dangerous as any it had ever known.

THE SPECIAL PERIOD

In June 1990 Fidel Castro announced the "Special Period in a Time of Peace." The defense plan for a Special Period in Time of War, a national planning document related to the conduct of a spirited and long-term defense of the island, was thus amended for a peacetime effort. Belt tightening as never before applied would become the rule as the nation reeled from the economic crisis detailed in other chapters of this book.

The FAR had of course been something of the spoiled child of the Soviet and Warsaw Pact connection. Although Cuba had never joined the pact, a policy decision which might well have brought U.S. direct intervention, the island benefited enormously from its special status with Moscow and several other pact members. Over some thirty years the military had enjoyed a generosity on the part of the Soviets that left the FAR almost completely in the Soviet style of armed forces. Cuban divisions were organized along Soviet lines, the FAR's tactical and strategic doctrine was closely modeled on the Soviet equivalents always given that the island's strategic situation was of course vastly different from its European friends, equipment had long since become virtually completely Soviet, and training was not only along Soviet lines but its senior and more complicated elements were usually conducted in the Soviet Union itself. And while Cubans were careful not to allow the Soviet instructors in Cuba to have excessive access to the rank and file of the FAR, their policy of "training the trainers" left deep marks on the Cuban military from which even now they have not moved very far.

Virtually overnight this connection was broken with the new Gorbachev policy of "cash and carry," meaning that Cuba could not even obtain vital spare parts for its equipment and weapons, never mind purchase anything new. Senior training in key tactical fields was abandoned or done with minimum resources. Fuel consumption took a nosedive with perhaps only a third of 1980s levels available in the first years after the rupture with Moscow. Exchanges of officers evaporated as did plum postings for FAR personnel abroad. While Cuba had already abandoned its forward policy in support of insurrections in Latin America and Africa, it now could not afford to do anything significant at all on the regional or international stage.

With little fuel, virtually no new spare parts, a nearly collapsed training system, poor availability of ammunition especially for training purposes, no new equipment or weapons, and a shattered world intelligence network formerly considered as the best in the Third World, Cuba's forces had little to look forward to. Attaché offices were cut to less than a dozen for a force the former envy of many developed countries for its widespread relations with armed forces almost everywhere.

The forces over the next three years were cut massively and career bottlenecks appeared at almost all ranks. From nearly 300,000 in fulltime service the FAR were soon to know a mere fraction of that figure, well under 100,000 and still falling. The defense budget, expressed even in the rapidly devaluing national currency, gave the lie to a serious effort to keep defense as a priority. The security and defense budget (called "defense and internal order" in national budgeting) received in 1990 $1.149 billion. But in the very first year of the Special Period it suffered a dramatic cut to $882.2 million. This sharp decline was to continue and in 1992 the sector received a mere $736.4 million. The next year, perhaps the deepest moment of the Special Period, some $712.8 million were given over to this sphere.

Significantly, the defense and security sector did not experience the recovery after these years that one could see in community services and sports. The year 1994 saw a continued decline to $651.2 million and even in 1995, usually seen as the beginning of real recovery from the worst of the Special Period, a further fall in the defense and security budget brought the figure to $610.1 million. Indeed, as late as 1996, with the recovery now under way, the security forces saw their portion of the national budget lose another quarter of its total, ending up with some $496.7 million. While almost all other sectors were by this time on the mend, especially education, public health, social security, and housing, the defense sector, far from being the darling of the government, was being asked to sacrifice most and longest.

The trend was only reversed in part in 1997, when the security sector received its first increase in the Special Period, reaching $637.5 million. But this was only some 55 percent of its pre–Special Period budget and was being allocated in a peso worth only a small fraction of its 1990 value. Even so, for 1998, the figure fell back to $537.1 million, only recovering a bit more seriously in 1999 with $752.3 million. In 2000, the last year for which "proper" figures are available, the total was $879.6 million, ten years after the beginning of the Special Period and still a mere 75 percent of the 1990 figure.[1]

With these vastly reduced resources in manpower, equipment, weapons, skills, and money, the FAR were asked to shoulder more, not fewer burdens within the Cuban recovery and survival plan as designed in the months and years after 1990. We can now look at the extraordinary utility their flexibility, loyalty, and discipline offered the Castro government in the now decade and a half of the Special Period.

THE ARMED FORCES AS MANAGER OF THE ECONOMY

The armed forces, as we have seen, were no strangers to a role in managing the national economy. From 1959 into the early 1990s, their role might have evolved but they were never entirely out of the field and as revolutionary armed forces accustomed to non-traditional roles, they quickly adapted to the tasks they received from their *comandante*. And from the mid-1980s that role was again expanding.

Thus the FAR cannot have been entirely surprised when they learned that they would have a special role again in the 1990s as a result of the vastly reduced circumstances of the Cuban state as of the beginning of that decade. But nothing surely prepared them for the scope of the jobs they were going to be given over such a short time. Essentially they were asked to do four things in contributing to the national effort of the Special Period:

- continue to deter attack and in the event it came, defeat it or at least inflict heavy losses on the aggressor but do so with greatly reduced resources;
- feed themselves from their own resources;
- take over the management of many key industries of the state, especially those with foreign exchange earning potential, bringing to them military discipline and efficiency; and
- maintain emergency services in the light of the increasing strains faced by Cuban society.[2]

Feeding themselves turned out to be rather easier than many expected. The forces had for long been involved in agriculture, especially at harvest time, and the *Ejército Juvenil de Trabajo* (Army of Working Youth), a specially established conscript force set up in 1973 which does basic training but then turns its efforts to the economy rather than strictly national defense roles, was reinforced, given better leadership and resources, and set to work even harder in the fields. Soon the armed forces were not only feeding themselves but also sending excess production into the agricultural markets of the towns and cities of the island.

Even more striking than the agricultural role was that in businesses earning foreign exchange. The military moved into control of even more of these industries than those where it had a foothold since the late 1980s or even before. While tourism is the best known of these, there are others such as telecommunications, real estate assistance, hunting lodge management, dredging, taxi companies, hotel construction and management, internal airline service, discotheques, restaurants, shopping centers, metallurgy, vehicle production, general construction, and of course arms and ammunition production.

In addition, military officers have in recent years been ministers of government departments as diverse as Fisheries and Merchant Marine, Communications, Transport, Sugar, and many others. Joint ventures with foreign capital became common with the military deeply involved in them. Only firms dealing with the direct production of defense material were excluded from such deals.

Through all these directly economic or largely economic roles the FAR have come to have an enormous influence on the day-to-day running of the state and its economy. Vital for earning foreign exchange, without which the crisis the revolution is currently facing would be immeasurably more serious, the forces are now inextricably linked with that economy and the national recovery plan as a whole.

THE POLITICAL ROLE

The Cuban armed forces are hierarchically organized, disciplined, present in regular or reserve form throughout the island, mobile, flexible, accustomed to planning and in particular to "worst case planning," constantly updating themselves as individual members and as an institution, *available* to the state, and *armed*. Their loyalty is unquestioned and they have never failed the revolution despite some ups and downs such as in Grenada, and with the Ochoa crisis of 1989. But this list of highly useful characteristics is the exclusive preserve of the FAR and no one else in Cuba.

No other institution can claim anything like this list. Only the Communist Party could in the past have made the assertion that it was in the same league in terms of influence in the country. And it no longer can do that. For the armed forces not only enjoy these otherwise unheard of advantages but many others as well. For a start, and as mentioned, they feed themselves and part of the rest of the population as well. In addition, they enjoy prestige in the country that the party can simply not match. They are not closely associated with the political ideology which much of the country, and especially the young, challenge. Instead, they are a source of pride for many Cubans *qua* Cubans as having a splendid reputation gained at home in events such as the Bay of Pigs and abroad in places such as southern Africa where their exploits in recent wars have brought much credit onto the institution.

In addition, they are probably the most important institution in earning foreign exchange and related to this, they probably come close to paying for themselves. For the other side of the drop in defense budgets during the Special Period is of course that to a considerable extent the FAR paid for their own operating costs. And while obviously it is easy to say this, it is nonetheless clear that only this ability made the FAR able to weather the current storm without collapse. The party does not pay for itself. MINFAR does. In a country as financially strapped as Cuba, this translates into real power and influence.

This is not to say that the party is altogether a spent force in Cuba. This is not the case and events such as the hurricanes of the early autumn of 2004, where the party did arguably a better job coming to the assistance of the public than did the FAR (far from the case normally where the forces do a superb job at disaster relief and bringing succor to the public), show that there is life in the old institution still. But compared to the forces, the party is increasingly less central to decisions taken on the future of the country.

The party's actual role in the control of the forces has been likewise weakened massively in recent years. It should be said that this control has been exaggerated by many analysts with a determination to make the FAR appear more like their Warsaw Pact former comrades than is warranted by the facts. For example, the political officers of the "commissar" type the rule in that alliance's members, following the early Soviet pattern of the post-1917 era, never existed in Cuba. There is no parallel chain of command in the FAR as was common elsewhere. The commanding officer of a unit is the unquestioned commander whatever the officer responsible for political training might think. In the early struggle for power between the FAR and the party the former had much the better of it.

In recent years the independence of the forces has grown apace. Fidel's turning to the FAR once again in time of crisis, and the growth of its already immense national role, has made controlling it from the party a virtual impossibility. This of course must always be analyzed with the point in mind that there is in Cuba no automatic division between party and army with so many senior officers, party members, and loyal ones, and with the links between the two so generalized in the state apparatus.

THE DOMESTIC DETERRENT ROLE

The role of the FAR in deterring foreign aggression is, of course, well known. Less considered is the nonetheless equally obvious role the armed forces have in deterring internal disorder. It is important to be clear on what is meant here. In Cuba the overwhelmingly key player in keeping the lid on popular discontent is MININT, the Interior Ministry, tasked directly with this responsibility. But the armed forces have a highly important if more indirect role in the job as well.

This is as a result of two factors that should be kept in mind. The Interior Ministry of Cuba is not an independent element of the state but exists under the command of the armed forces proper. The uniform may be slightly different. Procedures and priorities most certainly are. But administratively and in much more than that sense, the MININT belongs to the FAR. That there is a separate ministry should not hide this fact from analysis. In addition, since the shocking revelations or political maneuvers of the 1989 Ochoa scandal that connection and subordination has become more evident than ever.[3] Several trusted senior generals of the FAR were transferred directly into the MININT at the time and the purge they conducted left the weakened institution under more striking military control than ever.

Be that as it may, the useful fiction of a division between the two ministries is all to the FAR's benefit and this expresses realities of the military institution's self-image of great importance. For the FAR have been raised believing deeply that they are the nation in arms, a revolutionary army in a real sense expressing the belief of the people in the revolution's aims and far from the Latin American model of a repressive force at the service of a corrupt and exploitative state. The FAR take as an article of faith that "el ejército no tira contra el pueblo" (the army does not fire on the people) as is the wider Latin American tradition. Such behavior was left well behind when the Batista government fell and its army was disbanded. Under those circumstances the FAR are keen to be seen to be as far away from any repressive role as possible and the observation of this author is that this desire has been largely achieved. Respect for the armed forces is widespread and obvious. As mentioned, pride in the FAR's achievements is important and everyone has members of his or her family serving in the FAR or its reserve components and a huge percentage of the population has done so itself.

Despite this prestige and relative distance from a repressive role, it is obvious that Cubans, like other citizens of most states, know very well that the armed forces are the embodiment of the last bulwark of the state and that if that state were about to collapse they would act to save it. This is reinforced by a constantly reiterated public posture on the part of the FAR of absolute loyalty and devotion to the present government, its leaders, and its objectives and ideals. The ability of this force to mobilize, even now under the difficult circumstances of the Special Period, vast numbers of people for everything from disaster relief operations to reserve forces exercises of a more traditional kind, means that here as well the FAR have an absolutely vital political role in the maintenance of domestic order and peace. No Cuban this author has ever interviewed believes that the FAR would not act to defend the revolution. And the knowledge of this, generalized to the population as a whole, must be a central feature of domestic order in the long run.

THE TRANSITION

It is in this general context that one must see the potential role of the FAR in any likely transition scenario. We have already shown the vast advantages the forces have over other elements of the state when it comes to staying power in difficult situations. But it must also be said that they are the element of the state, apart from MINREX (the Foreign Ministry), which has the closest ties with the other key potential actor, this time an external one in the person of the United States, and specifically with the vital security forces of the United States, in any transition.

Quietly, but ever so surely, the FAR has established relations of some very limited closeness with the U.S. security forces almost across the board.[4] And while this is in many senses obviously an external element of the political utility of the forces to the Cuban government, its likely dimension in internal order in a transition makes it fully internal as well. Specifically, the FAR and MININT have established reasonably close relations with their U.S. counterparts, given the attitudes of their two governments as a whole, at a number of levels, relations which may well make their cooperation in time of crisis not only possible but potentially palatable to other key sectors of the political picture of the time.

MINFAR has close links with the U.S. military through the requirement to handle any number of delicate issues along the border between the U.S. base at Guantánamo Bay and Cuban territory proper. There are constant communications between the two local commanders *in situ* and a crisis management arrangement of some sophistication is in place. In addition, U.S. Coast Guard and occasionally naval forces have often worked, and still do so, with their Cuban counterparts in key areas of U.S. security concern, especially the anti-drugs "war" and anti-illegal immigration operations. There is a Coast Guard officer attached to the Interests Section the United States maintains in Havana. And the Drug Enforcement Agency of the United States has gone out of its way to try to influence U.S. opinion and government policy on the Cuba issue suggesting, not always subtly, that Washington has vastly more to gain from close cooperation with Cuba in this field than it does to lose.

Given the vast array of advantages, already seen, provided by the FAR to the Cuban state, and in consideration of this special potential to act as a bridge to the United States, an inconceivable role for the party or any other element of the Cuban state other than perhaps the academic community, one would be foolish to think that the forces will not have a central role in any transition. This alone makes their role for the future vital.

Just as interesting is the consideration of what this might mean for that transition. For the FAR are a revolutionary force beyond doubt, loyal to the revolution without question, but deeply exposed to the realities of the present world and its evolution. There is little doubt that many of the reforms of recent years, especially in the economy, originated from the ranks of the senior officer corps. Equally there is little doubt that Raúl Castro himself can think "out of the box" when he needs to. It is also important to keep in mind that the FAR are an institution with the usual institutional desires to continue to exist. Thus one may well find in the armed forces of Cuba a situation where, while not lacking in a desire to see the *logros* (achievements) of the revolution survive, those same forces are willing to make compromises in conformity with realities around them both on the global level and the domestic.

There should be no misunderstanding here. We have here a force deeply committed to the revolution and strongly revolutionary in its ideals. It will not happily part with the achievements of the revolution and it is worth mentioning that from its perspective the chief of those is the national sovereignty and dignity that was obtained through the revolutionary process. Thus there should be no imagining that somehow negotiating with the FAR in a transitional period would be easy. They will wish to ensure the survival of the best elements of the revolutionary government. And they will be keen to ensure their own future institutional existence. But they are extremely unlikely to "give away the shop." National sovereignty, general access to education and health services, and racial equality would not likely be on the bargaining table unless disorder were widespread and the situation close to desperate.

RECENT TRENDS

In the context of the present strategic situation of Cuba, the question on all Cuban lips is of course that of the chief utility presented as the *raison d'être* of the FAR: that is, its ability to deter. The growth in the perceived likelihood of an actual military attack on Cuba, in decline over many years among Cubans and especially the nation's young, is exceptional. The Cuban people now appear more united than for many years past in their determination to defend the island, and even the revolution, against any attack that might come. While this was frequently stated, even trumpeted, in the past, at the present this author is obliged to state that it appears to be actually the case. Castro no longer needs to do much to convince the public of the excesses of the government in Washington, and the generalized view of the Bush administration as "inhuman" or even fascist is widespread indeed.

This change in attitudes from indifference and doubt to at least much greater acceptance of Castro's assessment of Washington's actions, has been put to the test in the great national mobilization test of November–December 2004 known as "Bastión 2004." Air raid alarms sounded, long-disused underground shelters were re-opened, live-fire exercises took place in many places, vehicles were repaired and brought into operation, militia "fan-outs" (networks of calls to arms) dusted off and tried out, firing ranges made more active than in decades past, non-combat units tested on their often-aged skills in the field, naval craft put to sea, old uniforms put on again (often to the disappointment of middle-aged reservists who could now barely get physically into them), new ones issued, and all in aid of an attempt to see if the FAR's long-famed ability to turn out the people as a nation in arms was still a reality. The forces were indeed able to get the troops out and test them. This can only reassure the government that it still has a striking ability to mobilize the nation in time of crisis.[5]

Problems of course remain. Corruption at a low level, but nonetheless widespread, is as elsewhere but perhaps to a lesser degree, only too evident to the high command, itself often accused of being prone to it as a result of the great temptations of control of the tourism and other profitable industries. And while sentences for yielding to this temptation are severe indeed, there is little doubt that they have not been able to stamp out the phenomenon by any means. Anti-corruption courses, given to both forces and civilian personnel, likewise are not a panacea for this almost universal challenge.

FINAL THOUGHTS

The Cuban armed forces are the inheritors of proud traditions by any standards. They are loyal to the regime and to the country. They are vital to both. While doubtless not as able to deter attack as in the halcyon days of the Soviet alliance and hundreds of thousands of serving personnel, not to mention modern weapons and equipment, they are still a force to be reckoned with. They would surely give a good account of themselves in case of invasion.

In the absence of invasion, however, the issues are less stark. Many senior officers now know a great deal about business as well as soldiering. They have had to adjust many times to the demands of the real and nasty world of the Special Period. The armed forces they command, while central, are infinitely smaller than they have been at any time since the early 1960s. They are likewise much worse equipped and much less up-to-date than in the past. It is interesting then that despite all this, their political influence is not less but more than in recent decades.

It must be emphasized that these forces have an absolutely proven record of loyalty and usefulness to the Cuban state since before they took Havana those nearly five decades ago and at every stage of those passing years. Their flexibility in responding to their commander in chief's evolving and highly varied orders has been their hallmark and has been impressive indeed. In the future that flexibility may be tested again. It is virtually certain that their loyalty will be. There is little reason to think that this flexibility will not stand them in good stead in any circumstances. Their usefulness to the government of Fidel Castro is as great as ever. No one should think their loyalty is deficient. But they will want to look to the future as well. Proper handling of this key institution will be essential to providing a peaceful transition. Holding the ring while the politicians sort things out is alas a long-standing Latin American military role. The FAR have shed most of the traditions of the region's militaries. But it is not inconceivable that their ability to do that in the future may prove to have been their most useful contribution to Cuba, and to the *logros* of the revolution, to date.

NOTES

1. All these data for the state budget come from the 1995–2001 annual reports produced by Cuba, Oficina Nacional de Estadística, *Anuario Estadístico de Cuba*. They are given here with the caveat that like so many official state figures in Latin American countries, and especially those related to defense, they should not be taken at full face value. They do, however, suggest trends of great importance.

2. The formal structuring to achieve these ends came into being with Law No. 75 of National Defense of 1995 but it rather more confirmed things already done than added new ones. See *Gaceta Oficial de la República de Cuba*, Havana, 13 January 1995, pp. 1–14; and interview with General Orlando Almaguel Vidal in Luis Báez, *Secretos de generales*, Barcelona, Losada, 1997, pp. 234–47, especially 244–46.

3. The Ochoa Affair refers to the arrest and subsequent execution by firing squad of General Ochoa, a hero of the war in Angola, and of members of MININT charged with involvement in the illegal narcotics trade at a time when Castro was deeply concerned that the U.S. would be using that involvement as a justification for harsh action against the island.

4. This author has been able to elaborate on these linkages at more length in his *Confidence-Building Measures and the Cuba–United States Confrontation*, Ottawa, Department of Foreign Affairs and International Trade, International Security Research Paper, March 2000.

5. See the special edition of *Granma*, 20 December 2004, especially the article "Se ha demostrado nuestra capacidad de combate," pp. 3–6.

5

On Cuban Democracy

Cuba and the Democratic Culture

Rafael Hernández

When my daughter Patricia was a little girl, some peculiar cartoons, dubbed from Russian into Spanish and set in the African jungle, captivated her. The main characters were a philosophical monkey, a tiny elephant, and a monster named Tusa-Kutusa who hardly ever appeared on-screen. When, at the end of the story, the elephant ate some magic herbs and immediately grew to the right size, the Hispano-Soviet monkey, swinging from his branch, exclaimed, "I already told you. There's no such thing as a small elephant."

My daughter can still recite complete verbatim dialogues from that cartoon, engraved faithfully into her memory from childhood, that very short moment in life that accompanies one always. The saga of Tusa-Kutusa, the prophetic monkey, and the Soviet elephant are part of her infancy, not mine. Nevertheless, there is something in the ironic certainty of the monkey, who indulges in what former Marxist philosopher Roger Garaudy would have called boundless realism, that sticks with me until this very day: "Small elephants, there's no such thing."

Can a democratic system be developed on an island 90 miles away from a superpower that has relentlessly besieged it? Is democratic and pluralistic socialism, which might include a loyal opposition, imaginable next door to rampant capitalism? Is it conceivable in a country subject to U.S.-based financing and promotion of its own brand of "democracy"? The realistic monkey would not have hesitated in his response to these questions. I want to pause here, however, to examine these queries from a different angle. It's not that I am in total disagreement with such a realistic focus, but because the problem of democracy is almost never examined from the very real perspective of Cuban civil society and political culture.

HAS CUBA EVER BEEN SEEN AS DEMOCRATIC?

If the U.S. political system is taken as our point of reference, it's obvious that the island of Cuba contrasts sharply with its institutions and prescriptions. The Cuban system is one-party, while the North American system is two-party. We do have universal, direct, and secret suffrage, from local elections to those for the National Assembly. But we do not have political parties that compete with each other nor do we have U.S.-style electoral campaigns. Cuba has some legal restrictions on freedom of expression, organization, and movement—restrictions that do not exist as such in the United States. However, many more differences exist between the two societies, their political systems and civic cultures. These other factors are directly related to freedom and pluralism, as well as the development of a democratic culture, and are barely mentioned in reference to Cuba.

Historically, even when deep class divisions were the rule of the day, Cuban social relations have been perceived as less exclusive and more porous than those in the United States. For example, a North American visitor to Cuba in 1907 observed, "To the American at home, the negro as a social, political or even industrial equal is an affront, an offence, nothing less; to the Cuban, he is not. It is because [in Cuba the negro] is not everywhere confronted and made hard in thought and feeling by cold or resentful signs of contempt from the white man." (Lt.-Col. R.F. Bullard, "How Cubans Differ from Us" (*Century*, November 1907).

Other visitors from the North have considered that we Cubans have never had the capacity "to work out a republic and a constitution on a basis of universal suffrage"; thus, a republic could only be an imperfect experience in Cuba "with frequent lapses from the democratic ideal, with the accompaniment of a continuous commotion," and "under the somewhat indefinite but nonetheless effective suzerainty of the United States." (Sydney Brooks, "Some impressions of Cuba," *North American Review*, June 1914).

The perception that we Cubans are more socially egalitarian, more open in our cultural habits and, at the same time, less capable of governing ourselves democratically, is older than what one might imagine.

We also have tended to look at the question of liberties in the United States through a different lens. "What's this about not being able to smoke a cigar anywhere in this university, not to mention getting accused of sexual harassment if you just tell a department secretary that her dress is pretty; you can't even drink a beer in the park without being considered indecent," exclaimed a friend from Pinar del Río after visiting an illustrious East Coast university. Although from a U.S. puritanical viewpoint, my friend would be expressing "macho preferences of a tobacco addict," I suspect that most Latin and Caribbean visitors to North America would share some of his feelings about these limitations.

Many of us Cubans might agree with those pre-1959 visitors who observed that the republic alternated between dictatorships and corrupt governments, with a constant U.S. interference in domestic politics. And since the founding fathers of our independence in the 19th century to my friend from Pinar del Río, we do not identify with the North American version of democracy and civil liberties. Our present political system has (also) been a result of that history and perspective.

HAVE DEMOCRACY AND ITS PRACTICE CHANGED?

As my colleague the cigar aficionado likes to remind me, the defects of world socialism aren't necessarily included in the script, but have very often been a consequence of the *mise en scene*. Social justice, equality, and freedom are basic values embedded in the socialist political culture, as well as national sovereignty, popular mobilizations, solidarity, and the right to work, to education and health care. Perhaps a political analyst or legal expert could tell us that these are premises, properties, or expected consequences of a democratic system, as would be the routine alternation of power—but they do not constitute *democracy* itself as a political mechanism. Democracy is identified with—the experts would surely say—the real popular capacity to propose and freely elect their government representatives and to change them if they do not respond to citizens' interests. Democracy as a system would have to *represent* popular power, although it would also have to ensure real citizen *participation*. Hence, regardless of any specific institutional form, if we call democracy a system on which power is constructed and legitimated by citizen representation and participation, we can affirm that Cuba has developed that system, with both advances and setbacks.

In the last ten years, the course of Cuban democratic development has been influenced by three main factors: the economic and ideological crisis precipitated by the crumbling of Eastern European socialism; the reforms in the 1990s to confront the crisis; and the effect of renewed North American hostility with its eagerness to subjugate the country. These factors have acted directly on the domestic consensus, on the former linkage between the State and civil society, and have contributed to create a differentiated space for the production of ideas, as well as political activity.

What is more democratic in Cuba today than ten years ago? Power is more geographically decentralized within a system that is still highly centralized. Local governments have greater input into decisions and problem solving. Social development policy is more closely linked than ever to community work.

The generational change of leadership is highly apparent in all the provinces, governed by young people and, in some cases, women and blacks. The Central Committee of the Communist Party also reflects this new composition. Likewise, only three historic figures remain in the Political Bureau since 1965: Fidel and Raúl Castro and Juan Almeida, Council of State vice president and the highest ranking black leader in the country. The new members elected in 1997 were, on average, about fifty years old.

The 1992 constitutional reforms diversified types of property and established a more direct electoral system for the National Assembly. This representative body only meets twice yearly, but its commissions (equivalent to congressional committees) meet frequently in all the country's provinces to examine problems and make decisions.

The freedom to travel outside the country and to come and go for personal or work-related reasons is greater than ever after 1962. A growing number of citizens have received authorization to temporarily reside outside the island and be able to return—with the exception of those who go to the United States.

The space for debate about ideas, criticism, and public dissent has expanded. Questions such as those of racial discrimination and intergenerational differences, the crisis of moral and ideological values, the migratory wave of the 1990s and its motivations, the visions of way of life in the capitalist world, freedom of expression, civil society, and pluralism are debated in institutional public forums, and in magazines, novels, theater pieces, and films that circulate throughout the country.

Gradually, the information available to Cuban citizens is increasing. Television carries more information from foreign sources than before. In spite of economic limitations and administrative restrictions, Internet use has been expanding by institutions, organizations, and even individuals. Thousands of Cubans use e-mail and thus communicate more widely with the rest of the world.

What limitations are maintained on this democratic development? Political system institutions do not work as well as they should. For example, according to the powers given to it by law, the role of the National Assembly in the discussion and treatment of national problems is not critical in terms of the State's decision making. The representation of young people, women, and blacks in the political leadership is still insufficient. Public opinion laments the informative pablum provided by the mass media, demonstrating its ineptitude in reflecting public grievances. It's also questioned why there are still administrative restrictions on the travel of Cuban citizens to and from the island. The mechanism to nominate candidates, particularly to the higher representative bodies, could be improved.

Many of the political arguments for these restrictions have to do with the persistent meddling by the United States in Cuban domestic affairs, including its proactive sponsorship of opposition groups, its stated intention to use informational, academic, and cultural exchanges to destabilize the socialist system, and its eagerness to dictate the terms of the ongoing transition and to force Cuba on a capitalist track. These policies have had a counterproductive effect on democracy in Cuba. To the degree in which they have used the democratic banner to their own ends, they have made economic and political reforms more slow. Yes, Cuban socialism would be more democratic if the U.S. hostility would lapse. It's worthwhile to ask, though, if Cuban socialism has been weakened in relation to the United States because of democratic development and economic reform in the past ten years. Can these and some other future developments be postponed until these U.S. policies disappear? If, indeed, they would ever disappear entirely someday.

The advances and shortcomings of democratic development in Cuba can be illustrated through the theme of participation. It is a fact that the system has achieved a very high percentage of citizen participation in the country's political life, mainly through consultations and mobilization. Even during the crisis years, many proposed laws and economic policy measures were discussed in work places, schools, unions, and neighborhood meetings. The mobilizations to support them or to put a constitutional change to a referendum (as happened in June 2002) have been massive. However, this participation is less in regards to making decisions and to people's control over real policies. In spite of the decentralization and the diversification that has taken place in Cuban society and its economy, the bureaucratic mechanisms with their centralist style keep weighing on the system, emphasizing an essentially administrative concept of control.

Cubans on the island are not asking themselves if the system has established rules of political succession or whether citizens have the right to vote. They are not asking if elections are granted periodically or if the majority would vote or not for Fidel Castro or for socialism. There's no public outcry to allow organization of a multitude of political parties. The real problems—reflecting other contradictions—in regards to a more democratic system arise from a different social and cultural framework.

TO WHAT DEGREE DO WE HAVE A DEMOCRATIC CULTURE?

Possibly the most conspicuous of these contradictions arises from the primary democratic condition of the revolutionary socialist ideology, that of guaranteeing citizens free and complete access to education and culture.

Education still is today a top issue in the domestic political agenda. Even in the most marginal of neighborhoods in Cuban cities, the great majority of children attend school to at least the ninth grade. More than half a million Cubans have graduated from the university. In spite of the discontent created by the crisis, a greater level of culture permits a thoughtful civil society today. This right to think implies a capacity to reasonably appropriate and criticize the values of a socialist political culture, including that of democracy. The more educated and cultivated new generations are surely more capable than their parents of improving the socialist system and making it more democratic.

In relative terms, Cuba is further ahead in its democratic civic culture than any other society I've known. Democratic civic culture in Cuba is expressed when people say what they think and stand up for their rights and needs, despite the existence of an administrative structure of control (which is not that of a police state). That democratic civic culture is certainly larger and deeper than its institutional expression. My professor friends at certain private universities I've visited would dare only with difficulty to challenge the head of a department or a director, as I've seen happen in all the Cuban academic institutions with which I've collaborated. Recently, I went to José Martí Airport to say goodbye to a Caribbean researcher, who saw me argue with a policeman about a parking regulation. My colleague was so concerned that he called me at home a few hours later, convinced that something had happened to me. "Here in my country you might spend a night in jail for what you said to the policeman," he said. Many Cubans believe that the day that the government had to use the police or army to massively repress its citizens, there would be no socialism to defend.

In spite of those huge differences with other societies in the hemisphere, I think that we have our own problems, especially when we consider that the scope of a democratic culture cannot be reduced to the ballot box, the assemblies, and government bodies. For example, Cuban education, although universally accessible, in my opinion, is still rigid in its curriculum and authoritarian in its teaching style. Some might say that the schools reflect the vertical ideology of the system. I disagree, because I can remember private and public schools before 1959, and their style was not more democratic. Our family relations are also not exactly democratic. I believe that in order to consolidate a democratic culture, we must transform our educational and familial habits and the style of our social organizations, our mentality and the way in which we go about our daily lives.

Can a political system based on democratic socialist ideas possibly be fully developed, even if the society upon which it is built is not? Here, I'd say the wise monkey is right: "There's no such thing as a small elephant, is there?"

6

Successes and Failures of a Decentralizing Experience

Cuba's Local Governments

Haroldo Dilla Alfonso and Gerardo González Núñez

The purpose of this article is to discuss the particularities, successes, and short-comings of Cuba's most important decentralizing experience since 1959: the sub-system of local governments, considering both their exercise of a set of decentralized powers and their role as a niche for democratic participation. It is based on three years of research (1989–1991) conducted in four municipalities and focuses on the institutional scheme in practice between 1976 and 1992. Some changes, applied in 1992, modified certain procedures and norms, but they have not been so dramatic as to change the framework. The article is divided into four main parts. The first states the general goals and features of the original design. The second part considers the question of participation, both in the context of elections and as it bears on citizens' participation in decision making. The third part analyzes the institutions, focusing especially on the relationship between representative institutions and those in charge of executive and administrative tasks. Next, we assess the powers of local governments and their capacity to govern. Finally, we describe the changes which have taken place since 1992 and discuss the prospects for the evolution of local governments.

THE FORMAL DESIGN

The decision taken to establish a municipal subsystem in revolutionary Cuba was part of the modernization and democratization process of the political and administrative system known as the Process of Institutionalization, which occurred in the mid-1970s.

Such a decision posed various problems. It required, first, the creation of a set of institutions and norms to empower the recently founded local governments with the capacity to govern—and not simply to administer—over their territorial jurisdictions, in a context where the economy was centrally planned and property was for the most part publicly owned. Second, there was the intention to proceed in a sufficiently participative manner not only to fulfill the democratizing purposes embodied in the founding decision but also in order to achieve an acceptable level of popular involvement in various support tasks. Last but not least, the decision sought to break the political and administrative styles and procedures that had been the flesh and blood of the public bureaucracy and to replace them with a culture consistent with the new program.

The formal design of Cuba's municipal government rested on the belief that the core of local state power should be within the premier representative institution, the municipal assembly, which would be constituted of delegates elected in precincts by direct voting. The municipal assembly would have the power to elect, oversee, and dismiss both its executive committee and the administrative authorities. It had similar powers with regard to its representatives to the provincial assemblies and the National Assembly. Given that citizens had the capacity not only to elect but also to recall their municipal assembly delegates, there was thus a chain of successive subordinations in which the delegation of sovereign powers was conditional, while its effects were felt beyond the purely local setting. In every case, the right of voters to recall their elected representatives was coupled with the duty of the latter to account to the former and be open to public scrutiny.

The establishment of such a system had a powerful effect on community life, which for over thirty years has been an arena for multiple forms of popular participation, in which the classic distinction between what is private and what is public had become quite blurred. The new local governments not only absorbed the patterns of involvement and mobilization created over the years (activities to support social or productive endeavors) but they also opened new institutional channels, such as the nomination of candidates, elections, neighborhood meetings to oversee and debate municipal policies, and so on. All this affected the selection of local leaders and the opening toward a political socialization consistent with a democratic political culture (Hernández and Dilla, 1991).

In this framework, administrative bodies were supposed to be subjected to representative bodies, and both retained rights and resources that were considered essential to govern. Above all, there was an effort to give the new institutions supervision over a wide range of economic activities and services that heretofore had been managed directly by the central government or its subordinates. Ordinarily the activities whose control was transferred to the local governments dealt with basic social services (health, education, the supply of jobs, and aspects of social security) or with economic activities such as repair services, restaurants, cafeterias, building construction and maintenance, and so forth; productive activities, on the other hand, remained generally within the scope of the provincial or the central governments.

At the outset, planning for such a transfer of administrative powers had to address two problems. The first was how to reconcile the new margins of local autonomy, on the one hand, with the need for central planning, on the other hand, in order to avoid fragmentation, the waste of resources, or inequalities in development between regions. The norm adopted was called "double subordination": the central government set the procedures to be followed by the entities that would come under local control, while the local governments were vested with administrative authority. The second problem was how to reconcile the actions of municipal governments with economic activities within a given municipality, since there were also enterprises under direct central government control operating in the same municipalities. A set of norms was adopted giving local governments a limited role with regard to the enterprises under central control. Official documents typically described such a role as auditing and support, or often just as support.

Although a uniform, normative, and institutional framework was established throughout the country, the subsystem was affected by corrective actions taken by the central government or by de facto local adaptation within specific territories. All of this heterogeneity constrains the capacity to generalize responsibly. In any event, after more than fifteen years of operation one can observe successes and failures in the municipal government subsystem. Many of the presumed solutions found in the original design became themselves new sources of problems.

THE ELECTORAL DIMENSION

Up to 1992 municipal elections were the only ones where the population voted directly to elect their representatives, through whom higher representative organs were then elected. Municipal elections were organized in three stages. During the first, a series of neighborhood assemblies chose candidates for the delegate positions for each precinct; there had to be at least two and there could be as many as eight candidates. During the second stage, biographical information was given about the candidates through documents posted in public places. Finally, there was the voting (secret, direct, and equal); all citizens over sixteen years of age had the right to vote. No organization could campaign in favor of any candidate in any of these stages, nor could any candidate or any candidate's followers organize election campaigns (*Ley Electoral*, 1982).

The Electoral Commission organized the entire process. Presided over by a local leader of the Cuban Communist Party (PCC), it was constituted of representatives from grassroots organizations and of other persons or institutions that could provide effective material or organizational support. Besides managing the available resources and organizing the process, we observed that the role of the commissions was to guarantee the transparency of the process and the fulfillment of the law, for all of which the PCC's presence was considered vital. We did not observe any interference by the commission.

According to official statistics, (ANPP, 1987) municipal elections have enjoyed a very high degree of popular involvement. With regard to the assemblies to nominate candidates, the lowest percentage of attendance reported was 73 percent in 1979 while the highest was 91 percent in 1984. In 1989, attendance was slightly above 80 percent. Voting participation reached 95 percent in the 1976 election, 99 percent in 1984, and 98 percent in 1989.

Such statistics lead to very diverse interpretations, especially considering some of the most visible results, namely, that over 70 percent of the candidates and of the winners were members of the Communist Party or of its youth wing (UJC), even though such members represented only about 15 percent of the population with the right to vote. From a theoretical perspective this outcome has been perceived as an over-representation of militants (the term used in Cuba for members of the PCC or of the UJC) and, consequently, the result of a kind of Orwellian manipulation of the system in order to guarantee political loyalty in government institutions. At the other end of the spectrum, the outcome is interpreted as an indicator of popular support for the PCC, and thus as a clear act of identification with the political and ideological values that it supports. Even though they appear contradictory, both positions share some ground, especially the assumption that the vote—whether coerced or voluntary—was a conscious decision to support a militant.

Between March and May 1989 we carried out a study focused on the elections held in Santa Cruz del Norte, a small town some 50 kilometers east of Havana. Although not all of the findings from this study can be generalized across the nation, Santa Cruz is not an exceptional site, given its social, economic, and demographic indicators. As far as we could see, municipal elections there were not a coercive process, for there was enough of a climate of freedom for citizens to accept them as legitimate. This did not exclude, of course, the existence of certain coercive factors, such as the sense of civic duty or political-ideological commitments.

Nor were the elections a routinized liturgy. Over 50 percent of the delegates elected were not the product of re-elections, because some incumbents might not have accepted re-election (it is in fact an unpaid task that requires a considerable personal sacrifice) or because others lost the support of the electorate. On the other hand, over 80 percent of the voters we interviewed had already picked a candidate before the election and knew enough about the candidate for us to conclude that their vote was not a random choice.

One of the study's main goals was to inquire about the motivations and orientations of the votes, taking into account the issues already sketched. Of all the possible findings that could be identified within our empirical data base, the most important probably was the predominance of ethical over political-ideological criteria to explain the voting choice, as well as the influence of the former in the shaping of the latter. We carried out nearly 200 interviews with citizens who nominated candidates, others who argued over some nomination, or simply some who voted in the elections. In response to the question as to what the most important qualities are for a delegate to have, the majority of the answers referred to moral criteria such as "honesty," "solidarity with neighbors," "humane sensibilities," and so on, which were summarized in the single quality of "being a revolutionary." Fewer than 10 percent of those interviewed mentioned the quality "militancy in the Communist Party or in the Communist Youth Union" as a factor to take into account, and only one person believed that this was an important quality. On the other hand, of ten candidates up for election in the five precincts under study, nine were PCC or UJC militants.

Returning to the analytical question—Can the high proportion of candidates who were PCC-UJC members be understood in terms of the already-mentioned Manichean polarity of paradigms?—On the contrary, nothing found in Santa Cruz (or in other subsequent studies) so suggests. A large proportion of the voters did not even know that the candidates were PCC-UJC members, which is understandable if we recall that party cells are organized in work centers and not in residential communities. Finally all of the interviewees said that they had not received any indications on whom to nominate or for whom to vote. In any event, it is unlikely that such an attempt at imposition (or suggestion) could have had the desired result, given the secrecy of the vote, although one cannot rule out the probability that such attempts could occur (Dilla and Fernández, 1991).

The question of community participation should not be addressed with theoretical illusions or blinders. An appropriate interpretation should take into account the political-ideological factor but it should not reduce the understanding of community participation to such a factor; it is also important to add other features such as the feeling of belonging to a community, the emergence of local leaders, or the peculiarities of a new civic life—which has crystallized after over thirty years of living in a revolution—that embodies a set of political values, norms, and rules interwoven in the national tapestry.

To be sure, this mixture of values and political behavior in the selection of local leaders has had other undesirable effects in terms of the quality of representation. One obvious negative result has been a certain under-representation of some social sectors, such as young people and women. According to official statistics, since the first elections were held in 1976 the proportion of women candidates and of women elected as delegates has never reached 20 percent. The highest proportion (17.1 percent) was reached in 1986, dropping to 16.6 percent in 1989. This is paradoxical when taking into account that women were among those most engaged in community participation and that women had performed very good leadership roles when elected to public office.

Clearly, there are historical factors which greatly favor men, namely patterns of discrimination assigning to women a variety of reproductive roles which limit their free or flexible time to hold public office and which are manifest in the voting choice.

Certainly, there have been successes since 1976; women's participation in elected local posts has virtually doubled. But these gains have been so slow that more decisive affirmative action is needed. This would imply substantial changes in the dissemination of information related to the electoral system (which, as noted, was too limited) and a more active engagement of pertinent organizations such as the Cuban Women's Federation. Although it might seem odd to support actions that would sacrifice the effectiveness of popular representation for the sake of improving the representation of a given social sector, it is also improbable that Cuban society could reach more egalitarian and innovative levels if such corrective changes were left to the spontaneous results that might or might not occur over time.

PARTICIPATION AND DECISION MAKING

Beyond the voting choice, popular participation in Cuba's municipal subsystem took place at various times during the decision-making process, from the formulation of demands and the identification of problems to assessment of the decisions made. This participation occurred in different ways such as in neighborhood assemblies, in involvement in community activities that served public purposes, or in some oversight and auditing activities, such as belonging to commissions or participating in inspections at the local level. Perhaps the most important of all, because of their originality and widespread popular involvement, were the Meetings to Render Accounts (*Reuniones de Rendición de Cuentas*, RRC).

The RRCs were designed as a means to exchange information between the government and the community (formulation of demands on the part of the population and explanation on the part of the government of the extent and limits of its actions) and, at the same time, as a means of collective discussion of local problems and a search for solutions. Ordinarily, RRCs met every six months. They were presided over by the precinct delegate and typically featured the attendance of members of the government or the bureaucracy.

Although official figures indicated that more than 70 percent of voters took part in RRCs, according to our own observations actual attendance was slightly lower.

Ordinarily, between 50 to 60 percent of the electorate attended these community meetings, though attendance tended to drop off sometimes as the meeting proceeded. The meetings were in three stages, the first two being intended to supply information for the discussion regarding the government and the delegate. Debate rarely began before the government's report. The third stage, in contrast, was always more interesting; it allowed for the expression of new demands and a discussion of the community's most pressing problems. The length of the RRCs varied considerably from one site to the next, depending on the complexity of the issues, the number of problems to be discussed, and the delegates' ability to lead. They lasted generally 50 to 60 minutes. The most active participants typically were women and the elderly, who were most directly connected to the community and its problems.

How well did RRCs meet the objectives for which they were created varies a good deal. As with other community processes, it depended to a large extent on the community and its members, as well as on the ability and capacity of local leaders to mobilize resources and produce satisfactory outputs. Thus, it was not surprising that the RRCs were more dynamic and participative in small communities than in large urban centers, and especially in the city of Havana, where the very notion of community is more diluted and the problems more complex.

First, we could look at the RRC as a means to raise demands. We observed that the RRC was a legitimate means to make requests and provide inputs to the government. The issues reflected conflicts which existed in the municipalities. Although there were several channels to express demands (besides the RRC, demands could be presented directly to local or national officials or to delegates during their office hours), 68 percent of the 6,571 demands generated between October 1989 and April 1990 in the four municipalities under study had been communicated via the RRC. If we exclude those demands related only to family or personal matters (issues that people prefer to discuss in more private settings), this indicator could exceed 85 percent.

The success of the RRC as a vehicle for the expression and communication of demands implied the creation of a forum to debate the problems affecting the daily life of people and communities as well as an effective channel of information for the making of decisions by local and national government officials. A local government aspiring to a minimal degree of legitimacy cannot ignore the results of the RRC (or of other channels for the expression of demands); this was well known by citizens and their representatives.

We must recognize, however, that this is not the end of the assessment of the RRC even if it was its best success. With regard to the reverse flow of information—that is, from the government to the community—the results were less impressive because of the excessive formalism of the information given, which tended not to interest the ordinary citizen. In any event, this limited the ability of citizens to exercise their right to oversee public activities. Nor could it be said that the RRC became an effective setting for making agreements and for collective action. In fact, the RRC seemed to be a moment of community interaction that was isolated from other similar interactions in civil society. There were typically no prior agreements in smaller community entities (such as neighborhood, women's, or youth organizations) that had facilitated the collective articulation of demands. Ordinarily, these demands were formulated and presented as individual initiatives even if they reflected wider interests. Of the over six thousand demands that we studied in the four municipalities in the research project, only 6 percent had some dimension of prior collective agreement. Therefore, it was mainly during the RRC that it was possible to go beyond the individual character of demand-making and, even then, it depended on the delegates' leadership ability and capacity. Although it was not impossible to find community leaders who could build coalitions among the voters, obtain the support of political leaders, and launch self-starting projects without the prior approval of government officials, these were the exceptions. The more typical insufficiency of delegate leadership over-burdened municipal governments with demands and reduced the people's participatory potential.

Perhaps the existing imbalance between the successful performance of the demand aggregation function and the poorer performance of the oversight and agreement-making functions explains one of the major weaknesses of the community process: the endurance of a paternalistic pattern of participation and of a verticalistic relationship between the government, on the one hand, and the community and the citizens, on the other, which undermined people's self-confidence and the goals of a society which aspires to collective action and self-government.

INSTITUTIONAL HIERARCHIES OF MUNICIPAL GOVERNMENT

According to the constitution and pertinent regulations (ANPP, 1982), the assemblies of delegates were the highest state authority in each municipality. The designers of the Popular Power framework assigned to these institutions a set of powers to elect, oversee, and dismiss members of other municipal institutions—that is, the Executive Committee and the bureaucracy.

According to standard procedure, the Municipal Assemblies officially met twice a year but, in fact, they met more frequently. We observed that local governments had supplemented the standard procedures for legislative action by means of monthly informal meetings so that the delegates could discuss the community's problems and make decisions. The agenda of the assemblies was set by respective Executive Committees and presented to the delegates who had the formal power to change it, though they did so rarely, preferring to introduce the issues that concerned them in the actual course of the discussion. Only in unusual cases the higher national or provincial bodies indicated the need to include some topic of interest to them. We observed that Municipal Assembly meetings were characterized by long debates in which many participated, especially when the topics under discussion referred to daily life in the communities; much effort was made to organize and build a consensus to address issues.

Besides these meetings, the Municipal Assemblies had other channels to affect activities, the most important of which were the Permanent Work Commissions. These were specialized groups of delegates and ordinary citizens who were called upon to inspect and assess various economic and social activities in the municipalities. The commissions met regularly to analyze trends in production, in economic or social services, or in other areas of interest. They could act on their own initiative or at the request of the Municipal Assembly or of its Executive Committee.

They issued findings and recommendations that, once approved by the Municipal Assembly, became binding for all local state institutions. According to the available statistics, in 1987 some 32,000 people nation-wide (of whom 20,000 were ordinary citizens) were members of these commissions.

Municipal Assemblies constitute an important arena for discussion and decision making about public concerns. They also serve to represent the people's interests. Given the weakness of a sustained experience of representative institutions in Cuba's history, particularly since 1959, these assemblies can also be considered an important step forward in democratic development, especially at the local level. It would be unrealistic to say, however, that the Municipal Assemblies have become the key centers of government power. In daily life the intention to assume this role was affected by various variables, some quite independent from the political will of local officials.

One factor was the very membership of the assemblies. As noted, they were constituted by the delegates elected in precincts by means of a direct and secret vote by the people, for whom the efficiency or expertise of their representatives was not as important as their ethical and political stance. Of course, this was reflected in the composition of the assemblies. The delegates were people who knew how to represent the rights of their electorate but who had less expertise in how to govern. The most complex acts of government (such as the discussion of the Economic Plan for their municipality, the discussion of the profitability of large enterprises, or the election of judges) were beyond their comprehension. Thus issues of social services or those that affected the people most directly were discussed the most at assembly meetings; it also followed that delegates openly preferred informal sessions, with flexible agendas, devoted to a discussion of problems concerning voters' everyday life.

The limitations in the efficacy of the Municipal Assemblies as institutions for governing were made more acute by other circumstances. Two of them were the high rate of membership change that took place in the Municipal Assemblies after each electoral period (somewhat more than 50 percent of the members) and the short duration of each term of office (two and a half years). Thus each term became a learning and training process which was interrupted precisely when it was about to bear fruit.

A third reason for the limited role of the Municipal Assemblies as institutions of government was the Executive Committee's role. As noted earlier, it represented the Municipal Assembly between sessions. This had the legal effect of turning it into a permanent body representing the state's highest power since it was a decision-making and an administrative institution, as well as a representative institution.

In order to fulfill the executive and administrative purposes of the Executive Committee, each member became responsible for auditing and overseeing a set of social and economic activities in the municipalities. Such a person thus entered into direct relations with segments of the bureaucracy—whether subordinated to the local authorities or not—throughout the municipality. At the same time, to fulfill its representative purposes and its strict subordination to the Municipal Assembly, the framework's designers required that a member of the Executive Committee had to be a delegate first; to be elected by the Municipal Assembly to this highest local government position, an executive had to have been elected a delegate by popular vote first.

The Executive Committee's election was based on a list of candidates presented to the assembly by the Electoral Commission presided over by the PCC and composed of grassroot and other social organizations. The list always had 25 percent more names than the number of posts to be filled and it could be changed by the delegates. The Electoral Commission tried to include people about whom there was a consensus, who enjoyed enough prestige to gain the vote of the delegates, and who had enough capacity to be at least moderately successful in an executive post. From this list the delegates elected the Executive Committee's members by secret and direct vote; subsequently, the Executive Committee met in private and elected the three top officeholders: president, vice president, and secretary.

The procedure was too indirect to meet a satisfactory democratic performance, but the main point we wish to stress is that the typical outcome was a hybrid that was fully satisfactory neither in terms of representation nor in terms of executive implementation. It devolved more power than had been foreseen to the municipal administrative bureaucracy, which turned out to be the most stable and thus the most capable institution to impart continuity to local policies.

We could discuss an infinite number of alternative procedures and probably none would be fully acceptable. But in any event, if the goal is to achieve a more democratic and efficient institutional life, then the municipal governments surely need a clearer demarcation of the tasks of public entities and of their own constitution, and ought to rely on electoral procedures that are more open and participatory than those that currently exist.

To be sure, the question of the prospects for the municipal assemblies to become the highest state authorities in the municipalities cannot be limited to a discussion of the assembly's relations with other municipal institutions. It is directly connected to sensitive issues that bear on the extent of a municipal government's real autonomy to govern and not just to administer tasks delegated to it by the central bureaucracy.

THE CAPACITY TO GOVERN

To assess the real capacity to govern enjoyed by local government bodies, we must first compare the current situation to what prevailed before 1976. There was a great step forward in the decentralization of Cuba's public administration. Whatever their current weaknesses, which we are about to discuss, the local governments enjoyed important powers such as the possibility to affect the formulation of economic plans concerning the municipality and to control local budgets, adopt policies, and engage in actions that had a considerable impact at the local level, or to serve as local links for the development plans designed for the entire nation. This is especially important in a country where, two decades ago, everything was governed in a centralized fashion, or through institutions subordinated to the center.

As noted earlier, within the territory of a given municipality there coexisted various administrative levels. Besides the municipal administrative entities, there were others under the authority of the provincial or the national government. This resulted in a complex mosaic that had important effects on the actual operation of local government.

This presents the first dimension of conflict in terms of the capacity of municipal institutions to govern their own territory: the asymmetry of administrative powers within the municipality.

A national enterprise is an entity that ordinarily has material and human resources as large as or larger than those of any municipality, especially if the municipality is small. The municipal government could exercise limited influence over the national enterprise; that influence was officially called "cooperation" or "support." It was to be effected through specialized bodies such as the municipal departments in charge of finance, labor and social security, statistics, and so on. At the same time the municipality received some tax benefits from the enterprise's earnings. Something similar occurred with the provincial enterprises or departments, though the weight of the municipal government was somewhat greater in this case, given the nature of the services that they provide, which had ordinarily a greater local impact than that of the national enterprises or departments.

In practice, however, the relationship between the municipalities and the national enterprises had been more fruitful than had been expected. A national enterprise cannot in fact do without municipal services and other vital inputs, such as the labor supply; it also has enough impact on the local environment as to be affected by municipal needs. Such relationships grew spontaneously through the transfer of human and material resources to the municipalities to help them in works of social development, or in the use of enterprise by-products to satisfy certain demands evident in local markets.

There were a number of examples of relations between national enterprises and municipalities that showed positive impacts on the communities. The fact that these relations were essentially spontaneous, however, and the scope of legal municipal action, which was quite restricted, means that the municipal government's actual capacity to govern depended on variables, such as the local officials' capacity to bargain or the goodwill of national enterprise managers. These factors were not always present in every case; they could also be fragile. To be sure, the relationship between the municipal government and the national enterprise was also subject to yet another factor beyond the municipal environment, and was linked to a key issue in Cuba's economic organization: the extent of real enterprise autonomy to make the necessary decision to perform its tasks.

A second dimension of conflict was related to the powers of local governments to govern. As had been noted, local governments' activities were most directly connected to the needs of daily life: health, education, distribution of food products, housing construction, cultural and sports activities, and more. However, these activities came under a double subordination. The municipal government exercised administrative control but it had to follow a series of standard procedures set by the national government and overseen by the provincial government through parallel organizations.

The principle of double subordination was not absolutely mistaken. It was meant to prevent a waste of material resources or a low quality of services; it was also designed to allow new municipal officials some time to learn about their powers and responsibilities. The original conception, however, left little room for local initiative, although that could be explained in the context of the creation of new institutions.

Fifteen years later, however, the prerogatives claimed under the guise of standard procedures were clearly excessive given that municipal governments had demonstrated sufficient capabilities. The prevalence of the standard procedures had also strengthened centralizing tendencies in the provincial governments (though more so in some provinces than in others) that went well beyond the original design and that restricted municipal prerogatives in the name of an alleged administrative efficiency. Therefore, the principle of double subordination had become an obstacle to developing local capacities and initiatives.

In this context, local government capacity to carry on not merely with administration but also with governing, which had required its retaining sufficient capacity to decide and to coerce, had remained quite limited. In general, municipal governments had remained in charge of those tasks most directly connected to daily life, and most affected by popular demands, but they also had few resources with which to respond effectively. Their capacity to mobilize local human and material resources was limited by the standard procedures set by the central government and by the centralizing actions of the provinces. Local leaders and institutions, therefore, were in a delicate situation: their capacity to meet popular demands was increasingly at odds with the existing legal and normative framework.

One of the most remarkable "distortions" was the frequent interference of the Communist Party's local authorities in administrative matters. Contrary to what some might expect, the Communist Party's municipal committees played an important role in protecting and consolidating the authority of local government. The reason was very practical: the PCC was the only local institution whose jurisdiction reached over the entire economic system and which was empowered to make decisions over the whole municipality, affecting even the powerful national enterprises. Probably for this reason 77 percent of the sampled delegates indicated their satisfaction with the party's role with regard to municipal government, even though a third of the respondents believed that the party interfered in municipal tasks.

CONCLUSIONS: RECENT CHANGES AND PROSPECTS

The local government's scheme set up in 1976 was successful in many ways. It made local management more efficient, allowed for a more equitable regional development, created a participatory framework which gave citizens a greater say in decision-making processes, and demanded a higher degree of accountability from local officials. But, at the same time, there were enough shortcomings—institutional distortions, bureaucratic hindrances, and paternalism—as to lead to the conclusion that certain changes were necessary. That idea had been gaining ground among politicians, scholars, and citizens since 1986.

Consensus existed regarding the need for changes. It did not, however, as to why they were necessary and what their effects would be. At last a short term approach prevailed: changes were necessary in order to face the growing economic crisis and prevent political consequences. Therefore, different actions were taken in facilitating the allocation of scarce resources, decision-making concerning local affairs, and improving popular mobilizations. This perspective is clearly reflected in both the Law of Constitutional Reform (1992) and the new Electoral Law (1992).

The Law of Constitutional Reform gives the municipality a wider and more particular treatment, unlike the text approved in 1976 which basically focused on the local government bodies, with poor distinction between the province and the municipality. Consequently, the municipality is defined as "a local society, with legal status to all legal affect, politically organized as per the law" and "a territory defined by the required economic and social relations of its population, and with the capacity to meet the local minimum requirement."

Together with and subordinated to the municipality, a new entity has been introduced in the constitution, which was intended to promote development, the renewal of resources, and people's participation in the areas under its jurisdiction: namely, the People's Councils (*Consejos Populares*). This is a positive step since it not only strengthens the People's Councils—first created in 1988—as the grassroots body in charge of resource mobilization and control over the administrative activity, but also because it brings the councils into a stable legal and regulatory context.

Another significant change is the dissolution of the Executive Committee and consequent disappearance of many of the problems we have described. The Administration Councils (*Consejos de Administración*) were established in its place: they are bodies appointed by assemblies and headed by an executive body. Both the number and quality of the members of the new administrative bodies are within the jurisdiction of the municipal government, thus reflecting considerable variation from one place to another, according to the particular characteristics of each territory.

At the same time, other measures that have been implemented are aimed at increasing the influence of local governments on the territorial economy, including national and provincial enterprises located in its jurisdiction. Some of those measures have focused on improving administrative local bodies. Others have set up new territorial coordinating organizations in which local officials enjoy relevant positions.

On the other hand, the new Electoral Law does not provide for changes in the methodology and standards of the local vote. However, on introducing direct vote for the election of members of the national and provincial assemblies, the election functions which had so far been under the Municipal Assemblies in relation to the higher representative bodies are now affected. Municipal Assemblies lose those elective functions—now transferred to the population—but retain the capacity to approve the list of candidates prepared by social and political organizations—excluding the Communist Party—integrating the Candidacy Commissions.

Despite the fact that the changes so far discussed are still in the early stages of implementation, they appear to lead to the elimination of institutional malformations, the stabilization of new institutions, and the introduction of more democratic practices. They provide a positive potential which will strengthen and give impetus to municipal life and popular participation.

Finally, the relationship between local governments and the national framework is not limited to administrative and economic spheres. Community bodies and local governments are just segments of a larger society and political system, and the former shares with the latter not just their virtues, but also their constraints, which set the modalities and pace. As we explained earlier, excessive bureaucratic formality has produced negative results and encouraged a rather paternalistic relationship between local governments and citizens. A more powerful and dynamic process of popular participation at local levels will depend to a great extent on the advance of a pluralistic political style, combined with a more autonomous vote of popular organizations.

Far be it from us to assume that the answer to the numerous obstacles faced by the Cuban socialist project lies in the working of local structures—or, from a systemic perspective, in the construction of a more participatory, pluralistic, and decentralized system. Almost by definition, none of these proposals is unequivocal. What we wish to note is that no global solution will do without truly democratic and participatory goals. Rather than economic effectiveness or technocratic efficiency, the main guarantee of socialist continuity will continue to be its ability to consider the building process an imperative of daily life.

NOTE

This article is based on research funded by the International Development Research Centre. We want to thank Ana Teresa Vincentelli, Darlene Molina, and Armando Fernandez from CEA, Christopher Smart and Paz Buttedhal from IDRC, Andrés Pérez from the University of Western Ontario, Michael Kaufman from CERLAC, and Jorge Dominguez from Harvard University.

REFERENCES

ANPP (Asemblea Nacional del Poder Popular). *Normas reglamentarias de las asambleas provinciales y municipales*. Havana, Editorial de Ciencias Sociales, 1982.

———. *Información mínima sobre los procesos electorales en los Organos del Poder Popular*. Havana, June 1987.

Constitucion de la Republica de Cuba. Havana, Editora Política, 1992.

Dilla, H and A. Fernandez. "Las elecciones municipales en Cuba: un studio de caso." *El Caribe Contemporáneo* 23 (1991).

Hernández, R and H. Dilla. "Political Culture and Popular Participation in Cuba." *Latin American Perspectives* 18, no. 1 (Spring 1991), 38–54

Ley Electoral. Havana, Editorial de Ciencias Sociales, 1982.

———. Havana, Editora Política, 1992.

7

Society, Civil Society, and the State

An Uneasy Three-Way Affair

Damian J. Fernández

The search for civil society in Cuba resembles the quest for the Holy Grail. Everyone is after it, but no one knows exactly what to look for. Scholars do not agree on the location, origins, or characteristics of civil society. Some argue that state-sponsored mass organizations serve primarily as transmission belts for state and party directives.[1] Others see them as articulating limited sectoral interests.[2] Still others, and this was especially true in the earlier years of the Castro regime, consider them a socialist variant of interest representation.[3] The different theoretical and ideological positions of scholars largely explain this lack of consensus.[4]

There is little more agreement outside academic circles. While the Cuban government officially holds that state-sponsored mass organizations represent a uniquely Cuban form of civil society, not everyone agrees. Some members of the Communist Party of Cuba (PCC) and the state bureaucracy have argued for expanding and reactivating the public sphere inside the country.[5] Critics of the regime at home and abroad argue that civil society does not currently exist in any form in Cuba. Dissidents proclaim themselves as the standard-bearers of an incipient civil society. Regime supporters claim that civil society has already been achieved.

The definitional uncertainty continues into the policy realm as well, because it is often difficult to separate state and society in communist systems. The parameters of what is and is not civil society are contested, uncertain, and highly politicized territory. As a consequence, the problem of classification has great policy relevance to all interested parties. For activists at the grassroots level, the label of "non-governmental organization" (NGO) is an honor, although it carries more risks than benefits. The Cuban government confers official NGO status on dozens of branches of the state. Individuals and groups within these designated state NGOs have access to many highly coveted privileges, including foreign travel and international financial support. The presence of NGOs gives the Castro regime a measure of international legitimacy and access to hard-currency foreign assistance. For international organizations and governments, Cuban civil society provides an alternative forum to the state, and it is perceived as both an instrument and a cause of political change in an otherwise rather stagnant political environment.

Despite these obstacles, foreign governments and international non-governmental organizations still try to foster civil society inside Cuba, but without a clear understanding of which groups are independent and which are state-controlled. The United States, Spain, Canada, and Norway have all acknowledged the importance of nurturing civil society in Cuba. Yet Washington has had a particularly difficult time locating elements of civil society inside Cuba and, in an ironic twist, does not seem to realize that its policies have made the emergence of Cuban civil society more cumbersome and more distant.

This article attempts to clarify some of the questions related to civil-society formation in Cuba by offering an overview of the sources and status of organizations on the island. In the process it addresses several basic, although neglected, dimensions of the topic—namely the sources of civil society, the variegated nature of the institutions operating inside Cuba, and the potential for the civility or incivility of Cuban civil society in the future. The article poses several fundamental questions: What do we mean by "civil society"? How should the term be conceptualized for the socialist Cuba of the 1990s? Is civil society emerging in Cuba? If so, what are its sources? What is the process of civil-society formation? What will Cuban civil society look like in the future? What policy options are available to foster civil society inside the island?

These issues will be addressed in light of the multiple dynamics unfolding in Cuba since the 1980s. The advent of Gorbachev and his reforms, the collapse of Eastern-bloc trade subsidies, and the end of the Cold War all had repercussions for Cuba. The economy collapsed, and demands for responsive government increased, changes that often led to demands for reform in other authoritarian states.

The Cuban case should contribute to the growing body of literature on civil society, especially regarding its role in regime transition, post-transition, and change in one-party political systems. Civil society in one-party states tends to emerge from two surprising sources: the private sphere and the extensive bureaucracy of the party-state itself. The building blocks of civil society exist inside state institutions, including the state-sanctioned mass organizations, and in the unexpected consequences of state policies. This perspective challenges the traditional dichotomies of public versus private and state versus society that characterize most liberal discourse on civil society. In practice, the relationship between private and public, and between control by and autonomy from the state during transitions from one-party state systems, covers a wide spectrum.

IN SEARCH OF A DEFINITION

The meaning of the term *civil society* is not easy to grasp. It has several levels of meaning and a long genealogy stemming from different philosophical currents.[6] The definitional challenge is compounded by the normative dimension of the term. Civil society is a value, a project for society to undertake. In Eastern Europe intellectuals and labor unions like Solidarity used the term as a plan of action.

A minimalist orthodox definition portrays civil society as composed of voluntary and non-state associations that articulate different interests and identities from those of the state in the public sphere. To reduce it to its most basic unit, the members of civil society are nongovernmental organizations. Although this minimalist definition is useful to a point, the Cuban case will show that the relationship between civil society and the state is neither necessarily nor exclusively oppositional. Rather, the demarcation of "autonomy" is quite blurry, as is the relationship between civil society and the private sphere.

The notion of civil society also includes a broader, liberal subtext. The phrase is wrapped in liberal notions of individualism, privacy, pluralism, free market, and social class. As the empirical evidence presented below shows, civil society can form in non-liberal, corporatist ways and can emerge from socialist mass organizations, a nominally Marxist state, and a state-dominated economy. Civil society can also emerge from pre-political relations, such as networks of friends and family, or from organized religion.

To understand the process of civil-society formation, it is useful to disaggregate the concept, making it easier to handle with precision. In this narrow definition, civil society is separated from economic groups (businesses) and political actors (political parties), although in practice the three are intertwined. The disaggregation helps uncover the status of Cuban civil society with greater clarity, as the state monopolizes the economic and political sectors. However, it is precisely economic decentralization that has produced pockets of autonomous groups, primarily artisans and intellectual entrepreneurs, on the island, a process known as "destatization." The relationship between the economy and civil society works in another direction as well. Economic scarcity leads to the formation of alternative distribution networks that function outside of the socialist welfare state. Due to a number of social, political, and economic factors, including state policies, groups in Cuban society and components of the state are attempting to carve out spaces of greater autonomy to fulfill their identities and interests.

THE CONTEXT: CUBA IN THE 1990s

Contrary to the once-prevalent notion in the literature on socialist Cuba, Cuban society is not and has never been monolithic or homogeneous. Its sociopolitical and economic diversity has become even more evident in the past decade. Nevertheless, social diversity in and of itself does not a civil society make. Particularly since the 1980s (but much earlier as well), "society" has indirectly challenged the socialist regime by not conforming to the officially prescribed patterns of behavior. State-society relations in Cuba since 1959 point to the limits of state power and the long-term inefficiency of state-directed mass organizations, making it more difficult for the regime to sustain legitimacy and governability at the street level.

During the 1990s, many semiautonomous economic organizations emerged. However, although the collapse of the Cuban economy since the mid-1980s has spurred the transformation, it was by no means the only or initial cause. Political, economic, and social factors at the national and international levels combine to explain the recent redefinition of state-society relations in Cuba. The regime must adapt to changes in society, the state, and the world at large. The fluidity of the situation presents conceptual challenges as well as opportunities to illuminate how civil society emerges in one-party maximalist states.

Changes have occurred in three major areas: strengthening informal networks, creating or strengthening independent organizations, and establishing organizational autonomy in state and mass organizations (i.e., "destatization"). These interrelated phenomena are both a cause and an effect of the problems of legitimacy and governability facing the Cuban government since the 1980s.

(1) *Organizational Autonomy.* Since the mid-1980s specific social organizations, some within the purview of the state, others not, have challenged the regime by trying to increase their autonomy. A process of destatization has been underway that points to a disjuncture between the state, its components units, and the constituencies served by state organizations. The process has been in part a consequence of state policies that encourage decentralization, self-employment, dollarization, limited self-financing, mixed enterprises, and NGO status.

(2) *Independent Organizations.* Confronted with the reality that many Cubans did not seem as politically engaged as they had in the past, and facing a new international context emphasizing democratic governance, the government adopted a new discourse that legitimized diversity within pluralism and attempted briefly to create a "an atmosphere of discussion" (*una cultura polémica*) in the early 1990s. During these years, the government continued its rapprochement with the Catholic Church, lifted the restriction on believers joining the PCC, and amended the constitution to state that Cuba was a secular—not atheistic—republic. But beyond these reforms, the government did not undertake other significant measures to accommodate or encourage the incipient civil society. On the contrary, human rights groups and other independent professional associations have been dealt with severely, their leaders imprisoned, exiled, or harassed. This happened to Concilio Cubano and many others.

(3) *Informal Networks.* As the political and economic problems worsened in the early 1990s, state and party officials and ordinary Cubans responded by distancing themselves from the state. The mass organizations, specifically the National Association of Small Farmers (*Asociación Nacional de Agricultores Pequeños*, ANAP), and research centers affiliated with the party attempted to establish greater autonomy by acting as de facto non-governmental organizations. In doing so they were redefining the relationship between the state and its organs, pushing the limits of autonomy. At the social level, private homes were used for cultural events (*tertulaias*), home-based restaurants (*paladares*), or religious services. Public spaces were privatized in special ways. Artists such as the Arte Calle group exhibited in non-sanctioned public spaces, religious processions spilled into the streets, prostitutes beckoned potential customers on the main boulevards, and youth gathered to listen to rock music on the Malecón waterfront.

Pre-revolutionary organizations and transnational NGOs have also fed the incipient civil society in Cuba. Since the 1980s, Catholic, Protestant, and Afro-Cuban religious organizations have experienced a renaissance. Churches have become distribution points for food and medicine, replacing part of the social-welfare role of the state, and have helped human rights activists. The pope's January 1998 visit vividly underscored the popularity of the Catholic Church. But as the only autonomous social actor with a national reach, the church finds itself in a privileged but difficult position. The state restricts the number of priests allowed into the country, controls church access to the media, prohibits religious schools, and limits conspicuous religious services, such as open-air masses. Transnational NGOs have also opened new sectors outside the purview of the state. A number of foreign governments (including Canada and Spain) have tried to encourage the development of NGOs in Cuba, with modest results. The government responded by limiting the access of the NGOs to Cuban citizens and accusing them of being tools of imperialism.

CIVIL SOCIETY: SOURCES AND STAGES

The various studies of civil society do not explicitly pose a fundamental question: where does civil society emerge? The literature refers to the resurrection of civil society, its emergence, formation, and development, but not where it is located before it reaches institutional form—especially in one-party socialist states. Civil society does not form according to some natural, universal evolutionary logic. Rather it is a process undertaken by men and women within the constraints and opportunities dictated by existing political, social, cultural, and economic structures. Something cannot emerge from nothing. Therefore, civil society must have antecedents somewhere in society before the transition to democracy can begin. Finding the sources of civil society helps to uncover some of its qualitative aspects, for the character of civil society is influenced by socio-cultural elements.

The changes in state-society relations have resulted in increasing difficulties in individual-level governability, legitimacy, and the formation of a proto-civil society. The term "proto-civil society" refers to the increasing visibility and diversity of small and not so small groups and institutions articulating different interests and identities outside the control of the party-state. The top leadership's refusal to provide greater space for autonomous groups to coalesce prevents this proto-civil society from developing into full-fledged civil society. The restrictive opportunity structure, namely, the unwillingness of the government to endorse reforms that would allow greater space for these groups in society, thwarts greater expansion. The process of civil-society formation, and the emergence of proto-civil society, is slow, conflict-ridden, and pulled between small victories for those who favor openness and renewed attempts at control by hard-liners. Compared to the experience of Eastern Europe and the Soviet Union, civil society in Cuba is somewhere between a defensive stage in which private individuals and independent groups actively or passively defend their autonomy, identity, and interests vis-à-vis the state and an emergent stage in which groups take their limited demands into a wider social arena.[7] In making their public debut, social groups lose their ability to conceal their activities and goals.

Unlike the former socialist societies, Cuba lacks a reformist state. There is no political realm that provides the opportunity structure necessary for greater articulation, organization, and mobilization of self-constituted groups. The slow, zigzagging process of Cuban economic reform has been insufficient to generate significant social space for civil society. On their own, the market and private enterprise will not lead automatically to the creation of sociopolitical actors in civil society, as post-Mao China demonstrates.

Cuba displays a hybrid of the defensive and emergent stages identified by an increasing number of human rights, dissident, professional, religious, and single-issue organizations. New groups have actively defended their positions and made demands of the government, but most of the island's self-constituted associations are merely attempting to survive undetected by the state and have not formalized their activities.

Why is a proto-civil society emerging in Cuba? Where is it emerging? The reasons are sociopolitical and economic. The process is the result of state-related factors, international forces outside the control of the state, grassroots efforts, and factions within the party and state bureaucracy. The state-sponsored Center for the Study of the Americas has been a leading force, and its scholars believe that the concept of civil society holds a significant normative appeal. The discourse and praxis associated with the rise of civil society in formerly authoritarian and totalitarian countries resonates among groups inside Cuba, particularly as the gap between socialist promise and performance widens.

There are four sources of civil-society formation in Cuba. First, in the course of the informal relations of everyday life, small groups of family members and friends engage in a variety of non-state-sanctioned activities. Second, the bureaucracies, mass organizations, and policies of the state are generating new interests and cleavages that increasingly seek more space for autonomous actions. Third, there still are some traditional non-governmental organizations, primarily religious, that survived the revolution. Fourth, international NGOs are establishing contacts in Cuba, sponsoring affiliates or generating non-state activities with Cuban counterparts.

The informal behaviors of everyday life and networks of family members and friends at the grassroots are some of the building blocks of civil society. The "informal" realms of the private sphere, where friends and family interact, constitute an alternative source of norms to the state and state institutions. These groups of *socios* (buddies), friends, and family operate on the black market and facilitate all sorts of backdoor practices, resulting in a regime of *sociolismo* (connections), not *socialismo* (socialism). These networks form the infrastructure of the "politics of affection," politics that revolve around who you know, who you love, and are based on individual interests and rules. Human rights organizations, dissident groups, and independent professional associations also trace their origins to the politics of affection.

Knowing how to work the system—networking capital—was historically important in other socialist societies and became even more critically important in the transition and post-transition eras. But are these societies really "civil"? At the grassroots level, Cubans dealt with the economic crisis by resorting to a host of informal mechanisms and networks outside the purview of the state. Friends and family members facilitated black market transactions. The culture of illegality flourished as people tried to make ends meet.

The diffuse origins of civil society present a classic dilemma of collective action: How to expand the membership of groups based on particularistic criteria? Moreover, how to transform the political culture of the informal, which is usually associated with the illegal, and, as such, goes against the established rules of the state? And, will civil society eventually influence the institutions of governance?

The Cuban state and its policies, especially since the mid-1980s, have contributed unwittingly to the establishment of semi-autonomous groups in two ways. First, the state has granted NGO status to some of its agencies for financial as well as political reasons. They can secure funds from foreign sources and are held up as proof that an independent civil society exists on the island, foiling international attacks against the totalitarian Castro regime. The Cuban intelligentsia and the National Association of Small Farmers are engaged in a cautious process of distancing themselves from state control. Second, state policies have also contributed to the formation of independent groups outside the control (if not the regulation) of the state. The legalization of self-employment, dollarization, and the establishment of joint ventures, particularly in the tourist sector, has unwittingly opened more maneuvering room for independent and semi-independent economic units that in turn create their own sector-based interest groups. Economic reforms divorced from political reforms, however, do not help civil-society formation. The case of China is illuminating in this regard, as local and mid-level party and state bureaucrats benefit from the economic reforms.[8] Both these results—the presence of officially sanctioned NGOs and the small but important private or mixed economic sectors—provide a veneer of democratic pluralism within Cuban socialism and can become focal points of further change. Therefore, economic reforms might, in the short run, strengthen rather than weaken Party support.

A TYPOLOGY OF ORGANIZATIONS

Today there is a variegated institutional landscape on the island. In addition to the informal networks that operate day-to-day at the grassroots and informal levels, there are three main types of organizations in Cuba, separated by their degree of independence from the government. First, Controlled Governmental Organizations (CONGOs, not an official Cuban label) are the state-affiliated mass organizations and agencies that are slowly trying to distance themselves from the central command. Most still toe the party line. These include the Federation of Cuban Women, the Confederation of Cuban Workers, and the Union of Communist Youth. Second, a small number of Government-Oriented Organizations (GONGOs, also not an official Cuban label) are semi-corporatist in form. They enjoy some state privileges, such as legal recognition, but have greater autonomy than CONGOs. There are only a handful of GONGOs, of which the best-known are the Felix Varela Institute (now defunct) and the Martin Luther King Center. The Varela Institute dealt with new issues, such as gay rights, and sponsored novel events, such as open-air concerts and local development initiatives. Finally, the category of nongovernmental organizations (NGOs) comprises various religious, professional, fraternal, and dissident organizations. Caritas Cuba, the humanitarian group affiliated with the Catholic Church, is a prime example of an NGO operating inside Cuba. Many NGOs have links with international counterparts, including Cuban expatriates. NGOs are given little leeway and their activities are fraught with risk. Yet they continue to pursue their agendas, and new groups, albeit small, are being established.

THE OBSTACLES TO CIVIL SOCIETY

Several important factors militate against the expansion of civil society in Cuba. The principal one is the state. By foreclosing the sociopolitical space and opposing reforms, the Castro regime limits the possibility for groups to organize legally. The opportunity structure at present is not conducive to strengthening private groups and their influence in society. Sociopolitical factors, such as fear and the retreat to the private (what Albert Hirschman identified as the "cycle of shifting involvements") also conspire against civil society formation and consolidation.[9] The demands that an economy of survival places on individuals in terms of time and energy lead to a necessary self-centeredness. This attitude is not conducive to civic participation in independent organizations, particularly given the risks associated with such activities in contemporary Cuba. Not all Cubans are ready or willing to join alternative organizations. On the contrary, many Cubans have divided loyalties and seem confused and unsure about the future. To make matters worse, international factors, particularly Washington's statements and policies, tend to polarize Cuban politics, thus indirectly constricting the space for civil society.

The customary conflation of civil society and political society is not applicable to Cuba, because the party-state tends to indirectly control many "independent" activities. The state has not redefined the rules of the game and has not expanded the social space necessary for NGOs to thrive. In fact, the state seems to be steering in the opposite direction, toward greater control. Intellectuals from the Center for the Study of the Americas and the University of Havana have been repressed. There is rumored to be a draft law on associations circulating that would make it nearly impossible to establish new GONGOs. Since 1996, the pendulum's swing seemed to favor the hard-liners in the short run, but in the long term, structural and ideational factors were likely to conspire against their will and interest.

Sociopolitical factors, namely fear and the need to concentrate on day-to-day economic survival, mitigate the growth of independent associations. Cubans, tired of politics and mobilization, are retreating to the private, trying to avoid politics. Perhaps it is time to look beyond the transition phase to find ways to strengthen the civility of Cuban society well into the future. Perhaps it is time to start thinking about transformation, not merely transition, in the way Cubans relate to and conduct politics.

IMPURITY AS AN OPPORTUNITY FOR A NEW REGIONAL POLICY

In the past few decades, Cuban society has changed demographically, educationally, and economically, but the state has failed to adapt. The disjuncture seems to become more pronounced with time; as the government refuses to undertake reforms, the economy continues to falter, and the society resorts to mechanisms of informal resistance. The cleavages resulting from dollarization, youth disenchantment, and rising criminality are among many social features that point to the actual and potential problems of basic governance. Although corruption and rising social inequality erode the legitimacy of Cuba's socialist regime, it continues to exercise power and is firmly in control at the macro level of politics and society. At the micro level, however, the story is different. The gap between the theory and practice of Cuban socialism has never been wider, and it has shaken popular support for the Castro regime.

Cuban society is not organized to the point that it can mount a direct and orchestrated challenge against the government. The independent organizations and the mass organizations do not have the wherewithal to launch a campaign to redefine the political system from the bottom up. This is one of the major factors of social inertia that allows the regime to muddle through. The danger is that latent dissatisfaction may eventually erupt in riots. Furthermore, there is no group capable of providing leadership should the Castro regime collapse.

Nevertheless, Cuba's proto-civil society is important symbolically and practically. The organizations of the emergent civil society exert a demonstration effect that others will follow, pushing for reform and transition to what one hopes will be a more democratic political system. If the state ever provides an appropriate window of opportunity, public groups will proliferate. In and of itself this will not guarantee the civility of civil society, however. In addition to a quantitative/institutional dimension, civil society has a qualitative dimension that is defined by the society's political culture, the norms under which it operates, and its agenda. There is room for caution as to the nature of civil society in the future. The Cuban Communist Party may be replaced by a regime bent on accumulating individual wealth at any cost. In other words, the politics of civil society might reproduce the politics of the past, both inside and outside Cuba, in both the republican and the socialist periods, but in a new economic context.

The currency of the notion of civil society, the demonstration effect of other countries, the gap between theory and practice in Cuban socialism, and the economic crisis all indicate that civil society, regardless of how long it takes and what specific form it takes, will be established in Cuba. Once the state opens the door even a bit, civil society will expand. It is unlikely, though, that civil society by itself will be able to challenge the regime directly and redefine the Cuban political system. Such a scenario will have to wait until an initial period of reform allows the organizations of civil society to muster support and strength. The quality of civil society, however, is a more open and troubling question. Moreover, civil society in and of itself does not guarantee the operation of a democratic system if political society does not implement institutions and codes of conduct supportive of democratic governance.

NOTES

1. Juan M. Del Aguila, *Cuba: Dilemmas of a Revolution*, 3rd ed. (Boulder, Colo.: Westview Press, 1994).

2. Jorge I. Domínguez, *Cuba: Order and Revolution* (Cambridge: Harvard University Press, 1978).

3. Marifeli Pérez-Stable, *The Cuban Revolution: Origins, Course, and Legacy* (New York: Oxford University Press, 1993).

4. Gillian Gunn, "Cuba's NGOs: Government Puppets or Seeds of Civil Society?" Georgetown University, *Cuba Briefing Paper Series*, no. 7 (1995).

5. Haroldo Dilla, *La democracia en Cuba y el diferendo con los Estados Unidos* (Democracy in Cuba and the Differences with the United States) (Havana: Ediciones CEA, 1995); Haroldo Dilla et al., eds., *Participación popular y desarrollo en los municipios cubanos* (Popular Participation and Development in Cuban Communities) (Havana: Ediciones CEA, 1993); Aurelio Alonso Tejada, Church and Politics in Revolutionary Cuba (Havana: Editorial José Martí, 1999).

6. John A. Hall, ed., *Civil Society: Theory, History, Comparison* (Cambridge, UK: Polity Press, 1995).

7. Marcia Weigle and Jim Butterfield, "Civil Society in Reforming Communist Regimes," *Comparative Politics* 25, no. 1 (October 1992): 1–24.

8. Margaret M. Pearson, *China's New Business Elite: The Political Consequence of Economic Reform* (Berkeley: University of California Press, 1997); David L. Wank, "Bureaucratic Patronage and Private Business: Changing Networks of Power in Urban China," in *The Waning of the Communist State: Economic Origins of Political Decline in China and Hungary*, ed. Andrew G. Walder (Berkeley: University of California Press, 1993), pp. 153–84.

9. Albert O. Hirschman, *Shifting Involvements: Private Interest and Public Action* (Princeton, N.J.: Princeton University Press, 1982).

8

Cuba Poll

The Findings

Mimi Whitefield and Mary Beth Sheridan

A Miami Herald *poll in Cuba, the first independent, scientific survey there in more than three decades, indicates that a majority believe the revolution has yielded more achievements than failures—even though most people appear dismayed by the island's economic crisis.*

A significant number of Cubans interviewed mentioned the U.S. embargo—rather than the political system—as a reason for their economic misery. And a solid majority expect that 1995 will be a better year, following a series of highly popular economic reforms.

The poll was designed by the *Herald* and CID/Gallup, the Costa Rican affiliate of the Gallup polling organization of Princeton, New Jersey. It was conducted last month [November 1994] by fourteen Central American pollsters who canvassed 1,002 Cubans and 75 percent of the territory.

CID/Gallup co-owner Carlos Denton said he believed that Cubans gave honest answers to the poll takers, despite the government's history of repression. Other pollsters and experts cautioned, however, that some answers appeared to have been skewed by self-censorship.

Nevertheless, the experts said, the poll provides rare insights into Cubans' lives and points to significant trends.

Among the key findings:

- Only 3 percent of those interviewed identified politics as the country's main problem.
- One in five had been to church during the past month, a surprisingly high number in a country that officially repressed religious practice until 1985.
- Fifty percent favored equality over freedom, but 38 percent chose freedom as the most important value for society.
- Most of those polled expressed warm feelings toward exiles living abroad.

- Despite the fact that private enterprise has been largely illegal in Cuba for more than thirty years, more than half of those polled said they would be interested in starting their own businesses.

SOME CAVEATS

The Cuban government forbade CID/Gallup to ask about Castro and all "personalities." Nevertheless, the experts said, the poll offered some signs of declining participation in the one-party political system.

The experts also noted that some of the responses, particularly those related to the U.S. embargo, reflected thirty-five years of government propaganda and political indoctrination.

Asked to identify Cuba's biggest problem, the highest number of respondents—31 percent—picked the embargo, closely followed by lack of food. Follow-up responses repeatedly cited the embargo as a major culprit in the island's economic troubles.

"It's quite clear to me they are not in their situation because of the embargo. Cuba can trade with any country in the world except the United States," Denton said. "But the government has managed to take attention away from its failings and shift them to the embargo."

Denton's conclusion that Cubans "in the main are still willing to support their revolution" is based primarily on poll indications that politics wasn't an overriding concern and that of those surveyed, 48 percent identified themselves as "revolutionaries."

Fifty-eight percent of those polled said they believed that the achievements of the revolution—primarily listed as education and health care—outweighed its failures, Denton noted.

But other experts said a response that the revolution had achieved gains should not be translated automatically into support for the government.

"The lack of food and the U.S. embargo are political situations," said Rob Schroth, a U.S. pollster with experience in eleven Latin American countries. "It can't be deduced that people think the political situation is good" because they cited other concerns first.

DON'T ASK

Experts also cautioned that opposition to the government might be masked by Cubans' fear of it. For example, 46 percent of those polled said they didn't know or did not respond to a question about the principal failure of the revolution.

"The biggest group doesn't want to say anything at all to the most direct question of all, the one about judging the revolution," said Carmelo Mesa Lago, an economist and professor at the University of Miami.

"Actually, I'm surprised that so many—31 percent—said there were more failures (than achievements). You have to begin with the premise that people in Cuba aren't accustomed to responding to a survey, especially when conducted by foreigners. They are afraid," he said.

The poll asked few direct questions about the political system, in an effort to avoid putting the interview subjects on the defensive.

But some of the responses shed indirect light on politics.

Twenty-four percent of those polled described themselves as "not integrated" in the revolution—a term for those who are totally inactive politically. That percentage slightly exceeds the total of those who defined themselves as communists (11 percent) or socialists (10 percent).

The largest single group—48 percent—described themselves as "revolutionaries."

Denton said cross-checking his results showed the stereotypical "revolutionaries" to be mainly women between the ages of 25 and 49, living principally in rural areas, with higher education and more satisfied with their lives than the average Cubans.

"In Cuba, revolutionary is a very positive term," said Marifeli Pérez Stable, a Cuba expert from the State University of New York at Old Westbury. "But I don't think revolutionary today necessarily means a supporter of the government."

OUT OF THE LOOP

The "nonintegrated," on the other hand, tended to be city dwellers, either younger than 24 or older than 40, with only primary or high school education and not satisfied with their personal lives.

Only 36 percent said they had attended a political meeting in the past month—a surprising result in a country where meetings of everyone from young communists to workplace assemblies once touched practically everyone's life. Experts saw this as an indication of declining political activism.

Asked whether the law should promote economic and social equality, or promote individual freedoms, 50 percent chose equality—a cornerstone of Marxist ideology. "It's something the government has managed to insert into the belief system," Denton said.

But 38 percent chose freedom, which experts said denotes a possible erosion of belief in revolutionary tenets. "The idea that 38 percent chose freedom is astounding," Pérez Stable said.

Reflecting the weakness of nongovernment institutions, 23 percent of the Cubans, asked about who would aid or guide someone who disagrees with the government, replied "nobody"; 19 percent said they didn't know; 18 percent named the church; 17 percent cited the family; and 12 percent chose political and human rights dissidents.

"This is a measure of the disorganization of civil society," Pérez Stable added. "The church can maybe give you harbor, the family is your last bastion anywhere, so what do people really have in terms of independent leadership?"

Pollsters cautioned that the *Herald* poll simply provides a snapshot of attitudes when the poll was taken November 1–9, 1994—a time of optimism one month after the government increased food supplies by permitting farmers to sell their products at open markets.

HOW THE WIND BLOWS

Attitudes in Cuba during these trying economic times are indeed mercurial. They may have everything to do with whether the kids ate dinner, or someone spent three hours waiting for a bus that day, or the power was off for eight hours.

Back in September, an unscientific poll taken by Mexico's Televisión Azteca—400 people interviewed only in Havana—claimed to have found that Castro was unpopular and that Cubans were blaming the government more than the U.S. embargo for their economic problems.

But in November, the *Herald*'s pollsters found that while half of those surveyed said they were not getting enough food, and smaller numbers complained about the energy crisis and shortages of medicines and other basics, 60 percent believed that 1995 would be a better year for the Cuban people.

"I think the poll shows that with some of these (economic) reforms, the regime has bought itself some time," Denton said.

More than half of those polled said they'd be interested in starting their own business, 66 percent said they felt they would not be personally affected if foreigners bought property in Cuba, and 61 percent approved of the government's decision to allow foreigners to open businesses.

"Cubans feel that the way out of their economic problems now is foreign investment," said Donna Kaplowitz, a Cuba expert at Michigan State University. Cuba nationalized foreign-owned properties in the 1960s and began seriously courting foreign investors only in the late 1980s.

But Kaplowitz cautioned that many Cubans viewed foreign investment as a mixed blessing, with some resentful of what they see as privileges for the foreigners and profits mainly for the government.

In fact, the single largest group of respondents, 39 percent, felt it was the government that benefits the most from foreign investment. It wasn't clear if they believed it was good or bad.

NOT CASTRO'S MODEL

With 78 percent of respondents saying they own their homes, Denton said, Cuba will be a different place if the economic reforms continue.

"Cuba will then be a country of homeowners, small- and medium-size business proprietors, foreign investors and will not resemble the model Fidel Castro promoted for so many years," he said. "The question is whether Cubans themselves will note the contradiction."

On their relations with Cubans who left the island, most of those surveyed expressed warm feelings, and 75 percent said they regarded those Cubans who departed five or more years ago as political or economic emigrants; 15 percent said they were traitors.

Still, 32 percent expressed fear that if the Cubans abroad were allowed to return, they would bring "many problems." Forty-one percent said their return would mean the reunification of families, and 12 percent said they would bring money and jobs.

"That captures that Cuban ambivalence," said Gillian Gunn, head of the Cuba and Haiti Project at Georgetown University. "They love (relatives) and want to be with them, but they're afraid (they) might try to take things over with their superior wealth and marketing knowledge."

A surprisingly low number of those polled—13 percent—reported having received dollar remittances from relatives abroad; about half of those reported they received $100 or more per month.

An overwhelming 80 percent of respondents disagreed with President Clinton's decision last August to step up pressure against the Castro government by severely limiting travel and cutting off remittances to the island by Cuban Americans.

Three decades after the communist revolution vowed to attack racial discrimination, the survey also found a widespread feeling that the goal had been achieved. Ninety percent said skin color did not affect a person's opportunities and treatment.

Academic experts noted, however, that few blacks hold top positions in the government or the Communist Party.

GROUP PORTRAIT

The portrait of Cubans that emerged from the poll was of a sociable people, largely satisfied with their personal lives and given to watching television—especially the soaps.

Seventy-six percent of respondents were "very" or "somewhat" satisfied with their personal lives, something that the CID/Gallup analysis of the poll said held wider meaning.

"In poll after poll, it has been found that the more satisfied personally a respondent is with his or her life, the more likely that his or her opinions will be positive toward the government, the society and the economy."

The satisfaction level of Cubans was higher than that of Nicaraguans and Guatemalans who were asked the same question in recent polls, Denton said.

Respondents also said overwhelmingly—88 percent—that they were very proud to be Cuban. Denton said the response also was important, since measures of nationalism usually reflect a population's resiliency and openness to change.

"We put this question in because Cubans are obviously going through a crisis, which involves considerable change in the way they live," he said. "We wanted to measure their capacity for absorbing it."

Regarding their social lives, 36 percent of Cubans polled said they invite neighbors to their homes at least once a week to dance, talk, or listen to music.

That was higher than in many Central American countries, Denton said, possibly reflecting the fact that during the energy crisis it's difficult for Cubans to get transport out of their neighborhoods.

But the most popular leisure activity was watching television. Thirty-two percent of respondents said they primarily spent their free time in front of the tube—which Denton said is similar to the United States.

"People go about their lives in every society without making transcendental decisions about themselves and their families," Denton said, "and the Cubans are no exception."

9

Cuba's Catholic Dissident

The Saga of Oswaldo Payá

Tim Padgett

Dissident movements never get much traction in communist Cuba. That is partly because Fidel Castro is vastly more charismatic than the stone-faced apparatchiks of the old Soviet bloc and partly because his security apparatus would tax Orwell's imagination. Either way, *El Comandante* has always been able to put a lid on dissident leaders before their faces became as well known as Lech Walesa or Nelson Mandela.

But Cuban dissidents have never had much spiritual backup, either. In Poland, Walesa's Solidarity movement was sponsored by the Catholic Church from the start, a fact that automatically gave it the support of 90 percent of the population. History is full of evidence that faith can be a more resilient bond for democratic change than politics, and Fidel Castro is nothing if not a keen student of history. He proved this early in his dictatorship by purging Cuba of its Catholic clergy as well as its Catholic enthusiasm.

So it is not surprising to learn that Cuba's first bona fide dissident movement—one that has seen some seventy-five of its leaders imprisoned by Castro this year—can in many ways be traced to a small Catholic church, Nuestra Señora de los Dolores (Our Lady of Sorrows), on Cuba's Isla de la Juventud (Isle of Youth, formerly called the Isla de Pinos, or Isle of Pines). It was there that a teenage dissident named Oswaldo Payá spent his free time as a political prisoner for three years, from 1969 to 1972. But it was also a spiritual refuge, where Payá came to the conclusion that inept military actions like the Bay of Pigs were not the way to challenge Castro. The more effective approach in the long run, he reasoned, would be a nonviolent, grass-roots, faith-based campaign of opposition—the Christian Liberation Movement—which today has gained more support inside Cuba than any other since Castro took power in 1959.

Oswaldo Payá, in fact, is the first Cuban dissident ever to be compared with the likes of Lech Walesa. It's a premature likening, to be sure—especially since Castro essentially put Payá's top management out of commission last March with one of his most severe crackdowns in decades. But the fact that Castro did not jail Payá—

even Castro realizes what an international outcry that would provoke—is in itself proof that Payá is an unprecedented irritant for the Cuban regime. Just as important, however—and something that has gone largely and strangely unremarked upon in my profession—is the Catholic faith that fuels Payá's mission. Even less noticed, I believe, is the way Payá's mission has in turn helped strengthen a once moribund Cuban Catholic Church. "This," the 51-year-old Payá told me in a recent interview, "has finally become a duel between power and spirit in Cuba."

That standoff started early, but on a more personal level. Payá was born in a Havana parish called La Parroquia del Cerro, where his family were devout Catholics. Showing at a young age that he could match Castro for hard-headedness, Payá was the only youngster in his primary school who refused to become a member of the Communist Youth after the 1959 revolution.

Most Catholic clergy and laypeople had backed Castro's overthrow of the right-wing strongman Fulgencio Batista, but their attitudes turned when Castro adopted Communism. That, and the fact that Cuba's bishops had remained loyal to Batista, was bound to bring the communists' wrath down on the church. From 1960 through 1961 all Catholic media were abolished, Catholic schools were expropriated, and more than 3,500 priests and nuns were exiled. "Castro left about 200 priests to minister to six million Cubans," recalls Miami's Auxiliary Bishop Augustín Roman, one of the exiled priests. "It put Cuba's Catholics to sleep."

Not all of them. Payá was part of a small but tenacious crowd of activist Catholic youth who provoked ridicule and worse in their high school cafeterias. After publicly denouncing the violent Soviet crackdown in Czechoslovakia during the Prague Spring of 1968, Payá got hauled off to a work camp on the Isla de Pinos.

But it was there that Payá changed from "an aggressive boy, always hurling acerbic criticism of Castro's regime, into a more mature leader," says a longtime friend of Payá, the Reverend Armando Pérez, associate pastor at our Lady Queen of Martyrs in Fort Lauderdale, Florida. When Payá discovered Nuestra Señora de los Dolores in the island town of Nueva Gerona, he found it locked up. He sent a request to the Havana bishop for the keys and opened up a sanctuary that camp guards let him use as his prison home when he wasn't working at the island's quarry sixty hours a week.

Payá set up a virtual mission there, giving religious speeches, inviting in sick and elderly islanders, and pursuing what he calls a "more mystic life." It made him, he says, both tougher and more stoic—and more resolved to follow the methods he had heard about in the U.S. civil rights movement: fighting the system nonviolently from within the system. "He discovered a pacifist method more compatible with his Christianity," says Bishop Roman. "He realized that you can bring down a house in two ways—with a hurricane or with termites. The former just wasn't going to happen in Cuba, but the latter is still possible."

The best place for the termites to munch, Payá decided, was Castro's own constitution, which on its face, if hardly ever in its execution, allows for democratic niceties like multiple-candidate elections and referendums. But to be taken seriously as a patriotic Cuban politico, Payá had to thwart one of Castro's favorite modes of attack: accusing dissidents of being tools of the United States.

So even when he was offered a chance to escape to Miami during the massive Mariel boatlift of 1980, Payá instead opted to stay in Cuba for the rest of his life. He took a university degree in physics and became an engineer, specializing in the repair of hospital equipment—work to which he still travels by bicycle each day in Havana. (Many, in fact, speculate that the real reason Castro does not jail Payá is that, with Cuba's economy so ramshackle, the government cannot afford to lose talented medical technicians.)

Nor can Castro accuse Payá of promoting the U.S. economic embargo against Cuba. Payá does not call for abolishing it. But like the Catholic Church, he has repeatedly expressed opposition to those aspects of the embargo that hurt Cuba's 11 million people, especially the recently lifted U.S. ban on food and medicine sales to Cuba.

But the 1980's would turn out to be a decade of more religious than political significance for Cuba. After a quarter-century of dormancy, the island's Catholic Church got a whiff of smelling salts as Pope John Paul II hit the international scene. By 1986, the church in Cuba was deep into what it called the National Cuban Church Meeting, known by its Spanish acronym, ENEC (*Encuentro Nacional Eclesial Cubano*)—an exercise in soul-searching and revival that may have saved Cuba's church from irrelevance if not eventual extinction.

If Payá and other dissidents thought the ENEC would fuel their political activism, they were mistaken. Cuba's bishops, as well as the Vatican, decided that it made little sense for the church to confront Castro when the church in Cuba itself was still so threadbare. Cuba could not be Poland. As a result, the Cuban church opted for a controversial policy of accommodation with the communist regime as the only way to rebuild Cuban Catholicism—a policy that to a large degree still stands.

Characteristically, Payá pushed. The church, he argued, should not risk the impression that it cared more about its own corporate development in Cuba than it did about human rights—especially since that might end up actually alienating Cubans from the church. "The Castro government insists on protecting Cuba's sovereignty," says Payá. "My point is, by defending Cubans' civil rights, we are also defending Cuba's sovereignty."

Whether the church liked it or not, Payá would become its political voice in Cuba. In 1987, with church aid, he started up the magazine *Pueblo de Dios* (People of God), which regularly called on Cuba's Catholics to be in the vanguard of the human rights discussion. A year later, however, under intense pressure from the government, Cuba's bishops shut down the magazine. Undeterred, Payá immediately founded the Christian Liberation Movement, known by its Spanish initials, MCL.

By now Payá was married with three children—and a growing target for Cuba's security police, who often (and still do, he says) shadowed him on the streets from as close as a few feet away. But it was also a measure of Payá's growing popularity with Cubans that, while police often took him into custody for questioning, they never imprisoned him outright—even after he and the MCL began a grassroots "dialogue" on a national human rights referendum in 1991. "This is the first totally peaceful movement for change in the history of Cuba," says Payá. "They did not know how to confront that." Instead, Castro supporters ransacked Payá's Havana house and defaced it with graffiti that read "Traitor" and "CIA."

In 1992 Payá began his attempts to run for Cuba's parliament as an opposition candidate. He was, predictably, arrested; but again, he was never imprisoned. That allowed him to go on building a broader grassroots following, especially as Cuba's post–Soviet-aid economy hit rock bottom in the 1990s. By 1996 Payá and the MCL felt strong enough to start the Varela Project—a petition campaign to get the necessary 10,000 signatures that, under the 1976 Constitution, legalized a national referendum. Payá sought a plebiscite on five basic human rights issues: free speech, free assembly, multiparty elections, broader free enterprise, and the freeing of political prisoners.

But it was the project's name that was particularly shrewd. Varela was Padre Félix Varela, a Cuban Catholic priest who in the mid-nineteenth century helped spark the movement for Cuba's independence from Spain, which it eventually won in 1898, and freedom for black slaves. As a result, the Varela Project gathered all the more momentum, because it emerged on the eve of Pope John Paul II's historic 1998 visit to Cuba. That event further galvanized not only the Cuban Church but also Catholic dissidents like Payá—and the ongoing efforts of Cuban Catholics to win sainthood for Padre Varela. "It drove home for people," says Payá, "that we [the MCL] are first and foremost persons of faith. They realized that it's much harder—impossible, really—for a government to crush that sort of thing or keep it silent."

At this point, however, an important question arises. Who was gaining more energy from whom: Payá from the Cuban Church, or the Cuban Church from Payá? It's easy to imagine Payá taking sustenance from Catholicism's revival in Cuba; but it is hard to dismiss the notion that while Payá was out crusading for democratic reform in the name of Catholicism, his personal popularity helped draw more Cubans into the church's fold. More likely, says Bishop Roman, Payá and the church have been engaged in a symbiosis that is all too rarely acknowledged publicly: "The two receive too much from each other at this point to say otherwise."

Either way, Payá was on the verge of his most critical vindication. By 2002 the Varela Project had gathered more than 11,000 signatures, from Havana to Santiago in the east and Pinar del Río in the west. The most striking thing was that Payá had accomplished this by word of mouth, securing legal signatures through the island's catacomb-like system known as *resolver*—the Cuban expression for finding ingenious ways of solving problems like a chronic lack of food, auto parts, or access to mass media to promote an opposition campaign.

And then, during former U.S. President Jimmy Carter's equally historic visit to Cuba that year, Varela had its mass media moment. In a speech to Castro and a host of communist V.I.P.s in Havana, which Castro allowed to be broadcast nationwide, Carter not only mentioned the Varela Project but championed it. Suddenly every Cuban household knew about it—not only that there was a constitutionally sanctioned petition drive taking place on their streets, but that it was a Catholic-inspired campaign.

Overnight, Payá had gained Lech Walesa–style status both inside and outside of Cuba. Castro tried to counterattack by dismissing the Varela petitions as illegitimate—something not even the right-wing Chilean dictator General Augusto Pinochet dared do in the 1980s when the opposition successfully petitioned for a constitutional referendum on his rule. Castro mobilized massive marches in support of his government and held his own special referendum, which, not surprisingly, resoundingly affirmed Cuban socialism as the island's "irrevocable" system.

But it did little to dampen Payá's new fame. He won the European Union's Sakharov Prize for human rights last December. Vaclav Havel, who led the "velvet revolution" that toppled communism in Czechoslovakia, nominated him for the

Nobel Peace Prize. And this past spring, Robert DeNiro's Tribeca Film Festival canceled its screening of Oliver Stone's Castro documentary, *Comandante*, and showed instead a documentary on Payá. More important, within a year after Carter's visit, the Varela Project claimed to have garnered an additional 30,000 signatures.

Eventually, Castro had to strike with a harder fist—hence the arrests, convictions, and lengthy prison sentences, as many as 28 years, for 75 Cuban dissidents this past spring, more than 50 of whom were Payá lieutenants. They were accused of treason for taking aid from the United States, which Castro insists is poised to invade Cuba now as it invaded Iraq.

The crackdown makes it easier to understand why Cardinal Jaime Ortega of Havana recently insisted that the Cuban church cannot and will not "be on the side of the opposition, the same way you cannot ask the church to support the government." Ortega's critics, however, say he is essentially aiding the latter by being so indifferent to the former.

All of which makes this the most triumphant and yet the most precarious moment in Payá's dissident career. Critics both inside and outside Cuba have suggested that Payá unnecessarily provoked Castro by flaunting his international celebrity. But Payá insists that his movement has let a genie out of the bottle that will eventually succeed, either during Castro's lifetime or shortly thereafter—meaning that democratic change post-Castro might be easier now that a nonviolent, grassroots reform spirit has finally penetrated into the island's civic veins, largely through the Varela Project. What's more, as Payá showed during a visit to Miami this year, most of the once bellicose exile community has signed on to his strategy. "We've helped destroy the myth that a majority of exiles are war mongers," he says.

Meanwhile, the Cuban church and Payá will continue their delicate partnership. The church has in fact been building a stronger social backbone of late. Shortly before last spring's wave of arrests. Cardinal Ortega did make an unusually impassioned call for Castro to address the increasingly bleak economic straits of Cuba, where most workers make about $15 a month. Last month, he and Cuba's thirteen-member bishops' conference urged "clemency" for the jailed dissidents and criticized Castro for making his "official ideology" even more intolerant of late. But Cuba's bishops still seem as hoarse about human rights under Castro as they were under Batista. Payá may be right when he claims that despite Castro's crackdowns, his movement will keep growing. The question is whether the spiritual backup his movement needs, now more than ever, will grow as well.

PART III

ECONOMICS

For two hundred years, Cuba was the paradigmatic case of a monocultural export economy, dependent upon the production of one primary commodity—sugar—for sale to one principal trade partner—Spain during the early colonial period, the United States during the nineteenth and early twentieth centuries, and the Soviet Union after 1960. Overcoming dependency was high on the agenda of economic reforms pledged by the leaders of the 1959 revolution. Yet despite a promising start in the 1960s and early 1970s, Cuba could not easily escape the twin afflictions of sugar dependence and a dominant trade partner. Only the collapse of European communism freed Cuba from dependent trade relations with the Soviet Union and its Eastern European allies—albeit at the cost of enormous economic disruption.

In the late eighteenth century, sugar displaced tobacco as Cuba's principal crop, and comparative advantage soon made the island the dominant producer in the world market. For over a century, sugar brought Cuba prosperity, dulling the economic conflicts that fueled the wars of independence in Spain's other New World colonies. The rise of sugar also linked Cuba to the United States. When a collapse in international sugar prices in 1884 pushed many Cuban sugar mills into bankruptcy, capital from the United States poured into the island, consolidating and modernizing the sugar sector. In 1898, Washington's desire to protect these new economic interests contributed to the decision to intervene in Cuba's war of independence. The subsequent U.S. occupation of the island tied its economy ever closer to the United States as U.S. military governors promulgated laws giving U.S. firms concessionary access to the Cuban market. By the late 1920s, U.S. firms controlled 75 percent of the sugar industry and most of the mines, railroads, and public utilities.

The revolution of 1959 was animated in part by a nationalist desire to reduce Cuba's dependency on the United States. By 1960, Cuba's revolutionary leaders had concluded that the path to economic independence and development was a socialist one, and before the year was out, $1 billion of U.S. direct investment had been nationalized. Cuba's revolutionary government could not have survived Washington's declaration of economic war without external assistance. With the help of the

Soviet Union, Cuba's international economic relations were radically transformed. By 1962, trade with the United States had fallen to zero, and trade with the Soviet Union, negligible before 1959, had jumped to half of all Cuban trade.

Having ended Cuba's dependency on the United States, the revolutionary leadership next took aim at sugar. Their first development strategy, pursued until 1963, planned for balanced growth based on agricultural diversification and rapid development of both light and heavy industry. By 1961, bottlenecks associated with the shift from the market to central planning began to appear. Reduced sugar production (as called for in the diversification plan) led to a severe balance of payments crisis. Rapid industrial growth was beyond the capital-generating capacity of the Cuban economy, and the Soviet Union was unwilling to finance consistently huge deficits. In mid-1963, returning from a trip to the Soviet Union, Fidel Castro announced a return to specialization in sugar. The new strategy focused on exploiting Cuba's comparative advantage in sugar to generate hard currency that would then be used to finance the development of the rest of the economy. By the turn of the decade, Castro pledged, Cuba would produce ten million tons of sugar annually. Meeting the target of ten million tons of sugar in 1970 became enshrined as a matter of political prestige and regime legitimacy. Economic rationality took a backseat. Despite Herculean efforts that disrupted every other sector of the economy, only 8.5 million tons of sugar were produced.

The economic reforms that followed this failure marked the beginning of a more intimate economic relationship with the Soviet Union. A planning process modeled on the Soviet system was installed in exchange for increased Soviet economic aid. Cuba's reward for adopting the Soviets' less romantic vision of socialist construction was reflected in a series of five economic agreements signed in 1972. To reduce Cuba's perennial bilateral trade deficit, the Soviets agreed to pay higher preferential prices for Cuban sugar and nickel. Future trade credits were extended interest-free, and the repayment of Cuba's existing debt was deferred for thirteen years. In 1972, Cuba was admitted to the Council of Mutual Economic Assistance (CMEA), becoming one of the main sugar suppliers to the trade bloc.

The attractiveness of these arrangements was undeniable. Cuba was assured a reliable market for its exports, favorable terms of trade, significant development assistance, and an expansive line of credit allowing it to live beyond its means. As the oil crisis swept across the globe in the 1970s, sending the price of petroleum soaring and triggering financial catastrophe in much of the Third World, Cuba was immune because it purchased petroleum at a set price from the Soviet Union. But cheap oil reinforced the disincentive for Cuba to diversify its exports, or to develop energy-efficient production. The combination of low oil prices and high sugar prices hid the real costs of sugar production, making it seem more lucrative than it was. These structural weaknesses in the Cuban economy would only become apparent when the system of subsidized prices disappeared in the 1990s.

Overall, Soviet aid and the concomitant changes in Cuba's domestic economic policy had a salutary effect in the early 1970s. The economy enjoyed a robust recovery, with double digit average annual growth through 1974. In the late 1970s, however, a new economic crisis was precipitated by Cuba's attempt to expand its trade with the West. In 1974, an upward spike in the world market price for sugar gave Cuba an unexpected hard currency windfall, enabling it to expand imports from the West. Anticipating that higher sugar prices would last, and enticed (as were many Third World countries) by the easy availability of credit due to the global glut of petrodollars, Cuba took on four billion dollars of debt to expand imports even faster. By 1978, however, the world market price for sugar had declined to more traditional levels, saddling Cuba with a serious hard currency debt. By 1982, Cuba could no longer maintain regular debt service. After several attempts to restructure its debt, Cuba declared a moratorium on debt payments in 1986.

Cuba's hard currency crisis forced it back into an even closer and more exclusive economic relationship with the Soviet bloc. With little hard currency and no credit, Cuba could not buy much from the West. Trade with the Soviet Union ballooned from just 41 percent of total trade in 1974 to 69 percent in 1978 and remained at or above 60 percent until the Soviet Union collapsed. Cuba's trade dependence on the Soviet bloc also reinforced its dependence on sugar. Under the socialist division of labor that characterized relations within the CMEA, Cuba was designated as the group's primary sugar provider in 1981.

By the mid-1980s, Cuba's economic situation had become precarious. Despite the preferential prices Cuba received from the Soviet bloc, the balance of trade deficit expanded as domestic production of export commodities fell short of planning targets. In early 1986, Fidel Castro announced a new direction in economic policy. Criticizing the Soviet-sponsored socialist management system for fostering inefficiency, corruption, and profit-minded selfishness, he called for the "rectification of errors and negative tendencies." The Rectification campaign focused on recentralizing economic planning authority, dismantling material incentives and market mechanisms, abolishing the free farmers' markets launched in 1980, and combating corruption. The Rectification campaign did not solve Cuba's economic problems; if anything, it compounded them. The retreat from market-based material incentives hurt productivity, just as it had in the 1960s, so much so that Cuba's trade deficit grew, despite the austerity measures aimed at controlling it.

Thus Cuba's economy was already vulnerable when it was hit by the shock of European communism's collapse. The post-communist regimes insisted on trading at world market prices, refused to tolerate Cuba's trade deficits, and shut down their aid programs. The preferential prices and aid Cuba had enjoyed amounted to several billion dollars annually. Without the subsidies, Cuba's capacity to import shrank by 75 percent, causing severe shortages of energy, raw materials, and food. The resulting depression slashed gross domestic product by at least 35 percent, closed hundreds of factories, and left tens of thousands of Cubans unemployed. By one estimate, real wages shrank 80 percent between 1989 and 1995.

Faced with the worst economic crisis in the history of the revolution, Castro announced the beginning of the "Special Period in a Time of Peace" in 1990. Its strategy was that of a war-time economy: first, to reorient trade relations toward the West, attracting foreign investment capital to substitute for the lost subsidies, and second, to produce enough food to avert serious malnutrition. Initially, the government sought to weather the crisis without significant domestic economic reforms. By late 1993, the inadequacy of this approach had become clear, since the crisis was deepening rather than abating. Thus the second phase of policy initiatives included a series of market-oriented reforms, including the reestablishment of free farmers' markets, the devolution of many state farms to cooperatives, sharp reductions in subsidies to state enterprises, the legalization of self-employment, and—most significantly—the legalization of dollars.

In this section, Cuban economist Pedro Monreal describes the dimensions of the economic tsunami that hit Cuba in the early 1990s and the policies adopted to cope with it. Unlike the structural adjustments undertaken in the eastern bloc or elsewhere in Latin America, Cuba's policies placed a priority on maintaining its system of free health care and education, and on providing a basic minimum of consumption for all. As sugar declined in importance, tourism rose to take its place. The Cuban leadership invested heavily in this sector because it had the potential for rapid growth, thereby rescuing the economy from depression. Monreal examines Cuba's new development strategy during the Special Period and the ways in which even domestic sectors of the economy are affected by Cuba's need to compete in the world market. The focus on tourism and nickel exports was essential for economic survival, Monreal concludes, but these sectors are not dynamic enough to generate sustained development. "Cuba needs . . . a development strategy that replaces exports based on the intensive use of natural resources with technologically advanced exports," he argues. Cuba needs to base its economic competitiveness on its highly educated people, not its sunny beaches.

Mauricio de Miranda Parrondo's assessment of the problems the Cuban economy faces going forward focuses more on the limits of the economic reforms Cuba's leadership has been willing to undertake. His critique of Cuba's reliance on tourism and nickel to replace sugar as its main export echoes Monreal, but Miranda Parrondo also notes that Cuba's infrastructure has become badly decayed during the Special Period for want of domestic reinvestment. Foreign investment has lagged because of the political and bureaucratic maze investors must still navigate. In recent years, the government has begun to scale back some of the market-oriented reforms introduced in the mid-1990s, suggesting a degree of official complacency about prospects for future growth which Miranda Parrondo does not share.

Fidel Castro was always uncomfortable with the market-oriented reforms his government was forced to adopt in the early 1990s at the depth of the Special Period. Speaking on August 6, 1995, he explained to Cubans why it was necessary to "introduce elements of capitalism into our system." It was not, he assured them, because he wanted to unleash market mechanisms in the Cuban economy. "We have gone down this road basically because it was the only alternative for saving the revolution," he said. Indeed, this speech marked the beginning of a retrenchment of sorts. Although the market reforms introduced in the preceding two years were left in place, no further reforms were undertaken once the economy began to recover.

Phil Peters examines the gradual decline of the Cuban sugar sector and the impact of the decision in 2002 to radically downsize the sector, replacing sugar with tourism as the central pillar of the Cuban economy. Once Cuba had to pay world market prices for the petroleum to run its sugar industry and had to sell its sugar abroad at world prices, the obsolescence of a large part of the industry became unavoidably clear. For several years, Cuba continued subsidizing sugar production in many rural areas where sugar constituted the only source of employment and income. But in 2002, the day of reckoning arrived and half the island's mills closed down. "Sugar's pre-eminent position in Cuba's economy has been broken," Peters concludes. "Sugar will be an important factor, but no longer a determining factor in Cuba's economy."

Tourism, after a meteoric rise, has taken sugar's place, as Marguerite Jiménez describes. Before 1959, tourism was an important component of the Cuban economy, second only to sugar, but in the 1960s, the revolutionary government neglected tourism because of its association with the social ills of prerevolutionary Cuba, especially gambling, prostitution, and foreign domination. In the 1980s, as Cuba looked for new sources of hard currency, the tourism sector was revived, and became a critical component of the recovery strategy during the Special Period. Tourism was able to attract foreign investors willing to help rebuild a sector in which Cuba enjoys a strong comparative advantage. Since the 1980s, the number of tourists visiting Cuba annually has increased more than fivefold and tourism has become the leading sector in earning hard currency. Its rapid growth has also made it a key engine of domestic development in linkage industries.

Minor Sinclair and Martha Thompson examine the agricultural reforms introduced early in the Special Period as part of the government's effort to boost food production. The system of large state farms dependent on expensive equipment and high petroleum consumption, built up through the 1960s and 1970s, was replaced by small producer cooperatives called Basic Units of Cooperative Production (*Unidades Básicas de Producción*, UBPC), in which individual families had land use rights. Moreover, the government reintroduced free farmers' markets, in which both private farmers and UBPCs could sell produce to the public at market prices. An earlier experiment in the 1980s with farmers' markets had been ended by Fidel Castro when it began to produce income inequalities. In the Special Period, the need to stimulate agricultural production took precedence.

Another concession to the market was the decision in 1993 to legalize self-employment (*trabajo por cuenta propia*). Energy shortages after 1991 forced the closure of many factories, producing significant unemployment for the first time since 1959. Unable to provide jobs, the state was forced to recognize the reality that many Cubans had begun working in the informal sector to make ends meet. Legalizing self-employment gave the government an opportunity to license, regulate, and tax the activity. Ted Henken's account of the rise and fall of family restaurants (*paladares*) provides a microcosmic representation of how Cubans manage to *resolver* in the face of changing state policies toward private enterprise.

A key element in sustaining the ability of ordinary Cubans to get through the Special Period was support from abroad in the form of remittances. The Cuban government had to manage structural adjustment without the support of the International Monetary Fund, World Bank, or any of the other international financial institutions that cushion adjustments elsewhere. But, as Susan Eckstein recounts, ordinary Cubans lucky enough to have relatives abroad found a lifeline through remittances. In 1993, in hopes of increasing the flow, the Cuban government legalized the possession of dollars and opened dollar stores (*Tiendas de Recuperación de Divisas*) for Cubans to purchase imported goods. The policy succeeded; over the next decade, the remittances sent to relatives by Cubans abroad rose to over $1 billion annually. At the same time, however, the purchasing power of the Cuban peso receded, creating a two-class system of consumption: those with access to dollars (from remittances, work in the tourist sector, or the black market), and those without.

In 2004, the Cuban government "de-dollarized" the economy by prohibiting transactions in dollars. This forced Cubans holding dollars to exchange them for "convertible pesos" with a fixed exchange rate of one to one. Now, however, the government charges a tax on dollar exchanges, which constitutes a de facto tax on remittances. The move away from dollars was motivated by the government's desire to acquire dollars that Cubans were hoarding, so as to increase its capacity to import, and to mitigate its deteriorating terms of trade as the dollar declined in relation to the euro. Washington had also begun harassing international banks holding Cuban assets denominated in dollars.

Looking ahead, Cuba has begun to develop two high-technology sectors with the potential to take advantage of its highly educated population. Cuba has made extensive investments in biotechnology, and has had some success developing export products that have found a market in other developing countries. The Cubans have also begun to form partnerships with major pharmaceutical companies with the aim of getting over the complex regulatory hurdles blocking access to markets in the United States and the European Union. Cuba's information technology industry is newer than its biotechnology complex, but since 2000 it has received the same sort of sustained attention and strategic investment. Cuba's challenge, going forward, is how to develop its economy using the human capital the revolution has produced, and improve efficiency enough to effectively compete in the world market, while at the same time retaining the social gains in health care, education, and social equity that have been priorities of the socialist economy since 1959.

Development as an Unfinished Affair

Cuba after the "Great Adjustment" of the 1990s

Pedro Monreal

The Cuban economy endured the most profound crisis of its peacetime history during the first half of the 1990s, a crisis precipitated by the collapse of "really existing socialism" in Eastern Europe and the Soviet Union. Approximately one-third of the total gross domestic product simply evaporated in just four years, and foreign trade contracted by almost three-fourths. At some point in that period, the economy was unequivocally in free fall. Levels of consumption were severely reduced, social programs were negatively impacted, and there was a very real danger of a massive reversal of the achievements recorded during the thirty years of the Cuban Revolution.

Government policies to deal with the crisis were markedly different from the pattern of economic adjustment that other countries have adopted. Essential social services such as education and health care were provided universally and at no cost even in the worst moments of the crisis. Subsidized food—although in relatively reduced amounts—guaranteed a minimum level of nutrition, while other important social programs were designed to support particular social groups. Adherence to norms of fairness and social justice was the hallmark of Cuban adjustment policies during the 1990s. Resolving the crisis was a matter of survival, and various programs and policies were implemented to achieve that goal under severe time constraints and intense political pressure, including the tightening of the U.S. blockade.

A crucial aspect of the "Great Adjustment" of the 1990s was the adaptation of the Cuban economy to a new international context in which it would have to evolve—for the first time in several decades—in the absence of the special arrangements with the countries of the vanished "socialist bloc" of Europe. In this sense, the reinsertion of Cuba into the world capitalist economy was a key component of survival. Plans for long-term development were part of the general matrix of economic policy, but priority was clearly given to short-term programs aimed at inducing rapid recovery.

The political agenda was concentrated throughout most of the 1990s on survival, a relatively narrow agenda, though crucial for the country's future, and this left scant room for reflection on transformations taking place within a broader framework. By 1995, however, the worst of the crisis was over and the economy had begun a steady process of recovery. Consequently, the survival strategy that had prevailed during the first half of the 1990s was replaced by a "strategy for upgrading" (*estrategia de perfeccionamiento*) that became more prevalent as actors gained confidence about the durability of the economic recovery. The latter part of the decade did not see an end to the logic of resistance and survival but superimposed upon it a series of notions and programs that reintroduced the question of development into academic and policy debates.

TRANSFORMATION IN THE NAME OF SURVIVAL

The pattern of development that prevailed during the first thirty years of the Cuban Revolution (1959–1988) was import-substitution industrialization. This model was grounded in the progressive expansion and diversification of a national agro-industrial system that was financially, technologically, and commercially supported by the so-called socialist world, a structure that was severely shattered by the demise of "really existing socialism" in Europe during the late 1980s and early 1990s. Amidst the profound resulting crisis, measures were immediately adopted in order to cope with the new international context in which the Cuban economy had to operate. Modifications were introduced in the pattern of development, particularly the pillars and mechanisms of international integration, but they did not represent a radical transformation of the previous pattern. Import-substitution industrialization was not abandoned as the central component of a long-term vision of the country's development. What did change was the mechanism for connection with the international environment in which that industrialization would have to be conducted in the future.

The adjusted economic structure that emerged during the 1990s was characterized by activities aimed at external markets such as tourism and mining. Other economic sectors have also been favorably influenced by the expansion of domestic markets in which transactions are conducted in foreign currency, driven to a large extent by tourism and transfers from abroad (basically family remittances) and other income sources in currency associated with the "ripple effect" of tourism, and the establishment of incentive schemes, in foreign currency, for part of the labor force.

The transformation of an economic structure aimed at development in an open economy[1] like the Cuban one takes place in a framework of limitations that cannot be ignored. First, this structure should guarantee the efficient integration of the country into the international economy. There is no room for isolationist impulses, the consequences of which would be devastating.

Nonetheless, integration into the world economy will remain problematic (though not impossible) as long as the country is under the economic embargo imposed by the United States.

A second limitation is that for the purposes of designing development strategies, the "country" is not perhaps the most suitable unit of analysis. The advancement of the country through trajectories of technological and organizational learning is currently a function of its progress in the context of global commodity chains rather than of the self-centered promotion of "national" industries.

A third limitation is the need to restructure the economy as a part of a broader process of social change that goes beyond the partial reform of the traditional mechanisms of a centrally planned economy. In the absence of significant transformations of basic economic institutions and property relations, the likelihood of a successful reorientation of the economic structure of the country is not very great (Carranza, Gutiérrez, and Monreal, 1995).

Finally, another important limitation is that social and political considerations will strongly influence the identification, selection, and promotion of the sectors and activities that will constitute the new economic structure. No transformation of the economic structure will be sustainable in the long term if made at the expense of the well-being and expectations of the majority.

During the early 1990s, there was a change—significant in some respects—in the pattern of development that Cuba had been following since the mid-1970s. In 1975, the industrialization of the country was the central axis of the Cuban development strategy. This was a project that fifteen years later had not yet been accomplished but that undoubtedly established a relatively important role for industry, diversified industrial production and extended its supporting infrastructure, extended and concentrated the entrepreneurial network, at the same time creating its management capability, and fostered the expansion of a qualified industrial labor force.

The consequences of the changes in the pattern of development during the 1990s have been impressive in terms of the country's balance of payments (net income from tourism took over the dominant role that sugar had played for more than two hundred years as the country's main source of foreign currency), but in reality the old agro-industrial structure still prevails with regard to total production, despite evidence that much of it is no longer feasible or compatible with the requirements for Cuba's future development.

At the end of the 1990s it was clear that the transformation had not reached an end, and to the unfinished character of the changes was added ambiguity about the new configuration of the economic structure. Developing tourism—important as it has certainly been in the short term—does not necessarily bring the country a redeeming "tertiarization" of the economy (dominance of the tertiary sector, particularly services), nor can the expansion recorded up to now in a select group of activities be considered a permanent solution. The main challenge is to change the country's economic structure substantially through increasing international specialization. The implications of the changes made during the 1990s for the future development of the country can be clearly seen in an evaluation of two important dimensions: international reintegration and development strategy.

THE GREENER PASTURES OF TOURISTS' PLAYGROUNDS

In retrospect, it could be said that the Cuban economy pursued international reintegration in the 1990s in three ways: intensive use of natural resources for export promotion, access to external revenue (family remittances), and the limited entry of loan and investment capital.

Since the 1990s, the links between the country and the international economy have changed. Tourism has replaced sugar as the main source of hard currency, and foreign investment and family remittances have partially replaced the transfers that previously came from the socialist bloc. However, the pattern of development still bears an amazing resemblance to the previous one in that it continues to be essentially one of industrialization through import substitution.

From the second half of the 1970s to the late 1980s, the explicit emphasis of the development strategy was industrialization, particularly aimed at import substitution.[2] Another important element of the pattern of development was the promotion of exports of primary commodities or semiprocessed products (sugar, minerals, citrus fruits, tobacco), which were considered basically as a source of financing for industrial investment and as a starting point for new industrial products aimed at import substitution in the future (e.g., sugarcane derivatives or iron and steel products from mineral reserves).

A third element in that development pattern, the promotion of industrial exports, played a secondary role with scant results. During the five-year period from 1976 to 1980, 115 new export lines were established, but they had no significant weight in the country's total value of exports (Pérez, 1982). What crumbled at the beginning of the 1990s was basically import-substitution industrialization, the component that became most unfeasible without the external compensating mechanisms that had made it possible. The second element of the pattern—the export of primary products—was insufficient to serve as a source of accumulation for industrialization in the absence of the preferential prices formerly paid by the socialist countries, and this component also crumbled as a consequence of the commercial and financial dislocations resulting from the collapse of socialism in Europe. The third component, industrial exports, was marginal to the functioning of the development pattern.

In the midst of the crisis and as a consequence of the severe restrictions imposed by the balance-of-payments deficit during the 1990s, import-substitution industrialization could not be accomplished as a new industrial investment. Maintaining this strategy became a question of preserving as much of the existing industrial structure as possible by introducing the necessary changes while awaiting more favorable conditions that might allow the resumption of new investment in this type of industry. The high priority given to export sectors such as tourism, nickel, and pharmaceuticals was conceived not as a significant change from import-substitution industrialization but as the creation of better conditions to continue with it later on.

This implied making relatively important adjustments in the other two components of the development pattern. Exports needed to be increased, and it seemed that this would be possible only by trying to include new export lines on the basis of the intensive use of natural assets, primarily the utilization of coastal resources, climate, and geographical location to expand tourism, and by trying to "jump a step forward" in one or a few industrial exports, mainly high-tech activities such as pharmaceutical products with a biotechnological base and medical equipment. The unexpected rate of growth of tourism during the 1990s (20 percent annually) showed that this activity—frequently referred to as the foundation of a supposed "new service economy"—had been added to the export group of primary or semiprocessed products also involving the intensive use of the natural resources.

This is not to say that tourism should not be promoted. On the contrary, Cuba presents unquestionable competitive advantages in connection with this activity, and besides, in the short term it has been the only sector of the Cuban economy capable of acting as a leading sector of development. Nonetheless, from a long-term perspective, the success of tourism in the 1990s has been more an extension of the export component associated with the use of natural resources than the emergence of a new ingredient of the development pattern grounded in assets such as a qualified workforce, science, or technology; this is something that has to be taken into account because, in the long term, it is important that the economic structure "move upward" through technological and organizational learning trajectories—a process for which the sectorial composition of the economy is not "neutral."

The bet on industrial exports basically focused on the pharmaceutical industry. Although a range of export activities was carefully selected, expectations at the beginning of the 1990s decreased considerably later on. The industrial structure created before the crisis of the 1990s worked during the first years of the decade at very low utilization levels and in fact experienced a decapitalization that was particularly acute for some sectors of the economy. It had not been created to compete internationally (and therefore could not count on external markets for its supply) and was extremely dependent on imports, which prevented it from producing for the internal market because of the severe restrictions of the balance of payments. However, part of this industrial structure was favored by the expansion of what are known as "exports within the borders," consisting of domestic markets operating in foreign currency to meet the demands of an increasing number of national, foreign, and mixed enterprises that conduct business in foreign currency, basically related to tourism, and of the part of the population that possesses foreign currency because of family remittances and income associated with "spillovers" from tourism and, in some cases, salary schemes. It is scarcity of foreign currency, not of other productive assets, that is generally the bottleneck for economic productive processes in Cuba. "Exports within the borders" have allowed the leveling, in terms of the direct availability of this critical resource, of industries originally designed to replace imports and exporting sectors.

The fact that an increasing proportion of the supply of domestic enterprises has been called "exports within the borders" shows the importance of foreign-currency availability for the correct functioning of an economy such as Cuba's. This term should not yet be understood as being part of a process of export promotion, since it has actually been a mechanism for facilitating import substitution in the new context. Theoretically, domestic markets operating in foreign currency might act as a "springboard" to generate actual exports, but this has not happened in Cuba. New productive links have been created and older ones have been adjusted because of the demand associated with these distinctive domestic markets; "exports within the borders" have fostered the creation of "backward linkages" and entrepreneurial networks that have allowed the reactivation of some of Cuba's import-substitution-oriented industry.

The experience of "exports within the borders" is instructive on two counts. First, relatively inefficient industries have been able to recover and even modernize to a degree mainly because their sales take place in domestic markets that do not require the level of efficiency that would be required in the world market. Second, "exports within the borders" have acted as a significant mechanism for social and political stability during the 1990s because of the rising employment rate that results from the lesser efficiency required in comparison with an alternative pattern in which actual exports prevail.

Having clarified that the modifications introduced in the pattern of development were focused mainly on mechanisms of international integration rather than on industrializing the country by replacing imports, it is advisable to identify in a precise way some of the most outstanding characteristics of this integration process.

1. Cuba's insertion into the world economy during the 1990s consisted basically of expanding exports of products that intensively utilize natural resources, particularly through the promotion of activities with underutilized potential such as tourism.
2. The performance of the different activities within this group has been heterogeneous. While income from tourism increased tremendously during the 1990s, sugar exports decreased in the same spectacular way. Losses due to the decline of the sugar sector largely absorbed the positive effects of the increasing contribution of foreign currency from tourism.
3. Tourism dethroned sugar, but the country is still, as it has been for centuries, an exporter of natural resources. Services based on natural resources constitute the novelty introduced by tourism at this level. The share of Cuban exports in activities based on other types of assets (i.e., transforming industrial plants, labor qualification, or the use of science and technology) is still minimal. The expectations surrounding the medical and pharmaceutical sectors during the first years of the 1990s were never fulfilled.
4. The type of international integration achieved shows an amazingly low level of efficiency regarding the use of the main economic asset of the country: a labor force that is highly qualified and, above all, has high learning potential.
5. Under the effect of severe balance-of-payments constraints, a decrease in the total export capacity of the country has led to a kind of "import substitution" through recession; in other words, imports have lost relative weight in the total product as a consequence of the "compression" of imports (CEPAL, 1997). This problem was particularly serious during the first half of the decade, and though the situation has improved, it is far from being solved. The export level during the 1990s did not ensure the levels of financing required for the functioning of an industrial capacity created to replace imports.
6. The partial reorientation of that industrial capacity toward what some authors call "closed-cycle schemes" (i.e., direct access to hard currency at the level of enterprises) has allowed a kind of limited reindustrialization of Cuba through "exports within the borders" (González, 1997). This means that the demand created by institutional and individual holders of foreign currency connected to mechanisms of international insertion (tourism, foreign investment, credit access, family remittances) has reactivated the industrial base and levels of employment, also serving as a source of investment for modernizing and restructuring national industrial sectors aiming at internal markets.
7. Tourism has played an important role with regard to this limited reindustrialization. Not only has it generated foreign currency and employment but also it has been the only sector of the Cuban economy that meets the three conditions for qualifying as a leading sector: presence of a potential demand that has not been sufficiently made use of, a relatively large-scale business and ample potential for intersectoral links, and an "exogenous" growth rate that is relatively independent of the average growth of the national economy.

The contribution of tourism as the leading sector has been more significant than its strict contribution as an exporting sector. Tourism-induced "backward linkages," particularly with industry and other services of greater technological complexity, such as air transportation, telecommunications, information technology, and technical projects, might facilitate an improvement of the country's economic structure and its labor force. Thus, tourism, a service of low technological complexity in some of its main activities (i.e., lodging and catering), that is based on the intensive use of natural resources, might trigger the development of industrial activities and services technologically more advanced and more remunerative for the country.

8. Foreign investment has focused on activities related to the use of natural resources (tourism, mining, oil, agriculture), infrastructure development (telecommunications), and some industrial products for "exports within the borders" (light industry and food). Its direct impact in terms of the use of the installed industrial capacity and the available labor force has not been significant.

IN SEARCH OF A NEW PATTERN OF DEVELOPMENT

Sometimes development strategies have been clearly identified from the beginning as in the case of Cuba in the mid-1970s; at other times, what could be classified as a development strategy is actually the result of a far different process, as seems to have been the case of Cuba during the 1990s. Development strategies are not necessarily part of integral economic plans; most of the time they tend to be the result of practical and fragmented decisions aimed at solving immediate crises and short-term problems rather than the result of strategic considerations (Gereffi, 1990). Some specialists say that the majority of political actions that have been considered development strategies have actually been "discovered" as such solely through time; studying them retrospectively has given some coherence to economic programs that originally were only policies devised to respond to a crisis (Dore, 1990).

From a conceptual perspective, there is a great difference between a development strategy and a pattern of development; a strategy always refers to an ideal representation at the level of policymakers, while a development pattern is a given sequence of socioeconomic events and their results. The distinction is relevant in that a great deal of the debate over strategies turns around what governments can do; thus, studying the past (patterns of development) reveals what governments were or were not able to do and makes possible the use of that knowledge as a starting point for new strategies (Dore, 1990).

It will be clear, then, that the summary that follows is not a review of the Cuban development strategy during the 1990s. Rather than evaluating the ideal representations in the minds of policymakers, it refers to judgments regarding the pattern of development of that period. Analyzing some of its characteristics may well be a starting point for some preliminary considerations about the problems of development in Cuba during that period.

1. At the beginning of the decade, the Cuban economic strategy consisted of a series of principles, rationalizations, and assumptions aimed at "facing and

overcoming the effects of the crisis by distributing as equally as possible its impact on society while creating conditions for reinserting Cuba into the world market," but this resistance strategy—undoubtedly very important—must not be confused with a totally new development strategy, namely, an ideal representation of development that radically departs from the previous paradigm (Rodríguez, 1996).

2. What has occasionally been considered as a development strategy in Cuba during the 1990s is in fact more closely related to the strategies just mentioned that acquire coherence only retrospectively. In this sense, what is often called the "development strategy" of the late 1990s may have been the result of measures taken gradually from the resistance strategy that characterized the early 1990s.

3. More than a totally new pattern of development, the 1990s could be said to have witnessed a different phase of the pattern of development prevailing since the middle of the 1970s. If the development phase from 1975 to 1990 might be identified as industrialization through import substitution under conditions of high external compensation (to summarize: compensated import substitution), a new phase—based essentially on the old pattern—started in the 1990s that might be called combined reindustrialization (export-oriented reindustrialization plus import substitution).

4. The new phase reveals that industrialization by means of import substitution is still the most important component of the development strategy. What has become absolutely necessary under the new circumstances is to redesign the industrial structure to make good use of newly created domestic markets operating in hard currency, foster a few new exports capable of becoming sources of accumulation and axes for the articulation of productive linkages that might allow a partial reindustrialization, and include foreign investment as a means to gain access to financing, technology, and markets. Although new emphasis has been given to the creation of new exports in the short term, it is impossible to identify, in the new phase of the Cuban development strategy, any radical change in the industrialization paradigm grounded in import substitution.

5. The new combined reindustrialization phase has, despite its limitations, the virtues of almost any policy designed and executed under pressure: practicality and great flexibility. And although the paradigm of industrialization through import substitution (something that does not correspond to the current need for a newly based international specialization of the economy) has been maintained at the core of the strategy, it provides a relatively significant opportunity for reorienting the economy toward exports that certainly might be a platform for a different industrialization paradigm in the future. The emphasis of the development pattern of the 1990s is in the wrong place, but it has great potential because of the model's "combined" character.

6. The new development-strategy phase has two significant limitations. First, the absolute levels and rate of growth of hard currency and the potential productive linkages that the leading sector (tourism) can provide are considerably lower than the requirements for reactivation and reconfiguration of the current industrial base. A significant part of the potential supply of goods corresponding to this industrial base is unattainable under the current cir-

cumstances. The idea that a general reindustrialization aimed at import substitution would be applicable in Cuba in the foreseeable future cannot be considered a valid proposition for an economic program that aims to optimize the existing productive plant and labor force. As an extension of the previous development strategy it would be a dead end (see Brundenius and Monreal, 2001). Second, the export orientation of the 1990s is grounded in activities that, except for tourism, have no significant expansion potential, precisely because the natural resources they depend on have insurmountable physical limitations (i.e., mining or fish stocks) or market-imposed limitations (e.g., the limited call for an exclusive product such as Havana cigars or the relatively stagnant world demand for sugar).

At the end of the 1990s, as at the beginning of the decade, a new opportunity to restate the development strategy of the country opened. I am of the opinion that import substitution should be replaced though not excluded by a stronger emphasis on the exporting element of the strategy.

Cuba's development requires, among other elements, the reindustrialization of its economy (see Monreal, 2000).This should not be understood as a reconstruction of the industrial base aimed primarily toward the reactivation and diversification of the supply to the internal market. Cuba is a very open economy in need of increased international specialization based upon the availability of a valuable asset: a skilled labor force. Under the new circumstances in which Cuba must operate, the internal base needed for the systematic development of the country's productive forces must be the result of a reindustrialization process aimed at appropriating part of the industrial base of contemporary world production. Cuba needs reindustrialization by means of export substitution—a development strategy that replaces exports based on the intensive use of natural resources with technologically advanced exports. The development pattern seen up to now would radically change, since exports would become the core component of the pattern and be produced in a relatively broad spectrum of activities. Although this idea is not new, this is, as far as I know, the first time it has been applied to the Cuban case.

It is important that this concept not be identified with "export diversification," at least as this term is used in Cuba. The island must indeed follow the path of export growth, but raising the level of exports and diversifying the portfolio of exports is not necessarily the key to industrial upgrading. Efficient diversification must not be construed solely in terms of indiscriminately adding export headings but also as an absolute and relative increase in exports based on technological factors and the intensive use of a qualified labor force. It could be said that export substitution corresponds to export diversification only when diversification is produced in this direction.

I am not trying to propose a new strategy of outward-oriented industrialization in apparent opposition to an old strategy of domestically oriented import-substitution industrialization. First, historically, a combination of the two strategies has been present in the majority of industrialization processes worldwide, though it is true that at a certain point the emphasis has been placed on one or the other. In the long run, the two strategies have been shown to supplement each other (Gereffi, 1990). Regarding Cuba, export substitution could be the core of a new strategy that would benefit from factors associated with a preceding pattern of development in which import substitution was the center of the country's development strategy.

Second, the success of the industrial export orientation in many regions, municipalities, and countries turns around product and service clusters that are aimed at external markets but also favor the expansion of internal markets as part of their input structure. In other words, a cluster allows the expansion of domestic supplies that serve as a basis for externally oriented production. From the perspective of clusters, the boundaries between producing for "internal" and producing for "external" markets are unclear.

Third, under the prevailing import-substitution industrial structure, an attempt to reorient a part of the industrial supply toward exportation cannot be construed as neglecting production for internal markets.

CONCLUSION

The economic transformations that occurred in Cuba during the 1990s cannot be considered the best solution to the huge task of changing the country's economic structure in order to achieve development. Cuba's economic reconstruction is, despite the transformations of these years, a highly indeterminate and incipient process whose solution is still pending.

For an open economy like Cuba's, structural change in the direction of development takes place within a limited framework, partly inherited and made worse by the U.S. embargo, that cannot be ignored. Even under these circumstances, however, development is still possible.

The argument made here is plain: the soundest development strategy for Cuba under the current circumstances must consider reindustrialization with skill- and technology-based export substitution, allowing the country to progress in ascending trajectories of organizational and technological learning.

NOTES

1. "Open" in the technical sense that the sum of exports plus imports represents a relatively large share of gross domestic production.

2. "The principal task of industrialization consists in creating the internal base necessary for the systematic development of the productive forces; supply industry, farming and cattle-raising with equipment and raw materials; raise exportable resources; replace imports and produce varied articles to be consumed by the population" (Partido Comunista de Cuba, 1976: 77).

REFERENCES

Brundenius, C. and P. Monreal. 2001. "The future of the Cuban model: a longer view," 129–50 in C. Brundenius and J. Weeks (eds.), *Globalization and Third World Socialism: Cuba and Vietnam*. London: Palgrave.

Carranza, J., L. Gutiérrez, and P. Monreal. 1995. *Cuba: La reestructuración de la economía, una propuesta para el debate*. Havana: Editorial de Ciencias Sociales.

CEPAL. 1997. *La economía cubana: Reformas estructurales y desempeño de los noventa*. Mexico City: Fondo de Cultura Económica.

Dore, R. 1990. "Reflections on culture and social change," in G .Gereffi and D. Wyman (eds.), *Manufacturing Miracles: Paths of Industrialization in Latin America and East Asia*. Princeton: Princeton University Press.

García, A., H. Pons, J. Somoza, and V. Cruz. 1999. "Bases para la elaboración de una política industrial." *Cuba: Investigación Económica* 5 (2): 45–94.

Gereffi, G. 1990. "Paths of industrialization: an overview," in Gereffi and Wyman, *Manufacturing Miracles.* Princeton: Princeton University Press.

González, A. 1997. "Economía y sociedad: los retos del modelo económico." *Cuba: Investigación Económica* 3 (3-4): 23–47.

Monreal, P. 2000. "Estrategias de inversión sectorial y reinserción internacional de Cuba," in Mauricio de Miranda (ed.), *Reforma económica y cambio social en América Latina y el Caribe: Cuatro casos de estudio: Colombia, Costa Rica, Cuba y México.* Santa Fe de Bogotá: Tercer Mundo Editores.

Partido Comunista de Cuba. 1976. *Plataforma Programática del Partido Comunista de Cuba: Tesis y resolución.* Havana: Departamento de Orientación Revolucionaria del Comité Central del Partido Comunista de Cuba.

Pérez, H. 1982. "La plataforma programática y el desarrollo económico de Cuba." *Cuba Socialista,* no. 3, 21–32.

Rodríguez, J. L. 1996. "Cuba 1990–1995: reflexiones sobre una política acertada." *Cuba Socialista,* no.1, 20–37.

II

The Cuban Economy

Amid Economic Stagnation and Reversal of Reforms

Mauricio de Miranda Parrondo

INTRODUCTION

In the past few years, the Cuban economy's moderate rate of growth has been insufficient to pull the country from the severe crisis which affected it from 1989 to
1993. From 1993 to 2003, the average annual growth of the gross domestic product
(GDP) was only 3.3 percent. If this growth is projected forward, Cuba will recover
its 1989 GDP level in 2006—that is, seventeen years later. This is an exceptionally
slow recovery from an economic crisis for a country in peacetime.

The reasons for this slow rate of economic growth are the structural characteristics of the Cuban economy, Cuba's inability to integrate into the international
economy, the difficult international context in which the country operates, and its
leaders' lack of political will to modify in depth the mechanisms that drive the
economy.

THE PROBLEMS OF CUBA'S ECONOMIC STRUCTURE

The Cuban economy continues to depend excessively on primary production for export, while industrial production is unable to meet the domestic market's demand
for goods. This has deepened the country's economic underdevelopment and exacerbated its internal dependency.

Sugar: Sugar is still a significant item in the Cuban economy and in the country's exports. However, this industry has been plagued by a severe crisis in production, and has been facing a precarious situation within international markets.

Despite the downsizing (*redimensionamiento*) process to which this industry
was subjected in search of greater efficiency, there are still no signs that its efficiency has been improved. In the 2003–2004 harvest season, total sugar production
was only 2.2 million tons. The government acknowledged that the result had been
influenced not only by poor weather, but also by organizational problems and fi-

nancial pressures which interfered with efforts to ensure the timely supply of in-puts necessary for the harvest (Rodríguez, 2003). This volume of production was the lowest figure in the socialist era of the Cuban economy, and it was only slightly higher than Cuban sugar production in 1933.

Industry performance has matched the levels reached at the beginning of the 20th century, while income from exports has decreased significantly, so that in 2002 it accounted for only 19.5 percent of the foreign currency income earned by this sector in 1991.

In the process of downsizing this industry, the number of sugar mills and the area of sugar cane plantations were reduced by half, with attendant reductions in the sector's workforce. However, the displaced workers did not join the unemploy-ment lines, but were by and large incorporated into the education system; their salaries were charged to the budget, without the backing of production of goods and services, a measure which can be supported because of the low levels of real income of the Cuban labor force.

Nickel and the Exploration of Other Natural Resources: The nickel industry is another mainstay of the Cuban economy. Nickel's importance as an export has grown significantly in recent times, so that it alternates with sugar at the top spot. However, in 2003, the production of nickel was 71.7 million tons, below the levels of 2001 and 2002. Although export income data are not available for 2003, official sources announced that income had increased as a result of favorable international prices (Rodríguez, 2003). In 2002, this sector's contribution to Cuban exports rose to 412.5 million pesos, slightly below the value of sugar industry exports.

The nickel industry has attracted foreign capital as a result of promising calcu-lations of reserves of this mineral. If production increases and market conditions improve, nickel could become the country's main export product.

Other mineral explorations on the island have increased in recent years, basically in response to the interest of foreign investors. Although there has been prospecting for copper, chromium, magnesium, and zinc, results in all cases have been modest to date. On the other hand, crude oil and natural gas exploration has yielded significant increases in production levels, even if these still fall short of demand.

Tourism: Tourism has become the main driver of Cuba's limited economic growth, but it still depends on imports for a considerable percent of its inputs, which limits its efficiency as a means of earning foreign currency. Also, in the last few years this sector has reported less gross income per visiting tourist. Whereas in 1995 gross income per tourist was 1,475 pesos, in subsequent years this indicator declined steadily, until it reached a low of 1,037 pesos in 2001, with only a slight recovery to 1,049 pesos in 2002.[1] This situation reflects the fact that the tourists who arrive on the island are of low to middle income, and travel within low-cost packages. In spite of this, the overall gross income from this sector has increased, even if in recent years there has been a slight decline, stemming from the fall-off in international travel after September 11, 2001.

The fundamental problems of tourism in Cuba are a shortage of options beyond the enjoyment of sun and beach, the limitations in complementary infrastructure that result from underdevelopment, and the high cost of transportation, telecom-munications, and financial services systems.

Industry: Over the past decades, Cuban industrial activity has undergone a cer-tain diversification. Except for sugar and related goods, nickel and tobacco, industry focuses basically on meeting internal market demand, at quality levels that prevent it from competing in international markets. Generally, Cuban industry is not intensive either in capital or technology, but it is in labor. There is virtually no machinery production, except for the assembly of transportation equipment (which has been in a state of paralysis since the 1990s), and a very limited production of sugar mill equipment.

In the past few years there has been significant growth in the production of crude oil, gas, and fuel oil. Cuban crude oil has been able to supply about 90 percent of the country's domestic energy generation, maintaining levels close to those attained at the beginning of the last decade. This considerable increase in production is largely due to investments made by foreign companies involved in crude oil exploration. However, domestic crude oil is excessively heavy and difficult to use, given the technology of Cuban thermoelectric plants.

For other items, especially those that address domestic consumer demands, production levels are below those attained in 1990, even if increases reported last year are taken into account. As a result, there is a high level of unmet demand for such products.

Throughout 2004, new economic difficulties have arisen. The breakdown of an important electric power plant led senior Cuban leaders to adopt emergency measures which included the temporary closure of several industries, so as not to decrease excessively the supply of electricity to the population. This will undoubtedly affect not only the economic growth figures for 2004, but also budgetary and monetary balances because, for political reasons, the temporary closure of production enterprises in Cuba does not entail a suspension of salary payments. The budget will be affected by the payment of salaries, while income will decrease as production decreases.

Transportation and Communications: Cuba's transportation and communications infrastructure continues to be one of the most serious problems in the country's economy. Passenger transportation does not meet the population's basic needs. While Cuba's population increased from 10.8 million to 11.2 million inhabitants between 1991 and 2002, the total number of passengers transported dropped by 47.6 percent in the same period, from 2,014.7 million in 1991 to 959.7 million in 2002 (ONE, 1998 and 2003). Undoubtedly, the situation was even more difficult at the critical point of the crisis in the 1990s, but recovery efforts have not improved this indicator significantly in recent years. Two sets of additional figures help illustrate the difficult situation in this area: In 1991, there were 3,997 urban-service buses in Cuba, but in 2002 there were only 940. The number of trips made by the urban-service buses went from 11.5 million in 1991—when they already failed to meet the demands of the population—to just 2.9 million in 2002 (ONE, 1999 and 2003).

The underdevelopment of Cuba's urban and intermunicipal transportation system is today one of the problems that most seriously affects the national economy and the life of the country's inhabitants. This problematic situation translates into losses in working and leisure time for Cubans, who must allocate an excessive amount of time to travel between home and workplace. At the same time, it has negative effects on work productivity and on people's emotional health, since the majority of people do not have their own means of transportation.

Freight transportation has also declined. The total freight transported in Cuba in 1991 was approximately 72.5 million tons; in 2002, it dropped by 30.3 percent to 50.5 million tons (ONE, 1999 and 2003).

There has been some progress in communications in recent years, as the number of telephone lines installed in the country went from 611.1 thousand units in 1991 to 811.6 thousand in 2002. However, telephone density per 100 inhabitants has increased only slightly, from 5.7 in 1991 to 5.9 in 2002 (ONE, 1999 and 2003). Cuba still has one of the lowest per capita number of computers and Internet connections in Latin America and the costs of this service are among the highest in the region (UNDP, 2004). The Cuban government has banned the personal importation of computers, except in those cases where an official authorization has been given.

CUBA'S DIFFICULTY IN INTEGRATING INTO THE INTERNATIONAL ECONOMY

The Cuban economy has always been very affected by the behavior of its foreign trade. Historically, Cuban exports have set the pace for rest of the economy. In the past few years, however, exports have noticeably decreased, and are now centered on a few primary products of limited value added. In 2002, Cuban exports contributed only 4.6 percent to the GDP. Sugar industry products accounted for 31.9 percent of the total, while mining made up 30.8 percent and the tobacco industry 10.1 percent.[2]

Over the past four decades, Cuba's foreign trade has shown a persistent trend toward deficits compared with the country's trade balance before 1960. Imports, which shrank during the worst years of the economic crisis, have recovered to a certain extent in recent years, although they declined again in 2002, to 4.13 billion pesos.

Although more recent figures are unknown because they have not been officially reported, existing figures indicate some interesting changes in the geographic breakdown of Cuba's foreign trade. In 2002, the island's main trading partners were the members of the European Union, which represented 33.4 percent of Cuba's total foreign trade, followed by Latin American and Caribbean countries with 28.0 percent of the total. However, a breakdown by individual countries shows that the ten main trading partners were Venezuela (13.5 percent); Spain (12.7 percent); China (10.7 percent); Canada (8.0 percent); the Netherlands (6.5 percent); Russia (6.4 percent); Italy (5.3 percent); France (4.7 percent); Mexico (4.1 percent); and the United States (3.1 percent) (ONE, 2003).

It is interesting to note the significant rise of the United States among Cuba's trading partners, considering that this trade consists only of imports (the U.S. economic embargo laws do not allow Cuba to export its products to that country). Sales to Cuba have rapidly increased since 2000, when the American government authorized the sale of food and medicines, provided that the transactions are paid in cash, before the goods are unloaded at Cuban ports. The United States has become the main supplier of food to Cuba, with products such as live cattle, rice, eggs, chickens, corn, and milk, among others. Imports from the United States have risen in recent years, reaching to about $260 million in 2003, the island thus becoming an important buyer of items such as rice, chickens, condensed milk, and beans (Progressive Policy Institute, 2004).

It appears that purchases from the United States have become a political priority for the Cuban government in attaining an end of the economic embargo against the island through the application of pressure in Congress from political groups associated with American farmers. To meet its obligations to U.S. suppliers, payments have been delayed to European and Latin American suppliers; some of these have begun to face serious financial problems, because their businesses are relatively small and are concentrated on Cuba. Nevertheless, considering that the country's international reserves are at minimum levels, it can be assumed that the first destination of foreign currency in the hands of the Cuban economic authorities will be to fulfill agreements with American suppliers.

Cuba's position in the international economy is closely related to its economic structure, the terms of its foreign trade, the role of direct foreign investment, its external financing situation, and the state of its institutions.

As indicated, Cuba's economic structure is built on intensive exploitation of its natural resources using relatively low-skilled labor. The island has been unable to adequately benefit from the competitive advantages of a labor force with relatively high qualifications, and has maintained a high degree of dependency on a few basic products—sugar, nickel, and tobacco. As for tourism, Cuba attracts individuals of relatively low economic level, and their expenditures do not substantially exceed those included in their tourism packages.

Over the past few years, the current account item of Cuba's international balance of payments has shown a tendency towards chronic deficits. This is due, above all, to the deterioration of the trade balance which, itself, runs a deficit, and to a persistently negative income balance. These are not compensated by the balance of services—traditionally positive—nor by the increasing current transfers, among which include family remittances, which carry a significant weight.

The increase in the relative weight of current transfers shows that the Cuban economy is slowly becoming more dependent on foreign donations, especially family remittances. In Cuba, as in several Latin American and Caribbean economies, family remittances have become one of the country's most important foreign currency income items.

Foreign direct investment in Cuba faces a series of difficulties. One is the uncertainty that results from systematic changes in economic policy, particularly those related to the market. Another is the limitation of the domestic market, which is small, low-income, and segmented by Cuba's monetary duality; these characteristics discourage foreign investment in economic activities oriented towards this market. A final difficulty is the external pressure created by the Helms-Burton Law.

A comparison of the officially acknowledged flow of foreign direct investment in the 1997–2001 period with the accumulated balance of income (repatriated profits plus interest) in the same period shows that while the foreign investment accumulated rose to 1,313.8 million pesos, the balance of income accumulated a negative result of –2,570.1 million pesos. Thus, the inflow of investment capital failed to compensate for the outflow of capital.

The lack of international financing is one of the main factors that prevents Cuba from thriving in the world economy. This situation results from Cuba's non-membership in international financial institutions such as the International Monetary Fund, the World Bank, and the Inter-American Development Bank. Added to this are the negative pressure exerted on the island by the U.S. embargo, and Cuba's failure since the mid-1980s to meet its international financial obligations.

Cuba's foreign debt is one of the highest per capita debt levels in Latin America and the Caribbean (ECLAC, 2003). In convertible currency, this debt has been estimated at about eleven billion dollars, but this figure does not include the debt owed to Russia, which was originally written into rubles, and which for several years has been the subject of litigation.

A DIFFICULT INTERNATIONAL CONTEXT

In recent years, Cuba's international relations have deteriorated significantly. Besides the permanent confrontation with the United States (and in spite of the increase of limited trade links between the two countries), Cuba has also had conflicts with the European Union (EU), its main global trading partner. The EU's Common Position regarding Cuba, ratified at successive summits, has made democratization and respect for human rights *sine qua non* conditions for the establishment of closer ties with the island, and for the granting of the advantages enjoyed by less-developed countries in Africa, the Caribbean, and the Pacific. On two occasions, the EU's position has led Cuba to decide to withdraw its candidature to join the Cotonou Agreement. The EU's recent eastward expansion has placed additional pressure on Cuba, given the clear undertaking of several ex-communist countries, such as the Czech Republic, to engage with Cuban dissidents.

The subject of human rights and democratic opening has also distanced Cuba from Canada, one of its main trading partners and an important source of direct foreign investment.

Furthermore, this issue has also led to a deterioration of relations with some Latin American countries. Diplomatic incidents have resulted in the breaking of diplomatic relations with Uruguay, and the temporary recall of ambassadors from Mexico and Peru. At the same time, Cuba's ties with Venezuela have been strengthened, and this country is today the island's main trading partner and fuel supplier. Thanks to the excellent political relations between their two governments, the island receives Venezuelan crude oil at preferential prices in return for Cuban support in areas such as public health, education, and the training of political activists. Although in recent years the relations with Brazil and Argentina have noticeably improved, following electoral victories of leftist coalitions in those countries, good political relations have not led to preferential economic relations because of these countries' limited commercial interests in Cuba.

To this picture must be added the limitations imposed on the country by the United States. The American embargo both prevents the export of Cuban products to the United States, and hinders its access to commercial credit. In addition, the Helms-Burton Law affects third country enterprises interested in doing business with Cuba. Nevertheless, even if the American embargo was lifted, it is quite unlikely that Cuban exports could increase significantly because of the structural limitations affecting their supply.

REVERSAL OF REFORMS

In the past few years, the reform process started in the 1990s has not only stopped but has been reversed. There have been new trends towards centralization of economic decisions, while the so-called business efficiency system (*sistema de perfeccionamiento empresarial*), put in place in the late 1980s, has not resulted in true economic autonomy for state enterprises.

One example of the trend to centralization is the government's decision to limit access to dollar accounts of Cuban enterprises that operate in foreign currencies. The government decreed that the so-called convertible peso—denominated as equivalent to the U.S. dollar—must be used for internal transactions by these enterprises. The government also imposed state control over U.S. dollar accounts; the objective of this policy is to concentrate the availability of foreign currency in the hands of the Foreign Currency Central Commission.

Steps have also been taken to reduce self-employment by slowing down the granting of new licenses, or by withdrawing existing ones, for certain types of work. On October 1, 2004, a resolution of the Labour Ministry came into force, suspending the concession of licenses for forty self-employment activities. The country's authorities justified this measure by indicating that the state is capable of performing those functions. This would show that this type of measure is a response to a specific crisis, rather than a strategic conception of the economy's operating mechanisms aimed at promoting the consolidation of market relationships.

On the other hand, some recent economic policy modifications have weakened fiscal policy by increasing the fiscal deficit. The fiscal deficit's share of the GDP rose to 3.4 percent in 2003, from 3.2 percent in 2002 and 2.5 percent in 2001 (ECLAC, 2004). The increase in the deficit—which in 2002 was already 996.5 million pesos—is the result of a greater increase in expenditures than in income. Items showing greater increases in 2002 include subsidies for losses posted by enterprises and social assistance.

Also, the salaries of certain labor categories have increased systematically in recent years, in response to the weakened purchasing power of salaries in Cuba. Because there has been no corresponding increase in productivity, these salary increases do not solve the mismatch between income levels and the actual value of the basket of goods and services that meet the needs of the population.

Monetary policy, in turn, is restricted to the control of money through the printing of currency. Other instruments of monetary policy continue to be disregarded, and the use of credit is limited to a certain type of credit for consumption. ECLAC reported a significant decrease in the monetary supply in 2003 (–11.4 percent) as the population increased its purchases of foreign currency, and term deposits increased while sight deposits and circulating cash decreased. It is, however, interesting to note that a 5.0 percent increase in inflation was reported in 2003, following a 7.0 percent increase in 2002. In a context of monetary supply reductions, it is contradictory that prices should increase. The explanation is that the measurement of inflation in Cuba has a serious defect because it does not incorporate price increases that take place in foreign currency shops, which in fact offer products that are part of the basket of the goods and services needed by the population.

The elimination of the U.S. dollar for internal transactions and its replacement by the convertible peso—currency that was already in circulation in the country, equivalent to the U. S. dollar—was unexpectedly announced in October 2004. At the same time, the government announced the collection of a 10 percent tax on dollar-sale operations in the country, starting on 15 November of that year. Cuban authorities have declared that the measure is aimed, among other things, at countering the pressures exerted by the American government, and to recuperate the country's "monetary sovereignty." As this chapter was being written, no data had been provided about exchange operations. However, the government has announced that those dollars will serve to back the circulation of the convertible peso, artificially revalued by the previously mentioned tax. If this is the case, the Cuban convertible peso system would resemble the Argentine convertibility system put into practice in the 1980s. This system's unfortunate fate is known worldwide, and has been severely criticized by many economists on the island.

As long as the Cuban currency is not backed by the production of goods and services that can be sold internationally, it will not be really convertible.

IN SUMMARY

At present, Cuba's economic situation offers limited prospects for change. The economy is close to stagnation, but official public statements convey the message that the worst and politically most dangerous moment of the crisis has passed. It is not possible to expect deeper reforms to liberalize and decentralize the Cuban economy as long as the threat of a new collapse is not taken seriously. This lack of action will translate into continued slow rates of economic growth, and even possible recessions.

NOTES

1. Data calculated based on ONE. Anuario Estadístico de Cuba, 1998 and 2002.
2. Data calculated based on ONE, 2003.

REFERENCES

Nova, Armando: "Redimensionamiento de la agroindustria azucarera cubana. Historia y actualidad" ("Resizing of the Cuban Sugar Agroindustry. History and Current Situation"), in Reflexiones sobre la Economía Cubana (Reflections on the Cuban Economy), Pérez Villanueva, Omar Everleny, ed., Ciencias Sociales, Havana (being published).

Oficina Nacional de Estadísticas (ONE) (National Bureau of Statistics): Anuario Estadístico de Cuba (Cuba's Annual Statistics), 1996, Havana, 1998.

——. Anuario Estadístico de Cuba (Cuba's Annual Statistics), 1998, Havana, 1999.

——. Anuario Estadístico de Cuba (Cuba's Annual Statistics), 2002, Havana, 2003.

Progressive Policy Institute: www.ppionline.org.

Rodríguez, José Luis: Informe sobre los resultados económicos del 2003 y el plan económico y social para el 2004 (Report on the Economic Results for 2003 and the Economic and Social Plan for 2004), Havana, 2003, www.granma.cu.

United Nations Development Program (UNDP): Informe sobre el desarrollo humano, 2003, 2004 (Human Development Report 2003, 2004), www.undp.org.

United Nations Economic Commission for Latin America and the Caribbean (ECLAC): Balance preliminar de las economías de América Latina y el Caribe, 2003, 2004 (Preliminary Overview of the Economies of Latin America and the Caribbean, 2003, 2004) www.eclac.cl

——. Cuba: evolución económica durante 2002 y perspectivas para 2003 (Cuba, Economic Evolution in 2002 and Prospects for 2003), Mexico, 24 July 2003.

Cutting Losses

Cuba Downsizes Its Sugar Industry

Philip Peters

INTRODUCTION

The May 2002 announcement that Cuba would dramatically downsize its sugar industry made definitive a change that had been coming for years, and was forced by international market conditions. With sugar prices falling steadily, and having lost the Soviet bloc subsidies that for decades made sugar exports artificially lucrative, Cuba faced a choice: to attempt to revive the industry with subsidies and large investments, or to cut its losses and try to restructure it to make it profitable.

Cuba chose the latter course, to the immediate benefit of the national balance sheet. But a large set of challenges remains: completing the closure of half the nation's sugar mills and the conversion of massive amounts of land from sugar to other uses; caring for the people involved; raising productivity in the downsized sugar sector; and producing derivatives that will pull profits from cane and its waste products.

Sugar has an indelible place in Cuba's history and culture, but as an economic proposition it has lost its starring role. The downsized sector is no longer a proxy for the health of the Cuban economy. More time must pass before the sugar industry's retooling can be fully assessed, but even as the plan gets under way one can examine the plan's design, how it is proceeding, how Cubans view it, how it affects them, and the long-term implications.

SUGAR THEN AND NOW

The cultivation of sugar in Cuba dates from the seventeenth century. It forms, as Cubans readily and fondly say, part of the national identity. Sugar determined patterns of land use and ownership across the island. It caused the importation of slaves. Its production cycle set a rhythm of rural life that lasted for centuries. Sugar produced surges of wealth that made Havana and smaller urban centers such as

Matanzas flourish, financing waves of architectural riches. The sugar industry brought railroads to Cuba and new technology year by year. At different times, and for better or worse, sugar trade figured prominently in Cubans' relations with Americans and Russians. At the turn of the twenty-first century, sugar was still being produced in nearly every municipality—everywhere but Cuba's western tip and the Isle of Youth—and by sustaining nearly half a million jobs, sugar was putting food on the table of one in five Cubans.

Cuba's socialist government profited handsomely from the sugar-for-oil trade that it conducted with the Soviet bloc. Especially since the 1970s, Cuban sugar purchased Soviet oil at prices that were far above market levels; in some years Cuban sugar traded at the equivalent of 40 cents per pound, well more than double market prices, yielding an effective subsidy of $3 billion per year. In some years, Cuba could afford to re-export some of the oil that its sugar earned. "Nothing was more favorable than sugar production," a Cuban economist says. "It was reality, but it was virtual reality."

The demise of the Soviet bloc robbed Cuba of more than a subsidy. It left Cuba with a large, mechanized sugar industry designed to fit a customer that no longer existed, and dependent on sources of tractors, fuel, fertilizers, and other supplies that also ceased to exist. Repeated in many sectors, this experience plunged Cuba into a severe economic crisis.

Cuban sugar production dropped nearly three million tons, plummeting 39 percent between 1992 and 1993. Lower revenues caused investment and maintenance to falter, leading to a de-capitalization of the industry and further drops in output. Faced with these new difficulties, Cuba could not afford to maintain the large-scale, heavily mechanized farm techniques that produced the bulk of Cuba's sugar on large state farms.

In response, Cuba restructured its agricultural production—sugar and nonsugar—by breaking up state farms and creating smaller cooperatives. In the sugar sector, great emphasis was placed on relatively large cooperatives called UBPCs for their Spanish name meaning Basic Units of Cooperative Production. Unlike smaller varieties of cooperatives that still had the participation of private farmers working lands they own or once owned, UBPCs derived from state farms. Workers and managers were given production incentives, but they had no original connection to the land.

By 2000, fully 72 percent of sugar cane was grown in UBPCs, and the results were not promising: Cuba's average yield per hectare had dropped 38 percent in one decade, and according to the U.S. Department of Agriculture, per-pound production costs in the mid-1990s were 50–70 percent above world market prices. As a Cuban expert described it, "The organizational changes in production have not adjusted sufficiently to meet the high costs and low market prices of the sector."

Meanwhile, conditions in the international marketplace virtually dictated that Cuba downsize its sugar industry. Cuban sugar production had fallen 56 percent between 1989 and 2002, and Cuba's world rank as a cane producer fell from third to tenth. World sugar production grew 22 percent during those years, and consumption grew at an equal rate, but world stockpiles of surplus sugar nonetheless increased by 12 million tons.

These trends combined to exert downward pressure on prices: a pound of sugar sold for nearly 13 cents in 1989 and barely six cents in 2002.

As Cuba considered its possibilities in the world market, it saw new, efficient competitors with surging production. Brazil was foremost among these, with more than twice the production in 2002 than it had in 1989. And Brazil's "exports of raw sugar continue remorselessly," according to a London commodity newsletter. Brazil's 2002 exports of 11.6 million tons were greater than three times Cuba's entire production. And other sweeteners, such as high fructose corn syrup, were increasingly cutting into the market for sugar. Cuba's productivity, meanwhile, lagged far behind that of most competitors. Crop yields in Brazil, China, Thailand, India, and Australia, for example, were more than double that of Cuba.

What if Cuba were to export again to the United States? Even under the most optimistic scenario where U.S.-Cuba relations would improve and trade relations would be restored, there is no prospect that large-scale U.S. imports could revive Cuba's sugar sector.

The U.S. sugar market is highly controlled and distorted by government intervention. The domestic price is artificially maintained currently at a level more than three times the world price, and quotas determine how much the United States imports from individual countries.

Before Cuba's revolution, the United States purchased the lion's share of Cuba's sugar crop. In 1959, the U.S. sugar quota for Cuba was 2.9 million tons—an amount roughly equal to today's total production in Cuba. If the United States were to restore only one fourth of Cuba's 1959 quota, it would displace all U.S. sugar imports from Latin America and the Caribbean. The 2004 U.S. sugar quota for the entire world is 1.12 million tons.

With that hypothetical avenue cut off, Cuba's sugar industry was bound by a stark fact: to regain profitability in an environment of high oil prices and low sugar prices, it would need to increase its efficiency quickly and dramatically—and that result could not come about without large amounts of capital invested to modernize every stage of the sugar production process.

However, Cuba opted to invest elsewhere. Throughout the 1990's, with sugar prices declining year by year, tourism and other sectors had a higher claim on Cuba's scarce investment capital. The sugar industry would receive not new money, but a new direction.

2002: THE BITTER DECISION

"The question was posed," a Cuban economist said in 2001, "does it make sense for Cuba to continue as a major sugar producer given the world price of sugar and the cost of capital?"

The question was answered on April 10, 2002, when an executive order directed the sugar ministry to cut cane production and milling capacity approximately in half, to increase production of derivatives, and to achieve greater efficiency, from the ministry itself to every unit of production.

At its root, the decision was simple: "We had to act or face ruin," Fidel Castro told a gathering of sugar workers in May 2002, pointing out that $200 million would be saved in the first year of downsizing. In February 2003 he told a group of visiting Americans that the decision is in keeping with Cuba's policy of not protecting industries from foreign competition. "It's crazy to make an effort to produce something that costs more to make than to import," he said. He called Cuba's action a "rationalization" of the industry.

In fact, the 2002 "rationalization" culminated a process that was already under way. The appointment in 1998 of a new sugar minister, Ulises Rosales del Toro, led to a 73 percent reduction in the ministry's staff from 1300 to fewer than 400. Regional offices of the ministry cut half their personnel. The structure of 289 enterprises belonging to the ministry was streamlined, leaving 192 in operation. Enterprises were encouraged to enter a reform process that was being conducted in many sectors, forcing the enterprises to forgo subsidies, adopt standard accounting procedures, pay workers according to results, and achieve profitability.

The new minister also idled inefficient sugar mills; more than forty were taken out of production between 1998 and 2002. The 2002 decision led to the definitive closure of seventy mills, which are now being dismantled. Seventy-one continue to produce sugar and fourteen are producing honey. In addition to closing inefficient mills, a massive amount of land is being taken out of sugar production. Cane fields were ranked according to their soil quality and productive potential, and only the most productive will remain planted with cane. Ministry officials hope this process will help Cuba to raise its current average yield of 32 tons of cane per hectare to 54 tons per hectare.

In terms of land area, 827,000 hectares will remain planted with sugar cane, and 1,378,000 hectares will be converted from sugar cane to produce other crops—more than the 967,000 hectares that are now used for all other crops combined. The sugar ministry estimates that the restructured sector will produce enough sugar to cover Cuba's annual domestic consumption of 700,000 tons and have a maximum productive capacity of 4 million tons of sugar per year.

These momentous changes were explained exhaustively to sugar industry workers nationwide. The process began with a three-hour speech by President Castro to 10,000 workers on October 23, 2002. It continued with a series of assemblies across the country where officials discussed the changes and their impact with workers throughout the industry—a total of 7,850 assemblies were reported to have been held, often on several occasions in the same workplace, with a total of 942,000 participants.

A "programmatic document" prepared by the sugar ministry served as the basis of presentations at these workers' assemblies.

This document

- begins by tracing the history of sugar production in Cuba from the colonial era through the 20th century.
- explains the trading arrangement with the Soviet bloc that allowed Cuba to sell its sugar at preferential prices, and the shock Cuba suffered when it was forced onto the international market—because of fluctuating oil and sugar prices, a 100,000-ton increase in exports in 2002 brought $120 million less revenue than in 2001.
- explains that at six cents per pound, "the current world market's trash bin prices for sugar have reached the point where sugar production brings no real profit, no real income for the country; rather, it implies losses."
- states that in the first half of the 20th century, sugar demand grew an average of 5 percent per year; in the second half it grew at 1 percent. "However, until

1991 Cuba did not suffer the consequences of this because of its relations with the socialist camp."

- describes how other developing countries have reduced sugar production, noting that in other countries the workers "have personally suffered the consequences of this dramatic situation, left completely to their own devices, as is usual in capitalist countries." (This theme is repeated frequently in state media; in an October 2003 article, the labor newspaper *Trabajadores* said that in other countries when there are plant closures and layoffs, "some receive severance pay, and after that they have to solve their own problems—that's all.")
- says that while the Cuban government subsidizes electricity and other basic needs, "We cannot allow ourselves the luxury that rich countries have, of subsidizing their producers so they can be competitive in world markets."
- says that the goal of the restructured sector will be to "accelerate net income through a process of deep cost reduction"—a process in which no worker will be abandoned, all will have their salaries guaranteed, all have the option to return to school for new degrees and training at full salary; and all services in the *bateyes*, the communities that surround sugar mills, will continue.

In late 2002, when Sugar Minister Rosales del Toro discussed these measures in the National Assembly, Cuba's legislature, he said that the workers' highest concern was for the continuity of services in their communities. The minister guaranteed that the services would not be reduced, although over time these services—from clinics and food service to funeral parlors—might be administered by an organization other than the sugar ministry.

Taken together, the changes in the sugar industry represent "the most far-reaching economic transformation in the last 100 years," according to one Cuban scholar. The decision was taken for liquidity and foreign exchange reasons, and a restructured industry could lead to profitability. Greater capacity to produce derivatives, one economist noted, would allow Cuba to calibrate its production to world market trends, increasing sugar output when prices are high, and producing more alcohol for use as a fuel additive when sugar prices are low. "But you cannot confuse this strategy with the idea of putting sugar back as the cornerstone of the Cuban economy," he said. "It's not like oil in Venezuela."

DISMANTLING SUGAR MILLS

Throughout the Cuban countryside, sugar mills can be noticed from a distance by their tall smokestacks that stand out high above the seas of sugar cane fields. Closer, the mill itself looms on the horizon, a large industrial building. Approaching the mill, one sees that it is enveloped by a settlement, the *batey*, a collection of housing, administrative buildings, clinics, and other installations that are the home to a community of a few thousand workers and their families.

The mills and *bateyes* have been modernized over time, but many are centuries old, especially in western Cuba where sugar production prospered most due to the introduction of railroads in 1837.

Asked when a mill in Artemisa was built—a building whose construction materials and equipment were clearly from the 20th century—its director responded,

"Around 1700." His reference to the original settlement rather than the mill now standing reveals the deep ties between the industry, its people, and Cuba's distant past.

The *bateyes*, the Cuban sugar industry's version of the rural company town, are the places that are bearing the brunt of the sugar industry's restructuring.

Some mills remain in operation, undergoing modernization and adjusting to the new land use patterns.

Where the mills are closing, the workers are making a difficult transition as they watch the mill at the center of their community slowly be dismantled, until only the smokestack will remain.

The Julio Reyes mill near the town of Jovellanos in Matanzas province is one such mill; it was built a century ago, was idled in 1995, and is now being taken apart, its useable parts being sold to mills still in operation. One worker, a former boiler operator at the mill, now spends half his time working on the dismantlement, the other half studying to be an agronomist. He retains his full salary of 398 pesos per month.

"People took it very hard" when the mill's closure was announced, he said. "They told us that with the situation in the world and in the country, we couldn't make money anymore, but if sugar prices rise maybe we can build a new one."

Some of the workers in the *batey* have always been engaged in food production, he said. "It used to be just food for our own consumption, but now we sell to the farmers' markets," he explained. The workers are producing cattle, fruits, lettuce, beets, tomatoes, root vegetables, and other crops. He is studying math, science, history, and computers, raising his educational level from 10th grade to 12th grade. He is not sure how or where he will work as an agronomist, he said, but "that's what surrounds me—I can't do aviation."

A second worker at the mill is studying full time, at full salary, and expects to have an accounting degree in three years. But he too is uncertain where he will be placed once he has his degree. It's sad to see all this go,' he said, looking at the half-dismantled mill. "People had love for their work here, and they are industrial workers, not farmers."

Southeast of Havana near the town of Artemisa, the Eduardo García Lavandero mill is also being dismantled. Raúl Suárez García, its director, says that five cycles of meetings were held with the workers to explain the changes in the industry and in their community of 3,000. "Here, people worried about services continuing—ambulances, water, electricity, transportation . . . we explained that all those services would continue as before."

Garcia explains that 35 of the railroad workers now work at a nearby mill; 455 technicians also migrated to other mills; 12 work in the *organopónico*, the community's large organic garden.

Garcia now runs a new agricultural and livestock enterprise, created in January 2003, that is attempting to re-employ mill workers and farm cooperative members who are no longer growing sugar cane. "We started with the mentality of cane growers," he said. "We didn't know other crops, but every day we are getting better, we are studying, and we can learn the new techniques because we have illiterates [*sic*] here." He said he and his colleagues are discovering that "we have to dedicate more time to other crops than to sugar cane."

However, the enterprise is off to a good start. Its various units produce fruits, vegetables, poultry, and pork, and some of these products are being sold in hard currency to state enterprises that supply the tourism industry. "We are going as fast as possible" in the development of all the enterprises, Garcia explained, "so people don't have to suffer too much."

In a building in the shadow of the partially dismantled sugar mill, a new school was established in October 2002 for the more than 400 workers who opted to improve their education. Some are taking general courses that provide the foundation later to study accounting, agronomy, information technology, mechanics, and other specialties. A teacher at the school says that while all are entitled to stay in school until they earn a university degree, most want to be certified as a "mid-level technician" in their field—a degree that implies about four years of study after ninth grade.

This education program, officials say, reaches every sugar industry worker affected adversely by the restructuring and every official discussion of the program reiterates that the workers retain their full salary while in school. "As an economist, I see it as an investment," a sugar ministry official says. "They were being paid for doing something that was losing money and now they are doing something more useful." According to sugar ministry surveys of more than 213,000 workers whose mills or farms are being idled by the industry's restructuring, 58 percent of the workers are remaining in the ministry's enterprises, 20 percent are studying full-time, 10 percent are moving into non-sugar agricultural production, 8 percent are retiring or leaving for other fields, and 4 percent are working full-time dismantling sugar mills.

THE RESTRUCTURED INDUSTRY: A WORK IN PROGRESS

How is the restructured industry progressing? After one season, the changes are only beginning to bear fruit, and in critical areas the industry is still taking one step back before it takes two steps forward.

Sugar production. Sugar output is down in 2003; estimates of the first year's sugar production after restructuring are about 2.1 million tons, compared to 3.6 million tons in 2002.

Cuban officials attribute this result to three factors: lack of financing that delayed the purchase and delivery of herbicide and fertilizer, organizational difficulties related to the new patterns of land use and mill operation, and excessive rain. Independent observers fault the centralized, state-directed nature of the sugar industry and a lack of sufficient monetary incentives for sugar workers.

However, officials also point to signs of increased productivity. In 2003, the number of UBPC cooperatives that attained the goal of producing 54 tons of cane per hectare nearly quadrupled from the year before; 250 of the 708 UBPCs reached that goal, as compared to 64 in 2002.

However one explains the 2003 harvest, it is clear that the 2004 harvest, which officials are naming "the harvest of restructuring," will be a major benchmark for the reshaped industry. If the ministry has correctly chosen the least productive lands and mills for withdrawal from production, and if organizational difficulties are overcome, one can expect improvements in output, especially if incentive payments and other management improvements become more widespread. Reduced production is yielding cash savings—but if Cuba's foreign exchange crunch prevents timely spending on critical inputs, production levels may not recover.

New agricultural production. The success of agricultural production managed by the sugar ministry also remains to be seen. "We are a second ministry of agriculture," a sugar ministry official says, referring to the challenge of managing new production on more than 1.3 million hectares of land that once grew sugar cane. Nearly half this land will be devoted to forestry, the rest to crops, and a small portion to aquaculture. The sugar ministry will manage this production, officials say, because they want to carry their workforce through to new livelihoods rather than abandon sugar workers and turn them over to a new organization.

Derivatives. Cuba has used sugar cane to make products other than sugar for decades, but production fell dramatically in the 1990s as fuel costs increased and the general effects of the economic crisis hit this sector. Production of honey, fiberboard, and pulp for paper fell more than 60 percent in the decade, while alcohol production increased modestly.

In the industry's new strategy, with Cuba paying world market prices for energy, a selective approach is being taken. The industry is emphasizing the products where energy and other production costs are affordable; where it is profitable to substitute domestic products for imports; where there is a hard currency market for the product; or where foreign investment might be attracted to modernize production facilities and to link Cuba to new export markets.

Energy production is an important part of this strategy. Sugar production generates massive amounts of bagasse, the waste product from crushed sugar cane that can be burned to produce energy. The goal is to turn each year's sugar cane processing from a net drain on the country's electricity supply to a net contributor. Improvements are being achieved as modern turbine generators are installed in sugar mills. Eighty of these generators are on-line now, and more are being installed for the 2004 harvest. In 2003, seven mills reportedly achieved self-sufficiency in energy.

The sugar ministry is actively seeking foreign investors to boost production of derivatives, and officials use Cuban workers' educational level and the nation's scientific infrastructure, low production costs, location, and the markets' growth potential as selling points. They say they see substantial interest among potential partners. "There are more foreign capitalists that come to make offers than those we seek out," claims one official.

Ten joint ventures have been formed with foreign investors (where the foreign investor owns part of the business and shares profits), and fifteen cooperative production agreements have been reached (where the foreign partner contracts to assist production and earns a share of revenues, without ownership). The joint ventures include alcohol production (Spain), chemicals (Mexico), and specialty papers (Italy).

An example of a joint venture can be found at Quivicán in Havana province, where a Cuban-Italian joint venture's production facility is located alongside one of four of the ministry's research institutes. The joint venture was formed in 1997. Now in its first phase, it has $2 million in new equipment for cutting and packaging adhesive tapes and specialized papers for sale in Cuba and for export, and expects to reach $3 million in sales in 2003. The research center has used material derived from sugar cane waste to develop specialty papers, water filters, animal feeds, and ingredients for veterinary medicines that are produced and sold by sugar ministry enterprises. One product about to go to market is a water filter unit that can be fitted onto home plumbing and will sell for about five dollars. The institute also performs contract research on a consulting basis for the food, pharmaceutical, and other industries.

THE REVAMPED SUGAR SECTOR IN CUBA'S FUTURE

While the restructuring of the Cuban sugar sector is at an early stage, some implications of the restructuring are clear, and some large issues remain to be resolved.

First, it is clear that sugar's pre-eminent position in Cuba's economy has been broken. Sugar will be an important factor, but no longer a determining factor in Cuba's economy, and can no longer be used as a barometer for the island's economic health.

There is a historical irony in this development. During the revolutionary conflict, Fidel Castro criticized the "monoculture" that sugar represented for Cuba—an industry that dominated the Cuban economy and made it vulnerable to international market swings was itself dominated by foreign investors and owners, and caused workers to labor under allegedly unjust conditions.

Sugar production was thus de-emphasized during the early years of the revolutionary government, but with the Soviet bloc's preferential trade available to Cuba, policy shifted in 1969 to return sugar to its central position in the economy. Ironically, in the ensuing two decades the sector remained as dominant as ever. The Cuban saying, "Without sugar, there is no country," was never as true as during the 1970s and 1980s under the socialist government.

Sugar's reduced profile thus accomplishes an economic restructuring that was part of the revolution's original political program. It was delayed by unusual international economic circumstances, and it was finally forced upon Cuba by the economic conditions of today.

Second, it seems clear that a reduced emphasis on sugar is healthy for Cuba's economy. During the 1990's, investments that could have gone to sugar were directed to tourism, nickel, energy production, biotechnology, pharmaceuticals, and infrastructure needs such as telecommunications. These investments have created a more diversified economy that capitalizes on Cuba's natural resources and comparative advantages. With sugar prices remaining near six cents per pound, these were clearly sound investment decisions. In 2003, in spite of the lowest sugar harvest in seven decades, Cuba's economy is registering modest positive growth led by a recovering tourist sector and very high nickel prices. The outcome of other issues related to sugar's restructuring are less clear.

Productivity is a major question mark. Cuba's sugar production remains concentrated in the more collectivized units of Cuban agricultural production, the UBPC cooperatives. Savings have been realized by taking the least productive lands out of sugar, and the "industrial" part of the sector—the mills—will benefit from the fact that fewer mills will be competing for scarce resources. But state management of this sector of the economy will be challenged to develop management and incentive schemes that will bring production levels up to the industry's new targets.

Employment is another major challenge. The employment effects of sugar's downsizing have been cushioned by the fact that so many idled workers have returned to school. At least for a few years, this cushion will continue to function. But workers will need jobs upon graduation, and scores of communities need to be sustained after losing the industry and organization that has been at their center for centuries. The economy will also feel a slowdown in the industries that provide goods and services to the sugar sector.

Finally, the impact on Cuban agriculture remains to be seen. The sugar ministry will now manage non-sugar agricultural lands that are larger than the lands devoted to all non-sugar agriculture today. In time, this could result in vastly increased food production for domestic consumption and export, and it could lead to development of a large forestry sector and the positive ecological change that large-scale reforestation implies. In theory, it could lead to models of ownership, organization, and production that differ from those of the agriculture ministry today.

The jury is still out on these questions, but it is clear that as Cuba has moved decisively to restructure a formerly protected industry, it has done so without causing social unrest to date, and Cuba's economy will feel the effects of this decision for years to come.

13

The Political Economy of Leisure

Marguerite Rose Jiménez

More than two million international tourists visited Cuba in 2006. It marks the third year in a row that the total has surpassed this mark, which places Cuba far ahead of any other Caribbean island.[1] Cuba's return to the international tourism market has profoundly affected the revolution in the last twenty years. Consider that only 275,000 tourists—about one-eighth the 2006 figure—came to the island in 1987, when the government approved a law allowing joint ventures with foreign investors in tourism-related projects such as hotels.[2]

The decision to rely on tourism for hard currency earnings was not taken easily. Cuban leader Fidel Castro's reluctance to promote tourism was rooted in memories of pre-1959 Cuba, as an all-inclusive hedonist playground for affluent North American tourists, accompanied by prostitution, corruption, and gambling casinos run by organized crime syndicates. These pathologies were largely eliminated in 1959 or shortly thereafter. As a result, images of Cuba's pre-revolutionary past complicated the discourse on possibilities for Cuba's economic recovery. But the unwanted saviors, international tourism and its unavoidable bedfellow, *dollarization* of the Cuban economy, became increasingly palatable as the Cuban economy spiraled downward in the first years of the Special Period.

During the first decades of the revolution, tourism and foreign investment remained disdained by the fiercely independence-minded government. By the late 1980s and early 1990s economic necessity had caused the government's previously hard-line position to soften considerably. Thanks to the Cuban government's focus on developing the tourist industry, tourism to Cuba has grown exponentially over the past decade. Between 2000 and 2005, for example, tourism increased nearly 20 percent annually, helping Cuba become the eighth most frequented tourist destination in the Western Hemisphere.[3] Thanks to this growth, tourism has gradually replaced sugar as Cuba's top earner of foreign exchange. According to Cuba's Minister of Tourism, Manuel Marrero Cruz, the tourist industry employs some 80,000 people directly, 20,000 of whom have some form of higher education.[4] Philip Peters of the Washington D.C.–based Lexington Institute estimated in 2002 that there were 200,000 Cubans additionally employed in support sectors such as agriculture, communications, and other light productive industries.[5] Peters argues this support sector has been created by increased demands for goods and services that can be provided by state enterprises. Cuban economist Pedro Monreal elaborates that tourism has helped a "limited reindustrialization" process within the Cuban economy, reactivating the "industrial base and levels of employment, also serving as a source of investment for modernizing and restructuring national industrial sectors aiming at internal markets."[6] The benefits of this process are clearly evidenced by the drop in imports linked to the tourist sector. Ten years ago only 12 percent of the products needed for the tourist sector (fruits, juices, linens, uniforms, etc.) were purchased from local Cuban enterprises. By 2002, 68 percent of the necessary products came from Cuban sources.[7]

Along with the beneficial side effects of tourism's rise to economic dominance, there are several potentially problematic consequences as well. By jumpstarting the economy with an infusion of hard currency from tourists and foreign investments, the Cuban government set off a chain reaction which has contributed to a gradual deterioration of many of the institutions and ideals on which revolutionary Cuba was founded. Prior research about Cuba's turn to tourism has focused on aspects related to its impact on Cuba's economy or development. What has been often excluded from the discourse on tourism until recently is its political nature. This article examines sociopolitical issues inherent in the tourism industry—such as oppression, unequal power relations, and social injustice—which raise questions about the viability of tourism serving as the means to sustain Cuban economic development and the revolution's political goals simultaneously. The detrimental long-term side effects of tourism are likely to result from five factors which this article will outline: (1) the re-creation of class conflict within the dual economy; (2) the renewed objectification of Cuban women; (3) the reemergence of explicit race-based discrimination; (4) new laws governing the relations between international tourists and Cuban citizens, which have given rise to the term "tourist apartheid"; (5) the increasing commodification of Cuban culture.

DUAL ECONOMY OR DUEL ECONOMY?

By 1993, tourism had emerged as "the only sector of the Cuban economy with the capacity to act as a 'leading sector' for the country's development," according to Monreal.[8] It seemed to be an obvious choice because of Cuba's abundance of natural resources, which provided a competitive edge over her Caribbean neighbors. Cuba has more beachfront than all of the other Caribbean islands put together.[9] Other assets, as stated by Charles Suddaby, are Cuba's "geographic diversity, enormous range of existing and potential attractions, cultural and architectural history and combination of educated workforce and low incidence of crime,"[10] which make Cuba a desirable destination for pleasure-seeking travelers.

In order to remove obstacles for potential foreign investors in Cuba, major shifts in economic policy were required. Two key reforms emerged from decisions taken by the October 1991 Fourth Congress of the Cuban Communist Party. The first one, a 1992 constitutional amendment, provided protection for foreign-owned property, and permitted foreign companies to own a 49 percent share in joint ventures located in Cuba. The second shift occurred in 1993 when the government legalized Cubans' use of U.S. dollars with Decree Law 140. Dollars, which began to circulate freely, came mainly from Cubans who worked in the tourist industry, or from those with family abroad who sent monthly remittances. Their access to dollars enabled them to purchase material goods that were unavailable to Cubans who had no dollars. Thus developed the "dual economy," consisting of the *peso* economy, where *moneda nacional* (national currency or *pesos cubanos*) is used, and the dollar economy, where only foreign currency or *pesos convertibles* (convertible pesos or *divisas*) are acceptable. National currency can be used to ride a bus, pay for some state services, and buy basic foodstuffs (bread, rice, beans, vegetables, milk, and meat) and a meal in some restaurants. But it cannot, for the most part, be used to buy imported goods (toiletries, gasoline, electrical appliances, most clothing, or goods that can be exported for hard currency). The failure of the *peso* economy lies in the average Cuban's inability to buy necessities with the national currency. This inability has increased the pressure for most Cubans to find ways of obtaining "hard currency," though access to the tourist economy is difficult for most to acquire. The dual economy has produced several problems, the most prominent of which may be the re-emergence of significant inequalities in the population.

CONFRONTING CLASS IN A CLASSLESS SOCIETY

After the exodus of wealthy Cubans emigrating in 1959 and the early 1960s, class disparity was kept to a minimum through wage controls and the nationalization of property, which began in 1960 and was extended to the remaining privately held businesses with the "revolutionary offensive" in 1968. From its inception the revolutionary government espoused an ideology in which no Cuban would have the need or ability to accrue or possess a disproportionate share of the country's wealth in any form.

In Cuba today there are no large landowners controlling thousands of plantation acres. Mafia money does not grease the palms of puppet politicians who own opulent estates with teams of Afro-Cuban servants to maintain them. Now, foreign companies within the tourist industry and other sectors ripe for investment are re-staking a claim in the Cuban economy. Ironically, given Cuba's former colonial relationship with Spain, a Spanish corporation established Cubanacan, the first joint venture in Cuban tourism, in 1991. Since then Spanish companies have amassed the largest number (101) of joint ventures with the Cuban government. Those from Canada and Italy rank second and third, with 56 and 42 joint ventures, respectively. In addition to joint ventures, Spanish firms also have the highest number of management contracts and cooperative production contracts.[11]

Over the past decade class differences have re-emerged in a different, more subtle fashion, with the divide occurring between Cubans who work in the tourist industry or private sector and those who don't. Economist Carmelo Mesa-Lago illustrated this discrepancy by comparing the average salaries of Cubans employed by the state and those employed in the private sector. In 2001, a university professor earned a state salary of 300–560 Cuban pesos (approximately US$12–22) per month, while a family that rented rooms in its house could earn between US$250–4,000 per month. Cubans without access to hard currency are often barely able to meet basic needs. This is partially a result of decreases in real wages and their purchasing power, along with reduced state subsidies and monthly rations.[12]

ENTERTAINMENT OR EXPLOITATION?

One of the many attractions drawing tourists to Cuba is the entertainment industry dominated by music and dance. The tourist-oriented entertainment industry has contributed largely to the hyper-sexualized image and objectification of Cuban women. The use of women in the promotion of tourism in Cuba was epitomized at the very beginning of the Special Period when *Playboy* was allowed to tour the island and run a feature on Cuban women. Sociologist Susan Eckstein observes, "The government's interest in hard currency led it to play on its pre-revolutionary reputation and to reverse its earlier puritanical stance on such matters."[13]

Immediately after the revolution, the Cuban government made efforts to eradicate prostitution by rehabilitating and educating former prostitutes, incorporating them back into the new Cuban society as productive workers.[14] According to ethnic studies professor Elisa Facio, "The revolutionaries aimed to free women from sexual exploitation in all sectors of society."[15] Azicri further explains, "The government enforced policies directed at women to facilitate their progress and incorporate them into the overall development programs, so their gains would be parallel to men's." Between 1960 and 1990, women significantly increased their participation in the Cuban economy. Women's percentage of the labor force more than doubled, from 14 percent to 34.8 percent; the percentage of women becoming "economically active" rose by 223.9 percent from 1970 to 1990.[16] During these years prostitution in Cuba all but disappeared.

Coincident with the start of the Special Period, prostitution and sexual tourism re-emerged. Cuban authorities have tended to place a large share of the blame for the rise in prostitution directly on women involved in these sectors, rather than on the men who take part, or on the economic circumstances that at times seemed to require such self-degradation. Facio argues:

> To succeed, sex tourism requires Third World women to be economically desperate enough to enter prostitution. . . . The other side of the equation requires men from affluent societies to imagine certain women, usually women of color, to be more available and submissive than the women in their own countries.[17]

It is unclear if materialism or genuine necessity drives these women to prostitution. Eckstein notes, "A lust for dollars, meals in dollar restaurants, and gifts from the dollar stores outweighed the social stigma, the degradation, the health risks and the fear of arrest."[18]

Prostitution in Cuba is not only a problem because of the exploitation of women. The rise in prostitution has also exposed and perhaps exacerbated a racial divide within Cuban society. Tourists seeking sexual relations on the island apparently prefer darker-skinned consorts which is more problematic still, based on preexisting economic disadvantages experienced by many Afro-Cubans. Facio explains, "The combination of foreign men seeking sexual partners who are racially and culturally different, coupled with the sexual double standard's separation of women into 'good' versus 'bad' ones, reinforces the desirability of darker-skinned Cuban women as sex objects."[19]

THE COLOR-BLIND REVOLUTION

The dream of a colorblind Cuba was a dominant concept in José Martí's vision for the country. As Alejandro de la Fuente reports, the decrease in the material inequalities after 1959 disproportionately benefited Afro-Cubans because of their pre-revolutionary conditions.[20] Clarence Lusane, a scholar of comparative race relations, disputes this position. "Cuba eradicated institutionalized racism," he explains, but "racial prejudice and individual discrimination continue to occur at other levels."[21] While a decrease in the material gap between the races did occur in socialist Cuba, since 1991 class inequality has once again coincided with racial inequality. The reintroduction of tourism into the Cuban economy appears to have exacerbated the racial inequality on the island, as Afro-Cubans have significantly less access to jobs in the legal tourist industry which place them in direct contact with visitors likely to tip for services rendered. In the late 1990s, 60 percent of the Cubans involved in legal tourism were "light-skinned."[22] This phenomenon is strengthening the racial divide, as Afro-Cubans have less access to hard currency and less opportunity in the tourist industry. The discrepancy in access to hard currency would be problematic on its own because of its impact on Cuba's goal of creating an egalitarian society. It is compounded by the fact that Afro-Cubans had been the most economically disadvantaged segment of pre-revolutionary Cuban society, and had not achieved equality when the Special Period began. As Lusane points out, the revolutionary leaders did not initiate programs targeted at overcoming the effects of racial discrimination beyond the first several years of the revolution. They assumed, he explains, "that a rising tide would lift all boats, and that a broad distribution across all of Cuban society would necessarily benefit Afro-Cubans." Their assumption was problematic in the first instance, he argues, because "it reduced racial discrimination to material relations."[23]

In spite of the disproportionately negative impact the economic crisis has had on many Afro-Cubans, race is still not commonly addressed in official discourse. De la Fuente notes that the "official silence" about racism in Cuba has enabled negative racial stereotypes to continue and to be reproduced throughout the population.[24] In fact, the tourist industry has included these in advertising depicting Cuba as an exotic destination. Writer Eladio Secades notes, "The tourist is a type . . . who has become tired of civilization and seeks the primitive. To create the primitive where it does not exist is one of the ways to promote tourism."[25] This can be seen in the mass marketing of Afro-Cuban spirituality via reenactments of religious ceremonies, along with traditional song and dance forms packaged for tourist consumption.

TOURIST APARTHEID

People in areas where tourism is common often try to preserve their cultures and the normalcy of their daily activities by keeping much of their life hidden away from the gaze of tourists eager to explore exotica. By conducting many of their traditions and rituals or even basic aspects of their daily lives out of the tourist arena, they are able to express their culture as they choose without worrying about whether it fits the tourist's vision of how their culture ought to appear. This concept has been explored by anthropologist Laurie Medina, relating to interactions between tourists and local Mayan populations near Cancún, Mexico:

> The host population confronted with the arrival of tourists in their midst, protect and insulate their culture by dividing their lives into "backstage" areas, where they continue meaningful traditions (and go about their everyday lives) away from the gaze of tourists, and "front stage" areas, where they perform a limited range of activities for a tourist audience. This makes available portions of host culture for guest consumption, while it protects other parts from commoditization.[26]

In this sense, official regulations governing tourist-Cuban interactions facilitate efforts by Cubans to preserve their culture. To be sure, another motive of these rules is to ensure that most of the tourists' hard currency goes to the Cuban government, not to private individuals. A third objective is to insulate tourists from the exigencies of Cubans' daily life. The average tourist does not spend time in the homes of Cubans, visit Cuban schools, travel by distinctly Cuban transportation, or participate in Cubans' recreational activities. Few tourists thus experience blackouts, wait hours for overcrowded buses, or experience material shortages of any kind while in Cuba. Photojournalist Fred Ward noted, "Generally, living in first-class Cuban hotels is convenient and pleasant. Tourists are spared almost all the everyday problems plaguing citizens."[27]

However, there is a fine line between self-segregation and government-imposed segregation. The division in Cuba between Cubans and tourists has been codified in some instances by laws or regulations dictating the permissible boundaries for Cuban-tourist interactions. The restrictive nature of these practices, reminiscent of aspects of racial segregation in the United States, has led some to use the charged phrase of "tourist apartheid" to describe the barriers to contact between Cubans and non-Cubans.

With the resurgence of tourism in the late 1980s and early 1990s, the Cuban government grew concerned about the negative impact of tourism for the maintenance of revolutionary values such as collectivism, egalitarianism, and inclusiveness. As a consequence, the government began a campaign to root out social ills seemingly associated with tourism by limiting the opportunities for Cubans to interact with tourists. One of these laws, for example, required most tourist facilities to accept payment only in hard currency. Another prohibited Cubans from entering the residential areas of tourist hotels, or other specifically designated guest areas. Restrictions such as these eliminated the average Cubans' opportunity to stay in hotels regardless of their ability to pay for services in hard currency. In practice, the restrictions have been enforced inconsistently, and rarely with any substantive punishment. The Ministry of Tourism approved the most recent set of regulations—Resolution 10—in February 2005, which included restrictions on accepting gifts or invitations to socialize from foreigners, or consorting with foreign employers outside of the designated place of employment.[28] It is unclear whether some elements of the code of conduct for Cuban-tourist interactions are *de facto* or *de jure*. Yet there is no question that the Special Period has witnessed a significantly increased effort to govern the ways in which Cubans and tourists are allowed to interact.

REDEFINING CULTURE

> Attention is patterned by worldview. What you see when you look at anything, whether a person, a building, a city, or a country, is only a reflection—your world-view—coming back slightly colored. The best quality of an observer is empathy, which has to come with your worldview. No amount of immersion or adventure can take the place of empathy.—Andrei Codrescu, *Ay, Cuba!*[29]

There is perhaps no other country in the Western Hemisphere that evokes such romanticized images as Cuba. Tourists traveling to the island often come with de-tailed fantasies, which undoubtedly would include old cars, exotic women, cigars, rum, salsa music, *Buena Vista Social Club*, Latin dancing, and beaches. It is easy to see how tourist promoters would begin their effort, based on such preconceived no-tions of their potential clientele. They lay out Cuban culture, or what tourists be-lieve Cuban culture is, for consumption. Such promotions are evident in and around the major hotels or tourist establishments. In Central Havana, for example, miraculously preserved prerevolutionary American cars, waiting for tourist passen-gers, line the streets in front of the high-end hotels surrounding the *Parque Central*. More than merely the pride of their owners and a source of hard currency, these cars also embody the expectations of tourists. Travel writers and movies depicting pre-revolutionary Cuba create such expectations with their lyrical elegies and imagery. Cuban-born novelist Cristina García observes:

> There is a name for the gorgeous old American cars that continue to hum, rattle, and roll through the Cuban landscape: *cacharros.* Normally the word means broken-down jalopy. . . . But in the case of these Yankee beauties . . . cacharro is whispered softly, tenderly, like the name of a lost first love.[30]

The *Buena Vista Social Club*, both the documentary and soundtrack, gave un-precedented exposure in North America to Cuban "traditional" music. While the group could rightly attribute its success to the breathtaking musical talents of its members, it also succeeded by resurrecting a romanticized pre-revolutionary Cuban fantasy, with octogenarian musical phenoms being "rediscovered" by foreign musi-cians and producers. Such music is less dominant in Cuba today, yet the *Buena Vista Social Club* has come to epitomize Cuban music for many foreigners. As such, many tourists expect to hear songs featured in the documentary, sung by grandfatherly Cubans in fedoras smelling of Cuban cigars. In order to meet these ex-pectations, Cuban musicians have committed the film's soundtrack to memory, and regularly reproduce the tourists' desire for nostalgia upon request. This is con-sistent with a pattern that social scientist D. J. Greenwood has described: "Culture is being packaged, priced and sold like building lots, rights-of-way, fast food, and room service, as the tourism industry promises that the world is his/hers to use."[31]

One consequence of such packaging is the "commodification" of culture: that is, cultural practices are transformed into something whose value is measured by sales in the marketplace. In order to attract a steady tourist clientele it is necessary to create and provide a "desirable" tourist experience. Tourists rarely travel to someplace about which they have no preconceived notions or expectations as to what they will encounter. Tourist researcher S. Papson explains:

In order to induce the tourist to visit a specific area. . . government and private enterprise not only redefine social reality but also recreate it to fit those definitions.
This process is both interactive and dialectical. To the extent that this process takes
place, the category of everyday life is annihilated.[32]

Indeed, in Cuba as well as other tourist-dependent developing nations, it is apparent that local artists tend to skew their own social reality so that it conforms to
tourists' expectations. Yet in much of the scholarly literature on tourism, the host
population is rarely included in analyses about internal cultural changes or adapta-
tions, even though it is the agent of change. Historian Louis Pérez's description of
the way in which pre-revolutionary Cuban society was impacted indicates why
Cuban leaders were so reluctant in the 1990s to embrace tourism as a solution to
the special period's economic problems:

The expanding tourist presence introduced changes that were both profound and
permanent, transformations to which the Cuban people adjusted as a normal part of
daily life. . . . This involved a complex transaction by which the North American
notion of "Cuban" acted to change or otherwise modify Cuban self-representation
as a means of success and advancement.[33]

TOURISM: SAVIOR OR DESTROYER?

In order to survive today, the average Cuban needs access to hard currency. For
many Cubans without a family abroad to send remittances, working with tourists
is the only viable option for acquiring hard currency. Recognizing the need for some
adjustment, the government has begun to offer hard currency compensation along
with workers' state salaries in certain sectors of the Cuban economy. The government has found itself once again in a battle of moral versus material incentives. If
Cubans cannot legitimately gain access to hard currency through occupations
which provide for the common good—such as medicine or education—they will
have less incentive to educate themselves. This could result in a serious drain on
Cuba's well-trained professional population; a group that has been one of Cuba's
defining strengths throughout the revolution thus far. Mirén Uriarte, writing for Oxfam, describes this risk as "the 'inverted pyramid', a phenomenon that reflects the
devalued return on education and professional preparation in the new economy."[34]

Cuba cannot afford to lose the professional and productive sector of its economy. Such a loss would undermine many of the progressive elements upon which
Cuban national identity has developed, such as health care, education, and cultural
production. Of even greater concern, this loss of human capital would cripple
Cuba's prospects for development beyond the tourist industry. L. Richter in a study
on tourism in Asia noted,

In most countries, the [tourist] industry's health is assumed to be the best indicator
of a successful policy. This should not be so. A tourism policy in a developing nation, particularly, should be judged by its net impact on the economic, social, and
political life of the people. Since net economic benefits, as opposed to overall receipts, and social and political factors are seldom considered quantifiable, in many
countries they are simply left out of the policy equation.[35]

Regardless of claims about positive trickle-down effects of tourism, it is unlikely to generate greater equality or renew a spirit of egalitarianism. Tourism by its very nature creates distinctions between those who serve and those who are served. In many developing countries, it is an industry built on and fueled by the exploitation of inequality. Unless the inherent contradictions and potential risks of promoting tourism are more openly recognized, and greater precautions are taken to address them, contemporary Cuba could increasingly resemble prerevolutionary Cuba, complete with glaring social inequalities and other trappings of dependency.

NOTES

1. Cuban Ministry of Tourism, "Cuba celebrates the two millionth visitors in 2006," press release, December 1, 2006, www.gocuba.ca/en/news.asp?055.

2. Philip Peters, "International Tourism: The New Engine of the Cuban Economy," Arlington, VA: Lexington Institute, December 2002.

3. Stanley Turkel, "Cuba: Tourism Thriving Despite the U.S. Trade Embargo," *Hotel Interactive*, October 4, 2006.

4. Luz Marina Fornieles Sánchez, "The State of Cuban Tourism with Statistics," *Havana Journal*, April 15, 2006.

5. Peters, "International Tourism," 2.

6. Pedro Monreal, "Development as an Unfinished Affair: Cuba After the 'Great Adjustment' of the 1990s," *Latin American Perspectives*, Issue 124, Vol. 29, No. 3 (May 2002): 83.

7. Peters, "International Tourism," 7.

8. Pedro Monreal, *Development Prospects in Cuba: An Agenda in the Making*, Institute of Latin American Studies, University of London (2002): 15.

9. Julio Cerviño and María Cubillo, "Hotel and Tourism Development in Cuba: Opportunities, Management Challenges, and Future Trends," *Cornell Hotel and Restaurant Administration Quarterly* 46, No. 2 (2005): 225.

10. Charles Suddaby, "Cuba's Tourism Industry," *Seventh Annual Meeting of the Association of the Study of the Cuban Economy*, Miami, Florida (August 7-9): 123.

11. Jorge F. Pérez-López, "Foreign Investment in Cuba: An Inventory," *Cuba in Transition*, Association for the Study of the Cuban Economy (2004): 110–13.

12. Carmelo Mesa-Lago, *Growing Economic and Social Disparities in Cuba: Impact and Recommendations for Change*, Cuban Transition Project, Institute for Cuban & Cuban-American Studies, University of Miami (2002): 5, 23.

13. Susan Eva Eckstein, *Back from the Future: Cuba Under Castro*, Princeton University Press (1994): 105.

14. Oscar Lewis, Ruth M. Lewis, and Susan M. Rigdon, "The 'Rehabilitation' of Prostitutes," in *The Cuba Reader: History, Culture, Politics*, eds. Aviva Chomsky, Barry Carr, and Maria Smorkaloff, Duke University Press (2003): 395.

15. Elisa Facio, "Jineterismo During the Special Period," in *Cuban Transitions at the Millennium*, eds. Eloise Linger and John Cotman, International Development Options (2000): 57.

16. Max Azicri, *Cuba Today and Tomorrow: Reinventing Socialism* (Gainesville: University Press of Florida, 2000), 87.

17. Facio, "Jineterismo During the Special Period," 71.

18. Eckstein, *Back to the Future*, 123.

19. Facio, "Jineterismo During the Special Period," 69.

20. Alejandro de la Fuente, "Race and Inequality in Cuba, 1899–1981," *Journal of Contemporary History*, Vol. 30 (2005): 133.

21. Clarence Lusane, "From Black Cuban to Afro-Cuban: Issues and Problems Researching Race Consciousness and Identity in Cuban Race Relations," in *Cuban Transitions at the Millennium*, eds. Eloise Linger and John Cotman, International Development Options (2000): 87.

22. Alejandro de la Fuente, "Recreating Racism: Race and Discrimination in Cuba's Special Period," *Georgetown University Cuba Briefing Paper Series*, Vol. 18 (1998).

23. Lusane, "From Black Cuban to Afro-Cuban": 94.

24. de la Fuente, "Recreating Racism": 133.

25. Eladio Secades, quoted in Louis A. Pérez Jr., "Image and Identity," in *Inside Cuba: The History, Culture, and Politics of an Outlaw Nation*, eds. John Miller and Aaron Kenedi, Marlowe & Company (2003): 144.

26. Laurie Kroshus Medina, "Commoditizing Culture Tourism and Mayan Identity," *Annals of Tourism Research*, Vol. 30, No. 2 (2003): 353–68.

27. Fred Ward, "Havana, 1977: Welcome Tourists," in *The Reader's Companion to Cuba*, ed. Alan Ryan, Harcourt Brace Publishers (1997): 252.

28. Archibald Ritter, "Economic Illegalities and the Underground Economy in Cuba," *FOCAL Background Briefing on Cuba*, March (2006): 8.

29. Andrei Codrescu, *Ay, Cuba! A Socio-Erotic Journey*, St. Martin's Press (1999): 199.

30. Cristina García, "Cacharros," in *Inside Cuba: The History, Culture, and Politics of an Outlaw Nation*, eds. John Miller and Aaron Kenedi, Marlowe & Company (2003): 147.

31. D. J. Greenwood, "Culture by the Pound: An Anthropological Perspective on Tourism as Cultural Commoditization," in *Hosts and Guests: The Anthropology of Tourism*, ed. V. Smith, University of Pennsylvania Press (1989): 171–85.

32. S. Papson, "Spuriousness and Tourism: Politics of Two Canadian Provincial Governments," *Annals of Tourism Research*, Vol. 8 (1981): 220–35.

33. Louis A. Pérez, *On Becoming Cuban*, University of North Carolina Press (1999): 395.

34. Mirén Uriarte, *Cuba: Social Policy at the Crossroads, Maintaining Priorities, Transforming Practice*, An Oxfam America Report (2002): 27.

35. L. K. Richter, *The Politics of Tourism in Asia*, University of Hawaii Press (1989): 63.

Going against the Grain

Agricultural Crisis and Transformation

Minor Sinclair and Martha Thompson

The breakup of socialism first in Eastern Europe in 1989 and then in the Soviet Union in 1990 created a major crisis in Cuba known as the Special Period. Cuban agriculture was particularly vulnerable. In the 1960s and 1970s the revolution had reshaped agriculture under the principles that the state is the central force and that mechanization would raise the dignity of human labor. Three-quarters of the arable land was held by large state farms, which predominantly produced a single crop: sugar. Agriculture depended heavily on chemical inputs. In fact, Cuban farms used more fertilizer than U.S. farms. Before the economic crisis Cuba imported 1.3 million tons of chemical fertilizers (Murphy, 1999); today the figure is not more than 160,000 tons (Gutiérrez interview, May 2001). Before the crisis, Cuba used 17,000 tons of herbicides, and 10,000 tons of pesticides (Murphy, 1999); today Cuba uses 1,900 tons (Gutiérrez interview, May 2001). Farms were also heavily mechanized at a level comparable to the United States. One cooperative president told the authors, "We had more tractors than we could use." He added, "When the ministry told us to go to the port to pick up a new tractor, we said that we were too busy. We never went."

Many have compared the Cuban model to the Soviet model of collective farms. Although there were similarities, unlike the Soviet Union, Cuba never forced collectivization and retained a high percentage of private farmers. Cuban agriculture was similar to both the Soviet and U.S. models in that it was large scale, oriented towards export, subsidized, heavily mechanized, and dependent on chemical inputs. This made the Cuban model extremely vulnerable to dramatic changes in the trade and aid environment.

Although the infrastructure for capital-intensive agriculture still existed, in 1990 the Cuban agricultural model began to collapse as one problem after another halted production.

Imported inputs vanished—no chemical fertilizers, animal feed, tools, seeds, wire, or animal vaccines. Fuel for tractors and irrigation systems was practically unobtainable, as were tires, batteries, or spare parts. Cuban-produced goods such as feed, pipes, tools, fertilizers, and pesticides dried up because of the same litany of problems: no raw materials, no electricity to run the factories, no functioning trucks, and no petroleum.

The rural economy in Cuba slowed and then practically stopped. Tractors stood useless in the fields, electric pumps went dry as crops wilted in the fields, and animals died or were slaughtered for food as their feed disappeared. According to the Economists Intelligence Unit's (2000) evaluation, the agricultural sector began to contract by 10.3 percent in 1992, then by 22.7 percent in 1993 and by 4.9 percent in 1994. By 1994, agricultural production had plummeted to 55 percent of its 1990 level. Production decline was only half the story. Without resources to distribute, refrigerate, or store them, crops spoiled or rotted in the field.

The impact on food security was disastrous. Daily per-capita caloric intake fell from 2,908 in 1989 to 1,863 calories in 1995, according to the U.S. Department of Agriculture (USDA), and protein intake dropped by 40 percent. Some estimated that the average Cuban lost 20 pounds by 1994.

Throughout the worst years, 1993 to 1995, two basic government policies kept the food crisis from emergency levels: food programs for the vulnerable population (the elderly, children, and pregnant and lactating mothers) and the state food distribution system through the ration card (although drastically reduced compared to levels in the 1980s). Social unrest has been minimal even though the differences have increased between the haves and the have-nots in a society where those differences had been successfully reduced. Government policies and farmers' practices have revamped production and distribution systems and regained a basis of food security. This type of widespread change would be remarkable in normal times, but the fact that the Cubans were able to achieve it with the overwhelming shortages and scarcities of the economic crisis is unique and should be closely studied.

THE CUBAN REVOLUTION TRANSFORMS THE COUNTRYSIDE: LAND REFORM

In 1959, the new Cuban government set out to create social and economic equity by the radical redistribution of wealth, including restoring Cuban ownership of Cuban assets. In the countryside, this began by redistributing farmland through the land reform.

The first agrarian reform in May 1959 limited the land one person could own to 405 hectares (1,000 acres). By expropriating 12,000 farms with compensation offers of twenty-year bonds at 4 percent interest, the government obtained 44 percent of the farm and ranch land. As a result, the number of small farmers more than tripled (from 45,000 to 160,000), and state farms replaced the large plantations. Former sharecroppers and small farmers were deeded as much as 27 hectares of free land, and their incomes steadily improved (Rosset & Benjamin, 1995).

Concurrently, the government developed the state agricultural sector. The large expropriated properties became state farms and employed the seasonal workers as permanent employees. Life improved dramatically for the former seasonal workers, who received year-round employment, social security, sick leave, accident insurance, free schools, medical care, and day care. A second agrarian reform in 1963 reduced all private land ownership to 67 hectares and expanded the state farm sector.

By 1965 the rural landscape was radically transformed. No longer could foreigners dominate the Cuban economy—or even own an acre of land. State farms worked 63 percent of the arable land. More than 160,000 small farmers owned and worked about 20 percent of the arable land. The vast majority of small farmers joined farmers' associations, which were the precursors of today's cooperatives.

- **The credit and services cooperatives (CCSs)** today number 2,556 cooperatives and account for about 12 percent of the arable land (1,013,290 hectares). They range from ten to forty members who own and farm their land individually with family members or hired help, but who deal collectively with the state for inputs, credits, and services. CCS land can only be transferred through inheritance by a family member willing to farm it or sold to the state. Members elect the president and directors of the cooperative.
- **The agricultural production cooperatives (CPAs)** today number 1,133 entities and account for approximately 10 percent the arable land in Cuba (710,428 hectares). The CPAs vary in size from about 40 to 300 members. All CPAs own the land and farming assets collectively and relate to the state on credits, inputs, and commercialization. Members receive daily wages called an advance, and profits are divided annually among the membership. Members receive services such as housing, transport, and recreation from the cooperatives. Members elect the president and directors of the cooperative.

The CCSs and CPAs are part of a cooperative federation known as the National Association of Small Producers (ANAP), which claims a total membership of 239,217 farmers. ANAP provides cooperative training, agricultural extension, and an array of services to its membership. The federation also represents the interests of farmers in Cuba and often negotiates directly with the government on prices, credit, and other issues. ANAP farmers produce 52 percent of the vegetables grown in Cuba, 67 percent of the corn, and 85 percent of the tobacco. There is a third group of private, unaffiliated farmers (about 20,000 small producers) who own their own land but are not part of a cooperative. They control about 1 percent of the agrarian land, about 66,100 hectares.

REFORMING CUBAN AGRICULTURE

While the rural infrastructure, services, and standard of living were dramatically transformed in the first four decades of the Cuban Revolution, Cuban agriculture had not lost its taste for producing, milling, and exporting sugar. The Cuban model—characterized by large state farms, mono-cropping, heavy use of mechanization and chemical inputs, centralized planning, and dependence on imported agricultural supplies and imported foodstuffs—was sustained only through highly generous terms of trade of Cuban sugar for Soviet oil. By not producing food for domestic consumption and by not addressing its high input and low productivity problems, Cuban agriculture became very vulnerable to a rupture with its Soviet and eastern bloc trading partners.[1]

"Luckily—and I choose my words carefully—luckily the roof caved in for us in 1989," said Mavis Alvarez, a leader in the Cuban farmers' movement. "It made us pay attention to more rational methods." (Sullivan, 2000). Now, ten years later, the economy is slowly reemerging. The GNP has grown every year since 1995, reaching 6.2 percent for 1999 and an estimated 4.6 percent for 2000. Employment is up, productivity is up, and exports are up. In agriculture, certain sectors, including production of fruits, vegetables, and tubers for domestic consumption, have turned around completely. Caloric intake rebounded to 2,473 and 51.6 grams per person—not great compared to the 1980s, but still a 33 percent increase compared to 1994.

Neither the World Bank nor the International Monetary Fund nor other international lenders came to Cuba's aid. The recovery in agriculture came from internal reorganization—new policies, new actors, new systems. The goal, according to Cuban Vice Minister of Agriculture Alfredo Gutiérrez, is that "Cuban agriculture has to stand on its own two feet. We need to overcome the myth that agriculture must be subsidized" (Gutiérrez interview, May 2001). The overhaul entailed major structural changes, such as

- decentralization Cuban-style, through the conversion of large state farms into thousands of smaller farmers' cooperatives and leasing land in usufruct to thousands of private farmers;
- urban gardening and ecological agriculture, which altered the topography of rural Cuba, introducing greater diversity and organic practices and greening the cities with thousands of micro farms;
- reforming distribution through introduction of markets, price incentives, and profitability.

These measures, taken as a whole, make up Cuba's "third agrarian reform," every bit as profound as the major land expropriations and redistributions of the first two reforms of 1959 and 1963.

DECENTRALIZATION OF PRODUCTION

In September 1993, the Cuban government unveiled a major reorganization in agriculture: restructuring state farms as private cooperatives. As President Fidel Castro explained in the Cuban newspaper *Granma* (12/29/93), "The state has not had success in large farm business." Decree 142 affected most of the state holdings, a total of 41.2 percent of the arable land in Cuba—2,756,000 hectares—and created 2,007 new cooperatives whose membership totaled 122,000 people.[2] Called Basic Units of Cooperative Production (UBPC), the cooperatives now make up the largest sector in Cuban agriculture. The new policy was based on the fact that smaller farms would be more easily managed and better able to take on sustainable agriculture practices, which was now vital given the lack of agricultural inputs. This was seen as a new formula promoting decentralized decision making about production but allowing centralized planning so essential for planned biological diversity, pest control at a regional level, and water and other resource management. Government planners and farm leaders alike believed that cooperative members would be positive about the change and be motivated to work. This assumption was verified in an early study by a leading American researcher, Carmen Diana Deere (1997).

Because they believe that they will be the beneficiaries, cooperative members are also working longer hours and putting in much greater effort. Moreover, it is apparent that as owners of the means of production, they take better care of their equipment and farm implements.

The members also feel empowered to a certain degree, for they are now participating in production decisions for the first time and have elected their own management, sometimes in contested elections—something quite new in the Cuban political scene.

Unlike the large state farms, the UBPCs are smaller enterprises, member-owned and member-managed. The cooperative, not the state, owns the production, and the cooperative member earns based on his or her share of the cooperative's income. The cooperatives also own the buildings and farm equipment purchased from the government at discounted prices with long-term, low-interest loans (4 percent interest). The greatest structural difference between the UBPCs and other cooperatives is that the state retains ownership of the land and leases the land on a long-term basis, rent-free, to the UBPC cooperative. As Deere has characterized the transformation, "The gigantic state farm sector was, in reality, privatized," although Deere and others recognize that the state reserves the right to "dissolve whatever UBPC . . . on the basis of the social or economic interest as determined by the Government" (*Gaceta Oficial*, 9/21/93).

Many expected that replacing state farms with "socialized" private enterprise would unleash entrepreneurial energy and reverse the low productivity found on the state farms. Now eight years after the founding of the UBPCs, the track record of new cooperatives is not as strong as was hoped. While no one calls for a return to the state farm era, difficulties continue to stymie their development. The UBPCs inherited a highly mechanized, high-input agricultural model at a time when inputs are scarce and costly (credit and extension services have also been reduced). The cooperatives were born not out of plenty, like the small farmers in the agrarian reform thirty years earlier, but out of scarcity, and they lack the means of production. In addition, UBPCs have shown difficulty in retaining their work force due to inadequate living conditions, working conditions, and pay. And without a federation to unite the individual UBPCs, similar to the ANAP cooperatives federation, the UBPC movement has been unable to articulate its interests and bargain with the state as a sector (as opposed to as an individual cooperative).

Another issue concerns the new cooperatives' independence from the state. Although the UBPCs are legally autonomous, the state continues to exercise considerable influence on the activities of many of the cooperatives. The government contracts with the UBPCs on what crops and how much land the cooperative should cultivate and on that basis sells agricultural inputs to the UBPCs. UBPCs produce predominantly sugar. More than three-quarters of all the UBPCs, for example, are given quotas for sugar production, which severely limits any other crops they might produce and sell in the agricultural markets, thereby restricting their options and their income. An April 2000 visit by the authors to six UBPC cooperatives in Ciego de Avila revealed different perspectives between the UBPCs and local officials with the Ministry of Agriculture. The officials tended to relate to the UBPCs as if the co-ops were still state farms, while several UBPC leaders listed the need for relative autonomy in decision making as a key factor inhibiting their progress.

Given the state influence, some researchers have called the UBPCs "state cooperatives"[3] or private-state hybrids.[4] Regardless of the name, the state influence on the cooperatives affects "their consciousness as new cooperativists, who are owners and therefore social actors in an economic context. . . . The minimal necessary conditions for the development of self-management still has not been created and a culture of cooperativism has not been extended" (Perez, 2000).

Creating a consciousness of ownership among former agricultural laborers cannot happen overnight, unlike the passing of the decree that created the UBPCs, but at the same time will require a more intentional hands-off approach by local ministry officials who still view UBPCs as part of their domain. Trends clearly point towards greater autonomy for the cooperatives. Interviews on the ground and with agricultural specialists confirm that local cooperative leaders are demanding greater decision-making authority and local officials with relatively few resources are increasingly ceding authority. Non-sugar UBPCs have won more of the battle.

LINKING WORKERS TO THE LAND

Within the UBPC cooperatives and the agricultural cooperatives (CPAs), a new practice of tying an individual's salary to his or her productivity may be one of the most vital, yet unheralded, reforms. Traditionally members of cooperatives get paid based on the number of days they work (through an advance and an end-of-year share of the earnings). This practice pays everyone equally, no matter how hard, how long, or how productively one works in the day.

By linking workers to a specific plot of land on the cooperative, the cooperative compensates members based on their productivity, not their timesheet. Members who clear more land in a day get paid more; individuals who produce more on their area get paid more. This represents a move towards decentralization and greater incentives within the cooperative, but still allows for the larger economies of scale, mechanization, and collectivist spirit which cooperatives offer.

The breakup of the large state farms has freed enormous acreage for other types of land use and the government has turned over land to farmers—nearly 170,000 hectares since 1989 (ECLAC, 2000). The government retains title to the land, but private farmers and agricultural cooperatives (CPAs) can farm the land rent-free for an indefinite time period. The only qualification for farmers such as coffee farmers in the east, vegetable growers in the central provinces, and tobacco farmers in the west is that nearby land be available and that the farmers show the potential to expand their production.

Given the food crisis of the mid-1990s and the current income-earning potential, many Cubans now view farming as an occupation very differently than they did in the 1980s.

Thousands of families have left the cities and towns to claim a farming stake and make their livelihood from the land. ANAP claims that its membership has increased by 35,000 over the past three years and characterizes the new farmers as young families, many of whom are college-educated; people who opted for early retirement; or workers who originally came from a farming background.

REFORMING FOOD DISTRIBUTION: AGRICULTURAL MARKETS

On October 1, 1994, the government opened 121 agricultural markets throughout the country. For the first time in four decades (except for a period from 1980 to 1986) producers could sell in an open market directly to consumers without the state serving as an intermediary.

Immediately the black market for basic foodstuffs practically disappeared. Consumer prices in the new open markets were much lower than in the former black markets (pork sold for 25 pesos per pound instead of 75 pesos per pound in the black market and a pound of squash for 2 pesos instead of 15 pesos, for example). Predictions that free markets would increase production as well as spur higher quality and greater diversity of produce have borne out. According to a 2000 study by the Lexington Institute, "By 1999 the sales volume [of the markets] exceeded three times the 1995 level, and the *agros* were regenerating more than 5 million pesos in tax revenue" (Peters, 2000).

Cubans reacted positively to the opening of markets because they increased access to food. "People love going to the *agros*," said one shopper. "The government would fall if they tried to close these down again." (The government indeed did close the farmers' markets back in 1986 after experimenting with markets for several years.)

However, Cubans resent the high prices in the agricultural markets resulting from supply-and-demand pricing. Compared to people's earnings today, goods are out of reach for many. Many products once readily available through the *libreta* cannot be purchased either in the agricultural markets or from nontraditional producers and are available only in dollars through government-run dollar stores. The exception to this is the liter a day of milk products that the government provides to all children through age 7, pregnant and lactating women, and patients who need special diets. Cubans who have the funds purchase items in insufficient supply, such as eggs and oil, in the dollar stores. The prices in the dollar stores are prohibitive for Cubans. A liter of oil costs $2.40 or the equivalent of 25 percent of a month's salary for the average person. According to an Interpress report, food purchases can take up to 66 percent of the average Cuban salary (Grogg, 2000). A consumer may pay as much as ten times the price for the same goods sold through the ration card. The rations, however, frequently last no more than ten to fourteen days of the month for basic items (rice, legumes, some protein, coffee, bread, sugar, and root crops). Vegetable oil, meats and meat products, cheese, fruits, and vegetables are seldom available through the ration card and then in small quantities. The only fruit available through the ration card might be cheap oranges, while in the markets there are pineapples, watermelons, bananas, and tangerines, all for those who can pay. Many in Cuba project that the *libreta* will never regain its earlier prominence and may disappear.

Some attribute the high prices of the agricultural markets to underproduction: more supply will drive down the price. It has been said that may be part of the problem—since their inception in 1995 the agriculture markets have been handling three times the volume and prices have dropped by one-third. Others place the blame on farmers for charging high wholesale prices. While farmers unquestionably have gained because of the markets, "the market prices are inflated because of the intermediaries," according to Juan Valdés Paz, a noted rural sociologist (J. Valdés Paz, personal communication, September 29, 2000). The problem stems from transportation shortages, which allow the relatively few individuals who own trucks to collude, paying producers little and charging high prices to vendors and consumers. A Ministry of Agriculture official suggested that these shippers may collar as much as 75 percent of the profit of a product sold. To combat the high prices, the Ministry of Agriculture is turning over used trucks to private cooperatives to encourage farmers to ship their own goods or use their own marketing representative. In addition, new government policy has state farms selling more of their produce at low prices in state agricultural markets in an attempt to drive down prices (Gonzáles Vásquez, 2000). From 1995 to 1997 state farms doubled their "market share" of produce sold in the agricultural markets from 21 percent of the vegetables and 20 percent of the meat products to 41 percent of the vegetables and 39 percent of the meats.

While the opening of agricultural markets has helped ameliorate the food crisis, tricky problems persist. Consumers have choice and availability but only those who can afford the high prices. By opening private markets, the government recognizes that less state operationality can be beneficial, but more government control against price-gouging and price collusion is needed. Markets too, so far, have offered little consolation for the vulnerable population unable to pay the high prices; while the ration card and lower-priced state markets may be part of the solution, a more comprehensive solution is needed.

A GUIDE TO FOOD SHOPPING IN CUBA

Before 1995 the government was in charge of nearly 100 percent of the food distribution, principally through the *libreta* or ration card and meals at the workplace. Highly subsidized and plentiful food through the *libreta* was one of the revolution's chief social achievements. Since the onset of the economic crisis, the monthly rations have been reduced and now no longer last more than ten days to two weeks. In response to the crippling of the *libreta*, the agricultural markets and the following other venues for buying food have emerged.

- La Libre: "Free" markets are government stands, often outside of the ration stores, which sell very cheaply overstocks and produce not included in the *libreta* ration cards.
- Urban Gardens: Vegetable stands that market the fresh produce from a nearby urban agriculture plot. The upside is that produce is usually organic, high quality, and fresh daily, and prices are 40 percent to 50 percent of the agricultural markets. The downside is that variety is limited to what the garden happens to produce.
- *Ferias*: State farms ship in fruits, vegetables, and small livestock for wholesale in state-sponsored fairs. Prices are deeply discounted (about 25 percent of

the agricultural markets), but the fairs are infrequent (only monthly) and held in only a few points in the city, making access difficult for most shoppers.

- Topped Markets: Open markets favored by state producers, where the prices fluctuate with supply and demand but have a limit. Prices are generally less than in the agricultural markets and the quality is not as good.
- Dollar Stores: Originally for diplomats and foreigners, dollar stores cater to Cubans and non-Cubans with imported and domestic canned goods, drinks, packaged meats, vegetable oil, cheeses, and so on. Prices are high, sometimes double the cost of agricultural markets.
- Peso Stores: Opened in 1998 to parallel the dollar stores, the stores carry the Cuban manufactured version of the imports. Prices are in pesos, often at 75 percent the equivalent of the dollar value in dollar stores.

PRICE INCENTIVES AND PROFITS

All farmers continue to sell a percentage of their produce to the state marketing board known as *Acopio*. While *Acopio* provides a guaranteed market and a floor price, which the farmers favor, *Acopio*'s service has suffered from inflexibility and unreliability. When *Acopio* was the only legal buyer, farmers had little option but resignation. Not only have the agricultural markets offered an alternative buyer, but also the Ministry of Agriculture recently has introduced a tiered and more flexible pricing regime of *Acopio* in an attempt to increase production.

Farmers who contract a *plan* with the government are now motivated to produce "in excess" of their *plan*. They can sell any food produced over their quota in the agricultural markets or at "differentiated prices," often twice the contracted price, to the government. Under this impetus, almost all farmers, it seems, have been able to produce "in excess," and, in most cases, double their *plan*, which triples or quadruples their income. Historically, one of the biggest problems in stimulating productivity has been that the government sets prices very low, and farmers, under obligation to sell to the state, feel little incentive to produce to capacity.

Export-oriented crops such as sugar, coffee, and tobacco have seen the greatest increases in prices paid, in part because the state wants to encourage production and in part because foreign investment and loans can be tapped. In addition to the higher prices paid in pesos, farmers in sugar, coffee, and tobacco receive production incentives called *estimulos*, paid in dollars for meeting production quotas. A tobacco farmer earns $4 to $5 per 100 pounds of tobacco produced, which makes for a considerable sum in rural Cuba. A sugar-producing cooperative receives $4.60 per 100 *arrobas* (25 lbs.) of sugar sold. The *estimulos* are paid in cash, in the case of individual tobacco farmers, or in credit at a local "dollar" store for coffee producers and members of cooperatives. The result has been impressive production increases in tobacco and coffee, though perhaps less so in sugar, as many factors other than prices affect the production level of sugarcane.

With the state looking to reduce its import bill of $235 million for the tourist industry, a new government measure now allows co-ops to market high-quality produce to tourist facilities, granted that two state agencies serve as intermediaries. The co-ops are paid with credit in dollars that can be redeemed at certain stores. In a 2000 pilot project, two dozen ANAP cooperatives were authorized to market their goods directly to hotels, and the farmers were paid directly in dollars from hotel operators. Part of the deal required these cooperatives to give up state subsidies in agricultural inputs and become entirely self-reliant. The Ministry of Agriculture is gradually unrolling these experiments in dollarization and with high success: the cooperatives produce more and become more self-sufficient, the tourist industry gains access to fresh, local produce, and the state saves on foreign currency.

COMBINING THE NEW AND THE OLD

Like most new systems, Cuba's new model of agriculture casts off some old practices, holds onto others, and mixes those with new ideas. Importantly, the new model retains the long-standing commitment to social equity as guaranteed by the state and tries to instill incentives, a regulated market, and new practices as ways of increasing production and improving distribution. What has not changed has been

- Land ownership: Except for the 20 percent of arable land owned by the ANAP cooperatives, the state formally owns the agricultural land and leases it rent-free to the UBPC cooperatives and other private farmers. Private farmers cannot sell their land, except to the state, but they can transfer their land through inheritance to family members. State ownership of land can be argued as an inhibiting factor on growth, but it effectively has prevented reconcentration of land.
- Centralized planning and state administration: The reforms brought about significant decentralization of agricultural management, particularly in the UBPCs. However, the state continues to play the central role in the overall planning and administration of food production and distribution. The state supplies all the inputs, decides production priorities, negotiates quotas and prices with the producers, provides insurance, and is the first and primary purchaser and distributor of food.
- Food distribution: The state continues to play the principal role in food distribution in four main areas: the basic food basket distributed through the *libreta* (inadequate as it is); food supplements to the vulnerable population; food imports; and controls on pricing through market systems.
- Reliance on export agriculture: Sugar exports have been the economic cornerstone since the 1800s. While the relationship of dependence shifted from Spain to the United States to the Soviet Union, Cuba's fix on sugar continued. The new model has brought shifts, however. While sugarcane still occupies more land area than any other crop, its dominance has lessened as exports of tobacco, coffee, and citrus have gained importance. And while the agriculture exports are still key to the Cuban economy, other sectors have risen in importance. For the first time, tourism has replaced sugar as the biggest hard-currency earner, and nickel exports and remittances figure highly.

MANAGING GROWTH WITH EQUITY

Cubans with fixed incomes and no access to dollars face a great difficulty in accessing sufficient food, which is a new phenomenon in Cuba. The gap between those who have access to dollars or higher salaries and those who do not is growing and poses the most serious equity problem to the Cuban state and Cuban society. It is also true that the gap between the two groups is much narrower than in most other countries and everyone has access to a very basic food basket.

In mapping its strategy for the reactivation of agriculture, Cuba has found relative success in managing a problem that has plagued Latin America and the Caribbean: how to achieve economic growth with social equity.

In Cuba the economic crisis did not cause serious dislocation in the rural sector. No Cuban farmer has lost land through the crisis; in fact, the opposite has occurred, as 25,961 new farmers with government-leased land (rent-free) joined ANAP in the 1990s. Nor have the reforms caused dislocation. Markets have not squeezed the farmer; instead, farmers have made profits and produced more for the market while filling their quotas for the state food distribution system. While cooperatives are pressed to become more independent and financially solvent, government support for farmers continues in practically all areas except for provision of imported agricultural supplies—albeit on a reduced scale. The government provides free agricultural extension, crop insurance, guaranteed markets, and subsidies on what little inputs it can provide (although government subsidies for farmers have dropped each year since 1994). In addition, the government has carefully used food imports to complement, not substitute, for domestic production.

These policies have promoted rural employment and encouraged rural livelihood so that rural youth can choose to invest their education and aspirations in rural life, rather than try their luck in the cities. The combination of state control and calibrated reforms has increased production, but not at the cost of wealth for a few and misery for the majority.

NOTES

1. Through the 1980s Cuba dedicated 57 percent of all arable land to export crops and only 43 percent to production for internal consumption, which meant that Cubans relied on Soviet bloc imports for much of their food, especially processed food; 90 percent of all fats and oils were imported, 80 percent of beans, 40 percent of rice, 24 percent of milk—in short, 55 percent of all calories consumed on the ration card.

2. The state still owns and operates 33 percent of the arable land, 2,234,500 hectares, including the sugar mills, agricultural companies, and other production enterprises. Part of the farmland classified as state land belongs to the military for agricultural production.

3. As formulated by Niurka Pérez, director of the Rural Studies unit at the Sociology Department of the University of Havana.

4. As considered by Victor Figueroa, an agricultural specialist at the Universidad Central de las Villas.

REFERENCES

American Association for World Health. (March 1997). "Denial of Food and Medicine: The Impact of the U.S. Embargo on Health and Nutrition in Cuba." A Report from the *American Association for World Health.*

Burchardt, H. (2000). La ultima reforma agraria del siglo: ¿cambio o estancamiento? In H. Burchardt (Ed.), *La última reforma del siglo* (pp. 169–192). Caracas, Venezuela: Nueva Sociedad.

Centro de Estudios de la Economía Cubana (CEEC). (2000). *La economía cubana coyuntura, reflexiones y oportunidade*s. La Habana: Cuba.

Deere, Carmen Diana. (1997). Reforming Cuban Agriculture. *Review: Fernand Braudel Center: A Journal of the Fernand Braudel Center for the study of Economics, Historical Systems, and Civilizations*. VXX pp. 649–668.

Deere, Carmen Diana; González, Ernel; Pérez, Niurka; and Rodríguez, Gustavo (1995). House hold Incomes in Cuban Agriculture: A Comparison of the State, Co-operative, and Peasant Sectors. *Development and Change, Vol. 26.* Published by Blackwell Publishers, Oxford.

Díaz Vázquez, J. A. (2000). Consumo y distribución normada y otros bienes en Cuba. In H. Burchardt (Ed.), *La última reforma del siglo* (pp. 36–55). Caracas, Venezuela: Nueva Sociedad.

Economic Commission on Latin America and the Caribbean (ECLAC). (2000). *La Economía Cubana: Reformas estructurales y desempeño en los noventa* .Washington, DC: ASDI.

Economist Intelligence Unit (EIU). Country Report: Cuba. (Jan., Aug., Nov. 2000).

Food and Agriculture Organization website, Food Balance Sheet and FAO STAT Database Results, Cuba.

Grogg, Patricia. "Food Still Expensive Despite Recovery." Newswire: Interpress Service. (19 May 2000).

González Vásquez, A. (2000). La nueva experiencia del mercado agropecuario en Cuba. In H. Burchardt (Ed.), *La última reforma del siglo* (pp. 135–141). Caracas, Venezuela: Nueva Sociedad.

Gutiérrez Yanis, Alfredo. "Interview with Alfredo Gutiérrez Yanis, Vice Minister for Development of the Ministry of Agriculture by Oxfam delegation." (May 2001)

Lobe, Jim. "Learn From Cuba, Says World Bank." May 1, 2001. Interpress Service.

Murphy, Catherine. "Cultivating Havana: Urban Agriculture and Food Security in the Years of Crisis." Food First, Development Report No. 12, (May 1999).

Oficina Nacional de Estadistícas (2000). *Cuba en Cifras* 1999. Habana, Cuba.

Nova González, N. (2000). El mercado agro pecuario. In H. Burchardt (Ed.), *La última reforma del siglo* (pp. 143–150). Caracas, Venezuela: Nueva Sociedad.

Pérez Villanueva, O. E. (2000). La reestructuración de la economía cubana. El proceso en la agricultura. In H. Burchardt (Ed.), *La ultima reforma del siglo* (pp. 71–102). Caracas, Venezuela: Nueva Sociedad.

Peters, Philip. (Oct. 2000). "The Farmers' Market: Crossroads of Cuba's New Economy." A Report from the *Lexington Institute*, pp. 1–15.

Rosset, Peter & Medea Benjamin, Eds. *The Greening of the Revolution: Cuba's Experiment with Organic Farming*. Ocean Press, 1995, p. 90–96.

Sullivan, Robert. "Cuba Goes Organic." Newswire: Earth Times News Service. (24 July 2000).

UN World Food Program, "Development Project—Cuba: Nutritional Support to Vulnerable Groups in the Five Eastern Provinces." (2 January 2001).

Valdes Paz, J. (2000). Notas sobre el modelo agrario cubano en los años 90. In H. Burchardt (Ed.), *La última reforma del siglo* (pp. 109–132). Caracas, Venezuela: Nueva Sociedad.

15

Vale Todo

In Cuba's *Paladares*,
Everything Is Prohibited but Anything Goes

Ted Henken

INTRODUCTION

As we went through the makeshift front door of Central Havana's *Paladar Las Doce Sillas* (The Twelve Chairs Restaurant), I noted the owner's exasperated expression. It turned out that Gregorio, my resourceful street guide, had brought in four Spanish customers not ten minutes earlier and the owner would now have to fork out another $5 commission on top of the $20 he already owed Gregorio for his services. Playing the fool, I inquired of Magalis, the waitress, how it was that I did not see lobster on my menu, yet noticed a large red shell lying empty on a plate nearby. She lowered her head and whispered, "You know we can't put that on the menu?" Turning toward a small, improvised service door that opened to the kitchen, she asked in a clear, confident voice, "Hey, is there any more 'L' back there?" She returned to me with a hot plate of "L" *a la plancha* and continued, "If they catch us with lobster, they can confiscate all our equipment, close the *paladar*, and charge us with 'illicit sales'." After counting the twelve chairs that filled the cramped dining room, I inquired about the name of the restaurant. Magalis admitted that it was the owner's way of poking fun at the ridiculous restriction against having more than twelve chairs in any *paladar*. She then proudly showed me a hidden room behind the kitchen that could seat another twelve diners. Before leaving, I spoke briefly with Orestes, the owner, who claimed, "Through this experience, I realized that I was born an entrepreneur. The only problem is that I was born in the wrong country!"

This article draws four lessons from the world of Cuba's private, speak-easy eateries—the island's infamous *paladares*. First, the policy of "legalization" of the island's private food service sector inaugurated in the summer of 1995 has been accompanied overtime by such a thick web of legal restrictions that, by design or default, the original aim of expansion has been lost. In fact, restrictions on private restaurants are so great and their taxes so high that they often overshadow the benefits of legal status itself, prohibiting the full development of these legal micro-enterprises and forcing them to utilize informal strategies or into outright clandestine existence, to make a living.

Second, every legal restriction put in place to control and limit the growth of these private enterprises has given rise to a corresponding (and often illegal) survival strategy. For example, restrictions against intermediaries, advertising, and employees have provoked the development of an extensive underground network of *jineteros* and fictional cousins. Menu and size restrictions have led to the proliferation of hidden rooms and forbidden foods.

Third, while often described as "islands of capitalism in a sea of socialism" (Pérez-López 1994; Jatar-Hausmann 1999), in practice these restaurants are anything but isolated from the rest of the Cuban economy. Deep and functional linkages exist between these well-known manifestations of Cuba's private economy, connecting them in various direct and indirect ways with other parts of the economy.

A fourth and final lesson that can be taken from the above anecdote is the sense that these enterprises face an unsure future. While most of the still-surviving *paladar* operators doubt that they will be closed down outright by the state (especially if they have learned "how to play the game," as Orestes would say), few believe that they will ever be able to grow beyond their current small size into true small- and medium-sized businesses. The aura of illegitimacy that accompanies any independent economic activity and the government's antagonistic attitude toward self-employment effectively condemn these private restaurateurs to an informal, provisional existence.

THE ORIGINS AND HISTORY OF THE PALADAR

Birth and premature death (1990–1995). Because it is one of the most visible manifestations of private enterprise to foreign visitors in Cuba, much attention has been given to the *paladar*.[1] The name *paladar*, meaning "palate," derives from a chain of private restaurants featured in the Brazilian soap opera, *Vale Todo* (*Anything Goes*), which was popular in Cuba in the early 1990s (Baker 2000: 153; LaFranchi 1996). However, while *Vale Todo* was making Cuban mouths water, the size of the legal self-employed sector was negligible and private restaurants were forbidden by law. Still, these speak-easy eateries began to sprout up through the cracks in the broken socialist system of food provision, responding to the growing scarcity of foodstuffs. Because these informal food service networks were providing an essential service to the Cuban population, they were largely tolerated. Their eventual legalization was an administrative response to a multitude of homegrown economic survival strategies (most of which were illegal) developed by the Cuban people (Whitefield 1993).

Essentially, the Cuban government was forced to legalize large sectors of the expanding informal economy because it had no way of preventing their growth and realized that underground activities were picking up the increasing slack left behind by the drastic contraction in state provisions, allowing Cubans (and ironically the socialist system itself) to survive (Domínguez 2001; Fernández 2000). In September 1993 the government issued a list of 117 self-employment activities. Included among the occupations were four food service activities, including what became known as the infamous *"et cetera"*—"producer of light snacks (refreshments, sweets, popsicles, et cetera)" (Decree Law 141, 1993: 4-5; Alonso 1993; CEPAL 1997).

In the months following the September announcement, scores of Cubans who were already active in the food service sector took out licenses to begin doing legally what they had up to then been doing clandestinely. However, in early December the government reversed its decision, since many Cubans who had obtained licenses were, in fact, running full-fledged restaurants under the broadest possible interpretation of *"et cetera."* Debates in the late-December 1993 National Assembly meetings over the offending *"et cetera"* declared it a mistake due to the *paladares'* encouragement of competition, dependence on pilfered supplies, and unlawful contracting of employees (Whitefield 1994a).

The refusal of many of Cuba's fledging restaurateurs to close up shop led to the first of many crackdowns against purported "illegalities, indiscipline, and abuses" in the self-employed sector in January and February 1994 (Scarpaci 1995; Scarpaci et al 2002; Whitefield 1994a, 1994b). Police raided and closed down over 100 *paladares* in Havana, charging their owners with illicit enrichment despite the fact many did possess a food service license (Scarpaci et al 2002: 234–259). In fact, despite the crackdown, the number of *paladares* was estimated at 4,000 nationwide in early 1994, with between 1,000 and 2,000 of these located in Havana (Whitefield 1994a; Farah 1994; Scarpaci et al 2002; Pérez-López 2001).

Resurrection and regulation (1995–1996). The second stage in the life cycle of the Cuban *paladar* began with the approval in June 1995 of Joint Resolution #4. This new law specifically addressed the previously suspended self-employment category of "producer of light snacks (*et cetera*)" and laid out three specific types of food service operations that would henceforth be allowed. The first category, *"al detalle,"* was intended for street vendors and required a monthly tax of 100 pesos. The second category, *"a domicilio,"* was aimed at caterers and required a 200-peso tax ($100 if business was done in dollars). The third category were true home-based, private restaurants, or *paladares.* Monthly taxes for these full-service peso-charging *paladares* were initially set at 500 pesos, while operations that charged customers in dollars were required to pay a tax of $400 per month ("Ampliación de actividades: Paladares" 1997). Finally, while no other self-employed activity is permitted to hire salaried employees, the state recognized that *paladares* had always operated with the help of a service and kitchen staff. Therefore, the law established a peculiar regulation prohibiting "salaried employees" on the one hand, while mandating that at least two "family helpers" be employed, on the other. Thus was born the fiction that *paladares* are family businesses.

At this stage the state placed severe limitations on the size and scope of the *paladares* in order to limit competition. The most well-known restriction is the seating limit of just "doce sillas" (twelve chairs). The law also restricted each household to a single self-employment license. Operators were forced to purchase their supplies and foodstuffs in the expensive state-run dollar stores or in private farmer's markets. There was no wholesale market available and no foods or ingredients from the state-subsidized bodegas could be resold in *paladares.* Because dollar stores were not prepared to provide customers with receipts, many entrepreneurs understood the requirement that they purchase supplies in dollar stores as the legal loophole that could be used to close them down at a future date (Scarpaci et al. 2002).

Along with the other legalized food service activities, *paladares* would be subject to unannounced visits from a number of different inspector corps. The restriction of employees to "family helpers" discriminates against those who lack kin and condemns *paladares* to continuous low productivity, forcing growth to take place through the proliferation of extremely small-scale units, wasting talent, and preventing economies of scale. Moreover, restrictions of access to credit and markets inhibit the natural growth of these businesses, while protecting state enterprises from competition (Ritter 2000; Dirmoser and Estay 1997: 485-487).

Statistics shared with the public at the time indicate that, after just one month in effect food service operations were already among the most common self-employed activities. *Granma* reported that in Havana, the five most common licenses were street vending and porch-front cafeterias, messenger, artisan, hair stylist, and private taxi drivers. By August 1995 Havana authorities had granted 278 *paladar* licenses out of 984 applications. However, perhaps signaling the beginning of a popular rejection of the new regulations, the overall number of registered self-employed workers in Havana dropped down to 58,000 by the end of 1995, from a peak of almost 64,000 in August. The number of registered self-employed workers in Havana would never again reach past the 60,000 mark, and by April 1997 had fallen to 35,171 (Martínez 1995: 2; Avendaño 1997; *DPPFA* 1997).

However, this drop in the number of licensed enterprises should not be interpreted to mean that Cubans had simply given up on this new opportunity to "resolve" their daily needs. Instead, my interviews with Havana's entrepreneurs indicate that many simply switched into clandestine operation since it seemed increasingly clear that the government was determined to use legalization as a mechanism of control. Thus, micro-entrepreneurs generally interpreted the new regulations as a signal that the government intended to make the rules all but impossible to follow. Such a conclusion, in turn, led many of them to develop elaborate survival strategies and turn more frequently to the black market to obtain expensive and scarce supplies.

Increased regulation and decline (1996–2000). Unfortunately for the operators of Cuba's *paladares*, the next few years of their existence coincided with a major shift in government policy. Whereas the period before December 1995 saw a gradual expansion of the number of allowed occupations from 117 to nearly 160, along with a concomitant rise in the total number of licensed operators (peaking at 208,786 in December 1995), few new occupations were legalized after that date and the issuance of new licenses in many areas was frozen indefinitely thereafter. The best gauge of the policy change is the precipitous fall in the numbers of registered self-employed workers and the near elimination of the once ubiquitous *paladar*. Legal and fiscal changes during these years included (1) the announcement in February 1996 of an increase in the monthly tax rates for many occupations, including the doubling of peso *paladar* rates to 1,000 pesos and raising dollar operations to $600, (2) the suspension of the granting of any new *paladar* licenses in Havana in April 1996, (3) a nationwide re-inscription of all self-employed workers begun in June 1996, and (4) a new comprehensive law aimed at strengthening the sanctions against the violators of self-employment regulations in June 1997 (Decree-Law #174, 1997).

New regulations for full-fledged *paladares* included a prohibition against having televisions, live music, or even a bar area where customers could have a drink while they wait for one of the proverbial twelve chairs to become vacant ("Sobre el ejerci-cio" 1996:4; Rodríguez Cruz 1996: 5). Additionally, all "family helpers" in the private food service sector would henceforth have to take out their own self-employment license and pay a monthly personal income tax equal to 20 percent of the tax paid by the *paladar* itself. In practice, this tax is usually paid by *paladar* operators them-selves, thus increasing their monthly tax once again to 1,400 pesos in the case of peso operations, and to $840 for dollar operations (Whitefield 1996a, 1996b; Mayoral 1996: 2; Lee 1996a: 2).

For example, in my interview with Patricia, the proprietor of *paladar "El Rin-concito,"* she explained that her monthly taxes had risen drastically over the six years she had been in business. Upon obtaining her license in 1995 she was required to pay just 500 pesos ($23) a month. Six years later, in January of 2001 when our in-terview took place, she was paying a total of $775 dollars a month to keep her li-cense (almost 34 times her previous monthly rate of $23). She also employed five people. However, only three of them were legally registered so as to avoid paying extra taxes.

When I asked Patricia how much she normally owed in taxes on top of her fixed monthly tax of $775, she laughed, saying that she paid just $15 on her 2000 tax return. Seeing my surprise, she explained, "Since the state is so aggressive in its en-forcement of the laws, we have no alternative but to respond with the same aggres-siveness when 'complying with' the law." She also justified her routine dissimula-tion, cheating, and misrepresentation by saying, "The system is set up such that it obliges us to lie in order to survive." The fact that there seems to be a law against everything has produced a climate where lawbreaking and cheating is commonplace and seen as part and parcel of doing business. "In order to survive, everyone is forced to become a 'criminal', leading to a generalized disrespect for law itself."

The final major law passed during this period, Decree-Law #174, outlined spe-cific penalties for self-employed workers who violated the law. For minor infrac-tions, fines range from 500 to 1,500 pesos, and were to be paid in dollars for busi-nesses operating in that currency. For more severe violations, in addition to the above fine, one's business license could be revoked for a period of two years. Finally, for the most severe violations, the government can revoke one's business license and seize all equipment (Decree-Law #174, 1997). Thus, while Cuban entrepreneurs are forced, almost without exception, into becoming "liars and hypocrites" out of frustration with unworkable restrictions, the state seems content to maintain the simplistic fiction that splits the self-employed into "honest and honorable" work-ers on one side and "abusive speculators and delinquents" on the other. This dual-istic image is propagated by the official press in an attempt to transfer blame for high levels of delinquency and corruption from impractical laws to "bad elements" within the private sector itself. Indeed, knowing that no registered operator wants to be grouped together with *macetas* (black marketeers), articles in the official me-dia often remind readers of their revolutionary duty to denounce the economic crimes of their neighbors to the proper authorities (Lee 1996c: 4).

Harsher laws, enforcement, and calls for vigilance against crime have paid off given the precipitous drop in the number of registered *paladares*. Of the 1,562 *pal-adares* that had successfully become registered by 1996, there were just 416 by Au-gust 1998 (just over half of them in Havana). Of these, only 253 were still left in 2000, two-thirds of them located in Havana. By 2003, various researchers and journalists have put the number of legally operating *paladares* at less than 200 in the entire country (Viño Zimerman 2001; Vicent 2000; Newman 2001; Duany 2001: 48; Escobal Rabeiro 2001; Jackiewicz and Bolster 2003). On my visit to Havana in April 2006, an anonymous government source confirmed that there were just 98 remaining licensed *paladares* in Havana (Lee 1998: 2; "No official market economy . . ." 2000: 4).

In the case of *paladares*, it is ironic that enterprises that have survived to date have been forced by legal limitations and high taxes to raise their prices, charging an increasingly exclusive (and almost exclusively foreign) clientele in dollars (Holgado Fernández 2000). This is a significant change compared with the initial relatively low peso prices and decidedly domestic function of most *paladares* in the first half of the decade. Such a shift is even more unfortunate given the great difficulty most Cubans already have in procuring enough food. It seems that Raúl Castro's surprisingly bold declaration in 1994, that "if there is food for the people, the risks do not matter," no longer applies, or at least not to the risks presented by private restaurants. Indeed, the fact that *paladares* no longer serve the consumption needs of the Cuban population may be the perfect pretext for the government to continue its repressive policies against them (Scarpaci 1995; Scarpaci et al 2002; Castro, R. 1997: 466).

Economic recentralization and offensive against self-employment (2001–2006). Since 2001, internal Cuban economic policy has gradually shifted away from the market reforms of the early 1990s toward more centralized control of the economy. The granting of new self-employment licenses in many occupations has been discontinued and many licensed micro-enterprises have been forced out of business or underground by a predatory tax structure and stepped-up public attacks on entrepreneurs as corrupt "new rich." The three areas of self-employment most directly affected by this new offensive and most commonly criticized in the official Cuban press are private transport (taxis, cargo trucks, and pedicabs), bed and breakfast operations, and *paladares*. In fact, since Cuba's economy stabilized by the late 1990s and has since shown signs of incipient growth, the government has been able to gradually scale back the opening in the domestic economy by limiting or wholly eliminating many internal economic reforms. The fate of self-employment is the clearest example of this retrenchment.

In the summer of 2003, new regulations were announced against bed and breakfast operators that included raising overall tax rates, requiring all operators to pay an additional 30 percent tax for providing meals to their guests, charging an additional tax on common areas of the home used by renters, limiting renting to a maximum of two rooms with just two guests per room, prohibiting hiring anyone from outside the family, revoking the right to rent out an entire apartment, and requiring that a family member always be present in the home. This laundry list of new regulations against a type of self-employment, only first legalized in 1997 (Henken 2002), was justified based on the conviction that "negative tendencies and behaviors have emerged in the exercise of this activity that distort the very essence of renting" (Resolución No. 270, 2003). At the same time, by 2003 the overall number of registered self-employment operators had dropped to a new low of 100,000 from 208,500 in 1995 and 153,800 in 2001 (Grogg 2003).

At the same time, a new set of self-employment restrictions was enacted that included the suspension of new licenses in forty occupations, including licenses for such specific and seemingly innocuous occupations as magicians, party clowns, sellers of used books, makers of crowns of flowers, masseuses, and newspaper vendors (Resolución 11, 2004). Also included on this list were all four food service occupations: street vendors, cafeterias, caterers, and *paladares*. This change reduced to 118 from 158 the number of self-employment occupations for which licenses were still available. Moreover, *paladar* operators were instructed that their required three (up from two) family helpers must have been members of the family or co-residents in the home for at least the three preceding years (Resolución 11, 2004).

Finally, towards the end of 2005, the Cuban government kicked off an ideological campaign that included a crackdown on corruption, theft, pilfering, and the "new rich." In a six-hour speech, delivered on November 17 to students at the University of Havana, an aged but energized Castro called for nothing short of a cultural revolution. He declared a return to an egalitarian society and hinted that this "total renewal" of Cuban society would include drastic moves to eliminate rising differences between Cuba's haves and have-nots. Castro also publicly disclosed the existence of a multi-pronged government "Death to Corruption Operation," authorizing military intervention in the Port of Havana, where the embezzlement of merchandise from arriving container shipments had become pervasive. Most surprisingly, he revealed that he had replaced all of Havana's gas station attendants over the previous month with as many as 28,000 young social workers in order to counteract what later turned out to be the systematic pilfering and black market resale of fully half of the city's gas. Similar government social worker takeovers were carried out in many of the city's bakeries and *bodegas* (rationed goods stores). The fall offensive also included raids against farmers' markets, illegal satellite TV access, and Old Havana's ubiquitous private pedicabs (Ritter 2006).

In his speech, Castro zeroed in specifically and repeatedly on the self-employed, attacking them as the backbone of the rising class of "new rich." He specifically singled out taxi drivers, bed and breakfast operators, and *paladar* owners as the most egregious flouters of socialist morality. "The abuses will end," railed Castro. "Many of the inequalities will disappear, as will the conditions that allowed them to exist." Stressing the seriousness of the threat of economic crime and corruption, Castro declared, "In this battle against vice, nobody will be spared. Either we will defeat all these deviations and make our revolution strong, or we die." Finally, referring to U.S. promotion of private enterprise in Cuba, he reminded his listeners that self-employment has no real future in a socialist Cuba. "The empire was hoping that Cuba would have many more '*paladares*' but it appears that there will be no more of them. What do they think that we have become—neo-liberals? No one here has become a neo-liberal" (Castro, F. 2005).

SURVIVING UNDERGROUND

For every unreasonable legal restriction placed on *paladares*, entrepreneurs have developed specific strategies to circumvent those restrictions. Quite literally, Cuba's *paladar* operators have taken inspiration from the Brazilian soap opera "*Vale Todo*" (*Anything Goes*), despite (or perhaps precisely because of) the many legal restrictions. The most common strategies that micro-enterprisers have developed in the face of the onerous legal requirements include the serving of forbidden foods, the use of hidden rooms with additional place-settings, the printing and distribution of business cards, and the increasingly common presence of *paladar* sites on the Internet. Also, *paladares* make common use of intermediaries (to whom they pay illegal commissions), rely on black-market goods, and purchase bogus receipts to account for those goods.

Because of the high retail prices and limited supplies in the dollar stores and farmers' markets, *paladar* proprietors often turn to the "wholesale" prices of the black market. In the case of the few remaining large-scale operations, more egregious violations are common. For example, while nearly all *paladares* employ non-family workers, large-scale operations are often staffed by a small army of employees, including professional cooks, private security personnel, taxi drivers, and troupes of musicians who entertain guests with live music. The availability of rooms for lodging, drastic underreporting of earnings, and special "arrangements" with the inspector corps are salient features of some of these high-end operations. One negative side effect of the use of such strategies is that it tends to push smaller operations that are unable to afford them out of business, resulting in the survival of a small number of lucrative and/or well-connected large-scale operations (Fernández Peláez 2000; Ritter 2000).

Taken together, the common use of most of the above survival strategies by licensed *paladar* operators contradicts the assumption that illegality is the result of a lack of adequate top-down control, a deficiency in revolutionary consciousness, or the delinquency of a few individuals out to exploit the masses and "live off the work of others." Undoubtedly, there are those who abuse the system for personal gain, but the vast majority of entrepreneurs help make a notoriously inefficient system work more effectively while providing jobs, goods, and services to a population in need. Instead of recognizing and encouraging the positive contribution that entrepreneurship could make to the country's economic recovery, the state's antagonistic legal framework creates an ideological environment where entrepreneurship, even when legal, is still not considered legitimate.

CONCLUSION: BETWEEN TOLERATION AND PATERNALISM

In an April 1997 *Granma* article citing the need to mobilize Cuba's Committees for the Defense of the Revolution in the battle against growing economic crime, National Assembly President Ricardo Alarcón expressed the following sentiment toward the island's *paladares*:

> We mustn't be confused by the "miracles" which they attribute to [self-employment]. The richest ones, such as the *paladares*, would do well to ask themselves first, in what home if not the one given them by the Revolution would they have been able to set up shop and second, if in a capitalist society, the owner of those houses would have permitted one of his tenants to set up a restaurant in one of his properties. If capitalism were to return to Cuba, it would sweep them away. (Lee 1997)

The lesson here could not be clearer. The Cuban state sees itself as a generous landlord (*estado patrón*) who has permitted his unappreciative tenants to go into business in what, after all, is not really their property, but the patrimony of the revolution

(Escobal Rabeiro 2001). Such an attitude reveals the profound paternalism with which the revolutionary leadership views Cuba's fledgling micro-entrepreneurs.

Similarly, in a November 1997 *Granma* article, Raúl Valdés Vivo, the director of the Communist Party's ideological school and a member of the Party's Central Committee, rejected claims that it was unfair to allow for foreign investment while prohibiting domestic capitalists to participate more fully in the island's economy. Comparing the latter group to "piranhas. . . capable in a minimum of time of devouring a horse down to the bones" (Rice 1997), Valdés Vivo stated that the leadership had been forced to resort to capitalist investments from abroad against its will and claimed that Cuban nationals could not have provided the necessary capital, technology, or markets brought by outsiders.

As this study of Cuba's fledgling *paladares* has shown, the Cuban leadership's characteristic paternalism seems determined to choke out all autonomous economic activities, seeing them as threats to its top-down control. Existing policy treats most of these entrepreneurs as an anachronism, whose role in the economy will decidedly decrease as the socialist economy recovers. Such an antagonistic policy only discourages the growth of *paladares*, drives most entrepreneurs out of business or underground, provokes tax evasion, and encourages operators to develop deeper links with the informal sector, all leading to an even greater distrust of the government and socializing entrepreneurs further in criminality as their only means of survival. The few large-scale operations which benefit from economies of scale and special government connections tend to thrive, while the majority are condemned to informality. Moreover, the conspicuous financial success of a select few operations in a context of generalized economic hardship and growing inequality has made it easy for the government to target them as "new rich" exploiters and justify new crackdowns and closings since the fall of 2005. In summary, the emergence of Cuba's *paladares* over the last decade teaches the following lesson: the state's paternalistic desire to regulate and restrict their growth has transformed what was hoped to be a true expansion of the private micro-enterprise sector into another mechanism of state control over the economy.

NOTES

An earlier version of this article was published in the proceedings of the annual conference of the Association for the Study of the Cuban Economy, under the title, "Vale Todo" (Anything Goes): Cuba's Paladares," *Cuba in Transition*, Volume 12, pp. 344–353, 2003. lanic.utexas.edu/project/asce/pdfs/volume12/henken.pdf. The names of all places and individuals have been changed to protect anonymity. Descriptions of individual enterprises are composite sketches of two or more similar enterprises. All translations from interviews, newspaper articles, or scholarly work were done by the author.

1. See especially the newspaper reports by Whitefield (1994a, 1994b, 1996a, 1996b) and LaFranchi (1996), as well as the more scholarly studies by Pérez-López (1995), Scarpaci (1995), Núñez Moreno (1997), Peters and Scarpaci (1998), Ritter (1998, 2000), Fernández Peláez (2000), Duany (2001), Scarpaci et al (2002), and Jackiewicz and Bolster (2003).

REFERENCES

Alonso, José. 1993. "An Analysis of Decree 141 Regarding Cuban Small-Scale Enterprises." *La Sociedad Económica Bulletin* 35, September 20.

"Ampliación de actividades: Paladares." 1997. Joint Resolution #4, June 8, 1995. In *Economía y reforma económica en Cuba*, edited by Dietmar Dirmoser and Jaime Estay, 485–487. Caracas: Nueva Sociedad.

Avendaño, Bárbara. 1997. "Trabajadores por cuenta propia. Incremento de las cuotas fijas mensuales." (*Tribuna de La Habana*, May 5, 1996). In *Economía y reforma económica en Cuba*, edited by D. Dirmoser and Jaime Estay, 496–497. Caracas: Nueva Sociedad.

Baker, Christopher P. 2000. *Cuba: Moon Handbooks*. Second edition. Emeryville, CA: Avalon Travel Publishing.

Castro, Fidel. 2005. "Discurso pronunciado por Fidel Castro Ruz en el acto por el aniversario 60 de su ingreso a la universidad," Havana, November 17. Available online in English at: www.cuba.cu/gobierno/discursos/2005/ing/f171105i.html.

Castro, Raúl. 1997. "Si hay comida para el pueblo, no importan los riesgos." (*Granma Internacional*, September 28, 1994). In *Economía y reforma económica en Cuba*, edited by Dietmar Dirmoser and Jaime Estay, 458–467. Caracas: Nueva Sociedad.

CEPAL (Comisión Económica para América Latina y el Caribe). 1997. *La economía cubana: Reformas estructurales y desempeño en los noventa*. México: Fondo de Cultura Económica.

"Cuba will not allow citizens to open businesses." 1998. *Caribbean Update*, January.

Decree-Law #141. 1993. "Sobre el trabajo por cuenta propia." *Granma*, September 9.

Decree-Law #174. 1997. "De las contravenciones personales de las regulaciones de trabajo por cuenta propia." *Gaceta oficial*, June 30.

DPPFA (Dirección Provincial de Planificación Física y Arquitectura). 1997. "Diagnóstico de Población," Havana, July.

Dirmoser, Dietmar, and Jaime Estay, eds. 1997. *Economía y reforma económica en Cuba*. Caracas: Nueva Sociedad.

Domínguez, Jorge. 2001. "Why the Cuban Regime Has Not Fallen." In *Cuban Communism*, Tenth edition, edited by Irving Louis Horowitz and Jaime Suchlicki, 533–545. New Brunswick: Transaction Publishers.

Duany, Jorge. 2001. "Redes, remesas y paladares: La diáspora cubana desde una perspectiva transnacional." *Nueva Sociedad* 174, July–August: 40–51.

Escobal Rabeiro, Vicente. 2001. "Las pequeñas y medianas empresas en Cuba," Instituto Cubano de Investigaciones Sociolaborales y Económicas Independiente, *CubaNet*. www.cubanet.org/sindical/docs/d10020001.html.

Farah, Douglas. 1994. "Speak-Easy Eateries Attract Diners with Dollars in Food-Short Havana," *Washington Post*, February 16: A9, A14.

Fernández, Damián. 2000. *Cuba and the Politics of Passion*. Austin: University of Texas Press.

Fernández Peláez, Neili. 2000. *Trabajo por cuenta propia en Cuba: Disarticulación y reacción*. Senior Thesis, Department of Sociology, University of Havana, July.

Grogg, Patricia. 2003. "Landlords on the Verge of a Nervous Breakdown," Inter Press Service, Global Information Network, July 4.

Henken, Ted. 2002. "Cuba's Experiments with Self-Employment during the Special Period (The Case of the Bed and Breakfasts." *Cuban Studies* 33, pp. 1–29.

Holgado-Fernández, Isabel. 2000. *¡No es fácil! Mujeres cubanas y la crisis revolucionaria*. Barcelona: Icaria editorial.

Jackiewicz, Edward L. and Todd Bolster. 2003. "The Working World of the Paladar: The Production of Contradictory Space during Cuba's Period of Fragmentation." *Professional Geographer* 55: 3 (August), pp. 372–382.

Jatar-Hausmann, Ana Julia. 1999. *The Cuban Way: Communism, Capitalism, and Confrontation*. West Hartford, CT: Kumarian Press.

LaFranchi, Howard. 1996. "Cuba's Enterprising Cooks Open Their Homes: Since Castro's government legalized small, private eateries, 'paladares' keep popping up," *Christian Science Monitor*, May 9.

Lee, Susana. 1996a. "Entra hoy en vigor Nuevo Reglamento del TPCP," *Granma*, p. 2, June 1.

———. 1996b. "Trabajo por cuenta propia: una reflexión necesaria," *Granma*, p. 4, September 13.

———. 1996c. "TPCP: hay que combatir el desorden," *Granma*, p. 4, September 19.

———. 1997. "La batalla contra las ilegalidades y las indisciplinas sociales no se ganará sin los CDR," *Granma*, April 25: 3.

———. 1998. "El impuesto de los 'paladares'," *Granma*, p. 2, November 12.

Martínez, Silvia. 1995. "Regulan ejercicio del trabajo por cuenta propia," *Granma*, August 17.

Mayoral, María Julia. 1996. "Comienza reinscripción de los trabajadores por cuenta propia," *Granma*, June 21: 2.

Newman, Lucia. 2001. "Cuba squeezes private business as economy grows," *CNN*, March 12.

"No official market economy for Cuba: sharp decline in numbers of small entrepreneurs." 2000. *Latin American, Caribbean, and Central American Report*, August 22.

Núñez Moreno, Lilia. "Mas allá del cuentapropismo en Cuba." *Temas* 11.

Pérez-López, Jorge F. 1994. "Islands of Capitalism in an Ocean of Socialism: Joint Ventures in Cuba's Development Strategy." In *Cuba at a Crossroads: Politics and Economics after the Fourth Party Congress*. Gainesville: University Press of Florida.

———. 1995. *Cuba's Second Economy: From Behind the Scenes to Center Stage*. New Brunswick: Transaction.

———. 2001. "Cuba's Socialist Economy: the Mid-1990s." In *Cuban Communism*, Tenth edition, edited by Irving Louis Horowitz and Jaime Suchlicki, 205–236. New Brunswick: Transaction Publishers.

Peters, Phillip, and Joseph L. Scarpaci. 1998. "Cuba's New Entrepreneurs: Five Years of Small-Scale Capitalism." Arlington: Alexis de Tocqueville Institution. Available at adti.net/html_files/cuba/TCPSAVE.htm.

Resolución No. 270. 2003. "Reglamento sobre el arrendamiento de viviendas, habitaciones o espacios." Instituto Nacional de Vivienda, June 5.

Resolución No. 11. 2004. "Reglamento sobre el trabajo por cuenta propia." *Gaceta Oficial Ordinaria*, No. 32—Ministerio de Trabajo y Seguro Social, May 11.

Rice, John. 1997. "Cuban official signals limits on capitalism," *Miami Herald*, November 28.

Ritter, Archibald R. M. 1998. "Entrepreneurship, Micro-enterprise, and Public Policy in Cuba: Promotion, Containment, or Asphyxiation?" *Journal of International Studies and World Affairs* 40:2 (Summer): 63–94.

———. 2000. "El regimen impositivo para la microempresa en Cuba." *Revista de la CEPAL* 71: 145–162, August.

———. 2006. "Cuba's Economic Reorientation." Paper presented at the Bildner Center symposium, "Cuba: In Transition? Pathways to Renewal, Long-Term Development and Global Reintegration," March 30–31, 2006. Proceedings edited by Mauricio A. Font and Scott Larson. Available at web.gc.cuny.edu/dept/bildn/cuba/documents/CITBookFMpdfbychapter_000.pdf.

Rodríguez Cruz, Francisco. 1996. "La cuenta propia también es cuenta nuestra," *Trabajadores*, June 3: 5.

Scarpaci, Joseph L. 1995. "The Emerging Food and *Paladar* Market in Havana." *Cuba in Transition* 5 (ASCE): 74–84.

———. Roberto Segre, and Mario Coyula. 2002. *Havana: Two Faces of the Antillean Metropolis*. (Revised Edition). Chapel Hill: The University of North Carolina Press.

"Sobre el ejercicio del trabajo por cuenta propia." 1996. Joint Resolution #1, *Trabajadores*, June 3: 4–5.

Vicent, Mauricio. 2000. "'Paladares' de La Habana," *El País*, December 10: 6–7.

Viño Zimerman, Luís. 2001. "Política de exterminio de la iniciativa privada," *CubaNet News*, No. 32, April 1.

Whitefield, Mimi. 1993. "Rapid changes push Cuba into unknown: Will reforms spin out of control?" *Miami Herald*, September 27.

———. 1994a. "Cuban home eateries refuse to close shop: Undeterred by government order," *Miami Herald*, January 7.

———. 1994b. "Cuba tries to reign in market abuses," *Miami Herald*, January 29.

———. 1996a. "A Taste of Capitalism," *Miami Herald*, May 19.

———. 1996b. "The taxman comes to Cuba," *Miami Herald*, June 9.

16

Dollarization and Its Discontents in the Post-Soviet Era

Susan Eckstein

Cuba's world changed in 1991 with the Soviet Union's demise. At the time, trade accounted for about half the island's gross national product, with the Soviet bloc accounting for 85 percent of that trade. In hopes of bringing the weakened regime to heel, Washington tightened the embargo. But partly because Castro put ideology aside and found ways to reintegrate into the hard-currency-based world economy, Cuba withstood the domino collapse of Soviet bloc Communism and stepped-up U.S. economic strangulation. Most important, ordinary Cubans sought solutions to their own plight, also by putting ideology aside. They reached out to family in the diaspora for help. After three decades of limited contact between Cubans who stayed and those who fled the revolution, ties resumed. Kinship bonds proved more durable than political commitments. In the process, life on the island became transnationalized and transformed. In place of integration into the "international socialist division of labor" at the state level, Cubans became absorbed into networks and norms spanning the Florida Straits at the people-to-people level. They did so at the same time that U.S.-Cuban bilateral relations remained, in the main, frozen in the Cold War. To a lesser degree and with fewer social and economic consequences, Cubans sought ways to secure dollars domestically, typically informally and often also illegally.

From the government's and party's vantage point, the informal dollarization proved a double-edged sword. In the post-Soviet era all international transactions shifted to hard currency, but state activity alone generated an insufficient amount to cover needed and desired imports and foreign debt repayments and to finance income-generating investments. Dollars islanders secured on their own that the state managed to access became an essential official convertible currency revenue source. However, the dollarization generated as well as resolved regime problems. It had the effect of eroding state sector productivity, socialist values, and socialist bases of stratification and legitimation. What was good for dollar recipients proved a "mixed bag" for the state. Contradictions between state and societal interests were not new to the 1990s, but the forms they took and the effects they had were new.

REMITTANCES: CUBAN AMERICANS TO THE RESCUE

Consistent with the general Latin American trend but breaking with the Soviet era situation, remittances became one of Cuba's main sources of hard currency. Latin American offices of the United Nations (the Economic Commission on Latin America and the Caribbean [ECLAC]) report that cross-border people-to-people money transfers surged from $50 million in 1990 to above $700 million at the decade's end.[1] By the turn of the century remittances brought in more dollars than any single island export and about twice as much money as the government attracted in foreign investment.

Castro's government had remained committed to social welfare provisioning, including rationing, to ensure affordably priced food for all. But official allotments throughout the post-Soviet era covered no more than half of monthly family needs. Domestic production had become so depressed that the government used its limited hard-currency revenue to purchase U.S. farm products that it made available to ordinary Cubans through the ration system, at highly subsidized prices: chicken and flour for three cents a pound, rice for four cents per pound, and eggs for two cents each in 2002–2003.[2] This was a political decision, one deepening the budgetary deficit that had been on the rise since the late 1990s. In the absence of such subsidies, however, Cubans would have faced even more difficulty feeding themselves on their salaries in the new economy, a situation likely to have been politically explosive.

Cubans sought their own creative solutions to declining homeland income-generating opportunities by reaching out to family abroad with whom they had had little contact for three decades as a result of opposing views toward the revolution. In the time of crisis, though, families divided by the revolution put their political differences aside. Overseas kin came to islanders' rescue.

Similar to other Latin Americans, Cubans used remittances mainly to finance family subsistence.[3] But some relatives in the diaspora also subsidized materialist consumption the revolution had scorned.[4] So too did some overseas relatives finance home improvements. The government continued to guarantee that no one paid more than 10 percent of earnings on housing, and 85 percent of Cubans owned their dwelling unit, therefore paying no rent whatsoever.[5] However, the housing stock was in severe disrepair by the 1990s.

Overseas kin on occasion also financed small businesses, in defiance of the U.S. embargo and sometimes also of Cuban laws. Cuban regulations restricted private business opportunities, whether or not remittance based. Although authorities expanded the types of private activity permitted as state sector employment options contracted with the crisis, they required businesses to be owner-operated, to employ only family members, and to pay high (and regressive) taxes, including in hard currency. As a result of the combined constraints, the self-employed, whether or not drawing on remittances, reportedly earned on average a mere thirty-four dollars monthly at the turn of the new century.[6] Such earnings may appear a poor return to so-called migradollar investment or base for capital accumulation on any scale. Yet, they contributed somewhat to macroeconomic growth and to reduced dependence of Cubans on the goodwill of family abroad. Moreover, when converted at the unofficial exchange rate at the time of the survey, average earnings of the self-employed equaled 650 pesos, about two and one-half times the then average state employee monthly salary.

As ordinary Cuban Americans reached out to their island family, Washington sought to contain the people-to-people monetary flows. It hoped thereby both to limit Cuban government access to dollars it desperately needed and to build up grassroots island pressure for regime change. Legislation set a three-hundred-dollar cap on permissible quarterly transfers (with Washington prohibiting all US.-to-Cuba income transfers for three years), at a time when Latin Americans remitted, on average, two hundred dollars eight times a year.[7] Washington imposed no remittance cap on other Latin American immigrants.

Cuban Americans appear to comply with Washington's dollar-sending ceiling. In 1999 the mean Cuban-American remittance was around seventy dollars monthly. However, the average includes both émigrés who send and those who do not send money. Interviews I conducted between 2000 and 2002 in Miami and Union City, the two main Cuban-American settlements, suggest that if Cuban Americans want to send more than permitted, they do so, but informally.[8]

At least 65 percent of remittance dollars are believed to be transferred in ways that bypass U.S. regulations[9]: on family visits or via *mulas*, neighborhood-based middlemen who as of the 1990s made a business of transporting unreported money (as well as goods) across the Florida Straits.[10] Less frequently, Cuban Americans send money through new neighborhood-based "minibanks," informal ventures that also circumvent U.S. and Cuban regulations; the unregistered "bankers" transmit money for a fee that Cuban family and friends can withdraw from island "bank partners" almost immediately. The informal transfer mechanisms not only are typically cheaper than officially sanctioned wire services but also leave no paper trail. The embargo officially requires affidavits for income transfers.

Ironically, Cuban Americans rely on informal remittance channels more than do immigrants typically from the less-regulated economies in the region not subject to embargo restrictions.[11] U.S. regulations have had the unintended effect of inducing Cuban Americans to prefer informal cross-border transfer mechanisms. Affidavits caused uneasiness among Cubans wary of government on both sides of the Florida Straits and limited the amount Cubans could send at any one time.

The remittance economy thus reflects a transnationally grounded society able and willing to operate according to its own networks and norms, in defiance of both U.S. and Cuban official regulations that stand in the way. As subaltern studies alert us to, ordinary people may undermine what seemingly strong states can do, in patterned ways informally, covertly, and illegally through so-called everyday forms of resistance. Cubans' turn to the diaspora, the way they acquired dollars, and the uses they made of the money, all reveal a stronger society and weaker state than theories of state socialism suggest and than a socialist state desirous of regulating the economy would choose. So too do they reveal limits to the influence of Washington even once it became the uncontested world superpower in the post-Soviet era. The dollar became Cubans' currency of choice while U.S.-Cuban bilateral relations remained largely frozen in the Cold War.

STATE REMITTANCE AND OTHER INFORMAL DOLLARIZATION-LINKED INITIATIVES

Although ordinary Cubans took the initiative to reach out to the diaspora for assistance, the hard-currency-needing Cuban government had its own interest in luring remittances. It accordingly sought to channel the people-to-people flows to its treasury, though with institutional and moral ambivalence. The leadership understood that the informal transnational dollar flows were difficult to regulate and embedded in social networks and norms that defied precepts of the revolution. The Communist Party Central Committee, for example, worried that dollars were ideologically contaminating, encouraging individualism and materialism.[12] Yet in this respect as well moral principles became a luxury authorities could no longer honor.

The government's most important remittance-friendly initiative was legalization of dollar possession, in 1993. Informal dollarization had become so pervasive that repressing it was nearly impossible, practically or politically. In making legal what had been transpiring illegally, the government could, in theory, regulate the activity better. And without fear of dollar confiscation and arrest, Cuban Americans could be expected to be more inclined to send money (or give it, on visits) and islanders to want the foreign money more. However, dollar legalization led islanders to covet the hard currency not merely through remittances but also through other means, such as through tourism and new wage supplements (offered even in state sector jobs to motivate labor).

Soon after legalizing dollar possession, authorities developed a strategy that simultaneously addressed islanders' consumer yearnings and state institutional interests in appropriating for its own use the foreign money informally circulating. Cubans gained the right to shop at official dollar stores previously reserved for diplomats and other foreigners, and the government expanded the range of dollar stores and their stock. Dollar stores offered items unavailable through the ration system, or not available in quantities islanders wanted (including in 2002, for the first time, U.S. name-brand processed food products). The very name of the dollar outlets, Hard Currency Recuperation Stores, made transparent the state's objective. Net dollars recuperated could finance imports, the foreign debt, and investments. And in recuperating the dollars the government could, in principle, regulate economic activity according to its priorities and plans.

In implementing the consumer strategy, the former antimaterialist regime, however, became a chief agent as well as a beneficiary of materialism. The consumer strategy became so important that, as of 1997, two-thirds of the state's hard-currency income from production was from sales at official retail stores, compared to 11 percent from exports, and 22 percent from supplies sold to the tourist sector.[13] And by the turn of the century sales at CIMEX stores, the largest state-linked retail chain, reached $420 million, nearly the same amount the government then grossed from sugar exports.[14]

By selling items at considerable markup, the government, moreover, profited from dollar store sales. Authorities justified what they claimed to be an ideal markup, 240 percent above cost (especially of imported items), on equity grounds[15]: a hidden tax on dollar-holder spending to support programs benefiting those without dollar access. Official rationale aside, the government manipulated prices at the dollar stores to its own fiscal advantage, at consumers' expense. In 2002, for example, the government raised prices in the official retail outlets to offset revenue losses from other sources. The price hikes contributed to an 8 percent consumer price inflation.[16]

The government also set up exchange booths, CADECAs (bureaus of change), that honored the informal "street level" dollar-for-pesos exchange rate. It hoped thereby to soak up dollars not spent at dollar stores. The "street rate" gave dollarholders more pesos, at the state's expense, than conversion at the official one-to-one exchange rate would. But insistence on the official exchange rate would have induced Cubans to exchange the foreign currency illegally and informally, as they had before legalization of dollar possession in 1993. Accordingly, the CADECA exchange rate reflects yet another state accommodation to society.

The government set up exchange booths in farmers' markets it reintroduced in 1994. Previously permitted private markets had been closed down during the period of "rectification of errors and negative tendencies" because they allegedly created inequities and too many millionaires. The food crisis led the government, however, to view markets where farmers could sell surplus they produced beyond their commitments to the state at unregulated prices as a necessary production stimulus.[17] Food scarcities fueled not only a runaway black market but also the largest public protest under Castro, in August of 1994. But the government required sales at the newly opened markets to be peso-based, to prevent dollars from continuing to circulate informally in the economy. At exchange booths located in markets, buyers could easily trade their dollars for pesos before making purchases.[18]

The government, in turn, modified savings and fiscal policies to capture dollars in people's hands. It instituted interest-bearing dollar bank accounts, to stimulate savings. And it introduced personal taxes on the self-employed, in hard currency as well as in pesos, to broaden its revenue base.

The government even entered the remittance business, to profit from cross-border transfers. Because of the embargo it could not set up direct wire or bank services in the United States. Beginning in 1999, though, it established partnerships with such internationally renowned money transfer businesses as Western Union, and then with the Canadian firm TransCard (affiliated with MoneyGram in the United States). The agencies charged remittance senders higher fees for transfers to Cuba than to Mexico, Central America, and elsewhere in the Caribbean.[19] The higher rates enabled the Cuban government to get a share of the service charges, at a time when the Inter-American Development Bank and other Latin American governments sought to lower transaction costs so that recipients received more of the money immigrants allotted for remittances and intermediaries received less.

For remittances to be forthcoming, overseas Cubans had to be convinced not merely to forgo earnings but to send money to a regime they typically despised politically. To temper hostilities, the government modified its public stance toward the diaspora, facilitated transnational bonding, and more openly supported economically motivated migration. Authorities redefined émigrés previously pejoratively portrayed as *gusanos*, worms, as the "Cuban community abroad." And the government opened a special office within the Ministry of Foreign Relations to foster ties with the diaspora.

The Cuban government, moreover, increased the number of Cuban Americans it allowed to visit and reduced restrictions on émigré visits. The government introduced multiple-entry visas and permitted longer visits than in the past. It also allowed Cuban Americans for the first time to stay with island relatives. Cuban Americans took advantage of the easing of restrictions. Their visits rose from an estimated 7,000 in 1990 to some 100,000 a decade later.[20]

Psychological and political barriers that had hampered cross-border bonding broke down as families divided by the revolution reestablished ties. The bonding, in turn, inclined overseas family to help island family economically. Cuban Americans do not visit empty-handed. They take money, as well as medications, consumer goods, and other gifts. And the informal bonding makes visiting family more likely to send money upon return to their adopted homeland. From the government's vantage point, however, the new visit permissiveness was politically risky if economically rational. Officials faced the possibility of "another Mariel," the 1980 mass exodus that followed the one previous large-scale travel opening. The deep economic recession and desperation for dollars led the government to take the political risk.

INDIVIDUAL AND INSTITUTIONAL FORCES SHAPING REMITTANCE FLOWS

The Cuban diaspora remains dominated, from the vantage point of remittance-coveting Cubans, by the "wrong immigrants."[21] For one, studies show recent émigrés to remit most. Second, studies show refugees to remit less to their homeland than economic immigrants. Many pre-1980 Cuban émigrés, who constitute about two-thirds of all Cubans in the United States, continue to envision themselves as exiles. The more recent émigrés, however, resemble the archetypal economic immigrant, predisposed to remittance sending. Indeed, island families now strategize to send a member with income-earning, and therefore remittance-sending potential, abroad.

Institutional differences further explain why Cubans have been less successful in transforming their transnationalized families into economic assets. Washington restricts Cuban but not other Latin American émigré homeland visits, as well as remittance sending. Meanwhile, the Cuban government sets barriers to transnational ties. Although Cuban authorities reduced, they never eliminated barriers to cross-border bonding, and they continue to restrict (along with U.S. law) diasporic investment. Cuban Americans accordingly have incentive to send money mainly only for consumption.

Furthermore, the Cuban-American community leadership discourages remittance sending. A "hard-line" minority, whom disapproving Cuban Americans call "radical exiles," at the turn of the century remained hostile to cross-border ties, even if increasingly more often in public discourse than in private practice. These exiles silenced Cuban Americans who disagreed with them. Émigrés who disapproved of the personal embargo, that is, of the ban on people-to-people cross-border contact, felt that radio talk show hosts refused to let them on the air and that newspapers refused to publish their editorials. Cuban Americans with media access discouraged transnational bonding and remittance sending.

Lingering effects of earlier cross-border political hostilities at the personal level further stood in the way of remittance sending, among families transnationalized before the 1990s. For three decades Cuban authorities convinced most islanders to sever or minimize ties with exiles who rejected the revolution and denied those with ties access to the party and to job promotions. At the same time, some exiles refused to maintain ties with communist island relatives. As a consequence, by the 1990s some transnationalized families were divided beyond repair. In such instances Cubans were without activatable cross-border networks.

Politics led other exiles, including "radical exiles," to respond only sparingly to island family appeals. This was true, for example, of a Union City journalist I interviewed in 2001, who in print opposed remittance sending, and of an embargo advocate Miami radio-show host interviewed on *60 Minutes* in December that same year. Neither practiced what he preached, but they sent island siblings only enough money that they "wouldn't die." Reflecting the continued reluctance among a considerable number of ordinary Americans to send money to kin in a regime they despised, 74 percent of the Miami-based diaspora surveyed in 2000 by Florida International University reported having close relatives on the island, but only 40 percent said they or other Miami relatives sent money.[22]

THE IMPACT OF INFORMAL DOLLARIZATION

The informal dollarization generated a range of consequences, many of which neither remittance senders nor recipients had foreseen or intended. Its impact was far more than economic, and economically its impact permeated the peso economy. From the state's vantage point, the informal dollarization eroded state control over the economy, society, and moral order, while generating much needed hard-currency revenue.

Remittances, which are embedded in social ties that transcend the country's borders, accounted for an estimated 70 percent of the dollars Cubans informally accessed as of 2002.[23] With the cross-border relationships and income transfers came new values, new contradictions, and new tensions. Meanwhile, a desire for domestically obtainable dollars further eroded the socialist order.

Informal dollarization, for one, generated new bases of inequality in a society that under Castro had been committed to leveling historical disparities. Access to remittances, as well as to other dollar sources, is heavily race based. The diaspora is predominantly white. As of the late 1990s, 96 percent of all Cuban immigrants in the United States classified themselves as white.[24] Blacks, who in prerevolutionary Cuba were the most disadvantaged group, benefited most under Castro—relative to their situation under Batista. For this reason they were disinclined to emigrate, a loyalty that put them at a decided disadvantage in the emergent cross-border-based informal dollarized economy.[25]

A report by the Center for Anthropology of the Ministry of Science, Technology and Environment found that one-eighth to one-third as many blacks as whites had access to remittances. Making matters worse, the study found whites also more likely than blacks to access dollars through tourism, including through so-called informal tourism, islanders' other main foreign source of hard currency. Informal tourism includes money made on the side, such as tips, through the formal tourist sector and other state sector jobs catering to visiting foreigners, and money made from private room rentals, family-owned restaurants, sales of handmade crafts, and prostitution catering to travelers. Whites were found to be 1.6 times more likely than blacks to receive tips and to hold 80 percent of the dollar economy employment while constituting 60 percent of the population.[26]

Remittance flows also are geographically concentrated, following patterns of emigration. Approximately 60 percent of remittances go to Havana, where a mere 20 percent of the island's population live, and mainly to selected neighborhoods there.

So too are other informal dollar earning opportunities concentrated in the capital. As a consequence, informal dollarization increased rural-urban as well as racial disparities Castro had fought to eliminate. Under the circumstances internal migration to Havana increased, a trend authorities tried to block.

How inequitable did income distribution become? Claes Brundenius estimates that the Gini coefficient rose from 0.22 to 0.41 between 1986 and 1999.[27] Whereas in the predollarized economy the ratio between the highest and lowest salary had been five to one, as of the 1990s some Cubans attained several hundred times more income than others.[28] Differential access to remittances, as well as to other dollar sources, contributed to the new income inequality. And consumption became more income-contingent than in the preceding decades of Castro's rule.

Some in the new upper-income stratum, which comprises high-level joint venture employees and the most financially successful participants in the mushrooming informal (and largely illegal) economy, as well as the largest remittance recipients, employ gardeners, housekeepers, baby-sitters, and drivers, as they flaunt material wealth. It used to be taboo to show that you were living better than others.

The materialism not only defies the revolution's egalitarian precepts but would have been considered socially egregious in the antimaterialist morally driven early years of Castro's rule. Consumerism had been so stigmatized during the first decades of the revolution that islanders used to hide money and goods they received from family in the States.[29] Accordingly, the dollarization is contributing to the restoration of mores reminiscent of the prerevolutionary social order, as the Communist Party Central Committee had feared. Indeed, by the turn of the century Cuban awareness of U.S. brand names became one of the highest in the non-English-speaking world.[30]

Cubans, through their transnationalized networks, came to embrace, and openly so, a consumer lifestyle to the point that the previous stigma of it disappeared. A mimicking of Miami materialism led islanders to yearn for dollars for far more than basic subsistence. Any remaining residues of "Che" Guevara's utopian vision of the "new man," who worked for the good of society, not individual gain, were relegated to the dustbin of history. Differences in lifestyle between families on the two sides of the Florida Straits began to hinge more on their pocketbooks than on their values.

Consumer disparities fueled resentments among the peso-dependent populace. Labor union and public forums made the resentment apparent.[31] Worker dissatisfaction, according to one study, rose from 27 to 41 percent between 1989 and 1999.[32] A de facto devaluation of the peso in 2001 intensified such dissatisfaction.

Cubans with dollar access have yet to solidify into a new privileged social class. For one, dollar access for many Cubans is erratic. Whereas some 62 percent of the population were believed to have dollar access in 2002, only around 27 to 35 percent were estimated to have continual access.[33] Two, Cubans differ in the amount as well as the regularity of dollar access. The dollar stratum accordingly is itself internally divided. Three, the government contained dollar-based capital accumulation, through restrictions on private economic activity and heavy taxation of private ventures. Four, remittance access did not reinforce political private ventures. Families of party members, as blacks, tended not to emigrate. Without overseas networks to tap into, political cadre were at a disadvantage in the new economy. And when senior-level government and party officials had family in the United States, Washington prohibited their households from receiving remittances.

Reliance on informally attained dollars, meanwhile, made Cubans more directly and personally vulnerable to the very market vicissitudes the revolution had sought to eliminate. Whereas prior to the revolution economic opportunities varied mainly with the impact of world sugar prices at the macrolevel, islander income in the new economy became subject increasingly to the impact global market conditions had on family abroad. As the United States experienced a recession which deepened after the September 11, 2001, terrorist attacks, overseas relatives sent fewer dollars.[34] Recent émigrés were particularly vulnerable to the economic downturn because they tend to be employed in business-cycle-linked jobs offering no job security.

Islanders also became vulnerable to the impact the world economy had domestically, for example, on informal tourism. The decline in the two informal sources of dollars, in turn, fueled a depreciation of the peso that drove up living costs for all Cubans.[35] Integration into the Soviet bloc had cushioned Cubans from the impact of global market downturns.

The new consumer culture, combined with unequal dollar access, stirred rent-seeking, corruption, and theft in turn. The peso-dependent populace turned to such illicit and immoral activity to access the dollar economy. Islanders pilfered, pirated, and illegally appropriated supplies from state jobs to sell on the black market, and they bribed authorities to gain access to jobs offering such opportunities.[36] Pervasive economic crime and corruption led the Communist Party and state-controlled media to campaign against them. So too did it lead the government to create a Ministry of Audit and Control, in 2001, to strengthen economic monitoring, and to reinvigorate the largely defunct Committees for the Defense of the Revolution (CDRs) to mobilize against crime, delinquency, and indiscipline.[37] But because the conditions that induced the illegal activity remained, official crackdowns may have stopped specific individuals from breaking the law but failed to eliminate the problem.

The new materialism even undermined the three-decade-old socialist base of stratification. Remittances, in particular, transformed as well as transnationalized the stratification schema. Remittance senders began to enjoy a new exalted status that the most recent immigrants in particular neither experienced before emigrating nor experienced, as humble people, abroad. Émigrés previously stigmatized as outcasts, *gusanos*, were reenvisioned increasingly as heroes. The migrant acquired new symbolic status conditional on retaining homeland ties and sharing economic assets acquired abroad. Because of differential earning power in the United States and Cuba, "bad jobs," unskilled work abroad, became a source of greater income, stature, envy, and respect than "good," skilled island jobs.

The emergent informal transnationalized status schema turned the former socialist stratification hierarchy on its head. Many post-1990 émigrés and their island families are lower class and have limited education. But they have access to a lifestyle inaccessible to peso-dependent professionals. Those who stayed in Cuba and worked their way up the socialist bureaucracy, the socialist system of stratification, experienced downward mobility under the circumstances.

IMPACT ON THE STATE

From the state's vantage point, the informal dollarization had contradictory effects. On the one hand, informally attained dollars the government managed to appropriate provided much-needed revenue. Without the funds, it would have been in more dire straits. Even with the additional source of dollars, the government imported less at the end of the 1990s than in 1990, a decade during which imports to the Dominican Republic and El Salvador nearly tripled.[38] And Cuba's foreign debt, which had increased 60 percent in the 1990s, in 2000 was two and four times greater than the Dominican Republic's and El Salvador's, respectively.

On the other hand, dollars informally circulating in the economy generated a series of problems for the state. For one, they fueled a black market the government could not contain. An unintended consequence of the government's official monopoly on the vending of most nondurables and all but fresh fruits, vegetables, and meats, was to spur black marketeering, to the point that illicit sales absorbed a higher portion of consumer spending than in-market economies where transactions typically transpire through legal private businesses. Illicit vendors who offered items to dollar holders at below official agency prices created a market for their products.

The informal dollarization also fueled a black market in housing that undermined state control over allocations both of dwelling units and of building supplies. Illustrative of this problem, in 2000 the government confiscated more than two thousand illicitly obtained homes in the capital and imposed fines amounting to more than $1 million.[39] Authorities targeted building supplies for the state-run hard-currency-generating tourist sector, but islanders with dollars illegally purchased home improvement supplies, involving goods workers stole from state jobs.

Two, the informal dollarization adversely affected state sector peso-based productivity. The peso economy remained the main source of employment and the base both for the cradle-to-grave welfare state, on which regime legitimacy rested, and for production of most foreign-exchange-generating exports. But in the new dollarized economy islanders calculated peso earnings in their hard-currency equivalency. Since few state jobs paid more than the equivalent of ten to twenty dollars a month, far less than average remittance earnings secured without any work effort whatsoever, incentive eroded to labor at most peso-paying jobs. Under the circumstances, peso-paid workers absented themselves from their state jobs with frequency, partly to pursue dollar-earning sideline activity in the underground economy. Labor motivation was highest in those peso-paying state jobs that provided access either to dollars (informally or formally) or to goods that could be pilfered for black marketeering.

Disillusioned peso-dependent skilled workers, in turn, stirred a state sector brain drain. With the government restricting work options for professionals, including private sideline activity, professionals not only absented themselves from work but left state jobs altogether, for low-skilled work providing informal access to dollars, in tourism especially. Meanwhile, university-educated women, women who would not have dreamed of selling their bodies for sex in the past, turned to dollar-earning prostitution in the tourist sector.

With peso jobs no longer attractive and restrictions imposed on work options for university graduates, the younger generation lost interest in higher education. One of Latin America's most educated populations became "deschooled" as well as "deskilled." Enrollment rates remained intact at the primary and secondary school levels, but the proportion of the school-aged population enrolled in postsecondary studies dropped from 17 percent in 1980 to 12 percent in 1997.

Three, the revenue-poor government was pressed to initiate some costly worker-incentive reforms to stimulate productivity and labor loyalty in the public sector. The most economically and socially valued state employers began not only to feed, clothe, and house their workers, but to offer performance bonuses and to pay employees a portion of their salary in hard currency, especially in a new so-called convertible currency with dollar value in Cuba. The government also raised base-pay peso earnings. In 1999, for example, the government announced salary increases of 30 percent for teachers, doctors, and police. Two years later 40 percent of the labor force received hard currency or convertible currency bonuses, up from 30 percent in 1997. Bonuses amounted to one to seven times the monthly base peso wage.[40] Such bonuses cost the state $228 million in scarce hard currency,[41] the equivalent of one-fourth to one-third of the estimated total remittance intake at the time (and a higher percentage, according to the most conservative remittance estimates). The added peso and hard currency outlays, which left the government reduced funds for investment, were spillover costs in the state economy that governments in market economies do not have to absorb.

Four, the government's dollar-absorbing consumer strategy put strains on hard-currency fiscal resources, strains governments in market economies do not experience as directly. By 2000 consumer goods accounted for one-fourth of the state's slimmed-down import bill.[42] While domestic light industrial output by then had rebounded to the point that half the value of sales in dollar shops was locally produced, industry drew on substantially more hard-currency financing than other economic sectors.[43] In addition, the government, as previously noted, imported food that it sold domestically below cost to maintain the welfare state on which its legitimacy was premised.

Government efforts to channel toward savings informally circulating dollars not absorbed through consumption, moreover, proved only partially effective. Most Cubans preferred to hoard dollars they did not use for immediate consumption, rather than deposit the funds in the new dollar bank accounts.[44] They feared possible government appropriation of their deposits, a fear with some historical base. Castro, upon taking power, had frozen bank accounts and confiscated other assets, such as land. Cubans also preferred that authorities not know their dollar holdings, often obtained in ways not fully compliant with the law. Meanwhile, low interest rates (of 0.5 percent annually for depositors of more than two hundred dollars) provided people with little incentive to bank money.[45]

The taxes initiated both to raise revenue for the cash-strapped state and to reduce dollar-/nondollar-holder income disparities also met with dollar-holder resistance. When the government, for example, introduced license fees, private activity went underground. The number of officially registered self-employed islanders (some utilizing remittances for their operations), who were expected to file income taxes, dropped 23 percent between the mid-1990s and the decade's end, after levies were introduced.[46] And, in 2000 personal income taxes accounted for a mere 3 percent of total tax revenue.[47] From the moment the government announced direct taxation, which was without precedent in Castro's Cuba, it encountered resistance.[48] Consequently, the government stepped up more regressive but more easily implemented indirect taxation: on consumption, raising prices at dollar stores (e.g., in the early 2000s).

Domestic along with international constraints generated economic and political problems. In the latter 1990s the government's hard-currency current account deficit increased more than fourfold, and in the early 2000s the economy was stagnant, with little evidence of a turnaround. At the same time, though, the government stepped up social programs, mainly programs that were peso-based.

CONCLUSION

Cuba weathered the storm of the domino collapse of Soviet bloc Communism. Formally, little changed. Informally, however, the economy, society, and normative order quietly underwent transformation. In even more ways Cuba "regressed" from Marx's utopian socialist and communist goals the regime prioritized during the first decade of Castro's rule. Cuba continued its "backward" slide from the idealized future, with no prospects of reversal. Yet, in the early years of the new century Cuba had not entirely reverted to the status quo ante of the Batista era. Castro, with the support of the party and government, remained committed to the cradle-to-grave welfare state, even if not as fully as when the Soviets helped keep the regime afloat.

Sources of capital to sustain the economy and welfare state were not sufficiently forthcoming for a combination of reasons. Cuba experienced global economic marginalization because the United States tightened the embargo in hopes of thereby bringing Castro's government to heel, because the country failed to create conditions attractive to foreign investors except in selective sectors, and because world market conditions eroded the value of the one commodity in which Cuba had a historical comparative advantage. But domestic conditions also were to blame. The government proved unable to make full use of its healthy and educated workforce.

The most dramatic break with the past under the circumstances was created by the informal dollarization of the economy and the changes it spurred, and the vitalization of transnational ties in which the key source of informal dollarization was embedded. State and societal interests in dollars from abroad partly coincided. Both wanted the hard currency for their own purposes. But both also wanted to maximize the dollars they accessed and the value of those dollars, and to minimize costs they incurred to access the money. Prioritizing its interests, the government tried to profit at dollar recipients' expense: through pricing goods at dollar stores high, through taxing dollar activity, and through imposing high service charges on transnational wire transfers. It also tried to regulate islander usage of dollars, including capital-accumulating investments.

While islanders benefited materially and symbolically from the dollars they informally accessed, even if not as much as they would have in the absence of official regulations, the impact at the state level was mixed. Dollars government agencies managed to appropriate provided revenue for the cash-swapped state, but the informal dollarization eroded the socialist moral order and the socialist basis of stratification, and it undermined state control over production and distribution. Moreover, the informal dollarization had adverse spillover effects in the peso economy. To address emergent problems in the peso economy the government incurred costs governments in market economies do not. This did not bode well for a government that faced fiscal problems already before the crisis caused by the breakup of the Soviet Union.

Cuba's experience in the post-Soviet era reveals more than ever a regime weaker than models of strong states–weak societies under communism suggest. Ordinary Cubans transformed the island socially and culturally and not merely economically. But the society of consequence in the new Cuba is transnational in scope.

The Cuban experience also shows that society has not been uniformly able to assert itself. Unequal access to dollars is causing new inequalities and new social tensions, including in ways undermining precepts of the revolution on which regime legitimacy heretofore has rested.

In sum, informal dollarization has eroded the social and cultural fabric of Castro's Cuba and planted seeds of economic transformation, quite independently of why people sought the hard currency. It had such system-erosive effects while generating regime-bolstering revenue. By the start of the new century socialism as historically constructed was transformed, even as Castro's authority remained publicly almost unchallenged.

NOTES

I have benefited in writing the epilogue from funding from the Andrew W. Mellon Foundation and the Mellon-MIT Program on Non-governmental Organizations and Forced Migration, from the Committee for Cuban Democracy, from the Ford Foundation and Institute for International Education, and from the American Council of Learned Societies. My thanks also to Lorena Barberia for research assistance that I draw upon in this chapter; and to Manuel Orozco, who graciously shared data with me; and to Emily Morris, who provided me with very informed, detailed comments on an earlier version of the chapter. And thanks also to William LeoGrande, Luciano Martins, Jorge Pérez-López, and Archibald Ritter for helpful comments.

1. Remittances are difficult to estimate and politically charged. With minimal official information, different sources vary in their calculations. I draw on United Nations ECLAC estimates. ECLAC is a respected international institution, and its remittance figures are widely cited. Its estimates are based on inferences from "net current transfers" in official balance of payments figures. The figures may include informal tourism earnings, such as tips, room rentals, and prostitution. Indicative of the range of estimates, the well-respected Cuban economist Pedro Monreal (in "Las remesas familiares en la economía cubana," *Encuentro* 14 (Fall 1999): 50), believed remittances in the latter 1990s to total around $500 million. Remittances, it should be noted, may also be in kind, such as medicines, consumer goods, and material inputs to businesses.

2. U.S.-Cuba Trade and Economic Council (hereafter UCTEC), *Economic Eye on Cuba* (January 26, 2003): 5.

3. Douglas Massey et al., *Worlds in Motion: Understanding International Immigration at the End of the Millennium* (Oxford: Clarendon Press, 1998); EIU, *Latin American Country Briefing* (October 23, 2001); *The Economist*, October 23, 2001: 23.

4. Susan Eckstein, "Family-Based Social Capital in the Globalized Economy." Paper presented at the American Sociological Association Meeting, Atlanta, August 2003.

5. U.S.-Cuba Trade and Economic Council (hereafter UCTEC), *Economic Eye on Cuba* (December 8, 2002): 6.

6. Economist Intelligence Unit (EIU), *Cuba Country Report (CCR)* (May 2001): 18.

7. Multilateral Investment Fund (hereafter, MIF)/Inter-American Development Bank (hereafter, IDB), "Remittances to Latin American and the Caribbean" (Washington: MIF/IDB), February 2002, n.p.; *International Herald Tribune*, July 13, 2001 (www.iht.com).

8. Based on research done with the assistance of Lorena Barberia. See Susan Eckstein and Lorena Barberia, "Grounding Immigrant Generations in History: Cuban-Americans and Their Transnational Ties," *International Migration Review* 36, no. 3 (Fall): 799–837, for a description of the survey.

9. Estimates by employees in wire service companies interviewed in the United States and Cuba, and personal communication with Manuel Orozco. In December 2002, however, a new Canadian web-based money transfer service that reduced commissions and increased the speed of transfers was introduced. Cuban recipients who register for the service receive a card with which to make cash withdrawals. In its first month of operation the service report handling $320,000 of transfer and registering ten thousand users. EIU (February 2003): 28.

10. An estimated 10 percent of Cuban Americans visited the island annually as of 2000 (Robyn, Reitzes, and Church, "The Impact on the U.S. Economy of Lifting Restriction on Travel to Cuba," i).

11. An estimated 70 percent of transfers to Mexico, in contrast, are made electronically. Orozco, "Family Remittances to Latin America: The Marketplace and Its Changing Dynamics." Paper delivered at the Inter-American Development Bank Conference, "Remittances as Development Tool," Washington, May 2001, 6.

12. See LeoGrande and Julie Thomas, "Cuba's Quest for Economic Independence," *Journal of Latin American Studies* 34, part 2 (May 2002): 325–64.

13. Monreal, 51.

14. Personal communication with Emily Morris of the Economist Intelligence Unit, April 4, 2003.

15. UCTEC (May 5, 2002): 4.

16. EIU, *CCR* (February 2003): 9.

17. Authorities also transferred state farms into farmer-owned cooperatives.

18. Preferring dollars, merchants did not, however, always insist on purchases in pesos.

19. Manuel Orozco, "Remittances to Latin America and the Caribbean: Money, Markets and Costs" (Washington, D.C.: Inter-American Development Bank/International Monetary Fund, 2002), n.p. (http://www.thedialogue.org/publications.html).

20. *Cuba Business* (May 2001): 6.

21. See Sergio Díaz-Briquets, Lisandro Pérez, and Jorge Pérez-López, "Refugee Remittances: Conceptual Issues and the Cuban and Nicaraguan Experiences," *International Migration Review* 31, no. 2 (Spring 1997): 411–37; Massey et al., *Worlds in Motion: Understanding International Immigration at the End of the Millennium*, and the reference therein.

22. Florida International University (hereafter, FIU), Institute for Public Opinion Research (hereafter, IPOR), *FIU/Cuba Poll* (Miami: FIU-IPOR, 2000), 53, 56.

23. UCTEC, "Economic Eye on Cuba" (March 17, 2002): 12 (http://www.cubatrade.org).

24. United States Bureau of the Census, *Current Population Survey, 1997* (March), table 61: Selected Characteristics of the Foreign-Born Population by Year of Entry. Washington, D.C.

25. See Alejandro De la Fuente, "Recreating Racism: Race and Discrimination in Cuba's Special Period," *Georgetown University Cuba Briefing Paper Series*, vol. 18 (1998).

26. EIU, *CCR* (February 2003): 12.

27. Claes Brundenius, "Whither the Cuban Economy after Recovery? The Reform Process, Upgrading Strategies and the Question of Transition," *Journal of Latin American Studies* 34, part 2 (May 2002): 365–96.

28. *The Economist*, September 23, 1999: 37.

29. Susan Eckstein, "Globalized Family-Based Social Capital." Unpublished paper, 2002.

30. *New York Times*, May 26, 2002: 4, sec. 3, 4.

31. EIU, *CCR* (November 2000): 18.

32. EIU, *CCR* (February 2001): 11.

33. UCTEC (March 17, 2002): 12.

34. *Florida Sun-Sentinel*, October 28, 2001, p. 1.

35. EIU, *CCR* (February 2003): 9.

36. Although scarcities alone might induce pilfering, and the like, the new dollar-based consumer culture made islanders covet more material goods at a time when peso earnings bought less.

37. EIU, *CCR* (August 2001): 13.

38. World Bank, *WDI*, 214.

39. EIU, *CCR* (May 2001): 19.

40. UCTEC (March 17 2002): 12, for slightly different figures, see UCTEC (December 8, 2002): 7.

41. See *The Economist*, October 23, 1999: 37; EIU, *CCR* (February 2001): 19, and (August 2001): 22; World Bank, *WDI 2001*, 48.

42. EIU, *CCR* (November 2001): 5.

43. Banco Central de Cuba, *Informe Económico 2000* (Havana: Banco Central, 2000), 33.

44. EIU, *CCR* (August 2001): 20, and *CCR* (June 2000): 19. In the early 2000s use of bank accounts, however, increased somewhat.

45. Archibald Ritter and Nicholas Rowe, "Cuba: From 'Dollarization' to 'Euroization' or 'Peso Reconsideration'?" *Latin American Politics and Society* (Summer 2002).

46. EIU, *CCR* (May 2001): 18. The number of registered self-employed workers declined even more in the early 2000s (UCTEC, May 5, 2002): 10. Of the 162,000 islanders registered to pay income tax, 89 percent paid in domestic currency, 11 percent in hard currency (EIU, *CCR* [May 2000]: 17.)

47. EIU, *CCR* (August 2001): 18.

48. Eckstein, "The Limits of Socialism in Capitalist World Economy," 142–47.

PART IV

FOREIGN POLICY

In 1991, as the Soviet Union neared its end and Cubans began to experience the hardships of the Special Period, a Cuban official wryly remarked to us that "history has yet to record whether Cuba has suffered more from U.S. imperialism or Soviet friendship." Indeed, both countries had a significant impact on Cuba and on its foreign policies during the Cold War, and ironically Cuba's relations with both countries had the qualities of a double-edged sword.

Soviet subsidies and military assistance enabled Cuba to pursue an egalitarian program at home and a revolutionary vision abroad. But the subsidies locked Cuba into the socialist trading bloc—the Council of Mutual Economic Assistance (CMEA)—and fettered Cuban development. The CMEA designated Cuba as a producer of basic commodities within the network—sugar, citrus, and nickel—and production of these goods had to take precedence over other development possibilities. More than 85 percent of Cuba's international commerce at the end of the 1980s involved CMEA countries. As a consequence, when the Soviet Union and the CMEA disappeared, the Cuban economy became very vulnerable to external pressures.

Cuba's special relationship with the United States during the Cold War also produced benefits and ultimately costs that intensified the risks it faced. Cuba gained the admiration of Third World countries in part because it was a model of resistance to U.S. domination, and it often was an essential ally in direct confrontations with U.S.-supported forces or agents in Africa, Asia, and Latin America. Meanwhile, the ongoing U.S. threat to Cuba's fundamental security justified the maintenance of a militarized state, which gave Cuba its capability to support Third World countries. Yet each peso or person devoted to national security was one less that could be directed to economic diversification and development. In addition, each new clash with the United States undermined nascent efforts to change the policy by U.S. opponents of the embargo. As a consequence, extreme right-wing Cuban Americans had little opposition in 1991 as they developed legislation which seemed capable of toppling the revolutionary regime.

The dire circumstances at the start of Special Period, which Jorge Domínguez details vividly in the second chapter of this section, make Cuba's foreign policy turnaround all the more impressive. By the midpoint of the twenty-first century's first decade, Cuba had established new trading relationships with a broad array of countries. Spanish investments in Cuba's leisure industries gave Cuba the capacity to accommodate more than two million visitors annually. Chinese financing promised to modernize Cuba's nickel industry and provide a new source for earning hard currency. Rumors abounded that deep-sea oil explorations in Cuba's territorial waters, financed partly by China, had detected bountiful deposits. Venezuela's cooperative agreements with Cuba provided it with affordable oil and enabled Cuba to send doctors and teachers to Latin American countries with a resulting triple benefit.

First the doctors and teachers help to carry out Cuba's self-proclaimed internationalist mission, by providing health care, education, and training to poor people who had never received such services, in countries such as Bolivia and Ecuador. In turn, the poor have bolstered governments in these countries opposed to neoliberalism, which has encouraged even moderates such as Brazil's president Luiz Inácio Lula da Silva or Argentina's Néstor Kirchner to champion alternative development strategies intended to reduce poverty and inequality in Latin America. Third, these missions reduce the risk of a brain drain, because they give Cuban professionals an opportunity to earn hard currency they cannot earn in Cuba. At the same time, they alleviate the glut of highly educated Cubans who cannot find jobs on the island for which they can use their skills.

Partly in response to this recovery, Third World countries once again acknowledged Cuba as a global leader by naming Cuba as the host of the 2006 Summit of the Nonaligned Movement (NAM), and consequently the NAM chair for the following three years. Founded in 1961 as a supposed neutralist haven for countries caught up in the East-West conflict, the NAM has achieved little more than to act as a sounding board for Third World ire about unfair terms of global trade, neocolonial exploitation, apartheid, and infringements on the rights of "self-determination" by powerful countries. Yet the NAM's 118 member states do represent most of the Third World. At a minimum, its selection of Cuba as host was a striking indication of Cuba's standing, because Havana already had served as host in 1979.

In the realm of foreign policy, the 1991–2007 period was "special" because it marked Cuba's first real experience with independence since the start of Spanish colonization five hundred years earlier. No single foreign power structured Cuba's political, economic, and foreign policy decisions. None could expect to determine the country's fate peacefully. Cuba's foreign policies enabled the revolution to survive enormous challenges in the early 1990s, and to chart a new direction in the twenty-first century. The articles in this section provide a basis to analyze this achievement and to answer three questions: (1) to what extent did Cuba both reinvent and maintain its revolutionary goals through its foreign policies; (2) what was Cuba's foreign policy strategy for confronting adversity; and (3) how has Cuba's tense relationship with the United States impeded fulfillment of its foreign policy goals?

REINVENTING REVOLUTIONARY GOALS

It has been said that during the Cold War Cuba was a little country with a big country's foreign policy. On one hand, the caricature accurately captures a distinguishing feature of Cuba's international behavior. Unlike great powers, small countries tend to focus narrowly, on their immediate neighborhoods and not on the globe. Great powers with large military forces tend to act with a greater sense of freedom than small countries, because they perceive that only another great power can truly threaten them. The array of meaningful threats is far greater for a small state. In contrast, Cuba focused globally. Cuban leaders shared with Fidel Castro a vision that their country should spearhead a global revolution on behalf of the poor. Cuba's party-controlled newspapers such as *Granma* or state-run television stations generally are no more informative than in-house corporate public relations newsletters. But they do provide broad coverage of world events, with a depth not commonly found in most U.S. media, which has encouraged ordinary Cubans to think globally, and to identify with the struggles of people in other Third World countries.

However, the subtle denigration of Cuba's foreign policy as being inappropriate for its size overlooks a key difference between Cuba's international orientation and those of most great powers. Cuba has never sought to dominate and control other countries, nor has it sought to exploit the resources of another country for Cuba's exclusive benefit. This is evident from this section's first chapter, in which Fidel Castro articulates Cuba's contemporary foreign policy emphasis. The Cuban leader in effect reinvented the global revolutionary agenda by asserting that environmental degradation and the proliferation of weapons of mass destruction "threaten the very survival of the species."

Though Cuba's particular global vision may have changed in the Special Period, regime survival remained as its leaders' primary goal, as Jorge Domínguez explains in the second chapter of this section. He finds that they were characteristically proactive, and relied on "some pre-1990 legacies" to achieve their objective, including intense engagement in multilateral institutions and the development of new defensive economic ties with emerging powers such as China. This strategy, Domínguez notes, was not merely an ad hoc "master plan born in an instant of political creativity." It was rooted in a consistent set of central concerns. Michael Erisman outlines the larger strategy for addressing these concerns in the chapter which then follows. This involved building a South-South coalition to provide an effective means of pursuing "counter-hegemonic" policies against wealthy countries, particularly the United States.

U.S.-CUBAN HOSTILITY

Seen in this light, Cuba's success in working with Venezuela to develop momentum for a resurgence of antineoliberal politics in Latin America, and to buttress the region's leaders in their efforts to resist U.S. domination of the Western Hemisphere's economic relations, is a serious challenge to U.S. objectives. University of Havana political scientist Soraya Castro argues that it is this fundamental conflict of interests between a small defensive power and a superpower, not a Cold War legacy kept alive by rabid right-wing Cuban Americans, which explains the continuing U.S. hostility towards Cuba. She does not dismiss the relevance of irrational factors which may contribute to particular U.S. policies. But she contends that Cuban leaders cannot base their plans on assumptions of irrationality alone, because U.S. policymakers do view Cuba as a real threat.

Daniel Fisk's 2004 speech provides evidence to validate his argument that the United States takes Cuba's challenge seriously. At the time, Fisk was a deputy assistant secretary of state for Western Hemisphere affairs, and Cuba was part of his portfolio. As a staffer for Senator Jesse Helms (R-North Carolina), Fisk was one of the principal authors of the 1996 Helms-Burton Act. He subsequently became President Bush's senior national security adviser for Latin America.

To be sure, Fisk's remarks do exhibit some qualities of a fantasy. They describe a Cuba where the regime is at the brink of collapse due to the weight of its repressive machinery, and a populace clamoring for U.S.-style democracy. On the basis of Fisk's assessment alone, it would have been difficult to imagine that the Cuban government would have survived Fidel Castro's long absence after his major intestinal surgery on July 31, 2006. The peaceful transition of power in Cuba should have shattered the pipe dreams of would-be Teddy Roosevelts in the White House. Indeed, Julia Sweig's assessment seems apt, that the regime's staying power and calm continuity without Fidel Castro at the helm was the Cuban leader's "final victory." Notably, she has been a long-time analyst of Cuban affairs, and is director of Latin American studies at the Council of Foreign Relations, the leading assemblage of foreign policy professionals in the United States. Publication of her article in the Council's journal, *Foreign Affairs*, was an indication that a broad spectrum of U.S. elites recognized the failure of U.S. policy toward Cuba.

In the face of such opposition, the Bush administration's refusal to reconsider its approach to Cuba suggested that irrationality rather than reason governed the policy. Indeed, the policy even created obstacles for the United States as it pursued other goals high on the U.S. agenda. Wayne Smith, who once headed the State Department's Office of Cuban Affairs and then served as chief of the U.S. diplomatic mission in Havana, points to several ways in which U.S. policy toward Cuba evidences a lack of logic—by generating results exactly the opposite of the ones desired. In calling for a new Cuba policy which would actually advance U.S. interests vis-à-vis Cuba, Smith demonstrates the negative spillover effects the current policy has on U.S. relations with countries besides Cuba. Implicitly, he also points to the danger that arises when a superpower becomes frustrated in its failed attempts to achieve a goal based on illusions.

Terrorism stands out as one issue on which U.S. policy towards Cuba has undermined an important U.S. objective. Consider the case of the Cuban Five. As renowned civil rights attorney Leonard Weinglass recounts, U.S. prosecutors succeeded in convicting five Cubans of spying on terrorists in the United States in 2001. Their trial, held in Miami, resulted in sentences ranging from fifteen years to two life terms plus fifteen years. Spending seventeen months in solitary confinement during the twenty-six months they awaited trial, they were not permitted to meet with an attorney for long periods. Because they were working on behalf of the Cuban government, they may have violated a law requiring foreign agents to register with the Justice Department, a crime for which the penalty often is no more than a fine. But none of the five Cubans either acquired or revealed any U.S. government classified information, and there is no evidence that they intended to do so. Their stated and apparent aim was to protect Cuba from terrorists living in the United States.

In contrast, Luis Posada Carriles was charged in 2005 only for illegally entering the United States. Though he had publicly acknowledged deep involvement in attacks on hotels in Cuba which killed an Italian tourist and injured many others, and there is considerable evidence that he planned the destruction of a Cuban civilian airliner that killed all seventy-three persons aboard, U.S. prosecutors did not present evidence to the court regarding his terrorist behavior. He was held in a minimum security facility with ready access to lawyers, as right-wing activists in Florida and New Jersey championed him as a heroic freedom fighter.

The case of the Cuban Five not only highlights U.S. hypocrisy in claiming to fight a war on terrorism while the United States itself harbors terrorists, but it also illustrates why Cuban officials continue to believe that the United States has not abandoned plans and intentions to violently overthrow the Cuban government.

BEYOND THE UNITED STATES

With its Soviet bloc trading arrangements in disarray, and with no expectation that U.S. antagonism would lessen, Cuba turned to Europe at the start of the Special Period. The initial response was tepid, but European investors saw new opportunities when Cuba revised its laws on foreign ownership in 1992. In part, the 1996 Helms-Burton Act was intended to scare these Europeans away by targeting investment capital for penalties. But the law had only a limited effect, as U.S. allies demanded that President Bill Clinton waive a key provision which could have been costly to several European corporations. It was the emergence of the conservative José María Aznar government in Spain that had a greater impact on Cuba's relations with Europe. As Joaquín Roy reviews in his article, Spain's efforts to condition loans and aid to Cuba on human rights criteria led to a series of angry exchanges which effectively reduced Cuba's ties to the European Union (EU). Castro viewed the EU demands as a renewed form of neocolonial intervention, and bluntly asserted in 2003 that Cuba "does not need the European Union to survive."

To be sure, this was a statement tinged with bravado. But it also marked a psychological turning point in Cuban foreign policy. Cuba would no longer concentrate on its relations with the great powers—the United States, the Soviet Union, or Europe. It would devote its foreign policy more intently toward the Third World, toward countries with which it could relate on the basis of mutual respect, not asymmetric requirements. Cuba's securing the position at that moment as host of the 2006 NAM summit was a further indication of its turn south.

Analysts give too little attention to the importance of mutual respect in international relations. "Realist" scholars prefer to emphasize the significance of power, and the ability of one country to force another to accept its preferences. Yet Cuba's relationship with Canada offers evidence for a contrary conclusion, as Peter McKenna and John M. Kirk make clear in their review of Cuban-Canadian relations. Though far wealthier and more powerful than Cuba, Canada has been able to maintain ties that benefit both countries by avoiding a posture of dictating terms to Cuba, and by assuming that both countries can find a common ground that will produce win-win solutions.

This suggests that the United States and Cuba are not doomed to an eternally hostile relationship. Many factors besides geographic proximity will keep the two countries close to each other. Susan Eckstein and Lorena Barberia highlight the one which probably is of greatest significance—the family ties between the 11.5 million people on the island and the 1.2 million people in the United States who were born in Cuba or are the children and grandchildren of Cuban immigrants. The key to turning the closeness between the two countries into a constructive relationship will lie in the ability of future U.S. administrations to give up ambitions of dominance, and the willingness of future Cuban leaders to believe that U.S. officials sincerely respect Cubans as equals.

Neoliberalism, Global Inequality, and Irreparable Destruction of Our Natural Habitat

Message to the 11th United Nations Conference on Trade and Development

Fidel Castro Ruz

The UNCTAD, an organization founded forty years ago, was a noble attempt by the underdeveloped world to create in the United Nations, through fair and rational international trade, an instrument to serve its aspirations of progress and development. There were lots of hopes then and the naïve idea that the former metropolises were aware of the duty and the necessity to share that goal.

Raul Prebisch was the main promoter of that idea. He had characterized the phenomenon of the unequal terms of reference as one of the great tragedies hindering the economic development of the peoples in the Third World. This was one of his most important contributions to the economic culture of our times. In recognition of his relevant qualities, he was elected the first Secretary General of this United Nations agency for trade and development. Today, the terrible scourge of the unequal terms of reference is barely mentioned in speeches and conferences.

International trade has not been an instrument for the development of the poor countries that today make up the overwhelming majority of mankind. For eighty-six of them, basic commodities account for over half of their export revenues. Meanwhile, the purchasing power of such products, except oil, is now less than one-third of what it was at the time of UNCTAD's inception.

Although figures tend to be repetitive and boring, oftentimes it becomes unavoidable to use their eloquent and irreplaceable language.

- Eighty-five percent of the world population lives in the poor countries but their share of international trade is only 25 percent.
- These countries' external debt was close to USD$50 billion in 1964, the year this United Nations agency was born, while today it is $2.6 trillion.
- Between 1982 and 2003, that is, in 21 years the poor world paid USD$5.4 trillion in debt service, which means that its present sum has been paid to the rich countries more than twice.

The poor countries were promised development aid and the steady reduction of the gap between the rich and the poor; they were even promised that it would reach 0.7 percent of the so-called GDP of those economically developed, a figure that if true would amount today to no less than 175 billion USD annually.

What the Third World received as official development aid in 2003 was only USD$54 billion. That same year, the poor paid to the rich $436 billion in debt service and the richest of them all, the United States of America, was the one farthest from meeting the set goal, as it allocated only 0.1 percent of its GDP to that aid. And this leaves out the enormous amounts taken away as a result of the unequal terms of trade. In addition, the rich countries spend every year USD$300 billion on subsidies that prevent the poor countries access to their markets.

On the other hand, it is practically impossible to measure the damage brought upon those countries by the kind of trade relations that, through the sinuous roads of the WTO and the Free-Trade agreements, are imposed on the poor countries, which are unable to compete with the sophisticated technology, the almost absolute monopoly over intellectual property, and the immense financial resources of the rich countries.

Other forms of plundering that add to this are the gross exploitation of the cheap labor force in assembly plants that come and go at light speed; the currency speculation in the range of a trillion dollars every day; arms trade; the seizure of goods belonging to the national cultural heritage; the cultural invasion as well as other actions related to theft and pillage that it would be impossible to list here. The classic books on economics do not show the most brutal transference of financial resources from the poor to the rich countries, as it has not been studied yet—that is, the flight of capital which is a must that characterizes the prevailing world order.

Everybody's money escapes to the United States to protect itself from the monetary instability and the speculative frenzy brought about by the same economic order. Without this gift that the rest of the world, mostly the poor, makes to the United States, it would be impossible for the present administration to withstand its enormous fiscal and trade deficits that in the year 2004 amount to no less than 1 trillion dollars.

Would anyone dare to deny the social and human consequences of the neoliberal globalization imposed on the world?

- If 25 years ago five hundred million people were going hungry, today over 800 million are starving.
- In the poor countries, 150 million children are born underweight, which raises their risks of death as well as of mental and physical underdevelopment.
- 325 million children do not attend school.
- Infant mortality rate under one year is 12 times higher than it is in the rich countries.
- 33,000 children die every day in the Third World of curable illnesses.
- Two million girls are forced into prostitution.
- Eighty-five percent of the world population made up by poor countries consumes only 30 percent of the energy, 25 percent of the metals, and 15 percent of the timber.
- There are billions of full illiterates or functional illiterates on the planet.

- How can the imperialist leaders and those who share in the plundering of the world speak of human rights and even use such words as freedom and democracy in this brutally exploited world?

A permanent crime of genocide is being committed against mankind. The number of children, mothers, adolescents, youths, and adults who could be saved and die every year for lack of food, medical care, and medicines is similar to the tens of millions who perished in any of the two world wars. This is happening every day, every hour, while none of the great leaders of the developed and rich world say a single word about it.

Can this situation go on forever? Definitely not, and for purely objective reasons. After tens of thousands of years, humanity has reached at this minute—and almost unexpectedly given the accelerated pace of the last 45 years when it more than doubled—a population of 6.35 billion and these people must be provided with dress, shoes, food, shelter, and education. That figure will almost inevitably grow to 10 billion within hardly 50 more years. By then, both the proven and the unproven fuel reserves that it took the planet 300 million years to build will no longer exist as they will have been thrown to the atmosphere, the waters, and the soils together with other chemical pollutants.

The imperialist system that prevails today, towards which the developed capitalist society unavoidably evolved, has already come to such a ruthlessly irrational and unfair world economic and neoliberal order that it is unsustainable. Many peoples will rebel against it. In fact, they have already begun to rebel. It is stupid to say that this is the work of parties, ideologies, or subversive and destabilizing agents from Cuba and Venezuela.

Among other things, this evolution brought with it the so-called consumer societies, also an unavoidable process within the framework and norms that rule the system. In these societies, their irresponsible and spendthrift tendencies have poisoned the minds of large numbers of people in the world that amid generalized economic and political ignorance are manipulated by commercial and political publicity through the fabulous media created by science.

These conditions in the rich and powerful countries have not been particularly auspicious for the development of capable and responsible leaders gifted with the knowledge, the political principles, and the ethics that such an extremely complex world demand. It is not their fault as they themselves are the result and the blind instruments of that evolution. Will they be able to handle with responsibility the extremely complicated political situations showing up in the world in growing numbers?

Soon it will be sixty years to the day that the first nuclear bomb was dropped on Hiroshima. There are tens of thousands of such weapons in the world today, which are scores of times more powerful and accurate; and they continue to be produced and perfected. There are even programs for nuclear missile bases in outer space. New more sophisticated and deadly arms systems are being produced.

For the first time in history man would have created the technical capacity for its own destruction. However, it has not been capable of creating a minimum of guarantees for the safety and integrity of every country, on equal footing. Theories are elaborated and even applied with respect to the pre-emptive and surprise use of the most sophisticated weapons, "in any dark corner of the world," "in 60 or more countries," that make the barbaric claims of the darkest days of Nazism go pale. We have already seen wars of conquests, and sadistic methods of torture that bring back to memory the images showed at the end of the Second World War.

The United Nations' prestige is being undermined to its very foundations. Far from being perfected and democratized, this institution has been left as an instrument that the superpower and its allies intend to use only to provide coverage to war adventures and appalling crimes against the most sacred rights of the peoples.

This is no fantasy or simply imagining things. It is a fact that in barely half a century two great mortal dangers have emerged that threaten the very survival of the species: one that derives from the technological development of weapons and the other coming from the systematic and accelerated destruction of natural conditions for life on the planet.

The dilemma into which humanity has been dragged by the system is such that there is no option now: either the present world situation changes or the species runs a real risk of extinction. You do not need to be a scientist or an expert in mathematics to understand this, as the simple arithmetic taught to grammar school children would suffice.

The peoples will become ungovernable, and no repression, torture, disappearances, or massive murders will stop them. Not only will the hungry of the Third World be in the struggle for their own survival and that of their children, but also the conscientious people from the rich world, both manual and intellectual workers.

It will be from the inevitable crisis that rather sooner than later thinkers, leaders, social and political organizations of all shades will emerge that will do their utmost to preserve the species. All the waters will converge in one direction sweeping away all obstacles.

Let's plant ideas, and there will be no need for all the weapons created by this barbaric civilization; let's plant ideas, and the irreparable destruction of our natural habitat will be prevented.

The question stands, is it not too late? I am an optimist, I say no, and I share the hope that a better world is possible.

Havana, June 13, 2004

18

Cuba and the *Pax Americana*

Jorge I. Domínguez

Their world crumbled. In 1989 Cuban leaders watched the dominoes tumble in Eastern Europe as one after another of Europe's communist regimes came to an end. In 1991, the Soviet Union collapsed.

The legacies of Cuba's past international behavior and the sudden implosion of the world that Cuban leaders had known shaped its government's response to the new *Pax Americana*—U.S. unchallenged primacy in military force, worldwide predominance in political power, dynamism in global economic reach, missionary zeal in propounding its ideological creed and combating international terrorism. Internationally, it designed four strategies to cope with the United States.

1. It made a neorealist diagnosis of the post-1990 international system, designing a foreign policy in the expectation that other governments would balance U.S. power as it pertained to Cuba. It drew on its legacy of deterring the United States effectively. It built on its long experience as an activist multilateralist to enlist international support.
2. It designed an international strategy to diversify political risk in its international economic relations. Unlike in its past, it would seek to avoid concentrating its international economic partnerships on one or a few countries.
3. It would actively seek instances of cooperation with the United States, especially on shared security interests, to address U.S. concerns and build some support within U.S. military and coast guard services.
4. It would exercise "soft power," promoting internationally the attractive qualities of Cuban society in order to develop a constituency abroad, especially in the United States, friendly to Cuba and its people.

INTERNATIONALLY INDUCED ADJUSTMENTS IN CUBA

The end of the Soviet Union and communist Europe knocked down three pillars that had supported Cuba's political regime.

Military support. The Soviet Union had dissuaded the United States from invading Cuba. The Soviet Union had also transferred vast quantities of weapons to Cuba free of charge from the aftermath of the 1962 missile crisis to the very end of the 1980s and provided politico-military cover and substantial resources to enable Cuba to display a global foreign policy, including the deployment of hundreds of thousands of troops to African wars in the 1970s and 1980s.

Economic support. The Soviet Union paid a very high price premium for Cuba's sugar and sold petroleum at a discount. It provided huge loans at low interest rates to finance perpetual bilateral trade deficits, and it postponed indefinitely the collection of principal and interest on those loans. The USSR also provided development credits for specific projects as well as manifold opportunities for advanced training for Cuban military and civilian personnel. The best measure of the worth of this support is what happened to the Cuban economy once these subsidies stopped in 1990. From 1989 to 1993, gross domestic product (GDP) per capita fell 37 percent. Imports dropped 75 percent while exports plunged 79 percent.[1]

Ideological support. Castro believes that he has an historic mission and that he has been on the forefront of the march of history. "In America and in the world, it is known that the revolution will be victorious," said the text he crafted in 1962 as the topic sentence for the so-called Second Declaration of Havana.[2] This faith in the ever-growing strength of communist regimes was enshrined in Cuba's 1976 Constitution (Preamble and Article 12, paragraph f), drafted at the apogee of the regime's consolidation. The collapse of the Soviet Union and the communist world in Europe shattered this ideological vision and the Cuban leadership's confidence that the future was theirs.

The international change at the start of the 1990s produced cumulative losses for Cuba's leaders. Cuba was newly vulnerable to U.S. and other pressures. The defense of Cuba would have to rely more on nonmilitary means. Market-oriented economic policies would no longer be resisted but welcomed to generate the resources to rescue the regime. And the search was on for new means of ideological and political legitimation. The Cuban government responded through its own version of structural adjustment. The leaders felt compelled to change. Cuba had been too dependent on an international system that no longer existed.

Military adjustment. Cuba's global military deployments ended nearly instantaneously as the Cold War wound down in Europe and as Cuba rapidly lost Soviet backing. In September 1989, Cuba completed the repatriation of its troops from Ethiopia. In March 1990, all Cuban military personnel in Nicaragua were brought home. In May 1991, the last Cuban troops were repatriated from Angola. Also in 1990 and 1991, Cuba brought back its troops and military advisers from other countries. By fall 1992, Cuba had suspended its military backing for revolutionary movements in other lands. Also in 1992, the last Russian ground troops departed; they had been stationed in Cuba since the 1962 missile crisis. In 2002, Russia shut down its electronic intelligence center at Lourdes, Cuba.[3] From 1989 to 1996, the military and internal security budget in nominal pesos fell 74 percent. Cuba had also lost the off-budget free weapons transfers from the Soviet Union. For those same years, the military budget's share of the total budget dropped from 9.1 to 3.9 percent, bearing a greater burden of adjustment than the civilian economy.[4]

Economic adjustment. The budget deficit fell from 33 percent of GDP in 1993 to 7.4 percent in 1994 and 3.5 percent in 2000.[5] Sugar had been Cuba's long-time prime foreign exchange earner. In 2000, revenues from sugar amounted to $453 million while tourism revenues were worth $1.8 billion. Revenues from tourism had become the main source of foreign exchange. The second most important source of foreign exchange was international transfers, valued at $842 million in 2000—nearly all of it remittances from Cuban Americans.[6] In 2002, the government shut down 45 percent of Cuba's sugar mills; their inefficiency was hopeless. Cuba was en route to becoming just one more Caribbean archipelago dependent on sunshine and its diaspora for its welfare.

Political adjustment. Cuba's downsizing of its armed forces was also a political adjustment, highlighting effective civilian supremacy. Cuba's economic strategy reorientation implied another political adjustment. Despite grumbling from many of its long-time cadres, the government dropped many policies to welcome direct foreign investment and establish cordial enough relations with the Cuban diaspora to generate remittances. Generational replacement was yet another political adjustment. Cuba's most important leaders belong to the Political Bureau of the Communist Party of Cuba. From 1965 through 1980, no member had been dropped from the Political Bureau. Yet after the 1991 Fourth Party Congress, two-thirds of the Political Bureau members were new. At the conclusion of the 1997 Party Congress, only six of the twenty-four Political Bureau members had belonged to this entity prior to the collapse of the Berlin Wall. The median birth year of the 1997 Political Bureau was 1943.

Ideological adjustment. The Fourth and Fifth Party Congresses and the new 1992 constitution justified the economic policy reorientation to save the Cuban nation from doom. The new constitution and new laws provided a measure of property rights to foster international investment. References to the Soviet Union and the international socialist community were purged from the constitution. The State would no longer be atheist though it would remain secular. Religious believers were welcomed into the Communist Party. Fidel Castro's personal leadership role was emphasized in ways not observed since the 1960s. These ideological adjustments could not prevent a substantial erosion of support for the political regime, however.[7]

CUBA'S INTERNATIONAL STRATEGY:
A MULTILATERALIST COLD WARRIOR

Fidel Castro's regime did not survive for so many decades by being reclusive or defensive. The Cuban government designed an effective international strategy for the post-1990 period. This was not a master plan born in an instant of political creativity. Rather, it resulted from a pro-active approach to problem solving. Some pre-1990 legacies mattered. One diplomatic legacy was engagement in the international system and in non-financial multilateral institutions, especially the United Nations system. Multilateralism is a weapon of the weak. (Cuba did not belong to the International Monetary Fund, the World Bank, or the Inter-American Development Bank.) Another legacy was well-established diplomatic and trade relations with many countries. The Cuban government also held two key foreign policy assumptions:

1. The political regime's survival was the fundamental goal. Economic or social performance would be secondary to the achievement of regime survival.

Relations with others would be sacrificed if they conflicted with the primacy of survival.

2. The U.S. government could be trusted to blunder as a hegemon in its relations with Cuba. Its actions would at some point alienate U.S. allies, lead them to oppose important U.S. policies toward Cuba, and reactivate the waning flames of Cuban nationalism.

The key characteristics of the political regime that the leadership endeavored to preserve were the preeminent roles of President Fidel Castro and Vice President Raúl Castro; a "hard shell" conception of sovereignty capable of warding off external influence over the regime's political features including respect for human rights; a single-party political system with state ownership and operation of all mass media; the Communist Party's leading role, namely across all sectors of human endeavor its right to vet all key administrative and managerial appointments, set the main lines of policy, and demand deference to centralist principles; a high priority to provide educational and healthcare services to the entire population.

Building on the legacies of a successful foreign policy during the Cold War, the Cuban government mobilized the skills of its diplomats in the United Nations General Assembly and other U.N. organizations, the Iberoamerican summits, and the Association of Caribbean States (ACS). Cuba's U.N. activism drew on decades of hard work by Cuban diplomats and the gratitude of many African states that had received Cuban assistance on generous terms in decades past. Membership in Iberoamerican summits was a culmination of long and sustained Cuban engagement with Spain and Mexico—the leaders in founding the Iberoamerican summits and hosts of the first two summits—and also with other Latin American countries to a lesser extent. ACS membership was a legacy of Cuba's political relations with Anglophone Caribbean countries since the early 1970s even though the ACS itself was founded in the 1990s.[8] Thus unlike most governments that believe in neorealist international politics, Cuba acts pragmatically through non-financial multilateral institutions. Its armies can no longer contain the United States; its diplomats may.

In the United Nations, one measure of broad and growing opposition to these U.S. laws has been the vote in the U.N. General Assembly on a Cuban motion to condemn U.S. economic sanctions on Cuba. Cuba's large, professional, and effective diplomatic corps has worked worldwide over the years to build support for Cuba's position. In 1992, this Cuban motion received the votes of 33 percent of all U.N. members. In 1994, it got 54 percent. In the aftermath of the enactment of Helms-Burton in 1996, the Cuban motion garnered support from 73 percent of U.N. members. In 2001, at the apogee of U.S. power during the war on the Taliban regime in Afghanistan, 88 percent of U.N. members voted for the Cuban resolution.

The European Union (EU) illustrates how U.S. allies balanced against U.S. policy. In the early 1990s, the European Parliament set the pattern: it condemned the *Cuban Democracy Act* yet it also called for Cuba's democratization. In 1993, the European Commission approved its first program of humanitarian assistance to Cuba. Yet, the commission refused to sign a formal "cooperation agreement" with Cuba—the only Latin American country with which it still lacks such an agreement. Beginning in 1995, the European Union fashioned a comprehensive policy toward Cuba, a "common position" approved in December 1996—the first time that the EU adopted such a mechanism in its relations with a Latin American country.

The EU opposed U.S. policy toward Cuba as embodied in the Helms-Burton and Torricelli acts. It also supported Cuba's democratization. It would continue humanitarian assistance. Consistent with this policy, the EU invited Cuba as an Observer to participate in the re-negotiation of the Lomé Convention that was about to become the Cotonou Convention. Through these means former European colonies in Africa, Asia, the Caribbean, and the Pacific Ocean receive certain EU preferential trade treatment and economic assistance. Yet, the EU's insistence that only a democratic Cuba could join the Cotonou Convention led Cuba in April 2000 to withdraw its request to join the Cotonou system.[9] The Cuban government accorded primacy to its survival as an authoritarian regime; it would reject democratizing pressures from the European Union (and others).

Parallel to those Cuba-specific actions, the EU contested the Helms-Burton Act, litigating before the World Trade Organization (WTO) while also negotiating with the United States. On 18 May 1998, the EU agreed to discontinue its complaint against the United States before WTO and to discourage investment in certain properties of doubtful title in Cuba. The United States pledged that the president would henceforth exercise his lawful right under the Helms-Burton Act to suspend every six months the enforcement of Title III—the guts of the act, applying to direct foreign investments in Cuba. The White House also agreed to seek a congressional amendment to Helms-Burton to eliminate its Title IV, which mandated the denial of U.S. visas to executives (and their families) whose non-U.S. firms invested in Cuba.[10] At the time of signing, the United States did not believe that the EU would discourage investments in Cuba and the EU did not believe that the U.S. Congress would repeal Title IV. Nonetheless, the result of this negotiation killed Helms-Burton *de facto*. President George W. Bush's administration honored this agreement, regularly suspending Title III and keeping enforcement of Title IV to a minimum. In U.S.– European Union relations, Cuba was a cheerleader for the EU's neorealist balancing but not a direct participant. In the end, the European Union neutered Helms-Burton and saved Cuba from potential risks.

Cuba played a more active role to break out of its isolation in the Americas. Iberoamerican summits have been held every year since 1991; the Spanish-American countries—Spain, Brazil, and Portugal—attend them. President Castro has attended them as well and hosted one in Havana. These summits regularly approve ringing endorsements of pluralist democracy, which Castro signs without blushing. Through these summits, the Cuban government widens its political relations and obtains a modicum of additional international legitimacy, even before its own people: Cuba does not stand alone, despite the differences between its domestic politics and those of other countries at the summit. Moreover, Cuba's active participation in these summits undermines U.S. attempts to isolate Cuba. The Latin American governments thus also exemplified neorealist balancing against U.S. policy.

The Cuban government's most successful efforts to undermine U.S. policy have taken place in the Anglophone Caribbean. Cuba first had to end its own Cold War in the Caribbean. From 1979 to 1983, Cuba provided substantial support to the New Jewel Movement—a self-styled Marxist-Leninist party—government in Grenada. In 1983, U.S. troops invaded Grenada, overthrew that government, and installed one more to its liking. Cuban-Grenadian relations were suspended. In May 1992, Cuba took the initiative to recognize and establish diplomatic relations with Grenada. A month later, the Caribbean Tourism Organization admitted Cuba as a member. In

December 1993, the Caribbean Community (CARICOM) signed a cooperation agreement with Cuba, notwithstanding severe U.S. pressure on CARICOM to require Cuba to democratize and respect human rights (the accession clauses that the European Union requires of Cuba for access to the Cotonou Convention). Cuba objected to such a requirement, and CARICOM did not insist. The Association of Caribbean States was founded in 1994, with Cuba as a charter member. Anglophone Caribbean governments are among Cuba's staunchest allies in the post–Cold War world, defying U.S. pressures in international organizations.[11] In the late 1990s and early 2000s, Cuban relations with Haiti, the Dominican Republic, and Suriname also improved.

Cuba had no alliances, however. Communist Asia did not replace Communist Europe, rescuing Cuba for an ideological cause, though Cuba's political relations with Asian communist governments were good and trade with China was important. The People's Republic of China was unwilling to replace the Soviet Union as Cuba's patron.

For small, threatened countries, neorealist multilateralism is the best they can do. Multilateral institutions served as key arenas for Cuba's international activity and means to mobilize the support of other governments. Because Cuba's approach to multilateralism was neorealist, it did not foster a liberal institutionalist agenda— that is, Cuba did not seek to invest institutions with greater powers to shape domestic rules within countries and it sought to stop any multilateral efforts that would constrain Cuba's freedom of action. Cuba's approach to multilateralism was fully within the clash of forces to be expected from an anarchic international system.

CUBA'S INTERNATIONAL STRATEGY: DEFENSIVE INTERNATIONAL ECONOMIC LINKS

As the 1990s opened, Cuba had to design a strategy to prevent the United States from manipulating its new economic vulnerability to accelerate domestic regime change. In 1986, Cuba had defaulted on its international debt to market-economy countries and remained unable to work out a rescheduling; as a result, it received no long-term lending. For political reasons, it obtained no "soft" loans other than $9.8 million from the People's Republic of China in 2000.[12] It relied on suppliers' credits at a high margin over LIBOR (London Interbank Offering Rate). Foreign direct investment developed the tourism sector effectively but the monetary value of such investment was modest. Cuba's international economic strategy did not generate a vigorous recovery or renew economic growth. In 2000, on the eve of the economy's new slowdown, GDP in constant prices remained 18 percent below its 1985 level.[13]

On the other hand, since 1990 Cuba has successfully diversified its international economic partners. In 1989, the Soviet Union purchased 60 percent of Cuban exports and supplied 68 percent of its imports. In 2000, Russia remained the most important buyer of Cuban exports but it only took 18 percent. Spain was the main supplier of Cuban imports but it accounted for just 16 percent. These outcomes did not occur by chance. The Cuban government no longer manages all international economic transactions, as for the most part it did prior to 1990, but its state enterprises continue to control all foreign trade and tourist partnerships directly or through association with international firms. The government gives prior approval to all foreign investment deals and only the government incurs international debts. Mindful of a legacy of dependency on a single country (Spain in colonial times, the United States from 1898 to 1960, and the Soviet Union from 1960 to 1990) and a single product (sugar), Cuban officials worked hard and with stunning success to diversify international economic partnerships since 1990.

CUBA'S INTERNATIONAL STRATEGY: COOPERATING WITH THE UNITED STATES

Well before 1990, the Cuban government had found areas of cooperation with the United States and reached agreement. In the 1990s, this strategy served two purposes. First, it addressed issues that mattered to both governments, such as migration, drug trafficking, terrorism, and relations around the U.S. naval base in Cuba's Guantánamo province. Second, given such Cuban responsible behavior, its government hoped to persuade U.S. officials that it was not a "rogue" state, much less a charter member of an "axis of evil."

Migration agreements signed in 1994 and 1995 greatly reduced Cuban illegal migration. The U.S. Coast Guard would return to Cuba those Cubans picked up on the high seas intending to enter the United States without documents; the United States also took steps to facilitate lawful Cuban immigration well beyond the terms agreed to in the 1980s. Most aspects of U.S.-Cuban migration relations would henceforth receive routine treatment. The coast guards of both countries came also to collaborate in search and rescue missions at sea, especially useful during the 1994 migration crisis.

In 1993, the U.S. and Cuban armed forces began to develop confidence-building measures in and around the U.S. naval base located in Cuba's province of Guantánamo. U.S. and Cuban forces started to notify each other in advance of military movements. The highest-ranking military officers from both sides established regular and periodic communication.

In the mid-1990s, the U.S. and Cuban coast guards also began to cooperate on an ad hoc basis to combat drug trafficking. The U.S. Coast Guard would supply the information; Cuban Guardafronteras would arrest the criminals in Cuban space. The U.S. Federal Bureau of Investigation started to inform Cuba about terrorist activities of some Cuban-origin persons in the United States.[14]

CUBA'S INTERNATIONAL STRATEGY: "SOFT POWER"

U.S. worldwide influence, Joseph Nye has argued, depends not just on U.S. military and economic power but also on the attractive qualities of U.S. society, its way of life, its means of organizing public and private life, its popular music, television, Hollywood films, fashions, the intellectual clout of its universities, the dynamism of its religious missionaries, and so forth. Cuban scholar Carlos Alzugaray has argued that Cuba has some soft power as well.[15]

The Cuban government invests actively in its soft power. Its policies are closer to those of governments of France that over the years have promoted the spread of the French language and culture in part to secure a leading role for France in the world. The Cuban government does not have a *laissez faire* attitude toward inter-societal relations. Its artists, athletes, or physicians cannot leave Cuba without an exit permit. Most travel abroad only as part of explicit agreements that the Cuban government has signed and often as part of clearly identified policies. The Cuban government understands that its soft power is about *power*, not just about good feelings.

Some of Cuba's soft power dates from the Cold War years. Cuba defied the United States in the 1960s. For many Latin Americans, not just for left-wingers, the Cuban Revolution exemplified courage, creativity, liberation, the opening of new vistas, and a praiseworthy Latinamericanist affirmation facing the United States. Cuba's defiance drew from the deep well of a long-lived Latin American tradition, culturally and politically at odds with the United States. Cuban soft power in the twenty-first century retains some of those themes but it gathered some appeal even within the United States.

Cuban athletes impressively win many medals in the summer Olympics and in the Pan American games. The *Buena Vista Social Club* film had a considerable impact on a segment of the U.S. public, charmed by its characters and their music. Cuba sends its orchestras and smaller musical groups on international tours, including U.S. tours. Cuba welcomes international visitors to large-scale art exhibits, each time with greater participation from U.S. art collectors. The subtle political message is this: Could Cuban art be so attractive and its popular music so much fun if its government were so bad? The Cuban government actively regulates, promotes, and distributes the products of Cuban artists and musicians.

Cuba continued to develop its medical diplomacy as one element of its soft power, hoping for influence in parts of the developing world. In 2001, 2,146 Cuban medical doctors and other health care personnel were posted in 14 countries. At the end of the 1990s, Cuba founded a new medical school to train Latin American medical doctors; in 2001, this school had 3,460 students from 23 countries.

CONCLUSION

In the 2000s, Cuba has no allies. It does not belong to the international financial institutions. Its authoritarian domestic political regime has turned it into a pariah in Latin America and causes continuing friction with the United States, Canada, and the European Union. The character of its domestic regime is the Cuban government's principal international liability. In the 1990s, this government was compelled to adjust to the changes in the international system and the rise of unrivaled U.S. hegemony. It felt the heavy cumulative weight of the loss of its international military, economic, ideological, and political support. It adjusted successfully to permit the survival of the political regime—yet without the ideological fervor that once had buttressed it. It did not succeed in reactivating the economy or returning the welfare of its people to the levels that prevailed in the mid-1980s. Cuba is a "poster child" for the meaning of constraint in the international system of the twenty-first century.

Yet, Cuba also exemplifies how a talented and committed political leadership can exercise a wide range of choice under very adverse international circumstances. To respond to the rising power of the United States in the 1990s, the Cuban government developed a four-pronged international strategy.

The *Pax Americana* is not the international system that President Castro and his older associates would have chosen for the waning years of their rule but they showed, in the twilight of their careers, an unusual skill—unparalleled by any other authoritarian regime in the post–Cold War international system—to advance their interests and preferences beyond the boundaries of their very small country, notwithstanding the overwhelming power of the United States.

NOTES

1. Computed from Banco Nacional de Cuba, *Economic Report, 1994* (Havana: Banco Nacional de Cuba, 1995), 4, 11.

2. Fidel Castro, *Obras escogidas, 1953–1962*, vol. 1 (Madrid: Editorial Fundamentos, 1976), 131.

3. www.cubaminrex.cu/informacion/DECLARCOFICIALesp.htm (28 December 2001).

4. Budget calculations from Comisión Económica para América Latina y el Caribe, *La economía cubana: Reformas estructurales y desempeño en los noventa* (Mexico: Fondo de Cultura Económica, 2000), tables A.13 and A.14. Hereafter CEPAL.

5. Calculated from Oficina Nacional de Estadísticas, *Anuario estadístico de Cuba, 1996* (Havana: 1998), 98, 99; and Oficina Nacional de Estadísticas, *Anuario estadístico de Cuba, 2000* (Havana: 2001), 105; hereafter *Anuario 2001*.

6. *Anuario 2001*, 128, 137; CEPAL, table A.30.

7. Juan Valdés Paz, "El sistema político cubano de los años noventa: Continuidad y cambio," in *Cuba construyendo futuro: Reestructuración económica y transformaciones sociales* (Madrid: El Viejo Topo/Fundación de Investigaciones Marxistas, 2000), 245, 247.

8. Jorge I. Domínguez, *To Make a World Safe for Revolution: Cuba's Foreign Policy* (Cambridge, Mass.: Harvard University Press, 1989), pp. 171–176, chapters seven and eight.

9. Instituto de Relaciones Europeo-Latinoamericanas, "40 años de revolución en Cuba: ¿Transición hacia dónde?," *Dossier*, 68 (Madrid: 1999), 38–39, 43; and the Cuban Foreign Ministry, www.cubaminrex.cu/politicaregional/REGAmeLat.htm.

10. Joaquín Roy, *Cuba, the United States, and the Helms-Burton Doctrine: International Reactions* (Gainesville: University Press of Florida, 2000), 151–155.

11. John Walton Cotman, "Cuba and the CARICOM States: The Last Decade," in *Cuba's Ties to a Changing World*, ed. Donna Rich Kaplowitz (Boulder, CO: Lynne Rienner, 1993); Canute James, "Caribbean Community, Cuba Sign Controversial Trade Pact," *Journal of Commerce*, 15 December 1993.

12. www.cubaminrex.cu/boletin/invextranj_colab_asistec.htm.

13. CEPAL, table A.2. See also www.cubagob.cubaweb.cu/des_eco/mep/cuba2000.htm.

14. *CubaInfo*, 7, no. 16 (20 December 1991): 1.

15. Joseph Nye, *Bound to Lead: The Changing Nature of American Power* (New York: Basic Books, 2000); Carlos Alzugaray, "La política exterior de Cuba en la década de los 90: intereses, objetivos y resultados," Paper presented at the International Congress of the Latin American Studies Association, September 2001.

19

Cuba's Counter-Hegemonic Strategy

H. Michael Erisman

TRADITIONAL PERSPECTIVES ON CUBAN FOREIGN POLICY BEHAVIOR: THE REALIST SCENARIO

The Realist school (or, as it is known, the power politics school) revolves around the notion that the essence of foreign affairs is the constant struggle among states for the power they need in order to be able to pursue and protect their vital national interests, the foremost being security.

Employing this framework over a broad historical timeline leads Realists to conceptualize Cuba's foreign affairs as basically a series of client relationships—first as a Spanish colony, second as a subordinate resident in Washington's "Caribbean backyard," and third as a protectorate or vassal of the Soviet Union.

Despite the widespread popularity of the Realist school among academics and especially international affairs professionals, many observers are not persuaded that its "sphere of influence" concept has any serious utility as a tool for understanding the essential nature and thrust of revolutionary Cuba's foreign policies. They contend that this perspective grossly underestimates the impact of the strong nationalist sentiments that have always permeated the island's political culture and have led most Cubans to be extremely wary of any external power that might represent a threat to their country's sovereignty and independence.

Turning to the policy guidelines set forth by the Realists, they can, for simplicity's sake, be condensed into the following admonition—be totally *pragmatic* in expanding and using your power to safeguard your vital national security interests. Cuba, like many other small developing states, has tended to adopt a two-pronged conceptualization of its security needs. The military side of this equation demands that Havana take the measures necessary to protect itself from armed attack, either direct or indirect. Equally important, however, are economic concerns, for less developed countries are often highly susceptible to trade warfare and other similar forms of externally induced destabilization that can represent as serious a threat to their sovereignty as can a military invasion.

Observers have often overlooked or seriously underestimated the pragmatic security dimension of revolutionary Cuba's foreign policies, with devotees of the messianic and personalismo schools (discussed later) being especially prone to this oversight in their zeal to demonstrate that it is either Marxist ideology or Castro's ego that is the driving force behind Havana's international behavior.

Take, for instance, the controversial question of Cuba's support for the armed struggles of various revolutionary movements, especially in the Western Hemisphere during the 1960s. The messianic school has employed a messianic interpretation to explain these policies, contending that Havana was simply putting into practice the Marxist exhortation to spread communism throughout the world. Others have proposed that such behavior could be better understood in terms of its security implications, especially with regard to the threat posed by Washington's hostility to the very survival of the Cuban Revolution.

Realist analyses such as these are predicated on the assumption that security is the central strategic premise shaping Cuban international relations and that any specific moves Havana in general or Fidel Castro in particular might make on the world stage should be seen as constituting the pragmatic tactical means to achieve that end. Others might prefer a more hybrid approach, such as Nelson Valdés's portrayal of Cuba's external affairs as an exercise in principled pragmatism (or principled opportunism), in which certain ideological tenets form an untouchable core of policy guidelines and goals that the Fidelistas then feel free to pursue by the most effective means available.[1]

CUBAN FOREIGN POLICY AS A REVOLUTIONARY CRUSADE

The great revolutions often acquire a messianic aura in the sense that their proponents tend to see them as representing not only a new but, more important, a superior social order, the relevance of which goes far beyond the boundaries of the countries that originally spawned them.

Cuba is somewhat different since the messianic quality normally has not, at least in the twentieth century, been associated with revolutions in smaller countries.

Admittedly there has always been an ideological element within Cuban foreign policy, manifested most dramatically in the mutually reinforcing notions of proletarian internationalism and anti-imperialism, both of which have had a major impact on the Fidelistas' view of their role in world affairs and both of which have certain messianic implications. Proletarian internationalism by definition engages the revolution in the political affairs of other countries and regions. Moreover, the concept in its most pristine form does not present such activity as a matter of mere policy choice but rather as an obligation that successful revolutionaries must recognize and accept in order to create the united front necessary to overcome the wide-ranging opposition mounted by defenders of the status quo. Specifically, at least as far as the Cubans have been concerned, such solidarity implies a commitment to resisting U.S. imperialism, since they are convinced that Washington's eagerness to impose a Pax Americana wherever it can is one of the main obstacles not only to necessary revolutionary change but also to the aspirations of progressive countries to control their own economic and political destinies.

A case can therefore be made in certain instances for the validity of looking at Cuban foreign policy as a revolutionary crusade. The Cubans have, of course, always insisted that in principle they have a right to pursue a policy of proletarian internationalism (and they continue to do so). But in reality this claim has not been transformed into concrete policy for some time.

Fidel and the Personalization of Foreign Policy

Irrespective of whether one admires or detests him, Fidel Castro must be acknowledged as one of the truly great political figures of the twentieth century. In addition to his impressive intellect and almost inexhaustible energy, he possesses one of the most elusive and desirable of all leadership qualities—charisma, the ability to relate to both individuals and the masses in a direct, emotional manner that generates intense loyalty and serves as a vehicle for mobilizing people behind a particular cause.

Given these qualities, it is tempting and indeed easy to look at the Cuban Revolution (with regard to both domestic and foreign affairs) as essentially an exercise in projecting Castro's ideas and personal preferences into the island's political arena. Illustrative of this tendency is the common practice of using the terms *Fidelistas* and *Fidelismo* as shorthand labels to describe the supporters of and, more important, the essential nature of the revolution. The tendency has been to see the revolution essentially as the externalization of Castro's personality. Basically this approach to analyzing and understanding the revolution's dynamics falls under the rubric of the classical "Great Man" (or Woman) theory of politics.

Fidel certainly wants to guarantee that the revolution that has been his life's work survives his departure from the political scene. It will not do so if it exists simply as an extension of his personality, popularity, and power. Rather, to assure its long-term viability, the revolution must inextricably be "institutionalized" into the fabric of Cuban society.

The Surrogate/Superclient Theses

These two views of Cuba's behavior on the world stage, both of which revolve around the nature of its Soviet connection, were very much creatures of the Cold War.[2] The key difference between them is that the superclient analysis saw Havana as having some control over the dynamics of its Moscow ties, whereas the surrogate school portrayed the island as essentially a pawn of the Kremlin in the USSR's superpower competition with the United States. Because both views are time-bound in the sense that they were interpretations of the Fidelistas' activities during the Cold War, they obviously have little relevance as explanatory tools today.

Developing the Concept of Counterdependency Politics

One unfortunate trait that Cuba shares with many other smaller countries is a vulnerability to external domination. As suggested in part I, the island has fallen victim to this phenomenon throughout most of its history, with Spain controlling it for almost 400 years (1511–1898) followed by a 60-year period (1898–1958) during which the United States to a great extent managed its political and economic life.

According to this view, the Third World nations could not expect to improve their relative position significantly in the global economic arena as long as they remained locked into trade relationships whereby they mostly exported a few low-priced commodities to the industrialized states while simultaneously importing expensive manufactured products from those countries. Certainly prerevolutionary Cuba fit this profile, with the United States representing the metropole that dominated the island's economy both in terms of trade and as a source of foreign investment. But after 1959 the island no longer fit the classical dependency mold, for the revolution's nationalization initiatives had succeeded in recapturing assets that had fallen under foreign (mostly Yankee) control, and the preferential treatment that it received from the Soviet bloc had neutralized most of its traditional trade imbalances. In the post–Cold War period, however, many of Cuba's basic economic vulnerabilities have reemerged, bringing with them the unpleasant possibility that the specter of dependency might once again appear on its horizons.

A central feature of each set of political/economic dynamics summarized here, according to the radical dependendistas, is the development of a cooperative, symbiotic relationship between some metropolitan and Third World elites. While both parties, they argued, will actively seek such an arrangement, the main initiative frequently comes from sectors of the national bourgeoisie in the LDCs (often called the *comprador* class) who are willing to serve as local agents for or junior partners of foreign capitalist interests in order to be assured an ongoing piece of the exploitive action. In short, this alliance is seen as being based on a convergence of class interests, which subjects the masses in a dependent LDC to a complex pattern of oppression involving both internal and external dimension.

The highest (and most controversial) stage of political dependency is reached when its purveyors go beyond the limited realm of decision-making participation based on an alliance with the comprador class and begin to use their power to prescribe the composition and nature of the government in a dependent country. At this point, the dominant center is usurping the right of national self-determination, which is a prerequisite for any people to exist as a truly sovereign nation.

Basically, then, dependency emerges as the modern manifestation of classical colonialism. Granted, the specific mechanisms of penetration and control have changed, but the essence of the imperial relationship remains unaltered and can perhaps be most simply described in terms of an informal empire:

> The weaker country is not ruled on a day-to-day basis by resident administrators or increasingly populated by emigrants from the advanced country, but it is nevertheless an empire. The poorer and weaker nation makes its choices within limits set, either directly or indirectly, by the more powerful society and often does so by choosing between alternatives actually formulated by the outsider.[3]

It is this specter of dependency and the threat of being incorporated into someone's informal empire (e.g., Washington's) that have rendered counterdependency concerns a leitmotif underlying many of revolutionary Cuba's actions on the international stage.

Key Elements of a Counterdependency-Oriented Foreign Policy

Obviously, the key to this whole counterdependency scenario hinges upon developing the wherewithal to prevent penetration and to reduce vulnerabilities. Although other formulas might be employed, the strategy that revolutionary Cuba (and others) have tried to use to achieve these ends involves two basic stages: first, the expansion of one's available political/economic space through diversification, and second, exploiting the opportunities that diversification presents to acquire and then assertively to wield (collective) bargaining power.

Moving once again onto the global stage, a developing country also may occasionally possess unusual bargaining power because another state is strategically dependent on it for something (e.g., industrialized Nation A relies heavily on a particular LDC to supply a scarce natural resource required by A's defense industries). In practice, however, it is rare to find such fundamental weaknesses upon which smaller countries like Cuba can capitalize. Consequently, a more realistic international approach for such a country is to try to strengthen its hand by negotiating collectively. Some forays in this direction have already been launched, the mechanisms employed ranging from regional vehicles (an example in the Western Hemisphere is the Association of Caribbean States, which was formed in July 1994 with Cuba participating as a charter member) to commodity cartels (OPEC, the International Bauxite Association) to large, multi-issue organizations with worldwide membership (the Group of 77, the Movement of Nonaligned Nations). A common problem such multilateral initiatives have had to confront is the fact that the participants have not always been able to arrive at consensus regarding their overall priorities, the result being serious susceptibility to retaliatory divide-and-conquer tactics as disgruntled members become increasingly prone to breaking ranks and making their peace separately with the more (economically) powerful nations. Conversely, the benefits that many former colonies of Western European states have achieved within the Lomé framework suggest that despite its faults, collective bargaining has immense potential as a means for nations such as Cuba to make major progress in pursuing counterdependency-oriented foreign policies.

The central concern is to probe the survival strategies Havana has been trying to implement—for example, economic diversification and initiatives to develop collective bargaining power via South-South coalition building—to deal in a general sense with the specter of dependency that has long stalked the island and in particular to neutralize the threat to the revolution posed by Washington's resurgent hegemonic pretensions.

NOTES

1. For a more detailed presentation of this characterization of Cuban policy as a combination of core ideological principles and pragmatism/opportunism, see Nelson Valdés, "Cuban and Angola: The Politics of Principles and Opportunism." Paper presented at the conference on the Role of Cuba in World Affairs, University of Pittsburgh, November 15–17, 1977.

2. The part of the following section dealing with the surrogate thesis is an abbreviated version of material that first appeared in H. Michael Erisman, *Cuba's International Relations: The Anatomy of a Nationalistic Foreign Policy* (Boulder, Colo.: Westview Press, 1985), 3–4, now out of print.

3. William Appleman Williams, *The Tragedy of American Diplomacy* (New York: Dell Publishing Company, 1964), 47–48.

Like Sisyphus's Stone

U.S.-Cuban Relations in the
Aftermath of September 11, 2001

Soraya M. Castro Mariño

INTRODUCTION

In the Greek myth of Sisyphus, the gods punish the sinner by condemning him endlessly to push a heavy stone up a hill. Whenever he succeeds in getting to the top, the stone rolls down the other side and he must begin again. From a Cuban perspective, our relationship with the United States since 1959 has felt like Sisyphus's stone, an endless punishment meted out by a country claiming to act on behalf of a deity. This perception has been especially vivid since September 11, 2001, because the U.S. "war on terror" permeates discussions in both Cuba and the United States about the countries' relationship. This chapter examines the ways in which that context affects how the two states relate to each other.

Even before the 1898 U.S. intervention into Cuba's war of independence, a fundamental clash emerged between Cuba's desire to be sovereign and the U.S. ambition to dominate Cuba. While Cuban visionaries spoke of independence around the time of the 1823 Monroe Doctrine, John Quincy Adams compared Cuba to an apple, saying the island would gravitate naturally to the United States just as "ripe fruit" has no choice but to fall to the ground. U.S. leaders already thought of Cuba as an extension of U.S. territory.[1] U.S. intervention in the formation of the Cuban state after the 1898 war became a tangible reminder of the differences between the two states.

As a condition for ending its military occupation of Cuba, the United States required Cubans to live under a Damoclean sword: the Platt Amendment. The provision in the first Cuban Constitution granted to the United States the unlimited right to intervene in Cuban internal affairs. This left an imprint on Cuba's national consciousness and a vision of the United States: under all circumstances, the potent neighbor would be a threatening power which Cubans had to take into consideration in creating any national design.

Present Cuban-U.S. relations embody a similar conflict of national goals. Cuba has asserted that its sovereignty is a goal of the highest priority, and it has labored vigilantly to safeguard its independence from external domination. Meanwhile, the United States has defined its national interests in accord with the claim that it has the undisputed right to dominate the affairs of all Latin America countries. This dichotomy—sovereignty versus domination—explains the continuity of a policy of punishment and hostility against Cuba which the U.S. government has pursued despite the end of the Cold War.

The Cuban Revolution's defiant resistance to U.S. pressure, even before its socialist character was proclaimed officially in 1961, posed a challenge to U.S. interests in Latin America and presaged future hostile relations. Yet provocative moves each country made also played a role in deepening the antagonisms. U.S. actions included unilateral measures designed to harm the Cuban economy; the severance of diplomatic relations; the 1961 Bay of Pigs invasion; the imposition of an economic blockade; prosecution of a low-intensity covert war known as Operation Mongoose; assassination attempts against President Fidel Castro; covert wars in Central America which threatened to spill over to Cuba. Cuban actions included the nationalization of property owned by U.S. citizens and corporations; allowing the Soviet Union to install ballistic missiles on the island; integrating the country into the Socialist trading bloc; sending 50,000 troops to fight in Angola and Ethiopia against forces supported by the United States; removing migration restrictions in 1980 which led 125,000 Cubans to cross the Florida Straits and enter the United States. Indeed the Cold War manifested itself in the Cuban-U.S. relationship through the continuing concentration on these points of enmity.

While the East-West conflict might seem like an appropriate framework for reviewing these events, it actually obscures the essential Cuban-U.S. conflict since 1959: Cuba's pursuit of sovereignty versus the U.S. pursuit of domination. Still Cold War ideology did provide the language and rationale for U.S. policy. Thus when the Cold War ended, and the Soviet Union collapsed, it seemed as if a thaw in Cuban-U.S relations could be possible, because a substantially new international context existed.

DOMESTICATING U.S. POLICY AFTER THE COLD WAR

The breakdown of the bipolar international system disengaged Cuba from the East-West axis and changed U.S. perceptions about the island. By 1991 most U.S. officials recognized, for the first time since the 1962 missile crisis, that Cuba was not a threat to U.S. national security. U.S. demands during the Cold War had focused on Cuba ending its close relationship with the Soviet Union and its activities in Latin America and Africa, allegedly in support of Soviet expansion. Once the Soviet Union ceased to exist, these U.S. concerns were no longer meaningful. Yet U.S. hostility towards Cuba continued.

In the immediate aftermath of the Cold War, domestic politics governed U.S. policy towards Cuba and accounted for increased tension between the two countries. The George H. W. Bush administration gave little attention to Cuba. At the same time, the executive's tendency to react to events in an *ad hoc* fashion, combined with a continuing consensus that Cuba needed to modify its political system, enabled right-wing groups in the Cuban community to monopolize the Cuban issue. They encouraged members of congress to step into the vacuum left by the president's neglect. Led by the Cuban-American National Foundation (CANF), the fiercest anti-Cuban lobby group, these special interest groups had developed into an experienced and unified lobby expert at playing the North American political game. Using campaign contributions and key alliances with other right-wing lobbyists, they shaped the debate on Cuba in midterm and presidential election years.

Their effectiveness was evident in the passage of the 1992 Cuban Democracy Act (CDA), also known as the Torricelli Act, which intensified the economic blockade. The intention was to push Cubans to overthrow their government, which had been weakened by the breakdown of the socialist trading system on which Cuba had relied for international trade. The CDA would ultimately provide the template for the 1996 Cuban Liberty and Democratic Solidarity Act, commonly referred to as the Helms-Burton Act.

The right-wing approach, adopted by congress and approved by President Bill Clinton in signing Helms-Burton, challenged the essence of Cuba's national sovereignty. It tightened the blockade, and then specified which changes had to occur in Cuba's political and economic systems before the blockade could be lifted. The CDA and Helms-Burton Law stated plainly their goals: to overthrow the Cuban government, or in the current vernacular, to bring about "regime change" in Cuba.

Cuba's economic challenge in 1992 was exacerbated by the increasingly globalized and interdependent world. It was not clear whether Cuba's resolute attempt to reinsert itself into the world economy, in order to overcome its severe economic situation, would be successful. That uncertainty, along with Cuba's relative loss of weight in the system of international relations, led U.S officials in effect to bet that an intensification of pressure, rather than a change of policy consistent with the end of the Cold War, would quickly bring about a collapse of the Cuban project.

The Clinton Administration took office in 1993 at a ripe moment for reexamining Cuba-U.S. relations, as the world system underwent a deep process of transformation. Yet the administration's political rhetoric repeated its predecessors' worn-out phrases about Cuba's need to change its economic and political system. To be sure, Cuba policy was not an exception to the general lack of new foreign policy thinking in the Clinton administration. The president's decision to focus on U.S. domestic policy limited the necessary and prompt articulation of U.S. foreign policy in the post–Cold War period.

The incoherence in Clinton administration policy was evident from three issues which arose in the 1990s: the 1994 Rafters' Crisis, the 1996 Cuban Air Force shoot-down of two "Brothers to the Rescue" aircraft, and the 1999 standoff over the disposition of Elián González Brotón, the five-year old boy rescued in the Florida Straits. In each case there was an absence of coordinating structures at the highest level of U.S. government decision making. The fragility of the structure of bilateral relations became apparent as small players—such as the well-organized Cuban right wing—were able to harm bilateral connections as well as elements of regional and national security. As a result, U.S. policy towards Cuba and U.S. foreign policy objectives were held hostage by an extremist ethnic group. Decisions in the Elián González episode, for example, should have been derived simply from migratory policy and precedents regarding parental rights. Instead, the Clinton administration allowed the case to become demagogic fodder for unscrupulous congressional and presidential candidates.

The absence of presidential leadership on Cuba policy not only emboldened the right wing of the Cuban-American community. Many senators and representatives, business associations, churches, humanitarian groups, academics, and governors underscored the need to shift the prevailing course in Cuba-U.S. relations for the sake of America's own political interests. This had enough political impact that both Republicans and Democrats in congress tried to change U.S. policy by weakening the blockade.

However, renewed popular fears about U.S. security after the tragic events of 9/11 inhibited these advocates for change. Additionally, the so-called "Bush doctrine," which champions subversion or "regime change" as a legitimate U.S. foreign policy instrument, amplified hostilities between Cuba and the United States, and produced restrictive interpretations of extant laws in order to obstruct exchanges between Cuba and the United States.

CUBA POLICY IN THE CONTEXT OF THE WAR AGAINST TERRORISM

The world system went through a transitional stage of about ten years after the 1991 collapse of the Soviet Union, as the United States assumed political and military leadership and attempted to play a hegemonic international role, which reached a pinnacle following the September 11 terrorist attacks. The slogan of a "global war on terrorism" and its conceptualization filled the vacuum created when the prior "enemy" disappeared with the disintegration of the Soviet Union.

The terrorist events and the consequent tragedy in human, material, and political terms of September 11, 2001, constituted unprecedented events in U.S. history. But as the Bush administration began a new "crusade against terrorism," it resurrected a classification of states developed in 1982 to label some as alleged "sponsors of international terrorism." Notably, in 2001 Afghanistan was not listed as such a state. But Cuba is a target of the anti-terrorist crusade in part because it is on the list, despite counter-evidence about Cuba's behavior which has fallen on deaf ears in the Bush administration.[2] U.S. officials such as James Cason, former chief of mission at the U.S. Interests Section in Havana, must believe that the repetition of a lie will lead the public ultimately to accept its validity. He has argued erroneously that Cuba "missed the opportunity to join the international coalition against terrorism," which, he says, will "solidify its status as a rogue state."[3]

In reality, the Cuban government officially condemned the terrorist attacks on the afternoon of September 11, 2001.[4] It then offered to provide the United States with all the medical and humanitarian aid it could muster, and the use of Cuban airspace for U.S. aircraft.[5] (The U.S. Federal Aviation Administration, for reasons of national security, closed U.S. airspace shortly after the attacks.) This was followed on September 22 by President Fidel Castro's categorical condemnation of terrorism as an "ethically indefensible phenomenon that should be eliminated." He also declared that Cuba was ready to "cooperate with all the other countries in its total elimination" and added "Cuba would never permit its territory to be used for this type of action against the U.S. people." He underscored emphatically that Cuba would declare itself "never to be an enemy of the U.S. people."[6] Five weeks later, after a terrorist anthrax attack on the U.S. Congress, Cuba offered to deliver to the U.S. government 100 million tablets of Cipro, an effective antibiotic against anthrax. On November 12, it offered low-cost, Cuban-made devices to detect and eliminate anthrax. These measures of support elicited little or no acknowledgment from U.S. officials. Most newspapers and news broadcasts also overlooked Cuba's offers of aid and concern for U.S. citizens in their time of distress.

When the U.S. government called for an international coalition in the struggle against terrorism, the Cuban government argued that the struggle should be waged through the United Nations (UN). In a letter to UN Secretary-General Kofi Annan, President Castro promised Cuba's complete cooperation with initiatives to eliminate terrorism undertaken through multilateral institutions. By October 2001, Cuba had ratified twelve UN resolutions against terrorism which had stemmed from the September 11 attacks.

Afterwards, on three occasions, Cuban officials offered assistance to the United States and presented proposals for cooperation in the areas of illegal immigration and the smuggling of persons, narcotics trafficking, and terrorism. The Bush administration rebuffed the offers in the first two instances, and did not respond in the third, indicating its lack of interest in discussing the proposed bilateral settlements suggested by the Cuban government.

As the war in Afghanistan began, the United States started to ship alleged "enemy combatants" to the U.S. Naval Base at Guantánamo Bay, which is located on Cuban territory. Though the base has been under U.S. jurisdiction since the 1898 war for Cuban independence, it was effectively isolated after the 1959 Cuban Revolution. U.S. possession of the base has been a longstanding point of disagreement between the two countries. Yet Cuba avoided a confrontation over its use as a prison camp. Cuban officials continued to criticize the inhumane and illegal detentions, but Cuba's measured response to the unilateral U.S. decision to use Guantánamo Naval Base was viewed internationally as a welcome moment of quiet collaboration and positive diplomacy between the two countries. General Raúl Castro Ruz, Minister of the Cuban Armed Forces, observed on January 19, 2002, that this small contribution was "an example of what could be attained in other such areas."[7] The Bush administration, though, had little interest in acknowledging the possibility of an accommodation with Cuba. It even ignored the irony of sending prisoners accused of terrorism to Cuba's disputed base at Guantánamo while the Department of State considered Cuba to be a state sponsor of terrorism.

Indeed, Undersecretary of State John Bolton intensified U.S. accusations against Cuba on the eve of former U.S. president Jimmy Carter's May 2002 visit to Cuba. Bolton claimed that Cuba had "provided dual-use biotechnology to other rogue states" and expressed his concern that this technology would be used to "support BW [biological weapons] programs in those states."[8] His charges were unsubstantiated, and the State Department's own 2002 report on terrorism made no mention of any Cuban biological weapons capability.[9] Carter himself stated publicly that Bush administration officials had repeatedly assured him that there was no evidence Cuba had supplied other countries with technology for manufacturing weapons of mass destruction.[10] It appeared that the only reason the Bush administration raised the alleged threat of Cuban terrorism at that moment was to undermine the possibility that Carter's trip might have helped to relax tension between the two countries.

Later in 2002, a new unsubstantiated allegation of Cuban perfidy arose when Daniel Fisk, deputy assistant secretary of state for the Western Hemisphere, charged that Cuban agents systematically had approached U.S. officials with false warnings "about pending terrorist attacks." His claim emerged again in the State

Department's *Global Terrorism Report*: "On repeated occasions, for example, Cuba sent agents to U.S. missions around the world who provided false leads designed to subvert the post–September 11 investigation."[11]

But foreign policy matters concerned President Bush less than politics at home as the 2002 election loomed on the horizon. In May he returned Cuba policy to the realm of a domestic electoral game by announcing a proposed *Initiative for a New Cuba*. The initiative was transparently a sop to the hard-line Cuban-American community in an attempt to gain its support for the 2002 reelection campaign of his brother, Florida Governor Jeb Bush, and for Bush's own 2004 campaign. Promising to veto any new proposal which would expand trade relations or would lift restrictions on travel to Cuba by U.S. citizens to Cuba, the president bellowed that "Fidel Castro ought to open Cuba's political and economic systems by allowing non-communist candidates to participate in next year's legislative elections and the development of independent trade unions."[12]

President Bush's veto threat also was intended to restrain members of congress who saw their own electoral fortunes tied to opening the Cuban market for their districts. Beginning in 2000, there was increasing pressure from Congress to change U.S. policy, and several Republican conservatives sponsored measures to relax economic sanctions against Cuba. They were the key actors in securing passage of the Trade Sanctions Reform and Export Enhancement Act (TRSA) of 2000, which was the most far-reaching attenuation of the blockade in more than forty years. The TRSA legalized the direct commercial export of food and agricultural products from the United States to Cuba.

Though the sales required special licensing procedures, and the products could be purchased on a cash-only basis or with financing obtained through a third country entity, an enormous barrier had been breached. From December 2001 to December 2002, U.S. agricultural sales to the island rose to more than $255 million.[13] This placed Cuba in thirtieth place of the 228 countries which import food and agricultural products from the United States, compared with 180th place in 2000 and 138th place in 2001.[14] By the end of the first quarter of 2004, the accumulated U.S. sales to Cuba since late 2001 was $718 million.[15]

A majority of both parties, in both chambers of congress, also had voted on different occasions to allow increased travel to Cuba, even if that meant barring the Treasury Department from enforcing the law. But unresolved differences in House and Senate versions, and a legislative sleight of hand by Republican Majority Leader Tom DeLay (Texas) in one instance, kept these proposals from final passage. In any case, President Bush evidently was not disposed to listen to the bipartisan clamor on Capitol Hill which favored the lifting of sanctions against Cuba. Instead, the White House hardened its animosity toward Cuba by resorting to rationales which were increasingly implausible.

RELATIONS BETWEEN CUBA AND THE UNITED STATES
AFTER THE U.S. INVASION OF IRAQ

With the U.S. invasion of Afghanistan and quick defeat of Iraq's armed forces, force was reborn as an instrument of power which the United States was willing to use against those states it unilaterally characterized as "rogue". U.S. officials claim that threats from non-state actors—supported by rogue states—legitimated U.S. aggression, which supposedly would be used to stop emerging threats before they materialized. Asserting that such preventive attacks by the United States are "pre-emptive" strikes, the Bush administration has sought to legitimate its crude seizure of territory for geoeconomic and geopolitical gains.

This overbearing philosophy, with its origins in neoconservative precepts about the necessity of demonstrating rapid and lethal power, leads to the unscrupulous use of pretexts such as the alleged threat which the Iraqi regime posed for U.S. security under the presumption that it held an arsenal of WMDs. The Iraq invasion illustrates how the Bush administration has camouflaged the core doctrine of "regime change" within the global war on terrorism. Such a posture allows little space for positive dialogue between Cuba and the United States.

The designated "rogue states" in both the "Axis of Evil" (Iraq, Iran, North Korea) and "Beyond the Axis of Evil" (Cuba, Syria, Libya)—along with Sudan—were the seven states the State Department deemed to label "state sponsors of terrorism." (Libya was recently removed from the list.) The invasion of Iraq established a clear warning to Cuba that the United States has moved to the ultimate extreme in its range of options against any government it unilaterally defines as an "enemy." The United States now operates at the fringes of international law, defying the UN and its Security Council, and there is no force capable of stopping it. Using the war on terrorism unilaterally to achieve hidden foreign policy objectives, the United States feels it can use or threaten the use of force with impunity, even when the country it attacks has no links to terrorism.

In addition to the list of state sponsors of terrorism, the United States has uni-laterally created four other black lists to reinforce its rhetoric and propaganda, and to provide an apparent justification for an aggressive policy of regime change. Cuba is on all four lists:

- Countries which possess "at least a limited, developmental biological weapons research and development effort."[16]
- Flagrant human rights violators.[17]
- Countries with aggressive intelligence operations on U.S. territory.[18]
- States trafficking in persons for sexual exploitation and forced labor (Victims of Trafficking and Violence Protection Act).[19]

Moreover, the National Intelligence Council and the CIA have identified 25 al-legedly unstable countries—one of which is Cuba—where U.S. intervention might be required.[20] Cuba also is characterized as an "outpost of tyranny,"[21] which makes it an opportune target under the terms of the Bush doctrine. The president declared in his second inaugural address that the "survival of liberty in our land increasingly depends on the success of liberty in other lands." His message to Cuba was clear: "The rulers of outlaw regimes can know that we still believe as Abraham Lincoln did: 'Those who deny freedom to others deserve it not for themselves and, under the rule of a just God, cannot long retain it.'"[22]

Cuba's trumped-up reinsertion into the U.S. security perimeter, and the at-tempts to hasten the end of the Cuban regime and to erode any succession plans on the island, are the cornerstones of U.S. policy towards Cuba. The Bush admin-istration defines "regime change" as the basis for expanding its global hegemony, unilaterally employing a series of public instruments and resources that leave little space for positive dialogue with Cuba, even with respect to vital issues.

THE SO-CALLED "COMMISSION FOR ASSISTANCE TO A FREE CUBA"

October 10 is the anniversary of the beginning of the Cuban War of Independence against Spain. President Bush pointedly used that day in 2003 to announce the formation of a Commission for Assistance to a Free Cuba (CAFC). Headed jointly by Secretary of State Colin Powell and Secretary of Housing and Urban Development Mel Martínez, who subsequently became a U.S. Senator from Florida and chair of the Republican National Committee, CAFC was given the charge to present proposals designed to hasten and plan for the "transition to democracy" in Cuba. President Bush accepted the commission's report (CAFC I) on May 6, 2004, in the midst of the presidential electoral campaign.[23]

At first the proposed sanctions were construed as a mere attempt to secure the Cuban-American votes in southern Florida in the 2004 presidential election. In fact, the commission's key recommendations were quickly transformed into federal regulations, which indicates that the report was not merely an offering to right-wing Cuban Americans.[24] The sanctions are evidence of U.S. imperialist aims and of the U.S. intention to change the political and socioeconomic regime in Cuba. Reminiscent of halcyon days in the early twentieth century when U.S. proconsul governors John R. Brooke, Leonard Wood, and Charles A. Magoon ruled Cuba, CAFC I recommends that a State Department representative would oversee an interim government's implementation of the commission's plans. It also calls for a "Transition Coordinator at the State Department to facilitate expanded implementation of pro-democracy, civil-society building, and public diplomacy projects for Cuba," as well as the creation of a U.S.-Cuba Joint Committee on Trade and Investment (JCTI), through which the Departments of State, Treasury, Commerce, USAID, Justice, Agriculture, and Housing and Urban Development would make basic decisions about the Cuban economy, including implementation of a required Free Trade Agreement (FTA) between Washington and Havana.

Such arrangements constitute an attempt to project not only the type of government which the United States would tolerate but also the detailed functioning of Cuba's economy and society. This would be even more arrogant than the Platt Amendment, and represents a twisted revival of the Monroe Doctrine and Roosevelt Corollary.[25] Though Larry Wilkerson, chief of staff to Colin Powell, called the commission's plans "the dumbest policy on the face of the earth,"[26] Secretary of State Condoleezza Rice followed them in July 2005, by appointing an obscure former employee of the House International Relations Committee, Caleb McCarry, as Cuba transition coordinator. The appointment indicated the seriousness of the Bush administration's goal of accelerating the end of the current Cuban regime. McCarry subsequently warned that a Cuban transition might be attended by violence, in which case the United States might have to intervene and undertake a project of nation building.[27] Consequently, any kind of Cuban-U.S. interaction—whether educational, religious, humanitarian, or commercial—which could lead to mutual understanding, would challenge the Bush administration's ambitions for Cuba.

CAFC II AND FIDEL CASTRO'S JULY 31 SURPRISE

Rice and Cuban-American Commerce Secretary Carlos Gutiérrez replaced Colin Powell and Mel Martínez, respectively, as co-chairs of CAFC. On July 10, 2006, they ceremoniously released the commission's second report (CAFC II). Joined by McCarry, they claimed that the 2004 measures had made progress towards achieving U.S. goals for Cuba, and they offered additional recommendations to insure that "the Castro regime's succession strategy does not succeed."[28] The hollowness of their claims was revealed in a November 15, 2006, audit released by the Government Accountability Office (GAO), an investigative arm of the U.S. Congress. The GAO study concluded that the programs had done little more than create an anti-Castro economy which financed activities in the United States—including what some analysts saw as electoral support from the Cuban-American community.[29]

CAFC II offered detailed plans for a U.S. occupation, from reorganizing the economy and the educational system to the holding of multiparty elections. Though the report's recommendations seemed to be the stuff of fantasy, Cuban officials could not dismiss them easily, because their publication coincided with organizational changes that began to institutionalize a belligerent U.S. policy towards Cuba. During the summer and fall of 2006, the Bush administration created six interagency working groups to monitor Cuba and to use increased funding to implement U.S. policies more vigorously in order to bring about "Cuban regime change." Three of the newly created groups—for diplomatic actions, strategic communications, and democracy promotion—were located in the State Department.[30] A fourth, which coordinated humanitarian aid to Cuba, was run by the Commerce Department. The National Security Council and the Department of Homeland Security were in charge of an interagency working group which focused on migration issues. The sixth group was chaired by the U.S. Attorney for the Southern District of Florida, and was comprised of members from OFAC, ICE, FBI, IRS, the Department of Commerce's Office of Export Enforcement, the U.S. Coast Guard, and the Field and Air divisions of Customs and Border Protection. Named the "Cuban Sanctions Enforcement Task Force," it was formed to investigate violations and enforce energetically existing U.S. economic sanctions against Cuba.[31]

At about the same time, the intelligence community restructured the way it monitored Cuba. In August 2006 Director of National Intelligence John Negroponte appointed CIA veteran Patrick Maher to be acting mission manager for a new unit which combined and coordinated two previously separate departments devoted to Cuba and Venezuela.[32] Organizational units often take on a life of their own, especially as professionals gain a vested interest in their new responsibilities. These administrative changes thus contribute to the maintenance of a hostile policy.

The most concrete recommendation in CAFC II was the creation of an $80 million fund—to be known as the Cuba Fund for a Democratic Future—to "promote democracy" in Cuba. The report called for at least $20 million to be added to the program every year after the initial two-year period, in addition to the $10 million a year which the State Department and the U.S. Agency for International Development (USAID) spend for other democracy-assistance programs.

Supporters of the Bush administration's strategy for dealing with Cuba—that is, "transformational diplomacy" and forcible democratization—saw the timing of

CAFC II as remarkably prescient. Only twenty-one days after it was published, on July 31, 2006, the Cuban government announced that its ailing leader, Fidel Castro, had provisionally ceded power to a collective leadership headed by Raul Castro. The possibility of a transition in Cuba instantly became palpable. But U.S prognosticators had not anticipated the scenario which unfolded, in which the Cuban leader stayed in the background while a group of seasoned policymakers coordinated the continuity of the Cuban Project.

Though the Cuban system showed no instability in the wake of President Castro's illness, the turn of events did force Washington to consider the real consequences of its policy. The question arose as to whether continuation of the Sisyphus-like punishment of Cuba served U.S. interests. The Department of Defense, for example, had balked at acting too aggressively for fear of igniting a crisis in the U.S. backyard at a time when U.S. forces already were stretched thin by the Afghan and Iraq wars. And if rumblings of instability did begin to emerge from Cuba, it was hardly clear that Bush's mindless chants, urging Cubans on the island to adopt so-called democratic reforms, offered the United States a meaningful guideline to deal with such a circumstance. Would the United States try to push the regime over the edge, or would it help the regime to survive in order to avert chaos ninety miles from south Florida?

What was clearer to Cubans, though, was the way in which four decades plus of inhumane economic sanctions, and a policy of increasing hostility, had undermined U.S. claims for a role in shaping whatever might unfold within Cuban domestic politics on the island. At the same time, the negative U.S. position in its historic conflict with Cuba engendered a spirit of Cuban nationalism, while the Helms-Burton law, which codified the sanctions, reduced Washington's options. Such limitations on U.S. policy options constitute an enormous problem. Credible scenarios leading to chaos and violence can be envisioned if there were an upsurge in interest from radical right-wing segments in the Cuban-American community. These extremists could well engage in provocations in order to draw the United States and Cuba into a direct conflict.

NOTES FOR REFLECTION

While policymaking in Cuba has always taken U.S. politics into serious consideration, Cuba has not been, in the short or medium term, a political priority for the United States. This fact has constrained the debate on U.S.-Cuba policy for more than forty-five years. As a consequence, those with narrowly focused interests tended to monopolize the discussion about Cuba in the United States. But globalization, with its contradictory processes of economic integration and the marginalization of states, nations, and social groups, has made it essential to face genuine and universal problems of terrorism, underdevelopment, pollution, migration, drug-trafficking, weapons proliferation, and human smuggling, as well as new challenges to national, regional, and international security. The geographic, economic, political, and cultural space that Cuba and the United States share cannot be ignored.

Therefore, agreement on subjects of common concern is in the short-term interest of both countries. For example, the United States and Cuba could readily engage in win-win negotiations over issues related to the environment, terrorism, immigration, and drug trafficking. Negotiations concerning matters covered by international laws also could be feasible in the medium term. They might address issues such as the property claims and counterclaims of the two governments, the status of Guantánamo Naval Base, and the lifting of trade sanctions and restoration of normal trade relations. This would open the way for consular and diplomatic relations.

But the *sine qua non* of negotiations for most people on the island is that the United States must respect Cuba's sovereignty and quest for independence. Any U.S. intent to restore domination over Cuba would violate a fundamental Cuban national interest. U.S. willingness to abandon such a goal would be an indication of how seriously Washington sought meaningful negotiations and a peaceful outcome to any Cuban transition. To be sure, Cuba also must take into account U.S. national interests and concerns about regional security. Thus the process by which the two neighbors could achieve constructive coexistence needs to begin with mutual respect.

NOTES

1. Jules Robert Benjamin, *The United States and Cuba: Hegemony and Dependent Development*, 1880–1934. Pittsburgh, University of Pittsburgh Press, 1977, pp. 4–5; Ramiro Guerra, *La Expansión Territorial de los Estados Unidos*, Cuba, Editorial Universitaria, 1964.

2. Anya K. Landau and Wayne S. Smith, *Keeping Things in Perspective: Cuba and the Question of International Terrorism* (Washington, D.C.: Center for International Policy, 2001).

3. James C. Cason, "Regional Impact of the September 11th Events: U.S. Security Concerns"; presented at the Stanley Foundation Policy Forum on Securing the Third Border: Cuba, the Caribbean, and U.S. Foreign Policy Options, Washington, D.C., November 1, 2001, 11–28.

4. Government of the Republic of Cuba, "Statement by the Government of Cuba," Cuban Interests Section, Washington, D.C., September 11, 2001.

5. Andrew Cawthorne, "Cuba Offers Aid and 'Solidarity' to the U.S.," Reuters, September 11, 2001.

6. Fidel Castro Ruz, "Speech," Havana, September 22, 2001; available at www.cuba.cu/gobierno/discursos/2001/ing/f220901i.html.

7. Raúl Castro Ruz, "Televised Comparisons," *Noticiero Dominical*, NTV, Cuba, January 20, 2002.

8. John R. Bolton, "Beyond the Axis of Evil: Additional Threats from Weapons of Mass Destruction," Heritage Foundation Lecture 743 (2002):1–8.

9. U.S. Department of State, Office of the Coordinator for Counterterrorism, *Patterns of Global Terrorism—2002*; released April 30, 2003, p. 76.

10. Kevin Sullivan, "Carter Says He Was Told U.S. Had No Proof Cuba Shared Bio-Weapons Data; State Dept. Official's Claim Contradicted," *Washington Post*, May 14, 2002, 14(A).

11. Daniel W. Fisk, "Address before the National Summit on Cuba," Washington, D.C., September 17, 2002, *Patterns of Global Terrorism—2002*, p. 76.

12. Karen DeYoung, "Bush: No Lifting of Cuba Policies; President Reaffirms U.S. Sanctions," *Washington Post*, May 21, 2002, 1(A).

13. David Luhnow, "Cuba, U.S. Firms Reap Harvest at Unprecedented Food Expo," *Wall Street Journal*, 14(A).

14. Angel Guerra, "Los nuevos socios de Cuba," *La Jornada*, October 3, 2002.

15. A. Rodríguez, "Yanquis' rubrican contratos millonario," *El Nuevo Herald*, April 17, 2004.

16. John R. Bolton, "The Bush Administration's Nonproliferation Policy: Successes and Future Challenges." Testimony before the House International Relations Committee, 30 March 2004.

17. U.S. Department of State, Bureau of Democracy, Human Rights, and Labor, "Cuba," in *Country Reports on Human Rights Practices*—2004; February 28, 2005. Repeated in subsequent years.

18. Bolton, "The Bush Administration's Nonproliferation Policy."

19. U.S. State Department, Office to Monitor and Combat Trafficking in Persons, *Trafficking in Persons Report*, 2003 (June 11, 2003). Repeated in subsequent years.

20. Pablo Bachelet, "'06 Elections Pose Trouble, Goss Warns a Large Concentration of Elections in Latin America in 2006 Could Potentially Cause Instability, CIA Chief Porter Goss Told Senators," *Miami Herald*, February 17, 2005.

21. Pablo Bachelet, "Rice: Cuba an 'Outpost of Tyranny,' Venezuela a 'Negative Force,'" *Miami Herald*, January 19, 2005.

22. Text of President George W. Bush's inaugural speech, Office of the Press Secretary, The White House, January 20, 2005.

23. U.S. Department of State, Commission for Assistance to a Free Cuba, "Report to the President," May 2004.

24. U.S. Department of the Treasury, Office of Foreign Assets Control (OFAC), "Revocation of OFAC Specific Licenses to Engage in Travel-Related Transaction Incident to Visiting Close Relatives in Cuba," June 30, 2004. www.treas.gov/offices/enforcement/ofac/comment.html.

25. The report also advocated reducing contact between Cubans and their U.S. relatives—as well as between Cubans and U.S. citizens in general—by redefining "close relatives" narrowly, and by dramatically restricting the frequency, length, and allowable cost of Cuban-American family visits to the island.

26. James Morrison, "Embassy Row: Not a GQ Guy," *Washington Times*, May 27, 2004, 17(A).

27. Guy Dinmore, "US Steps Up Planning for a Cuba without Castro," *Financial Times*, November 1, 2005.

28. Condoleezza Rice and Carlos Gutierrez, "Report to the President: Commission for Assistance to a Free Cuba," July 2006, www.cafc.gov/documents/organization/68166.pdf.

29. United States Government Accountability Office, *Foreign Assistance: U.S. Democracy Assistance for Cuba Needs Better Management and Oversight*, table 9: State and USAID Grantees and Awards that GAO Reviewed, p. 50.

30. Pablo Bachelet, "U.S. Creates Five Groups to Monitor Cuba," *Miami Herald*, September 13, 2006.

31. Jay Weaver, "Trade Embargo. New task force to target Cuba ban offenders—South Florida's top federal law enforcement official unveiled a task force to crack down on violators of the U.S. trade embargo against Cuba," *Miami Herald*, October 11, 2006, p. B01.

32. Eric Green, "New U.S. Intelligence Manager Named for Cuba, Venezuela. Intelligence Director Negroponte Cites Concerns about Close Cuba-Venezuela Ties," *Washington File*, Bureau of International Information Programs, U.S. Department of State, August 21, 2006.

21

Advancing the Day
When Cuba Will Be Free

Daniel W. Fisk

(Remarks to the Cuban American Veterans Association, Miami, Florida October 9, 2004)

INTRODUCTION

At the outset, I want to recognize the commitment and sacrifice Cuban Americans have made in service to this country. Your sacrifices have helped to secure the freedoms and values that we all hold dear. From those who served in Korea and Vietnam—including Brigade 2506 veterans—to those currently serving in Iraq, Cuban Americans have served their country with honor and valor—and the United States of America is clearly the better for it.

You are in many ways the best and the brightest of your generation, and but for a tragic twist of history your service could have been dedicated to building a free and prosperous Cuba. You are to be commended for keeping the flame of freedom alive for that enslaved island. Your commitment and selfless dedication to Cuba's freedom may not be appreciated in all quarters of the globe, but I believe that when the history of our times is written, those authors will recognize that you were right and Castro's supporters were wrong—and that your dedication helped keep alive the Cuban people's hopes for a better future.

I think most of you in the audience tonight would agree with me that President George W. Bush has a unique and intuitive understanding of Castro's nature and the tragic fate that has befallen Cuba. This president needed no learning curve on Castro. President Bush knew from the outset, just as Ronald Reagan knew, that the only way you treat a bully like Castro is by rejection, isolation, and pressure.

That pressure reached a high point earlier this year when the president's Commission on Assistance to a Free Cuba (CAFC), chaired throughout by Secretary of State Colin Powell, released the first comprehensive U.S. government strategy to assist the Cuban people in hastening the day of freedom in Cuba and to prepare the United States to support Cuba's democratic transition.

I was proud to participate in the preparation of that report, and tonight, some 150 days after its release, I am pleased to provide you with an assessment of where we are on the implementation of its recommendations, and to offer some details on the blow for freedom this administration has struck.

IMPLEMENTATION OF CAFC

To hasten the day of Cuba's freedom, the commission recommended a comprehensive approach—one that pairs a more robust and effective effort to support the opposition in Cuba with measures to limit the regime's manipulation of humanitarian policies and to undermine its survival strategies.

To that end, we have provided an additional $14.4 million—of a proposed $29 million in additional money—to support the development of civil society in Cuba and the empowerment of the Cuban people in their efforts to effect positive change. Six million dollars has already been transferred to USAID to dramatically expand its work with civil society groups.

We are also working with international partners to promote greater international involvement in helping civil society activists by channeling the remaining $8.4 million through a new process designed to tap into the innovative ideas of democracy activists around the world.

We have streamlined licensing requirements so that, for the first time ever, high-speed laptop computers can be delivered to Cuban civil society groups. These deliveries have already begun.

Of course, Castro's agents know this, and we run the risk that such items will wind up in the hands of the regime, but they won't be able to confiscate all of them; and that is why we will continue to move forward in sending this type of equipment to peaceful civil society activists. The regime's "esbirros" are fighting a losing battle, and they know it. We also have stepped up our efforts to mobilize international diplomatic and public diplomacy efforts to increase international support for Cuban civil society and transition planning. We applaud such initiatives as the International Committee for Democracy in Cuba, led by former Czech President Vaclav Havel. Recently, dozens of current and former political leaders from around the world participated in an unprecedented three-day event in Prague. The resulting "Declaration of Prague" called for the release of all political prisoners, and included harsh condemnations of the Castro regime. President Havel told the press, "Cuba is a giant prison. We have to put up alarm bells around the walls."

Another key component of our strategy is to break Castro's information blockade on the Cuban people and to bring a message of hope to the island. To circumvent Castro's jamming, Commando Solo, the C-130 aircraft equipped with a powerful electronic transmission capability, has so far flown four times, beaming Radio and TV Martí signals to the island. TV Martí is being seen on the island, by many Cubans for the first time. Indeed, there is a C-130 flying this weekend, beaming the truth to Cuba, breaking Castro's information blockade on his own people. And these flights will continue.

Yet another pillar in our strategy is to identify long-ignored revenue streams for the Castro regime and then move to degrade them: for example, tourism, which has replaced sugar exports as Cuba's main foreign-exchange earner.

We eliminated the concept of fully hosted travel and the provision allowing for the import of Cuban goods by U.S. travelers to the island.

We have limited educational travel, putting an end to such abuses as traveling to Cuba for one week to study the architecture of Cuban beach resorts.

The U.S. Coast Guard has been granted new authorities to restrict U.S. vessels, including pleasure boats, entering Cuban territorial waters. This new requirement has reduced U.S. pleasure-boat traffic at Marina Hemingway by 90 percent, further cutting into the regime's revenue stream. And, in a subject area that has drawn the most attention in the commission's report—we are moving to limit the regime's manipulation of and massive profiteering from U.S. humanitarian policies.

As many of you are aware, to continue to reduce the flow of resources that enable Castro to keep the Cuban people repressed, we have tightened our policy on remittances, gift parcels, and family travel to the island. These avenues had generated an estimated $1.5 billion annually in funds and goods sent to Cuba from those living outside the island. We recognize that there are some in the community who have expressed deep concerns about the new restrictions. What concerned us was that there existed no effective oversight on travel to the island by Cubans living in the United States. What had developed was a self-defeating situation in which many Cubans had in effect established commuter relationships with the island— living and working part-time here and living and vacationing part-time there—all the while serving as conduits of hard currency to the regime.

For example, of the 176,000 U.S. residents who legally traveled to Cuba last year—and spent about $500 million there—about 128,000 claimed to be visiting family. This was one of the most misused and abused travel categories. Now there are controls.

What is important to remember is that these are a means to an end: the end of the Castro dictatorship. What I want to emphasize tonight is that these measures are having a dramatic impact on Castro's ability to economically sustain his regime.

We estimate that, since the June 30th implementation of the new travel, remittance, and gift package measures, we have deprived the Castro regime of over $100 million dollars in hard currency. That's $100 million less that Castro has to repress his people and keep his grip on power.

Moreover, by projecting these numbers over a full calendar year, we estimate a net annual loss to the regime of some $375 million—and that's just from reduced travel. When factoring in the decline in all revenue flows, we estimate we will have denied the regime at least half a billion dollars that Castro would have used to support his security and intelligence apparatus.

A successful transition to democracy in Cuba also means working to undermine Fidel Castro's succession strategy, whereby Castroism would continue in Cuba without Fidel Castro.

The commission recommended efforts to place pressure on the ruling Cuban elite so that succession is seen for what it would be: an impediment to a democratic and free Cuba.

Among these pressure points is the establishment of a database of those involved in torture and other serious human rights abuses, including those involved in the torture of American POWs in Southeast Asia, to prevent these individuals from ever entering the United States.

And, finally, not to overlook the other 90 percent of the commission report, dealing with a post-Castro transition, we are actively reviewing the specific policy and legal issues that would arise in the early moments of such a transition. This review is consistent with our long-standing policy to provide support to societies in transition, such as assistance provided in Eastern Europe and the former Soviet Union, and to Central and South America as those countries moved from authoritarian dictatorships with command-style economies to new democracies based on the rule of law and a market economy.

Our goal is to position the U.S. government to respond effectively and agilely, should such assistance be requested by a free Cuba. The State Department Bureau of Western Hemisphere Affairs, working with the newly established State Department Coordinator for Reconstruction and Stabilization, is coordinating a comprehensive interagency action plan that could serve to inform policymakers. We are working today to ensure that the U.S. government is prepared to the greatest extent possible for the day of transition to a free Cuba, and the work of the commission was the most thorough and rigorous effort to date to prepare for this transition.

BEYOND CAFC

Our list of accomplishments is long, and it is one we are extremely proud of. Beyond the Cuba Commission report, let me just quickly review the rest of the record:

President Bush has repeatedly told Congress that he will veto any legislation that weakens U.S. economic sanctions against the Cuban regime—and he has yet to receive a bill containing any such language.

- We have instituted a policy to deny entry into the United States of Cuban performers whose appearances and sales enrich the regime.
- After years of coast-to-coast propaganda tours by Castro's officials, the Bush administration put an end to those trips. No more luncheons, no more meetings, no more rallies for Castro. We could not be less afraid of their message, and we have complete confidence in the American people to judge this failed and repressive dictatorship for what it is. The reason we stopped these trips is because U.S. personnel based in Havana cannot engage in similar trips in Cuba. If we can't travel, then Cuban officials shouldn't be able to, either.
- Since November 2002, we have expelled a total of nineteen Cuban spies from their Interests Section in Washington and the Cuban Mission to the United Nations. And, Ana Montes, for sixteen years a Castro spy in our intelligence community, was arrested, tried, and convicted. We will not turn a blind eye to Castro's extensive espionage operations in the United States.
- Further, we now treat Cuban diplomatic personnel in Washington on a reciprocal basis to the Cubans' restrictive treatment of U.S. personnel in Havana. We will know where they are going, when they are going, and what they are doing.
- We have directed U.S. Customs to tighten inspections of direct inbound and outbound flights to Cuba. We have accelerated the issuance of civil penalties by OFAC for those who illegally travel to Cuba.

- We actively supported and lobbied for a resolution critical of Cuba's human rights record at the 2004 U.N. Commission on Human Rights in Geneva, which passed over intense Cuban opposition. This was the fourth consecutive year that we have won approval for such a resolution.
- The U.S. Interests Section in Havana, ably lead by Jim Cason, continues to provide more support to the opposition than any other diplomatic mission or entity in Cuba. Through U.S.-funded programs, we have distributed hundreds of thousands of printed items, hundreds of magazine subscriptions, and several thousand radios in Cuba.
- In addition, more than 120,000 pounds of food and medicine have been provided to the families of political prisoners and other victims of repression, and we have helped support more than one hundred independent libraries inside Cuba.
- Because the Castro regime refuses to discuss several issues important to us, we declined to schedule the 2004 bilateral meetings on migration issues that had been held twice a year since 1994.
- We continue to oppose U.S. financing for Cuban purchases of U.S. agricultural goods, and we request records from exporters to ensure this condition has been met.
- We are actively investigating more than two dozen Helms-Burton Title IV visa sanction cases. The most recent Title IV trafficking determination was made in April. No visa sanctions were imposed because the Jamaican company terminated its commercial involvement with the confiscated property in question. This was the first determination in five years. The law was implemented; the law worked.
- We have no doubt that our continued vigilance on foreign investors in Cuba has had a great deal to do with the fact that investment has flat-lined in recent years. According to the Economic Commission on Latin America and the Caribbean, new net foreign investment in Cuba for the past two years has been zero.
- In yet another area, we are actively working to neutralize Cuban government front companies. We have established a Cuban Asset Targeting Group staffed by law enforcement officials from several agencies to investigate and identify new ways hard currency moves in and out of Cuba, and to stop it.
- We have instituted a policy to deny visas to Cubans involved in the March–April 2003 crackdown and sham trials of seventy-five peaceful Cuban activists. And to reinforce our objection to the continued wrongful detentions of sixty-eight of those seventy-five civil society activists, we recently denied visas to sixty-seven Cubans, all of whom are employed by the Cuban government in its so-called university system.

CONCLUSION

This, ladies and gentlemen, is what President Bush and his administration have done over the past four years to challenge the Castro dictatorship, to hasten the end of its repressive grip on the Cuban people, and to encourage the island's rapid, peaceful transition to a democracy that is strongly supportive of fundamental political and economic freedoms.

We are advancing the day when the Cuban people will be free.

We reject out of hand the belief that lifting travel and trade restrictions against Cuba and, in particular, opening up tourism to Cuba, is the answer. Lifting the sanctions now would provide a helping hand to a desperate and repressive regime. Easing sanctions should only take place after there is verifiable movement toward democracy. Anything less would create a financial and political windfall for a decrepit regime. We believe that the best way to encourage a rapid transition to democracy in Cuba is to close off the Castro regime's economic lifelines and aid the development of Cuba's growing independent civil society.

In approving the commission's recommendations, President Bush clearly laid out what motivates our policy: "We believe the people of Cuba should be free from tyranny. We believe the future of Cuba is a future of freedom. It's in our nation's interest that Cuba be free. It's in the neighborhood's interest that Cuba be free. More importantly, it's in the interest of the Cuban people that they be free from tyranny."

Ladies and gentlemen, we are indeed working for the day of Cuba's freedom and we are better prepared than ever before to help the Cuban people realize their dreams for a better future.

Thank you very much.

22

Fidel's Final Victory

Julia E. Sweig

CUBA AFTER CASTRO?

Ever since Fidel Castro gained power in 1959, Washington and the Cuban exile community have been eagerly awaiting the moment when he would lose it—at which point, the thinking went, they would have carte blanche to remake Cuba in their own image. Without Fidel's iron fist to keep Cubans in their place, the island would erupt into a collective demand for rapid change. The long-oppressed population would overthrow Fidel's revolutionary cronies and clamor for capital, expertise, and leadership from the north to transform Cuba into a market democracy with strong ties to the United States.

But that moment has come and gone—and none of what Washington and the exiles anticipated has come to pass. Even as Cuba-watchers speculate about how much longer the ailing Fidel will survive, the post-Fidel transition is already well under way. Power has been successfully transferred to a new set of leaders, whose priority is to preserve the system while permitting only very gradual reform. Cubans have not revolted, and their national identity remains tied to the defense of the homeland against U.S. attacks on its sovereignty. As the post-Fidel regime responds to pent-up demands for more democratic participation and economic opportunity, Cuba will undoubtedly change—but the pace and nature of that change will be mostly imperceptible to the naked American eye.

In Washington, Cuba policy—aimed essentially at regime change—has long been dominated by wishful thinking ever more disconnected from the reality on the island. Thanks to the votes and campaign contributions of the 1.5 million Cuban Americans who live in Florida and New Jersey, domestic politics has driven policymaking. That tendency has been indulged by a U.S. intelligence community hamstrung by a breathtaking and largely self-imposed isolation from Cuba and reinforced by a political environment that rewards feeding the White House whatever it wants to hear. Why alter the status quo when it is so familiar, so well funded, and so rhetorically pleasing to politicians in both parties?

But if consigning Cuba to domestic politics has been the path of least resistance so far, it will begin to have real costs as the post-Fidel transition continues—for Cuba and the United States alike. Washington must finally wake up to the reality of how and why the Castro regime has proved so durable—and recognize that, as a result of its willful ignorance, it has few tools with which to effectively influence Cuba after Fidel is gone. With U.S. credibility in Latin America and the rest of the world at an all-time low, it is time to put to rest a policy that Fidel's handover of power was already so clearly exposed as a complete failure.

CHANGE IN THE WEATHER

On July 31, 2006, Fidel Castro's staff secretary made an announcement: Fidel, just days away from his eightieth birthday, had undergone major surgery and turned over "provisional power" to his seventy-five-year-old brother, Raúl, and six senior officials. The dead of August, with its intense heat and humidity, is a nerve-racking time in Cuba, but as rumors sped from home to home, there was a stunning display of orderliness and seriousness in the streets. Life continued: people went to work and took vacations, watched *telenovelas* and bootlegged DVDs and programs from the Discovery and History channels, waited in lines for buses and weekly rations, made their daily black-market purchases—repeating the rituals that have etched a deep mark in the Cuban psyche. Only in Miami were some Cubans partying, hoping that Fidel's illness would soon turn to death, not only of a man but also of a half century of divided families and mutual hatred.

Raúl quickly assumed Fidel's duties as first secretary of the Communist Party, head of the Politburo, and president of the Council of State (and retained control of the armed forces and intelligence services). The other deputies—two of whom had worked closely with the Castro brothers since the revolution and four of whom had emerged as major players in the 1990s—took over the other key departments. Ranging in age from their mid-forties through their seventies, they had been preparing for this transition to collective leadership for years. José Ramón Balaguer, a doctor who fought as a guerrilla in the Sierra Maestra during the revolution, assumed authority over public health. José Ramón Machado Ventura, another doctor who fought in the Sierra, and Esteban Lazo Hernández now share power over education. Carlos Lage Dávila—a key architect of the economic reforms of the 1990s, including efforts to bring in foreign investment—took charge of the energy sector. Francisco Soberón Valdés, president of the Central Bank of Cuba, and Felipe Pérez Roque, minister of foreign affairs, took over finances in those areas.

At first, U.S. officials simply admitted that they had almost no information about Fidel's illness or plans for succession. President George W. Bush said little beyond soberly (and surprisingly) pointing out that the next leader of Cuba would come from Cuba—a much-needed warning to the small yet influential group of hard-line exiles (Republican Florida Congressman Lincoln Díaz-Balart, a nephew of Fidel's, prominent among them) with aspirations to post-Fidel presidential politics.

A few weeks into the Fidel deathwatch, Raúl gave an interview clearly meant for U.S. consumption. Cuba, he said, "has always been ready to normalize relations on the basis of equality. But we will not accept the arrogant and interventionist policies of this administration," nor will the United States win concessions on Cuba's domestic political model. A few days later, U.S. Assistant Secretary of State for Western Hemisphere Affairs Thomas Shannon responded in kind. Washington, he said, would consider lifting its embargo—but only if Cuba established a route to multiparty democracy, released all political prisoners, and allowed independent civil society organizations. With or without Fidel, the two governments were stuck where they have been for years: Havana ready to talk about everything except the one condition on which Washington will not budge, Washington offering something Havana does not unconditionally want in exchange for something it is not willing to give.

From Washington's perspective, this paralysis may seem only temporary. Shannon compared post-Fidel Cuba to a helicopter with a broken rotor—the implication being that a crash is imminent. But that view, pervasive among U.S. policymakers, ignores the uncomfortable truth about Cuba under the Castro regime. Despite Fidel's overwhelming personal authority and Raúl's critical institution-building abilities, the government rests on far more than just the charisma, authority, and legend of these two figures.

POLITICALLY INCORRECT

Cuba is far from a multiparty democracy, but it is a functioning country with highly opinionated citizens where locally elected officials (albeit all from one party) worry about issues such as garbage collection, public transportation, employment, education, health care, and safety. Although plagued by worsening corruption, Cuban institutions are staffed by an educated civil service, battle-tested military officers, a capable diplomatic corps, and a skilled work force. Cuban citizens are highly literate, cosmopolitan, endlessly entrepreneurial, and by global standards quite healthy.

Critics of the Castro regime cringe at such depictions and have worked hard to focus Washington and the world's attention on human rights abuses, political prisoners, and economic and political deprivations. Although those concerns are legitimate, they do not make up for an unwillingness to understand the sources of Fidel's legitimacy—or the features of the status quo that will sustain Raúl and the collective leadership now in place. On a trip to Cuba in November 2006, I spoke with a host of senior officials, foreign diplomats, intellectuals, and regime critics to get a sense of how those on the ground see the island's future. (I have traveled to Cuba nearly thirty times since 1984 and met with everyone from Fidel himself to human rights activists and political prisoners.) People at all levels of the Cuban government and the Communist Party were enormously confident of the regime's ability to survive Fidel's passing. In and out of government circles, critics and supporters alike—including in the state-run press—readily acknowledge major problems with productivity and the delivery of goods and services. But the regime's still-viable entitlement programs and a widespread sense that Raúl is the right man to confront corruption and bring accountable governance give the current leadership more legitimacy than it could possibly derive from repression alone (the usual explanation foreigners give for the regime's staying power).

The regime's continued defiance of the United States also helps. In Cuba's national narrative, outside powers—whether Spain in the nineteenth century or the United States in the twentieth—have preyed on Cuba's internal division to dominate Cuban politics. Revolutionary ideology emphasizes this history of thwarted independence and imperialist meddling, from the Spanish-American War to the Bay of Pigs, to sustain a national consensus. Unity at home, the message goes, is the best defense against the only external power Cuba still regards as a threat—the United States.

To give Cubans a stake in this tradeoff between an open society and sovereign nationhood, the revolution built social, educational, and health programs that remain the envy of the developing world. Foreign policy, meanwhile, put the island on the map geopolitically. The Cubans used the Soviets (who regarded the brash young revolutionaries as reckless) for money, weapons, and insulation from their implacable enemy to the north. Although the government's repression of dissent and tight control over the economy drove many out of the country and turned many others against the Castro regime, most Cubans came to expect the state to guarantee their welfare, deliver the international standing they regard as their cultural and historical destiny, and keep the United States at a healthy distance.

The end of the Cold War seriously threatened this status quo. The Soviet Union withdrew its $4 billion annual subsidy, and the economy contracted by 35 percent overnight. Cuba's political elite recognized that without Soviet support, the survival of the revolutionary regime was in peril—and, with Fidel's reluctant acquiescence, fashioned a pragmatic response to save it. Cuban officials traveling abroad started using once-anathema terms, such as "civil society." Proposals were circulated to include multiple candidates (although all from the Communist Party) in National Assembly elections and to permit small private businesses. The government legalized self-employment in some 200 service trades, converted state farms to collectively owned cooperatives, and allowed the opening of small farmers' markets. At Raúl's instigation, state enterprises adopted capitalist accounting and business practices; some managers were sent to European business schools. As the notion of a "socialist enterprise" became increasingly unsustainable, words like "market," "efficiency," "ownership," "property," and "competition" began to crop up with ever more frequency in the state-controlled press and in public-policy debates. Foreign investment from Europe, Latin America, Canada, China, and Israel gave a boost to agriculture and the tourism, mining, telecommunications, pharmaceutical, biotechnology, and oil industries.

These changes rendered Cuba almost unrecognizable compared with the Cuba of the Soviet era, but they also allowed Fidel's government to regain its footing. The economy began to recover, and health and educational programs started to deliver again. By the end of the 1990s, Cuba's infant mortality rate (approximately six deaths per 100,000 births) had dropped below that of the United States, and close to 100 percent of children were enrolled in school full time through ninth grade. Housing, although deteriorating and in desperate need of modernization, remained virtually free. And a cosmopolitan society—albeit one controlled in many ways by the state—grew increasingly connected to the world through cultural exchanges, sporting events, scientific cooperation, health programs, technology, trade, and diplomacy. Moreover, by 2002, total remittance inflows reached $1 billion, and nearly half of the Cuban population had access to dollars from family abroad.

In 2004, a process of "recentralization" began: the state replaced the dollar with a convertible currency, stepped up tax collection from the self-employed sector, and imposed stricter controls on revenue expenditures by state enterprises. But even with these controls over economic activity, the black market is everywhere. Official salaries are never enough to make ends meet, and the economy has become a hybrid of control, chaos, and free-for-all. The rules of the game are established and broken at every turn, and most Cubans have to violate some law to get by. The administrators of state enterprises steal and then sell the inputs they get from the government, forcing workers to purchase themselves the supplies they need to do their jobs—rubber for the shoemaker, drinking glasses for the bartender, cooking oil for the chef—in order to fill production quotas.

At the same time, the revolution's investment in human capital has made Cuba uniquely well positioned to take advantage of the global economy. In fact, the island faces an overcapacity of professional and scientific talent, since it lacks the industrial base and foreign investment necessary to create a large number of productive skilled jobs. With 10,000 students in its science and technology university and already successful joint pharmaceutical ventures with China and Malaysia, Cuba is poised to compete with the upper ranks of developing nations.

INFIDELITY

Although the George H. W. Bush administration ended covert efforts to topple Fidel, the United States today spends about $35 million a year on initiatives described by some as "democracy promotion" and by others as "destabilization." Radio Martí and TV Martí broadcast from Florida to Cuba; other U.S. government programs are intended to support dissidents, the families of political prisoners, human rights activists, and independent journalists. Although some Cubans do listen to Radio Martí, the Cuban government blocks the TV Martí signal, and without open ties between the countries, only a fraction of the support actually reaches Cubans living on the island; the lion's share is distributed through no-bid contracts to the anti-Castro cottage industry that has sprung up in Miami, Madrid, and a few Latin American and Eastern European capitals. The recipients of such federal largess—along with the Cuban intelligence agents that routinely penetrate the groups they form—have become the primary stakeholders in Washington's well-funded, if obviously ineffective, policy toward Cuba.

On the ground in Cuba, moreover, these efforts are generally counterproductive. U.S. economic sanctions have given Cuba's leaders justification for controlling the pace of the island's insertion into the world economy. The perception, pervasive in Cuba, that the United States and the Cuban diaspora are plotting regime change further strengthens domestic hard-liners who argue that only a closed political model with minimal market openings can insulate the island from domination by a foreign power allied with old-money elites. Dissidents who openly associate with U.S. policy and its advocates in Miami or the U.S. Congress mark themselves as stooges of the United States, even if they are not. Moreover, the Cuban government has successfully undermined both the domestic and the international legitimacy of dissidents by "outing" some as sources, assets, or agents of the United States (or of Cuba's own intelligence services). The 2003 arrest and incarceration of seventy-five dissidents was intended to demonstrate that Cuba could and would preempt outside efforts at regime change regardless of the consequent international outcry and U.S. congressional rebuke.

There are some genuine dissidents in Cuba untainted by either government and not weakened by infighting. One, Oswaldo Payá, is a devout Catholic who heads the Varela Project, which collected more than 11,000 signatures in 2002 for a petition calling on the Cuban government to hold a referendum on open elections, free speech, free enterprise, and the release of political prisoners. Yet it is only by resisting the embrace of the international community, and of the United States in particular, that Payá has maintained his credibility and autonomy. Meanwhile, below the radar screen (and throughout officially sanctioned Cuban institutions), there are scores of thoughtful nationalists, communists, socialists, social democrats, and progressives who may not yet have the political space to air their views publicly but who express dissent in terms that U.S. policymakers either do not recognize or do not support.

The upshot of a half century of hostility—especially now with ties severed almost entirely—is that Washington has virtually no leverage over events in Cuba. With no other way to make good on its campaign commitments to Cuban Americans short of a full-scale invasion, the Bush administration established the Commission for Assistance to a Free Cuba in 2003 and appointed a "Cuba transition coordinator" in 2004. To date, the commission, the membership and deliberations of which have been kept secret, has issued two reports, totaling over 600 pages, on what kind of assistance the U.S. government could, "if requested," provide to a transitional government in Cuba.

The basic assumption behind the commission's planning is that with outside assistance, Cuba's transition will be a hybrid of those in Eastern Europe, South Africa, and Chile. Those analogies and the policy prescriptions derived from them do not hold up. Unlike Eastern Europeans in the 1980s, Cubans, though enthusiasts of American culture and dynamism, regard Washington not as a beacon of freedom against tyranny but as an imperialist oppressor that has helped justify domestic repression. (Moreover, the United States had actively promoted travel, commerce, and cultural ties with the Soviet bloc before the transitions there began.) In the case of South Africa, the sanctions that helped topple the apartheid regime were successful because they were, in contrast to the unilateral U.S. embargo on Cuba, international in scope. And in Chile, the U.S. government was able to ease Augusto Pinochet out of power only because it had staunchly supported him for so long.

The second feature of Washington's vision for post-Fidel Cuba is more dangerous than a bad analogy. The Bush administration has made clear that its top priority is to interrupt the Castro regime's succession plans. The Commission for Assistance to a Free Cuba report released just before Fidel underwent intestinal surgery in July 2006 states, "The only acceptable result of Fidel Castro's incapacitation, death, or ouster is a genuine democratic transition. . . . In order to undermine the regime's succession strategy, it is critical that the U.S. government maintain economic pressure on the regime."

After the 2003 war in Iraq, Cubans closely observed the effects of de-Baathification there. Like membership in Iraq's Baath Party under Saddam Hussein, membership in the Cuban Communist Party is a ticket to professional advancement for devout believers and agnostic opportunists alike. Party members include sophisticated intellectuals, reform-minded economists, clergy, brash up-and-coming youth leaders, scientists, professors, military officers, bureaucrats, police officers, and businesspeople in the "revenue-earning sectors" of the economy. In short, it is impossible to know who among the roughly million party members (and 500,000 members of the Union of Communist Youth) is a real *fidelista* or *raulista*. Purging party members would leave the country without the skilled individuals it needs, whatever the pace of change. And should the United States, or a government that Washington deems adequately transitional, ever be in a position to orchestrate such a purge, it would then face an insurgency of highly trained militias galvanized by anti-American nationalism.

One encouraging development is that the Cuban American community is no longer of one mind with respect to Cuba's future and its role in it. For decades, a vocal minority of hard-line exiles—some of whom have directly or indirectly advocated violence or terrorism to overthrow Fidel—have had a lock on Washington's Cuba policy. But Cuban Americans who came to the United States as young children are less passionate and single-minded as voters than their parents and grandparents, and the almost 300,000 migrants who have arrived since 1994 are generally most concerned with paying bills and supporting their families on the island. Now, the majority of Cuban Americans, although still anti-Castro, recognize that the embargo has failed and want to sustain family and humanitarian ties without completely eliminating sanctions. Overall, many want reconciliation rather than revenge.

The State Department is starting to recognize these changes, and many members of congress must now answer to constituents from other Latin American countries who resent the outsized influence of Cuban Americans. But the hardliners and their allies in Washington will continue to fight any proposed policy overhaul. They worry that if Washington adopts a more realistic approach to the island, the policy train will bypass Miami and head straight for Havana—and they will have lost their influence at the moment when it matters most.

WASHINGTON'S MOVE

Even with the economy growing and new public-sector investment in transportation, energy, education, health care, and housing, Cubans today are deeply frustrated by the rigors of just making ends meet. They are eager for more democratic participation and economic opportunity. But they also recognize that Cuba's social, economic, and political models will change only gradually, and that such reform will be orchestrated by those whom Fidel has long been grooming to replace him. Washington, too, must accept that there is no alternative to those already running post-Fidel Cuba.

From the perspective of Fidel's chosen successors, the transition comes in a particularly favorable international context. Despite Washington's assiduous efforts, Cuba is far from isolated: it has diplomatic relations with more than 160 countries, students from nearly 100 studying in its schools, and its doctors stationed in 69. The resurgence of Latin America's left, along with the recent rise in anti-American sentiment around the globe, makes Cuba's defiance of the United States even more compelling and less anomalous than it was just after the Cold War. The Cuban-Venezuelan relationship, based on a shared critique of U.S. power, imperialism, and "savage capitalism," has particular symbolic power. Although this alliance is hardly permanent, and American observers often make too much of Venezuela's influence as a power broker, it does deliver Cuba some $2 billion in subsidized oil a year and provide an export market for Cuba's surfeit of doctors and technical advisers. (By providing the backbone for Venezuelan President Hugo Chávez's social programs and assistance in building functional organizations, Havana exercises more influence in Venezuela than Caracas does in Cuba.) Havana, without ceding any authority to Chávez, will optimize this relationship as long as it remains beneficial.

Nor is Venezuela the only country that will resist U.S. efforts to dominate post-Fidel Cuba and purge the country of Fidel's revolutionary legacy. Latin Americans, still deeply nationalistic, have long viewed Fidel as a force for social justice and a necessary check on U.S. influence. Latin Americans of diverse ideological stripes, most of them deeply committed to democracy in their own countries, want to see a soft landing in Cuba—not the violence and chaos that they believe U.S. policy will bring. Given their own failures in the 1990s to translate engagement with Cuba into democratization, and the United States' current credibility problems on this score, it is unlikely that U.S. allies in Latin America or Europe will help Washington use some sort of international initiative to advance its desires for radical change in Cuba.

Various actors in the United States and the international community have ready a set of demands for Cuba: hold a referendum and multiparty elections, immediately release all political prisoners, return nationalized property and compensate former owners, rewrite the constitution, allow a free press, privatize state companies—in short, become a country Cuba has never been, even before the revolution. Many of those goals would be desirable if you were inventing a country from scratch. Few of them are now realistic.

A "transition" government of the sort Washington is hoping for will not occupy the presidential palace in Havana in the foreseeable future. This means that the White House cannot responsibly wait for the happy day when the outlines of its commission reports can be put to the test. Instead, the current administration should immediately start talking to the senior Cuban leadership. Recognizing that Cuba and the United States share an interest in stability on both sides of the Florida Straits, the first priority is to coordinate efforts to prevent a refugee crisis or unforeseen provocations by U.S.-based exile groups eager to exploit a moment of change on the island. Beyond crisis management, Washington and Havana can cooperate on a host of other concerns in the Caribbean Basin, including drug trafficking, migration, customs and port security, terrorism, and the environmental consequences of offshore drilling in the Gulf of Mexico. The two countries have successfully worked on some of these issues in the past: each has bureaucracies staffed by professionals who know the issues, and even know one another. An end to Washington's travel ban, a move already backed by bipartisan majorities in the House of Representatives, would further open the way to a new dynamic between the United States and Cuba. Just as the first Bush White House formally ended covert operations on the island, this Bush administration or its successor should also affirmatively take regime change, long the centerpiece of Washington's policy toward Cuba, off the table.

By continuing the current course and making threats about what kind of change is and is not acceptable, Washington will only slow the pace of liberalization and political reform in Cuba and guarantee many more years of hostility between the two countries. By proposing bilateral crisis management and confidence-building measures, ending economic sanctions, stepping out of the way of Cuban Americans and other Americans who wish to travel freely to Cuba, and giving Cuba the space to chart its own course, Washington would help end the siege mentality that has long pervaded the Cuban body politic and, with the applause of U.S. allies, perhaps help accelerate reform. Cubans on and off the island have always battled over its fate—and attempted to draw American might into their conflicts, directly or indirectly. Lest the next fifty years bring more of the same, the wisest course for Washington is to get out of the way, removing itself from Cuba's domestic politics altogether.

Fidel's successors are already at work. Behind Raúl are a number of other figures with the capacity and the authority to take the reins and continue the transition, even after Raúl is gone. Fortunately for them, Fidel has taught them well: they are working to consolidate the new government, deliver on bread-and-butter issues, devise a model of reform with Cuban characteristics, sustain Cuba's position in Latin America and internationally, and manage the predictable policies of the United States. That these achievements will endure past Fidel's death is one final victory for the ultimate Latin American survivor.

23

Wanted: A Logical Cuba Policy

Wayne S. Smith

Perhaps the most striking thing about U.S. policy toward Cuba is the near-total disjuncture between stated objectives and the means chosen to achieve them. Not only do the means not serve the ends, they seem designed to work against them.

For example, the United States has made it clear that it does not want any more floods of refugees from Cuba. Yet the policy is designed to increase economic distress on the island, thus exacerbating the very conditions which cause Cubans to take to the rafts. As one observer put it, "If U.S. economic sanctions worked as well as their architects intended, the result might be a million Cuban refugees on Florida's beaches, exactly what we do not want."

And this is but an example. On a point-by-point basis, the policy is embarrassingly counterproductive. Significantly, not a single other government supports our policy toward Cuba. Indeed, it has caused serious problems with many of our most important allies and trading partners and has placed at some risk the viability of the World Trade Organization, a body which has served U.S. interests well. Thus, while with the end of the Cold War Cuba is of little importance to the United States, in an effort to punish it, the United States has placed in jeopardy relationships and initiatives which *are* of vital importance. Some would call that irrational. Surely the time has come to work for a policy that *serves* U.S. interests—or at least that does not undermine them.

DEFINITION OF INTERESTS

One nation's interests with respect to another are usually defined as those conditions or acts which contribute to the well-being and/or security of the first. They range from securing favorable terms of trade to making certain the other does not have weapons of mass destruction—or at least the opportunity and intention to use them. U.S. policy toward other countries should be based on the advancement of those interests, whatever they happen to be.

244

In the case of Cuba, it clearly is not. Rather, advocates of present policy argue that the United States must maintain its embargo and otherwise continue a hard line toward Cuba because Castro has not held free elections and has violated human rights. But this is an utterly specious argument.

Advancing the cause of a more open system and greater respect for human rights is indeed a legitimate U.S. interest, as discussed below, but it would almost certainly be better served by engagement than by continued efforts to pressure and isolate Cuba. If we can engage with China, Indonesia, Vietnam, Saudi Arabia, and a whole series of other states that are no more democratic than Cuba and that have even worse human rights records, why can we not engage with Cuba? The argument that engagement works with them but would not with Cuba is utterly lacking in substance. True, we have other compelling interests in those countries. Undersecretary of Commerce Stuart Eizenstat's response to the question of why we trade with China but not with Cuba is illustrative: "I could give you a billion reasons."

China does indeed offer a huge, nearly irresistible, market. Saudi Arabia and Indonesia have oil. If Cuba had a population of over a hundred million people, there doubtless would be no embargo. It would have been abandoned years ago. But it is an island with a population of only eleven million. And it exports no oil.

U.S. INTERESTS IN CUBA

Still, the United States does have interests there which should not be ignored. In approximate order of priority they are:

No Massive Flow of Refugees. During most of the Cold War, and especially after the 1962 missile crisis, U.S. interests with respect to Cuba were principally of a security nature, the first and foremost being to make certain the Soviet Union did not reintroduce offensive weapons systems. With the collapse of the Soviet Union and the end of the Cold War, however, Cuba has ceased to pose any threat to U.S. security. Security interests have been replaced by the same concern the United States has with respect to most other Caribbean nations: that the populations remain in place. The United States does not want floods of illegal aliens or refugees, whether from Haiti, Cuba, or any other state. Cuba represents the most pressing problem, however, because it is the largest island and (with the exception of the Bahamas) the closest. The United States had to make major efforts to close off the Camarioca exodus from Cuba in 1965, the Mariel sealift in 1980, and the flood of rafters in the summer of 1994. That it wants no more refugees is reflected clearly by the 1995 refugee agreement with Cuba, under which, if Cubans try to escape to the United States by raft or small boat, they will be picked up at sea by the U.S. Coast Guard and returned to Cuba. This is manageable so long as the Cuban government does its part to curb the flow. If it did not, if it simply lifted the gates, then we would face another refugee flood, as we certainly would if there were a major outbreak of violence or an economic disaster in Cuba.

But it is as if we forget from one of these periodic outflows to the other just how costly and disruptive they are. And we seem to have forgotten again, for if preventing another outflow is a major U.S. interest, one must ask how that interest is served by a policy which aims at sharply increasing economic distress on the island—indeed, at choking it to its knees. Does that not fuel the very conditions which cause

Cubans to wish to take to the boats? And can anyone imagine that Castro would allow economic deterioration to reach critical mass *without* again lifting the floodgates? Of course not. Long before economic collapse, he would react by allowing a million Cubans or more to take to the boats.

Senator Jesse Helms's response to this dilemma is to say that if Castro allowed such an exodus, the United States would consider it an act of war. Brilliant! And how would the United States respond to that exodus? By blowing the refugees out of the water? By bombing the beaches where they were gathering? By bombing other targets or perhaps by invading Cuba? Hundreds if not thousands of people would die in the process. Some solution.

Fortunately, neither the original embargo nor the Helms-Burton Act is likely to have a devastating effect in Cuba. They have done some damage and will continue to do, perhaps enough to reduce the growth rate by a percentage point or two, but by no means enough to make or break. This is a case in which the policy does minimal damage to U.S. interests only because it doesn't work very well.

Interdiction of Drugs. President Bush called the war on drugs the nation's top priority. Cuba lies directly athwart one of the main drug routes from South America. Effective cooperation between the United States and Cuba could do much to stem the flow. Yet, the United States has no interdiction agreement with Cuba, nor even any systematic means of cooperating with Cuban forces involved in the effort. The Cubans have on a number of occasions indicated their readiness to cooperate and there have even been one or two instances in which the two sides have worked together. But the United States seems to place the need to maintain an adversarial relationship with Cuba above any need to reduce the flow of drugs. It has therefore made no effort to systematize a cooperative anti-drug campaign with Cuba. At best, this is woefully shortsighted.

Advancing Human Rights. Encouraging a more open political system and greater respect for human rights are perfectly legitimate U.S. interests and objectives in Cuba, as they are throughout the world. The idea that human rights are strictly an internal affair has long since been abandoned, by the United States and by the rest of the international community. The question is how best to advance human rights in Cuba, not whether we should make the effort.

Here, it must be said, the logic of trying to advance the cause by isolating the island and choking it economically is difficult to understand. As Elizardo Sánchez, Cuba's leading human rights activist, has put it, "If you want to let some light into the island, then don't keep trying to keep all the windows shut." He has also said, "The more American citizens on the streets of Cuban cities, the better for the cause of a more open system." The logic of both statements would appear to be unassailable. Yet the United States continues to prohibit the vast majority of American citizens from traveling to Cuba and continues all its other efforts, however futile, to isolate the island.

Given the history between the two countries, Cuba will always react to new U.S. pressures and efforts at intimidation by adopting a defensive mode and calling for internal discipline and ideological unity. In other words, heightened tensions and pressures produce conditions that are the opposite of those that might lead to greater openness and respect for the rights of the individual. Only when tensions between the United States and Cuba are relaxed can progress be made. It is in part with that in mind that all Cuba's religious leaders and many of its human rights activists call for an end to the U.S. embargo and a reduction of tensions between the two countries. When the very people the United States says it wishes to help tell it that its policy is wrong, surely it should listen. But so far, it has not.

Economic Benefits. It was estimated some years ago that the United States and Cuba could do upwards of $3 billion a year in trade as soon as the embargo was lifted, with the overall figure increasing very quickly to some $7 billion. So much European and Canadian investment has gone in since that estimate was done, and so many trade agreements have been signed, that the figure would probably now have to be revised downward. Even so, two-way trade would not be insignificant. Cuba does not offer the huge and irresistible market that China does. But for some companies and regions, it would be important. Louisiana and Arkansas rice growers, for example, would like to sell to Cuba again, as they did before 1959. The United States could also sell machinery of all kinds and consumer goods at competitive prices. And with the dollars it would earn from U.S. tourists and from the sale of shellfish and nickel to the United States, Cuba would have the money to buy U.S. products. Again, it would not be a huge market, but the United States nonetheless has an economic interest in trading with Cuba, an interest which we ignore in order to maintain our embargo. U.S. hotel chains can only stand on the sidelines as they see their competitors building profitable hotels on the best sites on the island. U.S. oil companies can only watch as their foreign competitors drill on leases they once held.

The United States also has a small but clear interest in being compensated for the some $2 billion in properties nationalized by the Cuban government in the early 1960s. There is only one way that compensation will be obtained: through negotiation with the Cuban government. Cuba has indicated its willingness to work out a compensation agreement—and indeed has reached them with every other country that had claims against Cuba. For its part, the United States sidesteps the issue. The fact is that it does not want to sit down to negotiate such an agreement with Cuba. To do so, it fears, would be seen as a long step toward normalization and it is unwilling to take that step. And so it sacrifices compensation on the altar of an unbending embargo.

No Complications with Third Countries. As noted above, in terms of concrete U.S. interests, Cuba is of little importance to the United States—except in the negative context of avoiding more floods of refugees. It follows, therefore, that the United States should not allow its policy or attitudes toward Cuba to perturb or threaten its important relationships elsewhere.

And yet, with the Helms-Burton Act, it has done exactly that. Helms-Burton has been condemned by virtually every other government in the world and has resulted in a rash of retaliatory legislation and in a protest filed by the European Union in the World Trade Organization. If the United States ever implemented Title III of Helms-Burton (which allows U.S. citizens to sue foreign companies in U.S. courts over properties they lost in Cuba), it would cause chaos in international commerce and perhaps even jeopardize the future of the WTO. This, then, clearly is a matter of placing at risk what *is* important over what is not.

A Peaceful Transitional Process. The U.S. government frequently says that it is working for a peaceful transitional process in Cuba. But given the objectives set forth in the Helms-Burton Act, it cannot be, for the principal aim is to bring about a transitional government *without* Fidel Castro. In other words, the United States now openly states that its objective is to get rid of Castro.

But how does one accomplish that peacefully? Can anyone imagine that Castro will retire quietly and give up without a fight? That is not in the nature of the man. He would fight and a good percentage of the Cuban population and armed forces would fight with him. The result would be massive bloodshed, perhaps even civil war—with tens if not hundreds of thousands of refugees on our shores and intense pressures on the United States to intervene to stop the fighting. Intervention, however, could result in thousands of U.S. casualties. In short, a bloody conflagration in Cuba would have costly and painful consequences for the United States as well as Cuba. Yet our goal of ousting Castro carries us in precisely that direction.

The objective should be a peaceful transitional process *with or without* Castro. The key thing is to find ways to encourage movement toward a more open society. That is likely to be a lengthy and difficult process and Cuba may well not become a true democracy until after Castro passes from the scene by natural causes. But so long as movement is in the right direction, and so long as the process is peaceful, the interests of all sides would be better served by this kind of gradual transformation than by a bloody end game.

CONCLUSION

U.S. policy seems to result more from passionate rhetoric and political posturing than from hard calculations as to what would best serve U.S. interests. It is time to try a more logical approach—before more damage is done. That, however, is easier to say than do, for the Helms-Burton Act stands in the way of any significant improvement in relations with Cuba or even any meaningful change in policy. Perhaps the best tactic over the next few years will be to find ways to chip away at Helms-Burton and begin piece by piece to dismantle it. Legislation to lift the embargo on the sale of foods and medicines is a good beginning.

24

The Cuban Five and the
U.S. War against Terror

Leonard Weinglass

Five Cuban men were arrested in Miami, Florida, in September 1998 and charged with twenty-six counts of violating the federal laws of the United States. Twenty-four of those charges were relatively minor and technical offenses, such as the use of false names and failure to register as foreign agents. None of the charges involved violence in the United States, the use of weapons, or property damage.

The Cuban Five had come to the United States following years of violence committed by a network of terrorist groups drawn from the Florida Cuban-exile community. For over forty years, successive U.S. administrations had tolerated the presence of most of these organizations in the United States, and even had provided some with their initial funds. Numerous Cuban protests to the U.S. government and at the United Nations fell on deaf ears, though Cuba suffered significant casualties and property destruction at the terrorists' hands.

As Cuba struggled to establish a tourism industry following the demise of the socialist states in the early 1990s, Cuban exiles mounted a campaign of violence to discourage foreigners from visiting the island. Tourist buses and hotels were attacked, dozens of people were injured, and an Italian tourist died from an explosion at Havana's Copacabana Hotel. Fortunately, authorities were able to deactivate a bomb discovered in the Havana airport's international terminal.

The U.S. government charged that the Five were spies whose mission was to obtain U.S. military secrets. In fact, their mission was to monitor and report to Cuba the planned activities of the exile terrorists. The arrest and prosecution of these men for their courageous attempt to stop the terror campaign was not only unjust. It exposed the hypocrisy of America's claim to oppose terrorism wherever it surfaces.

Nothing reveals this more than the contrast between the U.S. government's handling of their case with its handling of the cases of two Cuban-exile terrorists, Orlando Bosch and Luis Posada Carriles. Both Bosch and Posada were self-confessed terrorists, and numerous documents point to their involvement in planning and organizing the plot to bomb a Cuban civilian airliner, which exploded in midair killing seventy-three people in October 1976.

When Bosch applied for legal residence in the United States in 1990, an official investigation by the U.S. Department of Justice examined his thirty-year history of criminality directed against Cuba and recommended his application be denied. Its report concluded that "over the years he [Bosch] has been involved in terrorist attacks abroad and has advocated and been involved in bombings and sabotage." President George H. W. Bush ignored the recommendation and official findings, and granted legal residence to Bosch.

The case of Posada is no less revealing. After working for the U.S. Central Intelligence Agency, he became a high official in the 1970s in *DISIP*, Venezuela's combined counterintelligence agency and secret police. Linked to extra-judicial murders and cases of torture, *DISIP* previously had intimidated judges who attempted to bring any of its agents to justice. Thus when Venezuelan prosecutors accused Posada of masterminding the 1976 bombing of the Cuban airliner, it was no surprise that two courts declined to convict him. But prosecutors persisted, and Posada was awaiting the determination of an appeals court when he "escaped" from a Venezuela prison in 1985. (He walked out the front door, after the warden allegedly received money from an official of Miami's Cuban American National Foundation.)

Posada twice publicly admitted that he was responsible for a series of bombings in Havana in 1997. He was convicted by a Panamanian Court in 2000 for "endangering public safety" as a result of being found with several dozen pounds of C-4 explosives in his possession, which he intended to use at a public gathering at the University of Panama in order to kill President Fidel Castro (along with what would have been hundreds of others, mostly students, who attended that meeting). His long career in violence and terror is undeniable.

Yet he, too, became the recipient of U.S. hospitality. After Panamanian President Mireya Moscoso pardoned him on her last day in office, allegedly with encouragement from U.S. officials, Posada found his way to Miami. Though he was on a list which nominally barred him from entering the United States, his illegal presence was an open secret. U.S. marshals took him into custody only after Posada's televised press conference made it impossible for U.S. officials to claim any longer that they had no knowledge of his whereabouts. Venezuela immediately requested his extradition, so that he could be tried for the prison escape and on the earlier charges of murder. The U.S. Justice Department refused the request, asserting that he would likely be tortured in Venezuela and could not receive a fair trial there. It then charged him with the minor offense of having inappropriate residential documents. Housed in a minimum security facility as he awaited trial, Posada was released on bail and returned to Miami because the Justice Department failed to provide evidence of his violent past or of his prior escape from prison.

Contrast Posada's treatment with that of the Five, who were arrested without a struggle and immediately were cast into solitary confinement cells reserved as punishment for the most dangerous prisoners. They were kept there for seventeen months until the start of their trial, which lasted seven months. In December 2001, in the wake of 9/11, they were sentenced to maximum prison terms: Gerardo Hernández received a double life sentence; Antonio Guerrero and Ramón Labañino were sentenced to life in prison; Fernando González and René González received sentences of nineteen and fifteen years, respectively.

The Five were then separated into maximum security prisons (some of the worst in the United States), each several hundred miles from the other, where they remain today. Two have been denied visits from their wives in violation of U.S. laws and international norms. The Bush administration simply dismissed the validity of protests from Amnesty International and other human rights organizations about the inhumane treatment of the Five.

THE LONG PURSUIT FOR JUSTICE

The Five immediately appealed their convictions and sentences to the Eleventh Circuit Court which sits in Atlanta, Georgia. Nearly four years later, on August 9, 2005, a distinguished three-judge panel of the court reversed the convictions and sentences on the ground that the Five did not receive a fair trial in Miami. In a comprehensive ninety-three-page analysis of the trial's process and evidence, the judges found that the fundamental rights of the accused had been violated, and they ordered a new trial. Notably, for the first time in American jurisprudence, a U.S. federal court acknowledged (on the basis of evidence produced by the defense) that terrorist actions emanating from Florida against Cuba had taken place. The court even cited Posada's activities, and appropriately referred to him as a terrorist.

The decision stunned the Bush administration. A federal appellate court had declared that Miami—with its 650,000 Cuban exiles who provided the margin of victory for Bush in the 2000 presidential election—was a venue incapable of providing a fair forum for a trial of these five Cubans, because of an atmosphere that was irrationally hostile to the Cuban government and supportive of violence against it. Moreover, it found that the behavior of the U.S. government prosecutors, in making exaggerated and unfounded arguments to the twelve members of the jury who decided the case, reinforced the underlying prejudice, as did media reporting before and during the trial.

The panel's findings corroborated those of the UN Working Group on Arbitrary Detention, which had concluded that the deprivation of liberty of the Five was arbitrary. The UN Working Group also called on the U.S. government to remedy the situation.

U.S. Attorney General Alberto Gonzáles responded by taking the unusual step of ordering prosecutors to file of an appeal to the full twelve-judge panel of the Eleventh Circuit, asking the court to review the decision of the three-judge panel. Such an appeal is both rare and hardly ever successful, especially when all three judges agree and express themselves with the kind of scholarly and lengthy opinion the Atlanta three-judge panel had issued. Yet in October 2005, the judges of the Eleventh Circuit agreed to review the panel's decision. In February 2006 they heard oral arguments, which focused solely on the issue of venue, and then on August 9, 2006—the first anniversary of the smaller panel's decision—the Eleventh Circuit reversed its three-judge panel, reinstating all of the convictions. Notably absent from the opinion was any discussion of the suitability of the Miami venue.

However, the appeal of the Five did not end there. The matter of venue was just one of ten issues raised originally. The case was sent back to the three-judge panel for consideration of the other nine issues. Lawyers submitted briefs on those issues in January 2007, and an extraordinary third round of oral arguments was scheduled for August 2007. None of the lawyers involved knew of any prior instance when three rounds of oral appellate sessions had taken place.

The seven-month duration of the original Miami trial had made it the longest criminal trial in U.S. history until that time. More than 70 defense witnesses testified, including two retired generals, one retired admiral, and a White House presidential advisor. The mammoth trial record consumed over 119 volumes of transcript. In addition there were 15 volumes of pretrial testimony and argument. The defense introduced over 800 exhibits into evidence, some as long as 40 pages. The twelve jurors, with the jury foreman openly expressing his dislike of Fidel Castro, returned verdicts of guilty on all 26 counts without asking a single question or requesting a rereading of any testimony, unusual in a trial of this length and complexity.

The two main charges against the Five turned on prosecution allegations ordinarily used in politically charged cases: conspiracy. A conspiracy is an illegal agreement between two or more persons to commit a crime. The crime need not occur. Once such an agreement is established, the guilt of the accused is complete. All the prosecution need do is to demonstrate through circumstantial evidence that there must have been an agreement. In the absence of evidence that an actual crime had been committed, juries often infer agreement in such political cases on the basis of the politics, minority status, or national identity of the accused. This is precisely why and how the conspiracy charge was used here. The first conspiracy charge alleged that three of the Five had agreed to commit espionage. The government argued from the outset that it did not need to prove espionage occurred, but merely that there had been an agreement to commit espionage at an unspecified time in the future. The media was quick to refer to the Five as spies. However, the legal fact, and actual truth, was that this was not a case of spying, but of an alleged agreement to do it. Thus relieved of the duty of proving actual espionage, the prosecutors set about convincing a Miami jury that these five Cuban men, living in their midst, must have had such an agreement.

PROSECUTED FOR EXPOSING TERRORISM

In his opening statement to the jury, the prosecutor conceded that the Five had not possessed a single page of classified government information, even though the government had succeeded in obtaining over 20,000 pages of correspondence between the five defendants and people in Cuba. Moreover, that correspondence was reviewed by one of the highest-ranking intelligence officers in the Pentagon. He testified that he could not recall seeing any national defense information among the papers. The law requires the presence of national defense information in order to prove the crime of espionage.

The prosecution chiefly relied on the fact that one of the Five, Antonio Guerrero, worked in a metal shop on the Boca Chica Navy training base in Southern Florida. The base was completely open to the public, and even had a special viewing area set aside to allow people to take photographs of planes on the runways. Guerrero had never applied for a security clearance, had no access to restricted areas, and had never tried to enter any. Indeed, the FBI had him under surveillance for two years before the arrests, and there was no testimony from any of the agents about a single act of wrongdoing on his part.

Far from providing damning evidence for the prosecution, the documents seized from the defendants were used by the defense because they demonstrated the non-criminal nature of Guerrero's activity at the base. His objective was to "discover and report in a timely manner the information or indications that denote the preparation of a military aggression against Cuba" on the basis of "what he could see" by observing "open public activities." This information, visible to any member of the public, included the comings and goings of aircraft. Surveillance also discovered that he had clipped articles from the local newspaper which reported on the military units stationed there. Former high-ranking U.S. military and security officials testified that Cuba presents no military threat to the United States, that there is no useful military information which could be obtained from Boca Chica, and that Cuba's interest in obtaining the kind of information presented at trial was "to find out whether indeed we are preparing to attack them."

Information that is generally available to the public cannot form the basis of an espionage prosecution. In his trial testimony, General Clapper agreed "that open source intelligence is not espionage." Nonetheless the prosecution repeated in three separate arguments that the five Cubans were in this country "for the purpose of destroying the United States." The jury, more swayed by passion than the law and evidence, convicted all five defendants of the charge on the basis of this fraudulent prosecution assertion.

The second conspiracy charge was added seven months after the first. It alleged that one of the Five, Gerardo Hernández, conspired with other non-indicted Cuban officials, to shoot down two aircraft flown by Cuban exiles from Miami as they entered Cuban airspace. The planes had been intercepted by the Cuban air force, which killed the four crewmen. The prosecution conceded that it had no evidence regarding any alleged agreement between Hernández and Cuban officials to shoot down planes or to determine where and how they were to be shot down. In consequence, the law's requirement that an agreement be proven beyond a reasonable doubt was not satisfied. The government subsequently filed papers in which it proposed to modify the accusation, because it faced an "insurmountable obstacle" in proving the charge against Hernández. The Court of Appeals rejected the government's request, the doubtful charge remained, and yet the jury convicted him on that count.

The case of the Five stands out as an historic episode in American jurisprudence. It is similar to the Nixon Administration's attempt to use the court to muzzle the *New York Times* and *Washington Post* when the newspapers sought to publish the *Pentagon Papers*, which exposed the lies supporting the Vietnam War and that failed U.S. policy. The Five were not prosecuted because they violated American law or harmed the United States. They languish in prison because they attempted to expose those who actually did hurt U.S. global credibility by committing terrorist acts which broke U.S. and international laws. Through their infiltration of the terror network, which continues to exist in Florida, the Cuban Five demonstrated the hypocrisy of America's proclaimed opposition to international terrorism.

25

The European Union's Perception of Cuba

From Frustration to Irritation

Joaquín Roy

In April 2003, an extremely serious crisis affected Cuba's international relations, and most especially its link with Europe. It was the result of the harshness of the reprisals against the dissidents and the death sentences imposed on three hijackers of a ferry. These developments pushed back a series of rapprochement measures maintained by the European Union and most of its member states with the expectation of contributing to facilitate the political transition at the expected end of the Castro regime. In spite of the fact that the Cuban government justified its actions in view of the perceived threat presented by the increased activity of the internal opposition and the backing provided by the U.S. government to the dissidents, the bluntness of the response (disproportionate imprisonment and summary executions by firing squad) was too much to swallow.

The measures generated an unprecedented worldwide protest not limited to the usual conservative sectors in the United States and the Cuban-exile community. Traditionally tame governments in Europe made explicit protests, while important backers of the Cuban regime abandoned their endorsement, changing it for a straight denunciation. In the European context, the serious deterioration caught the EU institutions flat-footed, with the result that once again a possible cooperative arrangement became doubtful.[1] After careful consideration, precluded by intended measures to be taken by several member states, the institutional framework of the EU acted accordingly. The European Parliament passed a resolution and the council adopted conclusions condemning Cuba. The commission announced on May 1, 2003, the freezing of the procedure to consider the admission of Cuba into the Africa-Pacific-Caribbean (ACP) Cotonou Agreement. In essence, this decision pushed back the EU-Cuba relationship to a low level similar to the one existing in 1996 when the EU voted a Common Position (CP) conditioning a full European cooperation package of reforms to be taken by the Cuban regime. This time it was not the Cuban regime's withdrawal of the application process, as it did in 2000, but the decision of the European Union not to continue with the negotiations. As expected, however, Cuba decided to withdraw again its application in order to avoid an embarrassing rejection. From a dubious attitude and the absence of a clear single policy on Cuba, now the EU appeared to have confirmed an effective common policy.

On June 5, 2003, the presidency of the EU (held by Greece) issued an unprecedented blistering declaration on Cuba's "deplorable actions" in "violating fundamental freedoms," demanding the immediate release of "all political prisoners," and calling on EU member states to limit high-level government visits to Cuba, to reduce the profile of participation in cultural events, and to invite dissidents to national day celebrations.[2] On July 21, the EU Council of Foreign Affairs issued a conclusion using some of the crudest terms labeling Cuba's latest actions, confirming the previously announced sanctions of a mostly political nature.[3] The EU demanded the release of political prisoners, denounced the manipulation of an anti-drug trafficking campaign for internal repression, condemned Cuba's demonstrations against European embassies, and expected a new attitude of the Cuban government, conditioning all future assistance to political and economic reforms. In sum, from a policy of persuasion, the EU had expressed first frustration in expecting signs of reform from Cuba, and finally issued unequivocal signs of irritation.

In contrast with the apparent cohesion of the EU's policies on Cuba, variation has been the order of the day regarding European national attitudes towards Cuba, explaining the lack of a cohesive, well-coordinated policy, to the frequent (behind the scenes) dismay of the staff of the European Commission.

In the meanwhile, the European media ceased to look at Cuba through the lenses of the Cold War, which has resulted in mixed views in the political analyses of the Castro regime. In general, European newspapers seem to recognize the advances of the Cuban Revolution, while they are more critical of the human rights violations and economic weaknesses of the regime. Understandably, this pattern has drastically changed since the incidents of April 2003. In terms of volume, Cuba seems to enjoy disproportionate attention in the European media considering the relative value of the country in global trade and economic terms. While the British press seems to be more objective, in Spain Cuban affairs can turn into the subject of debate at the level of internal politics. Political parties are equally subdivided into ultra-conservatives rejecting direct contact with Castro, far-left nostalgics retaining loyalties to the Cuban Revolution, and the majority of the rest favoring a critical dialogue as the best way to guarantee a peaceful transition. Most lively on Cuban affairs are the European NGOs (church organizations, universities, foundations) dealing with Cuba, as well as regional and local governments, especially in Spain and Italy.[4] Pax Christi, one of the most vocal and influential church-related NGOs, has issued critical reports on the European links with Cuba.[5]

On the economic scene, activities between Cuba and Europe have been increasing in the last decade. Trade has doubled. EU exports to Cuba topped €1.43 billion in 2001 (44 percent from Spain, followed by Italy and France). Cuban imports in Europe were in the amount of €581 million (54 percent in the Netherlands, followed by Spain). Two-thirds of Cuba's imports from developed countries come from the EU. Bilateral development aid and tourism are two of the most important sources of European involvement in Cuba. Almost 70 percent of cooperation assistance comes from Europe, led by Spain (16.8 percent), followed by the commission. Italian tourists are the leaders (13 percent) in a key sector for the Cuban economy. European direct investment in Cuba is over 50 percent of total foreign investment, with Spain covering 25 percent, followed by Italy with 13 percent.[6] Of the 400 investment consortia, 105 are with Spanish companies, followed by Canada (60) and Italy (57).[7] Considering this impressive level of engagement, it is not surprising that only Sweden does not have a bilateral cooperation agreement with Cuba, and ten European countries have investment protection agreements with Havana. Spain leads the European pack with the number of agreements of different kinds with the Cuban government, followed by Italy, the country that in 1993 inaugurated the investment protection pacts.[8]

THE ACP: A BACK DOOR TO THE EU?

Whatever is the evaluation of the relationship between Cuba and individual European countries, the stark reality is that Cuba is the only Latin American country that still does not enjoy a bilateral cooperation agreement with the EU.

This anomaly was further complicated when Cuba became a member of the ACP countries without being a signatory of the Cotonou agreements, successor of Lomé. Nonetheless, Europe as a whole has been Cuba's most important trade and investment source, replacing the Soviet Union as Havana's main commercial partner. With the vanishing of the Soviet bloc, Europe has been able to afford to accept Cuban exceptionalism and has developed what can be labeled as "conditioned constructive compromise" based more on the carrot than the stick. But, until very recently, Brussels has barely used its economic leverage to pressure Cuba on a political level. The peculiar political structure of the EU has helped reinforce this weakness. European persuasion has been reduced to the spirit and the content of the Common Position of 1996, which in turn owes its development to the aftermath of the confrontation between the EU and the United States over the Helms-Burton law.

The Common Position, approved under the Spanish conservative leadership in the fall of 1996, renewed every six months, is a precondition for a bilateral agreement between the EU and Cuba, a clause that has been explicitly rejected by Havana.[9] It calls for a pacific transition to a pluralist democracy, preferably led from the top, with the benefit of development aid being channeled through European and Cuban NGOs. Observers have noted that this Common Position is void in view of the volume of bilateral relations with the majority of the most important member states. It has been basically violated by Cuba's most important partner, Spain, both in terms of trade and aid, under both socialist and conservative governments. Only the Nordic countries seem to respect the terms of the position. The result of this mixed message is that Cuba has not taken seriously the tough attitude emanating from the EU common institutions.

Meanwhile, the weight of Cuba's international activity and concerns seemed to have tilted towards the Western Hemisphere, away from Europe, perceived as concentrating on more pressing issues such as enlargement, the rise of the right, and immigration on top of the crucial disagreements over the consequences of the attacks of September 11. This thesis was confirmed by the absence of Castro in the second EU-Latin American-Caribbean Summit held in Madrid on May 17–18, 2002, replicating his decision of not attending the Iberoamerican Summits held in Lima in 2001 and in the Dominican Republic in 2002, a yearly event where the Cuban leader has been the frequent main protagonist of polemics. Castro invested his political capital in courting his neighbors in the setting of CARICOM's summit held in Havana in December 2002, where Cuba would receive encouragement for a deeper relationship with the ACP group, an offer that the Cuban leader took upon himself with renewed energy.[10]

BEFORE THE STORM

The decision to reapply for membership in 2002 and its consequences need to be considered in a wider and more complex scenario before the crisis of 2003, according to the analysis developed in Brussels. First, there was the financial exhaustion of Cuba by an accumulation of external shocks in 2001 (Hurricane Michelle, September 11 attacks, closing the Russian military intelligence station, global economic slowdown, oil price increases), with the result that Cuba faced in 2002 a sensible shortage in foreign hard currency, estimated at around $500 million.

Cuba embarked, after striking a rather conciliatory tone with the United States following the September 11 attacks, on a double-edged strategy: pursuing a more confrontational course with the Bush administration and engaging in a deliberate offensive towards the growing U.S. anti-embargo lobby both in congress and in the business community. Following Cuba's narrow condemnation at the United Nations Commission on Human Rights in 2002, which was supported by several Latin American countries, including for the first time Mexico, relations with the neighbors became rather sour (with insulting remarks against Uruguay's president). Relations with the Caribbean have been less problematic, with Cuba having signed partial free-trade protocols with CARICOM in June 2001 and having joined CARIFORUM (the EU-ACP aid framework in the Caribbean area) in October 2001.

Because of the endemic economic crisis in Cuba, the regime was in 2002 interested in improving its relations with the EU. In spite of the Geneva confrontation and rejection of the conditions of the EU Common Position, a positive attitude towards Brussels developed. Allowing Oswaldo Payá to travel to Europe to receive the Sakharov Prize was apparently part of the strategy. In the context of this mild EU-Cuba "honeymoon," the commission was accurately perceived by Cuba as a major, cohesive force for a deeper rapprochement. In consequence, the EU Commission opted once again for a policy of "constructive engagement," as opposed to one based on coercion, hoping for preparing the foundations for change in the longer run. In this line of thought, the opening of the EU Delegation in Havana was supposed to serve as the proper setting for the inclusion of Cuba in the new Asia-Latin American (ALA) Regulation (in which Cuba is already inserted in its 1992 arrangement), including a technical framework agreement governing the implementation of EU aid.

THE (OTHER) EMPIRE STRIKES BACK

Right after the serious events EU observers and representatives of member states compiled a bleak picture submitted in reports to the different institutions for their subsequent actions. With this background, on the eve of the May 1 celebration, the European Commission, in its weekly meeting, considered the thorny topic of Cuba and decided to file the still-pending petition of Cuba to become a member of the Cotonou Agreement. The commission issued a statement indicating that the situation in Cuba "has strongly deteriorated in such a very serious manner that the Commission did not want to remain silent."[11] Commissioner Poul Nielson recommended delaying the process some months waiting for a change to be made by the Cuban government. Other members of the commission (led by Spain's Loyola de Palacio and the UK's Chris Patten, in charge of external relations) pressed for an indefinite ban on membership. Nielson declared that the reason for this drastic decision was that the cooperative agreement is not limited to commercial benefits, but it also includes the area of respect for human rights.[12] Moreover, Patten put the burden on Cuban authorities ("the ball is in their court") until they "repair the damage done to the most basic human rights." For its part, the EU Council acted with a speedy condemnation, warning Cuba not to expect European aid.[13] The Latin American Group of the Council decided to endorse an unsuccessful Nicaraguan censure motion against Cuba presented at the Organization of American States (OAS), to issue instructions to governments to limit contacts and participation in programs to be held in Havana, and to carry out a special evaluation of the Common Position on Cuba in place since 1996.

DAVID RESPONDS TO THE NEW GOLIATH

Cuban authorities replied to this criticism and opposition by using such hard expressions as "blackmail" and "soft" [on the United States] for the actions and attitudes of Europeans. The Cuban ambassador in Madrid branded Spanish politicians as "opportunists" seeking electoral gains.[14] Several European countries cancelled or considerably downsized the level of scheduled participation in programs and activities to be held in Cuba.[15] The French government, in spite of its spat with the United States over the war in Iraq, issued extremely critical statements against Castro, vouching for support of EU-wide measures, while intellectuals signed letters of protest.[16] The Italian Parliament and government, dominated by premier Berlusconi's party, announced their intention of proposing what they envisioned as a European-wide embargo on Cuba, in anticipation of tougher measures to be implemented when holding the EU presidency in the second semester of 2003, while reducing the diplomatic relations between the two countries to the level maintained with Pinochet's Chile from 1973 to 1990.[17]

Cuban Foreign Minister Felipe Pérez Roque responded to the EU's criticism in a three-hour press conference held on April 9, transmitted on Cuban television. He lamented that the EU was not making similar condemning statements on the situation on the imprisonment and trial of the Cuban security agents arrested in Miami. The Ministry of Foreign Affairs also claimed that the EU has never condemned the United States for a much higher annual number of executions. Pérez Roque also stated that recent sentencing of dissidents as well as executions were performed strictly according to Cuban law and were "a sad but absolute necessity for defending the vital right to national independence and sovereignty," as the United States "is looking for a pretext for an armed intervention" on the island, by "creating the conditions for a new massive exodus from Cuba." These arguments are consistently reflected in other official declarations and reflections in the Cuban media. Most of these arguments were reiterated by the address made by Fidel Castro on May 1, and reflected by Cuba's former ambassador to the EU, Carlos Alzugaray.[18] On May 16, the Ministry of Foreign Affairs of Cuba summoned the newly appointed chargé d'affaires of the European Commission in Havana and announced the withdrawal of Cuba's application procedure for membership in the Cotonou Agreement of the African, Caribbean, and Pacific (ACP) countries, and in fact renouncing benefits from European development aid.[19]

Then, accusing Spain of improperly using its facilities, the Cuban government announced the cancellation of the bi-national agreement for the Spanish Cultural Centre, a unique institution funded by Madrid since 1997 at an initial cost of over $3 million for the remodeling of a beautiful and centrally located building along the Malecón.[20] The EU Foreign Affairs Council rejected as "unacceptable" the insults from Havana, confirming the sanctions. Italy pressed for the termination of cooperation funding still enjoyed by Cuba, but Javier Solana, high representative for foreign policy of the EU, did not endorse the ending of humanitarian aid.[21]

In Cuba, the government was about to commemorate the fiftieth anniversary of the attack on the Moncada barracks. As an answer to the conditional message of assistance and the political demands given by the EU, Castro dramatically ended half a century of Cuban history confronting the United States by electing to target a new enemy—the European Union. Calculating the effective EU assistance to about an average of $4.2 million in recent years, reduced to less than $1 million in 2002, of which no funds had arrived yet, Castro pointed out that Cuba had imported European goods valued at $1.5 billion, while EU's imports of Cuban products only amounted to $571 million. He not only blamed Spain's Prime Minister Aznar for being the main instigator of the EU measures, but labeled Spanish education as a "banana republic disaster, a shame for Europe." In an apparent deviation from his previous selective critiques and kind references to different EU commissioners, Castro also accused the professional staff of the EU institutions ("a small group of bureaucrats") of drafting a resolution (a "cowardly and repugnant act"), allegedly without consulting their ministers. Claiming the EU was endorsing "the hostility, threats, and dangers for Cuba" of the "aggressive policy of the hegemonic superpower," he stated that Cuba "does not need the European Union to survive," and vowed that "neither Europe nor the United States will say the last word about the destiny of humanity."

CONCLUSION

The balance sheet of the experience of the European Union's policies and attitudes on Cuba shows a mixed picture. It is composed of a coherent script of measures intended in the first place for maintaining the communication line open, and secondly for contributing to facilitating the conditions for a sort of "soft landing" in the terrain of democracy and market economy in the event of a peaceful transition. This strategy does not come free of charge, as demonstrated by the persistent negative vote on Cuba in the UN Commission for Human Rights, and the maintenance of the Common Position imposed in 1996 conditioning any special cooperation and aid package to the implementation of political reforms.

This institutional framework contrasts, on the one hand, with the apparently uncoordinated policies of the member states that trade and invest in Cuba according to their individual interests. This has made the Common Position "neither common, nor a policy," in the words of sarcastic EU insiders. The European strategy can be labeled at its initial stages after the end of the Cold War as one based on good intentions and reasonable (if not high) expectations. But at the end of any serious attempt to condition an offer of a special status in the EU structure (bilateral agreement, Lomé, Cotonou), the result has been a high degree of frustration. With the latest development of the arrests and executions, this sentiment has been translated into blunt irritation.

Decision makers in Brussels and many European capitals have come to the conclusion that Castro's priorities place a conditioned relationship with the European Union at a lower level than the urgency to maintain a line of internal discipline at the cost of violating basic human rights. Moreover, the confrontation with the United States is considered by the Cuban regime as the ultimate *raison d'être* to justify the continuation of the system and the refusal to modify it, or even less to change it. This ever-present theme is obsessive in all communications and declarations of the Cuban government when dealing in public and in private with EU officials.

NOTES

1. AFP, "Prisión a disidentes traba acuerdos con la Unión Europea," *El Nuevo Herald*, April 1, 2003.
2. Declaration of the Presidency, on behalf of the European Union on Cuba, June 5, 2003.
3. EFE, "Europa prepara su crítica más dura contra Castro," *El Nuevo Herald*, July 12; AFP, "EU to launch new attack on Cuba," July 17, 2003.
4. IRELA, "Revision of European Policy on Cuba," pp. 25–26.
5. *The European Union and Cuba; Solidarity or Complicity?* September 2000. www.cubacenter.org/media/recent_briefs/paxchristi.html.
6. IRELA, "Revision," pp. 27–34; Comisión Europea, *Cuba y la Unión Europea*, 2003.
7. EFE, "Mayoría de inversores en Cuba provienen de la UE," *Diario las Américas*, February 9, 2003.
8. IRELA, "Revision," p. 34.
9. Eduardo Perera, "Condicionalidad y condicionamientos previos en la cooperación al desarrollo de la Unión Europea," in *Revista de Estudios Europeos*, Havana, number 53/54, 2000, pp. 3–33.
10. AFP, "ACP pide a UE estudiar 'sin condición previa' candidatura de Cuba a acuerdo de cooperación," December 11, 2002; EFE, "Apoyan ingreso de Cuba a pacto de Cotonú," *El Nuevo Herald*, December 10, 2002; Pablo Alfonso, "La diplomacia de La Habana hacia el Caribe anglófono," *El Nuevo Herald*, December 8, 2002.
11. EFE, "Congelan la petición cubana," *El Nuevo Herald*, May 1, 2003; Tim Johnson, "Senators want to let Americans visit and spend money in Cuba," *Miami Herald*, May 1, 2003.
12. Bosco Esteruelas, "La UE congela su relación con Cuba por la represión de disidentes." *El País*, May 1, 2003.
13. European Union. Council. General Comment before taking action on the Draft Resolution 'Human Rights Situation in Cuba,' April 16, 2003. Amadeu Altafaj, "La UE emite una condena unánime," *ABC*, April 15, 2003; Javier Jiménez, "La UE condena la tiranía de Castro," *La Razón*, April 15, 2003.
14. "Cuba ahonda su aislamiento y desprecia la relación con la UE," *El País*, April 20, 2003; "La embajadora de Cuba acusa a los políticos españoles de oportunismo," *El Mundo*, April 19, 2003.
15. "La Commission européenne aura la semaine prochaine un débat sur la situation à Cuba," Agence Europe, April 23, 2003; "La Unión Europea reduce sus contactos con La Habana," Reuters, *El Nuevo Herald*, April 24, 2003.
16. "Francia critica duramente las recientes ejecuciones en Cuba," AFP, *Diario las Américas*, May 2, 2003. "Cuba, 'la mayor cárcel del mundo para los periodistas'," AFP, *Diario las Américas*, May 3, 2003.
17. "Posible embargo de UE a Cuba," AFP, *Diario las Américas*, April 30, 2003; "Berlusconi wants EU to adopt Cuba embargo," *Sources Say* (Brussels), April 30, 2003; "Italia pide tratar a Castro como a Pinochet," AP, *El Nuevo Herald*, May 5, 2003.
18. "Nueva etapa en las relaciones entre Cuba y la Unión Europea," *Cuban Review* (Netherlands), 2003.
19. Anthony Boadle, "Cuba pulls request to join EU's Cotonou aid pact," Reuters, May 17, 2003.

20. "Castro retira a España la gestión del Centro Cultural en La Habana," EFE, *El País*, June 13; 2003; L. Ayllón, "Castro da 90 días al gobierno de Madrid para que abandone el Centro Cultural Español," ABC, June 15, 2003; Mar Marín, "Castro eleva tensión con España," EFE, *Diario las Américas*, June 15, 2003; "Cuba interviene en La Habana el Centro Cultural Español," AFP, *El Nuevo Herald*, June 14, 2003; Andrea Rodríguez, "Castro takes over Spanish Embassy cultural center," *Miami Herald*, June 15, 2003; "El Centro Español aguarda por la llegada de los nuevos administradores," *El Nuevo Herald*, June 15, 2003.

21. "Europa declara inaceptable la actitud de Castro," EFE, *El Nuevo Herald*, June 17, 2003; Bosco Esteruelas, *"La UE califica de 'inaceptables' los insultos del gobierno cubano,"* El País, June 17, 2003. "Solana en contra de suspender la ayuda humanitaria a Cuba," AFP, *Diario las Américas*, June 18, 2003.

26

Sleeping with an Elephant

Peter McKenna and John M. Kirk

At the turn of the twenty-first century, Canada's cordial relations with Cuba stand as a model of "constructive engagement" and "principled pragmatism," which other countries may wish to emulate. Rather than seeking confrontation, exclusion, and viewing the situation as "the Cuban problem," the political leadership in Ottawa has opted for strengthening relations with Havana in a wide range of policy areas. Unlike the United States, Canada's Cuba policy has moved beyond the Cold War dynamic, has recognized the reality of globalized markets, and has sought to bring about constructive changes in revolutionary Cuba through dialogue and interaction—without any U.S.-like preconditions.

It is important to recognize that Canada's long-standing position on the U.S. embargo not only sets apart Canada's approach toward Cuba from that of the United States, but it also helps to explain, in part, why relations between Ottawa and Havana are on such a solid footing. From the beginning, officials in Ottawa have made it clear to their U.S. counterparts that they agreed with Washington's overall quest to bring about constructive change in Castro's Cuba, but they have disagreed strongly over the means of achieving this objective. Imposing an economic embargo against the Cuban government, Canadian officials pointed out, would prove ineffective and only succeed in tightening Castro's grip over the country. It was also believed at the time that Canada stood to benefit economically should the U.S. go ahead with the embargo.[1] In addition, they argued that Canada could not support such a punitive step because it would contravene its commitment to an open and liberal international economic and investment system—which greatly benefited a trading country such as Canada.[2] Successive Canadian governments, then, have consistently expressed their dissatisfaction with Washington's repeated attempts to act unilaterally against Cuba—as witnessed most recently by the Canadian government's firm opposition to the Helms-Burton Law.

Clearly, Canada's policy toward Cuba has been radically different from that of the United States, although it is not something which Canadian governments wish to publicize. As a small to middling power, and one with no historical baggage of intervention or superpower interests to protect, Canada has been able to temper its Cold War preconceptions with respect to Cuba. In addition, because of its geographical distance from the Caribbean island and the absence of a vocal and influential Cuban-exile community, governments in Ottawa have crafted a more pragmatic and less ideologically driven position toward Castro's Cuba. Neither country, of course, has ever felt threatened by the other, and thus have been able to conduct their relations in a mutually respectful and constructive manner. Havana has adopted a positive attitude toward Canada and the level of political dialogue has been largely civilized, even when fundamental differences do exist between the two countries.

The cordial nature of Canadian-Cuban relations can be partly explained by the fact that both countries share a common foreign policy problem since both have to contend with living next door to a superpower. Undoubtedly, both countries are significantly—and often adversely—affected by what happens in the United States or, as former Canadian Prime Minister Trudeau once said, by the "twitches" and "grunts" of the U.S. elephant. Canadian and Cuban sovereignty—whether of the political, economic, diplomatic, or cultural type—are constantly being threatened, albeit to different degrees, by the superpower reach of the United States. As a result, the political leadership in Ottawa and Havana has sought to reduce their vulnerabilities by devising a host of political and economic strategies—for example, Trudeau's "Third Option" and Castro's "Rectification Program"—to bolster their countries' respective positions vis-à-vis Washington. For this reason, both Canada and Cuba have been able to locate some common ground, underscored by a strong anti-U.S. sentiment among their populations, upon which to construct a mutually beneficial bilateral relationship.

From a political standpoint, however, Ottawa and Havana have experienced a strangely "on-again-off-again" type of relationship since the 1959 Cuban Revolution. Progressive Conservative prime ministers, such as John Diefenbaker and Brian Mulroney—and to a lesser extent Liberal Prime Minister Lester Pearson—tended to be less endeared or rather cool toward revolutionary Cuba. During the years of Pierre Elliot Trudeau's Liberal governments, however, the political relationship seemed to flourish even to the embarrassment of some Liberal cabinet ministers at the time. Trudeau and Castro developed a very close personal rapport, and this obviously set the tone for the overall relationship.

Perhaps the highlight of this period was Trudeau's visit to Cuba in 1976, marking the first time that a NATO Head of Government ever set foot on Cuban soil. Two years later, though, a disappointed Trudeau suspended development assistance because of Cuba's continued involvement in the war in Angola. Interestingly, the Liberal government of Jean Chrétien and his globe-trotting Foreign Minister Lloyd Axworthy—both of whom have visited Cuba—seemed to have moved beyond the coziness of even the Trudeau years.

When one sets out to explain the key driving forces of Canada's policy toward Cuba in the late 1990s, it is not easy to weigh those factors in terms of their explanatory value or to rank them in order of importance. It is true that some of the factors which were present from the early 1960s still carry some explanatory value today. Accordingly, economic, trade, and investment considerations continue to underscore or drive Canada's overall policy response toward revolutionary Cuba, and this has been the case since the imposition of the U.S. embargo. Clearly, officialdom in Ottawa has consistently maintained its interest in continuing political relations with Havana as the key to expanding trade and investment opportunities in a Cuban market which is essentially closed off to the United States. Having said that, Canada's Cuba policy cannot be solely understood in economic terms, but must also take into account a variety of historical, idiosyncratic, political-symbolic, and external variables such as the policy of the United States.

While it is admittedly difficult to assess its exact importance, what has happened in the past with respect to Canada-Cuba relations has helped influence or shape what is currently happening with the relationship. Efforts by the Chrétien Liberals to strengthen the bilateral relationship, in a wide variety of policy areas, flow from a previous policy approach which eschewed severing diplomatic ties with Havana, criticized any tightening of the U.S. economic embargo, and opposed isolating Cuba in this hemisphere. To have undercut relations with Cuba would have marked a sharp departure from a previous pattern of Canadian foreign policy behavior. Thus Canada's present Cuba policy is partly a product of a position that has been adopted for forty years. The Chrétien government has built on a pre-existing historical foundation while adding its own specially crafted bricks and mortar.

In some ways, of course, the Chrétien approach to Cuba reflects a desire on the part of the Liberal government to carve out a role for itself on the world stage and to give Canada some international recognition and profile. Like Canada's leading role in banning the manufacturing, stockpiling, transportation, and use of anti-personnel land mines, it has sought to establish itself as distinctly different from previous Canadian governments on the Cuban question. In fact, a frequent criticism of Canadian policy during the Mulroney years was its constant imitation of Washington's policy and, in view of strong Canadian nationalism, it is an approach that Prime Minister Chrétien was exceedingly careful to avoid. Canada's relations with Cuba, then, provided the Chrétien government with an opportunity to put its unique stamp on Canadian foreign policy. It is one which will likely be reflected in any written history of the Chrétien years.

Furthermore, Foreign Minister Axworthy made a point of raising the profile of the Cuba file within the Department of Foreign Affairs and International Trade. Unlike previous Foreign Ministers, Axworthy has taken almost a personal interest in things Cuban, perhaps signifying his reputation as being on the left wing of the federal Liberal Party. His visit to Havana in January of 1997, even in the face of stiff U.S. opposition, was an obvious testament of his commitment to strengthening ties with Castro's Cuba.

Indeed, when one arrives in Cuba it is impossible not to be aware of Canada's growing trade and investment presence on the island. Both the airport at Varadero and the new terminal at José Martí International Airport's expanded facility, which was inaugurated during Prime Minister Chrétien's April 1997 visit, were constructed by Canadian companies. Sophisticated hotel reservation systems and landing equipment at Cuban airports, McCain's French fries, President's Choice Cola, auto parts, and compact discs are all being supplied by Canadian businesses. A number of other Canadian-based companies are providing everything from foodstuffs to paper products, engineering equipment, paint, medical technology, and a variety of items for the tourism industry. Finally, the number of joint ventures between the two countries has increased dramatically since the early 1990s, particularly in the mining sector where Canadian companies now dominate.

Given U.S. economic power, its proximity to the island, and long-standing personal ties, when the United States ultimately normalizes relations with Cuba, it will not spell good news for Canadian businesspeople. What is now somewhat of a "captive" market for Canada would eventually become one where fierce competition prevails—and a competition in which, in many areas, Canadians would likely lose out. If Canadian business interests are to survive the inevitable American onslaught, they would do so largely on the strength of their existing arrangements and on the accumulation of Ottawa's political capital in Cuba.

Notably, the Canada-Cuba dynamic is very much a win-win situation. It also benefits Cuba, with few, if any, major costs or risks involved. For instance, the Cubans are obviously interested in increasing trade relations with western, industrialized countries like Canada, to replace the trade it lost after 1991 with the Soviet Union and Eastern bloc countries. The Cuban economy has teetered on the brink of collapse. While the country has not fully turned the corner economically, trade linkages with countries like Canada have been very important during the Special Period. Canada has become not only an important supplier of high-tech and consumer goods, which the Cubans desperately need, but also a crucial source of much-needed foreign investment. Indeed, the more than forty joint ventures with Canadian investors have been instrumental in enabling Cuba to survive this incredibly difficult period of readjustment and transition.

For political and symbolic reasons, it is important for the Castro government to showcase its relationship with a member of the exclusive Group of Eight industrialized countries, one that is prepared to work with the Cubans. The high-profile manner in which Foreign Affairs Minister Axworthy was received during his January 1997 visit—the full Cuban media was present and there were meetings with senior members of the Cuban government and major photo opportunities with President Castro—reflected the symbolic importance that Cuba attached to the partnership and the message that it wants to send out to the rest of the world. In a world where the only remaining superpower, the United States, has made life exceedingly more difficult for Cuba, it helps to have a friend in Canada especially when it is known to have a very close relationship with Washington. Solid relations with Canada also add legitimacy to the Castro government. Struggling Cubans can feel somewhat reassured, and perhaps, heartened, by ties with Canada.

Clearly Cuban authorities are interested in strengthening political and economic relations with Canada out of sheer necessity. It does not hurt that Canada is Cuba's number one market for tourism, with some 600,000 Canadians every year traveling to Cuba and bringing much-needed hard currency into the country. Not only is Canada important from an investment standpoint, but it also provides the Cubans with valuable development assistance and technical expertise. For example, Canadian officials have been involved in improving Cuba's banking system, its tourism sector, its economic planning, and its overall tax regime.[3]

The Canadian-Cuban relationship represents an important model of cooperation for the rest of the international community. Both countries have shown that it is possible to have political differences and still have a productive and profitable bilateral relationship. By setting aside differing ideological philosophies and replacing them with a calculated pragmatism, Canada and Cuba have developed a framework for achieving progress on a host of issues. The two countries recognize that hostility, high-pitched rhetoric, and isolation of Cuba only serve to reinforce old stereotypes and actually reduce the likelihood for substantive change in Cuba. Through constructive engagement and dialogue, officials in Ottawa believe that they will—over a period of time—bring about positive political and economic reforms in Cuba. Since these are some of the same objectives that other countries around the world share, they may wish to learn from the Canadian approach. The old-style confrontational and isolationist approach has clearly not worked in the past and perhaps it is now time to try a new strategy.

NOTES

1. See John M. Kirk, Peter McKenna, and Julia Sagebien (1995), "Back in Business: Canada-Cuba relations after 50 years," The Focal Papers (March), p. 9.

2. See Kim Richard Nossal (1997), The Politics of Canadian Foreign Policy, Third Edition (Scarborough. Ontario: Prentice Hall Canada), pp. 73–74.

3. Confidential interview with a member of Canada's Department of Foreign Affairs and International Trade, December 12, 1997.

27

Cuban Americans and Their Transnational Ties

Susan Eckstein and Lorena Barberia

Cuban-American homeland ties must be understood in the context of Cuba-U.S. immigration history. Emigration rates have varied with U.S. law, Castro's tolerance and encouragement of emigration, and ordinary Cuban informal covert efforts to leave.

The approximately 672,000 émigrés who arrived before 1980 came to include, in rough chronological order, officials of the Batista government, the upper class, businessmen and professionals, small shop owners, and others of the middle class. Only about 15 percent of the arrivals during the first three years of Castro's rule had been unskilled or semi-skilled workers in Cuba, and another 17 percent were skilled workers. With the exception of laborers, the emigration entailed a class exodus. Indeed, the island class base of large and medium farmers and businessmen, and then of small businessmen, disappeared with the radicalization of the revolution and increased nationalization of property ownership during the first decade of Castro's rule. Washington and Havana, in turn, permissive of family reunification, created a fairly contained émigré community, a community that remained rooted in pre-revolutionary values and memories.

Coming in the heat of the Cold War, Cubans benefited from privileges not offered most other émigrés. For one, under the 1952 McCarren-Walter Act, islanders, defined as victims of communism, were exempt from national immigration quotas in effect at the time. Second, Cubans benefited from some $957 million worth of official federal, state, and local level programs initiated to help their adaptation. They received food, clothing, and health care, assistance in finding jobs, financial aid, employment and professional training, bilingual education (including for adults), and college tuition loans (see Pedraza-Bailey 1985:4–52). Third, the 1966 Cuban Adjustment Act eased émigré qualifications for permanent residency status (and citizenship, in turn), and for benefits typically available only to U.S. citizens (such as Medicare). The privileges notwithstanding, both because of Castro's initial popularity among the "popular sectors" and Cuban government-imposed exit restrictions, emigration rates tapered off in the latter 1960s and especially in the 1970s.

By 1980, however, new emigration pressures built up. Fueling the desire to leave were visits by some 150,000 Cuban Americans. They had responded to Castro's first-ever tolerance of exile return trips, following a (temporary) thaw in U.S.-Cuba relations under President Jimmy Carter and an island government dialogue with Cuban-American moderates (many of whom had emigrated, as youths, at their parents' discretion, and who had come of age in the United States during the years of the civil rights and anti–Vietnam War movements). The visits led islanders to fantasize about how attractive material life in the United States would be. Cuban American–Cuban contact, in turn, stirred anti-regime sentiments. Unable to exit easily, wishful émigrés stormed the Peruvian Embassy. Seeking to defuse the political pressure, Castro unilaterally granted islanders permission to emigrate, from the port of Mariel. Some 125,000 Cubans made their way to the United States during the Mariel boatlift.

The so-called *Marielitos* in the main represented a different Cuba than earlier émigrés in their social and economic backgrounds and island experiences (see Bach et al., 1981; Díaz-Briquets and Pérez-López, 1981; Pedraza-Bailey, 1985; Fagen et al., 1968). They were less well-off and darker skinned, and they had been socialized in Castro's Cuba. They also included homosexuals, the mentally ill, criminals, and some political dissidents. Authorities loaded these government-defined undesirables onto the boats transporting islanders to the United States. (Pedraza 1995; García 1996).

With the "new Cubans" emerged a first-ever social divide within the émigré community. Earlier émigrés snubbed the new arrivals, whom they considered their social inferiors. While hostility towards *Marielitos* tapered off over the years, to date *Marielitos* and earlier émigrés socialize little with each other. Cross-cohort family ties are limited, and most activists in *municipio* (community-of-origin), Cuban-American professional and other groups are first-wavers. Moreover, *Marielitos* and earlier émigrés typically live in different neighborhoods in Miami.

Cuban emigration tapered off again after the Mariel exodus. The threat of ever more islanders leaving for the United States induced the two hostile governments to sign a bilateral agreement. The United States agreed to accept up to 20,000 island émigrés per year, at a time when other countries no longer were entitled to national quotas. The quota notwithstanding, by the early 1990s Washington granted entry visas to a fraction of the cap. In preventing entry of persons unhappy with Castro, pressure in principle would mount within Cuba for change.

But as in 1980, dynamics "on the ground" operated somewhat independently of government will and law on both sides of the Florida Straits. Cubans determined to come to the United States took to covert means when they could not come legally.

Contributing to the stepped-up informal emigration was the Cuban government's unilateral decision once again, when times were tough, to permit islanders to leave without respect for U.S. law. Castro renewed the option in 1994, against a backdrop of mounting economic and political tensions. Triggered by the sinking of a tugboat filled with islanders trying to escape and a short-lived occupation of diplomatic premises by 150 would-be emigrants, some 1,000 to 2,000 desperate, angry, and starving Cubans protested in downtown Havana. Islanders experienced a subsistence crisis as the supply of food reached rock bottom following the demise of Soviet aid and trade. While the logic of the U.S.-imposed embargo suggested that such a pressure-cooker-induced uprising would bring the regime to heel, Castro turned the situation around by opening up the option to exit. Some 38,560 islanders, known as *balseros* or rafters, took advantage of the opportunity and battled their way across the Florida Straits (U.S. Coast Guard, 2000). This time, though, Washington broke its three-decades-old policy of automatically accepting Cubans picked up at sea. In the post–Cold War context, support for privileging Cubans over other immigrants in the United States tapered off. Nonetheless, any émigré who reached U.S. shores retained the right to stay and qualify for resident status and ultimately for U.S. citizenship.[1]

With the threat of ever more balseros flooding the Florida Straits to make their way to U.S. shores, Havana and Washington signed yet another migration agreement in September of 1994. This time Washington pledged to grant a minimum of twenty thousand entry visas per year. Under the new accord, some islanders qualified for U.S. entry through a newly instituted lottery, others through family reunification prerogatives (see Nackerud, Springer, Larrison, and Issac, 1999).

Even more than the *Marielitos*, the 1990s émigrés bore little resemblance to those who first left—in social class, cultural background, and motives for emigration. The Immigration and Naturalization Service, for example, reported in their 1997 Statistical Yearbook that of the most recent immigrants for whom it had information almost half were operators and laborers, 16 percent were service workers, and 13 percent were craft and repair workers (Immigration and Naturalization Service, 1999). By contrast, only 9 percent had been executives, administrators, and managers. The demographic profile was a near-mirror image of the émigrés who came in the early years of Castro's rule.

Also, an even higher percentage of 1990s than Mariel émigrés had spent their entire lives in Castro's Cuba. Fewer knew the pre-revolutionary Cuba firsthand. More than *Marielitos*, they came for economic reasons.

The 1980–2000 émigré cohort thus experienced a very different Cuba than the first islanders to leave. They also had, in the main, different reasons for coming to the United States.

THE MAKING OF THE CUBAN-AMERICAN COMMUNITY

Cuban-American émigrés gravitated primarily to Dade County, Florida, but also to Hudson County, New Jersey. While Washington from the outset sought to disperse Cubans from South Florida (initially through the 1961 Cuban Refugee Program), its efforts proved to no avail. Over the years, the approximately 1.3 million Cuban Americans, émigrés, and their U.S.-born children became ever more centered in Dade County.

Our interviews with businessmen, clergy, politicians, group leaders, and journalists in both New Jersey and Florida reveal that Cuban Americans have come to dominate the smaller, less dynamic Union City as well as the larger, more dynamic Miami community. Other studies of Miami confirm Cuban-American dominance there (García, 1996:8). By the early 1990s, Cubans dominated Miami's city commission, and they accounted for nearly one-third of Dade County's delegation in the state legislature. Cuban Americans by then also served as mayors of several Florida cities, including Miami, as well as city and county managers, and two were elected to congress. All told, by 2000 Cubans held one-third of the top elected and appointed

Miami–Dade County positions. In addition, Cubans occupied top administrative posts in key Dade County nongovernmental institutions, including the *Miami Herald* and local colleges and universities, and they became a major entrepreneurial force (*Miami Herald*, September 4, 2000). Fifty percent of local firms came to be Latino-owned, mainly by Cuban Americans (U.S. Census Bureau, 1999:18).

The first-wave émigrés and their children, morally driven by anti-Castro Cuban nationalism, seek to speak for all Cuban Americans. They do so even though their interests and experiences typify an ever smaller portion of island émigrés. About one-third of all Cuban Americans have come to the United States since the 1980 Mariel exodus.

The first-wave émigrés project their values onto the communities, dominate the community public discourse, and advocate a U.S. foreign policy consistent with their political formation. It is they who deftly lobby at the local and federal levels. They were influential initially because they advanced Washington's Cold War anti-communist agenda, but more recently because they became wealthy well-organized lobbyists from states, especially Florida but also New Jersey, commanding large numbers of electoral votes in political "swing states."

The dominant first-wave core maintained its hold over the years through intimidation when normative means did not suffice. For decades Cuban Americans who disagreed with the community leadership feared making their views known. They feared social isolation within their community, and they feared discrimination in the world of work.

Whatever their antipathy to the Castro regime, the views of *Marielitos* and subsequent émigrés are grounded in the complexity of life in contemporary Cuba, and the lives of family members there, not in an imagined and idealized pre-revolutionary social order. They differ here from Cuban émigrés in the first cohort, especially those children of first-wavers who do not even know Castro's Cuba firsthand. Coming to the United States is mainly for pragmatic economic reasons, and not infrequently emigration is a family strategy, a way to earn money for kin left behind in the growing dollarized island economy. Recent émigrés put family first. By contrast, earlier émigrés, whose close relatives in the main are reunified in the United States, are well positioned to put politics and their personal principles first. Their contrasting social situation has predisposed them to oppose transnational ties they believe bolster the Castro regime.

TRAVEL TO CUBA

Cuban Americans who go to Cuba do so mainly to see kin, and family visits are the only routine travel Washington has permitted since imposing the embargo in the early 1960s. But Cold War anti-communist isolationist politics, and then effective first-wave émigré lobbying, resulted in the United States restricting even family visits. The Cuban government has similarly tightly regulated émigré visits. But its policies became more permissive in the 1990s as a result of a shift in institutional priorities and mounting pressure from ordinary Cubans.

In essence, our survey suggests that the Cuban-American leadership publicly opposing travel speaks increasingly less for the yearnings of the expanding émigré community. Our survey also suggests that U.S. travel restrictions are out of sync with the wants of ordinary Cuban Americans, especially second-wavers. However, we found that, on average, Cuban Americans traveled no more than once a year, consistent with Washington's cap in the years in the 1990s when it permitted travel.

The ripple effects of visits are multiple and far greater than most travelers intend or even understand. Travel humanizes feelings towards family abroad and softens views toward both countries. Accordingly, the growing number of trips is serving to strengthen transnational people-to-people ties and attitudes, in a manner having potential ramifications for bilateral relations. So, too, are visits having unintended macroeconomic, social, cultural, and, to a lesser extent, political consequences.

Reactions to visits vary first and foremost by émigré cohort. At one extreme, recent immigrants are unfazed by visits. On the other hand, there are first-wave émigrés whose visits confirm their preconceived views of Castro's Cuba and some grown foreign-born children of first-wave émigrés who are transformed by island encounters. Nearly all react well, though, at the people-to-people level.

Some Cuban Americans who came when young and who lived through the generational experiences of their American-born age cohort also came to question their parents' hostility toward the Castro government, even if they grew up in the main Cuban-American enclaves. Their historically grounded relevant generational experiences were U.S.- more than Cuba-based. The civil rights and anti–Vietnam War movements, in particular, led some Cuban Americans who came of age at the time to be more critical of the United States and more open-minded about Cuba than were their parents. Those who pushed for and engaged in the so-called Dialogue of the late 1970s typify this group.

Though poorer typically than first-wave émigrés and their children, *Marielitos* and especially post-1990 émigrés are more apt to travel whenever they can. Still adapting to the United States, they have fewer U.S. and more Cuban ties. For them trips are less traumatic. Since they grew up on the island, they are fairly unfazed by the visits. Their reactions are personal, not political.

Viewed from Cuba, visits by family who emigrated tend to be well received, although sometimes with ambivalence. In some instances, visits heal emotional wounds for Cubans who had resented abandonment by loved ones. Increasingly gettogethers are instrumental. Cubans have come to cultivate relations with relatives in the United States they previously rejected on political grounds once they became dependent on dollars for subsistence and other needs and wants.

Family visits are beginning to serve as building blocks for change at the group level. They are contributing to changes within Cuba as well as across national borders.

The building blocks are partially cultural. Liliana, whose first return to Cuba stirred a new commitment to the country she left at age one in 1959, decided to build on her professional as well as ethnic background to cofound a nongovernmental organization to support the arts in Cuba. The organization raises material resources in the United States to strengthen cultural development on the island. The group collects donations—dance shoes and outfits, music sheets, painting supplies, and the like. It also raises funds for nonpolitical cultural projects in Cuba.

Émigrés also build connections through religious activity. This is true of Catholics, Protestants, and Jews. Several Catholic Cuban Americans report visits to their former island parishes. Some participated in religious celebrations, meetings, and church reconstruction. A small but growing number of Miami priests also have begun to engage their more open-minded parishioners in informal "adopt a parish" projects. They encourage visits and raise funds for Cuban churches in disrepair.

Transnational ties are also of a political nature. Aside from first-wave anti-Castro émigrés who are cultivating ties with island dissidents and political prisoners, some Cuban Americans are promoting political engagement through "above ground" channels. An economically successful Miami businessman, moved by an early 1990s visit, seeks to promote interchange between political institutions on the two sides of the Florida Straits. On trips he has spoken with middle-level Cuban officials "who understand the need for change," and in the United States he works with a Cuban-American partisan political group. Elisa, the first-waver Catholic charities activist, also became involved in groups cultivating cross-border ties along with a loosening of the embargo.

Efforts to rebuild civil society that follow on the heels of visits first undertaken to see family remain in a nascent stage. But transborder ties, in part, are fueling a buildup of organizational activity independent of the state.

MACRO-LEVEL EFFECTS OF VISITS

While the cumulative long-term impact of the surging transnational people-to-people ties remains to be seen, the new bonds are serving to remake Cuba in ways that visiting family, motivated by kinship loyalty, had not intended and in ways the Cuban government can no longer control. Transnational kinship bonds are increasing émigré presence within Cuban society, challenging the state's ideological hegemony, reducing Cubans' dependence on the state, undermining the statist economy, and inducing state institutional reforms.

Aware of these changes, Cuban officials have redefined the immigrant experience, modified policies, reformed the state apparatus to accommodate émigrés, and sponsored programs to improve relations with the Cuban diaspora. Cuban functionaries as well as intellectuals today define national identity in terms of "shared culture," rather than narrowly in terms of state allegiance. And in 1994 the government institutionalized émigré relations through the formation of a special office within the Ministry of Foreign Relations. This same ministry sponsored conferences on the nation and migration. The 400-large second meeting addressed ways to normalize relations between émigrés, their island families, and the Cuban government. The increased flow of people, goods, information, and ideas, in turn, is challenging the Cuban government's ideological hegemony and stirring new ferment. In an authoritarian society, simple interactions between people can challenge a state's monopoly over knowledge and viewpoints.

Meanwhile, remittances, transmitted by émigrés on visits (as well as through official transfer agencies and other means), have become a key source of hard currency for the Cuban government. While the Cuban-American leadership core opposes remittance sending precisely because the money pumps up a bankrupt economy that might otherwise collapse, the generous informal transnational family dollar giving is economically and socially destabilizing. It is causing new inequalities, especially but not only race based, as well as resentments among islanders without remittance-giving relatives abroad. It is also distorting and undermining the official economy. Indeed, the influx of money sent to starving island relatives in the years following the collapse of Soviet aid and trade created such a dollar black market that the government, in its effort to rein it in, decriminalized possession of the U.S. currency in 1993.

The very legalization of the dollar, in turn, made law-abiding Cuban Americans more likely to send money to their Cuban kin. Anxious to capture the hard currency, the Cuban government instituted state-owned and controlled dollar stores, currency exchange facilities, and dollar bank accounts. State structures and state policies, accordingly, also changed as remittance flows picked up (for a discussion of other reforms as well, see Mesa-Lago, 1998; Eckstein, 1994; Pérez-López, 1995).

With peso earnings becoming worthless in the dollarized economy, islander motivation to work, in turn, plunged. As a consequence, the government came to have difficulty delivering the very services, education and healthcare, on which its legitimacy hinged.

The macroeconomic effects of remittances differ markedly from the familial motivations for dollar giving. Intended to help families in need, the hard currency infusion is serving to transform the economy. Paradoxically, the macroeconomic effects are consonant with the destabilizing goals of the Cuban-American leadership core who oppose transnational financial transfers as well as visits.

In essence, informal transnational ties are generating a range of unintended consequences. Family visits are serving to remake Cuba and to build up a new transnational social and cultural field.

NOTES

We wish to thank the Mellon-MIT Inter-University Program on Non-Governmental Organizations and Forced Migration, the Cuban Committee for Democracy, the Ford Foundation (above all, Cristina Eguizabal), and the Institute of International Education for research support.

1. This came to be known as the "wet foot/dry foot" policy. The "wet foot" component refers to the policy requiring the U.S. Coast Guard to return to Cuba all islanders picked up at sea unless they could prove that they were refugees in need of asylum. The "dry foot" component refers to the continued policy of allowing Cubans who made it to U.S. shores to qualify for resident status.

REFERENCES

Amaro, N. and A. Porter. 1972. "Una Sociología del Exilio: Situación de los Grupos Cubanos en Estados Unidos," Aportes, 23:6–24. January.

Bach, R., J. Bach and T. Triplett. 1981. "The Flotilla 'Entrants': Latest and Most Controversial," Cuban Studies, 11:29–48.

Díaz-Briquets, S. and J. Pérez-López. 1981. "Cuba: The Demography of Revolution," Population Bulletin, 36:2–41. April.

Eckstein, S. 1994. Back from the Future: Cuba under Castro. Princeton: Princeton University Press.

Fagen, R., R. Brody and T. O'Leary. 1968. Cubans in Exile: Disaffection and the Revolution. Stanford: Stanford University Press.

García, M. C. 1996. Havana USA: Cuban Exiles and Cuban-Americans in South Florida, 1959–1994. Berkeley: University of California Press.

Mesa-Lago, C. 1998. "Assessing Economic and Social Performance in the Cuban Transition of the 1990s," World Development, 26(5):857–879.

Nackerud, L., A. Springer, C. Larrison and A. Issac. 1999. "The End of the Cuban Contradiction in Refugee Policy," International Migration Review 33(1):176–192.

Pedraza, S. 1995. "Cuba's Refugees: Manifold Migrations." Paper presented at the Fifth Annual Meeting of the Association for the Study of the Cuban Economy.

Pedraza-Bailey, S. 1985. *Political and Economic Migrants in America: Cubans and Mexicans*. Austin: University of Texas Press.

Pérez-López, J. 1995. *Cuba! Second Economy: From Behind the Scenes to Center Stage*. New Brunswick, NJ: Transaction Publishers.

United States Census Bureau. 1999. Statistical Abstract of the United States: 1999. April 12, 2000, United States Census Bureau. November 22, 2000, www.census.gov, 1992 Hispanic-Owned Business Enterprises. April 12, 2000. United States Census Bureau. November 22, 2000, www.census.gov.

United States Coast Guard. 2000. Migrant Interdiction Statistics. August 30, 2000; November 22. www.uscg.mil hq/g-o1&opl/mle/links.btm.

United States Department of Justice, Immigration and Naturalization Service (INS) 1998, 1999 Statistical Yearbook, www.ins.usdoj/govlgrapbicslaboutins/statistics.

PART V

SOCIETY

When the Special Period was invoked, nobody could have imagined how radically Cuban society would change in subsequent years. Until the early 1990s, virtually everything of importance was decided by the government—from the amount of beans obtained with the *libreta* (ration card) at the corner store to the free funeral arrangements for all citizens, from egalitarian salary differentials (the top wage-earner could not by law earn more than six times the lowest-paid employee in the country) to the number of shirts one could buy on an annual basis. Pervasive, omnipresent, virtually omnipotent, the government literally regulated almost everything from cradle to grave. At that time too, largely (but not exclusively) because of Soviet largesse, these subsidies made for a safety net on which people could rely, and which was fairly comprehensive and generous. The ration book took care of most food needs, education and health care were both guaranteed and equitably distributed throughout the country, employment was secure for almost all Cubans, and the vibrant cultural scene was heavily subsidized and available to all. Prostitution was extremely limited until the early 1990s, and it was virtually impossible to encounter anybody who had ever seen or smelled marijuana, much less harder drugs. Indeed crime rates were—and in general remain—remarkably low by North American standards. In terms of basic socioeconomic conditions, most Cubans before the onset of the Special Period were far more comfortable than the vast majority of people in most other Third World countries.

There were, however, clearly delineated social limits, rooted in Cuba's revolutionary socialist political model, which embodied different values than those found in a capitalist society. Those values were evident in the objectives of the government, the services it provided the populace, and the philosophy behind the political system. For example, a higher priority was placed on achieving and maintaining relative equality among Cubans than in increasing productivity. Most aspects of daily living were micromanaged in order to ensure that a level playing field, on terms set up and protected tenaciously by the government, was respected and upheld by all. Thus until 1993, a Cuban found with "hard currency"—especially U.S.

dollars—could end up in prison, because access to hard currency was not available to everyone. Cubans avoided going near *diplotiendas*, stores stocked with imported goods at which diplomats and international visitors could shop with dollars.

Two anecdotes perhaps give some flavor to this context of control and imposed equality. On the cusp of change in the early 1990s, we went to a house three blocks from the imposing Soviet Embassy in the Miramar section of Havana, which we were told was a quasi restaurant. "¿Hay comida?" (Is there any food?), we asked the homeowner, who quickly brought us inside to her illegal *paladar*, or small-scale, home-based restaurant. The *paladares* were instituted by enterprising Cubans to make extra money by providing a needed service at a time of great economic uncertainty, and were enormously popular. They were, however, illegal at that time—the philosophy being that only state-run restaurants should operate. If discovered, the restaurant owner would have been severely fined for using her talent to buck the system. A few years earlier we were at a friend's house for dinner when a woman entered, glancing over her shoulder nervously. She had brought a superb cake, which she sold to the hostess. The trouble was that she was breaking the state monopoly on cake production, and could have faced disciplinary action if spotted by the local Committee for the Defense of the Revolution representative, because such entrepreneurship risked creating inequalities. The values and the benefits of the collective were to be protected at all costs, and private enterprise had no place in the socialist structure. And, while the interests of the individual were important, of necessity they were always subordinated to those of the collective.

What a difference a few years make. Today one cannot stay in a Cuban home without several irritating visits daily from people hawking everything from eggs to fish, or offering to stand in line—for a price—to pick up the (heavily subsidized) rationed goods. While there are many fewer *paladares* now than there were five years ago, they have become professionalized and generally deliver excellent (and sometimes even pricey) meals. The number of *casas particulares* (private guest houses) grew rapidly in the 1990s, though high taxes since then have caused several to close. Still, there are websites dedicated exclusively to advertising accommodations set up by enterprising Cubans.

On the streets, people vie to offer you their services as a guide, to sell you bootleg CDs and cigars, to lead you to Havana's "best" *paladar* (where they receive a commission from the owner), or even to introduce you to their family members. There are now numerous forms of transportation (both legal and illegal), and you can either travel in a *cocotaxi* (a two-person motorized scooter with a stylized coconut framework) or in a 1950s Studebaker, as well as on a *bicitaxi*, or in a wide array of legal vehicles ranging from sleek Mercedes to ragged Ladas. Even religion is not immune from this turn of events, with visits to Afro-Cuban Santería services offered by some unscrupulous intermediaries. Petty corruption has increased, despite vigorous government campaigns to eradicate its more visible aspects.

Two terms, commonly encountered before and now hardly used, illustrate the "new Cuba"—*guayabera* and *compañero/compañera*. The first refers to the loose dress shirt used throughout the revolutionary years as a reaction to the prerevolutionary dress code, when middle-class Cubans wore suits, despite the limitations of the weather. In "high society," women even wore fur coats at nighttime, desperately seeking to slavishly imitate customs in the North. *Guayaberas* were ubiquitous in the 1970s and 1980s, but today are worn mainly by functionaries and older

Cubans—and rejected by virtually everybody else. *Compañero/compañera*, meaning comrade, were terms of revolutionary solidarity which people commonly used in addressing each other. They, too, have disappeared, replaced by *señor* and *señora*. In terms of psycholinguistics, the disappearance of these terms from the popular lexicon speaks volumes of the vast societal changes that have occurred since the Special Period started.

How did such a radical about-face materialize? Simply stated, the Cuban government had two alternatives when it announced the advent of the Special Period. It could either adhere faithfully to its revolutionary principles (and undoubtedly see the revolution crumble), or it could make what Fidel Castro termed a "pact with the devil," introducing sweeping changes—ranging from the legalization of the dollar for Cubans to allowing foreign investment in Cuba.

The government chose the latter with extreme reluctance, understanding that the result would likely be severe social dislocation, a radical shift in the Cuban population's quality of life, and a major shock to the national psyche. But in order to retain the remaining, and still extensive, benefits of the revolution, it saw no alternative. Its primary goal was survival, and then it sought to turn the destruction of the old order into an opportunity for a new stage of development. Along the way, however, Cuban ideals have paid a high price, with some Cubans coming to live extremely well, and others struggling hard to get by. The articles in this section illustrate the agonizing challenges which Havana faced in plotting its survival strategy to secure the gains made by the revolution and to limit the concessions reluctantly given. Many of these strategies have in fact now become a regular part of the Cuban approach to development. The articles also demonstrate how Cubans have adopted new models—introduced at a time of crisis—to create a new stage of their revolutionary process. Taken together, the articles offer a detailed and broad view of the way in which Cuban society has changed during the past seventeen years.

Life in the early 1990s was extremely harsh for Cubans, who had to rely upon their ingenuity, their connections, and their family abroad in order to survive. (In an interesting play on words it was said that, to survive in Cuba, one had to *tener fe*—literally "to have faith"—although *fe* was also an abbreviation for the words meaning *family abroad*.) Fuel consumption was reduced drastically, supplies in stores were not replenished, and Cubans were forced to reduce electricity consumption significantly. Power cuts became a fact of life. Indeed they were so common that Cubans joked about having the occasional *alumbrones* (times when there was light) instead of *apagones* (blackouts). *No es fácil* (life is not easy) became the mantra for a decade.

The Cuban Revolution has traditionally pointed to two large social groups who have benefited substantially from the revolution—women and black Cubans. There is a lot of truth to this, as can be seen from the number of women and Afro-Cuban professionals, and the relative access to the political process (particularly at the middle levels). At the same time the Special Period placed great stress upon gains made to date, and there have undoubtedly been setbacks for black Cubans in terms of economic losses—as Alejandro de la Fuente illustrates well. Women too, described appropriately by María López Vigil as "the heroines of the Special Period," have seen their status challenged, and many of the gains previously made have suffered as a result. Raisa Pagés argues, though, that the status of women in Cuba remains higher than most other countries, and even continued to grow during the Special Period.

But it should also be remembered that this period has been—and continues to be—one of ongoing change. Indeed, were visitors to return to Cuba now after having been there last in 1994, they would have difficulty recognizing the place. At that time, prostitution was rampant, Cubans often went to bed hungry, and the most common form of transportation was heavy Chinese-made bicycles, bearing unlikely trade names such as "Forever" and "Flying Pigeon." By 2007, in contrast, prostitution had been significantly reduced—notwithstanding claims to the contrary by U.S. officials—the food distribution system had been improved, and hunger was no longer a problem. A fitting symbol is the death of the Flying Pigeon—whereas in the mid-1990s Havana was awash with Chinese bicycles, now there is hardly a bicycle on the streets to be seen.

Homophobia appears to be rooted deeply within Cuban identity, but Larry Oberg offers a compelling argument in his article that the situation of gays in Cuba has improved dramatically in recent years. The Cuban government has taken several steps to educate the Cuban population about the need to treat all Cubans as equals. The fact that the leading institute dealing with this campaign is headed by the daughter of Raúl Castro and Vilma Espín, who until her recnt death had been leader of the Cuban Women's Federation, has obviously been an enormous boost.

There are also misperceptions outside of Cuba about the government's promotion of "sex tourism." Reports on Cuba in the mid-1990s by the international media seemed almost duty-bound to include references to hordes of prostitutes roaming the tourist areas of Havana. (Prostitutes are colloquially referred to as *jineteras*, or "jockeys," since they take their tourist patrons for a "ride.") The Bush administration has repeatedly charged that the Cuban government encourages sex tourism, including the accusation in the State Department's report on human trafficking, and its annual human rights report. While prostitution was practiced openly and widely in tourist areas during the early years of the Special Period, it no longer is. Indeed, child prostitution and the exploitation of children for pornographic purposes is now a significantly greater problem in North America than it is in Cuba. Government sweeps of prostitutes started in 1998, and have continued.

To summarize the way in which Cuban society has evolved in the past fifteen years, one is brought back to the Spanish word, *resolver* (literally to resolve, to find a solution). That is precisely what Cubans have done, revealing great tenacity, an enormous capacity for innovation, and some temerity. The pieces by long-time Cuba-watchers Mirén Uriarte and María López Vigil set the stage well for understanding and appreciating the profound challenges facing Cuba at the outset of this era. The "guerrilla mentality" shown by the July 26th Movement in the struggle against Batista in the late 1950s, when against all odds they managed to rout an extremely large, U.S.-equipped army, has been well honed in the decades since.

Cubans often believe that they are invincible, that no obstacle can stop them, and that this is symbolized by the survival of their leader in the face of enmity from ten U.S. presidents for nearly five decades. As the Cuban Revolution itself survived, and indeed as Cubans have gone on to develop their own form of society, they can perhaps be excused for their "dreaming in technicolor." A significant facet of their national psyche is an extraordinary self-confidence, a conviction that there has to be a solution to their problems.

The dual peso–hard currency economy (made more confusing by the convertible peso, and the decision to accept the Euro at tourist destinations) was obviously a major catalyst for social change—much of it based upon the mad search for *fula*, or dollars. As foreign investors swept into Cuba in the early 1990s, and as tourism rapidly outpaced sugar as the spark plug (and major dollar-earner) of the Cuban economy, it was obvious that revolutionary morale would sag. In essence, many of the changes noted above are based upon the search for hard currency, and the question of whether key social values were lost in this process is an extremely pertinent question that readers will consider in their reading of many pieces found in this collection. This is certainly a question that has preoccupied religious leaders, whether from the mainstream Christian religions or those of the broadly based Afro-Cuban religious expression. Cardinal Jaime Lucas Ortega y Alamino is concerned with what many in the Catholic Church perceive to be a crisis of moral conscience, as his pastoral letter reveals. Margaret Crahan also reflects upon the role of organized religion in the midst of changing social trends.

To make matters worse, the twin jewels in the crown—education and health care—quickly became badly tarnished in the Special Period. There was simply not the money needed to buy school supplies, or maintain and replace simple diagnostic equipment. Doctors were faced with recommending treatments they knew were not available because of the scarcity of medicine. Schools fell apart without cleaning materials, books, and toys. Scarcity led to price inflation, which in turn spiraled into the rapid development of the black market, and the beginnings of illegal employment, as Robin Williams and Lavinia Gasperini explain in their articles, respectively, on health care and education.

The government replied with a variety of belt-tightening measures, while at the same time offering a guarantee that the burden of enforced adversity would be shared equitably, as would the benefits when Cuba emerged from the rigors of the Special Period. To some extent, many of these measures were introduced in reaction to the initiative already being shown by desperate Cubans themselves. For example, the legalization of the dollar resulted after anxious relatives in Miami had started to send large quantities of money to family members. Likewise, the legalization of dozens of professions where Cubans could become *cuentapropistas* (self-employed workers) was the result of many thousands of Cubans already working "under the table." Tales abound of Cuban professionals working as taxi drivers, selling coffee and cookies on the street, or making handicrafts.

Imagination—and the government reaction of taking advantage of these changing circumstances in order to harness the Cuban creative potential—have largely paid off, in that Cuban society was able to survive and reverse some of the worst consequences of the economy's sea change. The new model has also proved successful in ways that had been unexpected, as this section shows. Social indices, such as life expectancy as well as infant and maternal mortality rates, have continued to improve.

Again it is significant to bear in mind in all these cases that Cuba is a poor, developing nation, with a population of 11.2 million, and an official philosophy that is premised upon the need to provide the greatest amount of benefits to as many people as possible, and on an equitable basis. In a true revolutionary socialist system, access to money should not make any difference to the quality of life of individual citizens. In the real world of Cuba in the grip of the Special Period, the government has made major concessions—but wherever possible (as we see here) attempts to provide subsidized access to goods and services broadly. Understanding this basic principle is absolutely essential to a reading of the pieces in this section.

Innovations in the education field (Margo Kirk provides examples of reforms in the still well-functioning preschool system) have likewise challenged the Cuban populace, as the successful 1961 literacy campaign did. Many of the innovations have been introduced with volunteer, amateur labor, and as a result was initially of uneven quality—particularly during the early years. However, as the level of professionalism improved (as was the case with the literacy campaign), so has the delivery of the programs. Common to all these initiatives is an imaginative linking of impressive Cuban talent to the broadest delivery possible—and as equitably as can be managed—of these services. The benefit of the population as a whole is the objective, not pursuing a profit margin.

What began as a series of measures of basic crisis management in the early 1990s has thus evolved into a rational process of development *a la cubana*. In describing the state of social reform, for example, Mirén Uriarte insightfully observes that as new measures gradually took hold, Cuba was able to retain "a safety net, tattered but holding." In highly improbable circumstances, the Cuban Revolution has survived—and while the dollarization of the economy has led to far greater social class differences, fundamental social benefits remain remarkably and equitably distributed.

Revolutionary Cuba has always pursued its own path, often against the odds, and often too on a course that appeared foolhardy and initially destined to failure, especially to observers from advanced industrial nations. Despite significant adversity, this small country has made noteworthy progress on many fronts, and its self-reliance is quite extraordinary. But it is also clear that the genie is out of the bottle—notwithstanding the government's efforts to limit the differences between those holding hard currency and those without, there is no way that Cuban society can revert to the pre-1990 period of (subsidized) glory and the days of yore. Cuba is thus employing the basic tenets of capitalism to keep the essence of socialism intact. The report by María Isabel Domínguez on the social aspirations of youth is particularly pertinent in anticipating where this may lead Cuba in the future. Cuba faces another enormous challenge now, as it seeks to balance growth, political stability, social equity, and the delivery of enhanced social programs, while maintaining some free-enterprise pursuits and at the same time limiting the economic freedoms and individual self-reliance to which people have become accustomed. The post–Special Period promises to be another unpredictable stage—as has so often been the case—in the fascinating revolutionary process of Cuba.

28

In the Shadow of Plenty, Cuba Copes with a Crippled Health Care System

Robin C. Williams

I met the joyful young Cuban boy with bilateral retinoblastoma on a ward round at the National Institute of Oncology and Radiology in Havana. Although he had already lost his sight in one eye, he was a candidate for an implant of radioactive iodine to treat the other eye. The medical skills were available in Cuba, but the U.S. government had denied the pediatric oncologist a license to import the iodine because "the radioactive medication was a threat to U.S. security."

Thanks to humanitarian efforts, the child and his mother were being flown to the U.S. for the surgery and treatment at a cost that was astronomical compared with what it would have cost to import the isotope. The physician, however, was delighted to have access to the care and she wanted to show me what they had taught the young Spanish-speaking boy to say on his trip to the United States. The boy puffed himself up with pride at his newfound mastery of English and whispered "I love you."

I get a thickness in my throat even now as I write this, almost nine months after I was part of a delegation of physicians sent to Cuba to validate the findings of the American Association for World Health (AAWH) on the impact of the thirty-year-old U.S. embargo on sending health and nutrition supplies to Cuba. For me—a Canadian, a pediatrician, and a public-health physician—it was a week of mixed feelings: admiration for the work and energy of beleaguered physicians, sadness at the paucity of care and options for the sick, anger at the situation facing Cubans, and pride at the stand our federal government has taken.

THE TRADE EMBARGO

The factors that affect the Cuban economy are complex and numerous, and I am no expert in foreign policy. However, it was evident that regardless of other factors such as the economic collapse of the Soviet Union, Cuba's main trading partner, the tightening of the U.S. embargo since 1992 has had a devastating impact on the health of all Cubans. Three other developments have contributed to the desperate situation: an unexpected wave of mergers consolidating U.S. domination of the pharmaceutical industry, a ban on subsidiary trade (including food), and a requirement that U.S. government licenses be obtained before medicines and medical supplies are sent to Cuba.

Over a twelve-month period in 1995 and 1996 the AAWH traced the implications of the restrictions on health care delivery and diet in Cuba. A multidisciplinary research team reviewed key U.S. regulations, surveyed twelve American medical and pharmaceutical companies, and documented the experience of Cuban import firms. To assess the impact of sanctions on health care, the team visited forty-six treatment centers and related facilities and conducted 160 interviews with medical and other health care professionals, government officials and representatives from nongovernmental organizations, churches and international aid agencies.

The resulting three-hundred-page report was full of examples of how the embargo has affected Cuba. Waterborne disease rates have more than doubled, making diarrhea the second most common reason to visit a Cuban physician. The country's mammography program is crippled by a shortage of film and spare parts. Surgical rates are down because of a lack of supplies and equipment, including anesthetics. Drugs for leukemia patients and children with heart disease are not available, since the embargo effectively bans Cuba from purchasing half of the new world-class drugs on the market.

WALKING IN THEIR SHOES

My delegation was asked to validate the draft findings contained in that report. Having the opportunity to speak to physicians in a variety of urban and rural facilities allowed us to see their situation at a grassroots level and attempt to walk in their shoes. The terrific challenges they face were evident everywhere we went, yet these beleaguered and battle-weary physicians still managed to summon the energy to face and solve problems while showing little evidence of anger or vengefulness.

More than once I was overwhelmed as I thought about trying to care for pediatric patients without access to what Canadian physicians would consider to be the most basic medications and equipment. There was no acetaminophen, only basic antibiotics like penicillin and ampicillin were available, and there were no third-generation products of any type. Equipment such as ventilators and oxygen monitors lay in disrepair in a "neonatal nursery" because Cuba cannot get parts from the U.S.

Our group toured a variety of hospitals, including América Arias Maternity Hospital, Havana AIDS Sanatorium, Juan Manuel Márquez Pediatric Hospital, the National Institute of Oncology and Radiology, the Cardiology Institute, and the Nephrology Institute. Many facilities were dilapidated: paint and plaster were in poor shape, windows were dusty or broken, and furniture was often broken, worn, and very basic. The latest journals and books in the hospital libraries dated from the 1970s and 80s. One pediatric ward "playroom" we visited had not a single toy, piece of paper, or pencil. Patient charts consisted of microscopic handwritten entries jammed on every square inch of mismatched and reused paper. Isolation apparel was thin, torn, worn, and shabby.

My understanding of the state of the Cuban economy came from the AAWH study, conversations with physicians and others, and from our guide, an affable young man who spent long hours with our group and described life at his parents' home.

He considered himself fortunate, since his interpreter's job provided not only a small income but also tips in U.S. dollars. During our week in Cuba, he ate as many meals as possible with us so his food rations could be used by his hungry parents and siblings. At one point he produced his ration book, which allowed for four ounces of beef twice a year, eight ounces of poultry eight times a year, eight ounces of cornmeal six times a year, three ounces of bread each day, and two pounds of fish and six pounds of sugar a month.

The Cuban physicians we met could have been from any academic institution in North America. The profession is dominated by women, some of whom spoke freely of their long, six-day workweeks; only on Sundays do families have time together at home. Water supply and treatment is a serious problem. Cuba is not able to produce enough chlorine to disinfect the water supply, and water-treatment problems are compounded by distribution difficulties. The infrastructure for delivering the water was developed with American pipes and gauges. Attempts have been made since 1958 to introduce European equipment, but much of the delivery system continues to be in disrepair because American parts to repair pipes, pumping stations, pipe locators, and the like are not available. Because of these problems, 8.5 percent of Cubans don't have "drinking-water service." Even those that do have water face restricted service: in 1993, residents of Havana had drinking water for only eight hours a day.

A MAMMOGRAPHY PROGRAM DIES

Cuba's concern for women and children was once exemplified by an organized and comprehensive mammography program. Two units in Havana and fifteen mobile units canvassed the island annually, screening women over thirty-five years of age. Over the last five years the program has faced many disruptions because of parts shortages. In 1994 it was disrupted for two months when the country ran out of x-ray film; it was shut down again in 1995 when film developer couldn't be obtained.

Now the screening program has been permanently discontinued because of equipment failure, inability to obtain the Kodak mammography film that requires a lower radiation dose, gasoline shortages for generators and the mobile units, and lack of film developer.

Another reason for discontinuing screening concerns the lack of resources for surgical and medical breast cancer therapies. The interpretive pathology examination of tissue required samples to be transported by a family member from the operating room to a pathologist with a functioning cytology laboratory across town; sometimes surgical closure would be required before lab results could be obtained.

On one ward round I trailed behind a prominent neurosurgery professor from Cleveland and our host, a Cuban neurosurgeon. The latter had just returned from an international medical meeting in Rome. The surgeon presented two complex cases and was seeking advice regarding surgical approach and management. Next we discussed an infant with hydrocephalus who required surgical treatment with a shunt; the neurosurgeon described his inability to obtain a valve for the child. He told of his despair as he begged for help at two drug company displays in Rome; although both initially talked business, they became cool and refused the sale when they learned where he was from. They explained that it would be too dangerous for their companies to deal with Cuba. To this day, I'm not sure how, or if, he obtained the valve.

THE VIEW FROM CANADA

On returning to Canada I once again became involved in our community process to plan for hospital restructuring in the Niagara region. Like other communities we face dilemmas: there is an aging population with 418,000 people spread over a wide area, with hospital care being delivered through eight acute-care facilities.

But the situation in Cuba underscores how fortunate we are to be "just tinkering" with our system. I hope that increasing awareness of the plight of that country will encourage governments and medical suppliers to search for a short-term rescue operation while the politicians and people sort out a long-term solution.

On quiet evenings, when I poke my head out of my own local trenches and look beyond our problems, or when I catch a glimpse of "Cuba" in a newspaper headline, I am thrown back to that week last October [1996] and the tragedies I witnessed. I am left to wonder what any single person can do to make a difference. It is easier to wallpaper over these concerns with an energizing trip to a local elementary school's "Health Fair Day," where I witness the opulence and the vibrancy of our Canadian kids. The forces that continue this embargo against Cuba seem mammoth, complex, and immovable. I wonder if sending money, medical supplies, valves, or journals— all of which I've done—helps in any meaningful way.

29

Social Impact of the Economic Measures

Mirén Uriarte

The introduction of market-based reforms, which quickly began to heal the Cuban economy during the Special Period, had the same effect as in market societies—a sharpened economic inequality—and gave rise to a host of the emergence of new social problems. Even as the success of the measures was becoming evident, the Cuban government often expressed reluctance at having to implement them. "Some of these measures are unpleasant," said President Fidel Castro in July of 1993. "We don't like them." Throughout, the measures were projected as "necessary evils," as temporary, emergency measures that would be reviewed once the crisis was over. "It's a risk that government leaders have decided to take . . . because they have no other alternative," explained the Agencia de Información Nacional in 1998, "but also because they are confident that these are transitory circumstances." But as the measures proved to be permanent, many people raised serious concerns about the effects of the reforms on Cuban society. "There will be those who will have privileges, while others do not," explained President Castro. And this, indeed, was the case.

INCOME INEQUALITY

The most critical effect of the reforms has been the increase in income inequality, propelled primarily by the transformation in the structure of the labor market. "The greatest income inequality in the population," writes Cuban economist Angela Ferriol, "responds to the new characteristics of the labor market, which is related to the opening to foreign capital and with the adjustments and reforms we have undertaken." Although there had always been a "private sector" in Cuba, it was small and had been shrinking. The measures introduced in the early 1990s reversed that trend. Currently the labor market is privatizing rapidly, as joint ventures and the Cuban public/private entities developed to service them continue to grow. Many of these are "new economy" jobs in the tourism industry, in areas with heavy foreign investment, and in private national industries and agencies created to service this sector (like Cubalse and Corporación CIMEX). Others are self-employed workers, independent farmers, and farmers working in cooperatives. Close to one-quarter of Cuban workers were employed in the emerging private sector in the year.

The difference between the working conditions and the rewards for workers in the state and in the "new economy" sector (except the self-employed workers) is significant. Workers in the emerging sector have access to technology, office supplies, and comforts (such as air conditioning) that are often lacking in state enterprises. Aside from the regular salary in pesos, these firms would reward workers with needed "extras" that were hard to come by during the Special Period, such as clothes, toiletries, and some specialty foods. In time, some of these enterprises offered workers—both under the table and legally—at least some of their salaries in dollars.

Prior to the Special Period, the highest-paid Cuban workers—mainly professionals such as doctors or engineers—were paid only 4.5 times as much as the lowest-paid workers. This built in a significant equity based on income. But during the Special Period, this was greatly altered in an unusual way. Now it is possible for a waiter in a tourist hotel, which is one of the lowest-paid jobs in Cuba, to obtain a set of rewards—salary in pesos, tips in dollars, the "extras," and improved working conditions—worth many times more than the rewards that could accrue to a top professional who works for the state and earns a top salary, but only in pesos. Cubans call this the "inverted pyramid," a phenomenon that reflects the devalued return on education and professional preparation in the new economy. The immediate result has been the exodus of public service workers into low-level service jobs in the tourism industry. During 1993–1994, for example, almost 8 percent of teachers made this leap.

Income inequality has also risen as both the economic crisis and the subsequent restructuring of the old economy displace workers. From 1990 to 1998, 155,000 workers became unemployed. The initial policy, begun in 1991, was that, when factories stopped production or state entities were restructured, workers continued to draw at least 60 percent of their salary. There has been an effort to relocate workers to other jobs, and in fact, most have been relocated. Those who have not are protected by unemployment for a period of six months to three years depending how long they had worked for the state. Many of these workers have entered the ranks of self-employed.

Retraining workers for new jobs is ongoing as are the special programs to support the entry of young people, particularly young women, to the labor force. But this has not succeeded completely in stemming the flow of female workers out of the labor force. In 1997, male unemployment amounted to 4.4 percent while that of females reached 10.1 percent. Zulema Hidalgo, who runs a self-esteem group for women in the neighborhood of Atarés in Havana explained:

> (Women) told us that they received little result from their work: that they spent almost as much going to work, having lunch, and maintaining themselves there as what they earned. . . . In addition, the women also had to spend a lot more time in domestic tasks, getting food and solving problems due to the lack of resources available. These limitations led many women to leave their jobs.

Finally, another salient factor contributing to the growing inequality is the unequal access to dollars that the new structure provides. About one-half of the population has access to dollars in some way. Many earn dollars through their work: according to newspaper reports, about 35 percent of Cuban workers receive some remuneration in dollars. Some of these are state workers, a small percentage of which receive part of their salary in hard currency. But the majority of Cubans with access to dollars earn them as part of self-employment, formal and informal—in *paladares* (home restaurants), as unofficial taxi drivers, performing different services, or selling goods in the black market.

Employment is not the only way Cubans have access to dollars. Remittances come from across the world, but mainly from Cubans living in the United States. Estimates range between $400 and $800 million per year, now a major source of hard currency for the country and of income for many families.

The importance of dollars to everyday survival has produced great differences in conditions between those who have family abroad and those who do not, between salaried and self-employed workers, and between salaried workers in different sectors of the economy. Among the most economically vulnerable households are those that depend solely on the wages of low-paid state workers, on the fixed incomes of retirees, or on social assistance—that is, households where no member has the means to increase his or her income through private enterprise. Persons without access to dollars through remittances or employment are also very vulnerable. Vulnerability is most characterized by lack of access to alternative possibilities for the purchase of food and goods outside of the subsidized ration card. This can happen if the family does not have access to dollars or has a level of income in pesos that does not permit it to purchase food in the higher-priced agrarian markets or in the gouging black market.

EFFECTS ON FAMILIES

Increased economic vulnerability has made the situations of many families quite difficult. These difficulties result not only from the problems that arise from lack of income, but also from the problems that come from the way that the emergent economy affects families. Members of the family often work for the state but have additional ways of earning dollars, usually informally.

This can range from selling arts and crafts, to renting out a room in their home, to running a *paladar*. Working adults in families are extremely busy managing the problems of getting to and from work with a badly deteriorated transportation system, obtaining the necessary food and supplies for the home, and, in many cases, having a second job. This is contributing to less attention being paid by adults to the daily family life at home, including the supervision of children.

The new economy has also made for very deformed economic relationships within the family. Many different forms of participation in the economy can coexist in a family: most continue to be salaried workers working for the state, but increasingly, members of the family will work in the firms and businesses of the emergent sector, while others are self-employed working in both the established and the informal economies. Under the new conditions, a teenager can earn more money in one afternoon showing a tourist around Old Havana than his father earns in a month working in his government job. Parents complain that they have lost authority over their dollar-earning children, especially their teenagers. Parents feel pressure from children to purchase items in dollar stores when they may have no or very limited access to dollars. Families are under a great deal of pressure to raise children under very new and very different circumstances; this has led to significant family stress and dysfunction.

One indicator of the stress placed on families by these new situations is the increase in the divorce rate, which climbed from 3.5 percent in 1990 to 6.0 percent in 1993. By 1998, this rate had stabilized at the 1990 level. Another is the reappearance of children begging from tourists or doing small jobs as unofficial tourist guides. Political scientist Sheryl Lutjens from Northern Arizona University writes that a 1996 report on education in the City of Havana identifies over 20,000 children living in conditions of social disadvantage and vulnerable to the pull of street life. Lutjens further reports, for example, that in the *Casco Histórico*, the renovated historic section of Old Havana, most children working in the streets were boys between 5 to 11 years old, and that authorities had identified over 2,200 children in this situation in 1996.

An additional burden for families is the fact that some long-disappeared social problems have returned. Illicit street life has reappeared in a very public way in high tourist areas. Prostitution has increased significantly in cities with high tourist traffic, often in very blatant forms and involving young women. Petty crime has also increased involving mostly but not exclusively tourists. Although Havana's streets are still relatively safe compared with those of large urban areas elsewhere in the hemisphere, the reappearance of social problems and crime has been very troubling to a population that believed these social ills were problems of the past. In many ways Cuba spent the first part of the decade focused on the economic crisis with very thoughtful, measured, and, in the Cuban context, unexpected initiatives. But the second half of the decade has required a different response: managing the impact of these measures in Cuban society. For the first time in forty years, Cuba is contending with a growing set of social differences emerging from the new economy and their consequences for vulnerable groups, for families, and for communities. And this is happening in an environment of extremely reduced resources and options. It is still too early to foretell the policy prescriptions that Cuba may adopt to face these challenges, but all indications show their intention to hold to the strong values that have shaped Cuba's social policy in the past and build on the considerable strengths of both their social programs and their communities.

A SAFETY NET TATTERED BUT HOLDING

Where Cuba differed from other countries undergoing liberalizing reforms was the political will to shield the population from the most pernicious of these effects as well as from the impact of the crisis itself. Cubans sought to maintain the basic values of the Cuban social policy: universality, equitable access, and government control. This meant protecting social expenditures as much as possible in a rapidly shrinking budget. The basic outcome indicators, some of which were reviewed earlier, show the deterioration of some gains in health and education. The increase in low birth weights and the decrease in the nutritional status of young children, although they did not affect the infant mortality rate, were great concerns. Notable also were the reappearance of diseases such as tuberculosis, the increase in mortality from some infectious and parasitic diseases, and increases in incidence of contagious diseases, such as hepatitis and sexually transmitted diseases. Finally, the appearance of epidemics, such as the optic neuritis epidemic in 1992, underscored the effect of the economic crisis on people's health.

In education, the most affected indicators were enrollments and dropout rates. Enrollments decreased slightly in post-secondary schools and more sharply in higher education. In 1990 to 1991, 94.5 percent of the graduates from secondary schools (ninth graders) went on to further education; by 1994 to 1995, that figure had dropped to 86.4 percent. Moreover, whereas in 1990 most of these students went on to pre-university high schools, most were now going on to technical schools. This shift may represent a choice but most likely indicates tighter enrollments at the university level. University slots are highly linked to available positions in the Cuban economy, which was greatly reduced during the 1990s. As a result, enrollments in higher education dropped from a high of 21 percent in 1990 to 12 percent in 1996; dropout rates from high school also rose, particularly for students enrolled in pre-university education. These schools, which are almost all located in the countryside, represented a lot of hardship for students as food became scarcer and problems in transportation prevented teachers from reaching the schools.

The decrease in the quality of services also had an effect on health and education outcomes. The crisis led to the physical deterioration of hospitals, clinics, and schools; the absence of medical supplies and equipment and disinfectants; and the declining quality of education due to the lack of supplies and an exodus of teachers to jobs in emergent sectors.

In the area of social security, the most notable impact was the erosion in the buying power of pensions and social assistance. As the buying power of wages and pensions decreased and the subsidized ration goods covered less of a person's needs, those with fixed incomes, such as pensioners, became increasingly vulnerable economically. Nevertheless, the difficulties of daily living under the crisis made it very hard for persons to maintain employment; many older workers retired, increasing the number of retirees and the expenditures in social security.

In response to the crisis, the Cuban government has strongly reaffirmed the basic values of Cuban social policy and has reasserted the political will to maintain its social development model. At the same time, the government has begun to transform aspects of the model, particularly in the area of service delivery, in order to guarantee its reach and effectiveness.

MAINTAINING BASIC PRINCIPLES AND POLICIES

A review of the current writing in social policy makes evident that the basic principles of Cuban social policy have remained in place. First of all, there continues to be a clear commitment to equity in access by maintaining all services free of charge, as has been the history of health, education, and other benefits in Cuba. Although some fees have been instituted, these are minimal and affect services that are not central to the mission: for example, fees for school lunches in high schools and fees for some adult education. Cuba did not use the crisis to revoke the basic benefits of free, socialized medicine and public education.

It is also clear that the commitment to universal accessibility has been re-tained. Cuba did not approach the current funding crisis by excluding sectors of the population from basic benefits and services, and there is no evidence of serious efforts to curtail benefits with new eligibility criteria or time limits, even in areas like social assistance. The commitment to universality is strong, although this does not mean that no consideration has been given to developing targeted programs, directed toward the most vulnerable.

Finally, in spite of the thrust to decentralization existent in Cuba in the last decade, the government's role as the main actor in this sphere remains unchanged. The central government continues to be responsible for funding, developing, and providing the benefits and services of the Cuban safety net.

PROTECTING SOCIAL EXPENDITURES

In the midst of the crisis, the commitment to social benefits—education, health care, social security, and social assistance to the poor—was maintained. In fact, social expenditures increased in absolute terms through the period of 1990 to 2000, from 3.816 to 4.705 million pesos. With the exception of education, which experienced a reduction in 1990 to 1994, expenditures in all areas increased through the period.

Social expenditures also held their own as a proportion of the gross domestic product (GDP). As the GDP dipped by 40 percent between 1990 and 1994, overall expenditures remained constant but social expenditures increased slightly. As the GDP began its slow recovery in 1996, total expenditures were actually reduced, as part of the campaign to reduce the deficit, but social expenditures continued to increase. By 1998 they were 23 percent higher than they had been in 1990.

The fact that social expenditures increased even as the GDP decreased tends to indicate a strong protective inclination toward social expenditures (though it may be also due to the inherent resistance to change of items such as pensions). In fact, social security showed the sharpest increase in relation to the GDP, surpassing education in 1993 as the largest social expenditure. But increased allocations to education and health care and, to a lesser extent, social assistance also demonstrated a clear commitment to and protection of these areas.

Cuban social expenditures as a share of GDP are nearly double the average in Latin America. In 1990 Latin American countries devoted an average of 10.4 percent of their GDP to social programs; Cuba's share was 21 percent. By 1998, after a decade of crisis, Cuba's financial commitment to social programs, at 32 percent of GDP, was still the highest in Latin America. Like Cuba, other Latin American countries experienced a rise in the share of GDP dedicated to social expenditures during this period; but at 60 percent, Cuba's rise has been much more pronounced than those of other Latin American countries, which experienced an average rise of 30 percent. Only Paraguay and Colombia had higher rates of increase of social expenditures in relation to GDP.

In spite of this clear financial commitment, the negative impact of the economic crisis on services was evident, due to two critical factors. The first was a decrease in the allocations in convertible currency (i.e., U.S. dollars) toward education, health, and, in fact, all areas of life in Cuba. In 1994, for example, the allocation in convertible currency for the health sector was 39.6 percent of what it had been in 1989; by 1997 the allocation had risen to only 49.4 percent of that available in 1989. These restrictions limited the importation of such necessities as medicines and medical supplies, materials needed for the production of medicines, building materials for the repair of hospitals and clinics, and tires for ambulances. A similar situation took place in education, which was left without supplies and without paper to print books. Only funding for personnel, who are paid in pesos, was unaffected.

The second factor that tended to undermine the government's financial commitment to social benefits was the decreased buying power of the peso. Although government ministries received the same or even more pesos during the 1990s, the fact was that, except again for personnel, the real purchasing value of the peso had dropped.

TRANSFORMING THE DELIVERY OF SERVICES

Even as Cuba has reaffirmed its social development model and sought to protect the funding of social services, the government has felt the need to transform the delivery of services. In the past, Cuba has created service effectiveness by placing large amounts of funding behind a universal coverage for all services, without strong regard for efficiency. But this logic faces critical challenges at this time. Outcomes along many social indicators are not yet at levels achieved in the late 1980s. Although their amounts have been sustained and even increased, budget investments in social benefits have not completely prevented their deterioration, signaling that a much stronger financial investment will be required to reach the levels of 1989. All this takes place in a context of increasing demand: not only are more retirees requiring pensions, but more families are put at risk by the economic pinch. More attention is needed for pregnant women, more support is needed for families with less income, more work is needed with adolescents facing temptations to stay out of school—the list is long.

There is also great pressure to improve the quality of services. A large gap separates the service system as conceived by policymakers and providers and what is actually delivered today. This gap is becoming an increasing concern of users and will become even more critical as services begin to represent a more important survival element for those in need. The timeliness of a pension check, for example, takes on a different meaning when the recipient population is so economically stretched, as it is today. In many ways, the now decade-old crisis appears to have underscored the need for transformations in the implementation of social programs. Without abandoning the basic values that have shaped policy, Cubans now look for ways in which social policy can be delivered both efficiently and effectively.

30

Cuban Youth

Aspirations, Social Perceptions, and Identity

María Isabel Domínguez

Cuban society in the nineties was marked by the profound economic crisis that swept the country and by the important changes that resulted from the strategy adopted to overcome it. This strategy had to improve economic efficiency while minimizing the effects on the levels of social justice that had been achieved. The social consequences of this have had a harsher or more direct impact on youth. These consequences, however, also resulted from pre-crisis conditions, particularly the existing level of social integration and the extent to which the population was prepared to face the crisis.

Unquestionably, the most positive elements of the pre-crisis conditions were the strong consensus around basic values, such as equality and justice that has sustained most people's commitment to the social project, and the capacity for creativity and resistance inherent in the Cuban identity. The main negative elements were deficiencies in the socialization of youth, with the attendant impact on values and decreased participation, and the development of an egalitarian attitude that caused expectations not related to employment to soar among different social groups as a result of a weakened work ethic.

The magnitude of the economic collapse drastically reduced the Cuban population's standard of living; for example, in just three years (from 1989 to 1992), per-capita household consumption dropped by 18.5 percent. But it should also be noted that, in contrast to neoliberal approaches, the readjustment strategy adopted focused on equitably distributing the effects of the crisis. In other words, it avoided imposing strictly economic measures at the expense of particular groups, such as indiscriminate streamlining of labor or commercializing basic social services, while simultaneously attempting to compensate the most affected sectors by reinforcing social security. For example, a comparison of the employment rate among the working age population in 1996 with the same rate in 1987 shows a reduction of barely 5 percent during the worst years of the crisis, even though this population segment grew by 650,000 people. Likewise, social security and social assistance spending grew by 40 percent from 1990 to 1996, representing an increase from 17 percent to

24 percent of the total budget. This means that even in the worst moments, efforts were made to preserve a level of social justice that would prevent any one group from being crushed.

SOCIAL INTEGRATION OF YOUTH

The nature of the crisis, and the type of recovery strategy that emerged as feasible, given the domestic and international circumstances in which it occurred, inevitably had a number of effects, some of them structural. These have had implications in terms of social integration, particularly of youth, if integration is understood from the standpoint of three basic elements: employment, education, and sociopolitical participation.

Employment

The diversification of forms of ownership that accompanied the opening up of the economy to foreign capital, the establishment of the Basic Units of Cooperative Production (UBPC) and other forms of cooperative labor, and the growth in self-employment have had major repercussions on the living and working conditions of significant sectors of the population. They have also brought about a reorganization of the social class structure in which the generational aspect has been particularly relevant. First, there have been changes in the employment structure in the formal sector of the economy. In the second half of the nineties alone there was a notable increase in the total number of workers employed in sectors such as mining, electricity, gas, and water; tourism and trade; financial activities in insurance and business services; and agriculture and livestock production. There was a simultaneous decrease in the number of people working in the construction, transportation, and manufacturing industries. Precise data are unavailable regarding the age structure involved in these changes, but one can assume that the influence of younger members of the work force is significant.

Second, although it is extremely difficult to estimate underemployment, much less to understand the particular characteristics of the groups involved, young workers were most likely strongly affected in this regard during the early years of the crisis, since the industrial sector (which employs the highest proportion of people under thirty) was among the hardest hit. However, given the inherent characteristics of this age group, and its high qualifications, it is likely that young workers have managed to reinsert themselves in more vigorous economic areas featuring lower levels of underemployment more quickly than other groups of workers. Growth in the informal sector of the economy represents an employment option that accounts for some percentage of youth, and the rise in cooperativism includes youth participation in agricultural work at much higher levels than before. But young people also have less interest in securing stable employment, and more of them are disengaged from the labor market. Since 1991 there has been an observable decline in the economic activity of youth and women.

According to studies conducted in the mid-nineties, 79 percent of a representative sample of youth disengaged from the labor market reported having someone who could support them and 71 percent found no economic incentive to work. This situation began to change in 1996, at the same time that unemployment rose to between 6 percent and 7 percent; 60 percent of the unemployed were youth, the largest proportion were women, their skill level was average or average-high, and most were of urban origin.

The considerable presence of these segments of unemployed and disengaged youth spurred the implementation of a number of social programs to incorporate them into various work and study alternatives. These programs aim to restore the value of education, provide opportunities for continuing education, and reinsert youth into socially worthwhile jobs. They offer intensive vocational and technical education programs that prepare youth for work as well as for advanced studies at municipal-level university affiliates that facilitate classroom study through specially designed, student-centered programs. These programs, although still incipient, have begun to reverse some of the trends of the preceding decade and have significantly reduced youth unemployment and disengagement.

Education

Education had always been a priority in young people's expectations. It is important to recall that for three decades the education system was a genuine vehicle for the integration of different social classes, racially diverse groups, and especially women. Despite an enormous effort to minimize the impact of the crisis and the readjustment on education and to maintain universal coverage at the primary and secondary levels with fewer resources, there were objective or structural effects, particularly in the internal structure of middle and high school education. These included reductions in college preparatory instruction, expansion of polytechnic education (mostly in the agricultural field), and the strengthening of pre-university vocational programs as a means of access to the universities. At the same time, general enrollment in higher education declined, although unevenly across disciplines.

This was accompanied, in turn, by the subjective impact in terms of the social perception of the role of education. Education suffered a certain decline in stature in the nineties. It was no longer the channel par excellence of social mobility, nor the main route to a higher standard of living, nor an essential mechanism for achieving social status once other paths to higher earnings became available (employment in the emergent sector, self-employment, remittances from abroad, illegal activities, and so forth). This is the case even though these changes did not occur evenly, but rather fluctuated throughout the decade with marked differences among various social groups.

Sociopolitical Participation

Another essential area for evaluating levels of social integration in society is sociopolitical participation. This is particularly important with respect to youth, a generation typically excluded from decision-making process by most existing institutional models and, in recent years, by its own apathy and political withdrawal most everywhere in the world. In Cuba, macrosocial indicators showed the continued participation of young people in various social and economic activities, including government and political leadership roles, despite declines in some indicators. Membership in youth organizations remained high (all students belong to the Federation of Middle School Students (FEEM) or to the University Students Federation (FEU)). There was a high percentage of activists in political organizations, which had experienced a certain decline throughout the decade due to increased apathy among some youth toward social and political activities, but which has shown signs of renewed growth over the past three years. Except for the initial term, in which youth participation was nearly 30 percent, the proportion of youth representatives in local government (provincial and municipal) fluctuated between 12 percent and 23 percent over the nearly twenty years that the Popular Power system (Poder Popular) has been in existence. Twenty-six youths were elected [in 2000] to the Parliament, accounting for 4.3 percent of deputies. Data on organizational membership, however, are not the only valid indicators of sociopolitical participation, which has become increasingly heterogeneous in general. Structural heterogeneity and the resulting diversification have led also to diversification at the level of individual attitudes, particularly in terms of social perceptions, expectations, and values.

YOUTH ASPIRATIONS AND CONCERNS

As expressed in recent studies, youth aspirations, satisfactions, and concerns center primarily on four basic areas from the standpoint of the individual: family, social mobility, employment, and material living conditions. Essentially these refer to the satisfaction of basic personal needs. First, the family is given the highest priority and is central to the subjective experience of youth, as both a determinant and a result of their attitudes. The other three spheres remain in top positions, although the order changes in function of different groups. Second, measured in ten-year periods, youth aspirations reveal an interesting dialectic between stability and change. A past-present comparison (the eighties compared to the nineties) shows increasingly diverse aspirations as new ideas have entered the scene or as notions previously only vaguely sketched for isolated individuals in the preceding period have gained new currency. The most salient trends over the decade show that aspirations increasingly emphasize the individual-family significance. Socially oriented notions, such as world peace, international solidarity, and the future of humanity, which figured among the aspirations of youth in the late eighties, have declined in importance. Aspirations for the future (around the year 2010) do not differ substantially from the present: priority is placed on family, work, material living conditions, and particularly the ability to have one's own home, although individual spirituality and health are also considered of interest. In this sense, the vision of the future also tends to reinforce the main individual-family aspirations.

The vision of the problems facing society becomes even more interesting when compared to how youth view the specific core objectives of the social system that, if achieved, would provide solutions to their main problems. In this regard, priority is placed on economic development of the country, which is absolutely consistent with the view that all the country's problems are rooted in the economic situation. Indeed there is a tendency toward optimism that the future of Cuban society will be better than the present, but this improvement is contingent upon a series of internal and external economic, political, and social factors. At the same time, there are some more pessimistic viewpoints, albeit in the minority, and a sense of uncertainty expressed not only by those who believe that the future is unpredictable, but also that perspectives for an optimistic future are in the long term.

The search for spirituality emerges for the first time as a significant aspect of the aspirations expressed by youth, perhaps in response to the tensions experienced in society during a protracted crisis period. In addition to this, the perception that religion offers an opportunity for education, culture, and information has led some segments of youth to identify it as an avenue for social integration. Aspects related to migration, both internal and external, are particularly relevant in terms of social integration, and indicate a strong desire for permanence among young people, not just in the country, but also in their specific place of residence. Of the youth interviewed, 4 percent reported emigration abroad as an aspiration; most of these were white males from the capital, who were self-employed. The motives behind this aspiration primarily related to finding better opportunities for an improved standard of living and personal development. Those who did not place high value on the emigration option asserted that they were satisfied with their life in Cuba and with being Cuban, and had no desire to leave their place of origin and family ties. There was, however, more interest in short-term travel to see other countries, to get ahead, or for work-related reasons (mostly among students and professionals).

Besides these trends, other interviewees regarded emigration as something they had considered at one time or another, mainly for family or economic reasons; they had not discarded the idea entirely, but were waiting to see how circumstances evolved. The social image that today's young Cubans have of emigration abroad has become increasingly neutral and depoliticized, and it is accorded a certain amount of space in individual and groups strategies; this is particularly true of temporary migration.

YOUTH SELF-IMAGE AND NATIONAL IDENTITY

Another important characteristic of Cuban youth today is a strong sense of national identity and its association with historical, social, and political factors. Young Cubans are widely and rapidly able to define themselves and to maintain a positive self-image. The profusion of positive traits described can be grouped into seven categories, in order of importance based on the frequency with which they were mentioned: good character and attitude toward life; amiability, solidarity, and the ability to form good interpersonal relationships; courage; capacity for work, effort, sacrifice, and creativity; revolutionary, patriotic, and ethical principles; intelligence, ability, and education; and deep feelings and emotions.

Negative traits, while comparatively few in number (representing about one-fifth of the characteristics described), span the spectrum of adjectives mainly alluding to arrogance and self-importance, informality and lack of responsibility, and lack of formal education (bad manners, rules of respect, courtesy, and civility); these are similar to traits reported in earlier periods. Nonetheless, some responses reflect more recent negative changes, such as "have become self-interested" or "have lost their Cubanness."

The generational self-image is consistent with the national image. It is particularly significant that the primary trait defining this self-image is the capacity of youth to confront and solve problems, to work, and to exert themselves, above and beyond those traits relating to good character that are attributed to the Cuban population as a whole. Significantly, youth perceive more differences than similarities among themselves as a group in terms of social and cultural factors, values, behaviors, and economic and political considerations. These differences complicate the development of a solid and widely shared generational identity, even though a large segment mentions the presence of common traits associated with this age group that are conducive to similar tastes, interests, aspirations, and experiences. This explains why it is difficult to observe a sense of identification between youth belonging to different age subgroups.

There is a particularly wide gap between those 25 to 30 years old and the rest, which calls into question the validity—and this dates back to the late eighties—of defining youth so broadly. These disparities are intensified greatly when one considers the vastly different significance of living through the nineties—the economic crisis and readjustment period—as a child, or at different stages of young adulthood. This is corroborated by the fact that the 25-to-30-year-old subgroup stresses the differences between today's youth (excluding itself from this assessment) and previous generations. They attribute to the former unfavorable connotations in areas such as moral values, character traits, culture and formal education, and political values, in that order. This indicates that this subgroup identifies with older age groups and is distanced from the youngest segments, thus reinforcing the hypothesis that a new generation (from the sociological standpoint) emerged in the nineties creating a fracture within the social group currently defined as youth.

All of the above, coupled with the recognition of significant differences vis-à-vis youth in other countries and a highly positive, although not absolutist or apologetic, self-image bring interesting perspectives to the interpretation of generational identity among Cuban youth today as a relevant aspect of their subjective experience. A general reading of the subjective experience of youth must not overlook distinctions based on membership in different social groups. Unquestionably, social class and geographical location, in that order, are the two critical distinguishing factors, although there are other significant differences based on gender and age subgroup (particularly between the oldest segment and the rest, as already mentioned) in nearly all areas.

CONCLUSION

The unique evolution of events in Cuban society in the nineties, in my view, has influenced the subjective experience of today's youth in several major directions:

The rupture of close ties with the former Soviet Union and the rest of Eastern Europe has returned Cuba to a closer relationship with its Latin American context and compelled it to reinsert itself internationally through broadened contacts and interrelationships.

The goal of preserving a socioeconomic model as an alternative to capitalism, following the disappearance of "real socialism" as a reference point, has led to a deeper exploration of Cuba's own historical, national roots and to the modernization of its own social thinking.

Increased tensions with the U.S. government in the context of growing pressure to force a change to a capitalist system have reinforced feelings of independence and sovereignty. The impact on the population's economic, living, and working conditions has fueled contradictory behaviors that coexist in present-day society. On the one hand there is a spirit of resistance and survival under the most severe conditions that reinforces national cohesion and self-esteem; and on the other, there is a competitive spirit and search for alternatives that reinforce individualism and could change that self-image.

The economic situation, the social reorganization strategy, and some of the individual strategies adopted have led to the emergence of heretofore nonexistent social inequalities. This creates a certain heterogeneity in Cuban traits and perceptions that surely will influence national and generational identity. The process will interact with the main strengths and weaknesses of contemporary youth. Their strengths—advanced educational levels and high expectations—could have a galvanizing effect in the direction of a greater effort. The main weakness relates to a certain concentration of those expectations at the individual-family level, at the expense of the social level.

The generation of the nineties features greater structural heterogeneity than preceding generations, stemming from a certain reorganization of the class structure and the strengthening of certain territorial differences associated with the rhythm of economic recovery and the presence of an emergent sector. This has also led to increasing heterogeneity from the subjective standpoint, particularly in terms of social perceptions, expectations, and values, which is expressed in a broad spectrum of interests and in greater diversity with the attendant impact on identity development.

It is not possible to overlook the more global influences of the times, marked by increasing technological and direct human interaction. This has changed and informed today's youth by creating commonalities that transcend national borders. Such processes have contradictory effects in that they simultaneously accentuate fragmentation and facilitate integration within the generation. This in turn has an interesting impact on intergenerational dynamics. The common traits acquired during the socialization of today's young people in the social context that prevailed at a key moment in their formation as a generation, together with the largely similar influences they have experienced, have left their mark and distinguish this generation from previous ones. This has resulted in the integration of a youth identity that is more forcefully manifested than in the preceding decades.

In a general sense, there are signs of the emergence of a new generation of the nineties, concerned with what goals—individual and social—it can aspire to with any real hope of achieving them; goals that make it possible to strike a balance between expectations of personal fulfillment and social needs. This in turn requires greater clarification of the avenues available for achieving such a balance. This segment of young people is embarked on a quest and a process of adaptation unlike any faced by previous generations, albeit one that is ill defined and contains contradictory currents. It is a panorama in which the institutions involved in socialization do not have all the answers and one in which the long-standing values of Cuban national identity can be a valuable guidepost.

31

The Cuban Education System

Lessons and Dilemmas

Lavinia Gasperini

The Cuban educational system has long enjoyed a reputation for high quality. Recent studies comparing achievement tests scores from Cuba with those from other Latin American countries have further highlighted the achievements of the Cuban system. Cuban students score significantly higher than do students in other Latin American countries.

The Cuban education system has performed most satisfactorily on other conventional measures as well. According to official data, for example, 98 percent of Cuban children of the appropriate age attended preschool in 1997–1998. The enrollment rate for 6 to 16-year-olds was 94.2 percent, and primary school gross enrollment exceeded 100 percent. Repetition rates were 1.9 percent in primary school, 2.8 percent in secondary, and 1.8 percent in pre-university school. Age-grade distortion was about 2.5 percent in primary, 3.7 percent in basic secondary, and 0.9 percent in pre-university. In the mid-1990s there were 241,000 illiterates, out of a population of 11 million. In 1959, in stark comparison, half of Cuba's children did not attend school at all, 72 percent of 13- to 19-year-olds failed to reach intermediate levels of schooling, and there were over one million illiterates [out of a population of 6.8 million].

Cuba's schools have been remarkably successful in achieving gender equity, reaching rural and disadvantaged populations, and fostering community participation, even in the context of rapidly dwindling resources. Cuba is a poor country, and the past decade has been particularly difficult economically. Yet the success of its schools flaunts conventional wisdom: education in Cuba is entirely public, centrally planned, and free, in a global reform environment of privatization, downscaling of the state role, and cost recovery.

The Cuban education system is characterized by

- Sustained and high levels of investment in education;
- Consistent policy environment and political will in support of education for all;
- Quality basic education, including early childhood and student health initiatives, literacy, adult, and non-formal education programs;

- Universal access to primary and secondary school;
- Complementary educational support systems: early childhood and student health, literacy, adult, and non-formal education;
- Highly professional, well-trained teachers of high status;
- Ongoing professional development of teachers;
- Low-cost instructional materials of high quality;
- Creativity on the part of local educators in adapting and developing instructional materials;
- System-wide evaluation;
- Solidarity within schools and classrooms and competition among schools and classrooms;
- Significant community participation in school management;
- Compensatory schemes for disadvantaged and rural children;
- Clear connections between school and work;
- An emphasis on education for social cohesion.

Cuba devotes about 10 percent to 11 percent of its GDP to education, a very high percentage compared with the rest of the region or with the 6 percent recommended as adequate by UNESCO. Of course, the size of GDP allocated to education alone is insufficient to define an effective education system.

Cuba has invested substantial resources in non-salary items. Until March 1999, 60 percent of the Education budget was devoted to teachers' salaries with the remaining 40 percent for non-salary items used to support instruction. Both of these policies correspond to current understandings of best practices in education finance. Unfortunately, it will be difficult to maintain such a high percentage of expenditures on non-salary items. In March 1999, teachers received a 30 percent salary increase, a move that decreases the resources available for non-salary costs. Teacher motivation and retention are also threatened by decreases in the purchasing power of salaries and the attractiveness of new professional activities especially in tourism and in foreign firms, as evidenced by teacher attrition of 4 to 8 percent per year in the eastern provinces where tourism is more developed.

As in many other socialist countries the Marxist-Leninist philosophy of praxis inspires the objectives of the education system of educating a "New Human Being" to

> assume its most basic social duties, to educate this being to produce material and spiritual goods that will serve society in a way that every human being participates in material production in order to eliminate the contradiction among school and society, producers and consumers, intellectual work and physical work, and among cities and rural areas.

These objectives were set, of course, by the same party that has run the country for almost forty years. Continuity of educational policy and strategy—quite unusual in most countries of the region—has contributed to the achievement of goals set by party and government. The different components of the education system are articulated around common objectives subject to constant evaluation with the participation of the broader educational community and centered in the classroom.

In many Latin American countries, frequent political changes may impede the development and consolidation of educational strategies and achievements. The

Cuban experience suggests that measures are needed to protect the education system from the disruptive effects of continuous changes in strategies and plans. Education is a long-term investment requiring consistent policies and political stability to grow. This stability, however, was achieved at the cost of one-party rule.

The great emphasis placed on education and the high degree of collective control ensure that access to education is effectively universal. The high levels of investment permitted an emphasis on both equity and quality. Comprehensive early childhood and student health services, widespread literacy, adult, and non-formal education programs support the objectives of basic education for all.

32

Early Childhood Education in Revolutionary Cuba during the Special Period

Margo Kirk

"Nothing is more important than a child."

—Cuban billboard

A tourist or casual observer might dismiss this commonly seen slogan as government propaganda. Such skepticism would be reasonable, especially during the Special Period. Would it even be possible for the Cuban government to support this basic philosophical statement, specifically with respect to early childhood education?

Remarkably the answer is a qualified "yes." Even representatives of international, free-market-oriented organizations, such as the World Bank, have spoken favorably in recent years about Cuba's comprehensive early childhood programs. As well, Cuba has been warmly praised by UNICEF for its contribution to educating very young children. Such praise suggests the Cuban system must be doing something unique with respect to children's education. This chapter will examine those special aspects of the Cuban educational system.

At first glance it would seem somewhat incongruous for accolades to be bestowed on an early childhood education system during a time of severe austerity. Usually in times of financial crisis our governments cut, reduce, and entrench—yet clearly Cuba did something quite dramatically different. Throughout the most critical years (1990–1993), it became apparent that, while social policies—one of the main features of Cuba's socialist revolution—remained a major government priority, the funds were no longer in place to provide the same level of support. "Doing more with less" now became the government's mantra. Clearly, no sector in Cuba could avoid feeling the impact of the Special Period—including the early childhood education sector. The fact remains, however, that even during the Special Period, an expansion of early childhood education options actually occurred. The result is that approximately 99 percent of children in the 0–6 age group throughout Cuba currently have access to an established, state-supported early childhood program. Why is this so? How did this become a reality?

EDUCA A TU HIJO

Recognizing the value of early childhood education (ECE), and the need to provide a basic framework in a cost-effective manner throughout the country, researchers began to examine new ways to improve availability of this education—and in an economical way. This was to be made available to all children, regardless of social origin, color, or geographic location (child care centers were available to working mothers only, recognizing their extra responsibilities). Educators looked beyond the traditional or formal child care center as a delivery mechanism for early childhood education, relying on an approach that used a non-formal education as a means of reaching even more children than had been the case before the onset of the Special Period.

There were already some precedents for this. In 1981–1982 an experimental pilot project for non-formal education was launched in the municipality of Palma Soriano in the province of Santiago de Cuba, and in 1984–1985 a more specific program was outlined to support early childhood education in rural areas in general. This specific research project actually ran from 1983 to 1993, under the direction of the Instituto Central de Ciencias Pedagógicas (Central Institute of Pedagogical Sciences) and was based on two main premises: a) children with formal child care experiences or children who attended preschool (a non-compulsory program for five-year-olds) demonstrated superior results in primary school; and b) the family was the natural unit to prepare children in this program.

This research formed the basis of a national, UNICEF-sponsored non-formal early childhood education system called *Educa a tu Hijo* or "Bringing up your child." The program, inaugurated in 1992, just as the Special Period was starting, was to "support the education of children in their own homes, together with the advice and support of qualified personnel, and with broad community support" (Pérez Valdés and Pérez Travieso, 1995, p. 5). With its base as the family, the local *círculo infantil* and the community at large were all called upon to participate, and to help in spreading this approach throughout the country. There had been an interest in extending early childhood education throughout the country through non-formal programs for a decade already. With the advent of the Special Period, it now became a necessity.

FAMILY INVOLVEMENT

As a key facet of this program, a second and more concise version of the 1987 "Educa a tu Hijo" booklets was published in 1992 (Ramos) with the help of UNICEF (fourth reprinting, 1998), and was distributed throughout the country through neighborhood associations, unions, and other mass organizations. The revamped format in each booklet in the current edition (a series of nine) is presented in a less formal manner while remaining largely in the format of questions and answers. The booklets are widely available. Information pertaining to the health and developmental needs of a child within a specific age range, from birth up to six years of age, appears more accessible at a glance, in the bullet-accented presentation. The language is simple and straightforward, and the specific advice for parents is illustrated by clear drawings. Both parents (from a variety of racial backgrounds), as well as grandparents, are seen actively involved in all aspects of nurturing and raising the child. The role of the extended family is clearly defined.

Parenthood is depicted as a privilege, and the education of a child as an obligation. It is clearly the responsibility of every parent to understand child development and recognize the stages as the child grows. The booklets engage the parents, explaining to them in clear terms precisely how their child is growing and their role in promoting this development. Therefore, activities which promote adult-child interactions and which stimulate all aspects of development are provided. The booklets also address the parents directly with statements such as "You will have seen already." The resulting effect is that the readers (i.e., the parents) are drawn in, making them full partners in the process. Each booklet ends with a short checklist and parents are told to observe their child for these achievements, while being cautioned not to worry if the competencies shown are not fully met by the child.

The emotional development of a child is undoubtedly of paramount importance. Each booklet asks the questions: "What can you do in order for your child to grow up and develop healthy and happy?" In addition, "being affectionate" is consistently stated in the initial section, continuing throughout as a recurring theme. While expressing the stages and expectations of social and emotional development, these booklets are unquestionably educating parents in a clear and concise manner about child development and psychology. Parents are called upon to provide a loving and secure environment, while explanations on child behavior and suggestions for positive management approaches are being made. Redirection, modeling, positive reinforcement, praise, the avoidance of child frustration, and consistency are continually featured as ways to manage and support the child. Parents are repeatedly reminded not to shout and to be patient.

Sections are, of course, devoted to the intellectual and physical development of a child, as well. The play-based approach is clearly outlined and suggestions are concrete. Expensive toys or gadgets are not required. The use of questions also plays an important part. "Doing more with less" is illustrated in practical, and realistic, terms.

In addition to the emotional, physical, and intellectual development, health and safety issues form a continual thread throughout the booklets. Personal hygiene of all family members is explicitly stressed. For example, each booklet recommends a specific number of hours of sleep for the respective age group, and parents are coached on the importance of good nutrition as well as a clean house. Parents are urged to take the children to the family doctor regularly for check-ups and immunizations, and to raise any questions about the child's development.

The "how, why, and when" as presented in this series of booklets not only give parents an accurate baseline of child development, but also reinforce the philosophy that education is for all (including infants). Furthermore, and just as important, the booklets emphasize the parents' role in supporting the child's educational development and the necessary proactive role they must play.

COMMUNITY INVOLVEMENT

Significantly, however, the generally accepted philosophy of education went far beyond the home, and the publication of a set of booklets. Pérez Travieso (1997) joined other colleagues in stressing the community-based nature of the program which provided a format for "the development of children by means of non-formal education in the region where they live. In this way, the basic principle that education is a task which belongs to all is carried out" (p. 14). And, while the roles and responsibilities of the "collective" and the "community" versus those of the "individual" in raising and educating a child were repeatedly stressed, researchers did not lose sight of one of the fundamental objectives of the program, namely to prepare a child for success in primary school. Therefore, in an attempt to integrate home and school, children between the ages of two and six years of age, along with their parents, participate in activities organized in the community. The practical side of the program, as seen in the booklets, is thus carried out with extensive community involvement.

This outreach type program was described in practical terms in a twenty-four-page manual. The guide, *Manual del Promotor: Vías no Formales de la Educacion Pre-escolar* (Manual for the Animator: Non-Formal Education Methods in Pre-School Education) was directed toward those coordinating this national, community-based undertaking. The guidelines were clear: work directly with parents and children, be organized with initiative and good verbal and written communication skills, sensitize the community to the different aspects of the program, educate the volunteers in child development, and mobilize the resources of the community. The manual included the role and responsibilities of the coordinator, as well as a process for evaluation.

A similar publication appeared in 1994. This issue was also written in a question and answer format and was published with the support of UNICEF. The objective of this publication, *Cuba: Una Alternativa no Formal de Educación Pre-escolar* (Cuba: A Non-Formal Alternative of Pre-School Education) (Pérez Valdés, Pérez Travieso, Siverio Gómez, and Rivera Ferreiro, 1994) was to

> show, in a novel style, how a social program developed in our country can provide educational care to children between 0 and 5 years who for different reasons do not attend a child care center or a pre-school group, as a new non-formal way of pre-school education. This program is characterized by the combined work of the family and the community (Back cover).

Coordinating community bodies included representation from the Ministries of Public Health, Education, and Culture and Sport as well as the Committees for the Defense of the Revolution and the Union of Young Communists. The Federation of Cuban Women, as has traditionally been the case in all matters relating to women and children, also had a significant role. Pérez Valdés, Pérez Travieso, Siverio Gómez, and Rivera Ferreiro (1994) explained that the approach "is conceived as a social program in which members of the community will organize and co-operate collectively to contribute to the development of activities for children and their families" (p. 10). In short, the onus upon rearing children, of supporting their growth, of developing an awareness of identity, was to fall upon the community as a whole. Gym activities, patriotic celebrations, collective birthday parties, and cultural events in art, music, and dance were suggested as areas in which the active participation of parents, neighbors, and other community members could take place.

Significantly, an important resource was indeed the *círculo infantil* or daycare center itself, the formal wing of the early childhood education system, which was now also to be drawn into the non-formal program. The centers were assigned the task of providing learning resources for the non-formal program, and were seen as possessing the extensive potential to train members of the community at large. As established in the original pilot project of the 1980s, preschool-age children (four and five year olds) not enrolled in a formal program continue to participate in weekly visits to their local *círculo* to participate in activities held there.

Television plays a role as well. Weekly programs are aired on the state education channel, one of four official channels available to the general Cuban population. (Significantly, two channels are dedicated solely to educational matters.) Children are encouraged to watch either with their families or with a group of children, at the *círculo*, for example. Different programs target different age groups as I noted from a personal research visit to Cuba in May of 2002. The particular twenty-minute show aired at 10:00 a.m. EST on May 14, 2002, was designed for four- and five-year-olds. A significant portion of the show was aimed at creative expression. A child danced to classical music. Puppets interacted with the children, and a child played the role of a doctor. A facilitator also told a story to all the children sitting in a circle. Lending a helping hand seemed to be the central theme of this particular program. These television programs are produced by the Ministry of Education, and are broadcast throughout the country.

In sum, the complete "Educa a tu hijo" project has therefore three main scenarios for implementation: the home environment (where the extremely helpful pamphlets are used), the community at large, and the *círculo*. Indeed, this non-formal educational program relies on the resources of all three bodies. Yet, clearly this non-formal program is valued as a credible form of early childhood education demanding professional input and monitoring going beyond merely "recreational" status.

SUCCESSES AND FAILURES DURING THE SPECIAL PERIOD

As is to be expected, the sweeping economic crisis faced by Cuba in the 1990s also had a major impact upon the early childhood education system. In general, the formal system of the *círculos infantiles* during the Special Period and the infrastructure were well established and remained sound. All facilities operated, albeit in a more austere environment. Textbooks, pencils, notebooks, and other educational materials were in short supply and the facilities fell into disrepair. In addition, both the quality and quantity of food allotments to these schools and childcare centers were reduced. The professional journal, *Simientes*, first published in 1962, and specifically designed to target the field of early childhood education, was discontinued in 1992. Curriculum texts, previously printed in book form, have been reprinted in segments only, in booklet form (e.g., *Educación Preescolar: Programa Segundo Ciclo*, reprinted 1999). Materials remain in short supply. Despite the impact of the massive financial crisis, however, the Cuban government insisted that not a single school or child care center be closed, a policy also applied to hospitals. This policy was respected and in fact there was even a slight increase in the number of centers, as can be seen from Gasperini's (2000) estimate that 1,156 child care centers were in operation in 1994—up from the 1,116 centers in 1990.

A second conclusion to be drawn is that during the Special Period, the implementation of the national, non-formal program called Educa a tu Hijo seems to have been efficient, although the need exists for more detailed study. Gasperini (2000) commented on official Cuban figures, which revealed that in 1997–1998, an extraordinarily high percentage (98 percent) of Cuban pre-school children were served by either the formal or the non-formal system of organized early childhood education. The child care center program alone could only reach about 20 percent of that figure, which shows that the non-formal program carries an enormous responsibility.

CONCLUSION

It is without a doubt that the 1990's in Cuba were complex and extremely difficult. It may well be impossible for those outside of Cuba to truly understand the impact of such a far-reaching economic crisis. The very infrastructure on which the Cuban economy was founded, and had been encouraged to plan, suddenly collapsed. In addition, the United States tightened the embargo with passing of the Torricelli Bill of 1992 and the Helms-Burton Bill of 1996, also causing further economic hardship. This crisis was so severe that fully a decade later, the country is still facing hardship.

Yet, despite this crisis, universal education remained a firm commitment and in the midst of economic turmoil, an expansion of early childhood education opportunities, in actuality, did occur. The human resources of the country were organized in an innovative fashion to meet the new pressing social needs, and in this way the government facilitated the formation of the backbone of a national, non-formal system of early childhood education, called "Educa a tu Hijo," designed to reach in a cost-effective way, the 80 percent of preschool children who could not attend the *círculos infantiles*. In 2002, Gonzalez reported that of the 885,368 children from birth to six years of age, approximately 250,000 attend a *círculo infantil*, while another 610,171 are served by the non-formal system. By mobilizing the general population through community-based organizations, this expansion no doubt required minimal capital cost investment. Specifically, the plan was also supported by UNICEF.

There have undoubtedly been "growing pains" in the system. Poor distribution of materials and advertising of the program's goals were seen—particularly in less accessible regions. Some areas also had low participation rates in the initial years, in part because of a lack of understanding of the importance of the program—and the need to resolve the many difficulties of life during the Special Period. The involvement of the *círculos de abuelos*, the neighborhood groups of seniors who meet daily, has helped to meet some of the program's needs. Other non-formal channels of information have been implemented, and have been successful—such as the daily visits by the family doctors.

Currently in Cuba, education in general has taken on a renewed focus. Fidel Castro reiterated his conviction that Cuba's future lies in an educated population and initiated major reconstruction and rejuvenation projects. The commitment toward education, which was established at the beginning of the revolution, has remained high, and during the 1990s this commitment was confirmed with ongoing government support and the implementation of ingenious strategies. It would appear, then, that Cuba has made a significant attempt to demonstrate that indeed "Nothing is more important than a child."

REFERENCES

Gasperini, L. (2000). The Cuban Education System: Lessons and Dilemmas. *The World Bank Country Studies: Education Reform Management Publication Series 1(5)*, 1–36.

Gonzales, A. (2002). Preschool education in Cuba. *Childhood Education*, International Focus Issue.

Pérez Traviesco, I. (1997). "Direccíon y organizacion del círculo infantile y vías no formales de la educacíon preescolar (Management and organization of the child care center and non-formal methods of pre-school education). Unpublished paper.

Pérez Valdés, M., I. Pérez Travieso, (1995). Monitoreo y evaluacion de la educación preescolar por vías no formales en Cuba, 1994–1995 (Monitoring and Evaluation of Non-Formal Preschool Education in Cuba, 1994–1995). Paper presented at the *Congreso* Pedagogia 1995, Havana, Cuba.

Pérez Valdés, M, I. Pérez Travieso, A. Siverio Gómez, A., and I. Rivera Ferreiro. (1994). *Cuba: Una Alternativa no Formal de Educación Preescolar* [Cuba: A Non-Formal Alternative of Pre-School Education]. Havana, Cuba: Editorial Pueblo y Educación.

Ramos García, M. (Ed.). (1992). *Educa a tu Hijo* [Bringing up Your Child] (2nd ed.). Books 1 through 9. (Reprinted 1998). Havana, Cuba Editorial Pueblo y Educación.

UNICEF. (2001). *The State of the World's Children 2001*. Retrieved July 18, 2002, from www.unicef.org/media/sowc2001/reporteng.pdf.

33

Heroines of the Special Period

María López Vigil

When the walls of Eastern Europe began to fall in 1989 and the Soviet Union began splitting up into separate republics, everything in Cuba began to enter into crisis. The crisis in Cuba, known as the Special Period, is indeed "special," not in any festive sense but rather because it is so particular to the island. Suddenly everything—or almost everything—changed for a population that was used to acceptable standards of living, personal security, and social stability.

Above all, the Special Period means uncertainty. In 1989, the majority of Cubans viewed the past with pride, the present with security, and the future with optimism. But overnight, food, electricity, water, transportation, work, salaries, even the straight line of the horizon began to waver.

It is generally agreed that women bear the main daily burden of this prolonged crisis, and that their sacrifices, solidarity, and creativity have been most responsible for cushioning its impact.

SACRIFICES FOR FAMILY AND COUNTRY

Some women have been forced to give up their permanent or temporary jobs to tackle the crisis at home, where they have to improvise some kind of breakfast, lunch, and supper, stand in line for hours to buy what there is whenever it becomes available, work out how to deal with the shortages and care for old or disabled parents and in-laws on shrinking resources. Many of those who continue to work can only do so because there is another woman at home helping out. A lot of women are retiring before the age of fifty-five or putting aside their professional aspirations to take any job where they can earn dollars.

Perhaps the most "special" thing about this crisis is that the majority of Cuban women are making all these sacrifices not only for the survival of their family and their children—as is the case in any country—but also for the survival of the revolutionary project.

309

Although Cuba's economic adjustment is "special," it has resulted in structural unemployment, just like in other countries. Many factories have shut down, and the country is fighting hard to maintain quality levels in health care and education. Since women were traditionally a minority among laborers and the majority in the health sector (80 percent of mid- and higher-level technicians) and in education (87 percent of primary school and 54 percent of secondary school teachers), they have been less affected by unemployment. The high level of their participation in the priority sectors of tourism (44 percent) and in research (42 percent) has also helped restrict female unemployment. Most women who are currently unemployed were working in various sectors of the country's light industry. Women are 46 percent of the "available" workers, as the unemployed are known in Cuba.

ARE VALUES BEING LOST?

With the inequalities created by legal currencies, the state is seeking to maintain other essential qualities. If, for example, bath soap (imported or national) is sold to some Cubans in dollars, that hard currency can guarantee a daily liter of milk to all children under seven years old through the ration card at only 25 *centavos*—almost nothing.

Many do not understand this "aboveboard" state tactic, which creates some equality at the cost of other inequalities. What many see today is that it is not like it was before; the playing field is not at the same level for everyone. And in Cuba's political culture, nothing is as irritating as inequalities.

Legalizing the now-omnipresent foreign currencies created some inequalities, because egalitarianism was slashed with one stroke. But Cuba's new mixed economy made that slash irreversible. Has the revolution thus lost consensus? The earlier situation, with its extensive black market, had already created many "clandestine" inequalities, though everyone knew it. The stagnation of that unresolved situation also eroded consensus. The relief brought to many Cubans by legalizing the dollar justifies the measure. The values sown in Cuba over thirty years soften in thousands of ways the hard-edged individualism sown and harvested by capitalism in other latitudes. "You know," a thirty-two-year-old engineer selling artisanry for dollars told me, "I suffer because I can't help my neighbor; I don't have enough. I'm horrified by what he's going through. I refuse to conform. We cannot lose our values."

But it's a critical time, and those values could be lost because they need to be sown and re-sown and permanently tended. Equality has collapsed. Everyone in Cuba is talking about it, no matter the topic of conversation. Equality was presented as a value for many years, but now it's not. The goal is equity, and the value is solidarity. When equality fell, the media and official discourse failed to reflect this. They also failed to make a permanent, intelligent, attractive call to solidarity among Cubans, between those who have and can do more and those who have less. Nothing is as urgent as cultivating this value.

34

The Status of Cuban Women

From Economically Dependent to Independent

Raisa Pagés

- 66.1 percent of Cuban professionals and intermediate-level technicians are women.
- In 1953, women constituted 19.2 percent of the work force and now represent 43.6 percent of public employees.
- During the Special Period, the number of women employed has increased.
- Plots of land have been handed over in usufruct to more than 11,200 women.

They traveled to space, to the depths of the sea, were awarded the Nobel Prize, and were entered into the Guinness Book of Records, set Olympic records, held presidential posts. In short, women have dispelled the myth of the weaker sex during the 20th century.

A THRONE WHICH NO ONE DISPUTES

A woman ascends a throne which no one disputes, queen of the home, who makes life more comfortable for the rest of the family at the cost of her own social potential, her health and life, say experts in this subject from the Federation of Cuban Women (FMC).

According to a census carried out in Cuba in 1953, women made up only 19.2 percent of the work force in the country. They carried out chores of minimal social status, unskilled work, as domestic workers or in small family businesses, secretaries or teachers at best, and victims of a high rate of unemployment recorded in Cuba prior to the triumph of the revolution in 1959.

Cuban women took full advantage of the revolutionary government's initiatives aimed at opening the doors to improvement and reintegration into the country's socioeconomic life in terms of education, health care, employment, and projects with the goal of attaining full gender equality. It was due to this process that between 1970 and 1990 the female labor force grew by 22.4 percent, while the male sector only increased by 4.2 percent in the same period. While in 1990 women represented 38.9 percent of the work force, they now represent 43.6 percent, which is the equivalent of more than 1.417 million in the public sector.

HIDDEN SKIRTS

Women's participation in the Cuban economy during the Special Period did not decrease. During the last four years [1996–2000], the female workforce has increased by 36 percent. The explanation for this phenomenon, contrary to the trend in other countries undergoing economic crises, owes to the fact that 66.1 percent of professionals and intermediate-level technicians are women. Also, the greatest shortages of resources were in production sectors which are traditionally male-dominated. Half a million Cuban women are engaged in highly skilled technical and professional activities.

Currently, there is a great deal of talk about the feminization of poverty. On a global level, seven out of every ten poor people are women or girls, according to a study carried out by the World Food Program (WFP). Nevertheless, in Cuba there has been a feminization of the technical and professional work force. Women represent 45 percent of the scientific and technical sector. More than 70 percent of bank employees are women, while they represent 43.9 percent of the workforce in joint ventures and have proven their abilities, skills, and efficiency.

More than 50 percent of the workforce in the Ministry of Public Health is female and women many hold key posts, from primary care within the community to high-ranking positions in polyclinics and hospitals. Female creativity can also be seen within the National Association of Innovators and Rationalizers (a nationwide group of people seeking innovative technological solutions to Cuban productive challenges), and women have won outstanding prizes in the national forums held by this organization.

However, female involvement in the tourism industry does not tally with the dynamic growth within this sector in the current phase of economic recovery, which is explained, according to female management, by the incorrect methods employed within the technical schools that train personnel for tourism. To reverse this process, the FMC is promoting measures aimed at obtaining equity in terms of gender among those selected to enroll in tourism training schools.

The Cuban government's approval of a range of self-employment activities has currently enabled 42,267 women to earn a living on their own; more than 50 percent of them were previously housewives.

WOMEN LANDOWNERS

While thousands of women throughout the world are calling for a plot of land to farm, in Cuba more than 11,200 women are now using land in usufruct to grow tobacco, coffee, cacao, and garden vegetables, thanks to an initiative begun in 1993 which continues to expand. The majority of these farms are in mountainous areas, meaning that inhabitants of these parts now have an opportunity to improve their food and earnings. The number of women in agricultural work has grown by more than 51,200 over the past three years, in addition to the fact that the increase in industrial processing of tobacco created some 12,000 new posts for women in 1998 and 1999.

IMPACT OF THE SPECIAL PERIOD

Even though statistics indicate that the Special Period did not decimate female participation in the workforce, we must not forget the social impact and suffering it entailed for women and their families starting in the early 1990s. The home and the family have been damaged by the double blockade: that of the United States and that which occurred with the sudden demise of the Soviet Union and the Eastern European socialist bloc. At the start of the Special Period, owing to the severe transportation problems, which have not yet been resolved, many women workers had to change jobs in order to be closer to home. In addition, those services aimed at alleviating the domestic burden suffered cutbacks.

All this took its physical toll on women. Their strength and perseverance are evident in the many schemes and initiatives developed to alleviate the effects of the Special Period, both in their working life and in the family. They confront widespread shortages bravely and are very creative when it comes to ensuring that their families are adequately fed and that their children attend school clean and in uniform.

Women showed a great ability to adapt themselves to temporary work when workplaces had to close down because there weren't enough raw materials, fuel, or electricity. Now that the process of economic recovery within Cuba is progressing smoothly, women are reaping the benefits of the resultant improvements.

The fact that construction of daycare centers came to a halt due to lack of materials influenced the reintegration of young mothers into the work force. This difficulty, which still prevails, has compelled those with young children to become reliant on retired women or housewives who offer their services as babysitters. But this option is not open to everyone, since prices set in the private sector are higher than the minimal prices established in state-owned daycare centers, where food and educational programs are coordinated by skilled personnel with the aim of educating children prior to their enrollment in elementary school.

At the same time, material shortages in daycare centers, even though they are given priority for the limited resources available in the country, are the cause of temporary closures of these facilities, which has negative repercussions on the work patterns of many mothers. To mitigate these effects, informal educational projects have been set up in the community involving housewives or retired women who are trained and guided by the Ministry of Education and the FMC to care for and educate children. In rural areas, improvised centers have been founded which care for children of female agricultural workers and laborers living in remote or isolated regions.

THEY BEAR THE HEAVIEST BURDEN

A number of experts from the FMC's Women's Studies Center indicate that women are the ones who have been hardest hit by the difficulties of daily life in the Special

Period. However, they point out that the involvement of other family members in domestic chores is increasingly seen. One doesn't have to look at statistics to note that there are men who, when confronted by the need to care for a sick child, will decide to stay home if their wives make a higher salary. Of course, this is not the norm, but this kind of behavior can be seen more and more, thus breaking the stereotypical chauvinist relationship prevalent until now.

Unequal relationships within couples, experts argue, have not changed to the same degree as the current social role of women, even when the woman contributes a substantial part of the family income. The excess tension unleashed by women in the domestic sphere is often a source of conflict, without underestimating the pressures resulting from male chauvinism, according to Carolina Aguilar, Perla Popowski, and Mercedes Verdeses in a study carried out by the Women's Studies Center.

PROSTITUTION: A PHENOMENON WITH MULTIPLE CAUSES

A subject which has been played to the hilt in the foreign press and the focus of public debate by Cuban journalists—the resurgence of prostitution in Cuba during the Special Period, a social stigma eradicated by the revolution through its program of social justice—is a phenomenon with multiple causes. It cannot be seen as the only option to resolving economic difficulties. This profession, which is as old as humanity itself, is present throughout the world. Economic motives cannot be dismissed, but analysis must also encompass the gender perspective, on account of the discriminatory perception and self-perception of the woman as a sex object, as well as the distortion of values arising out of an overemphasis on material possessions.

Experts in this area agree that behind the return of prostitution in Cuba is the search for easy earnings by young people avoiding work and social and family responsibilities. At the start of the Special Period the activities of the so-called *jineteras* was more open and had a certain degree of impunity. However, the program of preventative action aimed at halting its spread has had an impact on the public practice of prostitution.

THE PYRAMID OF POWER

Officials and experts in the national leadership of the FMC say, "We are the majority of the economic base but a minority in power." While in 1996, 30 percent of women held leadership positions, the percentage last year [1997] rose to 32.2 percent. Three women are at the head of important ministries: domestic trade, foreign investment, and technology, science and the environment.

Within the Communist Party of Cuba, women are in the Central Committee and the Political Bureau and two women are first secretaries of this political organization in two vital economic regions: Matanzas and Pinar del Río, both in western Cuba. Within the National Assembly, 27.6 percent of the deputies are women. Cuba is twelfth in the list of women parliamentary representatives, surpassed only by those nations which have set minimum quotas for women representatives.

Reina Muros, FMC official in promotion and mass media, says, "We are still not satisfied because there is a great deal of ability and intelligence which are not being utilized." She emphasizes, "It is not the case that women restrict themselves as some argue; rather, they have a double shift, at home and in the workplace, that prevents their access to leadership positions." Almost half the Cuban population and women electorate are still not fairly represented in the highest administrative, political, and legislative spheres.

After the World Conference on Women in Beijing, Cuba initiated a government program incorporating more than eighty measures directed toward improving the situation of Cuban women, with the participation of all state bodies and institutions involved in the search for solutions to the range of problems remaining. The throne of the queen of the household is a scepter which the majority of the family, particularly men, do not wish to share, even when their partners are women who are increasingly more educated and efficient.

35

Recreating Racism

Race and Discrimination in Cuba's Special Period

Alejandro de la Fuente

"Race," an Afro-Cuban-American businessman wrote in the Miami press not long ago, "is at the heart of Cuba's crisis." Although statements like this are not unheard-of, most analyses of the Cuban transition or the so-called Special Period treat the country as if it were a racially homogenous entity. This is not particularly surprising. A candid discussion of "race" is generally unwelcome among Cubans, particularly among white Cubans, who frequently claim that racism has never been a problem in the island and that its open discussion is not convenient and will only serve the divisionist purposes of the enemy, however defined. In addition to this patriotic silence—with deep roots in Cuban national discourse—studies about current social problems in the island face a total inadequacy of sources. If they exist at all, these sources are seldom published or accessible to researchers. The overwhelming literature about the transition concentrates, as a result, on economic and political problems. The social dimension remains less explored.

The revolution's impact on racial equality and the singularity of the Cuban case can be understood better in comparative perspective (another possibility is to use pre-revolutionary figures as a reference, but this is not always possible). Using census figures, I have estimated a number of indicators that can be compared with similar results in Brazil and the United States—thus putting the Cuban figures in a wider context. For instance, by 1981 life expectancy in Cuba was not only close to that of developed countries in absolute numbers, but this figure was actually as meaningful for the black and mulatto residents in the island as it was for whites. Although a white/non-white gap of one year still existed, it was significantly lower than in Brazil (6.7 years) or the United States (6.3 years). Life expectancy reflects broad social conditions, including access to nutrition, health care, maternal care, and education, thus the significance of these differences.

This is true for educational achievement as well. Illiteracy was basically eliminated in the island in the early 1960s, but by 1981 inequality in education had disappeared all the way up to the university level. The proportion of blacks and mulattos who had graduated from high school (11.2 and 9.6 percent, respectively) was in fact higher than the proportion of whites (9 percent), an indication that blacks had made good use of the opportunities created by the revolutionary government in this area. Conversely, in the United States in 1987 (at the college level where 10.7 percent for blacks and 20.5 percent for whites graduated) and Brazil, in both high school (5.3 percent and 13.9 percent for blacks and whites respectively) and college graduation (1.0 percent for blacks and 9.2 percent for whites), large differences according to race remained.

The expansion and socialization of education eventually influenced the racial composition of the occupational structure. [According to the 1981 census, 66 percent of the population was white, 12 percent was black, and 22 percent was mulatto.] The index of dissimilarity (a summary measure of inequality) in the Cuban labor market was in the early 1980s three to four times lower than in the United States or Brazil. The proportion of blacks and mulattos employed in the professions (one-fifth of the labor force) was virtually identical to whites in the island, whereas in Brazil it was three times lower. Thirty-one percent of workers employed in the Cuban medical sector were blacks and mulattos, a proportion only slightly lower than their share of the population. But the distribution of the racial groups in the different occupations was still somehow unequal. Although blacks and mulattos were not greatly over-represented in blue-collar jobs (35 percent), their proportion in some sectors, such as construction, was larger than their population share (41 percent). Likewise, whereas 13 percent of whites worked in managerial positions, the proportion of blacks (7 percent) and mulattos (9 percent) was lower. Even taking these qualifications into account, however, it is safe to state that the incidence of race in the Cuban labor market was limited, particularly in the case of the mulattos. Furthermore, since these figures are not age-specific, at least part of the remaining differences could be attributed to historical factors and past discrimination.

Even in the area of black representation in leadership positions—an area in which the Cuban government has been frequently criticized—inequality had decreased significantly. According to a census conducted in 1986, 27 percent of management positions in the government at the national level were occupied by blacks and mulattos, a percentage only slightly lower than their proportion in the total population.

THE SPECIAL PERIOD

Data to analyze this process are far from satisfactory, but some important trends can be discerned. To begin with, a careful analysis of Cuban society in the 1980s reveals that, despite the improvements mentioned above, some structural conditions did suggest the possibility that a crisis would unequally affect people according to the color of their skin. Racial inequality had been greatly reduced in areas in which government performance had been successful: health care, education, and employment. But in areas of limited success, racial inequality remained much wider.

For instance, despite efforts to the contrary, a strong correlation between race, the regional distribution of the population, and the quality of the housing stock persisted through the 1980s. A traditional geography of race and poverty had not been dismantled, not the least because of the government failure to provide adequate housing to all the population. No neighborhood was racially exclusive—this was true, for the most part, in pre-revolutionary Cuba also—but in the most dilapidated areas of the big cities the proportion of blacks and mulattos was greater than that of whites. In Havana, the municipalities of Habana Vieja and Centro Habana exemplify well the persistence of these residential patterns. Blacks and mulattos represented 36 percent of the city's population in 1981, but they amounted to 44 and 47 percent of the residents in the aforementioned municipalities. Whereas 13 percent of the residents in the city lived in tenement houses, in Habana Vieja and Centro Habana their proportion was three to four times higher. Only 14 percent of the city's population lived in these municipalities, yet they contained 47 percent of the houses with structural damages in the whole city. The proportion of houses in which sanitary services were collectively used was also three to four times higher in Habana Vieja (36 percent) and Centro Habana (24 percent) than in Havana as a whole (9 percent). Households in these municipalities also ranked consistently lower than the provincial average in the availability of appliances.

These residential areas, characterized by high densities of non-white population and a physically deteriorated environment, are frequently deemed to be also dangerous and with high rates of criminal activities. There is a geography of crime which remains tied to race and poverty. Thirty-one percent of the areas officially classified by the Policía Nacional Revolucionaria (PNR, National Revolutionary Police) to be "criminal centers" (focos delictivos) in Havana (1987), were located in the three municipalities with the highest proportions of blacks and mulattos in the city: Habana Vieja, Centro Habana, and Marianao (which comprised only, however, 20 percent of the city's total population). These focos included some shanty towns, such as "El Palo," "Isla de Simba," "Las Yaguas," and "Isla del Polvo" in Marianao, or tenement houses such as "Mercaderes 111" in Habana Vieja and "Romeo y Julieta" in Centro Habana.

The persistence of racial inequality in the criminal system and the association between race and crime remained obvious in other ways. According to a MININT (Ministerio del Interior) report, the yearly average number of criminal acts between the periods of 1976–1980 and 1981–1985 increased nationally by 11 percent. The growth in some of the provinces with a large black and mulatto population was significantly higher: 57 percent in Granma, 29 percent in Santiago de Cuba, and 50 percent in Guantánamo. In the same period, the yearly national average of murders increased by 46 percent, from 216 in the 1976–1980 five-year period to 315 in 1981–1985. The increase in three provinces mentioned above amounted to 70 percent.

Impressionistic reports assert also that blacks and mulattos are overrepresented in the prison population. According to an organization of political prisoners in the Combinado del Este prison, in the late 1980s eight out of every ten prisoners were black. This, they concluded, destroyed "the myth proclaimed by the Cuban revolution that it has established racial equality." A U.N. Commission which visited two Cuban prisons in 1988 reported that "a large number of prisoners were black," a reality that was acknowledged by the vice president of the Council of State who accompanied the visitors. The functionary explained that the number of blacks in prison was disproportionate in relation to their population share because, despite "the substantial achievements of the revolution," blacks were still in a majority in the poorest strata of society. This, he claimed, "is by no means the expression of a policy of racial discrimination, but a left-over from the past."

Whether these racial differences can be explained as "left-overs" is of course open to question, but it seems safe to state that, just as in pre-revolutionary Cuba, blacks' delinquency rates remained higher than those of whites through the 1980s. A provision contained in the penal code which can be particularly telling about racialized perceptions of crime is that of *peligrosidad social* (social dangerousness). In other words, a person whose conduct was deemed to be "manifestly against the norms of socialist morality" could be deprived of freedom even without committing acts defined as crimes in the law. Included among these pre-criminal behaviors were habitual drunkenness, vagrancy, drug addiction, and other forms of "antisocial conduct."

Such a lax, broad definition of antisocial behavior created enough room for racialized notions of proper conduct to be enforced more freely than under the specific provisions of the penal code. Data to assess the racially differentiated impact of the "social dangerousness" provision are scant, but the results of a study commissioned by the Attorney General of Cuba in 1987 are indeed revealing. Out of a total of 643 cases of *peligrosidad* submitted to the courts in Havana city between May and December 1986, 345 were black subjects and 120 were mulattos. Nonwhites represented a staggering 78 percent of all the individuals considered to be socially dangerous. This proportion was more than double their share in the total population. Whereas there were 5,430 white adults living in the city for each white person facing charges of social dangerousness, the ratio among blacks (excluding mulattos) was one in 713. Blacks (again, excluding mulattos) were declared to be socially dangerous 7.6 times more often than whites, and 3.4 times more often than mulattos. Social dangerousness was essentially used to typify the conduct of blacks, particularly of young ones. Eighty-four percent of the socially dangerous subjects were between the ages of 16 and 30.

Despite its inadequacies, the information reviewed here provides a picture about the role of race in 1980s Cuban society which is more complex, contradictory, and nuanced than frequently assumed. The structural changes implemented by the revolutionary government did benefit large sectors of the black population, but such gains were concentrated in areas in which the revolution had been particularly successful and which had received generous government spending. Conversely, the government's failure to meet housing demands allowed for the survival and reproduction of traditional residential patterns which combined race with poverty and marginalization. This also limited the impact of the revolution's educational program, high rates of schooling notwithstanding. The chances for young blacks to grow up in these poorer areas remained significantly greater than for whites. Likewise, the chances for young blacks to be socialized in what Cuban criminologists referred to as the criminal micro-environment were also significantly larger. In summary, the achievement of racial equality was largely dependent on government performance.

But capacity to perform is, precisely, what the Cuban government has lacked under the Special Period. The Cuban government was forced to introduce a number of market-oriented measures, including foreign investment, to foster productivity and stimulate Cuba's stagnant economy. Measures like the legalization of dollars, self-employment, foreign investment, and "free" agricultural markets carry with them, as Cuban authorities themselves recognize, a heavy social cost: they unavoidably provoke increasing inequality and resentment in a population which is used to living in a highly egalitarian social setting. As Carlos Lage, vice president of the Cuban Council of State, remarked, "This will create differences among people, greater than what we have now and greater than we are used to having since the revolution . . . the inequality or privilege that can be created are realities we must allow."

These economic changes affect large sectors of the population, regardless of race, education, and other socially relevant variables. As Cubans in the island themselves recognize, the origins and nature of the crisis are not racially defined. "The issue isn't race," a black scientist asserted in 1993, referring to the crisis. A black female physician agreed: "Here there are not black and white differences. We are all living through the Special Period." A similar perception was prevalent among respondents to a survey conducted in Havana and Santiago de Cuba in 1994. Although a higher percentage of blacks (22 percent) than whites (7 percent), considered the crisis to have racially differentiated effects, the dominant view was that it affected blacks and whites equally.

Yet some of the reforms introduced by the government affect different social groups dissimilarly and do have racially differentiated effects. The most obvious example is that of the legalization of dollars, which has tended to fragment Cuban society along the lines of those who have access to dollars and those who do not. For the most part, Cubans receive hard currency from two main sources: family remittances and through links to the Cuban dollar economy, represented mainly by tourism and by the joint ventures and foreign companies that have opened businesses in the island. Workers in some productive sectors have also received dollar payments in the last few years, but these amounts are small compared to what can be obtained in tourism jobs or through family remittances (for instance, workers in the bio-medical research sector have received $70 once or twice a year). Some artists, artisans, writers, and scholars also obtain dollars through their work.

Family remittances are probably the most important source of hard currency for ordinary Cubans. Economic officials in the island estimate that annual remittances amount to 600 to 800 million dollars. Given the racial composition of the Cuban diaspora, it is reasonable to assume that blacks' access to these funds is rather limited. According to the 1990 U.S. census, 83.5 percent of Cuban immigrants living in the United States identify themselves as whites. Assuming that dollar remittances are evenly distributed among white and non-white exiles and that they stay, roughly, within the same racial group of the sender, then about 680 out of the 800 million dollars that enter the island every year would end up in white hands. What this means is that per capita remittances to the island would amount to about $85 per year among whites. The comparable figure for non-whites would be less than half this amount.

Given their limited participation in the remittances, blacks' opportunities to participate in the dollar economy are basically reduced to the competitive tourist sector. The desirability and attractiveness of tourist jobs is such that a large number of professionals have abandoned their occupations to seek employment in this sector, the most dynamic and lucrative in the Cuban economy. Consequently, competition for these jobs has escalated.

Tourism is a sector in which blacks should have had privileged access, for in the early 1980s they comprised a significant proportion of the labor force employed in hotels, restaurants, and similar services. Thirty-eight percent of those employed in "services" were, according to the 1981 census, blacks or mulattos—a percentage slightly above their population share. Yet there is widespread consensus that non-whites are currently under-represented in the tourist sector and face significant obstacles to both finding jobs and getting promotions.

Two additional factors tend to further increase the racially differentiated effects of the crisis and to fuel growing racial inequality under the special period. Because of blacks' relative concentration in areas which are overcrowded and with a dilapidated housing stock, the opening of *paladares* (family-operated restaurants) is not an economic option for many black families. The other lucrative sector in which blacks are under-represented is the private agricultural sector. Since the early decades of the century, the black peasantry was displaced from land ownership, so Afro-Cuban rates of urbanization have been consistently higher than those of whites. According to the Agricultural Household Survey, conducted by a University of Havana research team in 1992 in a sample of rural communities across the island, whites represented 98 percent of private farmers and 95 percent of members in the agricultural cooperatives.

Most of these racially differentiated effects are clearly unintended and escape government control. Government policies to cope with the crisis have provoked social polarization—including a fast-growing income gap—but they are racial only in their consequences, not in their design. The dollarization of the economy, for instance, has multiplied income differences according to race, but the government has no control over the distribution of the dollar remittances that the overwhelmingly white Cuban-American community sends to their relatives in the island every year. Yet, this does not explain blacks' under-representation in the tourist sector or in foreign corporations. As mentioned above, by the 1980s blacks had obtained levels of education comparable to those of whites and shared with them the benefits of expanded opportunities in white-collar employment. If anything, blacks' slight overrepresentation in service jobs should have given them a competitive advantage in the expanding tourist economy.

Despite its anti-discriminatory position and egalitarian social policies, the revolutionary government failed to create the color-blind society it envisioned in the 1960s. The Cuban authorities believed that with the elimination of the "material bases" of capitalism and class exploitation, the ideologies and mores from the past would automatically disappear. It would take time for racial stereotypes to wither away, but the "new man," formed in the principles of communism, would not know racism. Consequently, the issue of race was silenced in public discourse since the 1960s; precedence was given to the imperative of unity in the face of numerous internal and external threats. Race became a taboo in public discourse, its open discussion tantamount to an act of divisionism.

This official silence contributed to the survival, reproduction, and even creation of racist ideologies and stereotypes in a society which, particularly in the 1960s, was still far from being racially equal. What disappeared from public discourse found fertile breeding ground in private spaces, where race continued to influence social relations among friends, neighbors, co-workers, and family members. Supposedly harmless racist jokes reproduced in fact traditional images of blacks as criminals, dirty, lazy, and genetically inferior. Racial ideologies were reproduced within the family and enforced in multi-generational households.

Still, the extent to which these racial ideologies permeate Cuban society and the intensity of racial prejudice in popular consciousness is somehow surprising.

Seventy-five percent of respondents to the survey conducted in Havana and Santiago in 1994 by myself and Glasco agreed that prejudice is rampant in the island. The study conducted in Havana by the Centro de Antropología in 1995 found that 58 percent of whites considered blacks to be less intelligent, 69 percent claimed that they do not have the same "values" and "decency," and 68 percent opposed interracial marriages.

The state-sponsored media have also contributed to the persistence of some of these racist images. Black actors are conspicuously absent from television and are frequently relegated to stereotypical roles. "When I worked in television," a black female script writer asserts,

> I told the national director once that blacks' situation in TV was hopeless, because television does not reflect the reality of blacks. If the programs referred to the past, blacks appeared as maids or *santeros*, but it was not like that, there was a class of black professionals . . . The same today, with the black professionals created by the revolution. Blacks are always portrayed as marginals . . . I would write a script with a black character and they changed it and put in a white.

Likewise, whereas movies set in the past, particularly during times of slavery, have treated Afro-Cuban religions and culture as positive examples of popular resistance (*La última cena* [1976], for instance), those dealing with post-revolutionary realities (for an example, see *De cierta manera* [1974] and its characterization of *ñáñigos*) have portrayed the same practices as decadent forms of cultural expression that generate marginality and prevent integration into the socialist project.

This ideology was not created under the Special Period, but it has acquired visibility and growing social acceptability over the last few years. Indeed, despite its failure in eliminating racial prejudice, the impact of government propaganda, which claimed since the 1960s that all Cubans are equal and deserve full access to all sectors of national life, should not be underestimated. This campaign created an ideal of egalitarianism that was shared by vast sectors of the population. Its complexities and contradictions notwithstanding, the post-revolutionary social environment was decidedly anti-discriminatory. Public discourse equated racism with a past of capitalism and class exploitation—a trait of the antinational, pro-American, white elite which had been displaced from power. To be racist was to be counter-revolutionary. Real revolutionaries were not supposed to be racist—at least in public.

The association between revolution and racial fraternity/equality is a double-edge sword, however. It links the unacceptability of racism to the legitimacy, popularity, and support of the revolution—as represented by the government. But legitimacy, support, and popularity are, together with economic resources, what the government has lost the most in the 1990s. The erosion and deepening crisis of legitimacy of the current political system thus creates new spaces for racist ideas and practices to operate and flourish. What used to be social and political anathema restricted to private spaces has become increasingly acceptable and public. These ideas, to use the graphic expression of one of my collaborators in the island, are not confined to "people's heads" anymore. As the example of the tourist sector shows, they result in concrete practices which are discriminatory in nature. Diminishing government control over the hiring and promotion of personnel in the expanding private sector creates additional opportunities for these racially discriminatory practices to operate unhindered.

FIDEL'S "SECRET WEAPON"?

The revival of racism and racially discriminatory practices under the Special Period has led to growing resentment and resistance in the black population, which suddenly finds itself in a hostile environment without the political and organizational resources needed to fight against it. In this context, events such as the Malecón "riot" of August 5, 1994, begin to make sense. These spontaneous outbursts of rage and anger are typical of politically disorganized groups who perceive their situation as hopeless. Symptomatically, participants in this street protest stoned dollar stores while calling for "freedom" and political changes. As I have argued elsewhere, the surprise of the Cuban government concerning the racial composition of the rioters—according to an official report leaked to the press, blacks and mulattos were in the majority—is more a function of its own prejudice and expectations than of any concrete sociological reality. The government expects young blacks to behave as passive "beneficiaries" of revolutionary gains, not as active protagonists for their own well-being and future.

Perhaps because of these expectations, the reaction of the Cuban government to this process of racial polarization has been slow and inadequate. Given the lack of official action, it is even questionable whether in official circles there is awareness about the existence of a problem at all. The program of the Fifth and most recent (1997) Congress of the Communist Party (PCC) contained an element of hope: while claiming that the revolution "eliminated the institutional bases of racism" and worked to incorporate all Cubans, regardless of race, into the country's life, it called for maintaining "the just policy" of increasing black representation in positions of command. Even if fully implemented, the impact of this policy would have been limited: positions within the government bureaucracy are not, for the most part, as desirable as they were in the past and they certainly do not provide material benefits comparable to those in the dollarized sector. Yet, a visible increase of blacks in the power structure would have sent an unequivocal message to managers in the private sector that the government opposes racial exclusion and that racially discriminatory practices would not be tolerated. Instead, the Party Congress elected a Political Bureau in which non-whites represent only 21 percent of the total (this is an improvement compared to 1991, when it was 16 percent). Their proportion in the Central Committee is even lower: it amounts to only 12 percent. The upper echelons of the party are actually whiter today (87 percent, including Central Committee and Political Bureau) than in 1991 (84 percent) or 1986 (72 percent). The proportion of blacks and mulattos among the candidates to the National Assembly of Poder Popular in the 1997 elections was higher than in the PCC (about 21 percent), but still considerably low considering their share in the total population. Furthermore, this figure does not show a significant improvement over the racial composition of the candidates in the elections of 1993 (it was then 19 percent).

CONCLUSION

In a September 2000 speech at New York's Riverside Church, Fidel Castro empha-sized the Cuban Revolution's aspirations for social equality. Yet he also stated,

> I am not claiming that our country is a perfect model of equality and justice. We be-lieved at the beginning that when we established the fullest equality before the law and complete intolerance for any demonstration of sexual discrimination in the case of women, or racial discrimination in the case of ethnic minorities, these phenom-ena would vanish from our society. It was some time before we discovered that mar-ginality and racial discrimination with it are not something that one gets rid of with a law or even with ten laws, and we have not managed to eliminate them com-pletely, even in 40 years. . . . I told you that our country is on its way to a new era. I hope someday to be able to speak to you of the things we are doing today and how we are going to continue to do them. . . . I have faith that we will succeed because that is the endeavor today of the leaders of our youth, our students, and our people. I shall not say more, I am simply saying that we are aware that there is still mar-ginality in our country. But, there is the will to eradicate it with the proper meth-ods in order to bring more unity and equality to our society.

The available evidence suggests that race relations have deteriorated in Cuba under the Special Period. Not only has racial inequality increased along with other forms of social inequality, but racist ideologies and prejudices seem to be operating with greater freedom than before the crisis started. Declining government control over the economy and lack of government action to enforce color-blind hiring and promotion practices have opened new spaces—and expanded old ones—for racist ideas to result in discriminatory practices. The case of the tourist industry is a prime example of this process. In this sense, one could argue that race is indeed "at the heart" of the Cuban crisis.

It is more difficult to agree with the belief that Afro-Cubans represent a source of support for the current government. This assertion might be as inaccurate as its opposite—that whites oppose the government en masse. The limited evidence available suggests that it is more accurate to analyze "support" in generational, rather than racial lines. Older Cubans, regardless of race, are more concerned about a political change that might destroy what is left of the safety net created by the government to protect the elderly. This concern is less relevant for younger Cubans, who are also, as a rule, better educated than previous generations. Furthermore, the belief that blacks are Fidel Castro's "secret weapon" rests on the assumption that they fear the return of discrimination and racism to the island in a post-communist future. In fact, there is convincing evidence that race discrimination is a reality that blacks already face in Cuba. In summary, Afro-Cubans should not be automatically seen as uncritical supporters of the government.

However, the assertion that blacks are loyal supporters of the government is not surprising—and not only because of the mobility experienced by Afro-Cubans after 1959. Linking blacks to crumbling political regimes seems to be a regularity in Cuba's post-colonial history. In previous moments of transition, blacks have been always portrayed as supporters of governments whose falling is perceived as immi-nent. This happened under the dictatorial regimes of both Gerardo Machado (1925–1933) and Fulgencio Batista (1952–1959). The statement that "los negros" are

Fidel Castro's "secret weapon" is essentially identical to Machado's belief that he would stay in power with "his army and his negros," or to Batista's vision that blacks should expect nothing from the white revolutionaries of the M-26-7 ("July 26 Movement": the organized resistance against Batista, named after the date on which Fidel Castro stormed the Moncada barracks in 1953, the symbolic date for the beginning of the Cuban Revolution).

From a historical perspective, the racialization of the Special Period is hardly special. Race has been central to every major crisis in Cuba's modern history, and constructs similar to those currently used have emerged before. The 1990s crisis is just another instance in the long and contradictory process of defining how racially inclusive the Cuban nation should be. Race remains central to the definition of Cuban nationhood—it is not possible to define a new Cuba without addressing the issue of race. That another "new" Cuba is about to be born is beyond dispute—it is already in the making. What this will mean for Cubans of different "races" is uncertain. As in previous transitions—late 1890s, 1930s, 1959—the current crisis is fraught with racial tensions, social dislocation and competing notions of what la Patria should be.

As in previous transitions, blacks will not quietly acquiesce to displacement or exclusion from a nation that they helped create. It is interesting that some of the concerns voiced about the role of blacks in the current transition are essentially identical to those of the previous *fin de siècle* transition. In their introduction to the anthology *Afrocuba*, Pedro Pérez Sarduy and Jean Stubbs wrote that "no matter what happens . . . black Cubans are a force to be reckoned with." In 1899, an American observer of the Cuban situation stated in an almost identical language: "The existence of blacks must be reckoned with in every phase of the reconstruction of the island." Times might be different, but our concerns remain the same.

36

The Status of Gays in Cuba

Myth and Reality

Larry R. Oberg

Based upon a memoir by the late self-exiled Cuban writer Reynaldo Arenas, the film "Before Night Falls," released in 2000, chronicles the author's coming of age and repression as a homosexual and artist by Cuban authorities in the early days of the Cuban revolution. Arenas wrote his memoir in New York shortly before his death from AIDS in 1990, some ten years after leaving Cuba in the Mariel exodus. Apart from any artistic considerations, questions have arisen concerning the accuracy of Arenas's descriptions of the past persecution of Cuban gays and the usefulness of the memoir and film as guides to the current status of gays and lesbians on the island.

Between March 2000 and April 2002, I spent more than four months in Cuba on four separate occasions, working as a librarian on a range of research projects with my Cuban colleagues. Most of that time was spent in Havana, but also in numerous other cities, including Matanzas, Trinidad, and Santiago de Cuba. As a gay man, I was motivated to find out as much as I could about the status of Cuba's gay and lesbian population. What I experienced, read, and was told made me suspect that Arenas's portrayal of his personal life as a gay man in the early years of Cuba's revolution may have been exaggerated. For example, his fantastic claim, arrived at by "complicated mathematical calculations," to have bedded some five thousand men by the age of twenty-five is hardly plausible and, if we are to believe him, every young stud on the island was constantly on the alert to jump his bones. Well, perhaps not.

Interestingly, Arenas's apparently insatiable sexual appetite does not come through in Julian Schnabel's sanitized film version of the memoirs, in which he is depicted as little more than an inveterate flirt. I cannot claim to know whether Arenas's description of the repression that he and other gays suffered during that particular moment in Cuban history is accurate. But, whatever the truth of the matter, I can attest to the fact that the condition and status of gay men and lesbians on the island today can only be described as much improved.

To prepare for my visits, I read Canadian Ian Lumsden's 1996 introduction to Cuban gay life, *Machos, Maricones, and Gays: Cuba and Homosexuality*. Lumsden, a lukewarm supporter of the Cuban Revolution, provides us with a useful history of the treatment of gays during the early days of the revolution and surveys their status in contemporary Cuban society. I also watched Sonja de Vries's 1995 documentary, "Gay Cuba," which consists of a series of interviews with gay men and lesbians who speak frankly of their lives and relationships with friends, family, and coworkers. (One of the producers of the film, an interviewee himself, now works as a tour guide and gave me useful background information on the film.) "Gay Cuba" was shown at the annual International Festival of New Latin American Cinema in Havana to public and critical acclaim. Nonetheless, some of the Cuban gays with whom I spoke expressed reservations about the film, suggesting that, while it is generally accurate, it nonetheless presents an incomplete portrait of gay life in the island nation.

"Gay Cuba" is not, however, the only filmed account of gay life in Cuba. Several other documentaries are available. A particularly interesting one, released in 1996, is "Mariposas en el andamio" (Butterflies on the Scaffold). Mariposa, a metaphor for drag queen, is used here to refer to someone who transforms himself into something beautiful to be admired by all. The film documents the daily life and performances of drag artists in a Havana neighborhood called La Guinera. At my request, I was invited to La Guinera for a private show. Extremely poor before the revolution, La Guinera today is recognized by the United Nations for exemplary community development, but remains what might be called working class. Many of these drag shows are sponsored by the local CDRs (Committees for the Defense of the Revolution), and all play to large and enthusiastic audiences.

What I found during my time in Cuba was a gay community with many parallels to those of Europe and North America, as well as a number of differences. For one thing, all laws that discriminate against Cuban gays have been removed from the books. Earlier efforts to legislate behavior in Cuba gave rise to the Public Ostentation Law. Enacted in the 1930s, it was used effectively for decades to harass gay people who refused to remain closeted. Aimed at those who "flaunted" their homosexuality, the law defined public and even private homosexual acts that might be witnessed involuntarily by others as offenses punishable by fine and detention. The Public Ostentation Law was repealed by the revolutionary government in 1988. The legal situation of gays in Cuba today is usefully contrasted with, for example, that of the United States, where many states retain outdated anti-sodomy laws, and repressive legislation aimed at gays increasingly is enacted at the state level and proposed at the national level.

While in Cuba, I spoke with scores of gays, mostly men, and encountered none who said that their government was persecuting them, although many older gays did talk about the "bad old days." Most, however, reported incidents of private discrimination by individuals, and all resented the residual *machista* attitudes that remain stubbornly embedded in some levels of Cuban society. Nourished for centuries by Spanish colonialism, the Catholic Church, and a quasi-reverential attitude towards the traditional heterosexual family, these attitudes not only perpetuate prejudice against gays but also result in more highly polarized sex roles than generally exist in North American and European societies. No one with whom I spoke, however, reported active or systematic repression by the state.

One question that I asked many of my informants was, "Would you feel comfortable holding hands with your boyfriend on the street?" Several responded with a qualified yes and a few stated that they do just that. Indeed, two men or two women holdings hands is not an altogether uncommon sight, at least not in Havana. But some also stated that they would stop holding hands at the approach of a police officer. Urban Cuban police forces recruit a high percentage of young *macho* males from the provinces, many with a chip on their shoulder against gays.

It is important to put Cuba's past record of mistreatment of gays into perspective. While context rarely excuses negative behavior, it is worth remembering that Cuba was scarcely alone in its anti-gay attitudes and actions. For example, in the Boise, Idaho, of the 1950s, scores of gay men were persecuted, driven from their homes, pursued when they fled to other states, and imprisoned in what came to be known as the Boys of Boise scandal, one of the most infamous anti-gay actions in United States history. Florida, home to so many Cuban expatriates, has a dreadful record of gay rights abuses, and in 1990, in Adrian, Michigan, the police staked out a public park for months on end before arresting nearly twenty men on charges of public indecency. Almost all were married and self-identified as heterosexuals. Many were arrested in their homes in front of wives, children, and in a couple of instances, grandchildren.

Cuba's past record on gay rights may be no better than that of most western societies, but it can be argued that gay people in Cuba are better off today than those in any other Latin American society and even in parts of North America and Europe. It wasn't too long ago, for example, that death squads in Rio de Janeiro were sent out to cleanse the city of its "queers." In the United States, the problem is more likely to be private violence underpinned by a pervasive hatred of gay people, as in the murders of Matthew Shepard, Brandon Teena, Billy Jack Gaither, and countless others.

Like North American and European societies, Cuba is undergoing a profound review and reconceptualization of its attitudes towards gays and lesbians. The 1994 film "Fresa y Chocolate" (Strawberry and Chocolate) is the first Cuban film to deal openly and directly with homosexuality. Directed by Tomás Guitérrez Alea, the film has been widely praised. What is less well known is that it was also wildly popular across the island, playing simultaneously at ten or twelve Havana theaters to lines several blocks long. Its popularity was, no doubt, a response to a repressed desire on the part of Cubans to talk more openly about this issue.

Another seminal incident along the road to acceptance for Cuban gays occurred in 1996. Pablo Milanés, a Cuban nova trova singer who has achieved quasi-sainthood among the island's population, wrote a song about love between two men entitled "El pecado original" (Original Sin). Pablito, as he is affectionately known, dedicated the song to all Cuban homosexuals. Introduced at his annual holiday concert held in the vast Carlos Marx Theater in the Miramar neighborhood of Havana, "El pecado original" took the audience and the country by storm and did much to advance the cause of gay acceptance. It is of interest to note that, in the 1960's, Milanés was briefly confined to one of the UMAP (Military Units for Aid to Production) work camps set up to rehabilitate prostitutes, gays, and others considered to be delinquents. Although short-lived, the UMAP camps represent the low point in revolutionary Cuba's treatment of its gay and lesbian citizens.

One of the most striking things about Cuba is the vitality of its cultural and intellectual life throughout the island, particularly in Havana. Gay themes are prevalent in the theater, in lectures, and in concerts. In December, 2000, I attended a play entitled "Muerte en el bosque" (A Death in the Woods), produced by the Teatro Sótano in Havana's Vedado neighborhood. Based upon the acclaimed novel *Máscaras* (Masks), by Leonardo Padura Fuentes, the play follows a police investigation into the murder of a Havana drag queen, a plot device that allows for an examination of Cuban attitudes and prejudices towards gays at every level of society.

On a lighter note, a group called La Danza Voluminosa, which features large dancers, produced an alternately amusing and touching ballet version of Racine's Phèdre. The director opted for gender-blind casting and, indeed, a man danced the title role. A one-man—yes, one man—stage version of "Strawberry and Chocolate" played to considerable success a few years ago. And, at the 22nd International Festival of New Latin American Cinema held in Havana in December 2000, perhaps half of the films shown had gay themes or subtexts. In 2001, Emilio Bejel published *Gay Cuban Nation.* The book is a fascinating scholarly study of the impact of homosexuality on Cuban politics, society, and culture, as seen through the writings of its gay artists, both past and present.

A striking contradiction in Cuban society today is the contrast between the rich cultural and intellectual life that is widely available and easily affordable, and salaries that make the purchase of a pair of shoes an event for which one must plan. Cubans purchase theater tickets in pesos (MN, i.e., *moneda nacional*; valued at approximately five U.S. cents). Tickets for the National Ballet cost Cubans five pesos; theatrical plays, eight; musical extravaganzas and ballet festival performances, ten. Admission to first-run films costs two pesos. Foreign tourists pay in convertible pesos (more commonly known as CUC or tourist dollars, valued at approximately 1.25 U.S. dollars). Admission to the National Ballet costs tourists 20 CUCs. For most other theatrical events tourists pay the same amount as Cubans, but in CUCs, not Cuban (national) pesos. Tourists are allowed, however, to pay at the cinemas in Cuban pesos.

In Havana, gay-run and gay-clientele restaurants are not hard to find. Try, for example, the elegant French cuisine at "Le Chansonnier" or "La Guarida," the latter located in the apartment in which "Strawberry and Chocolate" was filmed. Until its recent closing, the famous, indeed somewhat infamous, Fiat bar on the Malecón attracted hundreds of gay twenty-somethings who, on weekend nights, spilled across this emblematic Havana thoroughfare to line the sidewalk along the sea wall. Midnight mass on Christmas Eve at the Havana cathedral and any performance by the National Ballet at the Gran Teatro de la Habana attract scores of Cuban gays.

Gay culture in Cuba without doubt was repressed, sometimes severely, during the period described by Arenas in "Before Night Falls." But where was it not in that pre-Stonewall era? This, however, is not the reality that I found in today's Cuba. Indeed, it is unlikely that the slick and trendy "Out" magazine would feature Havana as "The new gay hot spot . . . hot boys, drag-heavy bars, and a whole lot more" in its February 2001 issue, if Cuba were as repressive as its critics would have us believe.

It is ultimately unproductive to hold Cuba to an abstract standard that no other country in the world, certainly not my own, can claim to have reached. It is more useful to view this small island nation within the context of current reality. How well is Cuba doing compared to the rest of Latin America? How well is it doing relative to our own countries? How much progress has been made over the past forty years on a variety of fronts—literacy, education, health care, housing, the status of women, and of course gay rights? When we respond honestly to these questions, we see a vision of Cuba that is sharply different from that propounded by Cuba's detractors.

37

Civil Society and Religion in Cuba

Past, Present, and Future

Margaret E. Crahan

Before 1959, Cuban civil society had developed into one of the most advanced in Latin America in spite of periodic government attempts to regulate it both legally and through repression. Civic, fraternal, and religious organizations were common in Cuba as early as the nineteenth century and they continued to proliferate throughout the twentieth. Since 1959 the revolutionary government has tried, largely through executive orders, to limit the autonomy and development of associative organizations. Laws adopted from 1976 to 1985 to institutionalize the revolutionary process codified the state's efforts to control civil society. Nevertheless, in recent years there has been a revitalization and expansion of civic and other organizations not dominated by the government. Indeed, there is a sense of mild ferment within Cuban civil society. Critical elements within the autonomous sector of Cuban civil society are religious groups that are increasingly occupying public space. Given that a good number of recent studies suggest that the nature, strength, and resources of a civil society help determine a country's direction, a better understanding of the role of religions, past and present, in the evolution of Cuban civil society could help clarify the island's future.

THE PAST

The tendency to regard religions as being relatively weak in Cuba flows, in part, from a focus on formal participation, levels of activism, and direct political influence. It is true that attendance at services and participation in religious groups was historically relatively low in Cuba and political influence was evaluated rather superficially. What has not been sufficiently studied is the very real penetration of Cuban society by indigenous, Judeo-Christian, and spiritist religions that have made the vast majority of Cubans believers and popular religiosity widespread. In addition, religious beliefs have permeated Cuban culture and molded societal values. At the same time, the very multiplicity of religions and the weak presence of religious institutions and personnel, especially in rural areas, have contributed to low levels of practice and also to a great deal of syncretism and permeability in terms of both religious and secular belief systems. Weak institutional presence, chronic limitations in terms of material and human resources, together with considerable openness to other belief systems resulted in higher levels of secularism, as well as lower levels of institutional identification and loyalty, than in most Latin American countries.

Nevertheless, Cuban culture and society was and is permeated with religious symbolism, icons, referents, and popular religiosity. Belief in the divine has long been an integral part of Cubans' self-identification or *cubanidad*. Therefore, Cuba is somewhat contradictory in that while it is a nation of believers, institutional religion, especially Catholicism, is weaker than in most of Latin America's formerly Spanish colonies, thereby giving rise to the notion that religion in general has had relatively little sway in Cuba.

Hence, while the percentage of Cubans actually engaged in regular religious practice was not high, religious beliefs were widely held and influenced concepts of polity and society, as well as Cubans' involvement in civil society. Furthermore, the level of belief in the divine has remained remarkably stable in Cuba from the fifties to the present (approximately 85 percent), albeit formal religious practice remains low. This suggests that while institutional religion in Cuba has historically been somewhat weak according to such indicators as frequency of attendance at services, geographic reach, and resources, the influence of religions in the conceptualization of polity and society has been strong.

THE PRESENT

How have forty-five years of Marxist revolution affected the role of religions in civil society in Cuba today? Largely marginalized in the sixties, institutional religions began to recoup in the seventies and eighties and experienced a resurgence in the nineties, particularly as the government became less capable of fulfilling the population's basic socioeconomic needs. The government had from the outset justified its policies and actions, including organizing civil society into government-created mass organizations, on the grounds that this was necessary to ensure equitable distribution of the benefits of a socialist economy. Redemption of the latter promise was at the core of the government's claim to legitimacy. Although religious leaders supported the revolutionary government's objective of greater socioeconomic justice, by the eighties, and particularly with the economic crisis of the nineties, they were increasingly questioning governmental policies and programs. Failure of the government's economic model to meet the basic socioeconomic needs of Cubans was linked by religious leaders to a lack of effective citizen participation in determining public policies and securing governmental accountability. The Cardinal of Havana, Monsignor Jaime Ortega y Alamino, stated in a 1994 visit to Rome that because the revolution had raised the hopes of so many and mobilized Cubans to create a more just society, the Catholic Church had a duty to help preserve the achievements of the revolution. At the same time, he argued, the Church had an obligation to help the Cuban people transcend the revolution's limitations, particularly through increased popular participation in government decision making. The latter, he posited, could best be achieved through intensifying evangelization so that the laity would be better prepared to act through a mobilized civil society.

In order to facilitate this, the Catholic Church adopted a Global Pastoral Plan for 1997–2000. Its principal objective was to promote evangelization via prophetic and acculturated communities that would disseminate the gospel message in order to promote human dignity, reconciliation, and the construction of a society characterized by love and justice. This would require the strengthening of faith-based communities in which all individuals would be regarded as children of God and therefore treated justly. This required substantial resources, both in terms of monies and personnel, which were in short supply. Some clerical and lay leaders felt that the plan was too general and not sufficiently proactive.

A group of priests issued a public critique arguing that a basic prerequisite had to be overcoming the profound passivity of citizens inculcated by the existing political system. In addition, they felt that calls by both the Catholic and other churches for a national dialogue were flawed as they were premised on the government's willingness to dialogue. Some priests proposed that what the Catholic Church should do instead was create a national dialogue that included a broad coalition of civil society sectors including other churches, fraternal organizations, and autonomous groups. Neither of these proposed national dialogues has been undertaken as the government is resistant and organized civil society not sufficiently strong to sustain such an initiative. This is further evidence of the fact that there has not yet been the necessary strength and unity of purpose within either the Catholic Church, nor the religious community more generally, to adopt a consensual agenda together with a strategy to implement it. Although some have suggested that the Varela Project, which calls for constitutional and other reforms to make Cuban political life more participatory and pluralistic, could serve as a basis for such a consensual agenda, to date there has not been broad-based mobilization in support of it.

There are real impediments to the religious community mobilizing civil society. Virtually all religions in Cuba suffer from a scarcity of resources and face increasing demands for humanitarian assistance from the Cuban populace. Most of the material resources available come from abroad and are subject to government regulation and control, thereby encouraging caution on the part of churches and other religious organizations. Foreign religious donors have also been careful not to become identified with some of the more autonomous or dissident sectors of civil society. Even so, the increased role of religions in responding to the socioeconomic needs of the population has expanded the role and credibility of most religions within civil society. Overall, while religions are emerging as critical elements of a slowly revitalizing civil society, there is an understandable desire on their part not to precipitate serious conflicts with the government.

THE FUTURE

In recent years, religions have been recognized as often serving as a stimulus for the growth in activism of civil societies, particularly in countries experiencing substantial pressures for change. In Cuba, where the revolutionary government has attempted to subsume organized civil society into the state and marginalize religions, the possibilities for religions to assume a major leadership role via civil society in determining Cuba's future is unclear. Nevertheless, given that there is currently a "ripening" of civil society in Cuba, the potential is there. In order for that potential to be realized, and for religions to play an influential role, there are a number of prerequisites both for the religions themselves, as well as civil society.

One such precondition is that there must exist sufficient space to allow for generalized pressures for a greater role for civil society to be effectively exerted, together with an increasing capacity on the part of civil society to effectively occupy it. In Cuba there has been some progress in this area. The government since the late seventies, for example, has increasingly allowed some autonomous civic, cultural, and religious actors to move away from the margins of society, to which they had been relegated in the sixties. This is partially a result of the government's need for assistance in meeting the basic needs of the population, as well as its efforts to compensate for the erosion of support from some other sectors.

The government's inclination to accord more public space for religious actors was confirmed in the early nineties by the elimination of the prohibition against believers being members of the Communist Party, which had blocked religious activists from holding influential positions in government or in education. In 1992 a constitutional amendment transformed Cuba from officially an atheistic state to a lay state. There has been a concurrent ceding of public space by the government, the assumption of greater autonomy by some official organizations, and the mild revitalization of some historical organizations, including religious ones. The result is obviously increased ferment as such groups very tentatively attempt to exert more influence over politics and society. Few are questioning the socialist nature of the government, although a fair number are challenging the government to deliver more enjoyment not only of socioeconomic, but also of civil/political rights. The upshot is that the government's claim to legitimacy rooted in the guaranteeing of greater freedom resulting from increased socioeconomic justice is also being challenged. There are some indications that this is striking a responsive chord among the population in general, but it is in the nature of agreement rather than mobilization.

Such a situation raises a critical question: that is, can the principles and norms that sustain a free civil society be a basis for the incorporation of self-organized groups into a socialist system, thus making it more pluralistic and participatory? If a pluralistic civil society is deemed compatible with socialism, then a program of reforms would have to focus on expanding structures of participation in such a way that they would not be totally subsumed by centralized political or economic structures. Furthermore, it is not clear that religions in Cuba are disposed to work for such incorporation. There is, at present, considerable difference of opinion on this point.

Some analysts posit that Cuba could deepen the autonomy of mass organizations as a way of allowing civil society to help rebuild social and political consensus. Others question the realism of a pluralistic concept of civil society in a context where forty-five years of governmental ideological hegemony has resulted in a fairly high degree of suspicion of ideological and political heterodoxy. A second issue concerns the fact that the Cuban political class has restricted the debate about civil society and limited the broadening of the public sphere arguing that civil society could become a "fifth column" on behalf of the United States. A third issue results from the effects of globalization on Cuba, particularly the penetration of non-socialist norms and behaviors, including those transmitted by new religious actors. Indeed one of the most notable developments in contemporary Cuba is the intensification of international exchanges between religious organizations at both the macro and micro levels. This has been stimulated by a variety of humanitarian efforts, as well as the natural impulse to build community with one's counterparts. It has resulted in more discussion of the need for religions to formally undertake a role in promoting reconciliation, including developing a theology of reconciliation, among Cubans on the island and with Cubans abroad.

Given that religions in Cuba are increasingly playing an intermediary role (both formally and informally) between state and society in meeting the latter's basic needs, can religious actors gradually assume a mediating role in the current transition? Does increasing governmental and societal dependence on religious actors, national and international, provide a real opportunity for religions to influence the direction of society? The indications to date are that the government would resist such a possibility, but there is no guarantee that it will continue to be able to do so. To what degree, then, will relatively weak religious actors be able to take advantage of the situation? Furthermore, given the broad spectrum of opinions within the religious sector over the nature of the transition and the extent of the restructuring to be undertaken, would there be a consensus that goes much beyond the need for change? And to what degree would a civil society with strong strains of secularism be willing to accept a substantial leadership role by religions even if the latter have the most extensive institutional resources and networks?

In short, what is the disposition of Cuban citizens to accept the leadership of religions in building the Cuban society of the future? While there has been an upsurge in church attendance and involvement in religious groups in recent years, it is possible that if there were more secular associational alternatives, the current popularity of religious involvement might decline. Furthermore, there are no strong indicators that nascent Cuban civil society is committed to according religions a major role in a resurgent civil society, even if they are one of the strongest elements within it. In order for the desires of civil society in Cuba to become clearer, it would be necessary for the right of association to be exercised more broadly. Consensual agendas could then be more easily arrived at and pursued. At present there is no acknowledged leadership of autonomous civil society. Identification of such leaders requires a critical mass of proactive citizens, albeit not necessarily a majority. That does not appear to have happened yet in Cuba. Whether the development of such leadership can be facilitated by religious groups is a question. There have been some efforts by various religions to train community leaders, professionals, youths, and others to take a more active role in civil society, but there has not been a coalescing of such individuals around a consensual agenda. While there has been some acquisition of leadership skills, they do not appear as substantial as those developed through government mass organizations.

In short, there is a lack of clarity about whether or not there is an emerging consensus about what forms Cuban society and polity should take in the future. Although there has been some discussion of this within the nascent civil society, the proposals circulated to date tend to be quite schematic. The topic has been explored to a degree in religious publications, conferences, and courses, but again without any strong indication that there is a consensus about what form Cuban political, economic, and social organizations might take in the future. This reflects the degree to which civil society is somewhat adrift conceptually. Religious actors do not, generally, feel in a position to lead such a discussion that would result in greater consensus. Hence, while Cubans have a history of strong associationalism, together with a tradition of religious beliefs informing civil society, neither appears to have sufficient force to guarantee that civil society and religions could determine the outcome of the transition that is currently underway in Cuba.

38

There Is No Homeland Without Virtue

Cardinal Jaime Lucas Ortega y Alamino

Excerpts from "There is no homeland without virtue," the pastoral letter by Cardinal Jaime Ortega Alamino, Archbishop of Havana, released on Feb. 24, 2003, the 150th anniversary of Father Félix Varela's death.

Many of our brethren turn to the Catholic Church in Cuba, asking for a word about the future, because the Cuban people experience a diffused and generalized fear of the future. How will events transpire in our nation? Will our living conditions improve? With there be a reconciliation among all Cubans? It's always the best and the most restless Cubans who express this concern.

What's missing in Cuba are proposals that will raise people's spirits and increase their hope, that will encourage projects in their personal and community lives in which all may feel involved.

- Abortion has been practiced openly in Cuba since the first half of the twentieth century. Added to the frequent suppression of life in the womb is the existence of the death penalty. This creates the concept that death is a solution to many problems. Contempt for life also brings with it the unchecked violence that leads someone to kill or assault to rob or to settle a quarrel.
- At a certain age and depending on the place of residence, parents do not have options for their children because the only possibility that minors have to study is in boarding schools.

Let us listen to Father Varela's warnings about this period of adolescence: "The lack of sound judgment when guiding youngsters through the most dangerous period of their lives is the cause of the demoralization of many." And "the period we can properly call dangerous is between fifteen and eighteen years of age."

It is precisely at this stage of young people's lives that Cuban teenagers live outside the home. Cuban parents facing this situation fear early sexual initiation among boys and girls, early pregnancies, violent quarrels, frequent robberies, and so on. In addition, the absence of Catholic schools in Cuba always has been a thorn in the heart of the church.

Although education and health care are free in Cuba, wages do not generally adjust to the cost of living. Professionals, employees, and workers who do not receive financial aid from relatives or friends living abroad are forced to perform some sort of legal or illegal work activities, in addition to their regular jobs, to bring them some financial benefit. Think of the effort invested—but also the anxiety, fear, and disquietude felt—by those who cannot pay the high taxes to legitimize their activities.

Priests listen to the people's concern with a frequency greater than anticipated. "Is it a sin to act thus when we feel that the expenses exceed our income?" the faithful ask. I understand these grave concerns. We hear the stories from the families of elderly people visited by Cáritas volunteers, or by people who occasionally come to our dining halls or by the great number of needy people who knock at our doors.

So I ask myself—and leave the question to those who can answer—isn't it possible to rationally reduce the high rate of taxes so the illegal can be made legal and anxiety may disappear?

Why can't we give a greater degree of participation to personal and family initiative in a legal manner and conveniently reward the industriousness and creativity of our people in agriculture, handicrafts, services, jobs of various sorts, even allowing people to associate legally to earn their sustenance with dignity? This is the best way to prevent corruption.

People's lack of confidence in the possibility of greater financial ease, without surprises or anxiety, leads many to emigrate by any means possible. More and more we hear the cases of a member of a family who emigrates to help support those he leaves behind, not to mention the marriages, divorces, applications for foreign citizenship, invitations to one-way travel, and so forth, used to leave Cuba.

The Cuban family finds itself harshly affected by an emigration of dramatic proportions that includes the risk of leaping into the sea one way or another to reach the United States. Cubans ought to live in a climate of confidence that allows them to think about a possible project for their personal and family lives and gives them the hope to reach with serenity a better future in their own homeland.

Despair is the leading cause of emigration today. The Cuban family is gravely harmed by the fractioning that emigration produces, and emigration is also the cause of suffering for those who choose it or are forced to pursue it.

- Notwithstanding political options and painful confrontations, the Catholic Church in Cuba does not cease to recall the unity in love that must exist among all children of this earth. To do this, the church always turns in prayer to the Virgin of Charity, Our Mother, asking Her to plead to God for the gift of brotherhood among Cubans, which must entail—when necessary—a serious effort at reconciliation.
- It shouldn't be only the pastor's or the bishop's eyes that turn mercifully to the crowd; the leader's eyes, too, should.

The time has come to go from the avenging state that demands sacrifices and settles accounts to the merciful state that is ready to lend a compassionate hand before it imposes controls and punishes infractions.

I am not referring here to the necessary actions against homicidal crime, drug trafficking, and anything that corrupts or harms others, but to a consideration of the kind of power that leaves room for love, despite major social ills.

It is true that I am using a language not frequently found within the existing economic and political systems. My language is that of the social doctrine of the church.

- Only a man who is truly free can make the choice that will put him in an ethical posture of this kind. For this reason, Father Varela was passionate about the freedom of man. He, who denounced slavery as the great moral evil of Cuba in the nineteenth century and died wishing to see Cuba free in the concert of nations, was an educator of freedom for every Cuban, beginning with his students at the San Carlos Seminary.
- We have to educate young people for freedom; they must learn to think. There is too much memorization of facts, historical text, phrases taken out of context, and slogans. What is lacking is the internalization and willingness to understand and act on what the words say.

Repetition and passive acceptance of memorized text is ideology; to discover and exercise the reflexive ability to make decisions is thinking. The possibility of assuming an ethical stance depends on the basic freedom of every human being.

Civilian laws must guarantee freedom, but freedom does not originate in civilian laws; man is free because God has created him thus. Therefore, respect for freedom is sacred. National independence and freedom are the children of individual freedom.

We are commemorating the 150th anniversary of the death of Father Varela, who, as he left, passed the torch to José Martí, born the same year of Varela's death. We remember them together because both were fighters not only for the freedom of Cuba but also for the freedom of man. Only free men can build the homeland of their dreams.

PART VI

CULTURE

Culture is a term that is particularly difficult to define—as a glance at any good dictionary will show. Yet culture is an enormously important reflection of the broader changes that are occurring in the larger social context—as can be seen from an understanding of jazz and blues music in the early twentieth century United States, or the impact of the Beatles in the changing England of the 1960s. It helps us to appreciate in a different way the changes taking place, to feel both the triumph and the anguish of a nation as expressed through the sensitivity of the cultural voice.

Cultural expression is also a phenomenon that is constantly evolving—changing to reflect the transformation of the society around it. Social, political, and economic developments cast a long shadow upon the way we see ourselves—and accordingly our cultural voice reflects that evolution. At times it appears as if cultural icons have become fixed in our consciousness, and appear permanent reflections of our reality—until we discover different symbols, apparently more pertinent for the new context. For example, the music of Bob Dylan and the groups associated with the Tamla Motown label in the 1960s spoke loud and clearly to their constituencies, but are out of date forty years later. By understanding the thoughts behind expressions of popular culture at a particular time, we come to appreciate better the historical moment in which they appear.

Cuba is no different. The popular expressions of culture—from jazz to literature, from rap to cinema—are important for understanding Cubans' fear and aspirations. There has been an extraordinary change of focus in Cuba's national cultural expression in recent years, as one would expect. The onset of the Special Period and the enormous challenges in its wake have resulted in Cubans needing to adapt to extraordinary circumstances, often using ingenious coping mechanisms. As this section shows, the original response of adapting to the new reality out of necessity has now resulted in a firmly established, self-confident cultural voice. (That said, many talented cultural figures—particularly in the plastic arts—have preferred voluntary exile to remaining on the island, a process which has understandably had a deleterious effect on the richness of cultural expression.) The shock to the body politic as the Soviet Union imploded, and the largesse from the socialist countries evaporated, was enormous. The reaction to this has had an immense influence on virtually all levels of cultural expression. A cruel new world had been unceremoniously ushered in, shattering many dreams, and a new harsh cultural tone emerged, reflecting a profound identity crisis.

Cuban culture has changed more since 1991 than in the previous thirty-five years, passing from a stage of frustration and anger to a stage of maturity and self-confidence. Much of the anger can still be found—from the music of rap artists to the cinema of young film makers—but there is now a strong sense of self, an awareness of the value of each artist's contribution, which had been lacking previously. By contrast, cultural life prior to the Special Period (with some exceptions) was dependent almost totally upon the state, and as a result artists were often loathe to bite the hand that fed them. Although almost never descending to the depths of traditional Soviet dogma on the arts, cultural expression was generally orthodox, and not overly challenging to the status quo. Cuban writers, film directors, artists, and songwriters were as talented and professional as those found anywhere—but as is also the case anywhere else, were careful not to alienate those who paid their salaries.

Assessing the degree of change in Cuba in recent years is a complex challenge. For three decades prior to the Special Period, a dominant cultural model was maintained in Cuba. Its basic parameters came from an observation to Cuban intellectuals more than forty years ago by Fidel Castro—"Dentro de la revolución, todo; contra, nada" (Within the revolution, everything is permitted; against it, nothing). Unfortunately these broad guidelines were not developed, and self-censorship often followed because of fear about crossing the invisible line. At the same time there was an undoubted cultural effervescence—most notably (and paradoxically) in the 1960s, as Cuban cultural figures experimented widely, seeking a made-in-Cuba voice after depending upon North American icons as the dominant models for so long. To a certain extent, that determination to present a distinctive Cuban culture—even when influenced by revolutionary values—resulted in a strong indigenous voice.

It is therefore important to point out that, although resolutely affirming a socialist revolutionary paradigm, Cuban cultural expression never fell into the trap of socialist realism found in the Soviet Union. Cubans are outspoken, indeed garrulous, lively, and energetic. They are also rebellious, not easily given to parroting empty clichés. Cubans have traditionally practiced a more irreverent, free-thinking cultural expression, typified by their vibrancy and *chispa* (spark). The bright colors of a Portocarrero painting, the jazz fusion of Chucho Valdés, the flamboyant acting of Jorge Perugorría, all reflect the ethos of Cuban culture.

This degree of vibrancy varied, according to the particular cultural expression. Music, for instance, has traditionally been significantly less restricted than literature (particularly the narrative), and as a result has usually been more experimental, and less controlled. The plastic arts for many years have likewise enjoyed a degree of autonomy that was never found (and is not today) in Cuban newspapers or television or radio. Cuban literature until the 1990s, by contrast, was consistently more in line with the positions advocated by cultural commissars. Writers who strayed from the straight and narrow were often not published, though even within these bounds authors such as Pablo Armando Fernández, Miguel Barnet, Antón Arrufat and Nancy Morejón produced world-acclaimed poetry, novels, and plays. In general, then, Cuban cultural expression never imitated or followed slavishly the parameters from the Soviet Union—although the quality of the narrative left a great deal to be desired, and the extremely poor television was rather sad. Indeed, one could often tell when Soviet or Bulgarian films were being shown on Cuba's limited TV channels because most Cubans, hopelessly bored by the ponderous propaganda, were usually on the streets. By contrast, when a game of *pelota* (baseball) or a *telenovela* (soap opera) was on television, the streets were deserted.

While the revolutionary government has never been able to fully control the outspoken, lively, and irreverent Cuban culture, there have been pendulum swings, so that censorship and self-censorship were pervasive at some points more than at others. The low point in cultural freedom came in 1971—when the *quinquenio gris* (literally the "five-year gray period") started. In actual fact, it lasted a lot longer than that, and was a period typified by an autocratic, dogmatic approach to culture, administered by functionaries who were more concerned with ideological purity than anything else. Following the show trial of the talented Cuban poet Heberto Padilla in 1971, cultural bureaucrats tightened their grip on expression. Writers such as Arrufat and Fernández were denied permission to travel abroad. Their work went unpublished and they were given menial jobs. Others—such as Reinaldo Arenas—chose to flee the country.

Very little remains of the dominant cultural influences of that time. Within twenty years of the gray depressing 1970s, there was a sea change in the variety and breadth of cultural expression, and the political space which had been won. Several of the formerly repressed writers became lionized and received highly prestigious national literary awards in Cuba. Today, Cuban literature includes works which are extremely critical of the many paradoxes and contradictions that abound throughout the country.

The superb detective series of Leonardo Padura Fuentes, or his masterful novel, *La novela de mi vida* (*The Novel of My Life*), constitute an excellent starting point to begin to appreciate the freedom now exercised by Cuban writers. Padura Fuentes's observations in this section on the greater freedom of expression illustrate the vastly different scenario now encountered in Cuba. Abel Prieto, the irreverent, Beatles-loving Minister of Culture, has contributed much to this flowering of cultural expression. The fact that he is a published author, highly regarded for his narrative, speaks volumes of the maturity of the Cuban cultural scene. True, there are severe limitations still in place, but the harsh dogmatism of the 1970s is long gone. The dominance of stiff functionaries began to wane with the arrival of Armando Hart as Minister of Culture. While he deserves credit for initiating the process of cultural *apertura*, it has been on Prieto's watch that it came to fruition.

Films such as *Fresa y chocolate* (*Strawberry and Chocolate*), *Guantanamera*, *Lista de espera* (*Waiting List*), *Amor vertical* (*Vertical Love*), *La vida es silbar* (*Life Is to Whistle*), *Madagascar*, and *Suite Habana* are examples of the newfound freedom in the air, and the rich vein of cinematic talent that has recently been tapped. Without doubt, *Suite Habana*, by the enormously talented Fernando Pérez, has emerged (after *Fresa y chocolate*) as the expression of the Cuban cinema this past decade. Sad and wistful, always emotional and full of empathy, critical and yet in its own way supportive, the film's images are so clear that its lack of dialogue is hardly noticed.

To some extent, the production of such outspoken cinema is largely due to economic circumstances beyond the Cuban government's reach. Indeed, the harsh realities of the Special Period, and the desire of cultural figures in Cuba to continue their cultural production wherever and however they could, led to a number of joint venture agreements with foreign music and film producers, international publishing houses and agencies (particularly in Spain and Mexico). Cuban artists now sell their wares extremely successfully outside Cuban boundaries. It became impossible for the Cuban government to control the resulting cultural explosion—which flowed over the banks that had been so carefully protected for three decades. There was still an awareness of producing cultural expressions that remained "dentro de la revolución," but largely gone now were the strict guidelines, and the fear of straying too far.

In many ways, the rapid and radical changes that permeated Cuban society can be seen in the microcosm of cultural expression in that country. Changes in intellectual life, mirroring those of the broader social stage, have continuously pushed the frontiers back since the early 1990s. For a country of 11.2 million people, its cultural footprint is truly immense, and the listing of Cuban cultural talents is exhausting.

Dance has traditionally been a forte of Cuban culture—and it is no surprise that the rumba, cha-cha-chá, and salsa all originated there. In recent decades the ballet, still directed with an iron hand by the legendary Alicia Alonso, has been wildly applauded on European and North American tours, and has brought much thoroughly deserved respect to the island. The plastic arts—from the Santería-influenced motifs of Afro-Cuban religious expression of Mendive to the stylized heads of Roberto Fabelo—now fetch enormous prices throughout the world, and the biennial art exhibit in Havana is highly regarded in international art circles.

Cuban music, also with an enormously rich vein of talent, has evolved dramatically in a number of genres, from the jazz of Irakere and Chucho Valdés (who has received four Grammy awards) to the *Nueva Trova* (folk music often with political overtones) of Silvio Rodríguez, Pablo Milanés, and their heir apparent Carlos Varela. The lyrics of two Varela songs reprinted in this section illustrate the way this kind of music speaks for a new generation. It would be necessary to hear a young audience belting out the chorus of "William Tell," emphasizing their collective desire to be the subjects of their destiny, in order to appreciate its value as the hymn of a generation that wants to be taken seriously. The barely veiled reference to the paternalistic figure who for years has told his son (the young generation) what to do, and the rebellion of the son, speak eloquently to the aspirations of Cuban youth. The same could be said about the evolution of truly popular music, from the vibrant mixture of old and new of the veterans of the Buena Vista Social Club to the pointed social commentary of Cuba's young rap and hip-hop singers which Margot Olavarria's article in this section describes.

Wide international acclaim has resulted for this explosion of talent—all found, it must be remembered, on a relatively small island of just over eleven million people. Cuba's prowess is similarly impressive in one often-forgotten aspect of popular culture, international sport. Cuba won twenty-seven medals, for example, at the 2004 Athens Olympic Games, finishing in eleventh place—and first among Latin American nations. Still, this achievement was a noticeable decline from the heights of the 1992 Barcelona Olympics, when Cuba finished in fifth place with a total of thirty-one medals. Economic pressures had taken their toll even in the revered sports domain. In all cases, the advent of the Special Period has forced Cuban culture to look outside its traditional funding sources, and its former modus operandi, while pursuing international recognition through cultural (and sports) triumphs. The arena of international sports is no different, with Cuba exporting athletes and, especially, trainers to dozens of countries. In all cases of this broad cultural policy, the Cuban government has been delighted with artistic and sports triumphs, greater income for the national treasury, and heightened prestige abroad. Indeed, as the article by Paula Pettavino and Philip Brenner explains, the Cuban sports program has long served multiple goals. Popular culture is likewise an extremely powerful unifying force, reflecting the nationalism with which the state imbues it. This complex policy, implemented initially because of the disastrous economic situation in the early 1990s, is now officially embraced.

Perhaps nothing illustrates better the changing currents of cultural expression in Cuba over the past decade or so than the official treatment given the Beatles, not just in the Cuban media but also by the revolutionary leadership itself. It is important to bear in mind the context for this observation. Until the mid-1960s at the earliest, the Beatles were widely criticized, when they were not ignored by the Cuban media. In fact they were seen as examples of western decadence and ideological diversionism by the revolutionary leadership. Their music was banned from the radio, long-haired musicians were occasionally grabbed by militants and had their heads shaved. Silvio Rodríguez, the founder of the *Nueva Trova* folk music movement—and the cultural figure most closely identified with the revolutionary government—was even dropped from Cuban television because of his expressed admiration for the musical influence of Lennon and McCartney.

That had all changed by early December 2000 when a superb bronze statue of John Lennon was unveiled in a park located in the Vedado suburb of Havana. This was evident in the eloquent proclamation by Ricardo Alarcón de Quesada, the National Assembly president and a high government official for decades, in dedicating the park. It would always be, he said, "a testimonial to struggle, a summoning to humanism. It will also be a permanent homage to a generation that wanted to transform the world." Even more dramatic was the political symbolism involved in the unveiling of the statue—to the strains of "All You Need Is Love"—by Silvio Rodríguez and Cuban President Fidel Castro. Castro praised Lennon's vision and his contribution to humanity: "What makes him great in my eyes is his thinking, his ideas . . . I share his dreams completely. I too am a dreamer who has seen his dreams turn into reality," he noted.

The articles in the following section are intended to provide an overview of cultural change during the Special Period, an appreciation for the challenges artists faced and continue to face, and an understanding of the forces that contributed to the change and are reflected in the changing culture itself.

A Black Woman from Cuba, That's All

An Interview with Nancy Morejón

Nancy Morejón and John M. Kirk

This interview took place in Havana in 2000. The interviewer is John M. Kirk.

Q: Does the fact that you are a poet and a black poet mean that you have more responsibilities than a white woman?

A: I am always fearful of stereotypes. Of course, the very notion of being a white writer in Cuba is an exceptionally abstract concept. To a large degree my analysis is based on the fact that every Cuban is a person of mixed cultures and diverse racial origins. Every Cuban is a true cultural blend. I have read many books on feminist philosophy, and I think that we have to proceed with great caution when analyzing any stereotypes. At the same time I believe that, as a black woman, yes, indeed, I do have things of value to say. Because of those origins I come from a history of suffering, and I always have to be alert, to share that history, to have it felt by others. At the same time, I don't have to exaggerate.

Q: Is there still racial prejudice in Cuba?

A: Yes, because eradicating it is an extremely slow process. For me, racial discrimination is the exercise of those racial prejudices. To stop that, I believe that making people aware of their conduct, developing an ideological understanding of the problem, is far more effective than resolving the abuses solely through legal means. This does not mean that there should not be laws against discrimination—only that we also need to channel the true spirit of the revolution to all sectors.

Some people here say, "Don't talk to me about the race question." But we do have to examine this again, because it is an important matter here in Cuba.

At times people have been afraid to talk openly about it and have not known how to deal with it as they should. And that is why there are such gaps in our understanding, gaps which we hear more about all the time. That is why we need to

344

reconsider so many facets of our revolutionary traditions, because this problem of racism is a universal problem, one affecting all humanity, and not just Cuba. For example, if we analyze what has happened since 1989 in the former socialist community, we can see how the question of ethnic identity has been revisited. The proof of this can be seen in Bosnia-Herzegovina or in Chechnya. If we don't address this factor, if we do not study it and seek to resolve it, we may ultimately face unwelcome surprises. And so I think that we should examine in more detail the question of race relations.

Q: Do you, as a black woman, feel any responsibility to help in this process?

A: Yes, I do, and also from my perspective as a writer. But it has to be by means of a high-quality artistic expression, because no mater how good the message may be, it will be useless unless it is done well. But I also need to speak with others in the cultural milieu. I have already spoken with film directors and have suggested the need to make a film about this very issue. We cannot simply forget the racial question. We also need to see black characters somewhere other than in films about slavery. We badly need something more contemporary and more pertinent.

Q: A question on the concept of Utopia, which you describe well in your poem "Divertimento" (Amusement). In it you refer to Cuba in the following manner:
    "Between the sword and the carnation/I love Utopias/I love an island which lies piercing the throat of Goliath / like a palm tree in the center of the Gulf/I love a David / I love everlasting freedom?" How do your feelings of evident nationalism react to the "pact with the devil" that the Cuban government has undertaken in order to survive? How do you feel when you are faced by the near realities of tourism, prostitution, search for the dollar, and foreign investment?

A: It is a reality that in many ways is upsetting, in part because it was so unexpected. We need to be audacious if we are to function properly in this new context. We are convinced about what we need in order to survive. We also know well that the process cannot be stopped, since otherwise Cuba would remain completely isolated. In essence we have witnessed several developments over which we had no control, and as a result we had to reconsider many things. Now that tourism has returned to play such a major role in the economy, we have the opportunity to receive a fair amount of income for the national economy. At the same time we have to be careful about the type of tourism that we seek to develop. We can't develop the form that they have in Barbados, for example. We can have, for instance, a positive kind of tourism, one that does not need to use the bodies of our women as a hook to bring in male visitors.
    It is fair to say that we have been surprised by the kind of tourism that has sprung up in certain sectors. It has been painful for us in many ways. At the same time I don't believe that this situation will be resolved by repression. Rather, we need to reflect upon the whole issue of tourism, in order to see how it can be useful for our country and also what we need to confront in a vigorous fashion. We have discovered a very serious phenomenon, but again it seems to me that this cannot be resolved through repressive means.

Q: Have you written anything about this new reality of Cuba?

A: No. And that is not because I haven't wanted to, because I have thought a lot about this new reality (which in many ways I dislike). Rather, I haven't written anything because I don't want any of my comments to be misinterpreted. At times if you say something controversial, people think that you want to become some kind of famous dissident. And that is definitely not my case. I believe that I have had many opportunities to play the role of dissident, but I'm not the slightest bit interested in that game.

At the same time, I do believe that it is necessary to have a space where you can air concerns. We have to encourage people to study this reality and to be honest when facing the problems that we have. If that's not the case we are in trouble.

Q: In your opinion, what have been the major cultural successes of the Cuban Revolution? And what have been the failures?

A.   Often we see errors, but we don't realize just how serious they are until later. And we regret that they were made in the first place. But let's start with the positive elements. One can note there the tremendous potential which we came to see in ourselves. The revolution opened doors for us and allowed an enormous social mobility. Many walls that blocked communication were demolished, and taboos were cast out. At the same time there came a certain point when the idea of massive numbers of people pursuing cultural interests became a priority of the government, often above everything else. They forgot that, in order to appreciate art, people have to have some basic ideas about the need to recover the essence of beauty. It is very true that liberating social sectors as well as progress and social mobility clearly need not be limited to the individual. Just the opposite: They have to reaffirm it. The problem was that often, closely connected with this emphasis on such a massive approach to culture, there came the accompanying practice of justifying mediocrity, often in the name of a supposed form of equality. As a result, we have often protected mediocre cultural expressions, and I believe that we should be more rigorous.

Q: In every society there are absolute and limited freedoms. How would you describe the freedom that currently exists in the Cuban cultural forum?

A: I think it's important to take into account our reality. We are a country that is still under siege and one that has never been alone. We must always remember the hostility to which we have been subjected. There are other limitations that need to be considered. In this Special Period we have had limited paper and, of course, all sorts of limitations on cultural resources. This country has a very high level of education, and much of the money that we could have used for cultural purposes has instead been used to buy textbooks. We simply don't have the resources to do both. Very often people abroad see us talking about our free education as some sort of empty political slogan but in fact it is a reality and a priority. This element in the midst of the Special Period, has limited literary life enormously and as a result there are fewer journals, literary competitions, publications, et cetera. We need to recover all the lost terrain in this matter.

I feel that Cuban writers today are demanding things that simply cannot be conceded in a period like this, since we are facing difficulties as critical as the Bay of Pigs invasion or the missile crisis. This country has to survive. Moreover "freedom" has many facets, and many people think that they have to make demands on the state for their freedom. I think that there are, in fact, several "freedoms" and not just "freedom" in absolute terms.

And freedom here has to be conditioned, or affected, by the hostility that we have encountered in the last forty years. Now it is practically a psychological phenomenon. We are all subjected to the same tensions. I personally believe that a writer has to feel a major responsibility, resulting from the nation's identity as well as a major ethical responsibility in regards to the community. As a result of those twin factors one needs to know that there are things that can and cannot be done, because the revolution has the right and the duty to exist.

Of course; there have been many errors here, basically because we all have limited conceptions of what the revolution should be. To give you an idea, my parents had a utopian idea of the revolution. They would argue, for example, that a revolutionary shouldn't drink Amaretto liqueur. . . . As you can see, we have come to accept many stereotypes, and we badly need to struggle against that. We need to respect differences and diversity and precisely because of that fact I am certain that there were errors in cultural matters. Che, too, was a declared enemy of socialist realism, and I believe that we should respect his honesty. By all means we should have the freedom to criticize dogma and stereotypes, but we must always bear in mind the reality of our history.

40

Living and Creating in Cuba

Risks and Challenges

Leonardo Padura Fuentes

One of the problems facing Cuban culture is that it is significantly greater than the country from which it springs. This gigantic culture, whose origins can be traced back to the nineteenth century when national culture as such was just beginning, has been with us Cubans for so long that we scarcely notice it now. And so, when the revolution of Fidel Castro succeeded in 1959, Cuba was already an important cultural presence in the western world, with its creators and protagonists receiving recognition in the most diverse artistic circles. There can be no doubt that, from that point on, this solid artistic potential and this major cultural thrust received a tremendous boost in their development in Cuba. Government support helped to multiply that potential, turning it into a clear cultural reality that spread rapidly. Moreover, because of government support, culture was now available to all levels of society (as producers and consumers of our culture) and it achieved new levels of international prestige.

Other measures taken by the government helped to support and develop this new cultural reality. The 1961 Literacy Campaign was key to cultural development in the 1960s, as were the creation of schools of art and cinema, the production of books, and the development of music and theater. That decade had as its backdrop the cultural policy drawn up by Fidel Castro: "Within the revolution, everything is possible; against it, nothing is," he noted in October 1961. An atmosphere of genuine creativity exploded full of enthusiasm and massive participation. Its first discordant note sounded with the closing down of the weekly cultural supplement *Lunes de Revolución*, its first major schism came with the Padilla affair, and the process of officially imposed "cultural parameters" that ushered in a period of profound dogma following the 1971 Congress of Education and Culture.

If the 1960s was a decade of expansion, vitality, renovation, and open commitment with the revolutionary process on the part of Cuban artists, the 1970s have been judged as a dark, repressive period, one in which numerous cultural figures (the most notable being Lezama Lima and Virgilio Piñera) were officially marginalized. Artistic parameters similar to the inauspicious dogma of socialist realism were imposed in a more or less visible fashion. It is not by chance, for example, that out of nowhere there should appear the new genre of the "revolutionary police novel." This tendency was of dubious artistic value, presenting everything in terms of us versus them, and clearly written with the intention of defending the goals of the revolution while ignoring general aesthetic principles.

In the second half of that dark and somber decade, the Ministry of Culture was created to redirect Cuban culture. This came in the wake of several grave political errors by the government, both in the treatment of intellectuals and in the very definition of what artistic expression should be. Just a few years later, however, these new state structures began to assimilate the need for a more profound change of policy. This was not the result of a new interpretation of the cultural phenomenon per se. Rather, it was demanded by the artists themselves, who expressed their feelings clearly in their work.

As a result, from the early 1980s on, we can see the definitive rehabilitation of so many artists who had been marginalized by Cuban officialdom for almost ten years—and for a variety of reasons (perhaps because they were practicing Christians or homosexual; because their art was more of a questioning nature than one that reaffirmed official positions; or because in their literature they included clear social criticism). It was a time when a generation of Cuban cultural figures emerged. They brought a new approach to the traditional insular reality. They also felt relatively angst-free, an important development, since many of their predecessors felt burdened with the original sin of not having fought more directly in the revolution.

If the Cuba of the 1960s was a country in the midst of social and political effervescence, a country in which socialist institutionalization was taking its first steps in the midst of the struggle for control over the cultural apparatus, the 1970s was a period when the socialist cultural project was implemented with few concessions upon a population that had mainly shown its support for the revolutionary struggle. The result of this approach, however, wreaked havoc in cultural circles: artists were repressed, and culture was taken over by an official bureaucracy.

Despite this current, however, the internal dynamic of the country, together with its deeply rooted, potent culture, ended up showing a fair degree of independence in the 1980s. At that time painters, writers, dramatists, and even dancers and people involved in the cinema took fairly substantial risks and began opting for a less inhibited cultural expression. This decision was based more on identification with the aesthetic function of art than on any direct political expression of the content.

The maturation of this process took place during one of the most convulsive social and economic periods of Cuban history and indeed the most dynamic era of the revolutionary history since the 1960s. It constituted the first clarion call, and a dramatic one at that, of significant change in Cuba. This led to the dramatic 1989 court trials that would end in the execution of important figures of the armed forces and the Ministry of the Interior, the imprisonment of other officials, and the firing of dozens more.

As the Berlin Wall was tumbling down and the Soviet Union was collapsing, Cuba experienced a terrifying political and economic solitude. The government introduced the "Special Period in a Time of Peace," a title with which it baptized the harshest economic crisis that the country had ever lived through. Just a few years later, as the crisis worsened, the government felt obliged to introduce major economic changes—with immediate social repercussions—changes never before imagined.

Many of these benefits also brought significant social change. Prostitution and a network of pimps reappeared; some social sectors suddenly became extremely wealthy; Cuban society became divided between those holding dollars and those without; an exodus of professionals moving to work in the tourist sector became visible; Cubans moved to the far corners of the earth; and religious faith and religiosity noticeably increased, as did violence and delinquency. Symbolic of these changes was the disappearance of the term *compañero* (denoting solidarity and classlessness) in favor of the more traditional expression *señor*. All of this occurred in a society that lacked the most basic materials and where the U.S. embargo had drastically affected the economic and social life of the country.

In such a convulsive (and truly special) period, artistic and literary production could be no less convulsive and special—as in fact proved to be the case. As a result there was a distinctive change in the relationship between the cultural creator and the state. If I were asked to define the cultural characteristics of the 1990s, I would name three: the crisis of cultural production, the winning of space by the creators to express themselves, and the massive (voluntary) exile of Cuban artists.

The first of these factors has been analyzed on several occasions. It includes a drastic reduction in the number and types of Cuban books published, television programming and films produced, art exhibitions mounted, and plays staged. It is true that in the late 1990s these difficulties were steadily overcome. Nevertheless, we have been faced with a crisis of such magnitude, a crisis in which institutions were simply unable to respond with support to the productive demands of culture. This had a special connotation in a country like Cuba, where government support had been crucial. It provoked stagnation and a fundamental rupture of the artistic growth in quantitative, and indeed qualitative, terms in several areas of cultural expression.

Closely linked to these economic difficulties of the 1990s is perhaps the factor that had proved most important of all the cultural changes of this decade, namely the necessary opening up of space for artistic expression. It is true that there was always a certain level of ideological support for this phenomenon, and not for reasons solely linked to the economic crisis. Institutions like the Ministry of Culture, the Union of Writers and Artists of Cuba (UNEAC), and the Cuban Film Institute (ICAIC) have traditionally supported the need for their members to have access to a greater space for reflection, analysis, and criticism of themes that previously had been either censored or treated in a superficial manner.

With the economic crisis, however, the lack of institutional support to finance their projects meant that cultural figures actually gained in independence. This allowed them greater freedom of expression, and they responded with the badly needed sounds to fill the silent void that existed before. Their situation had cried out for artists and writers, film directors and singers, to voice their feelings. Yet in the midst of the previous institutionalization, this had been impossible. Now things had changed.

As a result, several alternative projects have emerged and have dealt head-on with areas previously ignored. This is seen most clearly in the Cuban cinema. To appreciate this development, one must remember that since the historic scandal surrounding the 1961 documentary "P.M.," the cinema industry has been centralized under the auspices of ICAIC and two or three similar production houses controlled by trusted institutions such as the Ministry of Education and the Armed Forces. Now that these state institutions were unable for financial reasons to take on any further projects, this created the possible space for some initial efforts by independent filmmakers—a phenomenon that previously would have been inconceivable—to produce their work in video format. Just as important, however, is the fact that even within the traditional structures Cuban cinema has developed an aesthetic vision of reality that it has been struggling to present for many years. In short, it now dealt openly with themes that it would have been impossible to examine even a decade earlier.

One film in particular clearly revealed Cuban filmmakers' urgent need to express themselves: *Fresa y chocolate* [Strawberry and Chocolate]. This film, directed by veteran Tomás Gutiérrez Alea in collaboration with Juan Carlos Tabío and based on a script of Senel Paz, has proved to be a truly significant aesthetic benchmark. It has staked out, like no other film, the claims and possibilities of Cuban art in the 1990s, one that is very different from the epic romanticism of the 1960s, the simplistic ideological presentation of the 1970s, and the critical stammering of the 1980s.

It is around this film that several others have developed, such as the controversial *Guantanamera* (at which Fidel Castro publicly lashed out), also made by Alea and Tabío; the most recent films by Fernando Pérez (*Madagascar* and *La vida es silbar* (Life is to Whistle), both of a distinctly existentialist flavor); *Amor vertical* (Vertical Love) Arturo Soto; and what was without a doubt the film that generated the bitterest controversy in recent years, *Alicia en el pueblo de Maravillas* (Alice in the Town of Wonder) by Daniel Díaz Torres. *Alicia* was condemned in the local media as a counter-revolutionary work and snatched from Cuban cinemas just three days after its premiere. Even during its limited showing, the cinemas were filled with "revolutionaries," sent there to avoid any demonstration that might support a film with such perverse political intentions.

Something similar happened with Cuban literature. Again, the lack of editorial support because of the economic crisis, changes in mentality in certain spheres of the state direction, and the need for writers to reflect upon a complex and difficult reality have all combined to mold a new form of literary production. This is particularly evident in the narrative, which has contributed to the destruction of several literary taboos, as well as to the literary treatment of several topics which previously had been totally disregarded or not "well regarded." It was thought in official circles that there was never an opportune moment to deal with such themes, including exile, narcotics, homosexuality, corruption, desperation, and suicide. What is curious about many of these works is that they arrived on the Cuban scene already possessing the pedigree of recognition from several international, and occasionally national, literary competitions. As a result, they were well known before they were distributed on the island.

And so what in happier economic times (albeit under more rigid ideological parameters) would have caused rumors and quarrels (if not full-blown scandals and possible punishment) has now been accepted as being a natural ingredient of a more open and flexible creative environment in Cuba. Perhaps the best adjective to describe this new policy is *intelligent*. And significantly all of this has come about despite the position of political protagonists (both outside and within the so-called cultural sector) who have openly expressed their opposition to this form of reflection and cultural expression, which to a certain extent they consider alien and indeed harmful to the goals of the Cuban government.

None of this means that the traditional phenomena of censorship and self-censorship have disappeared from Cuba. The freedom for all cultural figures on the island as (Cuban novelist and dramatist) Antón Arrufat has explained, is conditioned by the political and social reality of the country, which in turn imposes rules of game that those in the cultural world have learned well. That said, it is indeed true that the levels of permissiveness and the ceiling of tolerance have grown. Now, thanks to the economic crisis of the 1990s, Cuban culture has gained space: cultural workers now possess increased possibilities both to reflect and to express themselves, possibilities that simply did not exist before. These possibilities now extend as far as dealing with the thorny ideological and aesthetic challenges of working "within the revolution," a process which for many years had been reduced to working "in favor of the revolution"—and nothing else.

The economic context has also brought about another feature of Cuban culture that previously did not exist: the possibility of commercializing Cuban cultural work. As a result, several writers now publish their manuscripts in Spain, Mexico, and Italy before they appear in Cuba. Dozens of artists hold exhibitions of their work throughout the world and sell it before foreign galleries, often without the slightest involvement of the state apparatus. And Cuban actors work abroad for international companies.

The most complicated and heartrending of these end-of-the-century problems, however, against which the only bureaucratic measure has traditionally been repression, is undoubtedly the mass exodus of members of the cultural sector. This has notably impoverished Cuban cultural life. This fact of life, which, given the significance of the numbers involved, could be perhaps compared with the 1959–1961 exodus, is really quite different. Early in the revolutionary process, several key figures in the cultural realm left Cuba, including Jorge Mañach, popular singer Celia Cruz, ethnologist Lydia Cabrera, and television magnate Goar Mestre. The political process at that time, however, produced a dynamic of such tremendous growth, supporting the development of a radically new culture, that it was possible to overcome the loss of these figures.

The exodus of the 1990s was very different, however. It was produced by people who had been formed within the revolutionary cultural tradition, and it included some of its most notable representatives (the great historian Manuel Moreno Fraginals, the novelist and film director Jesús Díaz, the extremely popular painter Tomás Sánchez, musicians like Arturo Sandoval, the journalist and writer Norberto Fuentes, almost the entire generation of plastic artists trained in the 1980s, and finally a legion of television and film actors including Reynaldo Miravalles).

It is worth noting, however, that for the first time since 1959, cultural workers have left for both economic and cultural reasons. This is also seen in the public attitude toward the revolutionary process of these intellectuals. The "economic" exiles are able to maintain links with Cuban cultural institutions, to enter and leave the country, and to exhibit their work here in Cuba, a development which has meant that they have not broken completely with Cuba, even if their work for the most part is produced and distributed outside Cuba. By contrast, their "political" counterparts, definitively distant from the Cuban system, have become the last legion of political dissidents who are officially recognized as such. A significant part of their work—if not all of it—supports this definitive rupture, since it appears irreconcilable, at least given the parameters being debated at present.

Within the island an attempt has been made to build bridges between state institutions and Cuban exiles who do not maintain political positions that are hostile to the government. An example of this happens with the so-called Cuban Americans who left the island during their childhood. On the other hand, the tension is maintained, and indeed it has sharpened, between Cuban authorities and those who could be considered political dissidents. The official position toward them is the same as it has always been: to ignore them totally and, if possible, to alienate them from their cultural roots. Such an approach goes above political affiliations or political will. Guillermo Cabrera Infante is clearly a Cuban writer, even though government officials may not admit it, publish the fact, or even recognize him in Cuba. And even though Cabrera Infante himself might state that he doesn´t want to be considered a Cuban writer, or denies the fact (as he has done), he is clearly a Cuban writer.

The basic option of these dissidents, meanwhile, has been more or less the same: They increase their political opposition to the government in response to the system. In some cases, too, in works of doubtful artistic merit, they have condemned the Cuban government. This tactic is clearly the quickest way to develop an audience, and it is an approach that has led to their work being distributed widely, and to a fairly substantial income.

It is a fact that, for any nation in the world, the departure from circulation of a notable percentage of those working in the cultural sector leads to a serious loss for the country's spiritual life. And Cuba is clearly no exception. The surrounding cultural atmosphere is made up of figures who grow in that country, producing work that is inspired by daily experiences there, and leaving a legacy through their words, their work, by means of a necessary accumulation of visions and opinions. The absence of such figures, whatever their cultural stature, produces a vacuum that is combined with the other vacuum stemming from the crisis of production by national institutes. The end result is that Cuban culture is suffering from the presence of both these blows, different but at the same time complementary.

Despite the complex and dramatic features of the actual situation of Cuban culture, I believe that the country is living through a period of special creative effervescence. We see in Cuba today the flowering of the results of this small space that is now available for reflection, for creation, and for debate. If it is true that some sectors, and especially the newspapers and television, are little more than instruments of propaganda instead of information, we also need to recognize that today many people in the cultural sector are expressing themselves with greater depth within the space of "conditional freedom" that they have been winning in recent years. Doing so, of course, is not without risks (which can range from censorship to deliberately ignoring them or their work in the media). That said, risks and censorship can also be a challenge to the imagination.

Because of this complex context, it is no coincidence that Cuba has once again created a culture that is so much larger than the small insular territory from which it springs. People in several Spanish-speaking nations are increasingly speaking about the boom of the new Cuban novel, thanks to the work of a dozen or so authors from several generations whose work has received a number of prizes in international competitions. In addition, Cuban music (both traditional and modern) is at a peak in terms of creativity and financial return. This can be seen in international prizes being awarded at the highest levels, concerts given at the most desirable venues in the world, and impressive record sales, even in the United States.

The Ballet Nacional de Cuba has recently celebrated its fiftieth anniversary by touring Europe and North America, revealing in its productions its continuing vitality. The plastic arts, too, are now obligatory points of reference on the artistic and commercial circuits in Paris, Geneva, and New York, with Cuban artists increasingly winning international competitions. And finally the Cuban cinema, still badly affected by the economic crisis, continues to produce miracles, with prizes piling up in many international film festivals.

And so, in the midst of tensions and risks, with artistic expression produced both in Cuba and abroad, often with virtually no resources, Cuban culture has returned, larger in so many ways than the relatively small country that produced it. This process over the last forty years has been hard and complex. The rigors of censorship, the effects of being marginalized, and the current presence of a voracious marketplace for these talents—all have blazed the trail for today's cultural expression. Above all, however, and with so many of its talents living abroad, the cultural creativity of this small Caribbean island continues to be one of the greatest riches of the Cuban nation and, why not, of the entire world.

41

Visions of Dollars Dance
Before Cuban Artists' Eyes

Maria Finn

The theme of the 2003 biennial, "El Arte con la Vida" or "Art with Life," fore-shadowed the event itself, as the Prince Claus Foundation, a Dutch cultural fund that supported the biennial in the past, withheld its $100,000 pledge in protest against the imprisonment in April of seventy-five dissidents—primarily librarians, journalists, and organizers of a referendum calling for democratic reforms like free-dom of association and expression—sentenced to up to twenty-eight years in jail by the Cuban government.

This did not stop the show, but it may have contributed to the stunning disor-ganization of the event. Visitors milled around the headquarters of the organizer, the Wilfredo Lam Center in Old Havana, trying to figure out where they could find a schedule of the exhibitions, performances, and panel discussions taking place throughout Havana. The responses by officials to questions usually fluctuated be-tween "Come back tomorrow" and "I don't know."

But this barely slowed the momentum, because art has become big business in Cuba. Charter flights from the United States to Havana filled fast this year, as cu-rators, art buyers, gallery owners, and artists jockeyed for seats with large groups of travelers on cultural tours. While real-estate developers and tourist agencies in the United States cannot do business with Cuba, art collectors can, and works of art here are generally considered good investments.

This year [2003], people headed to the biennial, held from November 1 through December 15, with a heightened sense of urgency. After January 1, very few cultural licenses will be renewed by the Treasury Department. This is part of President Bush's plan to tighten the embargo on Cuba in an attempt to force Fidel Castro to introduce democratic reforms. United States officials sharply curtailed the cultural exchanges because they felt the trips were being abused by Americans simply look-ing to vacation in Cuba.

At the Taller Experimental de Gráfica, a print studio in Old Havana, Rebecca Schnelker, curator at the Tamarind Institute in Albuquerque, was on the lookout for talented printmakers to invite to workshops. With the changing climate between Cuba and the United States, she fears this will be difficult.

"A few years ago it took three weeks for a Cuban artist to get a visa to come to the States," Ms. Schnelker said. "Now, it's nearly impossible."

This year, a climate of uncertainty hangs over the events. Congress voted to end the travel embargo to Cuba, reasoning that a deluge of American citizens traveling to the island could be more effective in pressuring the communist government than the embargo. The president pledged to veto the bill and to use the Department of Homeland Security to track down violators. Two weeks ago, a Senate-House committee stripped the provision from an appropriations bill, but still, because of the bipartisan support for lifting the travel ban, many people think an end to it is imminent.

Whether hordes of American tourists descend on Cuba or tours are canceled altogether, life for artists in Cuba will change dramatically. Either they will return to trying to survive on the Cuban peso like most of the population, or the influx of American dollars could create a scramble to make ideologically neutral work, art that sells.

Younger generations of Cuban artists have become savvy about their careers. They know the rewards of being noticed during the biennial are fellowships to study in the United States, exhibitions in American galleries, gallery representation and cash from collectors. Meanwhile, American tour groups have been coming to Cuba to visit the homes of artists and buy their work. These artists have cachet in Cuba, and they also have financial clout as important attractions at a time when Cuba has come to rely on tourism as its primary industry.

Some people attending the biennial lament such commercialization. Teresa Iturralde represents several Cuban artists at her Los Angeles space, the Iturralde Gallery. "Young artists here are creating art to sell," she said. "They saw what happened at the last biennials, and they are making what they think people want to buy, and it's a little disappointing."

Among the Cuban artists Ms. Iturralde represents are Raúl Cordero, Fernando Rodríguez, and Juan Carlos Alom, whose works command prices from $1,000 to $10,000. In a country where surgeons earn approximately $20 a month, this is an enormous amount of money. To get these prices, an artist must have a name, an individuality that is in opposition to the values of socialism.

After the revolution of 1959, artists in Cuba like the painter Raúl Martínez or the multimedia artist Alberto Blanco contributed their talents to community projects. They designed posters and billboards to be disseminated around Cuba advertising Cuban films, giving health advice, and encouraging the sugar cane harvest. At the last biennial (which in Cuba does not occur every two years as the name implies; the last one was in 2000), groups of Cuban artists, brought together by René Francisco Rodríguez, collaborated on installations at El Morro, a sixteenth-century fort. This year, no such collaboration took place.

Mr. Francisco, whose biennial exhibition is at the Museo de Bellas Artes, has been invited to the United States several times for shows and to colleges as a visiting artist. He believes that for the Cuban artists the motivation is not just money but also international recognition.

"When the U.S. says 'yes' to your art, it matters," he said. "But it's too bad in a way. The work here used to be radical and more in the streets for the Cuban people. Now, the art is made more for New York City."

Because of his success as an artist, Mr. Francisco could live anywhere he wants in the world, but he stays in Havana because, he says, he has a much higher standard of living here than in New York or Berlin, where a small apartment costs much more than a nice house in Havana.

He also works as a professor at the Instituto Superior de Arte in Havana, saying he believes that he has a responsibility to the Cuban artists who came before him as well as to his students and to the role of artists in Cuba's development. Since the collapse of the Soviet Union in the late 1980s, Cuba has been left financially insecure and without a social model to follow. For perhaps the first time in Cuba's history, it has not had a larger country to rely on for help in surviving.

Mr. Francisco encourages his students at the institute to make art part of the community instead of just for themselves. He and his students rehabilitate buildings in Old Havana for impoverished families, repairing them and painting the walls. In this way, he says, art is not isolated but has a practical function in the community. Among the students involved in a 1990 project with Mr. Francisco were Los Carpinteros (The Carpenters).

They followed Mr. Francisco's idea of trying to forgo self-interest and creating a collective identity in which nobody signed his own name. This group of young men, Alexandre Arrechea, Dagoberto Rodríguez, and Marco Castillo, all now in their early 30's, traveled to New York for shows at P.S. 1 in Queens in 2001, the New Museum of Contemporary Art in 1998, and Art in General in 1996. The group is known for installations of shapes that reinterpret urban spaces, evoking movement and impermanence.

Los Carpinteros embody both the Castro era's values of Cuban art of the collective and the new sophistication of young Cuban artists who are less self-referential and more abstract. But their current show here proved to be the final collaboration for one member of the group.

While creating the biennial installation, "Fluido," large black nylon shapes resembling drops of liquids, Mr. Arrechea decided to leave. "As a Carpintero, I renounced my own persona for the experience of working as part of a group," he said. "Now I want to work in a different way, and I'm trying to recover my own identity."

At a small gathering apart from the biennial, Mr. Arrechea gave a presentation of a new video project. He had created a series of pictures resembling police sketches and projected one after the other onto the screen, sometimes showing pairs of faces in tandem. The men's faces looked like those made by forensic artists. Video representations of actual eyes animated the faces, creating isolated expressions of bewilderment and concern.

"These men possibly exist," Mr. Arrechea explained. "But it can't be confirmed. It's still a search."

At another exhibition apart from the biennial, on a beach near the burned-out shell of Casino de Santa Fe, Grupo 609, a collective of young women named for the dorm room they once shared at the institute, climbed into a shallow river under a low concrete bridge. With musicians accompanying them from shore, they performed a puppet show from behind a tarp. The puppets danced to whistling, grunting, hissing, and snoring noises that echoed from under the bridge. In this way, Grupo 609 mocked and condemned machismo in Cuban society.

For the grand finale, people standing on the bridge waved sparklers, and as if in response, lightning sparked behind thick clouds gathered over the sea. When the performance ended, a group of neighborhood boys collected their bikes, and as they mounted them, one commented, "I didn't really understand it, but I think I liked it."

Ballet

Split with Cuba Still Brings Pain

Enrique Fernández

Rolando Sarabia was speaking in Cuban. "No es fácil, esto," he said, using a phrase common on the island and among recent exiles—it ain't easy, this thing. He was referring to the life of a dancer, which at merely twenty-three has already cost him one ankle and two knee operations.

And his country.

Sarabia, an acclaimed principal dancer from the Ballet Nacional de Cuba, defected in July and will make his U.S. debut on Saturday and Sunday as part of the International Ballet Festival of Miami at the Jackie Gleason Theater in Miami Beach.

"I never wanted to leave," he said, his lithe and solid body gathering steam and tensing in a T-shirt and jeans at the Art of Classical Ballet, a Pompano Beach dance academy run by his former teacher, Magaly Suárez. "I just wanted to go dance for a season with the Boston Ballet and then come back and dance with my company."

Seven times he appeared before the head of Ballet Nacional, the legendary Alicia Alonso, to ask for a leave, "I was very respectful and polite," Sanabria said. And seven times she denied him. "End of story. Nothing else to talk about, so I went off to. . ." And he finished the sentence with a Cuban vulgarity.

In Mexico, where he was allowed to teach some ballet classes this summer, Sarabia went to the border. "I asked for political asylum," he said. "It felt terrible to have to do that. All the while, the guards there were asking me for my autograph and saying, 'A lot of your baseball players have come through here.'"

Sarabia had no idea whether he would be allowed back into Cuba to see family and friends. "I have friends who are artists and friends from the street who know nothing about dance, and all they can say is, 'Man, you can really jump high.'"

Worse, he had recently decided it was time to make space in his life for a relationship and had a girlfriend in Cuba. "No, don't print that," he said. Then he changed his mind. "What the hell, print the whole thing. I don't give a . . ." Thinking about being forced out of his country to pursue a career—"They threw me out," he said—was getting him riled.

Sarabia had reached the point in his career where he needed to expand—after all, Alonso herself had launched her own stardom in the United States. He wanted the same freedom. Recently, the *New York Times*'s Erika Kinetz wrote that "critics have called him 'the Cuban Nijinsky.'" And also quoting the *Times*, Pedro Pablo Peña, who heads the International Ballet Festival of Miami, said Sarabia had been compared to Rudolf Nureyev and Mikhail Baryshnikov.

Sarabia says the political tensions of defections like his held no interest for him because dance had been all-consuming: "Ballet is a very small world and you never leave it."

His father, Rolando Sr., was a principal dancer with the Ballet Nacional—"He's older now so he dances character roles," the younger Sarabia says. At age five, Sarabia Jr. was already a gymnast, but at home he would put on music and dance like his father. Soon he switched to ballet.

"Rolando was very studious, very dedicated," said Suárez, who has been hosting Sarabia in her home and studio in Broward County. "He's a great virtuoso, of course," Peña said, "a master of technique, but what he has is a nobility that is rare in someone that age."

Sarabia said he owes it all to top-level instruction. "Alicia Alonso is the head of the company, but the ones who made Cuban ballet dancers great were the teachers." And he named Suárez, who taught at Cuba's Escuela Nacional de Ballet for nineteen years, and others. "Thanks to them we have dancers who are now principals with the world's best companies, like Carlos Acosta with the Royal Ballet, José Manuel Carreño with American Ballet Theater, Joan Boada with the San Francisco Ballet, and Yosvani Ramos with the English National Ballet."

Peña, who says he invited Sarabia to participate in his festival because "there are many Cubans in Miami who follow ballet," says the Cuban ballet style is an amalgam of French, Russian, and American influences. Sarabia agrees: "Fernando Alonso [Alicia's ex and co-founder of the company] told us, 'I take a little bit from everywhere.'"

But Sarabia took the definition further: "What distinguishes the Cuban style is that the woman is very feminine and the man very masculine."

And then he added, in a tone resonant of a street boast, "We [male dancers] are very well trained in the way we handle the girl."

Sarabia says he is now certain he will finally be able to dance with the Boston Ballet, where his brother already is a dancer along with other Cubans. "The director of the company likes the Cuban style," Sarabia explained.

But even with his dreams coming true, and his career about to truly take off, an edge of exile melancholy had already crept in. He had family in Miami and after training all week in Suárez's Pompano Beach studio, he would come down for the weekend and they'd spend their time together, "remembering the old days."

Seeing that attitude in a mere twenty-three-year-old Suárez had to exclaim: "¡Ay, Rolandito!"

"There is nothing left for us," Sarabia insisted, sounding like a much older man, "but to live off our memories."

43

Cuban Cinema

Michael Chanan

Some commentators speculated that the "Special Period in a Time of Peace" implied the sort of restrictions on freedom of expression associated with times of war, but this is simplistic. The evidence suggests a battle between different tendencies and levels within the party. Although Fidel had criticized the timidity of the press in 1986, the media remained firmly under the thumb of the party's ideological overseers, while the cultural regime remained a liberal one. In testing the limits of this liberalism, the young artists provoked a backlash among hard-liners, whose position was strengthened as political tensions with the Soviet Union mounted. In 1988, the same year Fidel appeared at the UNEAC congress and asserted full liberty for artists in content as well as form, a number of shows were canceled or closed for various reasons that the artistic community interpreted as euphemisms for censorship.

A few weeks after the ban on the Soviet publications in 1989, a series of exhibitions by young artists in the Castillo de la Fuerza was shut down after some portraits of Fidel by Eduardo Pon Juan and René Francisco caused offense. One of them depicted Castro speaking in the Plaza de la Revolución to a myriad of reflections of himself; another, titled "Suicide," showed him on a shooting range again surrounded by mirrors. According to the art critic Gerardo Mosquera, writing in 1991, "It was the final cut, that show in 1989. From that time on to today, the cultural arena has been closing. . . . The visual arts were the first to open critical issues in Cuban culture. They have been enclosing that space and encouraging the artists to go."[1] ICAIC would come under attack for displaying a similar parodistic irreverence in the film *Alicia en el pueblo de Maravillas* (Alicia in the Town of Wonder) by Daniel Díaz Torres, and the Film Institute was precipitated, as we shall see, into the greatest crisis of its history when the film was attacked by the party faithful as counterrevolutionary, and banned.

The dismantling of the Soviet bloc and the collapse of the Soviet Union left Cuba in a crisis of double isolation. As the supply of everyday goods shriveled and the country spiraled toward near-bankruptcy, the Special Period became one of electricity blackouts, severe gasoline rationing, huge cuts in public transport, and bicycles from China. Dollars, which were illegal tender but came into the country with tourists and visitors from the exile community in Miami, fueled a growing black market, as the exchange rate on the street rose to 50 and then 150 pesos to the dollar.

Filmmakers, artists, and intellectuals all felt the consequences, along with everybody else. At ICAIC (the National Film Institute), although they managed to keep the annual film festival going, not only would they be forced to curtail production, but they also faced radical alteration in the economic regime that provided for their existence. In 1991, state companies involved in import/export were instructed to aim for financial autonomy in hard-currency dealings—in other words, no more subsidies. ICAIC's foreign income from distribution was never very great, but by dint of co-productions, the sale of services, and hire of personnel to foreign producers, which had all been growing during the 1980s, it was able to fulfill the new requirements and even bring in dollars. Yet now, the economic collapse of the country meant that home-based production without foreign participation would be drastically reduced, and filmmakers would become idle. The consequences included an erosion of the institute's personnel as its members began to disperse, seeking work in other countries (although some found useful employment at the international film school at San Antonio de los Baños); in 1993, after leaving ICAIC, García Espinosa would shoot a feature on video with students at the school called *El Plano* (The Shot) as a demonstration of how to make a virtually no-budget film.

The whole cultural sector suffered. Plastic artists were not only under political pressure to conform but lost the domestic market for their work that had opened up in the 1980s. With work piling up in their studios unsold, they quickly began to leave. Musicians, who continued to enjoy huge popularity while suffering the same privations as their audiences, took every opportunity for trips abroad. These opportunities were on the increase because the period coincided with the rediscovery of Cuban music by foreign audiences and promoters. By the mid-1990s, music had become Cuba's principal cultural export, far greater than film had ever been, embroiled in an ideologically ambiguous trade that inevitably transmitted certain stereotypes along with its apparently non-ideological joie de vivre. Worst hit were the writers, when the publishing industry was brought to its knees through a collapse in the paper supply.

Despite the growing crisis, ICAIC completed three features in 1990. It is notable that in all of them the central characters are women, carrying the suggestion that the representation of women was now recognized as especially fertile ground for investigation, although only one of these films had a contemporary setting. *Hello Hemingway* by Fernando Pérez is a sequel to his earlier *Clandestinos*, another youth film set in the 1950s, but here portraying the frustrations of the time from the perspective of Larita, a talented girl from a poor background struggling to win a scholarship to study in the United States, who happens to be a neighbor of the famous American writer.

ICAIC was thrown into political crisis by the other new film of the year when *Alicia en el Pueblo de Maravillas*, directed by Daniel Díaz Torres, was banned in Cuba after winning an award at the Berlin Film Festival. The crisis was compounded by the announcement around the same time of a scheme to merge ICAIC with Cuban television and the film unit of the Armed Forces, as part of a general plan of rationalization of human and material resources by the state, in the face of the greater economic crisis that had befallen Cuba with the collapse of communism in Eastern Europe. At ICAIC, following unprecedented protests by the film directors, the situation was resolved by the end of the summer. The institute survived, but the film remained banned, and the head of the institute, Julio García Espinosa, was replaced by the return of its founder, Alfredo Guevara. That we can still talk of Cuban cinema today is due to strong protests by Cuban filmmakers against the suppression of this film, which was seen as an act of censorship directed not merely against the film itself but, because of the accompanying threat against the film institute, against the right to free artistic expression.

First reports of the film, after its Berlin screening, suggested that it revisited the same terrain as *La Muerte de un Burócrata* by Tomás Gutiérrez Alea back in 1966, a black comedy about the sins of bureaucracy. Maravillas is a town lost in the crack between two provinces where a job as a community drama coach awaits the film's Alicia. In Maravillas, Alicia finds, nothing works properly and the people behave in the strangest way. A restaurant has chained the cutlery to the table to prevent it being stolen, and some of the chains are too short. Indoors and outdoors, wild animals roam around freely because when the zoo started, the animals came but cages never arrived. People spy on each other. At the Sanatorium for Active Therapy and Neurobiology, or SATAN for short, the patients drink sulfurous water and take mud baths; the whole town goes there.

This is a town where people are sent who have "problems." The exemplary worker caught distributing food from the back of his truck at an illegal beer shop, the bureaucrat involved in petty corruption. No one ever knows who sent them there, and to Alicia they all appear cowards. All this is communicated through vivid and at times hallucinatory images. The humor is black and scatological.

A complex film to shoot, *Alicia* was eight months in preproduction; filming was completed in February 1990, and postproduction at the end of the year. The country had changed considerably over this period. The Berlin Wall had fallen. Throughout Eastern Europe, communism had collapsed. In Moscow, Gorbachev was hanging on by the skin of his teeth. Cuba was isolated as never before. What had always doubtless been a risky project now emerged as a gloating satire on the *cavernícola*, or caveman attitudes of the party orthodoxy, at the very moment when everything seemed to be collapsing around them.

It was also unusually scatological in its sense of humor, and the shit hit the proverbial fan immediately after the Berlin Film Festival success. According to García Espinosa, *Alicia* aroused the ire in particular of the then senior party ideologue, Carlos Aldana, who had a number of video copies made of the film so certain people could see it. Copies of the film soon began to proliferate and all sorts of rumors started circulating about hidden connotations in the film, the satirical targets of its characters, especially the suggestion that certain gestures that Reynaldo Miravalles incorporated into the character of the director of the sanatorium were reminiscent of Fidel Castro himself, and that the film was a direct attack on the revolution. The timing of the episode could hardly be worse. To confront the mounting economic crisis, the government had decided on a program of administrative rationalization intended to save management costs. The decision was taken to merge ICAIC with Cuban television and the film section of the Armed Forces. The politicians were quite unprepared for the response of the filmmakers, who immediately, including those who were party members, signed an unprecedented document, declaring their total opposition to the plan. The unity of the film institute would force the government to back down.

In 1993 he returned to the screen with a film that was equally critical but made only the slightest allusion to Castro. *Fresa y chocolate* (Strawberry and Chocolate) was based on a short story by Senel Paz, who also wrote the script. Near the beginning of *Fresa y chocolate*, Diego, a gay photographer and art critic, puts on a recording of Maria Callas to entertain his guest David, a university student and Young Communist militant whom he has just picked up. "God, what a voice!" he sighs. "Why can't this island produce a voice like that? We need another voice so badly, huh? We've had enough of María Remolá!" Never mind who that is, for the Cuban audience there is an obvious double entendre. We are back in the irreverent and rebellious world of the young artists of the late 1980s—although the film is nominally set in 1979, shortly after the fall of Somoza, and evidently filmed in contemporary Havana, where the buildings are reaching an advanced state of disrepair. This deliberate blurring of the historical moment (which is noted by several commentators) has the effect of intensifying the film's sense of contemporaneity. The students in the university common room watch a documentary about the overthrow of the Nicaraguan dictator, which, according to the commentary, took place a few months earlier, but in the streets outside, a squealing pig being carried up a staircase to be slaughtered presents an image of the hardships of the Special Period.

If *Fresa y chocolate* caused a stir by making its central character, for the first time in Cuban cinema, a gay man, its phenomenal success—it ran in Havana for eight months—certainly suggests that it touched a deep nerve in the social body. As Ian Lumsden has written, "It unleashed a popular discourse about a culturally tabooed and politically repressed issue that went beyond the confines of the film itself."[2] It is not, however, a "gay" film in the regular sense at all, and not because the authors were straight. The tale of friendship between David, a young man of solid Marxist beliefs, and Diego, a homosexual poorly looked on by society, becomes the dramaturgical premise for something much more unfashionable, a hardcore political film, brimming with explicit dialogue about censorship, Marxism-Leninism, nationalism, aesthetics, and not least, sexuality. The narrative takes the form, as John Hess has observed, of a kind of Cuban *bildungsroman*—the education of an innocent in the ways of the world; in this case, the cultural, political, and sexual education of a patriotic young Cuban male growing up at any time since the revolution (hence with broad appeal across the generations), but with a twist: sidestepping the conventional expectations of the genre, it is a cultured "bourgeois" homosexual—although their relation remains unconsummated—who educates the ideologically challenged peasant student.[3]

If Diego (a flamboyant performance by Jorge Perugorría) flaunts his sexuality with outrageous good humor, he does so with a sense of political purpose. The crux is that to be gay for Diego is not just a question of sexuality; it is also to be in possession of a cultural tradition in which the father of Cuban nationalism, José Martí, rubs shoulders with the great Cuban writer Lezama Lima, whom he calls a "universal Cuban," whose novel *Paradiso* (*Paradise*) had been suppressed in Cuba because of its portrayal of homosexuality. His first criticism of the party is that what it tries to repress is imagination, and it can only think of art in terms of either propaganda or mere decoration. As he protests to his neighbor Nancy, "Art is not for sending messages, it's for feeling and thinking. Messages are for the radio." What he most opposes in the "system" is the regimentation of thought, as he declares in another scene to David:

> I also had dreams. When I was fourteen I joined the literacy campaign. Because I wanted to. I went to pick coffee in the hills, and studied to be a teacher. What happened? This head of mine thinks, and anyone who doesn't say "yes" to everything, they reject.

In short, Diego challenges David's assumption that because he's gay he couldn't be a revolutionary, and isn't patriotic—he defends the country "so that people know what's good about it. I don't want the Americans or anyone coming to tell us what to do"—just as he also dismisses the explanations of homosexuality that David draws from the political textbooks. Clearly *Fresa y chocolate* is not just about the homophobia of the Cuban Communist Party, but also a critique of its aesthetic Puritanism, and the suppression of artistic voices considered by authority as deviant.

Fresa y chocolate took top prize at both the Havana Film Festival in 1993 and in Berlin in 1994, and was bought by Miramax for distribution in the United States, allowing Hollywood to pay homage to Alea, who was ill with cancer, and at the same time send a message of solidarity to the beleaguered Cuban filmmakers by nominating it for an Oscar as Best Foreign Film. In many ways a breakthrough film, it played very differently, however, to audiences at home and abroad. In Cuba its runaway popularity gave it the largest-ever audience for a Cuban film in the shortest period of time, provoking a commotion that took on the dimensions of a sociological phenomenon.

However, *Fresa y chocolate* was not (and not intended as) a campaigning film, but as an intervention in a national debate that by the time the film was made had already begun to change significantly. As noted in a personal communication with the author, life for gays had improved long before the film was made. The government had reviewed the issue in the mid-1980s, and in 1988 repealed public ostentation laws that had been in force since 1938—long before the revolution. Police were ordered to stop harassing people for their appearance; the law now only prohibited homosexual acts that were violent, coercive, or with underage persons.

Four years later, as Alea started work on the film, a play by Senel Paz based on the same story opened in Havana, where it ran for two months. What Alea did was seize the moment to test the sincerity of this mood of liberalism by fixing it in the eye. It provokes reflections that go beyond the anguish of a particular marginalized community; in short, it was a highly liberating film.

NOTES

1. Cited in Jay Murphy, "The Young and Restless in Havana," *Third Text*, 20 (1992), 116.

2. Ian Lumsden, *Machos, Maricones, and Gays: Cuba and Homosexuality* (Philadelphia: Temple University Press, 1996), 194.

3. See John Hess, "Melodrama, Sex, and the Cuban Revolution," *Jump Cut*, no. 41: 120.

Two Songs

Carlos Varela

Translation by John M. Kirk

William Tell

William Tell didn't understand his son
Who one day got tired of having the apple placed on his head,
And started to run away.
His father cursed him—
How could he now prove his skill?

William Tell, your son has grown up,
And now he wants to shoot the arrow himself.
It's his turn now to show his valor with your crossbow.

Yet William Tell did not understand the challenge:
Who would ever risk having the arrow shot at them?
He became afraid when his son addressed him,
Telling William that it was now his turn
To place the apple on his own head.

William Tell, your son has grown up,
And now he wants to shoot the arrow himself.
It's his turn now to show his valor with your crossbow.

William Tell was angry at the new idea,
And refused to place the apple on his own head.
It was not that he didn't trust his son—
But what would happen if he missed?

William Tell, your son has grown up,
And now he wants to shoot the arrow himself.
It's his turn now to show his valor with your crossbow.

William Tell failed to understand his son—
Who one day got tired of having the apple placed on his head.

Tropicollage (Selection)

He left in a Havanautos rented car
Heading to the beach at Varadero,
Havana Club in the sand,
Smoking a cigar
And taking pictures,
Leaning against a palm tree.
Returning to the Habana Libre hotel,
He hired a Turistaxi to go to the Tropicana night club.
On the way to the airport,
He left believing
That he really understood Havana.
He took with him
The image they wanted him to have.
And in his Polaroids
And his head he carries
Tropicollage.

He never went to the real Habana Vieja
Nor to the barrios
Of workers and believers.
He took no photos
On the city reefs
Where a sea of people swim.
He never saw the construction workers,
Cementing the future
With bricks and cheap rum.
Nor did he meet those guys
Changing money 5 for 1.

That too is my country,
And I cannot forget it.
Anybody who denies it
Has their head full of
Tropicollage.

I know that dollars
Make the economy go around—
Just like flour makes bread.
But what I don't understand
Is that they confuse people
And money.
If you go to a hotel
And are not a foreigner,
They treat you differently.
This is happening here.
And I want to change it.
And anybody who denies this
Has their head full of
Tropicollage.

45

From the Heart of Cuba, a Love Song for the Crescent City

David Cázares

HAVANA—The troubling images of New Orleans left in chaos and pain by Katrina astounded people around the world, but it broke hearts here. Centuries of commerce, migration, history, and music bind these two cities, and musicians at this year's international jazz festival gave props to the Crescent City in their common language.

Two of Cuba's most prolific composers and internationally acclaimed bandleaders composed musical tributes to New Orleans and its people. Flautist Jose Luis Cortés of NG La Banda and jazz pianist Chucho Valdés want musicians and residents of New Orleans to know Cubans are with them as they rebuild.

Cortés, a black Cuban whose music blends a streetwise sensibility with jazzy sophistication, was particularly saddened that so many black people in New Orleans were among those most affected. "In New Orleans, there are black people," Cortés said. "In Cuba there are black people. Blacks came from Africa. We're all from the same place."

Cortés also wanted to reach out to his fellow musicians in New Orleans, who share his love of a treasured art form. "New Orleans is the birthplace of jazz," he said. "I want to look for the currents of jazz that are within the music of New Orleans as much as they are in the music of Cuba."

The bandleader's composition, which he hopes to perform soon in a country accessible to musicians from both nations, is written for symphonic orchestra and his big band. Intended as an inspirational work, it fuses classical music with Afro-Cuban dance music and Yoruban chants.

The piece will be an expression of solidarity with the musicians there "and above all with the black community," Cortés said.

New Orleans is beloved in Cuba because of the cultural, historical, and musical roots it shares with the island. Founded by Canadians working for France, New Orleans became a city under Spanish rule in 1762, and the first governor of Louisiana reported to the captain-general of Cuba. The Spanish gave New Orleans its structure and rebuilt the city after fires in 1788 and 1794 destroyed most of it. Even in the fabled "French Quarter," Spanish architecture predominates.

New Orleans had a profound cultural relationship with the port city of Havana, ties that continued well into the twentieth century, said Ned Sublette, author of the book *Cuba and Its Music: From the First Drums to the Mambo.* The island's habanera rhythm appears in the music of New Orleans in the first half of the nineteenth century and is the "Spanish tinge" that New Orleans jazz musician Jelly Roll Morton said was essential to the genre, Sublette said.

It is only fitting, Sublette said, that today's Cuban musicians would feel an affinity for New Orleans and its people. "New Orleans was the first important music city in North America," said Sublette, owner of New-York based Qbadisc, which specializes in music from the island. "The city that gave birth to jazz was in a constant, open circuit with Havana, and jazz was heard in Havana from early on."

Like New Orleans, Havana has played an important role in the development of jazz. Musicians in Cuba and the United States have long collaborated, particularly since the golden age of Cuban music in the 1940s and 1950s.

After Katrina, many Cuban musicians dedicated their concerts to New Orleans. "New Orleans is part of the Caribbean community and like Cuba, the city has a strong African culture. I can't forget that New Orleans is a port city and that sounds travel," said Dr. Michael White, a clarinetist in the legendary Preservation Hall Jazz Band. "It's a beautiful thing that Cubans are honoring New Orleans's musical heritage."

One of the most ambitious signs of support came from pianist Valdés, who helped close Havana's twenty-second annual international jazz festival with a work that honored New Orleans.

Performing with Cuba's National Symphony Orchestra, the Cuban National Choir, and his quartet, Valdés delivered a spectacular concert that fused the blues, classical music, gospel, Yoruban chants, and straight-ahead jazz.

In the tribute "A Song to God," the composer's sister, Mayra Caridad Valdés, sang an ode to the music of New Orleans, "so beautiful and lovely," and to its people: "How many sad stories must be forgotten," she sang.

Valdés told the audience at the Teatro Mella that his work was a song of love, of peace and humanity. "This is a tribute to New Orleans, its history, the place where ragtime and the blues were born—a tribute to Jelly Roll Morton, to Wynton Marsalis," he said. "It's for the musicians."

46

Rap and Revolution

Hip-Hop Comes to Cuba

Margot Olavarria

Half an hour's drive east of Havana is the suburb of Alamar, home to three hundred thousand Cubans. Built in the early 1970s, it is one of the largest housing projects in the world, made up of massive, Soviet-designed, walk-up buildings spread across sixteen zones divided by stretches of tropical vegetation. It was here that in the 1980s young residents would construct antennas to put out on their balconies to capture the sounds of "la moña," R&B and rap music from Miami radio stations WEDR 99 Jams and WHQT Hot 105. That is how the sounds of U.S. hip hop arrived on the island.

Young, mostly black Cuban men adopted the genre, first by imitating it and eventually infusing it with their own roots and reality, transforming it into a space for self-expression that both reflects and constitutes their identity. Today there are some two hundred hip-hop groups in Havana, and five hundred throughout the island. The lyrical depth of this music, evidence of the benefits of Cuba's educational system, speaks to the many ways in which race, gender, class, and national identity intersect and are in constant flux. Their articulate rhymes flow at machine-gun pace, fusing words with Afro-Cuban rhythms to make Cuban hip-hop a distinct art form.

While not all rap is politically charged, a number of groups have begun an important movement for cultural and social change, using rap as a vehicle to speak out about racism, prostitution, police harassment, growing class differences, the difficulty of daily survival, and other social problems of contemporary Cuba. While rap is not necessarily offering solutions to these problems, the movement has created an opening for freedom of expression under the threat and pressure of state censorship. It was certainly a struggle to bring this music out of the underground during the 1980s and early 1990s, when hip-hop concerts and parties—seen as carriers of capitalist, anti-socialist influences—were closed down by police, to a time when the movement has the attention of the local and international media. Cuban rap can now be heard on a weekly radio show, "Esquina de Rap," and seen on television Saturday afternoons. Now the government even promotes and supports, to the extent that it can, the yearly rap festivals held in (aptly) Alamar.

"Those are the best four days of the year for us," Julio Cárdenas and Yohan Linares of RCA (Rapperos Crazy de Alamar) told me in October 2000 as they showed me the amphitheater where the festivals are held. But the success of the festivals is only one step in a struggle that continues "por el suelo," they tell me, using a Cuban expression for crawling across the floor, as in avoiding the cloud of smoke lurking above in the middle of a fire.

Cuban hip-hop artists have had help in dissipating some of that smoke, clearing the way toward gaining a certain amount of legitimacy. Nehanda Abiodun, a U.S. Black Liberation Army activist in political exile in Cuba, began her involvement with Cuban rappers after arriving on the island in 1990. That was when Abiodun encountered thousands of young Afro-Cubans enjoying themselves and break-dancing to U.S. rap music at street parties.

> What made it exciting for me was that there were a number of brothers with X's carved into their hair. Once they found out I was here and that I was part of a movement, they began to ask me questions about the Black Panther Party, Malcolm X, what happened to Angela Davis. I found it very comforting and exciting after eight years living underground and even more than that struggling against racism back home.[1]

At the same time, Abiodun noticed Cuban rappers imitating U.S. "gangsta rap." The aggressive, mysoginist lyrics about the violence of U.S. inner cities did not fit the Cuban reality, so Abiodun began working with organizations in the United States to bring progressive U.S. rappers to perform in Cuba. Since then, Mos Def, dead prez, Black Star, Common, and other U.S. rappers have brought their politicized messages to Cuba and since 1998, the New York–based organization Black August has held fundraising concerts in the United States to support the Havana rap festivals and establish a hip-hop library and studio there. This bridge between the Cuban and U.S. hip-hop communities continues to strengthen, despite the U.S.-imposed embargo. The latest evidence of this has been the October 2001 visit of Cuban hip-hop groups Obseción, RCA, and Anónimo Consejo to New York City as part of this ongoing cultural exchange.[2]

On the island, the hip-hop movement found support in the mid-1990s from Grupo Uno, a collective from an East Havana cultural center, and rock promoter Rodolfo Renzoli, who set out to launch the festivals in 1995.[3] They allied with the Asociación Hermanos Saíz (AHS), an organization that promotes young artists and is linked to the Communist Youth Organization, and got official endorsement for the festivals. By comparing it to the Nueva Trova of the 1960s, Ariel Fernández of AHS sees the Cuban hip-hop movement as a revolution within the revolution. "The social role it is playing is very important," says Fernández. "Cuban rap is criticizing the deficiencies that exist in society, but in a constructive way, educating youth and opening spaces to create a better society."[4] The government began sponsoring the festivals and listening to what the rappers were saying. Cultural officials decide who gets to participate and perform in the festivals, however, and on occasion some groups have felt they have been unjustly excluded.

While competing to be part of the 2000 festival, for example, the group Free Hole Negro was asked to explain their name on television. They said that besides being an obvious pun (free hole = frijol = black bean), it was calling for a space where all black people could be free. This got a little too close to the sensitive issue of racism in a context where revolutionary discourse has declared it to be a non-issue (see, Alejandro de la Fuente, "Recreating Racism" in this volume). Free Hole Negro was not part of the line-up of artists featured in the festival that year. Other groups performing denounced their exclusion and Free Hole Negro got to perform the following year.

That Cuba is not a bastion of racial equality became crystal clear to me during my first trip in 2000. While renting a room from a white couple, I overheard the husband complaining about a coworker, whom he described as "one of those with bad hair." Then when visiting an Afro-Cuban friend I noticed a poster behind her door that listed "Ten racist expressions we should not repeat."[5] She pointed to number nine, "She is black but has a white soul" and told me she herself would use this expression even well after the revolution. Further, there were no black newscasters and few blacks in general on television.

Given the lack of public discourse on race and racism, and the continuing resonance of José Martí's "more than black and more than white, we are Cubans," it is not surprising that there is not a strong sense of belonging to an African diaspora among rappers. In "Afro-Cuban," the accent is on the Cuban. The reluctance to talk about race and racism is slowly wearing away, however, with youth taking the lead. Cuban rappers are cultivating a sense of blackness through their music, but they are doing it in a way that is specific to their own racialized context.

The media attention the movement is getting provides opportunities to get their expressions of racial identity to mainstream society. For example, hip-hop producer Pablo Herrera was asked in the Cuban press whether there were any white rappers. He replied: "Well, let's say there are lighter-skinned rappers, because no one in Cuba is white."[6] In a country where some official documents consider mulattos white, and many mestizos self-identify as white, Herrera's response is like dropping a bomb.[7]

Racial identity is also mediated by other factors. Most young Afro-Cubans recognize that racial prejudice was more pronounced during their parents' generation and that intermarriage is far more common today. For example, Doris Agramonte from Instinto, a female rap trio, identifies as both black and mixed race. "I am Cuban—I am black, very black but my grandmother was Phillipine and my grandfather was Catalán. I have the whole world in me."[8] Instinto feel they have been discriminated against not for being black, but for making music that originated in the United States and for being women who rap. "We defend our right to do rap, but we do it sensually," Janet Díaz told me. Instinto likes to rap to live drums—"catá, tambor, the sound of beating on goat skin and wood, mixing rumba and rap." Like the majority of groups, they mix Afro-Cuban rhythms, referred to by most as simply "traditional Cuban music" (that it is African in origin is assumed), with their rhymes.

Young Afro-Cubans also recognize that the police brutality against blacks is worse in U.S. cities than the police harassment they experience. They frequently asked me about the human rights abuses under the Rudolph Giuliani administration, especially about the Amadou Diallo and Abner Luima cases. At a party welcoming back to Cuba the delegation of groups that visited New York, Kokino from Anónimo Consejo confirmed others' belief that "African-Americans have had it worse than us."

At a presentation in an art gallery in East Harlem, Magia López of Obseción introduced a song about racism: "It is an undeclared racism. . . . There are people who reject blacks and we live this and feel this in Cuba."[9] The song speaks to racial codes that use notions of "decency" to exclude blacks.

Cuban rap often voices its criticism with satire, or with dispersed and double meanings. The Reyes de la Calle, for example, have a song about people who devoutly pray while still holding on to their prejudices, and their likely reaction if at the world's end, God turned out to be black. Lester Martínez of Free Hole Negro says that the use of satire is more than just about getting around censorship. "Cubans always laugh at themselves, at what is funny and at what is unfortunate," says Martínez. "We make music of the street to make people dance and think. We let the message be in the lyrics but in an ironic way. We feed off rap, timba, soul, son, and guaguancó."[10]

Another example of satire is a song by Alto y Bajo that says, "This is the most beautiful island that Cubans have ever seen/I am the Cuban hip-hop, the international one." The subtext here reads: Given the difficulty of travel for Cubans, Cuba is the only island they have ever seen. But the frequent references to Cuba and being Cuban are more often on a serious note. The Orishas, for example, rap about being unable to "stop the blood of love and homeland [patria] that runs through my veins" over the Buena Vista Social Club's "Chan Chan." These strong expressions of *cubanidad* could be interpreted as attempts to placate government paranoia that Cuba is losing its youth to globalized consumer culture. But they must also be understood as coming from an awareness of Cuba's marginalization within that global order and the consciousness that they represent Cuba in the cosmopolitan youth culture they also strive to be part of.

Despite Cuban rap artists' dissatisfaction with the hardships of everyday life and their frustration with lacking the resources and technological equipment necessary to make their music, they appreciate the gains of the revolution and criticize Cuba's rising individualism. All over Latin America, marginalized urban youth are taking hip-hop and reshaping it to express their own reality. In Cuba, hip-hop is a movement whereby black youth can celebrate and express themselves. To trivialize it as anything else would be to deny art's political potential.

NOTES

1. Interview with author, Havana, October 2000.

2. The project was organized by International Hip-Hop Exchange, a group of New York activists including actor Danny Hoch and Mairanieves Alba, director of Hip-Hop Leads, and the organizations Vera List Center for Art and Politics of the New School for Social Research and the Caribbean Cultural Center.

3. See Deborah Pacini Hernández and Reebee Garofalo, "Hip-Hop in Havana: Rap, Race, and National Identity in Contemporary Cuba," *Journal of Popular Music Studies* 11–12, 18–47.

4. Talk by Fernández at "Lenguas Libres" event at Mixta Gallery, East Harlem, NY, October 13, 2001.

5. Poster published by Grupo Identidad de la Mujer, Santo Domingo, DR.

6. Alessandra Basso Ortiz, "Rap: Por el amor al arte?" El Caimán Barbudo website, www.caiman-barbudo.cu/caiman303/page/rap.htm.

7. Eugene Godfried, "Reflections on Race and the Status of People of African Descent in Revolutionary Cuba," available through AfroCubaWeb, www.afrocubaweb.com/eugenegodfried/reflectionson-race.htm; Pedro Juan Gutierrez, "Razas Diferentes Pero Iguales," *Bohemia* 89, no. 2 (1997): 4–9.

8. Interview with author, Havana, October 2000.

9. Presentation by Obseción at "Lenguas Libres" event at Mixta Gallery, East Harlem, NY, October 13, 2001.

10. Interview with author, Havana, October 2000.

47

Home-Grown Virtuosos

Howard Reich

HAVANA—Without saying a word, teenager Yamila Cruz seats herself at the grand piano, places her slender fingers on the keyboard and, after a brief pause, unleashes a torrent of sound one might expect from a virtuoso twice her age and size.

Though the battered, perpetually out-of-tune instrument—made ages ago in Moscow—sounds as if its strings might pop at any moment, though the din of traffic outside rushes in through open windows on a sweltering afternoon, the sixteen-year-old has tuned everything out to turn in a masterful performance of Saint Saens' Piano Concerto No. 2.

Similar scenes are unfolding in practically every chaotic corner of the sprawling Amadeo Roldán Conservatory, a fabled institution in Central Havana that has trained some of Cuba's most celebrated musicians. Guitarists, drummers, flutists, percussionists, pianists, you name it, they're making music well beyond their years in the classrooms and hallways and sun-drenched courtyard of a three-story walk-up that looks as if it hasn't had a new coat of paint since Fidel Castro took power, at the end of 1959.

Yet in this decaying building, and others like it scattered across this impoverished city, Cuba is producing musicians of Herculean technique, many of whom have applied their intensive classical training to the art of jazz—and thus have come to tower over their counterparts around the world. Though the roots of Afro-Cuban music run deep in Havana, to the slave trade of centuries past, the last two generations have yielded larger-than-life jazz players whose mastery of their instruments and exalted level of musicianship enables them to conquer audiences wherever jazz is played.

Exactly why Cuban jazz musicians sound consistently brilliant may be a mystery to the outside world, but in Havana it is no secret: After Castro forged his alliance with the former Soviet Union in the early 1960s, the island quickly saw an influx of Russian and Soviet-bloc music teachers. They brought with them techniques that had been producing monumental classical virtuosos since the nineteenth century. And though the fall of the USSR in the 1990s meant that financial support from Moscow virtually vanished, the Russian methods had become integral to Cuban music education and remain so to this day.

The merger of Cuban musical tradition and rigorous Soviet teaching has produced some of the greatest jazz players of the past forty years. Yet for every Chucho Valdés and Gonzalo Rubalcaba, who have broken through the U.S.'s long-running embargo of Cuba to win acclaim in the United States and beyond, uncounted others feel doomed to a lifetime of obscurity. Unable to bring their gifts to the international marketplace because they have great difficulty getting into the States, where most of the world's musical stars are merchandised, the Cuban giants languish well outside the spotlight.

These musicians—some old and tired of battling against the effects of the embargo, others young, poor, and frustrated by their inability to make contact with U.S. listeners—are creating a music as complex and profound as anything available in jazz today. But they were not featured in the *Buena Vista Social Club* film, which in 1999 popularized a small group of aged Cuban musicians, and few listeners outside Cuba get to hear today's exceptional players.

With political tensions between Washington and Havana on the rise during the past couple of years, and with the United States granting entry visas only sparingly to Cuban musicians, the Cuban jazz artists realize that their prospects are getting worse.

"If Cuban musicians would have a chance to enter the great distribution of the United States, we could show everyone that some of the most important music in the world is being made here, in Havana," says the esteemed Cuban bandleader Jorge Gómez. Gómez has toiled for thirty years in the Cuban music industry but was allowed into the United States to perform just once, in 1986.

"Without us, the world is losing one of the most important roots of music as well as some of the most formidable jazz artists working today."

COMING OF AGE

Hernán López-Nussa, a forty-four-year-old jazz pianist revered in Havana but virtually unknown in the United States (despite a brief tour in 1999), can see himself in the faces of the gifted youngsters making music at the Amadeo Roldán Conservatory.

It was in this building, near the intersection of two dusty, noisy roads in Central Havana that López-Nussa spent more than a decade studying the harmonic intricacies of Bartok, the technical idiosyncrasies of Liszt and the keyboard poetry of Chopin. Though López-Nussa, like the students today, spent mornings studying math, science, and literature, in the afternoons he pored over musical scores, practiced ear-training exercises, and polished his technique at the piano.

He didn't realize it at the time, but López-Nussa was coming of age at an extraordinary moment in Cuban culture, the mid-1960s and 1970s, when the ancient traditions of folkloric Cuban music were being galvanized by the techniques of Soviet musicians who had been sent to the island by the Kremlin. Suddenly, students who attended the Amadeo Roldán Conservatory were being taught not only the noble works of Cuban composers such as Roldán and Ernesto Lecouna but also drilled in the ferociously difficult keyboard exercises of Anton Rubinstein, Nikolai Rubinstein and other giant Russian pedagogues. To López-Nussa, this Cuban-Soviet training seemed the most natural thing in the world, but it was unprecedented in Cuban history and laid the groundwork for a musical revolution yet to come.

"I cannot say that we students loved being here—we certainly never loved this building," says López-Nussa, who's greeted with hugs and kisses from students and teachers alike as he makes an impromptu visit to the conservatory, which trains preuniversity students.

"Even now, the conditions are terrible, the pianos are terrible, the noise from outside is terrible, the practice rooms are filled with distractions.

"To tell you the truth, I do not understand how the kids here learn to make music in such a difficult place.

"Yet somehow we forget about everything else and concentrate on the music."

In truth, the children have no choice, their teachers placing the same demands upon them as had been made on such earlier Russian supervirtuosos as Vladimir Horowitz, Sviatoslav Richter, Emil Gilels, David Oistrakh, Mstislav Rostropovich, and scores more.

"Something incredible happened in this building, and it continues to happen today," says Roberto Catalá de la Hoz, director of the conservatory, which opened on Oct. 2, 1903.

"When we got the great professors from Russia, and they joined with the great Cuban professors, the students started to play at an incredible level, unimaginable.

"The Russians have a tradition of tremendous technique—speed and accuracy and power on their instruments. And the Russian method became our method.

"It is very strict, very disciplined, and it is at the center of what happens here."

Adds Mayra Torralba, assistant director of the conservatory, "The Russians brought us the knowledge on how to study music, all the experience they had acquired in more than a century. And we adapted their methods into our reality."

That much is obvious in every studio in the conservatory, where young Cuban musicians still play from Soviet scores, the titles of works and the composers' names written in a Cyrillic alphabet that is impenetrable to the students. Moreover, the youngsters make music on grand pianos bearing the names not of Steinway or Baldwin but of Moscba (or Moscow) and Estonia. Compared with modern-day American and German instruments, the Soviet models sound dull, metallic, and poorly constructed.

Yet on these wrecks, as in López-Nussa's youth, the students fire off scales with phenomenal speed and accuracy, meanwhile playing melodic phrases with a degree of sensitivity and introspection one does not associate with Russian-school training. In effect, the young Cuban musicians are reaping the best of two worlds: monumental Soviet technique and ardent Afro-Caribbean melodicism.

As López-Nussa strolls through hallways of the Amadeo Roldán Conservatory, he knocks on individual practice-room doors, sticking in his head to hear one young musician bringing demonic rhythmic drive to a Bartok dance, another finding sublime lyricism in a Chopin ballade.

But these youngsters are practically beginners compared with the university-level students preparing to play on the international stage—should they ever get the chance.

Before Castro's revolution, the lush acreage along Calle 120, in an upscale neighborhood, was a country club, its rolling hills a golfer's paradise, its spacious main building a posh restaurant and plush hotel.

But after 1959 it was nationalized and transformed into the Instituto Superior de Arte (Institute of Superior Arts), the place where López-Nussa obtained his artist's diploma and new waves of great Cuban musicians have been trained.

Here, the students—who play on instruments not much better than the ones at Amadeo Roldán—are old enough to have found their calling in jazz. You can hear it by strolling past some of the practice rooms, where swing rhythms and blue-note scales intermingle with Beethoven's trills and Liszt's arpeggios.

In one practice room, two young marimba players are firing off syncopated riffs so complex and fast-moving you might guess that American vibes masters Bobby Hutcherson and Stefon Harris were wielding the mallets. In another room, a group of percussionists is laying down gently swaying backbeats of the sort that could keep a mambo jam session going for hours.

And in yet another, a young pianist takes a pause from practicing a Chopin ballade to talk about his heroes—jazz pianists Oscar Peterson and Chucho Valdés.

"I have one goal for after I graduate—to have a jazz band of my own," says Alejandro Vargas, 21. "Everyone at the school knows it. My professor knows it, and he thinks it's great.

"But when I am in his studio, I am not supposed to play jazz. I am to play only classical—Beethoven and Chopin and Debussy."

Indeed, no one graduates without mastering the classical repertory, which means that aspiring jazz players like Vargas pick up the art of jazz improvisation in the same way that American jazz musicians long have done: by listening to records and repeating what they've heard on the bandstand.

Since the embargo prevents them from buying the CDs, the youngsters befriend professional musicians in the nightclubs, then go to their homes to listen to the American jazz CDs the musicians have picked up during European tours. Then the young Cubans try out the tunes in the streets.

When they play American jazz, however, they cannot help but redefine the music with the Cuban dance rhythms and song forms they have heard all their lives. Played by the young Cuban jazzmen, tunes such as Miles Davis's "So What" convey gorgeous layers of rhythm and counterpoint, as well as the fluid technique and sophisticated harmonic sense the youngsters have learned in the conservatory.

Thus when emerging Cuban musicians take turns riffing with pros such as pianist Danilo Pérez during the recent Havana International Jazz Festival, the Americans are startled by what they hear.

"These kids have accomplished so much with so little," says Perez, after leading a master class with a roomful of gifted young players. "Their passion for this music is unbelievable."

CROSS-CULTURAL MUSIC

In essence, the nascent Cuban jazz players are following an artistic path established by artists such as Valdés and Rubalcaba and López-Nussa before them.

Valdés, above all, proved that the merger of Soviet-style technique and Afro-Cuban jazz could create a cross-cultural music so brilliant and powerful that it could pierce the wall separating Cuba and the United States. By establishing the great Cuban band Irakere in the 1970s and touring it first on the island, then around the world, Valdés and his followers brought Cuban jazz musicians a prominence not seen since the days when artists such as percussionist Chano Pozo and bandleader Mario Bauzá collaborated with Dizzy Gillespie in the 1940s.

But this time, the Cuban jazz revolution was homegrown, based in Havana and not dependent on the co-sponsorship of an American star like Gillespie. Moreover, emerging Cuban musicians in the 1970s were blessed not only with conservatory training but with the deep vein of Cuban folkloric music that they grew up hearing. From fantastically accomplished congueros such as Tata Guines and Changuito they learned to hear and reproduce the multiple layers of rhythm that are at the heart of Cuban music. From elder pianists such as the late Frank Emilio—whose tune "Mandinga, Mondonga, Sandunga" holds a place in Cuban culture roughly equivalent to George Gershwin's "I Got Rhythm" in the U.S.—they learned that jazz and Cuban music were as compatible as rum and coke. Historic Cuban musical forms such as danzón, son, rumba, and cha-cha-chá were easily integrated into American swing rhythm.

Perhaps it's no coincidence that so many of the classically trained Cuban jazz musicians who conquered the music world came from families already steeped in folkloric Cuban music and American jazz. Valdés's father, pianist Bebo, led the sensational dance band at the Tropicana nightclub, which from 1939 to this day stands as the most opulent showroom in Havana. Rubalcaba's father, Guillermo, was widely admired for the exquisite charanga dance bands he still leads around Cuba. And López-Nussa was the fortunate son of a pianist mother who often traveled to Europe and brought back recordings of Louis Armstrong, Charlie Parker, Oscar Peterson, Art Tatum, Count Basie, and John Coltrane.

When López-Nussa tells the young Vargas of the populist backgrounds of so many of the best Cuban jazz pianists, the twenty-one-year-old musician practically beams.

"My father plays in the jazz bands too," Vargas says. "Maybe I will be the next López-Nussa."

He's not the only one who's nurturing big dreams. In a nearby practice room, a young musician is struggling with Cuban dance rhythm, slowly playing dance beats while counting aloud—"One, two, three, four"—in endless repetition. But this is no Cuban musician—it's an American who has come to Havana to study with the masters.

"Havana is the heart of Latin music, and there's no better place on Earth to study rhythm," says Andrew Turpening, twenty-eight, of St. Paul.

"In a way, it's impossible to compete with the Cuban jazz musicians—their folklore and their training gives them the edge.

"I was lucky. I got a license to come here. When I get back to the States, the other musicians are not going to believe the rhythms that I'll be able to play. Then I'll have the edge."

The most remarkable music-making at the institute takes place not inside the great conservatory but outdoors, where the wind and brass students are playing to the heavens.

This is the norm in Cuban music education, which encourages students to play outdoors so that they can sound big and as bold as possible.

Put these same players in a jazz club or concert hall, and they sound as if their lungs are twice normal size. Perhaps this is why Cuban trumpeters such as Arturo Sandoval and Jesús Alemany (of Cubanismo) sound as huge as all outdoors.

"When we're not in class, we're always out here, practicing, blowing, trying to make our sound big," says Kervin Barretto, a twenty-year-old trumpeter.

Then Barretto puts his horn to his lips and begins a lightning-fast version of "A Night in Tunisia," a tip-of-the-hat to the great Gillespie, who wrote the tune.

Another young trumpeter a few feet away picks up the theme, the two quickly exchanging riffs as if having a conversation on the nature and meaning of jazz.

"This is the music that a lot of the students here want to play," says trumpeter Jorge Miguel Vistel Serrano, twenty. "But sometimes we feel that everyone in the world is trying to stop us, that everything is against us."

But it won't be until later in the evening, when Serrano has left the school to play at a Havana jazz club, that the depth of his frustration and the hopelessness of his situation will become fully apparent.

Until then, he tilts his horn skyward and lets out a great blast of sound, a mighty horn call if ever there were one.

López-Nussa listens admiringly, then shakes his head.

"Imagine what he could do if he could come to America."

48

The Dual Role of Sports

Paula Pettavino and Philip Brenner

As negotiations over a March 28, 1999, exhibition game to be played in Havana neared their end, the *New York Times* speculated that the Baltimore Orioles might not send their best players to compete against the Cuban national baseball team. This notion was nipped in the bud by an observer close to the team, who bluntly commented, "They aren't interested in losing."

The high quality of Cuba's baseball team was hardly news. Even those who are not sports enthusiasts know that U.S. professional teams have sought many of the island's best players. However, Cuba's sports expertise extends far beyond baseball. Cuban athletes in boxing, judo, fencing, cross-country, wrestling, and volleyball have won numerous medals in international competitions. Indeed, Cuba ranks first in the world in per capita medals won. Though it has only eleven million people, it is a sports powerhouse whose teams consistently achieve scores as high as those from the world's most populous countries. This success is hardly accidental. The Cuban Revolution devoted considerable resources to the development of athletes, and this allocation has continued during the Special Period of economic crisis in the 1990s.

Cuba's national sports program initiated in 1961 had two mutually reinforcing goals. International sports triumphs would provide a spotlight on the Cuban Revolution and symbolize its success. In addition to displaying Cuba's leadership to Third World countries, this would give Cubans themselves pride in the revolution and a sense of nationalism. It was seen as a way of enhancing the revolutionary government's legitimacy, especially in the 1960s during periods of terrible scarcity and deprivation.

At the same time, the sports program would promote internal development. In order to cultivate internationally competitive athletes, Cuba created an elaborate "farm" system for identifying those with extraordinary talents and funneling them to the highest levels for expert training. It did so by universalizing sports participation and making it an essential component of revolutionary activity. *Masividad*, or mass participation in sports, thus served domestic political goals.

Universal physical education underscored the revolution's commitment to eradicating class and racial divisions, provided a tangible benefit to everyone, and helped advance the general health of Cubans. The slogan, *el deporte es salud* (sport is health), became a theme of the revolution, and physical education was seen as supporting the development of the country by making individual Cubans stronger and ultimately better workers.

By 1991, the dual purposes of the sports program—serving Cuba's international and domestic goals—were well established. Then, however, conditions outside and inside Cuba changed. With the departure of Cuban troops from Africa, the failure of revolutionary movements in much of Latin America, and the loss of Soviet support, Cuba needed to reorient its effort as a leader of the Third World. Simultaneously, the collapse of the Council for Mutual Economic Assistance (the Eastern bloc trade organization) wreaked havoc on Cuba's domestic economy and ushered in the Special Period of scarcity. The country had to focus on reorganizing its system of industry and commerce, and consequently its social relations of production.

Under these new external and internal circumstances, it would have been expected that Cuba's sports program would also undergo changes. Nevertheless, that program's dual purpose has survived, so that the international aspects of Cuban sports cannot be neatly segregated from its domestic components.

Prior to 1959, Cuba rarely scored victories in international competitions, except in baseball, where success came earlier. There were Cuban professional teams even in the nineteenth century, and baseball flourished in Cuba—as it did elsewhere in the Caribbean Basin—with the arrival of the U.S. Marines. By the 1920s it was the national sport, and soon after Jackie Robinson broke the color line in 1947, Cuban athletes regularly joined U.S. teams. In the 1950s, the Havana Sugar Kings were a Triple A International League franchise. Boxing also was popular in Cuba before the revolution, especially as a route for talented Afro-Cubans to escape from poverty. But sports often mirrored the society's class and racial divisions. Several sports were associated with private clubs, and racial discrimination kept many of Cuba's best athletes off national teams. This partly accounts for the country's poor showing in international contests before 1959.

The pattern changed quickly with the revolution. The national sports program initiated in 1961 had two mutually reinforcing goals. International sports triumphs would provide a spotlight on the Cuban Revolution and symbolize its success. In addition to displaying Cuba's leadership to Third World countries, this would give Cubans themselves pride in the revolution and a sense of nationalism. It was seen as a way of enhancing the revolutionary government's legitimacy, especially in the 1960s during periods of terrible scarcity and deprivation.

The revolutionary government lost no time in putting sports to use as a political tool, both internally and externally. Over the past forty years, it has shifted its focus from one to the other of these dual goals, and back again, depending on the circumstances in the international, regional, and national political arenas. For the first several decades after the revolution, both efforts worked in tandem. Given the low level of interest in sports on the part of previous Cuban governments, any emphasis put on sports and health by the revolutionary regime had the potential to produce marked, consistent improvement. Cuban leaders referred to the links between physical culture, health, discipline, and defense.

The results within Cuba were seen almost immediately. The first reform measure of the revolutionary government was to open private sports clubs to everyone. By 1967, all charges for sporting events and participation had been dropped. Sport was seen as a right of the people and it was mentioned four times in the Cuban Constitution of 1976. Indeed, sport merited its own article under "Fundamental rights, duties and guarantees."

After several years, this emphasis on *masividad* began to bear fruit in the realm of international competitive sport. The first indication of this burgeoning success came at the 1966 Central American and Caribbean Games in San Juan. The Cuban athletes, forbidden by the United States to land by plane, traveled to Puerto Rico by boat and won seventy-eight medals (thirty-five gold, nineteen silver, and twenty-four bronze). The extent of Cuba's international success in sports was revealed to the world at the 1976 Olympic Games in Montreal. Cuba placed eighth overall, winning thirteen medals (six gold, four silver, and three bronze).

Although no formal limitation exists on participation because of race, class, or gender, some groups continue to be underrepresented. Women, especially older women, participate in sports less frequently than do other groups. In addition, there appears to be more emphasis on sports in the urban rather than in the rural areas. In the cities, sport is more organized and receives more staff, more facilities, and more equipment. Notably, the specialized sports secondary schools are located mainly at urban sites, although they are distributed so that there is one in each province. Still, the general growth of participation in all programs is impressive, especially when compared with the pre-1959 situation.

This success is attributable in large part to the organizational structure of the sports system that has been put into place by the revolutionary government. Although the Cuban system is modeled after that which existed in the former Soviet Union and Eastern bloc countries, the system has remained uniquely Cuban. For example, according to a former sprinter, even though intensive training is necessary for top-level athletes, care is taken so that athletes are not burned out by boring training sessions. Swimmers, for instance, play water polo to break the monotony. Runners play soccer, which naturally includes distance work and speed work all within the rhythm of the game. Presumably, if running or swimming is more enjoyable within the context of a game, then the athletes will do more of it and thereby derive more benefit from it than if it were just sprint intervals. In addition, there has been a continuing emphasis in Cuba on egalitarianism and mass participation for the benefit of the overall populace, not only to produce champions. Although all of the socialist countries asserted that healthy bodies were a necessary component of productive labor, Cuba maintained facilities for recreational sports that are not included in international competitions.

In the Cuban system of competition, an attempt is made to give every person with talent the opportunity to be discovered and to develop that talent. At every level, beginning with the individual schools, a championship team emerges. At the same time, another team, called a *selección*, is chosen from the best players from all the losing teams at that level. For example, if ten teams competed for the municipal title, a *selección* would be chosen from the remaining nine teams. In this manner, two teams actually move on to the championship. This process is repeated at every level up to the national, and there have been times when the *selección* has beaten the original champion. And with the *selección*, sports help to achieve a greater degree of integration. Athletes no longer identify with the old unit of school or factory. They begin to identify with the nation. This process supports the argument made by Raudol Ruiz, one of the founders of INDER, that "when the athlete goes abroad to compete, he competes for powerful reasons. People don't understand this. The force of ideology is much more powerful than any steroid or artificial drug that is given to an athlete."

Early efforts to encourage greater participation were formalized in February 1961, when a single unified administrative structure for Cuban sports and physical culture was established—the Cuban National Institute for Sports, Physical Education and Recreation (*INDER* in the Spanish acronym). At the same time, Voluntary Sports Councils (Consejos Deportivos Voluntarios, CDVs) were set up to form the grassroots base of Cuban physical culture. INDER is responsible for everything connected with sports: physical education, competitive athletics at all levels, as well as recreation and use of free time. It is also responsible for the national athletes and their training and for sports research. Central INDER offices are located in Ciudad Deportiva (Sports City), a huge complex of sports facilities on the outskirts of Havana. Also in the same complex are the Instituto Superior de Cultura Física (ISCF), the Instituto de Medicina Deportiva, the National Training Center, and the Industria Deportiva (Sports Industry), where most of the athletic equipment for the country and for export is manufactured. INDER also controls all national coaches, the specialized sports schools, the Voluntary Sports Councils, and its own provincial branches. INDER reports directly to the Cuban Olympic Committee, which is headed by José Ramón Fernández, a vice president of the Council of Ministers and the Politburo member responsible for sports.

The development of champion athletes is seen as too important to be left to chance. For that effort, the Cubans have developed a parallel structure of specialized sports schools that follow the regular curriculum at the same time as they intensively train top-quality athletes for national and international competition. At the first level are the specialized sports secondary schools called Escuelas de las Iniciación de Deportivas Escolares (EIDEs). At the next level are the Escuelas Superiores de Perfeccionamiento Atlético (ESPAs), and at the highest level are the two Centros de Alto Rendimiento (CEARs), at which athletes prepare for international competitions. Both CEARs are in Havana.

In the Cuban system, as soon as a child shows a particular talent, he or she is given every opportunity to develop it. Participation in the competitive track brings with it access to special facilities, special training, a more balanced diet, and the resources of specialized sports science. Despite this inequality, compatibility between the dual goals of sports is believed to be possible as long as the aim of sport for the masses is never abandoned once top-level talent is found. "The more people practicing (sport)," the manager of the Cuban delegation to the Central American and Caribbean Games observed in 1975, "the more people from which to choose."

The rapid decline in the Cuban economy in the first half of the 1990s impacted all aspects of Cuban society, including sports. Soon after the pace of victories on sports battlefields began to slow, however, Cuban officials began to take a long, hard, realistic look at the "system". As they recognized the shortfalls and pinpointed the causes of problems, they began to change the system, and the efforts seem to have paid off.

By the turn of the decade, the sports system actually was paying for itself. Self-financing came from prize money won in international competitions, from the export of sports equipment, from the contracting of Cuban coaches to rival athletic programs, and from charges for interviews with athletes and officials. In addition, other countries helped to finance Cuban sports. The Italian government paid for the Cuban baseball team to go to Barcelona in 1996. The Australians covered the cost of sending 300 Cuban athletes to Sydney in 2000.

Soon after the 1991 Pan American Games, however, the Special Period began to take its toll. In 1993, at the Central American and Caribbean Games in Puerto Rico, approximately fifty Cuban athletes—from a delegation of 667—sought asylum and chose not to return to Cuba. Cuban officials also found that they had to tighten their belts as a result of the economic crisis. To conserve electricity, night baseball games were canceled. A shortage of newsprint resulted in a reduction in sports coverage. Most important, while the Cuban sports system continued to receive funding, the resources that were available were directed toward the higher level of competitive sports. Sports facilities and equipment for the masses were relatively neglected.

This short-term solution to the economic crisis, however, soon led to a slump in performance at international competitions and a general decline in morale within the athletic community, according to one knowledgeable Cuban official. As a consequence, Cuba experienced severe setbacks in Olympic and Pan American competitions. In the 1996 Atlanta Olympics, the total number of medals dropped to twenty-five and the team came in ninth overall. And whereas the Cubans won 265 medals, 140 of them gold, at the 1991 Pan American Games in Havana, they received only 238 medals total (112 of them gold) at Mar del Plata in 1995.

Baseball defections have received the greatest attention in the U.S. media because of the visibility of players leaving for the riches of the U.S. Major Leagues. Perhaps the most famous (and likely the most embarrassing) departures are those of brothers Liván and Orlando "El Duque" Hernández. The former signed a multimillion-dollar contract with the Florida Marlins and helped them win the 1997 World Series, gaining the Most Valuable Player Award. El Duque signed the next year with the New York Yankees, and they proceeded to win the 1998 World Series. In the last half of the 1990s, more than fifty high-quality players left the Cuban Major League either to play in the United States or to play on "loan" in other countries, especially Japan.

Some of the best baseball players were allowed to "retire" early, to play in other countries such as Colombia, Japan, Italy, Nicaragua, and El Salvador. More than fifty players, most still at the top of their game, left to take advantage of what *New York Times* reporter Larry Rohter described as a "new, government-authorized plan that allowed them to earn hard currency by playing abroad."

Although as much as 80 percent of their earnings had to go to the Cuban government, their salaries still exceeded the twenty dollars per month that they would have earned in Cuba. More often than not, they were replaced by players with more "revolutionary spirit" (i.e., unlikely candidates to defect) than baseball talent.

The wake-up call came in August 1997, when Cuban baseball's ten-year string of victories in the Intercontinental Cup was broken, with an 11–2 loss to Japan. Another tournament in Spain saw Cuba lose 16–6. The Cuban sports bureaucracy quickly moved to address these growing concerns, and it began by purging itself. INDER also ended the policy of permitting good players to "retire" to play in other countries, and it scrapped the system of playing two seasons a year and returned to the single, longer season. There are now ninety-two games played in a season stretching from November 15 to March 26. In addition, night games are being played again in the larger cities. The government also provides "material incentives" to the nominally amateur national baseball team players, who receive a car, a home, and the right to earn hard currency, commensurate with their record. Players also receive personal items such as uniforms, equipment bags, all necessary equipment, including batting gloves, and toiletries such as toothpaste. Further, the national team was strengthened by removing the *sembrados*, those who seemed "planted" in their place on the team only by prior reputation. Beginning in 1998, players earned a place only by virtue of their actual record.

Sports equipment still comes from the Industria Deportiva, located in the Sports City just outside of Havana. In general, the factories at the Industria Deportiva appear to be grossly underutilized. Only about 65 percent of production capacity is in use. The main obstacles to further production are poor technological quality of manufacturing techniques and a shortage of primary materials. There are 7,500 different raw materials used in producing sports equipment, some of which must be imported, and foreign investors have shown little interest in the sports industry. In 1998 the industry produced 70,000 baseballs, with 60,000 reserved for domestic consumption. Overall, the industry produces equipment for 38 sports, and 95 percent of the equipment used in Cuba at the turn of the century came from the domestic sports industry.

On occasion, Cuban teams are sent to other countries as a team, and then are divided up to play on various teams there. They also come together to practice as a team and sometimes even compete as a team. The volleyball team goes to Italy and Greece; handball to Hungary and France; basketball to Argentina; and track and field to Spain. Each country signs a contract with the Cuban Sports Federation, not INDER or individual players.

The hard currency goes to the Cuban Sports Federation, and the players earn some of it. The volleyball team earned prize money worth more than $1 million in hard currency last year. The money covers the team's expenses first, and then some goes to each player (about one thousand dollars each). The system of specialized sports schools continues to operate. There is still one EIDE in each province and every province but Sancti Spíritus has an ESPA. There are two CEARs, each of which has about seven hundred athletes and which also train some foreign athletes. One of the CEARs also has facilities for teaching regular academic subjects, because many of the swimmers and tennis players there are young teenagers. There are twenty-five thousand students in the EIDEs and ESPAs, and fifty-four thousand teachers of sports throughout the country. Female athletes have made significant progress. Internationally, there are more opportunities for women athletes. Cuba has increased its emphasis on sports for women, which now include water polo, volleyball, badminton, beach volleyball, and soccer. At the start of the 1990s, 30 percent of the students in EIDEs, ESPAs, and CEARs were female. Ten years later, the number stood at 45 percent.

Baseball and other sports continue to be important vehicles for Cuba to realize its international objectives. Havana sees sport as a way of demonstrating to other poor countries that it is still a significant world actor. Especially since the passage of the 1996 Helms-Burton Act, sports achievement has been one way that Cuba visibly indicates that it is weathering continued U.S. hostility. Its export of trainers, coaches, and athletes provides it with a source of ambassadors to athletes who are revered in their own countries. As these Cuban emissaries work with European teams, they attempt to build goodwill in a region that is important to Cuba economically. Success in international competition also strengthens Cuban nationalism and contributes needed support to the government during a period of economic scarcity. Cuba's sports victories thus serve domestic purposes in a period of declining morale. Mass sports participation can provide an outlet for frustrations that young Cubans are experiencing and demonstrates a continuing government commitment to dispensing services universally. Cuba continues to see sports in a dual manner: *masividad* domestically and high-level competition internationally go hand in hand and reinforce one another.

The Cuban Media

María López Vigil

In August 1994, the waters of the Florida Strait teemed with Cuban rafts, and wire services teemed with interpretations of what was happening. Once again, Cuba and the future of Cubans was lead news in the international media. And, as always, the news appeared in two stark colors: black and white.

NO AUTHENTIC CULTURE OF DEBATE

One of the challenges perpetually facing the Cuban Revolution is its image. It's a huge challenge, since the majority of news images circulating around the world are fashioned by the United States. With its abundance of teachers skilled at simplifying historical and human realities, the United States is home to the most ardent adversaries of the process that radically changed things in Cuba thirty-five years ago.

But Cuba's image also depends on Cuba. The Cubans, too, have an image factory, whose product is presented in their own media. Perhaps the time has come for Cubans to put their media on trial, because it is not equal to the current situation. Its "specialty" in the current Special Period seems to be little more than accentuating the many faults that already existed during the "normal" period.

This issue of the media is not a minor one. It goes to the very heart of Cuban political practice, which, more than party pluralism, needs a plurality of opinions, of voices—an authentic diversity. The media problem is longstanding, but today, when Cubans' social consensus regarding the revolutionary project is undergoing such a severe crisis, it becomes central.

The palette in Cuba has the same two colors: black and white. Sorely lacking in Cuban society is an authentic culture of debate, as is reflected with utter clarity in the teaching of social sciences and communications. This grave deficiency is at the root of many of the subjective problems that limit the capacity of Cuba's economy and society to transform itself today. The only thing the Cuban people can hang on in order to survive with their human values intact in this "new world disorder" is to know, discern, and contrast, so they can make choices. And all discernment must be based upon debate.

DEBATE: THE UNKNOWN VARIABLE

"Why have I been unable to find even one creative discussion with distinct points of view regarding the waves of raft people in the Cuban media?" I asked one editor colleague. "*Chica*," he argued, "that's a very thorny subject, and the situation is very delicate right now. We can't risk it." But even with other, less thorny, subjects, and even when conditions were far more stable, the Cuban media has never really been open to debate.

No topic is laid out as a problem, a dilemma, a multisided issue. Certainly not the transcendental political ones that some want to see appear in Cuba (e.g., Should there be one party or many? Who will replace Fidel?). Nor are the less weighty topics perked up by suggesting a "for" and "against" position (e.g., Is it better to be a bellhop in a hotel today because of the tips than to be a teacher?). And certainly not the small day-to-day topics (e.g., Is it better to nurse or bottle feed?). Since a truly open debate is, in principle, a dangerous and distracting enterprise, no distinct voice is heard in the media, nor even as a "theatrical" way of exploring the dimensions of a topic. Any "debate" in the media usually has, aside from the moderator, one or two specialists who stake out the correct position and always have the last word.

Nor is there room for "error," which explains the fear of live programs and improvisation in front of the microphones. It's why so many programs are read straight from scripts. The sacred and revolutionary right to err in public simply does not exist—either for journalists or for the population at large. Only the official line can backtrack. A high political cost has been paid for this ideological monopoly.

In the Cuban media, official discourse has the first and last word; only intermittently is anyone allowed to get a word in edgewise. The Cuban media understands—and defends the position—that if it presents a "debate" on breast-feeding, it is not to think about the issue collectively, much less give rise to fear or doubts, but exclusively to encourage women to breast-feed their babies.

"Wouldn't it be more efficient to reach the same conclusion by opening a real debate so women can express their concerns, hear others, then decide for themselves whether or not to breast-feed?" The question in itself seemed to disconcert the journalists. "What would be the point, then, of talking about this nonsense? So in the end each person goes off and thinks what she or he wants?" commented one. "Listen! We've got priorities here!" was the response of another. But Cuba today is submerged in the details of daily life. And they are not debated.

Are the great priority items too complex? Are the daily issues of the Special Period too delicate? If so, then the radio could use a debate forum for any of a thousand and one topics. Should a boy play with dolls? Why doesn't anyone like soy? How do you pick a name for your child? Are humans really descended from monkeys?

With virtually any topic, radio and tv could begin to exercise their thought muscles and, more than anything, unblock public expression of thought. The lifting of *this* blockade falls to Cuba.

THOUSANDS OF SUGGESTIONS FOR IMPROVEMENTS

In 1989 and 1990 the Call to the Fourth Communist Party Congress was discussed, based on a text that was stellar in the history of the revolution for its sincerity and provocativeness. This discussion did not happen in the media but in a massive participation of grassroots party members and independents. People made thousands upon thousands of suggestions for improvements in all aspects of the country. They were particularly critical of the media.

People perceived the media as apologist, boring, routine, and triumphalist, and emphasized the gap between the media line and reality: the news would say that plantain production for a given year had surpassed its goal, while none were to be seen in the markets. That's how it went with virtually everything. People insisted that the media be the channel for criticizing government officials and improving services. The topic of the media was among those that sparked the greatest number of comments and suggestions.

Growing out of these demands, a number of decisions were made to expand information formats that had already started to appear. In particular, radio stations were given the essential task of mediating between state officials and individuals or groups from society who, over the radio, could make not just complaints but also suggestions.

Such programs have become increasingly popular throughout the world. They are, in effect, a safety valve, an efficient channel of information regarding very real problems and one through which a good number of these problems can be resolved. They are also a step towards the democratic task of relinquishing control and management power to society, to the people as a whole, whether they are organized or not.

These sorts of programs came late to Cuba, but they came. Right on their heels, however, came the disintegration of the Soviet Union. The island found itself in a Special Period, with shortages, uncertainty, realignments in all areas of the economy—another Cuba in another world. New and excruciating problems arose, and many of the suggestions made at the time of the congress were shelved.

The media, which had barely begun to make changes toward filling this mediator role, took a big step backwards. They became more monochromatic than ever. The reason given? "What's the point of saying what's bad if we can't correct it? It only creates more dissent, and tends to demoralize people." And that was that. "What demoralizes us is to see a truck pulling up with a literally rotting load of grapefruit, but nobody does anything about it. And nobody says anything!" was the angry opinion of a housewife. But she could no longer say that on the radio. And that's that.

RADIO: SPECIAL PROTAGONIST

The Special Period also caused other upheavals within the Cuban media. The paper shortage (Cuba had long depended on the socialist camp for paper) forced the closure of several specialized periodicals and dramatically reduced the circulation, frequency, and number of pages of those that survived. Of course, school and university texts and notebooks were also affected. *Granma* doesn't even look like a newspaper anymore; it often comes out with only two pages.

Is there any bright side to the crisis? Abel Prieto, president of the National Union of Cuban Writers and Artists, admitted to local journalists during a visit to Argentina last July that the Cuban press was "dreadful," but said the crisis had "improved" it: with less paper, it has less opportunity to show how bad it is. The reality is that people in Cuba are eating and reading less and less—in terms of both quality and quantity. This is a sad and weighty reality for a population that had previously been so well fed and well educated by the revolution.

Rationing of the country's electricity supply due to a shortage of petroleum and obsolete machinery reduced the two television channels' broadcast hours to six, slightly more on the weekends. They had previously broadcast from the morning hours on. The long power cuts further reduced these hours in practice, cutting severely into the few hours of distraction available to people

CINEMA: A HAPPY EXCEPTION

The valuable exception is the Cuban Institute of Cinematographic Art and Industry (ICAIC), which enjoys hard-won autonomy. Even though it is formally within the straitjacket of the party structure, it has never allowed itself to be controlled or permitted its creative work to be inhibited. The moral authority and lucidity of Alfredo Guevara, the guiding light of Cuban film, has a lot to do with winning this autonomy, but it hasn't been easy.

Cuban film director Humberto Solás ("Lucía," "Cecilia," "Un hombre de éxito,") recently talked about this in Costa Rica.

> We have forced the state to accept self-criticism in the sphere of cinema. Of course, we haven't done this in a coercive way, because it's very hard to make a state bend, and would be particularly difficult for a group of film artists to do so. But I'm very proud of being a Cuban filmmaker, because, even though we can only make two films a year now, due to the Special Period, we've won a very important space in Cuban society. I think film is the one area of culture that has been capable of caustic, biting and thus constructive criticism from within the revolution.

That can clearly be seen in a glance at Cuban film over the last three decades. The recent "boom" of *Strawberry and Chocolate* is neither coincidence nor state opportunism for export purposes, as some in Miami would have it. From the time of *Death of a Bureaucrat* to the more recent *Plaf!* or *Adorables Mentiras* (*Adorable Lies*), Cuban film has always been full of humor and life, as if it were a very challenge to debate. It is something of a creative factory of images in which all colors possible are used to paint the Cuban reality.

CUBAN MEDIA AND THE SPECIAL PERIOD

Cuba's ongoing financial, economic and ideological crisis contradicts the media. Many aspects of this rapidly changing reality are simply not reported. And because the media doesn't debate, they neither inform nor form in the sense of education. "Why doesn't the media deal with Cuba's new reality, one that is increasingly complex, and with such diverse points of view?" I put the question to a group of Cuban journalists, who, the younger they are, the quicker they are to recognize the media's deficiencies. For instance, why doesn't anybody really delve into the issue of the *jineteras* (prostitutes)? Everybody knows of at least one person involved in this and has formed some opinion about the issue. It is thus an ideal theme for open media debate. But, once again, the silence is deafening. "Why?" I ask. The journalists' responses vary, but all are symptomatic:

"With the revolution, prostitution was eradicated in Cuba and this is something else."

"Fidel has not spoken at length about this issue."

"Discussing the subject would actually promote it."

"The whole thing overwhelms me; I wouldn't even know what to say about it, so better I say nothing."

All these Cuban arguments lead journalism to silence.

WHAT IS OPINION?

They also reveal a journalistic style in which lies are not told and truths are not invented when dealing with controversial topics. But what is really happening isn't discussed either—unless the topic is such that it permits saying what should happen. There is a tight linkage between paternalism and voluntarism. The media preach a doctrine of what *should be* and offer neither information nor reflection about what *is*. The media are state authority's loudspeaker, not a space in which society's distinct actors are represented. Journalists are not society's critical consciousness, they are the state's uncritical pawns. They don't conceive of critically supporting the system, only of unconditionally identifying with it.

Thirty-five years after constructing a project in which each and every Cuban was offered so many opportunities in life—security, employment, food, work, education, free time, culture, sports—as well as a feeling for life itself, this communication model is indefensible. It is also unacceptable, now that Cuba is seeking integration with the rest of Latin America and has increasingly close relations with foreign tourists and investors, as well as with international journalists. From overprotecting the people—perhaps justifiably in the 1960s, when everything was still to be done and defended—the evolution has been toward underestimating the people as producers of their own thoughts, as capable of having mature opinions.

A journalist from the Cuban [news] agency Prensa Latina tells a joke that captures the problem poignantly. "An FAO (United Nations Food and Agriculture Organization) official was doing an international survey. He goes to Africa and asks: 'What is your opinion about the world food scarcity?' The African doesn't understand the question: 'Food? What's food?' He goes to Germany and asks the same question, but the German doesn't understand either: 'Scarcity? What's scarcity?' He finally gets to Cuba and repeats the question there. And the Cuban says, 'Opinion? What's opinion?'"

A change in the media—towards debate, participation, reality, pluralist opinion—would clearly go to the heart of power. It could put it at risk. But, shouldn't revolutionary power put itself at risk, within the revolution? Is that not possible? Won't it have to do so, sooner or later? Can't openings be made to pluralist opinion that doesn't mean caving in to the United States? With Cuba's reality so complex, how can there be only a single interpretation of events, and only one voice doing the interpreting?

"The worst opinion is silence," is one Uruguayan radio station's motto. "Worse than the dangers of error are the dangers of silence." Fidel told journalists some years ago, during the Fifth Communist Party Congress. Is there awareness of the risks of this silence in the media? While the revolutionary leadership decides this issue, silence continues to substitute for debate. The media, potentially an extraordinary tool to creatively accompany the people in this crisis, are rust-bound, Jurassic. They could be the channel for a massive consultation–survey–temperature-taking to find out what Cubans—people, not just leadership cadres—think or imagine is the way out of this crisis. But they are static, with their channel hatch closed.

It is not possible that the most educated population in Latin America, with so many intellectual resources, with thousands and thousands of professionals and technical experts, with such an extraordinary historical experience, could perish of hunger, could languish with the wings of its initiative cut, could remain silent. It is not possible that a now adult revolution could fear debate that much.

APPENDIX

Chronology of the Special Period, 1986–2006

1986

February 4: The Cuban Communist Party's Third Congress approves President Fidel Castro's proposal to begin the "process of the rectification of errors and negative tendencies." In calling for reforms aimed at returning Cuba to egalitarian and collectivist principles of the 1960s, Castro denounces decentralization and the profits earned in private farmers' markets. In May he orders the closing of private farmers' markets.

February 25: At the Twenty-Seventh Soviet Communist Party Congress, General Secretary Mikhail Gorbachev proposes economic reforms, including some limited free-market mechanisms, under his plan for *perestroika* (restructuring).

1988

May 3: The United States, South Africa, Angola, and Cuba begin four-party negotiations in London to end the civil war in Angola, as Angolan and Cuban troops declare a victory in the battle of Cuito Carnivale against South African forces.

November 15: The four-party talks conclude with South Africa agreeing to Namibia's independence, and with Cuba and South Africa agreeing to withdraw their troops from Angola.

1989

November 9: Berlin Wall falls. The reunification of Germany sets off a chain reaction of political and economic change in Eastern Europe and the Soviet Union.

1990

July 25: Gorbachev announces that trade with all members of the Council for Mutual Economic Assistance (CMEA), the socialist countries' trading pact headed by the Soviet Union, will be conducted on the basis of hard-currency exchanges, and that Soviet foreign assistance to developing countries such as Cuba will be scaled back significantly.

July 26: Castro declares the onset of a "Special Period in a Time of Peace," and he forecasts the sort of rationing, especially of energy usage, which occurs during wartime.

1991

June 28: The CMEA is formally dissolved; Cuba must pay hard currency for transactions with former members of the pact. Trade with the CMEA had accounted for 88 percent of Cuba's international commerce.

September 11: Gorbachev announces that the Soviet Union will withdraw all of its troops from Cuba and cut off military aid.

October 10–14: The Cuban Communist Party's Fourth Congress approves amendments to the Cuban constitution that allow for limited economic liberalization, fewer restrictions on local elections, and the right of religious believers to join the Communist Party.

December 21: The Soviet Union is dissolved, leaving Russia as the successor state. (Russian President Boris Yeltsin had indicated his antipathy towards Cuba with a 1989 visit to Miami as a guest of the Cuban American National Foundation.)

1992

July 10–12: The National Assembly of People's Power approves constitutional amendments which protect foreign investment in Cuba, permit foreign ownership of Cuban property, and legalize selected activities of some nongovernmental organizations.

October 23: U.S. President George H. W. Bush signs the Cuban Democracy Act, which tightens the embargo by restoring sanctions on trade for U.S. third country subsidiaries. It also eases the embargo to encourage people-to-people engagement. Dubbed "track two," these provisions were intended to "wreak havoc on the island," according to Rep. Robert Torricelli (D-New Jersey), the law's principal author.

1993

July 26: The Cuban government legalizes the free circulation of U.S. dollars, which leads to a dual peso and dollar economy.

September 9: Decree-Law 141 goes into effect, allowing self-employment in 117 new occupations. At its peak in 1996, 209,000 individuals (called *cuentapropistas*) were licensed to own a small business. In 2005, there were approximately 150,000.

December 31: The year ends with the Cuban economy in a severe decline. Malnutrition begins to appear for the first time in thirty years, as average caloric intake of the working population (age fourteen to sixty-four) falls to 57 percent of the World Health Organization's recommended level.

1994

June-August: An average of more than fifty Cubans per day attempt to cross the Florida Straits in makeshift rafts and small boats. During this *balsero* (rafter) crisis, nearly forty thousand people try to emigrate illegally to the United States.

July 13: Trying to prevent a hijacked tugboat from leaving Cuban territorial waters, the Cuban coast guard sinks the boat. Thirty-seven people on the boat drown.

August 5: More than five thousand demonstrators—the largest anti-government protest since 1959—converge on Havana's waterfront roadway, the Malecón, demanding the right to emigrate.

September 9: U.S. President Bill Clinton announces a U.S.-Cuban agreement to grant twenty thousand visas annually to Cubans. None of the nearly twenty thousand rafters whom the United States had detained at the Guantánamo Naval Base would be eligible for visas.

1995

May 2: As the Guantánamo detainees threaten to riot, U.S. and Cuban officials negotiate a new immigration plan which came to be known as the "wet-foot-dry-foot" policy: Cuban exiles rescued at sea would be repatriated to Cuba; those arriving on any U.S. territory would be permitted to stay and apply for asylum. The Guantánamo detainees are granted U.S. visas.

September 5: The Cuban government approves new laws allowing foreigners to own one hundred percent of a business.

1996

February 22: Several leaders of *Concilio Cubano*, an umbrella opposition organization, are sentenced to fourteen months in prison for allegedly using U.S. government funds to organize a February 24th conference of 130 Cuban groups seeking to change Cuba's form of government.

February 24: A Cuban air force plane shoots down two Brothers-to-the-Rescue planes in international airspace, killing four people. On previous missions, Brothers-to-the-Rescue planes had dropped propaganda pamphlets and trinkets over Havana. José Basulto, a Cuban exile long associated with anti-Castro terrorist activities, founded the organization in 1991.

March 12: In the aftermath of the February 24th shoot-down, and on the day of Florida's presidential primary elections, Clinton signs into law the "Cuban Liberty and Solidarity Act," known as the "Helms-Burton Act." The law codifies prior executive orders related to the Cuban embargo, and creates the opportunity for former owners of property in Cuba to sue foreign corporations in U.S. courts as repayment for their "trafficking" with stolen property.

August 4: Cuba finishes in ninth place with a total of 25 medals at the 1996 Atlanta Olympic games—down from fifth place at the 1992 Barcelona Olympics. The drop reflects the impact on Cuba's sports program of Special Period shortages. Cuba finishes in eighth place at the 2000 Sydney Olympics, and in eleventh place at the 2004 Athens games.

1997

April 12: A bomb explodes in Havana's Hotel Meliá Cohiba, in the first of a string of hotel bombings that wound several people and kill an Italian tourist. Luis Posada Carriles, a Cuban exile and former CIA operative who had been charged with blowing up a Cuban civilian airliner in 1976, later admits to planning the hotel attacks.

October 11: The Fifth Congress of the Cuban Communist Party concludes by installing new, younger members in key leadership posts, and by reducing the size of its Central Committee.

November 23: Jorge Mas Canosa, founder of the Cuban American National Foundation, dies.

1998

January 21: Pope John Paul II arrives in Havana, marking the first papal visit to Cuba. During his five-day visit he conducts several open air masses involving hundreds of thousands of Cubans, he criticizes the U.S. embargo, and he calls for improved human rights in Cuba.

September 12: Five Cuban intelligence agents (the Cuban Five) are arrested and charged with espionage against the United States. They had been attempting to monitor terrorist activities of extremist anti-Castro groups in South Florida.

October: Cuba inaugurates the Latin American School of Medicine (ELAM) in Havana. All of its students, primarily from Latin America and the Caribbean, receive full scholarships.

1999

March 28: In the first of two games, Cuba's national baseball team loses 3-2 to the Baltimore Orioles in Havana's Estadio Latinoamericano. The Cuban team wins the second game, 12-6, in Baltimore on May 3.

November 25: Five-year-old Elián González is found at sea, after his boat capsizes, killing his mother and other Cubans attempting to emigrate illegally. Disregarding the wishes of his father, who remained in Cuba, U.S. officials place González in the care of distant Miami relatives. The U.S. Justice Department allows the boy to return to Cuba with his father on June 28, 2000.

2000

October 27: Clinton signs a bill lifting some restrictions on the sale of food and medicine to Cuba, though it requires transactions to be paid in advance, without bank credits, making sales to Cuba difficult. This comes after a year in which the U.S. House and Senate approve several legislative proposals to relax the embargo.

November 17: Panama arrests Luis Posada Carriles and three other men outside of the tenth Ibero-American Summit meeting in which Fidel Castro was participating. They were found with a carload of C-4 explosives.

2001

June 8: After a tension-filled trial in Miami, the Cuban Five are convicted and later sentenced to prison terms ranging from fifteen years to "double life."

2002

January: The United States houses prisoners of war captured in Afghanistan at the U.S. Guantánamo Naval Base on the eastern end of the island. Cuba does not protest this use of the base.

May 10: Osvaldo Payá, head of the Varela Project, delivers a petition to the Cuban National Assembly signed by eleven thousand Cubans. It calls on the legislature to hold a national referendum to amend the Cuban constitution, permitting un-fettered public speech, an uncontrolled press, unrestrained private ownership of enterprises, and amnesty for political prisoners. The assembly rejects the Varela Project petition, and approves a Cuban government-sponsored petition calling for a constitutional amendment affirming the "irrevocable" socialist nature of the Cuban system.

May 12: Former U.S. President Jimmy Carter arrives in Havana for a five-day visit that includes meetings with Castro and a speech at the University of Havana in which he criticizes both the lack of political freedom in Cuba and the U.S. embargo.

June 13: Fidel Castro announces that the Cuban government had begun to disman-tle the country's sugar industry, closing down 71 of the country's 154 sugar mills, because of the low world price for sugar and the high cost of modernizing aging mills. In the following three years Cuban sugar production declines 70 percent, from 4 million tons in 2002 to 1.3 million tons in 2005.

2003

March 18: On the eve of the U.S. invasion of Iraq, the Cuban government arrests and accuses seventy-five regime opponents of treason and accepting U.S. financial support for their activities.

2004

May 6: U.S. President George W. Bush accepts the five-hundred-page report from his Commission for Assistance to a Free Cuba. The first chapter lays out a "proactive, integrated, and disciplined approach . . . that will help the Cuban people hasten the dictatorship's end."

June 30: Based on the Commission's recommendations, the U.S. Treasury Depart-ment imposes new restrictions on U.S. study abroad programs, educational ex-changes with Cuba, remittances, and family visits. More than three hundred U.S. universities immediately shut down their academic programs in Cuba.

November 8: U.S. dollars are taken out of circulation in Cuba, and replaced by Cuban Convertible Pesos (CUC) with a 10 percent tax on conversion from other currencies.

November 22: Chinese President Hu Jintao visits Cuba to discuss strengthening bilateral relations between the two countries. An agreement is reached for Cuba to annually ship four thousand tons of nickel sinter to China between 2005 and 2009.

December 14: Venezuelan President Hugo Chávez and Castro call for the "Bolivarian Alternative for the Americas," a hemispheric trade pact that would counter the U.S.-sponsored Free Trade Area of the Americas. They also announce that Venezuela will provide oil to Cuba at drastically reduced prices, and that Cuba will send doctors to Venezuela.

December 27: Cuba reaches its goal of two million visitors to the island in one year.

2005

July 28: U.S. Secretary of State Condoleezza Rice appoints Caleb McCarry as a Cuba transition coordinator, "whose mandate it is to design and implement a comprehensive strategy for advancing freedom in Cuba."

August 30–31: The trial of Posada Carriles, on charges of entering the United States illegally, opens in Texas. Venezuela asks the United States to extradite him in order to stand trial for his alleged role in the 1976 Cubana Airline bombing. He claims asylum as a former CIA agent and asserts that he would be tortured if he were returned to Venezuela.

December 30: Evo Morales, Bolivia's newly elected president, begins his inaugural tour by meeting with Castro in Havana. The Cuban leader promises health care and education assistance to Morales's government.

2006

July 10: President Bush's Commission for Assistance to a Free Cuba issues its second report, recommending increased enforcement of the U.S. embargo, and calling for an $80 million fund "to increase support for Cuban civil society."

July 31: As a result of major intestinal surgery, Cuban leader Fidel Castro "temporarily" turns over his responsibilities to six officials. Vice President Raúl Castro assumes the leadership of Cuba's Communist Party and Politburo, and becomes acting president of the Council of State.

September 11–16: Cuba hosts the Fourteenth summit of the 118-nation Nonaligned Movement (NAM), and becomes the chair of the NAM for the next three years. Castro is not well enough to attend the NAM summit or ceremonies in December to mark his eightieth birthday.

October 31: Cuba reports an economic growth rate in 2005 of 11.8 percent, based on measures that include estimates of the market value of free social services in Cuba and medical services exported to Venezuela and Bolivia. Cuba has deployed more than thirty thousand medical personnel to South America.

November 8: By a vote of 183–4, with one abstention, the United Nations General Assembly approves a resolution calling for an end to the "economic, commercial and financial blockade imposed by the United States of America against Cuba."

Index

About the Editors and Contributors

Philip Brenner is professor of international relations and history and codirector of the Inter-Disciplinary Council on Latin America at American University in Washington, D.C. He is the coauthor of *Sad and Luminous Days: Cuba's Struggle with the Superpowers after the Missile Crisis* (2002), and author of *From Confrontation to Negotiation: U.S. Relations with Cuba* (1988). A coeditor of the *The Cuba Reader: The Making of a Revolutionary Society* (1989), he has published numerous articles in journals and anthologies on U.S.-Cuban relations, Cuban foreign policy, and the Cuban missile crisis.

Marguerite Rose Jiménez is completing her master's degree at the School of International Service at American University in Washington, D.C. She has conducted research in Cuba on tourism as a McNair Scholar, and on music and social movements as an invited researcher at Casa de Las Américas. Her senior honors thesis, *Rhythm, Rhyme and Revolution* (2004) examined the political and cultural significance of hip-hop in Cuba. She is the coauthor of "U.S. Policy on Cuba: Beyond the Last Gasp" (*NACLA*, Jan/Feb 2006), and author of "The Answer Lies Within: Fixing Our Image Abroad by Fixing Our Democratic Deficiencies" (*Swords and Ploughshares: Journal of International Affairs*, Spring 2007). Her current research focuses on the development of national identity and political culture in Cuba.

John M. Kirk is professor of Latin American studies at Dalhousie University in Canada. He is the author of *José Martí, Mentor of the Cuban Nation* (1983) and *Between God and the Party: Religion and Politics in Revolutionary Cuba* (1983); coauthor of *Canada-Cuba Relations: The Other Good Neighbor Policy* (1997); and coeditor of *Cuba, Twenty-Five Years of Revolution, 1959–1984* (1985), *Transformation and Struggle: Cuba Faces the 1990s* (1990), *Cuban Foreign Policy Confronts a New International Order* (1991), *Cuba's Struggle for Development: Dilemmas and Strategies* (1992), *Culture and the Cuban Revolution* (2001), and *Redefining Cuban Foreign Policy: The Impact of the Special Period* (2007).

William M. LeoGrande is dean of the School of Public Affairs and professor of Government at American University in Washington, D.C. He is the author of *Our Own Backyard: The United States in Central America, 1977–1992* (1998) and *Cuba's Policy in Africa* (1980). He is coauthor of *Confronting Revolution: Security Through Diplomacy in Central America* (1986), and coeditor of *The Cuba Reader: The Making of a Revolutionary Society* (1989) and *Political Parties and Democracy in Central America* (1992). He has written widely on U.S. relations with Latin America for a variety of journals and newspapers.

CONTRIBUTORS

Lorena Barberia is a program associate at Harvard University's David Rockefeller Center for Latin American Studies, where she manages the Cuban Studies Program and coordinates projects for the Brazilian Studies Program. She has worked as a consultant to the World Bank examining the role of municipal governments in the promotion of local economic development in Brazil. She has authored a number of scholarly works and is coeditor of *The Cuban Economy at the Start of the Twenty-First Century* (with Jorge I. Domínguez and Omar Everleny Pérez Villanueva, 2004).

Soraya M. Castro Mariño is senior researcher and professor at the Center for the Study of the United States at the University of Havana, Cuba. She is the author of numerous articles in scholarly journals and anthologies on U.S.-Cuban relations, U.S. foreign policy, and the U.S. foreign policymaking process. Dr. Castro has been a visiting scholar at Harvard University, American University, Johns Hopkins University, and Uppsala University.

Fidel Castro Ruz is President of the Republic of Cuba, First Secretary of the Communist Party of Cuba, and Commander in Chief of the Revolutionary Armed Forces.

David Cázares is an assistant metro editor at the *South Florida Sun-Sentinel*, where he writes a weekly column on Latin America music and culture.

Michael Chanan is professor of film and video at Roehampton University in London. A documentary filmmaker, he is also the author, editor, and translator of books and articles on film and media, and on the social history of music. His article in this volume is excerpted from the second edition of *Cuban Cinema* (2004), which continues to be the standard reference work on the subject in English.

Margaret E. Crahan is the Dorothy Epstein Professor of Latin American History at Hunter College and The Graduate Center, City University of New York. She is the author and editor of dozens of books and articles, including *Wars on Terror and Iraq: Human Rights, Unilateralism, and U.S. Foreign Policy* (2004), *Religion, Culture and Society: The Case of Cuba* (2003), and *Human Rights and Basic Human Needs in the Americas* (1982).

Alejandro de la Fuente is associate professor of history at the University of Pittsburgh. He is the author of *A Nation for All: Race, Inequality, and Politics in Twentieth Century Cuba* (2001). His research focus includes Latin American and Caribbean history, comparative slavery and race relations, and Atlantic history.

Haroldo Dilla Alfonso is research coordinator at FLACSO Dominican Republic. Previously he was director of Latin American and Caribbean Studies at the Centro de Estudios sobre América in Havana. He is the editor of *Los Recursos de la Gobernabilidad en la Cuenca del Caribe* (2002) and author and coauthor of numerous other books and articles on decentralization, civil society, and social movements in Cuba and the Caribbean.

Jorge I. Domínguez is the Antonio Madero Professor of Mexican and Latin American Politics and Economics and vice provost for international affairs at Harvard University. From 1996 to 2006 he was director of Harvard's Weatherhead Center for International Affairs. A past president of the Latin American Studies Association,

Dr. Dominguez is the author or editor of dozens of books and articles, including *Cuba: Order and Revolution* (1978), *To Make the World Safe for Revolution: Cuba's Foreign Policy* (1989), *Democratic Politics in Latin America and the Caribbean* (1998), and *Between Compliance and Conflict: East Asia, Latin America, and the "New" Pax Americana* (2005).

María Isabel Domínguez is associate professor and scientific director of the Psychological and Sociological Research Center in Havana, Cuba, where she specializes in themes related to youth and generations. She holds a Ph.D. in sociology from the Cuban Academy of Sciences.

Susan Eckstein is professor of sociology at Boston University. Her research focuses on urbanization, immigration, poverty, rights and injustices, and social movements in the context of the Third World Countries. She has written extensively on Mexico and Bolivia, but focuses on Cuba. Selected publications include *Back from the Future: Cuba under Castro* (1994, 2003) and *Power and Popular Protest* (1989, 2001). She is also coeditor of *What Justice? Whose Justice?: Fighting for Fairness in Latin America* (2003) and *Struggles for Social Rights in Latin America* (2003). Her forthcoming book, *Diasporas: The Cuban Experience*, is scheduled for publication in 2008. Dr. Eckstein is a former president of the Latin American Studies Association.

H. Michael Erisman is professor of political science at Indiana State University in Terre Haute. His extensive work on Cuba's foreign relations includes *Cuba's International Relations: The Anatomy of a Nationalistic Foreign Policy* (1985) and *Cuba's Foreign Relations in a Post-Soviet World* (2000). Dr. Erisman also has coedited *Cuban Foreign Policy Confronts a New International Order* (1991) and *Redefining Cuban Foreign Policy: The Impact of the "Special Period"* (2006). He serves on the editorial boards of the *Journal of Latin American Society and Politics* and *Cuban Studies*.

Damián J. Fernández is vice provost of the Biscayne Bay Campus, professor of international relations, and director of the Cuban Research Institute at Florida International University. His research interests include Cuban politics, Cuban-Americans, and international relations of Latin America. He is the author of *Cuba and the Politics of Passion* (2000), coeditor of *Cuba, the Elusive Nation: Reinterpretations of National Identity* (2000), and editor of *Cuba Transnational* (2005).

Enrique Fernández is a columnist and reporter for the *Miami Herald*, writing about all aspects of culture, from classic film to fish shacks. A former professor of Latin American literature and columnist for *Billboard* and *Village Voice*, he was a senior vice president of the National Academy of Recording Arts and Sciences before joining *The Herald*.

Maria Finn is on the faculty of the English Department at St. Francis College in New York. She is the editor of *Cuba in Mind* (2004), an anthology of essays, poems, novel excepts, and short stories in English on Cuba, and *Mexico in Mind* (2006). Her articles have been published in the *New York Times*, *Los Angeles Times*, *Chicago Review*, and *Exquisite Corpse*.

Daniel W. Fisk is the senior director for Western Hemisphere affairs for the National Security Council. Mr. Fisk was serving as deputy assistant secretary in the Bureau of Western Hemisphere Affairs at the U.S. Department of State when he delivered the speech excerpted in this volume. He also has been a senior staff member and associate counsel for the Senate Committee on Foreign Relations (1994–1997).

Lavinia Gasperini is a senior officer in the Sustainable Development Department of the United Nation's Food and Agriculture Organization, where she is the coordinator of the Education for Rural People Partnership (ERP). ERP promotes policies, networking, advocacy, and programs to overcome the urban/ rural gap in education.

Gerardo González Núñez is professor of economics at the Universidad Interamericana de Puerto Rico/Metropolitano. His research focuses on Cuba–Caribbean relations as well as on economic issues facing the Caribbean region. His books include *El Caribe en la Política Exterior de Cuba* (1991) and *Cuba en Crisis, Perspectivas Económicas y Políticas* (1995).

Ted Henken is professor of Black and Hispanic studies and sociology at Baruch College, City University of New York (CUNY). Additionally, he is a fellow at the Bildner Center for Western Hemisphere Studies (CUNY Graduate School) and a member of the board of directors of the Association for the Study of the Cuban Economy. He is the author of *Cuba: A Global Studies Handbook* (2007) and has published articles on Cuba in journals such as *Cuban Studies, Latin American Research Review, Latino Studies, Encuentro de la Cultura Cubana*, and *Cuba in Transition.*

Rafael Hernández is senior research fellow at the Centro de Investigacion y Desarrollo de la Cultura Cubana "Juan Marinello" and the editor of *Temas,* a Cuban quarterly in the field of social sciences and the humanities. He has taught at the University of Havana and as a visiting professor at Harvard University and Columbia University. A scholar of Cuban and U.S. policies, inter-American relations, international security, migration, and Cuban culture, society and politics, he is the author of *Looking at Cuba* (2001) and *The History of Havana* (2006).

Margo Kirk is the executive director of the University Children's Centre at Dalhousie University in Halifax, Canada. Her Master's thesis at Mount St. Vincent University examined the early childhood education system in revolutionary Cuba. Her current research and advocacy work focuses on the development of educational policy and its impact on children.

Hal Klepak is professor of history and war studies at the Royal Military College of Canada. His research focuses on Latin American security issues, Canadian foreign and defense policy, and conventional strategy. He is currently an adviser on inter-American security to the Canadian Department of National Defence and the Department of Foreign Affairs and International Trade. His publications include *Canada and Latin American Security* (1993), *Natural Allies? Canadian and Mexican Views on International Security* (1996), and *Cuba's Military 1990–2005, Revolutionary Soldiers in Counter-revolutionary Times* (2005).

Saul Landau is a columnist for *Progreso Weekly,* a fellow of the Institute for Policy Studies, a poet, and an independent filmmaker. The first of his three films on Fidel Castro, *Fidel,* was released in 1968. His fiftieth film, *We Don't Play Golf Here and Other Stories of Globalization,* was released in 2007, and his fourteenth and most recent book is *Bush and Botox World* (2007). He has won the Letelier-Moffitt Human Rights Award, the George Polk Award for Investigative Reporting, the First Amendment Award, and an Emmy for *Paul Jacobs and the Nuclear Gang.*

María López Vigil is editor in chief of *envío*, a progressive monthly magazine published at the Central American University–UCA, which focuses on politics in Nicaragua and Central America. Born in Cuba, she has worked on popular education projects throughout Central America since 1990 and is the editor of several books, including *Don Lito of El Salvador* and *Death and Life in Morazan.*

Peter McKenna is associate professor of political studies at the University of Prince Edward Island, Canada. He has published widely on Canadian-Cuban relations, Canadian-Latin American affairs and Canada's relationship with the United States. He is the author of *Canada and the OAS: From Dilettante to Full Partner* (1995) and coauthor of *Canada-Cuba Relations: The Other Good Neighbor Policy* (1997).

Pedro Monreal is senior research associate at the Center for Research on the International Economy at the University of Havana and teaches in the university's School of Economics. He has extensively published in journals and magazines and is the editor of numerous books on the Cuban economy, including *Development Prospects in Cuba: An Agenda in the Making* (2002).

Nancy Morejón is one of Cuba's leading poets. Her work has centered on the themes of the Afro-Cuban experience and women, and on Caribbean culture. In 1986 she won the Cuban Critics prize for *Piedra Pulida*, and in 2001 won Cuba's National Prize for Literature. Morejón is the author of more than a dozen collections of poetry and several monographs.

Larry R. Oberg is a former university librarian at the Mark O. Hatfield Library at Willamette University (Salem, Oregon) and editor of *Moveable Type.* In March 2000, he traveled to Cuba with fourteen other North American librarians on a fact-finding trip investigating the Independent Libraries in Cuba Project, which provided the basis of a report to the American Library Association.

Margot Olavarria is the program director for the New York Immigration Coalition. She has served as the associate editor of the *NACLA Report on the Americas*, published by the North American Congress on Latin America, and has written on issues of political culture and racial identity in the Americas. She received her Ph.D. from The New School for Social Research.

Cardinal Jaime Lucas Ortega y Alamino is the Archbishop of San Cristóbal de la Habana. He was installed as Havana's Roman Catholic archbishop in 1981 and elevated to cardinal in 1994. Pope John Paul II named him Bishop of Pinar del Rio in 1978. Cardinal Ortega was President of the Cuban Conference of Catholic Bishops from 1988 to 1998.

Tim Padgett is the Miami and Latin America bureau chief of *Time*. He was a recipient of the 2005 Maria Moors Cabot Prize from Columbia University's Graduate School of Journalism for his coverage of Latin American politics, religion, dissent, and culture.

Leonardo Padura Fuentes is a Cuban novelist and journalist. He is best known for his series of detective novels set in the Special Period, the Havana Quartet, which feature Inspector Mario Conde. *Havana Red*, the third in the series, was awarded the international Dashiell Hammett prize for detective fiction in 2004.

Raisa Pagés is a staff writer for *Granma International*. She covers international affairs for *Granma*, the official newspaper of the Communist Party of Cuba.

Mauricio de Miranda Parrondo is the director of the Economics Department at the Universidad Javeriana Pontificia in Cali, Colombia. He has edited and coauthored several books, including *Cuba, Sociedad y Politica en Tiempo de Globalizacion* (2003).

Philip Peters joined the Lexington Institute as vice president in April 1999. He specializes in international economic programs with a focus on Latin America, U.S. policy towards Cuba, state enterprise reform, and information technology. His articles have been published in the *Wall Street Journal, Chicago Tribune, Miami Herald, National Geographic Traveler*, and specialized publications, and he has provided interviews and commentary on CNN, Univision, and numerous radio programs.

Paula Pettavino is the coauthor of *Sport in Cuba: The Diamond in the Rough* (1994) and several articles and chapters in journals and anthologies on international sports and politics. She has taught international relations and comparative politics at Marymount University and American University and was the coordinator and instructor for American University's study abroad program in Cuba for five years.

Howard Reich is the veteran jazz critic of the *Chicago Tribune* and the winner of many journalistic awards. A longtime correspondent for *Downbeat* magazine, he is the coauthor of the critically acclaimed biography *Jelly's Blues: The Life, Music, and Redemption of Jelly Roll Morton* (2003).

Joaquín Roy is the Jean Monnet Professor of European Integration and director of the European Union Center of Excellence at the University of Miami. He is the author of twenty-five books and more than two hundred articles published in Spain, the United States, and Latin America, including *Cuba, the U.S. and the Helms-Burton Doctrine* (2000).

Mary Beth Sheridan is a journalist with the *Washington Post* who has written extensively on United States domestic and foreign policy issues.

Minor Sinclair leads Oxfam America's Gulf Coast Emergency Program. He has served ten years with Oxfam, including a post as program officer for the Cuba program and as co-leader of Oxfam Canada's Caribbean program based in Havana. Prior to joining Oxfam, Mr. Sinclair worked for nine years on human rights and global issues focusing on Central America, the Caribbean, and domestic refugee policy. He has authored and edited several publications, including *The New Politics of Survival: Grassroots Movements in Central America*.

Wayne S. Smith worked as a career diplomat for twenty-four years until leaving the Foreign Service in 1982, due to his disagreement with the Reagan administration's polices toward Cuba. At the time of his resignation, he was serving as head of the recently opened U.S. Interests Section in Havana. Smith is currently a Center for International Policy Senior Fellow, director of the Cuba Program, and adjunct professor of Latin American Studies at Johns Hopkins University. He is the author of several books, including *The Closest Of Enemies* (1988), *Portrait of Cuba* (1991), and *The Russians Aren't Coming: New Soviet Policy in Latin America* (1992).

Julia E. Sweig is the Nelson and David Rockefeller Senior Fellow and director of Latin America Studies at the Council on Foreign Relations. She is the author of *Inside the Cuban Revolution: Fidel Castro and the Urban Underground* (2002) and *Friendly Fire: Losing Friends and Making Enemies in the Anti-American Century* (2006).

Martha Thompson is the manager of the Rights in Humanitarian Crisis Program of the Unitarian Universalist Service Committee. From 1995 to 1999 she developed and implemented the Oxfam International program in Cuba. She is on the faculty of the Sustainable International Development Masters of Arts program at Brandeis University and the School of Nutrition at Tufts University.

Mirén Uriarte is associate professor of applied sociology, Latino studies, and public policy at the University of Massachusetts at Boston. Her areas of expertise include institutional development in minority communities, the impact of social policies on Latinos in the U.S., and education, health care, and human services in the U.S. and abroad. Her publications include *Cuban Social Policy Responses to the Economic Crisis of the 1990s* (2004) and *Holding on to Basics and Investing for Growth: Cuban Education and the Economic Crisis of the 1990s* (2003).

Nelson P. Valdés is a professor of sociology at the University of New Mexico. His areas of expertise include Latin American society and politics, with a focus on Cuba. He was the creator and founder of the Latin America Data Base and since 1986 has directed the Cuba-L Project.

Carlos Varela is a singer-songwriter whose work is considered among the most representative of *la nueva canción cubana* (the new Cuban song). He became involved with the *nueva trova* folk music movement in 1980 and helped to develop *la novísima trova*, which is characterized by its politically charged lyrics and social commentary. He has performed in concerts worldwide, including in Spain, Mexico, Venezuela, Colombia, Chile, Sweden, Ireland, Canada, and the United States. He lives in Havana, Cuba.

Leonard Weinglass has been a civil rights attorney and activist for nearly fifty years, representing defendants in prominent political trials, such as the Pentagon Papers case and the case of the Chicago Eight. Currently he is the attorney for Antonio Guerrero, one of the five Cubans the U.S. government has imprisoned for their alleged espionage activities. He is the coeditor of *Superpower Principles: U.S. Terrorism Against Cuba* (2005).

Mimi Whitefield is the business enterprise editor of the *Miami Herald*. A reporter and editor at the *Herald* since 1985, she has won awards for reports on drug trafficking in Latin America, human rights in Cuba, and money laundering in the Caribbean. She was part of the *Herald* team that won the 2001 Pulitzer Prize for coverage of Elián González.

Robin C. Williams is the medical officer of health and commissioner of public health for the Regional Municipality of Niagara, Ontario. He visited Cuba as part of a medical delegation verifying the findings in a report from the American Association for World Health.